THE ORIGINS OF COMPANY LAW

This book provides histories of company law, uniting a variety of approaches from law, business and management, economics, and history.

What were the origins of company law? How did it begin? Why did it change? There is no single answer to these questions. Each discipline, and sub-discipline, has a different approach and method that brings different facets of study to the fore. This multidisciplinary endeavour is immensely valuable for debates taking place now among policy-makers in the UK and US about returning to historic modes of company regulation.

The book brings together Anglo-American scholarship that will not only shed greater light on the history of company law but also influence contemporary debates about our ability to return to, or learn from, the past. Historical research has great value here because it not only generates new insights into the evolution of present legal rules, but also corrects misunderstandings and misapprehensions about them.

The book shows how this body of law developed to become the rules with which we are now familiar. It showcases antecedents of present debates, reveals regulatory lessons from previous legal regimes, identifies instances of path dependency, unpicks pivotal legal events, and explains drivers for legal change. The chapters reevaluate the history of company law, and the knowledge gathered here will inform the law-making and policy-making agenda.

CONTEMPORARY STUDIES IN CORPORATE LAW

Series editors: Marc Moore, Christopher Bruner

Corporate law scholarship has a relatively recent history despite the fact that corporations have existed and been subject to legal regulation for three centuries. The modern flourishing of corporate law scholarship has been matched by some broadening of the field of study to embrace insolvency, corporate finance, corporate governance and regulation of the financial markets. At the same time the intersection between other branches of law such as, for example, labour, contract, criminal law, competition, and intellectual property law and the introduction of new inter-disciplinary methodologies affords new possibilities for studying the corporation. This series seeks to foster intellectually diverse approaches to thinking about the law and its role, scope and effectiveness in the context of corporate activity. In so doing the series aims to publish works of high intellectual content and theoretical rigour.

Titles in this series

The Foundations and Anatomy of Shareholder Activism
Iris H-Y Chiu

Corporate Governance in the Shadow of the State
Marc T Moore

Reconceptualising Corporate Compliance
Anna Donovan

Corporate Opportunities: A Law and Economics Analysis
Marco Claudio Corradi

The Making of the Modern Company
Susan Watson

Court-Supervised Restructuring of Large Distressed Companies in Asia: Law and Policy
Wai Yee Wan

Activist Shareholders in Corporate Governance: The Australian Experience and its Comparative Implications
Tim Bowley

Investment Management, Stewardship and Sustainability: Transformation and Challenges in Law and Regulation
Edited by Iris H–Y Chiu and Hans-Christopher Hirt

Diversity. Merit and Power in the C-Suite
Eleanore Hickman

Shareholders and Stakeholders: The Unrealised Promise of Company Law Reform in Post-War Britain
Joanne F Sonin

The Origins of Company Law

Methods and Approaches

Edited by
Victoria Barnes
and
Jonathan Hardman

•HART•
OXFORD • LONDON • NEW YORK • NEW DELHI • SYDNEY

HART PUBLISHING

Bloomsbury Publishing Plc

Kemp House, Chawley Park, Cumnor Hill, Oxford, OX2 9PH, UK

1385 Broadway, New York, NY 10018, USA

29 Earlsfort Terrace, Dublin 2, Ireland

HART PUBLISHING, the Hart/Stag logo, BLOOMSBURY and the Diana logo are trademarks of Bloomsbury Publishing Plc

First published in Great Britain 2024

A catalogue record for this book is available from the British Library.

A catalogue record for this book is available from the Library of Congress.

Library of Congress Control Number: 2024944237

ISBN: HB: 978-1-50996-444-4
ePDF: 978-1-50996-446-8
ePub: 978-1-50996-445-1

Typeset by Compuscript Ltd, Shannon

Contents

List of Contributors .... *vii*

Introduction 1
Victoria Barnes and Jonathan Hardman

1. *When did English Company Law Begin?* 7
Victoria Barnes and Sally Wheeler

2. *On Mistakes and Trajectories: Using History in Normative Company Law* 27
Jonathan Hardman

3. *New Approaches in Corporate Law History: History as a Resource for Navigating Uncertain Times* 49
Sarah Wilson

4. *The Unexpected Origins of the US Limited Liability Partnership* 71
Harwell Wells

5. *Upending the State's Power to Regulate Corporate Separateness* 91
Robert B Thompson

6. Salomon *and* Sequana*: The Central Significance of Separate Legal Entity* 117
Susan Watson

7. *Three Regimes: Corporations and Regulation in US History* 141
Naomi R Lamoreaux

8. *Early American Corporations and the Public Purpose* 161
Eric Hilt

9. *Capitalism as Personal: Brunner, Mond & Co Ltd (1881–1926)* 183
Lorraine Talbot

10. *The Corporate Share: From Membership to Financial Interest to Contractual Design* 209
Ron Harris

11. *Natural Unity? The Origins of the Principle of Inseparability of Voting Rights from Shares across Jurisdictions* 229
Jennifer Trinks

12. *From Managerialism to Shareholder Primacy: The Role of the Cohen Committee and the Bank of England* 249
Andrew Johnston

13. *'A Few Pike in a Trout River'? Hostile Take-Over Bids and Dividend Restraint: The Debate in Government in the 1950s* 273
Neil Rollings

14. *The Right to Repose in Peace: The Making of Modern Company Law* 295
Paddy Ireland

15. *Epilogue* 327
Victoria Barnes and Jonathan Hardman

Index 335

List of Contributors

Dr Victoria Barnes is a Reader in Commercial Law at Queen's University Belfast and Honorary Reader at Brunel University London.

Dr Jonathan Hardman is a Senior Lecturer in Company and Commercial Law at the University of Edinburgh and an Honorary Associate Professor at the University of Auckland.

Professor Ron Harris is the Kalman Lubowsky Professor of Law and History at Tel-Aviv University.

Professor Eric Hilt is Professor of Economics at Wellesley College.

Professor Paddy Ireland is Professor of Law at the University of Bristol.

Professor Andrew Johnston is Professor of Company Law and Corporate Governance at the University of Warwick.

Professor Naomi Lamoreaux is a Senior Research Scholar at the University of Michigan and the Stanley B. Resor Professor Emeritus of Economics and Professor Emeritus of History at Yale University.

Professor Neil Rollings is Professor of Economic and Business History at the University of Glasgow.

Professor Lorraine Talbot is Professor of Company Law in Context at the University of Birmingham.

Professor Robert Thompson is the Peter P. Weidenbruch Jr. Professor of Business Law at Georgetown University.

Dr Jennifer Trinks is a Senior Research Fellow at the Max Planck Institute for Comparative and International Private Law, Hamburg.

Professor Susan Watson is Professor of Law and Dean of Business & Economics at the University of Auckland.

Professor Harwell Wells is the Richard H. Walker Chair in Law at Temple University.

Professor Sally Wheeler OBE is Vice-Chancellor of Birkbeck, University of London and Honorary Professor of Law at the Australian National University.

Dr Sarah Wilson is a Reader in Law at the University of York.

Introduction

VICTORIA BARNES AND JONATHAN HARDMAN

I. USES OF THE PAST

THIS EDITED COLLECTION emerged from the Society of Legal Scholars' Annual Seminar, which was hosted in York in 2022. This workshop was, like most workshops, several years in the making. Then the relationship between law and capitalism was being recast. This is what brought the group of scholars, who were working at the crossroads of company law and history, together. The key tenets of company law were being questioned often using ideas from the past. Politicians, policy-makers and members of the public alike, debated the virtues of economic history. In 2019, then democratic presidential candidate, Elizabeth Warren proposed to introduce a system of corporate chartering.[1] This would require big businesses to apply to the United States (US) federal government for corporate rights and mark a return to the system of company regulation of the seventeenth and eighteenth centuries.[2] At roughly the same time, Boris Johnson sought the advice of business leaders for his proposal to undertake regulatory change in the United Kingdom (UK).[3] This would undo the changes brought about over the course of the last half century, through the UK's membership in the European Union (EU).[4] In the Anglo-American sphere, regulation of the corporate form became seen as a logical way of shaping company behaviour, but age-old methods seem to be preferred over novel or untested ideas. The time felt ripe to revaluate the history of company law and for business organisations, more generally. These debates, of course, continue today.

This collection comprises some of the papers presented at that event. It brings together scholarship that aims to inform those debates about the past, which are taking place in the present. The contributors are largely Anglo-American in

[1] T Newmyer, 'Elizabeth Warren Takes on Corporate Giants as She Lays 2020 Marker' *Washington Post* (17 July 2020) www.washingtonpost.com/news/powerpost/paloma/the-finance-202/2018/08/16/the-finance-202-elizabeth-warren-takes-on-corporate-giants-as-she-lays-2020-marker/5b746bc91b326b7234392946/ accessed 29 April 2024.

[2] See chs 7, 8 and 10.

[3] D Thomas and G Parker, 'Boris Johnson Vows to Business He Will Seize "Opportunities of Brexit"' *Financial Times* (18 January 2021) www.ft.com/content/1c4942da-5849-4082-b15e-ea78f73c7f9b accessed 29 April 2024.

[4] See ch 11 for European insights.

focus. Historical research is essential here not only because it provides a more informed view about the present legal rules, but also because it corrects misunderstandings and misapprehensions about the past. This collection examines the historical origins of company law to show how this body of law developed to become the rules which we are now familiar with. This involves showcasing periods as antecedents of present debates.[5] Such explorations reveal regulatory lessons from previous legal regimes that policy-makers now seek. They also show instances of path dependency,[6] which remain useful for those in the present seeking to make change or to understand where or when this policy began. Aside from this, chapters here also unpick pivotal legal events and explain drivers for legal change.[7] The knowledge gathered about the evolution of company law from this collection informs those engaged in law-making and the policy-making agenda looking to understand the past.

It also brings together scholarly work and different viewpoints on the development of company law. Since (at least) the Companies Act of 2006, company law in the UK at least is no longer seen as a disparate and eclectic set of principles, doctrines and rules.[8] As a body of law, however, company law has far longer historic roots. In the sixteenth and seventeenth centuries, governments granted a small number of firms monopolies on trade within an industry or sector.[9] The Industrial Revolution of the eighteenth and nineteenth centuries is often seen as a fulcrum for modern commercial law with the rise in enterprise, every day commercial transactions and arbitration.[10] The emergence of big business in the twentieth century, too, resulted in fundamental changes in structure of socio-economic relations, such as the development of managerial hierarchies,[11] the separation between ownership and control,[12] an increasingly impersonal relationship between employer and worker,[13] and substantial inequalities in wealth and power.[14] These events all brought about shifts in the relationship between law (including corporate law) and the economy. The corporate economy was seen as a development of a liberal ideology and political vision.[15]

[5] See chs 5, 6, 12 and 13.

[6] See chs 1, 2 and 3.

[7] See chs 4, 9 and 14.

[8] P Hood, 'Directors' Duties Under the Companies Act 2006: Clarity or Confusion?' (2013) 13 *Journal of Corporate Law Studies* 1; D Ahern, 'Codification of Company Law: Taking Stock of the Companies Act 2006' (2014) 35 *Statute Law Review* 230.

[9] WR Scott, *The Constitution and Finance of English, Scottish and Irish Joint-Stock Companies to 1720*, vol 1 (Cambridge, Cambridge University Press, 1911).

[10] R Cranston, *Making Commercial Law Through Practice 1830–1970* (Cambridge, Cambridge University Press, 2021).

[11] AD Chandler Jr, *The Visible Hand* (Cambridge, Harvard University Press, 1993).

[12] AA Berle, and GC Means, *The Modern Corporation And Private Property*, 1st edn (New York, MacMillan, 1933).

[13] L Hannah, *The Rise of the Corporate Economy*, 2nd edn (London, Methuen, 1983).

[14] T Piketty, *Capital in the Twenty-First Century* (Cambridge, Harvard University Press, 2014).

[15] WR Cornish and G de N Clark, *Law and Society in England: 1750–1950* (Oxford, Hart Publishing, 2019) 266.

Company law is one such topic that has frequently lacked systemic historical attention and so its historical development has usually been under theorised. This is in part due to the fractured nature of company law as a field of law. Company law is a relatively new area of law. What we understand now to be company law would have historically been thought of more commonly as the law of equity and trusts in England. This lack of distinct or clear identity has stymied the development of company law as a standalone topic or a singular field of inquiry. Early company law commentators had to work out where to fit their unit of study within law's taxonomy before they could commence full conceptualisation of it. Another reason which helps to explain the slow emergence of scholarly research on the history of company law is the confines of disciplinary thinking.[16] This collection gathers those leading scholars working in a doctrinal and socio-legal method. This in itself is not always simple. Yet, it also brings in another group, namely those without a legal background, such as economists, historians, sociologists and management scholars working on related themes. These diverse scholars are brought deliberately into the mixture. Differences in disciplinary approaches will spark innovative debates about doctrinal evolution in company law and also about the uses and abuses of the past in contemporary debates.[17]

The title reflects our aim to bring together discussions about the origins of company law from a variety of different disciplines. The use of the word 'origins' suggest that the scholarship contained within the collection is historical in nature, but it is distinctly different from 'legal origins' and the literature therein.[18] It also makes it distinguishable from a straight forward historical account. Although these chapters are all discussions about the beginnings of company law, the methodologies used here push beyond a simple or singular history of company law.

[16] Some see fields or areas of law as disciplines. This suggests that they have a distinctive method in their own right. One example is comparative law. It is difficult to see such an approach in company law.

[17] This literature has not yet been integrated into legal scholarship. The seminal methodological text in history is: M MacMillan, *The Uses and Abuses of History* (London, Profile, 2010). More recently, economic historians have begun exploring lessons from history or the memorialisation of past events as a method of learning. See J Mokyr, 'The Past and the Future of Innovation: Some Lessons from Economic History' (2018) 69 *Explorations in Economic History* 13; Y Cassis and CR Schenk (eds), *Remembering and Learning from Financial Crises* (Oxford, Oxford University Press, 2021); MA O'Sullivan, 'History as Heresy: Unlearning the Lessons of Economic Orthodoxy' (2022) 75 *The Economic History Review* 297. Other business and economic history challenge the use of the past and see the use of history more cynically as a story that can be abused. See C Lubinski, 'From "History as Told" to "History as Experienced": Contextualizing the Uses of the Past' (2018) 39 *Organization Studies* 1785; RD Wadhwani and others, 'History as Organizing: Uses of the Past in Organization Studies' (2018) 39 *Organization Studies* 1663; V Barnes and L Newton, 'Visualizing Organizational Identity: The History of a Capitalist Enterprise' (2018) 13 *Management & Organizational History* 24.

[18] There are some limited methodological similarities between the debate about legal origins and this collection. These similarities are methodological rather than substantive ones. The legal origins literature uses quantitative and global or international and comparative frameworks and several of the chapters employ them here too.

These chapters provide histories (in the plural) of company law. Our intention is to bring together those different histories of company law; to embrace and showcase the different manners and ways of conducting legal and historical research. We now turn to discuss the rationale behind this approach in more detail.

II. OPENNESS AND DIVERSITY IN METHODS

Each contributor was asked to be upfront about their argument, aims and methods. Historians predominately engage in the creation of narratives. The chapters here are deliberately a mixture of aims and methods, although, it would be fair to say, that they mainly tell stories about law in the past. How is a narrative about law constructed? What are its value and limitations? The following sections examine the various methods on show here and their advantages for answering certain questions in research.

The value of historical narratives is perhaps best explained by the seminal text by EH Carr. To start this discussion, he cited the work of Sir George Clark, who stated that:

> Historians … expect their work to be superseded again and again. They consider that knowledge of the past has come down through one or more human minds, has been 'processed' by them, and therefore cannot consist of elemental and impersonal atoms which nothing can alter … The exploration seems to be endless, and some impatient scholars take refuge in sceptism, or at least in the doctrine that, since all historical judgements involve persons and points of view, one is as good as another and there is no 'objective' historical truth.[19]

Carr disagreed with this sentiment as he saw too open a contradiction as often being 'flagrant' leaving the 'field open to inquiry'.[20] He lamented some of the disagreements he saw in the field on the grounds that they present a picture of a weak field. Both Clark and Carr were, in their own ways, entirely correct. History, and law, for that matter, is not a science. It cannot be falsified in the same way a scientific experiment can be falsified. How can one have proof that something did not happen? That proof does not exist. We can simply prove that an event did happen. Carr did not disagree entirely with Clark, but he simply urged scholars to exercise some caution in how they discuss the work of others. He acknowledged explicitly that historians interpret. Lawyers, of course, do the same. He states that:

> History consists of a corpus of ascertained facts. The facts are available to the historian in documents, instructions and so on, like fish on the fishmonger's slab. The historian collects them, takes them home and cooks and serves them in whatever style appeals to him.[21]

[19] EH Carr, *What Is History?: The George Macaulay Trevelyan Lectures Delivered in the University of Cambridge January March 1961* (London, Penguin, 1987) 8.
[20] ibid 8.
[21] ibid 9.

In Carr's view, there was – and is – very naturally some variation between historians and among histories. Scholarly discourse has, of course, changed substantially since then. Carr wrote in 1961 and Clark in 1957. The challenge brought by postmodernism came to history in the 1980s.[22] It reduced the value of historical narratives; lamented them as 'subjective' or 'teleological' and thus not particularly meaningful. Historians have responded perhaps more slowly than other disciplines.[23] Although some did embrace postmodernism, few were keen to embraced postmodernist thinking and some responded strongly against it.[24] Historians with their emphasis on empiricism are less likely to be swayed by high theory. Some of the methodological advice on dealing with postmodernism is simply to select more reliable sources.[25] Is law, perhaps, somehow or in any way different to history? Most would be hard pressed to argue that law resembled the hard sciences.[26] Lawyers often engage in a process of interpreting words, whether that be words in a statute, judgment or other document. Common lawyers, at least, present those interpretations in a court room, where they build that interpretation into an argument. Their interpretation and overall argument are those most favourable to their client. Judges, as well as those in the courtroom, decide on which of the two arguments has the most merit and is the most persuasive.[27] In this sense, there is very little difference between the work of the historian and the work of the lawyer. Except, perhaps, for the fact that the lawyer expects his, her or their argument to be one of several different interpretations.

The academic world in both law and history is also no longer small nor is it as personal as it once was. With the increase in the size of law schools,[28] success is not simply built on prestige or reputation alone. Formal metrics and policies have been introduced to measure outputs. These are, in many ways, levelling. They allow individuals to be judged fairly without biases creeping in. As such, they are good for minority groups. They improve diversity or, in the words of Marxist critique, they act as a counterbalance for hegemonic replication. They have been accompanied by an increase in size and the formalisation of policies around hiring and promotions. Whilst in most ways this has been a force for good, it also places greater pressures upon individuals, as 'success' in the field and suitability for progression have also become more quantified and more standard. This, in turn, discourages heterodox work.

[22] M Bevir, J Hargis and S Rushing (eds), *Histories of Postmodernism* (Abington, Routledge, 2012).

[23] E Breisach, *On the Future of History: The Postmodernist Challenge and Its Aftermath* (Chicago, University of Chicago Press, 2003); K Yilmaz, 'Postmodernism and Its Challenge to the Discipline of History: Implications for History Education' (2010) 42 *Educational Philosophy and Theory* 779.

[24] One might look to Richard Evan's book as a good example: R Evans, *In Defence of History* (New York, Granta Books, 2001).

[25] L Jordanova, *History in Practice*, 2nd edn (London, Bloomsbury Academic, 2006).

[26] Branches of law and, indeed, history, might well.

[27] J Herring, *How to Argue: Powerfully, Persuasively, Positively* (New Jersey, Pearson, 2012).

[28] A Hudson, 'Two Futures for Law Schools' (2021) 55 *The Law Teacher* 101.

Take, for instance, the seminal work of Brian Simpson on landmark cases in the 1990s, with a stated aim to 'show that we can obtain greater enjoyment' from them.[29] As he was writing this work, he was at this point at the height of his career.[30] He could afford to write fairly luxurious pieces about legal history that were openly fun, fanciful and amusing. Such a blasé approach is plainly likeable, intellectually honest and commendable. Sadly, it is probably no longer tenable. Nowadays, academics in the UK, at least, are asked formally to justify their work to internal assessors in terms of its originality, significance and rigour. This is the framework used by the Research Excellence Framework. The simplest way to claim to be original is to lament failings in the work of others, or to 'challenge' it. This play may help individuals score highly in internal school-based assessment,[31] but does nothing to help promote the field or area of law, history or legal history as a whole. It can undermine an entire area of research, as Carr says. This is a field where scholars write on top of one another and they quite naturally have different interpretations of events.

This collection aims to build bridges among new interpretations of the past and new historical narratives. It constructs a research agenda that is not coherent. Indeed, it does not intend to be so. But what this collection does do is embrace difference in a positive way. This is a body of scholarship that we understand from the start will be different – and we acknowledge that explicitly and clearly. Studies which yield different results are commended. The broad interdisciplinary approach advocated here is not new nor is it in itself ground-breaking. Yet, the explicit nature of the claims here across this collection about the positive value of difference are useful. Overall, difference in opinion is seen here to be beneficial and it gives fertile ground for the growth of a research field. This is an area where diversity in approaches and methods should be seen as complementary. The combination of them enhances an area of scholarship.

[29] AWB Simpson, *Leading Cases in the Common Law* (Oxford, Clarendon Press, 1996) vii.

[30] For more on Simpson's path, see D Sugarman, 'Brian Simpson's Approach to Legal Scholarship and the Significance of Reflections on "The Concept of Law"' (2012) 3 *Transnational Legal Theory* 112.

[31] The individual scores given the REF panel, which matter, are, of course, not given out individually. Individuals remain anonymous. Only aggregate scores for a unit are publicised.

1

When did English Company Law Begin?

VICTORIA BARNES AND SALLY WHEELER

I. INTRODUCTION

MOST HISTORIANS ARE of the view that modern company law came into being with the Joint Stock Companies Act of 1844 and/or the Limited Liability Act of 1855.[1] For those who see the 1844 Act as being a pivotal moment, it is because the 1844 Act created the possibility of incorporating a company by registration and gave shareholders a standard set of rights, which was not evident for deed of settlement companies. Rix considers that the 1844 Act 'marked the end of a phase rather than a beginning, with its emphasis less on [the] facilitation [of] new enterprise [but rather] on the regulation of unincorporated joint stock companies of the type that then existed'.[2] Others see the passage of the limited liability legislation as ushering in the modern business form. Bryer remarks that '[i]t is widely agreed that the coming of limited liability in the Joint-Stock Companies Act of 1855 marked a revolutionary change'.[3] Similarly Rob McQueen explains

> [u]nlike some other institutional reforms of the nineteenth century, corporation law is an area of reform in which a precise event apparently delineates the 'new' from the 'old', the 'modern' from the 'past' – this event being the introduction of the Limited Liability Act of 1855 and the Joint Stock Companies Act of 1856.[4]

[1] Another of interest is the Companies Act of 1862 and Companies Act of 1856.

[2] See MS Rix, 'Company Law: 1844 and To-Day' (1945) 55 *The Economic Journal* 242, 242. See also G Todd, 'Some Aspects of Joint Stock Companies, 1844–1900' (1932) 4 *The Economic History Review* 46; AC Storrar and KC Pratt, 'Accountability vs Privacy, 1844–1907: The Coming of the Private Company' (2000) 10 *Accounting, Business & Financial History* 259; M Freeman, R Pearson and J Taylor, *Shareholder Democracies?: Corporate Governance in Britain and Ireland before 1850* (Chicago, University of Chicago Press, 2011).

[3] RA Bryer, 'The Mercantile Laws Commission of 1854 and the Political Economy of Limited Liability' (1997) 50 *The Economic History Review* 37, 37.

[4] It is worth noting that while describing this view, McQueen argues against a teleological account of company law. R McQueen, *A Social History of Company Law: Great Britain and the Australian Colonies 1854–1920* (Farnham, Ashgate Publishing Ltd, 2013) 8.

There is a longstanding tradition of viewing legislation as a tipping point and so by definition it marks the beginning or the end of a study.[5] In the context of company law it is obvious that this is one way to understand the roots of contemporary company law. Both the 1844 and 1855 Acts were two lengthy pieces of modern statutory law[6] giving a standard shape and structure to the companies incorporated under them.

This chapter takes a different and novel approach to explaining the origins of modern company law. It identifies the tranche of landmark cases that come together to shape the field of company law. These are often forgotten by those who see the beginnings of modern company law in legislation. Our approach does not intend to place statutory intervention at the edge of company law or suggest that it is entirely non-material. Explaining the origins of company law through cases compliments the existing legislative histories of company law. As legal instruments, legislation has many advantages over common law, particularly if the user group or audience are not legally trained. Codes are much easier to digest.[7] This is the case with the Companies Act 2006. Its users are not just lawyers but businessmen, entrepreneurs and traders. However the length and the sheer breadth of the Companies Act 2006 is testament to the general difficulties of codifying complex areas of common law in the context of a consolidated legislative instrument.[8] It is important to acknowledge that the Acts of 1844 and 1855 gave foundational structures. There was a vast body of case law that preceded these rules. The doctrines they reflect were once encapsulated by the

[5] For in depth studies of the passage of limited liability legislation, see HA Shannon, 'The Coming of General Limited Liability' (1931) 41 *The Economic Journal* 267; BC Hunt, *The Development of the Business Corporation in England, 1800–1867* (Boston MA, Harvard University Press, 1936); PL Cottrell, *Industrial Finance, 1830–1914: The Finance and Organization of English Manufacturing Industry* (London, Methuen, 1980) ch 3; CE Amsler, RL Bartlett and CJ Bolton, 'Thoughts of Some British Economists on Early Limited Liability and Corporate Legislation' (1981) 13 *History of Political Economy* 774; M Gillman and T Eade, 'The Development of the Corporation in England, with Emphasis on Limited Liability' (1995) 22 *International Journal of Social Economics* 20; D Loftus, 'Capital and Community: Limited Liability and Attempts to Democratize the Market in Mid-Nineteenth-Century England' (2002) 45 *Victorian Studies* 93; J Taylor, *Creating Capitalism: Joint-Stock Enterprise in British Politics and Culture, 1800–1870* (Suffolk, Boydell & Brewer Ltd, 2006) ch 4; McQueen (n 4) ch 4; DC Smith, 'The Mid-Victorian Reform of Britain's Company Laws and the Moral Economy of Fair Competition' (2021) 22 (4) *Enterprise & Society* 1103. For studies that begin in 1856, see PL Payne, *The Early Scottish Limited Companies, 1856–1895: An Historical and Analytical Survey* (Edinburgh, Scottish Academic Press, 1980).

[6] The Repeal of the Bubble Act 1825 was no such statute. With only two sections, which were lengthy, it represented the statutory drafting of a fore gone era. There is also a good body of work examining both the drafting of the Bubble Act, its impact and its repeal. See AB DuBois, *The English Business Company after the Bubble Act 1720–1800* (London, The Commonwealth Fund, 1938); R Harris, 'The Bubble Act: Its Passage and Its Effects on Business Organization' (1994) 54 *The Journal of Economic History* 610; R Harris, 'The Bubble Act: Its Passage and Its Effects on Business Organization' (1994) 54 *The Journal of Economic History* 610; R Harris, 'Political Economy, Interest Groups, Legal Institutions, and the Repeal of the Bubble Act in 1825' (1997) 50 *The Economic History Review* 675; M Patterson and D Reiffen, 'The Effect of the Bubble Act on the Market for Joint Stock Shares' (1990) 50 *The Journal of Economic History* 163.

[7] M Arden, 'Time for an English Commercial Code?' (1997) 56 *The Cambridge Law Journal* 516.

[8] R Goode, 'The Codification of Commercial Law' (1988) 14 *Monash University Law Review* 135.

common law alone. Some of these historic cases remain influential now and so they have a close relationship to current legal thinking. If we are to understand the evolution of concepts and categories, though, there are good reasons to examine waves of case law as much as key legislative interventions. Other cases have fallen into disuse. They are outdated and perhaps even obsolete. They are representative of commercial practices that no longer occur or, indeed, age-old doctrinal thinking. These legal ideas have no place in the present and as such there is a weak relationship to today's commerce and society.

To identify those historic cases, which are still commonplace and used in contemporary legal thinking, this chapter examines cases cited in the latest editions of five leading textbooks. This creates a cumulative dataset of over 6,000 cases. In adopting an empirical approach, this chapter builds on a stream of work that has both informed and transformed debates in company law in recent years. At a macro level, studies of interlocks (board to board ties) and elites as directors and executives have informed discussions around boardroom diversity and directors' duties[9] using tools such as network analysis.[10] Perhaps from a more intensely 'law' perspective, there is the extensive literature surrounding the 'law matters' thesis[11] and variations upon it,[12] which whilst it might be critiqued from methodological[13] and comparative law[14] perspectives, has nevertheless placed empirically informed work in a stronger position within company law than it enjoys in any other field of law outside possibly international law[15] and those areas where socio-legal studies now provide the

[9] See, eg, E Heemskerk, 'The social field of the European corporate elite: a network analysis of interlocking directorates among Europe's largest corporate boards' (2011) 11 *Global Networks* 440 and G Davis, M Yoo and W Baker 'The small world of the American corporate elite, 1982–2001' (2003) 1 *Strategic Organization* 301.

[10] European lawyers have created a lively debate on the use of network analysis to track the influence of particular decisions in the ECJ, see M Derlen and J Lindholm, 'Is it Good Law? Network Analysis and the CJEU's Internal Market Jurisprudence' (2017) 20 *Journal of International Economic Law* 257 and 'Goodbye *van Gend en Loos*, Hello *Bosman*? Using Network Analysis to Measure the Importance of Individual CJEU Judgments' (2014) 20 *European Law Journal* 667; *cf* J Frankenreiter, 'Network Analysis and the Use of Precedent in the Case Law of the CJEU – A Reply to Derlén and Lindholm' (2017) 18 *German Law Journal* 687.

[11] R La Porta, F Lopez-de-Silanes, A Shleifer and R Vishny, 'Legal Determinants of External Finance' (1997) 52 *Journal of Finance* 1131.

[12] D Cabrelli and M Siems, 'Convergence, Legal Origins, and Transplants in Comparative Corporate Law: A Case-Based and Quantitative Analysis' (2015) 63 *American Journal of Comparative Law* 109 and L LoPucki, 'A Rule-Based Method for Comparing Corporate Laws' (2018) 94 *Notre Dame Law Review* 263.

[13] J Armour, S Deakin, P Sarkar, M Siems & A Singh, 'Shareholder Protection and Stock Market Development: An Empirical Test of the Legal Origins Hypothesis' (2009) 6 *Journal of Empirical Legal Studies* 343 and B Cheffins, 'Does Law Matter? The Separation of Ownership and Control in the United Kingdom' (2001) 30 *Journal of Legal Studies* 30.

[14] M Siems, 'The Web of Creditor and Shareholder Protection in 25 Countries: A Comparative Legal Network Analysis' (2010) 27 *Arizona Journal of Comparative and International Law* 747.

[15] See, eg, W Alschner, 'The Computational Methods in International Law' in R Deplano and N Tsagourias (eds) *Research Methods in International Law* (Cheltenham, Edward Elgar, 2021) 203 and S Fobbe, 'Introducing twin corpora of decisions for the International Court of Justice (ICJ) and the Permanent Court of International Justice (PCIJ)' [2022] *Journal of Empirical Legal Studies* 491.

dominant tradition; family law and criminal justice are good examples. At a more micro level and focusing on the UK, there is the excellent work of Alan Dignam and Peter Oh[16] on collating and codifying the circumstances in which courts have been prepared to disregard the principle of corporate separate legal personality finally articulated by the House of Lords in *Salomon v Salomon*[17] which itself draws on earlier empirical studies in the UK and US.[18]

By examining the historic cases cited by these five textbooks, we consider:

- When did modern company law, as we understand it today, begin?
- Which cases are relevant in understanding modern company law?
- When were the principles of modern company law were settled and recognisable?

Using this dataset, we reveal the cases, doctrines and principles that are widely perceived to be the origins of modern company law.

We find diverging views on when company law began. With some cases dismissed and others included, we suggest that there is room for more theorisation, discussion and consensus on the usefulness of these first mover and pioneering cases. At times the dividing line between when historic cases can be used fruitfully to explain principles of modern company law, and whether they should be deemed obsolete, is a fine one. This chapter engages critically with these cases and their potential use and abuse in company law.

II. HISTORIC CASES AND THEIR FUNCTION

This section explores ideas on when and how to use cases. It develops the criterion on which cases are seen to be of importance, ranking them from low importance to high importance. An important feature here is the reception of those cases and the discussion of them. We describe these cases as 'forgotten', 'obsolete', 'key' and 'seminal cases'. This taxonomic categorisation avoids using the term 'landmark case' for the reason that this is now highly contested term with a multitude of different meanings.[19] This chapter does not intend to unify or challenge presumptions in the literature on 'what a "landmark" case is' not

[16] A Dignam and P Oh, 'Disregarding the Salomon Principle: An Empirical Analysis, 1885–2014' (2019) 39 *Oxford Journal of Legal Studies* 16.

[17] *Salomon v Salomon & Co Ltd* [1897] AC 22.

[18] C Mitchell, 'Lifting the Corporate Veil: An Empirical Study' (1999) 3 *Company Financial & Insolvency Law Review* 15 and R Thompson, 'Piercing the Corporate Veil: An Empirical Study' (1991) 76 *Cornell L Rev* 1036.

[19] The *Landmark Case in …* series has, for example, over 10 volumes with more planned. These books focus on foundational cases and typically cover fields of law, such as contract, property, torts, as one might well expect but also now also extend to the more specialist and idiosyncratic areas of law, namely, medical law, intellectual property law and so on.

least because this subject is often approached as a closed question. The distinction between 'landmark' case or not is narrowing in a way.[20] This section instead attempts to broaden this thinking and add to, diversify, and widen the language that might be used to discuss the status of historic cases. It provides a layering up process through which cases are rank.

A. Forgotten Cases

Our first and lowest grouping is forgotten cases. Forgotten cases are cases, which are reported. This is the first requirement and an essential one – because not all cases are reported.[21] Unreported cases were not remembered in the first place, simply put. Unreported cases were especially common in the era before the formalisation of law reporting. Where there was no barrister present in the courtroom to listen, make notes and turn them into a fully-fledged law report, no law report could be made. Without a consistent or solid method for reporting cases, barristers would make notes of cases and use them as precedents even in instances when they did not develop or push common law doctrines. Cases were not reported thereafter, when law reporting became formalised, often because the case did not make new law. Forgotten cases were, therefore, once important and used. They are ordinary and perhaps illustrative of a wider rule, but they are now no longer meaningful in any way.

B. Obsolete Cases

Obsolete cases are the second lowest tier and distinctly different to forgotten cases. This is because they are now what we might describe as 'bad' law. They were once examples of good law. As such, we use them but not to discuss present law. These cases are of use predominantly to legal historians because they apply to the operations and practises of a historical society in the past. They show an old rule that has been overturned or regulate a commercial practice that has now ceased. These cases have no relationship to present day law. The case itself is a relic of a time now passed and its use is confined to understanding historical development of an area of law.

[20] Chapters in the *Landmark* series commonly consider whether the case really is a landmark and whether it deserves the status that it has achieved.

[21] Law is recorded in different sources. One example here is judicial notebooks, which are private resources for judges, but these are rarely thought to have any precedential value. HR Medina, 'Trial Judge's Notes A Study in Judicial Administration' (1963) 49 *Cornell Law Quarterly* 1; CJ Stiegler, 'The Precedential Effect of Unpublished Judicial Opinions under Louisiana Law' (2013) 59 *Loyola Law Review* 535.

C. Key Cases

Key cases are legal precedents that still stand today as 'good' law. They are memorable, but they are not pivotal case for that doctrine or area as it stands, today. They are a cases that stand firmly and clearly for a proposition of law. This might be a case with a judgment that is developed and insightful, but is also limited in its scope. This point is, of course, relative. In order to establish that a case has gaps or is confined to a certain point, there must be another case which provides a better assessment of the area or limits the particular rule to a set of factual circumstances. A key case might also be useful for the *obiter dicta* it contains or for clarification of points that were previously agreed. Key cases are typical pioneers for an area. They are the first mover or 'origin' cases for a certain doctrine, which begin to develop an area of law but do not settle it.[22]

D. Seminal Cases

The final and highest category here are seminal cases. These are the leading cases for a particular doctrine. They are legal precedents sitting on the tip of the tongue. Seminal cases are extensive in their judgments and application. They have defined a doctrine, challenged settled thinking or made sense of a complicated doctrine stemming from an incoherent set of cases. They are naturally from the highest courts and most eminent legal minds because of the hierarchical nature of courts in common law thinking. This is of course rather tongue in cheek – not all cases are held in such high esteem and not all deserve such high praise. However, a good number remain fundamental in our understanding of the landscape of modern law.

Table 1.1 Categories for cases

Category	Importance	Characteristics
Forgotten	Low	Reported but no longer cited widely
Obsolete	Low	Bad law
Key	Medium	Good law that remains of some practical utility and in current circulation
Seminal	High	Good law that is exemplary of a principle, doctrine or rule and defines it in its current state

[22] An obvious modern example of this is *Aluminium Industrie Vaasen BV v Romalpa Aluminium* [1976] 1 WLR 676. The principle of reservation of title clauses was first judicially approved here but later cases such as *Clough Mill Ltd v Geoffrey Martin* [1985] BCLC 64 and *Hendy Lennox (Industrial Engines) Ltd. v Grahame Puttick Ltd.* [1984] 1 WLR 485 are of much more significance in developing and delineating the application of these clauses in English law, see C Kelly and J Davey, 'Romalpa and Contractual Innovation' (2015) 42 *Journal of Law and Society* 358.

There are several ways to classify cases according to their importance and relevance today. Table 1.1 provides a brief overview of our categorisation of these cases. It ranges from cases of low importance to those which define (or redefine) a doctrine. We now turn to explain how we have identified the cases in current circulation through company law textbooks.

III. METHOD

To construct our sample of important cases in the history of English company law, we used the following five textbooks:

1. Dignam & Lowry, *Company Law*,
2. Hannigan, *Company Law*,
3. Mayson, French & Ryan, *Company Law*,
4. *Pettet, Lowry & Reisberg's Company Law*, and
5. Sealy & Worthington, *Text, Cases and Materials in Company Law*.

We do not include *Gower's Principles of Modern Company Law* in this sample because one of the authors, Sarah Worthington, is also the author of *Sealy & Worthington's Text, Cases and Materials in Company Law*. To ensure that the sample contains the widest range of views possible, the selection of leading textbooks should include those written by as different and diverse voices as possible. We opted for *Sealy & Worthington's Text, Cases and Materials in Company Law* over *Gower's Principles of Modern Company Law* because, simply put, the former, as the title suggests, ought to contain more cases. We do not examine the *Anatomy of Corporate Law* or any other comparative company law textbook within this sample because they ostensibly focus on company law from different jurisdictions; they are not principally concerned with the development of English law. The latest editions of these five textbooks were all written in the last seven years. Those written by Hannigan and Mayson, French & Ryan were published in 2021. Dignam & Lowry's textbook was published in 2020, Pettet, Lowry & Reisberg in 2018, and, finally, Sealy & Worthington's textbook was published in 2016. These editions provide us with most recent interpretations of the law as it is seen today.

The table of cases in each of these five textbooks is then used to construct a database. To make this list, the tables are first turned into machine readable data. The individual entries are broken down into four fields: case name, year, reference, and the citations within the textbook. For those cases with two years, the first year is taken (eg, 1874–75 becomes 1874). Although this is not the case among all of the textbooks, for the most part, the report of appeal decisions and earlier decisions are listed separately. This list, therefore, contains both in some cases. We first discuss the volume of historic cases before considering their importance within the landscape of company law.

IV. VOLUME OF HISTORIC CASES

This section explores the extent to which cases reported before or at the turn of the nineteenth century appear in the dataset. Figure 1.1 shows the number of cases cited from the period 1700–1900. Mayson, French & Ryan use the most historic case law and they cite around 350 cases reported in this time period. Hannigan and Sealy & Worthington employ a similar number of historic cases. Dignam & Lowry and Pettet, Lowry & Reisberg are at the lower end of this spectrum. Pettet, Lowry & Reisberg only use around 50 cases from this period in their textbook. This number is, however, somewhat misleading as a marker of the relevance they ascribe to historic case law. If we look at this number as a percentage of the total number of cases cited in their text, as Figure 1.2 shows, rather than just the volume measure shown in Figure 1.1, the idea that Pettet, Lowry & Reisberg do not see historic case law as being relevant is not sustainable.

Figure 1.2 shows the number of historic cases cited as a percentage of the overall cases cited. This allows us to see the temporal makeup of the cases in the textbook and how much of their focus is on early or historic cases, relatively speaking. Citing around 650 cases in total, Pettet, Lowry & Reisberg use the smallest number of cases in comparison to the other four textbooks. Pettet, Lowry & Reisberg's textbook favours the discussion of legislation; it is best described as statute heavy and case law light. Hannigan and Sealy & Worthington use around 1,200 and 1,400 cases respectively. Mayson, French & Ryan contains the highest number of case citations. With around 2,000 cases cited, it uses around three times the number of cases of Pettet, Lowry & Reisberg and twice as many as Dignam & Lowry.

Not only do Mayson, French & Ryan use the largest number of cases, Figure 1.2 shows they also include the largest proportion of historic cases. Around 18 per cent of the cases included in Mayson, French & Ryan are from the period 1700–1900. When we look at the total volume of cases compared with the proportion of historic cases, Pettet, Lowry & Reisberg are more reliant on historic cases than Hannigan. If we use this comparison measure for Dignam & Lowry, they engage least with historic case law as only 7 per cent of the cases they use are from this early time period we selected.

This section has shown the extent to which historic case law is used by each of the five textbooks. Whilst historical cases are present and well noted by each of the textbooks, their relative proportion of the total number of cases cited varies considerably. Each of the textbooks uses this formative case law to a differing extent and are to varying degrees elucidating principles of company law using principles from history. Mayson, French & Ryan's textbook is the clear outlier in this group and the heaviest user of historic case law. The following section examines the cases which are thought to be at the very beginning of modern company law.

Figure 1.1 Number of cases cited dating from 1700 to 1900

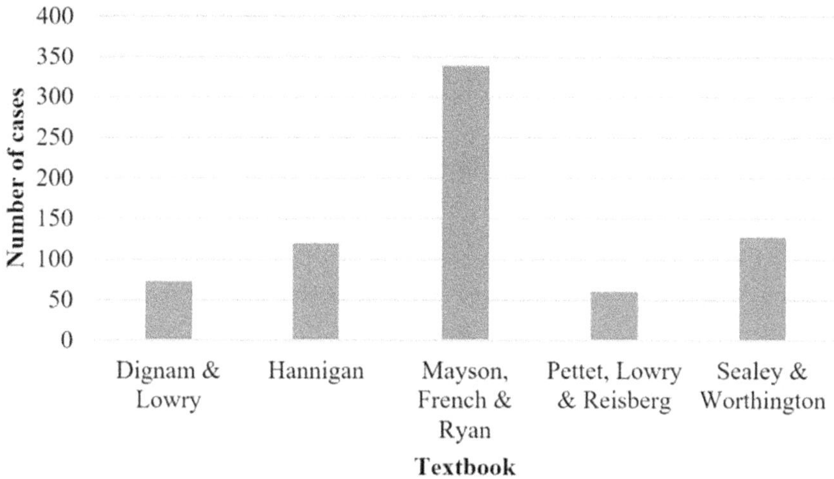

Source: Dataset.

Figure 1.2 Percentage of cases cited dating from 1700 to 1900

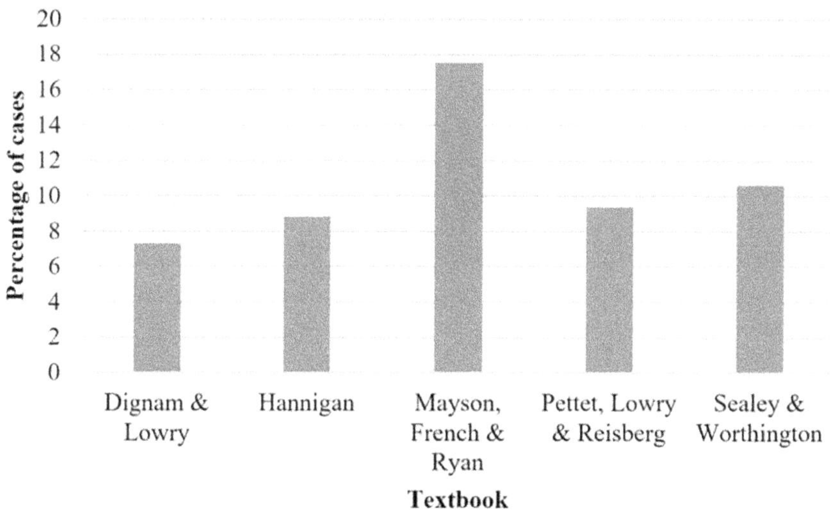

Source: Dataset.

V. THE FIRST COMPANY LAW CASES

This section provides an overview of the first six cases in company law. We elect for six because we can provide an in depth analysis of these cases with detail on the case itself and their currency in the scholarly literature surrounding the field. Table 1.2 lists the first six cases in our period chronologically and shows which textbook each is cited in. It shows that the first case was reported in 1714 and the last in 1812. This suggests that the seventeenth century is largely thought to be bereft of useful cases for company law. It is also perhaps unsurprising that the textbook with the greatest use of historic cases cites the most of these early cases. Mayson, French & Ryan cites four out of six of the first cases and is the only textbook to cite more than two out of the six.

Table 1.2 First six cases

Case name	Year	Citation	Textbook
Wilson v Tooker	1714	V Brown 193	Mayson, French & Ryan
Keech v Sandford	1726	Select Cases Temp. King 61	All
Charitable Corpn v Sutton	1742	2 Atkyns 400	Dignam & Lowry
R v Pasmore	1789	3 Term Reports 199	Mayson, French & Ryan
Wolff v Horncastle	1798	1 Bosanquet and Puller 316	Pettet, Lowry & Reisberg
Carlen v Drury	1812	1 Vesey & Beames 154	All

Source: Dataset.

A. *Williams v Tooker* (1714)

This case is cited only by Mayson, French & Ryan. The House of Lords heard *Williams v Tooker* in 1714.[23] It involved the sale of exchequer annuities, which were assigned by way of mortgage. After repeated demands for repayment, the annuities were sold on the market. The House of Lords decided that the sale was valid in law and that there was no necessity of previously foreclosing the equity of redemption. This case involves secured transactions and as such has a relationship to finance.

B. *Keech v Sandford* (1726)

For all the textbooks examined here, company law begins with *Keech v Sandford* (1726).[24] The case stems from a dispute over a lease and it discusses the role

[23] (1714) V Brown 193.
[24] (1726) Select Cases Temp. King 61.

of a trustee involving the principles of equity and trust law. The rule from *Keech v Sandford* (1726) can be expressed *simpliciter* in a single line: a fiduciary must account for profits. The judgment provides an explanation for the rule, namely that it does not depend on fraud or detriment to beneficiary, but arises from the mere fact of a profit having been made from office. For company lawyers, the case is important because they are at the base of the rules around director's duties now contained in sections 171–175 of the Companies Act 2006.

C. *Charitable Corpn v Sutton* (1742)

The case involved a charitable corporation set up for the purposes of assisting 'poor persons with sums of money by way of loan, to prevent their falling into the hands of pawnbrokers'.[25] A committee of 50 people was responsible for the running of the company. A number of unsecured loans were made which were not repaid resulting in a substantial loss of £350,000.[26] The committee members were alleged to have committed a breach of trust, fraud, and mismanagement.[27] Lord Hardwicke said of the role of committee '[b]y accepting of a trust of this sort, a person is obliged to execute it with fidelity and reasonable diligence; and it is no excuse to say that they had no benefit from it, but that it was merely honorary (ante, 60); and therefore they are within the case of common trustees'.[28] *Charitable Corpn v Sutton* (1742) is, therefore, like our first case of *Keech v Sandford* (1726), associated with the law of equity and trusts. It underpins the modern day understanding of fiduciary duties, especially those associated with negligence (or to phrase it more positively, care and skill).

D. *R v Pasmore* (1789)

The case of *R v Pasmore* (1789) involved the expiration of the corporate charter for Helleston.[29] Helleston is in Cornwall better known now as Helston.[30] The facts of the case are complex; it involved the renewal of the town's charter as well as the roles and duties of individuals associated with it. The case was heard in the Court of Common Pleas. Lord Kenyon gave the leading judgment. Here, he was clear that 'in doing so I do not confine my observations to Helleston alone, but they are applicable to corporations in general, where they have conclusive jurisdictions from the rest of the county'.[31] He explained that 'Corporations are

[25] (1742) 2 Atkyns 401.
[26] (1742) 2 Atkyns 402.
[27] (1742) 2 Atkyns 400.
[28] (1742) 2 Atkyns 406.
[29] (1789) 3 Term Reports 199.
[30] See Pigot's Directory of Cornwall (Cornwall, Pigot & Co, 1830) 145.
[31] (1789) 3 Term Reports 240.

the creatures of the Crown: and on their dissolution their franchises revert to the Crown. But if the King choose that all their rights shall be revived, it is competent to him to do so.'[32] The Court confirmed the Crown's role in determining corporate privileges.

E. *Wolff v Horncastle* (1798)

The facts in *Wolff v Horncastle* (1798) are complicated,[33] not in the least by the number of parties involved in the transaction. The litigation concerned a marine insurance policy. The ship *Fahrsund's Wharf*, was carrying 574 sacks of moss from Fahrsund in Norway to London. The seller of the moss was a Jochum Brink Lund. His general agents in the UK were a firm called Messrs. Wolffs and Dorville. Wolffs and Dorville insured the moss on Lund's behalf with Horncastle. Lund drew a bill of exchange from his agents, Wolffs and Dorville. The shipment was rejected first by the Cudbear Company and then lost by the perils of the sea. Wolffs and Dorville (together with those involved with the goods on the ship) sued the defendant, who underwrote the policy for the ship. The defendant appeared to object to paying out on the insurance policy on the basis that: (1) the policy was not made by the order of Lund, nor by the plaintiffs as his agents, and therefore was void; and (2) the plaintiffs had no insurable interest.[34] There were some discussion as to the applicability of the Marine Insurance Act 1788,[35] especially with regard to the way in which the documents had been filled out, the Act having been enacted to mitigate the rigorous demands of the Insurances on Ships Act 1785 in this area which it replaced.[36] Buller J, in giving one of the judgments in the Court of Common Pleas, said that the 'Plaintiffs therefore accepted the bill for 300*l*. drawn by Lund upon them on the faith of the consignees accepting the bill drawn for the value of the goods, not on the faith of the goods arriving.'[37]

F. *Carlen v Drury* (1812)

Carlen v Drury (1812) is a case cited by all five textbooks.[38] The case is famous in company law not least because of the dictum of Lord Eldon. 'This Court', Eldon said, 'is not to be required on every Occasion to take the Management

[32] (1789) 3 Term Reports 241.
[33] Sometimes spelled Wolf. This is the case in Pettet, Lowry & Reisberg's textbook, for example.
[34] (1798) 1 Bosanquet and Puller 318.
[35] 28 Geo 3 c 56.
[36] H Bennett 'The Three Ages of Utmost Good Faith', in C Mitchell and S Watterson (eds), *The World of Maritime and Commercial Law* (Oxford, Hart Publishing, 2020) 63–88.
[37] (1798) 1 Bosanquet and Puller 320.
[38] (1812) 1 Vesey & Beames 154.

of every Playhouse and Brewhouse in the Kingdom'.[39] As this line suggests, the litigation involved a brewery. The shareholders sued the firm's management over a number of unresolved issues, ranging from allegations of mismanagement to self dealing and to fraud. The firm itself was a joint stock company; a partnership with large numbers of shareholders who were unlimited in their liability. The case is used to show that courts are reluctant to engage in corporate governance disputes; judges refuse to interfere in company management. This point of law is now embedded firmly in judicial thinking.[40] It has not yet been taken into statutory form.

Having examined the facts of the cases and the rulings in them, we now turn to examine the value that these cases bring within company law.

VI. CLASSIFYING THE FIRST SIX CASES

Three of the six cases remain a point from which modern law is derived. *Keech v Sandford* (1726) has a strong relationship to current law, applicable to this day.[41] Yet, it has been overtaken now as a leading authority on fiduciary duties by other cases, such as *Industrial Development v Cooley* and *Regal (Hastings)* (1972).[42] It is used to explain the law which stems from *Boardman v Phipps* (1966).[43] It follows that *Keech v Sandford* (1526) builds the bank of cases in company law, which stem from the law of trusts and fiduciary duties. The rule in *Charitable Corpn v Sutton* (1742) is now encapsulated by section 174 of the Companies Act 2006. It is, as the company lawyers Jennifer Hill and Matthew Conaglen describe it, a 'watershed' decision.[44] It 'measured', they say, 'the standard of care and diligence required by directors against the lowest standard available at that time, one of "gross neglect" or crassa negligentia"'.[45] The standard has evolved since then. The principle from *Carlen v Drury* (1826), which gives rise to the rule that judges should not interfere in corporate governance disputes, has ties to

[39] (1812) 1 Vesey & Beames 158.

[40] V Barnes and J Oldham, 'Carlen v Drury (1812): The Origins of the Internal Management Debate in Corporate Law' (2017) 38 *The Journal of Legal History* 1.

[41] M Pawlowski, 'The Modern Application of the Rule in Keech v Sandford' (2022) 28 *Trusts & Trustees* 200. It has been a starting point for doctrinal analysis. In 1905, WG Hart, who the Hart workshop at IALS is now named after, traced trust law as it developed following this case in 1526. WG Hart, 'Development of the Rule in Keech v. Sandford' (1905) 21 *Law Quarterly Review* 258.

[42] *Industrial Development Consultants Ltd v Cooley* [1972] 1 WLR 443; *Regal (Hastings) Ltd v Gulliver* [1942] 1 All ER 37. See H Rajak, 'Fiduciary Duty of a Managing Director' (1972) 35 *The Modern Law Review* 655; JP Lowry, 'Regal (Hastings) Fifty Years On: Breaking the Bonds of the Ancien Regime' (1994) 45 *Northern Ireland Legal Quarterly* 1.

[43] M Bryan, 'Boardman v Phipps', in C Mitchell and P Mitchell (eds), *Landmark Cases in Equity* (Oxford, Hart Publishing, 2012) 604.

[44] JG Hill and M Conaglen, 'Directors' duties and legal safe harbours: a comparative analysis', in in D Gordon Smith and AS Gold (eds), *Research Handbook on Fiduciary Law* (Cheltenham, Edward Elgar Publishing, 2018) 306.

[45] ibid 306.

stronger and more prominent legal authorities today. The principle has been confirmed by *Foss v Harbottle* (1843),[46] *Mozley v Alston* (1847)[47] and *Burland v Earle* (1902).[48] The three cases of *Keech v Sandford* (1726), *Charitable Corpn v Sutton* (1742) and *Carlen v Drury* (1826) then fall into our categorisation of a key case. For any of them to have qualified as a seminal case on our taxonomy, they would need to have defined the area in the judgment that was given.

Aside from this point of agreement on the value and use of *Keech v Sandford* (1726), there is little consensus on which cases from this century matter or not within our textbook set. All of the other four cases from the eighteenth century are only cited by one of the textbooks. Mayson, French & Ryan use *Wilson v Tooker* (1714). It is a case that has attracted minimal scholarly attention. It has some use in the specialist finance literature.[49] This case lacks much in the way of judicial or scholarly commentary. It was popular in the nineteenth century, when there were fewer legal precedents.[50] Apart from its appearance in Mayson, French & Ryan's book, there is very little written about the case in the last century. As such, it falls within our category of 'forgotten' cases.

R v Pasmore (1789) is the only other case cited by Mayson, French & Ryan from the seventeenth century. *R v Passmore* (1789) occurs at a time when the corporate form was restricted and offered as a privilege by the monarch. Corporate charters were typically given then for cities.[51] They were also sought after in the seventeenth century for canal companies.[52] Entrepreneurs could create limited liability companies freely after 1855, but there was the strongest uptake after the failure of the Glasgow City Bank, which revealed the weakness of unlimited liability arrangements.[53] The specific historical context means that this case has little use for company lawyers today. It remains useful for those who seek to recreate an understanding of the way in which law was made at this point in time. We might see it as forming part of the jurisprudence that supports the concession theory of the corporation in which there has been contemporary interest but as a source of support it is outcompeted by cases that do not have the distraction of charters in their facts.[54] It has something of a life within legal history. James Oldham, for example, has used the case to illustrate the

[46] 2 Hare 461, 67 ER 189.

[47] 1 Ph 790; 41 ER 833.

[48] AC 83.

[49] PR Wood, *Comparative Law of Security Interests and Title Finance* (London, Sweet & Maxwell, 2007) paras 20–027.

[50] N Lindley and WB Lindley, *A Treatise on the Law of Companies, Considered as a Branch of the Law of Partnership*, 6th edn (London, Sweet and Maxwell, 1902) 634.

[51] RL Raymond, 'The Genesis of the Corporation' (1906) 19 *Harvard Law Review* 350.

[52] J Reeder, 'Corporate Loan Financing in the Seventeenth and Eighteenth Centuries' (1973) 2 *Anglo-American Law Review* 487.

[53] GG Acheson and JD Turner, 'The Death Blow to Unlimited Liability in Victorian Britain: The City of Glasgow Failure' (2008) 45 *Explorations in Economic History* 235.

[54] See J Hardman 'The Making of Corporate Legal Concession Theory' [2024] *Oxford Journal of Legal Studies*.

diverse sources of law used by judges in the courtroom.[55] As the powers of the monarch were an integral part of constitutional law and municipal regulation, the legal historian Kevin Costello examines this case to understand the relevant rules.[56] The case also features in Douglas Hay's biography of one of the judges in the case, Ashhurst J.[57] Judicial biography is an important method in legal history for understanding who, how and why the law developed in the way that it did.[58] As the case centres on the old system of corporate chartering, it, therefore, remains of primary use to historians and represents an example of a rule that is now 'obsolete'.

Wolff v Horncastle (1798) could also be classified as 'obsolete' because it turns on an old legal authority, the Marine Insurance Act 1788. Yet, owing to Buller's judgment, the case is more commonly associated with good faith in financial law.[59] Pettet, Lowry & Reisberg are the only textbook to cite *Wolff v Horncastle* (1798). Its lone citation is an indicator that the case is not well used. That said, as the section above indicates, the case is much more strongly linked to financial law as opposed to company law. For some, such as Pettet, Lowry & Reisberg, company law includes corporate finance. For others, represented by the other four textbooks here, it does not. Just like agency law,[60] finance can be seen as a standalone subject. It can also be part of the curriculum in commercial law.[61] The law of agency is again the same in the sense that it either appears in the company law or commercial law syllabus.[62] Given the limited use of *Wolff v Horncastle* (1798) and its position as used only if company law is defined more widely to include corporate finance law, this case is classified as 'forgotten'. It is at the periphery rather than the centre of company law.

This section has applied the classification system to the first six cases cited by leading textbooks in company law. It shows that while there is a mixed variety of cases here, none of these first cases were 'seminal' cases that defined a doctrine. Three of the six lay the ground work and the doctrine(s) evolved through later cases. These first three cases were, however, central to our understanding of the development of legal rules. As such, they are 'key' cases. Two cases are

[55] J Oldham, 'The Indispensability of Manuscript Case Notes to Eighteenth-Century Barristers and Judges', in A Musson and C Stebbings (eds), *Making Legal History: Approaches and Methodologies* (Cambridge, Cambridge University Press 2012) 39–40.

[56] K Costello, 'Mandamus and Borough Political Life, 1615 to 1780' (2021) 42 *The Journal of Legal History* 171.

[57] D Hay, 'Ashhurst, Sir William Henry (1725–1807), Judge' www.oxforddnb.com/view/10.1093/ref:odnb/9780198614128.001.0001/odnb-9780198614128-e-784.

[58] C Smith, 'The Disruptive Power of Legal Biography: The Life of Lord Phillimore – Churchman and Judge' (2020) 41 The *Journal of Legal History* 164.

[59] YQ Han, 'Conclusions: (Utmost) Good Faith and Pre-Contractual Duties Globally in the Twenty-First Century', in YQ Han and G Pynt (eds), *Carter v Boehm and Pre-Contractual Duties in Insurance Law: A Global Perspective After 250 Years* (London, Bloomsbury Publishing, 2018) 449.

[60] See the textbook H Bennett, *Principles of the Law of Agency*, 1st edn (Oxford, Hart Publishing, 2013).

[61] Finance is covered in E Baskind and others, *Commercial Law*, 4th edn (Oxford, Oxford University Press, 2022).

[62] Agency is also covered in the commercial law textbook: Baskind and others ibid.

'forgotten' on the basis that they are excluded from company law and have lost their core connection to it. Only one is 'obsolete' and demonstrates an outdated understanding of the law.

VII. HISTORIC CASES AND THEIR VALUE

In this final section, we explore the potential reasons for the rise and fall of cases. Why have some cases, like *Keech v Sandford* (1726) and *Carlen v Drury* (1812) retained their status, while others have faded from view? One factor that we can discount for the difference in notoriety is the method or mechanism for law reporting. All of these six cases were heard in an era before the modern system of law reporting was conceived. All six cases were taken from the Nominate Reports into the later English Reports. This adds to their importance to the common law. First, by taking them into these reports, they were (and are) more accessible to lawyers. The English Reports filtered out some cases of lesser importance. Second, by including the cases in the English Reports, the report went through another stage of editing.[63] This included adding or correcting details.[64] The attention given to the case gives the user an increased sense of confidence about its accuracy.

The movement towards standardising and authorising law reporting came in the late nineteenth century.[65] It involved rationalising the number of cases reported and discarding unwanted and duplicate reports. It was a shift towards efficiency that was in some way motivated by the deluge of cases; the burgeoning legal literature made legal research more frustrating, cumbersome and time consuming.[66] Those writing about law at this time also sought to construct doctrines, principles and rules. This interest in developing principles, concepts and legal theory stemmed from the growth of natural sciences as a popular discipline and the connection between theory and application within it.[67] In this guise, some common lawyers, therefore, complained of the 'case lawyer', who knew nothing of legal concepts and could not distinguish fact from principle.[68] With a clear set of guidance about when a decision should be reported, only those cases that advanced new legal thought were included in law reports.[69]

A second factor that may explain the longevity of *Keech v Sandford* (1726) and *Carlen v Drury* (1812) is the breadth and depth of scholarship on these cases.

[63] Some nominate reports also did this. See the first and second edition of the report in Vesey & Beames. *Carlen v Drury* (1812) 1 Vesey & Beames 154.

[64] Footnote 1 of *Williams v Tooker* (1714) indicates some errors in reporting, which was typical of the time.

[65] WTS Daniel, *The History and Origin of the Law Reports* (London, Wildy, 1969).

[66] RA Danner, 'Cases and Case Lawyers' (2016) 35 *Legal Reference Services Quarterly* 147.

[67] C MacMillan, 'Sir Edward Fry: Law, Science and Religion' (2020) 41 *The Journal of Legal History* 122; V Barnes, 'Interrogating the Self-Told Narrative: Lord Lindley's Autobiography, His Life and His Legal Biography' (2020) 41 *The Journal of Legal History* 143.

[68] Danner (n 66).

[69] N Lindley, 'History of the Law Reports' (1885) 1 *Law Quarterly Review* 137.

The social and economic context, which is missing in the law report, matters to the reader in terms of aiding understanding.[70] These two cases and the rules within them, while fundamental to understanding company law today, reflect the time and place in which they were constructed. The context is not necessary for readers of the same generation or temporal zone and so becomes lost to those reading the report decades or centuries later. Some of these cases have received scholarly attention that has brought in details from economic and social history in order to explain the decisions of actors. Joshua Getzler has researched *Keech v Sandford* (1726) and its context.[71] A history of the rule in *Keech v Sandford* (1726) has been written from several perspectives, including a comparative one. The American legal historian John Langbein has considered the case as a pivotal source of English law in the later codification of trust law in the US.[72] Archival research has revealed the background of *Carlen v Drury* (1812).[73] These studies help to correct misshapen narratives by bringing together copious amounts of sources and reveal forgotten detail that makes the case comprehendible. They do this in a way that the textbooks cannot. Textbooks represent an overview of a whole area of law which is from a bird's eye view. They are primarily digested by undergraduate students and this is the target audience. They are primers on a subject. Monographs and articles make for a specific study with a targeted research question or focus. Cases are often the sole focus. These case studies help the case survive and be understood by law students. They add to the case's notoriety and help promote it within legal scholarship. Indeed, they should be seen a catalyst for further legal development around the case. Yet, the sign of scholarly focus is also a sign that the case has achieved some status in the first place.

Table 1.3 Summary of case details

Case name	Category	Court	English Report Citation	Length (words)
Wilson v Tooker	Forgotten	House of Lords	2 ER 622	2,000
Keech v Sandford	Key	Chancery	25 ER 223	500
Charitable Corpn v Sutton	Key	Chancery	26 ER 642	2,500
R v Pasmore	Obsolete	King's Bench	100 ER 531	24,000
Wolff v Horncastle	Forgotten	Common Pleas	126 ER 924	4,500
Carlen v Drury	Key	Chancery	35 ER 61	2,000

[70] R Auchmuty, 'Whatever Happened to Miss Bebb? Bebb v The Law Society and Women's Legal History' (2011) 31 *Legal Studies* 199.

[71] J Getzler, 'Rumford Market and the Genesis of Fiduciary Obligations', in A Burrows and A Rodger (eds), *Mapping the Law: Essays in Memory of Peter Birks* (Oxford, Oxford University Press, 2006).

[72] JH Langbein, 'Why Did Trust Law Become Statute Law in the United States' (2006) 58 *Alabama Law Review* 1069.

[73] Barnes and Oldham (n 40).

A third factor is the length and complexity of the law report itself. Table 1.3 shows that there is some correlation between length and 'key' case status. *Keech v Sandford* (1726), at 500 words, is not a report with a set of salacious facts nor does it contain an endless and detailed list of financial accounts. The judgment is also rather brief. Harry Rajak quips that it 'must be one of the shortest case reports in English legal history'.[74] His comment here is justified. In the English reports, the case stands at just two paragraphs long. The case was heard in 1726 before the Court of Chancery. The Lord Chancellor then was Peter King. The Lord Chancellor sat as the only judge in this court until the reforms in the nineteenth century and so he gave the only judgment in the report.[75] The absence of rival or dissenting judgments in *Keech v Sandford* (1726) also adds to the case's overall coherency. Chancery was unusual in the sense that it had a single judge and thus a single judgment. Both *Carlen v Drury* (1812) and *Charitable Corpn v Sutton* (1742) are cases from Chancery. The report of *Wolff v Horncastle* (1798), for example, contains three judgments (and four, if the Chief Justice's is considered), but all three concur raising the question which in today's parlance we might term 'added value'.

The observation about the simplicity of a case is important because cases are often distilled to single lines or a single proposition. This distillation can lead to negative consequences, namely a distortion of the rule. Take *Carlen v Drury* (1812), for instance. The famous quote – 'This Court is not to be required on every Occasion to take the Management of every Playhouse and Brewhouse in the Kingdom' – is deployed as a single line.[76] The meaning that the case has now is, however, far from what Lord Eldon meant with his oft cited line. The second part of this sentence added a great deal of nuance. It read: 'but, if the Case justifies the Interference of the Court it may appoint a Manager in the Interim, for the Purpose of winding up, and putting an End to, the Concern'.[77] Eldon was prepared to interfere. This point, of course, contradicts the wisdom supposedly given by this case. The wider judgment shows that he was prepared to act in his judicial capacity but only to dissolve the company and bond among the members.

Here we have suggested three reasons why some cases might enjoy more longevity than others. The first is the filter of law reporting. Inclusion in the English reports might allow for a case to be refined and even corrected increasing its utility as an authority. The second is the choices of the early treatise writers and their inheritors, the writers of the first texts. Their use of a case in the search for conceptual categories and theoretical propositions was key to keeping a case

[74] Rajak (n 42) 655.

[75] M Lobban, 'Preparing for Fusion: Reforming the Nineteenth-Century Court of Chancery, Part I' (2004) 22 *Law and History Review* 389; M Lobban, 'Preparing for Fusion: Reforming the Nineteenth-Century Court of Chancery, Part II' (2004) 22 *Law and History Review* 565.

[76] (1812) 1 Vesey & Beames 158.

[77] ibid.

alive leaving more contemporary writers to supply the often forgotten context of the decision. The third is more prosaic still; the length of a judgment and the stylistic presentation of facts matter.

VIII. CONCLUSION

Overall, this chapter has explored the cases thought to be at the beginning of modern company law. We have identified these pioneering cases by examining the citations to early case law in five leading company law textbooks. The textbooks themselves shows little in the way of agreement about which of these cases are useful in company law. Only two of the six first cases were cited by all five textbooks, for instance. The remainder of the cases were cited by just one of the five textbooks. Our analysis of these cases, for the most part, shares these findings. It shows that the importance of these six cases and their importance to the field is equally mixed.

To measure the importance of a case, we develop a new taxonomic framework. Our classification system ranges from 'forgotten' to 'seminal' cases (with 'forgotten' being the least important and 'seminal' being most important). None of the cases at the beginning of company law are considered to be 'seminal' cases. *Keech v Sandford* (1726), *Charitable Corpn v Sutton* (1742) and *Carlen v Drury* (1812) are identified in our framework as 'key' cases, at the position just below 'seminal'. The remaining three are rather peripheral to company law. This chapter also provides some explanation for why these age-old cases have remain in circulation and so strongly so at that. Survival, we argue, is about centrality to the key doctrines in company law, today. It also depends on the accessibility of the law report as well as the clarity of the reported judgment.

2

On Mistakes and Trajectories: Using History in Normative Company Law

JONATHAN HARDMAN

'You could almost always find a basis for your claims in the past if you looked hard enough.'[1]

I. INTRODUCTION

THIS CHAPTER WILL explore the argumentation structures through which historical analysis is deployed in modern debates in corporate law. Following the quote at the start of the chapter, it will argue that the deployment of any normative argument – focusing on what the *law should be* – inevitably contains a value-judgment being advanced by the commentator. History is pliable in its use in furthering the end goal identified by that original value judgment. This chapter will argue that such analysis tends to be deployed within one of two loose approaches. First, the trajectory argument identifies the direction of travel of corporate law and argues for a continuation of that trend. Second, the mistake argument identifies earlier approaches to a rule, argues that it was a mistake to move away from such a rule, and argues for a return to those approaches. Thus trajectory arguments tend to be incrementalist – they represent a continuation of current developments. Conversely, mistake arguments tend to propose a more radical break from modern developments, normally guised as a return to the past. The relative stability of UK company law on major matters means that trajectory arguments tend towards the status quo, whereas mistake arguments tend towards major change.

To advance this argument, this chapter will engage briefly with some theoretical discussion of the structures of academic legal argument, and some theoretical discussion in respect of how we view history. It will then connect these to the two argumentation structures. This chapter will argue that both approaches tie in to general themes applicable within corporate law. It will thus argue that these

[1] M MacMillan, *The Uses and Abuses of History* (London, Profile, 2010) 103.

structures naturally fit with other argumentation structures, and can be linked together into wider schools of thought. Exploring the strengths and weaknesses of trajectory and mistake approaches reveals that neither is inherently correct. As such, whilst such argumentation structures can augment an argument made elsewhere, neither will act as an ultimate 'trump card' in any debate.

The chapter will finish by contextualising the issues identified in the area of business vehicle choice. It will draw links to the horizontal 'market for incorporation' as between different jurisdictions, and argues for a vertical 'market for business choice' as between different legal forms within a jurisdiction. It will trace the development of business vehicle choice in the UK, and argue that it has liberalised, so that those establishing companies with a small number of residual claimants now have more flexibility (and lower state mandated regulation) than they used to. It will then identify both trajectory and mistake normative arguments that can spring from such analysis as a way of illustration of the arguments advanced above.

II. DEPLOYING HISTORY IN NORMATIVE LEGAL ARGUMENT

We are interested in this chapter in the deployment of historical argument in normative company law. As such, we care about 'norm selection',[2] how we choose which of an option of rules *should* govern any individual activity. We therefore care less about the pure description of the historical development of law.[3] This matters, of course, but only instrumentally for our purposes – we use different aspects of historical development to further arguments that we wish to make. This is not to undermine the importance and real world effect of making such arguments.[4] It is, though, to state that when we argue what the law should be, we are inevitably using a tool to argue for something that we already believe in.

This takes us into semiotics,[5] the study of signs.[6] In particular, using any particular individual argumentation structure presents a sign of wider connection to various schools of thought.[7] For example, if I argue that shareholders

[2] P Schlag, 'Normative and Nowhere to Go' (1990) 43 *Stanford Law Review* 167, 178.

[3] For a discussion of the difference between positive and normative, see M Friedman, 'The Methodology of Positive Economics' in *Essays in Positive Economics* (Chicago, University of Chicago Press, 1966) 30–43.

[4] See RM Cover, 'Violence and the Word' (1986) 95 *Yale Law Journal* 1601.

[5] T Sebeok, 'Semiotics: A Survey of the State of the Art' (1974) 12 *Current Trends in Linguistics* 211. I am grateful to David Kershaw for identifying that the themes I was raising in this chapter were reminiscent of legal semiotics.

[6] Semiotics interacts with a number of disciplines, see SW Tiefenbrun, 'Legal Semiotics' (1986) 5 *Cardozo Arts & Entertainment Law Journal* 89.

[7] See JM Balkin, 'The Hohfeldian Approach to Law and Semiotics' (1990) 44 *University of Miami Law Review* 1119.

should have more power,[8] or less power,[9] that tells readers how my views fit into wider theoretical arguments within corporate law: it can *signal* to other corporate lawyers the school of thought my arguments closest associate with. Semiotics therefore tells us about particular relationships between concepts. In law, we see not just established language used in legal arguments,[10] but *established argumentation patterns*, too.[11] The micro decision to advance a particular argument – with a particular normative end – is political in nature. The micro decisions to follow particular argumentation structures map out into wider plays – making a decision to argue A instead of B shows the reader how you will react to a debate between argument C and D – the same political choices play out repeatedly.[12] In each field where there are contrary political decisions to be taken (ie every field) there plays out a series of argument dyads to reflect that choice, swirling around each other in a giant double helix.[13] In the same way as taking a micro decision gives us insight into the wider political views of the arguer, we can also break arguments down into a series of 'argument-bites', consisting of the pairing of opposite and opposing arguments.[14] Choosing to deploy one argument bite over another also reflects a political choice, and also signals the views of the author. Personal political views therefore provide signals in terms of the normative aim identified and the argumentation structures used to advance that argument.

This is, of course, how academia functions – we listen to arguments that are close enough to what we know, with a 'minor heresy' that can be debated within wider frameworks.[15] Too close to our conventional wisdom, and there is a risk that we reject it as being not novel; too far and there is a risk that we reject it as being unconnected to existing debates. We signal to the academic community that we are part of them by following the same arguments and structures – both to the academy that we are part of them, and as between particular schools of thought as to how our thinking aligns (or opposes) them. We therefore demonstrate, in our writings, *repeated plays of similar moves.*[16] Of course, if both sides of any argumentation structure are playing repeated moves, then by their very nature there is no determination made by any particular move. We can never checkmate our game of legal normative arguments, just move along the

[8] eg, FH Easterbrook and DR Fischel, *The Economic Structure of Corporate Law* (Cambridge, Harvard University Press, 1991) 66–72.

[9] eg, SM Bainbridge, 'The Case for Limited Shareholder Voting Rights' (2006) 53 *UCLA Law Review* 601.

[10] See P Goodrich, 'The Role of Linguistics in Legal Analysis' (1984) 47 *Modern Law Review* 523.

[11] D Kennedy, 'Form and Substance in Private Law Adjudication' (1976) 89 *Harvard Law Review* 1685.

[12] JM Balkin, 'The Crystalline Structure of Legal Thought' (1986) 39 *Rutgers Law Review* 2.

[13] D Kennedy, 'A Semiotics of Legal Argument' (1991) 42 *Syracuse Law Review* 75.

[14] ibid 76–77.

[15] JK Galbraith, *The Affluent Society* 40th anniversary edn (London, Penguin, 1999) 9.

[16] JM Balkin, 'The Promise of Legal Semiotics' (1991) 69 *Texas Law Review* 1831.

treadmill. After all, it has been argued that arguments only have validity *because of the presence of a counterargument.*[17] The result, then, of advancing an argument is to expect a counter argument – just as the child wanting to stay up late appeals to the different types of arguments available to them, and expects and responds to counter-arguments.[18] In the company context, this constant use of established argumentation patterns towards normative ends creates a risk of circularity of argument: for example, does the company have standing because it is a person, or is it a person because it has standing?[19]

None of this undermines the role of normative legal argument, of course, which has a concrete effect in real life,[20] including providing legitimacy and bargaining boosts and chills to various actors.[21] We can avoid nihilism by having concrete aims that we wish to achieve[22] – and use accepted argumentation structures to advance those aims. This, though, inverts our traditional understanding of the legal discipline: rather than unbiasedly applying legal techniques to solve a normative problem, we pick our normative solution and then work out which legal techniques are most persuasive to achieve that end. There are limits to this analysis, of course, and we should not overplay the agency that individuals have in such analysis. In particular, facts do not lend themselves to every interpretation. White argues that whilst we may be able to plot what happened to JFK in Dallas as a drama or a tragedy, we are unlikely to be able to plot it as a comedy.[23] This is because interpretation of those facts have a viscosity that connects them to certain techniques and approaches.[24] Now, obviously, that partly means that we can ignore the facts that do not fit with our narrative to some degree – but there are limits to doing so. Similarly, the approach I have just presented implies that we chose the approach we want to achieve our ends, whereas it is equally possible that the ends are dictated by the approach that we use.[25] In addition to limits on our facts and our methods, there are limits on what is acceptable to the audience – in our case the wider academic community.[26] This can become entrenched in company law – for example, arguments that non-shareholder and director interests are and

[17] J Paul, 'Politics of Legal Semiotics' (1991) 69 *Texas Law Review* 1779, 1786.

[18] J Paul, 'A Bedtime Story' (1988) 74 *Virginia Law Review* 915.

[19] F Cohen, 'Transcendental Nonsense and the Functional Approach' (1935) 35 *Columbia Law Review* 809.

[20] SL Winter, 'Transcendental Nonsense, Metaphoric Reasoning, and the Cognitive Stakes For Law' (1989) 137 *University of Pennsylvania Law Review* 1105.

[21] RL Hale, 'Bargaining, Duress and Economic Liberty' (1943) 43 *Columbia Law Review* 603; RL Hale, 'Coercion and Distribution in a Supposedly Non-Coercive State' (1923) 38 *Political Science Quarterly* 470.

[22] JW Singer, 'The Player and the Cards: Nihilism and Legal Theory' (1984) 94 *Yale Law Journal* 1.

[23] H White, 'The Historical Text as a Literary Artefact' (1974) 3 *Clio* 277.

[24] eg, U Eco, 'The Theory of Signs and the Role of the Reader' (1981) 14 *The Bulletin of the Midwest Modern Language Association* 35.

[25] eg, D Kennedy, 'A Semiotics of Critique' (2001) 22 *Cardozo Law Review* 1147.

[26] Galbraith (n 15) 9.

should be governed by other parts of the legal taxonomy[27] imply strongly that attempting to focus on such interests takes us outside our traditional company law audience. Nonetheless, there is a degree of agency – we can choose which general schools we want to position ourselves within, and can do so by choice of facts, argumentation structures, and/or normative ends.

To recap, then, all normative arguments are pliable – we decide what argument we want to make, and follow a series of argument-bites – in substance or form – to advance the argument that we want. These arguments signify to academic colleagues that we belong in the academy, and which sub-schools we should be considered to be part of. History itself is equally pliable. Toynbee argued that we must start with a theory through which we then examine historical 'facts', rather than the other way round.[28] Historical facts, then, become 'things that have been made' – that is to say '"fictitious" things rather than "factual" things … [w]hether we call the phenomena data or call them facts, we are admitting that they have been given or have been made by somebody.'[29] White argued that history becomes something that cannot be studied objectively like a science – instead, we study the individual subjective understandings of past events.[30] Similarly, history does not quite belong in the arts, either.[31] Attempts to treat history as part of a fusion between the two leaves it open to methodological attacks from both sides. This can be resolved if one acknowledges that when we use history to make arguments about what the law should be, we tend to use history for a particular purpose rather than objectively. We can expect commentators seeking to achieve different normative ends to see different things in apparently the same set of facts, and to use them for different purposes, in the same way as

> we do not expect that Constable and Cézanne will have looked for the same thing in a given landscape, and when we confront their respective representations of a landscape, we do not expect to have to choose between them and determine which is the 'more correct' one.[32]

When we analyse history, then, we must interpret history, by excluding facts that we consider to be irrelevant, and interpolating actions that must have happened

[27] eg, AK Sundaram and AC Inkpen, 'The Corporate Objective Revisited' (2004) 15 *Organization Science* 350.

[28] AJ Toynbee, *A Study of History Vol. XII* (Oxford, Oxford University Press, 1961) 244.

[29] ibid 230.

[30] H White, *Tropics of Discourse: Essays in Cultural Criticism* (Baltimore, Johns Hopkins, 1985) 23. I am grateful to Akbar Rasulov for introducing me to Hayden White's work in 2007 (along, in fairness, to the work of Duncan Kennedy, Robert Lee Hale and Pierre Schlag. Come to think of it, there is a strong chance that I owe Akbar more than I usually credit …), and to Harwell Wells for pointing out that a lot of my views in this chapter overlapped with White's – there is nothing new under the sun.

[31] FW Nietzsche, *Untimely Mediations*, first published 1873, RJ Hollingdale tr, (Cambridge, Cambridge University Press, 1997).

[32] H White, 'The Burden of History' (1966) 5 *History and Theory* 111, 130, citing EH Gombrich, *Art and Illusion: A Study in the Psychology of Pictoral Representation* (Washington, Phaidon, 1960).

in order to fit facts that we know did happen: if the same army fought a battle in one place on one date, then another battle in another place on another day, then we interpolate that such army must have moved between the places.[33] The result is that whenever we use history, we construct a narrative by emplotting one from the various tropes presented to us.[34] As such we can no longer conclude that fiction is the opposite of fact, or that historical facts stand on their own without a bit of narrative assistance from the commentator.[35] Indeed, often we need to revisit our historical analysis when the facts upon which we had predicated our understanding proved to be verifiably incorrect: if our historical analysis was predicated upon X occurring, and it is subsequently proved that X did not occur, then our historical analysis needs to be changed.[36]

It is easy to see, then, why and how historical argumentation can connect into our normative arguments. When making our normative arguments, we use familiar argumentation structures, and apply pliable details to them. History itself is, ultimately, full of pliable details. Therefore we can use historical arguments as detail to apply to our familiar argumentation structures. More than this, though, the inherent pliability of historical concepts make it *natural* for us to do so. This allows us, effectively, two stages of moulding circumstances to our argumentation patterns: when outlining what the 'history' is, and also when applying that history in a normative sense.

I argue, then, that two of the most popular argumentation patterns within normative company law are to argue that history presents us with a logical trajectory from which we cannot particularly deviate, and that a mistake took place in the historical development of company law which needs to be put right now. I call the former the trajectory argument, and the latter the mistake argument. I will outline their usual tropes, patterns, and connections to wider concepts.

III. ARGUMENTATION PATTERN 1: TRAJECTORY IN NORMATIVE CORPORATE LAW

The first argumentation pattern is that of trajectory. It is, of course, possible to explore corporate law's trajectory generally, and from such foster a better understanding of the current state of legal analysis.[37] We are not concerned with this, but with what, normatively, is done with such trajectory. The argument being

[33] H White, 'Interpretation in History' (1973) 4 *New Literary History* 281, 281.

[34] White (n 23).

[35] H White, 'The Fictions of Factual Representation' in A Fletcher (ed), *The Literature of Fact* (New York, Columbia University Press, 1976).

[36] eg, MA O'Sullivan, 'History as Heresy: Unlearning the Lessons of Economic Orthodoxy' (2022) 75 *Economic History Review* 297; EJ Hobsbawm and T Ranger (eds), *The Invention of Tradition* (Cambridge, Cambridge University Press, 1983).

[37] For an excellent example of this, see BR Cheffins, *The Trajectory of (Corporate Law) Scholarship* (Cambridge, Cambridge University Press, 2003).

advanced with this argumentation pattern is that law has developed in a way that is optimal. Not just, then, is the current law a continuation, a logical trajectory, of what has gone before, but that future changes to the law should not deviate dramatically from that trajectory. Legal development is, therefore, used to plot this trajectory and map normative conclusions from it by extrapolating that trajectory. If company law had changed dramatically over the years, then trajectory arguments could be potentially dramatic in their effect (if yesterday it[38] was 2, and today it was 12, then the next day it could be 22 (by adding 10) or 72 (by multiplying by 6)). However, the fundamentals of UK company law have not changed much since 1856 (meaning that 100 years ago it was 2 and today it is 3, then we may not get to 4 until 100 years from now).[39] As such, trajectory arguments tend to favour, and as such be used to justify, the status quo. There are three sub-arguments that can be deployed within this larger pattern. First, it could be argued that the current law is optimal. Posner argued generally 'many legal doctrines rest on inarticulate gropings towards efficiency'.[40] It can therefore be argued that the trajectory of legal development has *got it right*. Second is the idea that law should – perhaps does – reflect the hypothetical bargain that the parties *would have struck* if they were bargaining, but it is cheaper for all if law just sets whatever-rule-we-are-talking-about at the level of where-it-would-normally-be-following-a-full-bargaining-process.[41] Either law currently does so, or is close to doing so under the normal deployment of this argumentation structure.

The third sub-argument that can be deployed is that of path dependence. This argument proceeds that the norm in question may not be the right one. However, either we did not (or could not) have known a superior norm in advance, or it would be too expensive and time-consuming to identify a superior norm. At its heart, the idea of path dependency is that matters cannot be looked at in the abstract, but instead have to be analysed by reference to how we got here: 'starting points matter'.[42] We can look at path dependence in a number of ways. Commentators generally outline three versions of path dependence – the weak, the semi-strong or the strong,[43] which can also be called the first degree, second

[38] The numbers here do not represent anything in particular, but are merely illustrations of trajectories at play.

[39] See LS Sealy, *Company Law and Commercial Reality* (London, Sweet & Maxwell, 1984) 1–2; P Johnson, *Making the Market: Victorian Origins of Corporate Capitalism* (Cambridge, Cambridge University Press, 2013) 110.

[40] RA Posner, *Economic Analysis of Law* 5th edn (New York, Aspen, 1997) 27. This book is currently on its 9th edn, but I have a particular soft spot for the 5th.

[41] See the debate between JC Coffee Jr, 'Mandatory/Enabling Balance in Corporate Law: An Essay on the Judicial Role' (1989) 89 *Columbia Law Review* 1618 and JR Macey, 'Courts and Corporations: A Comment on Coffee' (1989) 89 *Columbia Law Review* 1692.

[42] JC Coffee Jnr, 'Future as History: The Prospects for Global Convergence in Corporate Governance and Its Implications' (1999) 93 *Northwestern University Law Review* 641, 660.

[43] Mark Roe adopts this approach – M Roe, 'Chaos and Evolution in Law and Economics' (1996) 109 *Harvard Law Review* 641.

degree, and third degree.[44] In weak, or first degree, path dependence, my current decisions are based on historic decisions. Thus I may buy a house in the area that I currently live in not because it is objectively the best area, but because it is where I currently live. This decision, therefore, is inherently intertemporal. It is not automatically, though, right or wrong – it could be proved to be either. In second degree, or semi-strong, path dependence, I take a decision which is shown after the fact to be inefficient, but this could not be known in advance. For example, I move to a house, and then five years later a sewerage plant is built next to it. The decision is, with the benefit of the fullness of time and hindsight, regrettable. But this does not mean that it was wrong when made – we could not know about this at the time. Third degree, or strong, path dependence occurs where I take a sub-optimal decision due to intertemporal aspects, which I know to be wrong. For example, I could move into a street where I know that a sewerage plant is being built because my family live nearby. The continued use of QWERTY keyboards is often presented as evidence for third degree path dependence.[45]

The application of path dependence to law generally is evident.[46] The concept has also been used to examine the interplay between legal rules and corporate structures.[47] It can prove difficult to deviate from the current location of the path, or the trajectory of that path, because it can prove costly to replace existing norms for the optimal norm.[48] The information costs[49] required to be incurred merely to analyse the current norm, identify alternative norms, and analyse their putative superiority are likely to be significant, plus costs in changing and costs for market participants in adjusting to comply with the new norm. It is therefore unsurprising that changing norms – even where long-term advantages are agreed by all – can be very unpopular due to short-term costs. It can also be argued that what *is* optimal in the longer term is affected by inter-temporal issues as well.[50] The argument is not, of course, that no change is possible, nor

[44] This is the approach favoured by Liebowitz and Margolis – see SJ Liebowitz and SE Margolis, 'Path Dependence' in P Newman (ed), *The New Palgrave Dictionary of Economics and the Law*, Vol 3 (Basingstoke, Palgrave Macmillan, 1998); SJ Leibowitz and SE Margolis, 'Path Dependence, Lock-in and History' (1995) 11 *Journal of Law, Economics & Organization* 205.

[45] Although it may not be accurate – see SJ Liebowitz and SE Margolis, 'The Fable of the Keys' (1990) 33 *Journal of Law & Economics* 1.

[46] O Hathaway, 'Path Dependence in the Law: The Course and Pattern of Legal Change in a Common Law System' (2001) 86 *Iowa Law Review* 601; J Bell, 'Path Dependence and Legal Development' (2013) 87 *Tulane Law Review* 787.

[47] L Bebchuk and M Roe, 'A Theory of Path Dependence in Corporate Ownership and Governance' (1999) 52 *Stanford Law Review* 127.

[48] R Gilson, 'Corporate Governance and Economic Efficiency: When Do Institutions Matter?' (1996) 74 *Washington University Law Review* 327, 329–30.

[49] Which themselves form part of transaction costs – see RC Ellickson, 'The Case for Coase and Against Coaseanism' (1989) 99 *Yale Law Journal* 611.

[50] For a comparison between this and the 'adjustment costs' approach to path dependence, see RH Schmidt and G Spindler, 'Path Dependence, Corporate Governance and Complementarity' (2002) 5 *International Finance* 311. See also R Schmidt and G Spindler, 'Path Dependence and Complementarity in Corporate Governance' in J Gordon and M Roe (eds), *Convergence and Persistence in Corporate Governance* (Cambridge, Cambridge University Press, 2004).

that path dependence will affect different norms equally[51] – other factors are at play.[52] Within this analysis, though, there are positive (or descriptive) aspects, and normative aspects.[53] The former identify that the current position of rules is based on inter-temporal aspects; the latter uses this insight to make arguments as to the future direction of legal rules.

Path dependence is usually viewed temporally, but it is part of a wider argumentation structure that argues that the decision to select a preferred norm cannot be taken in isolation.[54] Another restraining factor can be pressures to align to norms appearing in other jurisdictions,[55] although such pressures can conflict with path dependence internally within a national jurisdiction.[56]

Path dependence, hypothetical bargaining, and law's natural efficiency arguments all point towards the same argumentation moves. They are all inherently incrementalist in their normative outlook for corporate law. The acceptable options for legal development through each of them are fundamentally limited. Within path dependence, the options available to us are limited by our current position on the path. Hypothetical bargaining is naturally bounded: existing legal options delimit what participants would choose (whether due to the familiar, the costs of change, or the lack of knowledge of potential options to change to). Law's natural efficiency is inherently against dramatic change. Each of these argumentation structures is able to present itself as value neutral. The current law is deemed superior not because the content of the rules is the best, but because inter-temporality makes it impractical to change, market participants would choose it, or it is part of the current law which is generally seen as efficient. These argumentation tropes are therefore able to present themselves as containing no, or limited, embedded political characterisations. Commentators can even argue, should they like, that they *would like to see change, but* alas, alack, alay, it is not possible to achieve due to inter-temporal aspects.

This belies, though, the inherently political character of the arguments being advanced. To advance a first degree path dependent argument, one is arguing that the decision in respect of which norm to apply *should* be made in the

[51] J Armour, S Deakin, P Lele and M Siems, 'How Do Legal Rules Evolve? Evidence from a Cross-Country Comparison of Shareholder, Creditor, and Worker Protection' (2009) 57 *American Journal of Comparative Law* 579.

[52] Roe (n 43).

[53] R Mann and C Milhaupt, 'Foreword: Path Dependence and Comparative Corporate Governance' (1996) 74 *Washington University Law Quarterly* 317; EB Rock, 'America's Shifting Fascination with Comparative Corporate Governance' (1996) 74 *Washington University Law Quarterly* 367; Gilson (n 48).

[54] R Gilson, 'From Corporate Law to Corporate Governance' in J Gordon and W-G Ringe (eds), *The Oxford Handbook of Corporate Law and Governance* (Oxford, Oxford University Press, 2018) 9–10.

[55] H Hansmann and R Kraakman, 'The End of History for Corporate Law' (2001) 89 *Georgetown Law Journal* 439.

[56] A Licht, 'The Mother of All Path Dependencies: Toward a Cross-Cultural Theory of Corporate Governance Systems' (2001) 26 *Delaware Journal of Corporate Law* 147.

context of past decisions, or *should* be based on our understanding of existing advantages. To advance a hypothetical bargaining argument, we are inherently arguing that the most typical parties should choose the norm applying to all.[57] To advance a 'law is efficient' argument, one must make a normative case as to why efficiency is optimal, and for who, and how it is tested. We may be told, for example, that markets expect a certain outcome.[58] For this to matter, of course, one must already hold the notion that this is the most important consideration in the analysis. Value judgments abound before such arguments can be advanced. An argument that trajectory results in a lack of political choice is thus a veneer – such choice is inherent in the choice to deploy the argumentation structure. The relatively fixed nature of major aspects of UK company law mean that trajectory arguments are against major change, and as such we can expect those who advance trajectory arguments to be supportive of the status quo, or making minor changes to the status quo.

If Balkin is right, and arguments advanced in one area follow similar patterns elsewhere in a recurring crystalline structure,[59] then we can expect the deployment of trajectory arguments to dovetail with existing perceived status quo arguments. Thus we can expect arguments within the trajectory school to dovetail neatly with concepts such as shareholder wealth maximisation,[60] even if achieved through other ends than shareholder primacy,[61] viewing the company as a nexus of contracts,[62] and arguing for low state intervention in corporate activity.[63] None of this, of course, is it to allege deliberate hiding of views of company behind veneers of legal analysis. It is, nonetheless, the effect. When opening an article written by any particular corporate law commentator, a reader is likely to know how the arguments will fit into wider debates in company law. Not necessarily the exact content, but the general shape and positioning of the argument within the wider field. This is because argumentation structures tend to be ways to achieve normative, political proposals that we wish to advance, and these themselves are inherently grouped with other argumentation structures. Thus we can tell (or at least make a strong guess), for any given normative company law issue, whether any particular commentator is likely to be pro- or anti- status quo based on their previous writings. From this, we can extrapolate

[57] For example, we can aim to protect those who most need protection, or require the sharing of knowledge by those with more – see I Ayres and R Gertner, 'Filing Gaps in Incomplete Contracts: An Economic Theory of Default Rules' (1989) 99 *Yale Law Journal* 87.

[58] For a discussion on the role that certainty – or uncertainty – plays in commercial decisions, see I MacNeil, 'Uncertainty in Commercial Law' (2009) 13 *Edinburgh Law Review* 68.

[59] Balkin (n 12).

[60] DG Smith, 'The Shareholder Primacy Norm' (1998) 23 *Journal of Corporation Law* 277.

[61] S M Bainbridge, *The New Corporate Governance in Theory and Practice* (Oxford, Oxford University Press, 2008) 23–73.

[62] See J Hardman, 'The Nexus of Contracts Revisited: Delineating the Business, the Firm, and the Legal entity' (2022) 34 *Bond Law Review* 1.

[63] eg, F H Easterbrook and DR Fischel, 'The Corporate Contract' (1989) 89 *Columbia Law Review* 1416, 1435–1436.

what their normative conclusion on any particular corporate law issue will likely be, and from this how they will deploy history within their argumentation structure. And we can tell this *before even reading the abstract of the new piece.*[64]

IV. ARGUMENTATION PATTERN 2: MISTAKE IN NORMATIVE CORPORATE LAW

Trajectory arguments are not the only option for argumentation structure available for the deployment of history in what company law should be. Indeed, semiotics tells us that trajectory arguments only exist as valid signs because of the presence of an opposite argumentation structure. This is the argument that there has been a mistake somewhere in the development of corporate law – that the path taken was the wrong one. It could have been wrong because it moved law away from a certain established position,[65] or because a reform opportunity was missed or suggestion not followed.[66]

We see here, then, a different role for the use of history. In trajectory arguments, history acts as a block on dramatic reform. It is a reason to retain the status quo, or not deviate dramatically from it. This is not because trajectory arguments are inherently status quo biased in every context. Instead, it is merely because company law (especially in the UK) has not made major changes: its trajectory is very status quo focused, with limited drastic reform of fundamental concepts, which means that trajectory arguments naturally fall within that concept. It is not inevitable that this argumentation pattern means the same within every aspect of law (or within every jurisdiction for a particular corporate law issue). Mistake arguments therefore claim that we should go back to, or pick back up, a *major* change to UK company law. We therefore should go back to revisit that mistake, and correct it now.

At first blush, it is unclear why history would be relevant to this argumentation structure. After all, if the intention is to achieve something novel, then why appeal to history at all? The answer is less about the actuality and more about the perception. It matters not whether a solution is truly novel or something that has been tried before. But using history can alter the *perception* of how dramatic and drastic the change is. By appealing to history we can make a change to corporate law seem *less* dramatic and drastic, and fit more naturally in with the existing schema of corporate law. There are two reasons that this argumentation

[64] It could be argued that there is path dependence in argumentation structure (I have previously argued A, so I am bound to argue A now). However, the insights from legal semiotics indicate that it is more likely that we start with the normative political outcome – itself part of a grouped family of potential outcomes – and work backwards from that.

[65] eg, SM Watson, 'The Significance of the Source of the Powers of Boards of Directors in UK Company Law' [2011] *Journal of Business Law* 597.

[66] eg, SM Watson, 'How the Company Became an Entity: A New Understanding of Corporate Law' [2015] *Journal of Business Law* 120.

trope can be helpful when proposing dramatic reform. First, the legal profession can be rather conservative, and dislike change. For example, it has been argued that the law of secured transactions in England remains unreformed due to substantial pressure from the legal profession.[67] Here, then, is a concern less about substance and more about form. It is the same concern identified in respect of path dependence. However, rather than conceding that adjustment costs make reform impossible, here we try to overcome adjustment costs by minimising them. If the concern is that something new is being attempted, then a mistake argumentation trope can reduce the perception of this novelty. It can be used to assuage fear in respect of implementation, and argue that the dramatic change has been seen before so is less dramatic.

This in turn adds to the second key use. In addition to reducing fear, mistake tropes in history can be used to *legitimise* change proposals. This is a particular issue for corporate law in the UK. Here, we have shareholder control embedded across corporate life.[68] Shareholders thus set the constitution,[69] can change it,[70] have a residual power to appoint directors,[71] have a statutory power to remove them,[72] and abilities to proceed against them in certain limited situations.[73] Changing any individual one of these features leaves the others intact. As such, changes that adjust any of these features can easily be dismissed for a lack of cohesion: any change will not be coherent with the rest of corporate law. The interconnected edifice of UK company law becomes difficult to chip away at. However, the bigger change that is to be made, the more controversial it will be. An argument trope that has the ability to make a dramatic change seem less dramatic is therefore a powerful part of the crystalline argumentation structure pushing for change. The mistake trope can identify any aspect of history to look at previous laws, or previous proposals for change that were rejected, or where reform opportunities were missed. It therefore has a broad range of possibilities to draw from. In the same way, then, that it is natural for those advocating for the status quo to justify this position based on the trajectory that law has taken, it is natural for those advocating for change to argue that a mistake has been made. It is helpful for them to be able to identify a sliding doors moment whereby this could have been rectified previously, if only the chance were taken.

This argumentation structure resists the fundamental tenets of the trajectory approach. Trajectory is not an inherent good; a mistake was made. This

[67] L Gullifer, 'Will the Law Commission Sink the Floating Charge?' [2003] *Lloyds Maritime and Commercial Law Quarterly* 125; H Beale, 'The Exportability of North American Chattel Security Regimes: The Fate of the English Law Commission's Proposals' (2006) 43 *Canadian Business Law Journal* 178.

[68] Hardman (n 62).

[69] Companies Act 2006, s 18.

[70] Companies Act 2006, s 21.

[71] Watson (n 65).

[72] Companies Act 2006, s 168.

[73] Companies Act 2006, Pt 11 in respect of derivative claims and Companies Act 2006, s 994 in respect of unfair prejudice.

thus appeals to third degree path dependence – mistakes were made, but we can remedy that now. Such mistakes may even have been accidental, or unknowable at the time. The important thing is that they can be remedied. This is because, once again, there is nothing determinative about the mistake argumentation structure itself. Any set of facts can be fed into the mistake argumentation structure, and we can be relatively certain that it will produce the result that we should have taken the other path, and whilst it may be regrettable that we did not, it is not too late. The 'we', in this situation, means state intervention. In the context of company law, we must appeal to the state to rectify historical mistakes. Thus this argumentation structure can be expected to fit with other arguments that justify increased state intervention in corporate life. It is possible that a mistake can be too *much* governmental intervention in company activities.[74] However, there are two reasons why this is unlikely. First, the state is not heavily involved in the regulation of UK company law.[75] Relatively low governmental intervention is thus the status quo – so if you believe in that, you will explore a trajectory. Second, a mistake argumentation structure needs the state to act to effect change. Thus you are unlikely to be wanting the state to amend the position if you want to see less of the state. There is an irony here, though – to argue trajectory arguments you must argue that the state has done so well in the past that it must do nothing now; to argue mistake arguments you must argue that the state which has previously made legislative mistakes is the best organ to fix things now.

To every set of historical facts (themselves malleable) we can apply either trajectory or mistake argumentation structures to achieve the normative goals that we would like. This means that the two argumentation structures exist as counterbalances. If I want change, I apply the mistake approach, to be told that the answer is a trajectory approach instead to justify the status quo. These argumentation structures thus do not resolve our issue at all. Why do we bother with them at all then? Because if we did not, the other side would win if they presented their argumentation trope. To advocate for the status quo, then, we *must* advocate trajectory tropes, as otherwise we are open to being trumped by an argument that the law has made a mistake. Conversely, to advocate change, we will be told that history is against us unless we advance a mistake trope. The two exist in a form of defensive counterbalance: advancing one does not prove the point, but it stops the other side's approach winning. Not only can we use

[74] There is certainly a recent trajectory of increased state intervention – see J Hardman, 'The Butterfly Effect: Theoretical Implications of an Apparently Minor Corporate Transparency Proposal' (2021) 50 *Common Law World Review* 180.

[75] It is more heavily involved than in the US – see MT Moore, 'Private Ordering and Public Policy: The Paradoxical Foundations of Corporate Contractarianism' (2014) 34 *Oxford Journal of Legal Studies* 693 – but the majority of state interaction in the UK is in respect of independent courts rather than executive governmental bodies – see D Gibbs-Kneller, D Gindis and D Whayman, 'Not by Contract Alone: The Contractarian Theory of the Corporation and the Paradox of Implied Terms' (2022) 29 *European Business Organization Law Review* 573.

these argumentation structures to buttress normative arguments that we would like to make, but we have to, in order to avoid those wanting to achieve contradictory normative outcomes from presenting history as a trump side for their side of argumentation. To stay silent based on nihilism, then, risks conceding the argument.

Further, a direct confrontation on the basis of the argument structure is unlikely, as it will evidence the indeterminancy of argument. Instead, then, the argument must move to the context of the argument – *why* the trajectory was achieved, *why* a change was rejected, and the application of those arguments to the modern concepts. It could also argue that the *perception* was false – the law was misunderstood, legal changes were political and so do not stand up to legal scrutiny,[76] or were otherwise irrationally made. Overall, though, doctrinal development on its own is likely to need contextual support. The argumentation structures on their own will need to be augmented by meta-arguments to support their applicability in any particular context. Thus whilst at the same time we must advance a particular argumentation structure, we are also likely to need to support it by drawing on contextual features in respect of the change.

V. A WORKED EXAMPLE: LEGAL FORM

So far, then, we have concluded that commentators are likely to either want to retain the status quo – or a recognisable variant thereof, at least – or change it. They will have decided which they want to do when deploying history in their normative arguments. Following such decision, they will choose which argumentation structure is most likely to produce that outcome. The result, as legal semioticians told us would be inevitable, is that neither is determinative. Neither acts as a trump card for the other. The presence of one argumentation structure does not prove a point. Indeed, worse, it indicates to us that there will *automatically be a counter argumentation structure* which uses history to achieve precisely opposite normative ends. We can thus choose which argumentation structure to deploy, depending on what the answer we want to achieve will be. We have the choice to deploy the argumentation structure that we consider to be best for achieving our ends, and this will normally be the same argumentation structure.

[76] This argument trope has been deployed inter alia in respect of the passing of the Bubble Act (M Patterson and D Reiffen, 'The Effect of the Bubble Act on the Market for Joint Stock Shares' (1990) 50 *Journal of Economic History* 163), the repeal of the Bubble Act (R Harris, *Industrialising English Law: Entrepreneurship and Business Organization, 1720–1844* (Cambridge, Cambridge University Press, 2000) 243), and the introduction of limited liability (eg, C Mackie, 'From Privilege to Right – Themes in the Emergence of Limited Liability' [2011] *Juridical Review* 294; D Loftus, 'Capital and Community: Limited Liability and Attempts to Democratize the Market in Mid-Nineteenth Century England' (2002) 45 *Victorian Studies* 93).

I will illustrate my point by looking at different ways that we can analyse the historical development for the market for entity choice. The market for incorporations concept is well known in corporate law literature.[77] This argues that states compete for incorporations, by providing jurisdictional differences between the laws governing companies. States compete to set their laws in a way that will attract companies towards them. We can see this as a horizontal market for incorporations, as it tells us that market participants will shop around between jurisdictions to find those that suit their needs best, and will avoid those who heavily restrict their activities.[78] Much work has also been undertaken on similar forces which drive competition between legal forms within a jurisdiction,[79] and between features chosen within corporate forms.[80] If there is a horizontal market for incorporations as between jurisdictions, then there must be a vertical market for incorporations *within* each jurisdiction. Within the UK, for example, one could incorporate a public company,[81] private company,[82] limited liability partnership,[83] register a limited partnership,[84] or carry out a partnership.[85] Each take a slightly different approach to different corporate features, such as the availability of limited liability for participants.[86]

A normative question, then, is the extent to which those looking to establish a business entity should be provided a free rein to choose their legal vehicle. Should the state funnel different types of business activity into specific legal forms depending on characteristics, or should it let those setting up the company choose between legal forms? The former is clearly more interventionist, and advocates for a role of the state in business choice; the latter is clearly more

[77] WL Cary 'Federalism and Corporate Law: Reflections Upon Delaware' (1974) 83 *Yale Law Journal* 663; LA Bebchuk and A Hamdani, 'Vigorous Race or Leisurely Walk: Reconsidering the Competition over Corporate Charters' (2002) 112 *Yale Law Journal* 553; J Hardman, 'Further Legal Determinants of External Finance in Scotland: An Intra-UK Market for Incorporation?' (2021) 25 *Edinburgh Law Review* 192.

[78] R Romano, 'Answering the Wrong Question: The Tenuous Case for Mandatory Corporate Laws' (1989) 89 *Columbia Law Review* 1599; R Romano, 'Law as a Product: Some Pieces of the Incorporation Puzzle' (1985) 1 *Journal of Law Economics & Organization* 225.

[79] JA McCahery and EPM Vermeulen, 'The Evolution of Closely Held Business Forms in Europe' (2001) 26 *Journal of Corporation Law* 855; J Hardman and G Ramírez Santos, 'Empirical Evidence for the Continuing Need to 'Think Small First' in UK Company Law' (2023) 24 *European Business Organization Law Review* 117.

[80] P Giudici, P Agstner and A Capizzi, 'The Corporate Design of Investments in Startups: A European Experience' (2022) 23 *European Business Organization Law Review* 787.

[81] Companies Act 2006, s 4(2). Of course, being a public company alone does not mean that your shares are listed, this requires an additional step – see J Hardman, 'Equity for Punks: Conceptual Issues with Public Protections in Offerings of Shares to the Public' (2021) 42 *Company Lawyer* 322.

[82] Companies act 2006, s 4(1).

[83] Limited Liability Partnerships Act 2000, s 1.

[84] Limited Partnerships Act 1907, s 4 – these are registered rather than incorporated – see J Hardman, 'Reconceptualising Scottish Limited Partnership Law' (2021) 21 *Journal of Corporate Law Studies* 179.

[85] These require no active state involvement in their creation – Partnership Act 1890, s 2.

[86] J Hardman, 'Fixing the Misalignment of the Concession of Corporate Legal Personality' (2023) 43 *Legal Studies* 443, 446.

contractual and involves deferral to private actors. I hope that readers therefore have a 'gut feeling' about which argumentation structure would be best deployed when analysing history in advancing to achieve the relevant ends.

I want to show how pliable the same set of facts about the doctrinal development of company law are to be deployed by different argumentation structures. To do so, I will explore how law used to approach the freedom of those establishing businesses to choose legal form based on the number of residual claimants[87] to the profit of the business vehicle – shareholders in the case of companies,[88] and partners in the case of partnerships.[89] I will outline how the state has become slowly less interventionist in its approach, increasing freedoms for market participants to choose between business forms. There are a number of other sub-divisions that we could choose – for example, whether there are any maximum number of shareholders in a private company.[90] It, though, tells the same story as the focus on different legal forms – in particular, the increased freedom that businesses have to choose their legal form. We will focus on the development of the maximum number of partners that a partnership can have, and the minimum number of shareholders that a company must have.

Originally there was no cap on the number of partners that a partnership could have,[91] and one was not included by the passage of the Bubble Act.[92] The basis for modern companies created by registration,[93] the Bellenden Ker Report,[94] recommended introducing a cap on the number of partners in a partnership to 15.[95] However, the 1844 act which introduced the concept of a company created by registration set the limit at 25.[96] This was reduced to 20 in 1856,[97] bucking the trend of that act which generally followed the liberalising tastes of its sponsor, Robert Lowe.[98] It was further reduced to 10 for banks, whilst retained at 20 for other businesses in 1862,[99] but returned to 20 for all

[87] EF Fama and MC Jensen, 'Agency Problems and Residual Claims' (1983) 26 *Journal of Law and Economics* 327.

[88] EF Fama and MC Jensen, 'Separation of Ownership and Control' (1983) 26 *Journal of Law and Economics* 301.

[89] BT Borden, 'Residual-Risk Model for Classifying Business Arrangements' (2010) 37 *Florida State University Law Review* 245.

[90] E Manson, 'The Evolution of the Private Company' (1910) 26 *Law Quarterly Review* 11, 15; R Harris, 'The Private Origins of the Private Company: Britain 1862–1907' (2013) 33 *Oxford Journal of Legal Studies* 339, 352.

[91] PL Davies, *Gower's Principles of Modern Company Law* 6th edn (London, Sweet & Maxwell, 1997) 21. Subsequent editions have truncated the rich historical detail on the early development of company law.

[92] 6 Geo. 1, c 18 (the Bubble Act), s 25 preserved expressly any partnership that would have been legal prior to its passing.

[93] See J Hardman, 'The UK Historical Viewpoint' in RS Thomas et al (eds), *Research Handbook on Shareholder Inspection Rights: A Comparative Perspective* (Cheltenham, Elgar, 2023).

[94] H Bellenden Ker, *Report on the Law of Partnership with an Appendix Thereto* (House of Commons, 1837).

[95] ibid 39.

[96] Joint Stock Companies Act 1844, s II.

[97] Joint Stock Companies Act 1856, s IV.

[98] PL Cottrell, *Industrial Finance 1830–1914* (London, Methuen, 1980) 52.

[99] Companies Act 1862, s 4.

company types in 1929.[100] The cap remained here through numerous restatements of company law,[101] until removed in 2002[102] – partnerships since then have been able to be of any size desired.

Similar trends can be seen in terms of the minimum number of shareholders. In 1844 there was no minimum, likely because there was no limited liability achievable by regulation.[103] In 1856 a minimum of 7 shareholders was introduced,[104] which was reduced to 2 by the introduction of the concept of a private company in 1907.[105] It was reduced to 1 in 2006.[106]

A simple pictoral representation of this information is set out in Figure 2.1

Figure 2.1 Maximum Partners and Minimum Shareholders Over Time

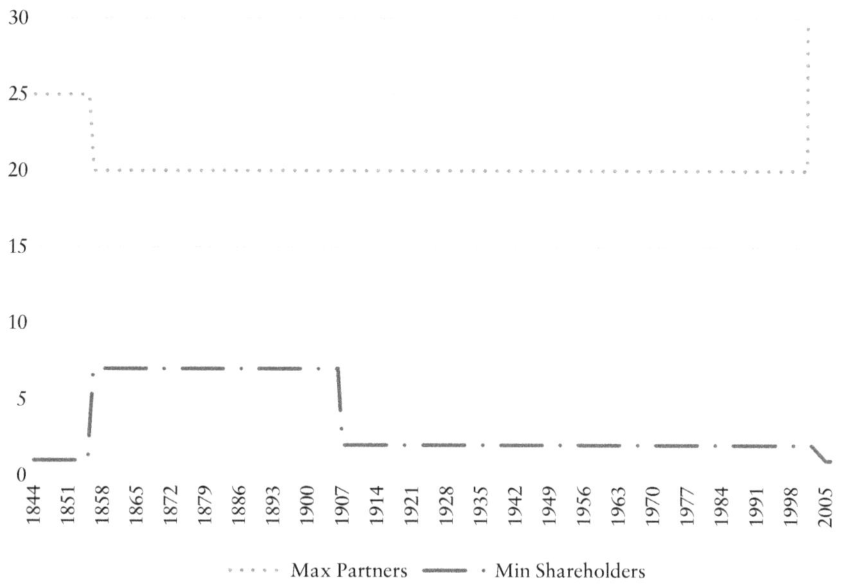

A few easy observations can be made. Above the dotted line are prohibited partnerships (therefore such number of residual claimants would mandate a company form), and below the dashed line are prohibited companies (therefore such number of residual claimants would mandate a partnership).[107] The gap

[100] Companies Act 1929, s 357.
[101] To 1985 – see Companies Act 1985, s 716.
[102] Regulatory Reform (Reform of 20 Member Limit in Partnerships etc.) Order 2002 (SI 2002/3203).
[103] MS Rix, 'Company Law: 1844 and To-Day' (1945) 55 *The Economic Journal* 242.
[104] Joint Stock Companies Act 1856, s III.
[105] Companies Act 1907, s 37(4).
[106] Companies Act 2006, s 7(1).
[107] At least on registration. The rules for what happened if shareholder numbers dropped below the minimum required for incorporation would introduce unnecessary added complications in comparison.

between the two lines initially narrows between 1844 (with maximum partners 25 and minimum shareholders 1) and 1856 (with maximum partners 20 and minimum shareholders 7), then slowly widens over time until there is no effective proscription on either from 2006 onwards.

This means that the flexibility for market participants to choose their preferred legal form slowly increased from 1862. In 1862, if you had 5 recipients of the residual claim, you must be a partnership, and if you had 21 recipients, you must be a company. There was, thus, a 16 person-wide 'overlap zone' in which participants could choose either form (narrowed from the original 25 person-wide overlap zone in 1844, although given the lack of limited liability,[108] the forms could be argued to not be analogous). In 1907, this widened to 18 (for private companies), and from 2002 onwards it has been nearly limitless (with only 1 recipient you could not be a company, and nor could you be a partnership), and from 2006 onwards it has been even closer to limitless (with 1 recipient you can be a company but you cannot, by definition, be a partnership[109]). In other words, the freedom that the state has allowed market participants with a small number of residual claimants in the UK to choose their business form has slowly grown since 1862, and is now near limitless. The converse of this, of course, is that state prescription as to business form based on numbers of residual claimants has reduced accordingly. The legal restraints as to the choice of business form[110] in the UK's vertical market for incorporation have decreased. Conversely, the amount of state control that has been exercised over the menu of options[111] available has liberalised: the growth in overlap-zone increased the flexibility that market participants could have when choosing their business form for a small number of residual claimants.

So what does this tell us if we were looking to ask the normative question of what level of prescription/freedom of choice of legal form there *should* be for business vehicles with small numbers of residual claimants' law? Well, by now you will have picked up my thoughts on the subject: it tells us *whatever we want to hear already*. For we can use this ostensibly neutral set of doctrinal developments to argue whatever we would like the result can be. We can thus advance trajectory arguments – in path dependence, hypothetical bargaining, and legal efficiency forms – and mistake arguments, depending on what we would like the answer to be. Intuitively, we can already see how these argumentation patterns will map into existing debates and discussions in respect of corporate law: trajectory arguments are likely to assist in a case against

[108] Which only appeared in 1855 – see HA Shannon, 'The Coming of General Limited Liability' (1931) 2 *Economic History* 267; R Harris, 'A New Understanding of the History of Limited Liability: An Invitation for Theoretical Reframing' (2020) 16 *Journal of Institutional Economics* 643.

[109] Partnership Act 1890, s 1(1) requires plural persons for a partnership.

[110] WA Klein, 'The Modern Business Organization: Bargaining Under Constraints' (1982) 91 *Yale Law Journal* 1521.

[111] I Ayres, 'Menus Matter' (2006) 73 *University of Chicago Law Review* 3.

state intervention; mistake arguments are likely to assist in a case in favour of state intervention.

Thus, on the trajectory side, a range of options is available. One could argue that law has reached its optimal position – there are upsides in terms of market participants and no evident downside. This would be overtly Posnerian in tone, justifying either the process for achieving this end, the substance of the norm itself on its merits (which is rarely undertaken), or (most commonly) merely arguing a version of *res ipsur loquitur*:[112] the thing speaks for itself. In other words, if one subscribes to the legal efficiency theory, then the law currently allowing an unlimited overlap (or, more accurately, not preventing any overlap) is evidence itself that it is the best rule. Versions of this logic can also easily be applied in respect of the hypothetical bargaining argument – participants would want choice. The use of the word 'participant' makes it *sound* all encompassing, as if this is the rule that everyone affected in the world would have chosen had they been asked. However, the focus of 'participants' in the hypothetical bargaining model is also inherently political – here, we really mean the holders of residual claim. It is perhaps unsurprising that they would vote to provide themselves with maximum freedom. Third parties who receive the brunt of the differentials between the two (in our case, for example, the presence of limited liability) may be less happy with such untrammelled freedom.

Finally under the trajectory perspective, we can appeal to path dependence. We can approach such argument from a number of different perspectives. First, we can argue that liberalisation has already occurred, and as such it should be followed regardless of its merits. This represents a form of first degree path dependence: the decision to liberalise was inter-temporal, and the die is cast. We could even go further and argue that such liberalisation was, somehow, actually *sub-optimal*, but it is too late to change that now. It may be too late because markets like the norm. This argument may, itself, play to the horizontal market for incorporation: given the horizontal market, any attempt to tighten up our vertical market will inevitably result in smaller businesses using legal forms from other jurisdictions.[113] Here, we could see second or third degree path dependence plays being made: either we did not know it was sub-optimal, or did not care because its sub-optimality was outweighed by advantages elsewhere. We could buttress these arguments with a plea for information. This would tell us that we cannot know whether the rule is optimal or not, it would cost too much to find out, and any advantages would be outweighed by the costs. As a result, the costs in terms of either adjustment costs, or costs to coherence with the wider evolutionary framework, would

[112] This legal doctrine is a tort one, and applies where the evidence of injury is used to evidence an actionable wrong that caused that injury – M Shain, 'Res Ipsa Loquitur' (1944) 17 *Southern California Law Review* 187.

[113] Romano (n 78).

outweigh the benefits of moving to a norm which would be superior in isolation. If we could find one. Which we couldn't, of course. Because it would be too expensive. Do keep up.[114]

Counter-arguments exist from a mistake perspective. An evident place to argue for a mistake was in 1856, when the overlap zone narrowed. We could argue that it did not narrow *enough* – this reform folded limited liability into the incorporation by registration mix, and thus could have narrowed matters even further to legally mandate businesses with a small number of residual claimants to utilise one form or the other. This argument would, of course, be interventionist as we assumed mistake arguments would be in corporate law. Mistakes could be identified at any stage of this development: it may have been a mistake to drop the minimum number of shareholders from 7 to 2 in 1985, or from 2 to 1 in 2006. It may have been a mistake to remove the cap on the maximum number of partners. It may have been that a proposal to increase the minimum number of shareholders or decrease the cap on the maximum number of partners should not have been rejected. As noted in the quote that starts this paragraph: whatever we want to argue the law should be, we can almost always find a basis for your claims in the past if you look hard enough.

Should a trajectory argument be advanced without a mistake argument being advanced, then the former will appear to have the weight of history on its side, and vice versa. Thus we must use history when we advance normative arguments in respect of company law. So long as we understand that we use them because they fit into wider normative arguments we want to advance, not because they prove them. We need to do more work to prove that we should be using this argumentation structure, by focusing on the context of the argument. Even then, though, we need to be aware that matters are unlikely to be determinative. If I believe that change needs to be undertaken, then I am more likely to attribute heuristic argumentation weighting to matters that justify that change, and vice versa.

VI. CONCLUSION

Normative arguments are pliable, as is history. This makes them natural bedfellows. This chapter argues that we pick the normative approaches to company law that we want to adopt, then find all tools that we can to justify it. History's natural indeterminancy makes it a logical tool to deploy in every situation. I have argued that in normative company law we adopt one of two approaches: we could argue that law should follow its current trajectory, or we could argue that a mistake has been made in the development of company law. The slow

[114] In the unlikely event that any reader has traced the legal semiotics readings, they will see that this is how those engaging in a certain type of legal semiotics seem to write. I must say it's growing on me, and so I may keep the approach going forward.

pace of change for UK company law naturally connects these arguments into wider themes that company law already advances, and so naturally dovetails to other normative arguments taking place. In a UK company law context, trajectory arguments justify the status quo, mistake arguments justify radical changes to the status quo. Both appeal to history for different, but connected, reasons. Of course, in other disciplines and other jurisdictions, these arguments may play out different. Entirely different tropes may be deployed. Importantly, though, there *will be* argumentation tropes deployed in respect of the use of history in normative approaches to law. These tropes will be connected to other parallel tropes. Deploying history within these crystalline structures is never determinative, but we still need to do it to avoid accidentally losing out.

This chapter illustrates this by tracing the maximum number of partners in a partnership, and minimum numbers of shareholders on incorporation of companies, over time. It tracks these on to normative arguments in respect of how the overlap (or lack of) between these two entities *should function*. Readers may find one potential argument more persuasive than another. They may find none of them persuasive. This chapter does not claim a major failure of the persuasiveness of legal argument generally,[115] or even that we have matters wrong within corporate law.[116] It does, though, identify that when we use history in normative corporate law, we have more agency than we may feel in terms of choosing our approach and normative outcomes. Readers may also find this chapter's overall argument persuasive, or not. Whatever the reader thinks, the meta-theme of this chapter is that it *probably matches what they already thought*.

[115] eg, P Schlag, 'Law as the Continuation of God by Other Means' (1997) 85 *California Law Review* 427.

[116] Contrast with Grant Gilmore's statement that Wesley Sturges was trying to argue 'that the North Carolina law of mortgages made no sense of any kind and could charitably be described as a species of collective insanity on the march' – G Gilmore, 'The Storrs Lectures: The Age of Anxiety' (1975) 84 *Yale Law Journal* 1022, 1035.

3

New Approaches in Corporate Law History: History as a Resource for Navigating Uncertain Times

SARAH WILSON

I. BACKGROUND AND CONTEXT: CELEBRATING CORPORATE LAW'S HISTORICISING TENDENCIES IN A WIDER SPHERE OF (AHISTORICAL?) TRADITION WITHIN LEGAL SCHOLARSHIP

IN THE UK context, Corporate Law scholarship has traditionally been regarded as a niche interest within legal scholarship. This remains largely the case notwithstanding the traction achieved, particularly in the past 30 years, for the view that there is a collective interest in understanding what corporations are and how they act, and how this should be reflected in the legal frameworks which are applied to them and wider societal understandings of them.[1] Here, the architecture of corporate law scholarship testifies to how this more recent trend is probably better understood as an intensification of longer standing concerns about the social significance of these strongly perceived economic entities[2] rather than as a new idea. Here, current directions in studies of corporate law suggest that longer-standing concern about the 'awesome collective power'[3] of corporations supports analysis of corporate law as a research imperative, rather than undermining this. In 1995, Lawrence E Mitchell proposed that as corporate law was an innovation of the twentieth century that the twenty-first would be the 'second century of corporate law'.[4] Through exploring 'new perspectives on law, culture, and society',[5] Mitchell and his colleagues presented a ground-breaking 'communitarian' vision for corporate law – a vision which

[1] See, eg, LE Mitchell (ed), *Progressive Corporate Law: New Perspectives on Law, Culture, and Society* (London, Westview Press, 1995).
[2] See Foreword from Joel Seligman, in Mitchell (n 1) ix–xi.
[3] Mitchell (n 1) Preface, xiii.
[4] ibid.
[5] As embodied in the very title of Mitchell's work.

could ensure that corporate law could serve new times well.[6] Although framed by, and written for, US experiences, the key reasoning and premises deployed are considered to have wider application and significance.

Mitchell proposed that corporate law of the twentieth century had served its times well, responding to the key elements of corporate activity which could be applied to economic growth goals, and gave corporate law's key customers (customers, and managers and shareholders) 'what they want[ed]'.[7] From this, it was argued that the second century of corporate law needed to take on board new realities of changing times, and the changed significance of the corporation. These changes had resulted in the corporation moving beyond being merely an 'instrument to facilitate our market economy', and to an institution with significant social and political significance, and one which in various ways leaves virtually no aspect of the everyday lives of ordinary people untouched. From this, according to Mitchell, it was important to challenge the historical treatment of the corporation as a 'public good in the private service'.[8] For Mitchell, the core idea that a new century for corporate law makes it necessary to 'evaluate the extent to which the corporate invention must be adapted to the tasks it now in fact performs'[9] is a familiar one for academic lawyers generally through how it intimates core ideas of legal change and its impetuses. What Mitchell's work demonstrates very effectively is how calls for legal change can come from places of understanding law in the present moment through reference to the past.

If US corporate law is a creature of the twentieth century, and this necessitates its review for changed times and changed significance for the corporation, then aspects of UK company law are even older still, making it a creature of the nineteenth century as well as the twentieth. For the UK, this certainly was the case until relatively recently. As discussed shortly, this was marked by the reform movement for moving away from law substantially put in place during the nineteenth century, and which had been revisited since in a piecemeal and ad hoc way, rather than by way of comprehensive revision, and which the nature of changing times and operating context for company law demonstrably required. The view that '[a]side from … governments and great wars few, if any, institutions or topics have been the subject of as much contemporaneous commentary as business',[10] will go some way to explaining the extent of scholarly interest in corporate law, even if this is overall niche in the UK. And perhaps it is because corporate law (in the US, like in the UK) retains strong connections with the early twentieth century (or even earlier) that its scholarship is overall well populated

[6] ibid xiii.
[7] ibid.
[8] ibid.
[9] ibid.
[10] GA Mark, 'Some Observations on Writing the Legal History of the Corporation in the Age of Theory' in Mitchell (n 1) 67; 68.

with historical perspectives of different types. Well populated, or at least better populated than much legal scholarship, which is strongly *ahistorical* in character. Much of what follows proposes that legal scholarship with historical perspective can enrich understandings of law, and moreover that undertaking this in particular ways can raise the profile of legal scholarship, through highlighting its capabilities for generating 'resource' insights for living through challenging and uncertain times. Given this, it might be asked why the corporate law emphasis is part of this proposed movement for change, given that as amongst legal scholarship, this sphere is recognisably significantly 'historicised'.

What thus follows is an emphasis on promoting historical enquiry undertaken *in particular ways*. This acknowledges that corporate law history is actually quite plentiful within a discipline which is considered largely ahistorical. Corporate law's position in respect of undertaking historical enquiry in *particular ways* is interesting and complex, but even proposing that law as a discipline might be considered ahistorical is far from straightforward. This is so given that within legal scholarship the longstanding and respected tradition of 'Legal History' is to be found. More is said about legal history and its relationship with the discipline of history shortly, and why even it might also be considered ahistorical. But for legal scholarship generally, whilst characterising it as ahistorical reflects that much legal scholarship lacks any historical perspective, it is also the case that legal scholarship's dominant disposition might also be described as *chronocentric*. In borrowing from the discipline of Criminology's self-characterisation of much of its scholarship, chronocentricity in analysis is said to manifest a presumed wisdom attaching to current conditions and context, where these considerations are regarded as being 'superior to that of their own predecessors'.[11] This suggests that absence of engagement with the past does not necessarily reflect lack of thought about the past on the part of legal scholars, and might reflect a conscious commitment to the importance of the present – and possibly even an ideological choice in privileging the perceived importance of the presence.

Whether or not legal scholarship recognises these characteristics of vesting the present with a conscious superiority, much legal scholarship *is* strongly present-focused, if not present-centric. It is here that whilst corporate law remains a niche interest, whether or not it should do, it is a field that is well populated with historical perspectives. In acknowledging this, this analysis looks first to encourage corporate law scholars to continue to embrace historical perspectives, and to continue to do so even in circumstances which transpire where laws become re-written, and thus become more obviously connected with the present. In giving corporate law scholars this encouragement, this analysis would also wish to encourage them to reflect on how differently historical perspectives could be written – differently from what is currently most

[11] P Rock, 'Chronocentrism and British Criminology' [2005] *British Journal of Sociology* 473; 475.

evident by way of approach – through greater conversing with the discipline of history itself. In this latter sense, the corporate law reference point might be considered one for showcasing a more ambitious historicising agenda across legal scholarship more generally. This is a truism, but this should not downplay the importance of the corporate law scholarship example; whether this is the second or third century for corporate law (or beyond), the twenty-first century shows the corporation as being at the heart of economic prosperity and wider 'social life' – across the western world, and beyond it.

Given its existing dispositions towards historical perspective, the corporate law reference point can be directed towards how different approaches to historical engagement can provide particular types of insight which merely referencing 'the past' is unlikely to. The corporate law reference point is also deployed to help to explain the capabilities of historical enquiry for generating resources for living through uncertain times, by way of introducing insights, and ways of thinking about and understanding prevailing conditions, and for living through them. This is pursued through showcasing particular approaches in history; ones which view past, present, and future as being on the same continuum of societal evolution and development, and as part of a 'trajectory … still unfolding', and where choices around future directions and possibilities can be made.[12] Through illuminating what this 'trajectory thinking' might actually mean, and how it is reasoned and theorised, the argument is made that 'being historical' amounts to more than engaging with the past, and instead involves doing so in particular ways. For legal scholars, the essence of the 'history as resource'[13] idea lies in proposing that 'being historical' in this way presents a pathway for possible further enrichment in understanding of law and its manifest importance for society which might not readily follow from taking a purely present-focused view of our subject matter, whatever this might be. Those holding this view are clear that the purpose of doing so is not to seek from the past precedents for future living,[14] and instead to use distinctive insights to explore possibilities and engage in self-reflection on how possibilities present scope for choices to be made.

The analysis engages with this line of thinking, and explains how it can combine with a core message from legal scholarship which is recognised as Legal History; namely that understanding law's past is a vital element for achieving sophisticated understandings of law, and that this is a vital element for achieving 'confident law reform'.[15] Many corporate law scholars will be familiar with the essence of the claim made in 1995 that in an age where interdisciplinary

[12] J Tosh, *The Pursuit of History: Aims, methods and new directions in the study of history* (London, Longman, 2015; 2010 edn) 40.

[13] M Zundel, R Holt, and A Popp, 'Using History in the Creation of Organizational Identity' [2016] *Management & Organizational History* 211.

[14] Tosh (n 12) 33.

[15] eg, D Ibbetson, *A Historical Introduction to the Law of Obligations* (Oxford, Clarendon, 1999) v–vi.

scholarship has been a hallmark of (twentieth century) legal literature, corporate law scholarship appeared 'oddly stunted'.[16] For the author of this US perspective, this state of being was especially significant given that the shift away from doctrinal approaches in favour of law and economics analysis alone could only provide partial contextualisation for corporate law analysis. In this instant analysis, it is a reflection which can help to make the case for greater emphasis of historical perspective in corporate law scholarship. In applying this also to the UK context specifically, the argument is made that legal scholarship generally has embraced the intellectual enrichment potential of history much less than it has done so with the benefits associated with conversing with key analytical approaches from other disciplines.

From this the case is made not only for greater emphasis of historical perspective in legal scholarship, but that this greater emphasis should come from conversing with the discipline of history, and doing so in particular ways. For this it is proposed not only that the discipline of history is a natural intellectual partner for the discipline of law, but that interdisciplinary study which embodies this can produce analyses which are particularly ambitious and profound, as well as ones which can help to question very fundamentally the discipline of Law's strongly present-focused or even chronocentric character, and thereby help to mainstream and normalise what has recently been termed analysing or theorising with 'historical sensitivity'.[17] Here the corporate law reference point now helps to illuminate some of the more abstract ideas surrounding encouraging legal scholarship more generally to be more historically inclined, and to do so by developing its intellectual curiosity for this in particular ways. For this, if it is to be argued that historical enquiry prioritising 'trajectory thinking' can deliver highly sophisticated accounts of law itself, and of societal choices, then explaining the perceived distinctions between this approach and what is known as legal history is essential. This is particularly so given that legal history does already consider that studies of law's past are vital for the pursuit of 'confident law reform' – and thus for framing laws for the future.

II. HARNESSING CORPORATE LAW SCHOLARSHIP'S HISTORICISING TENDENCIES AND PURVEYING A NEW VISION FOR HISTORICISING LEGAL SCHOLARSHIP

Because corporate law scholarship is already much more enriched with historical perspective than many other spheres of legal scholarship, any case which

[16] Even if they are unfamiliar with this particular source of this claim; see Joel Seligman's Foreword in Mitchell (nn 1 and 2) ix.

[17] M Del Mar, 'Philosophical Analysis and Historical Enquiry: Theorizing Normativity, Law and Legal Thought' in MD Dubber and C Tomlins (eds), *The Oxford Handbook of Legal History* (Oxford, Oxford University Press, 2018) 3; 4.

is made for this to be undertaken more extensively, or to be written differently, needs explaining. Indeed, as will become clear as the hallmarks of legal history scholarship are set out, the field of corporate law history already boasts an impressive range of approaches which are associated with the field of legal history, and recognised as its 'many faces'. Corporate law history is also recognised as having very long temporal reach as well as spatial reach, as perspectives look beyond typical, or even paradigm historical development timeframes (from especially the nineteenth century to the present)[18] and beyond paradigm jurisdictional reference points in common law and civilian traditions.[19] Moreover, corporate law *history* (and not simply corporate law scholarship) is also showing significant 'collection' potential for publication purposes.[20]

The ambition of this analysis is therefore to encourage corporate law history to embrace 'longer-view' histories. This does advocate analyses which are conducted across time, rather than attaching to specific points in time, or specific timeframes or recognised periods in history.[21] Here, ideas underpinning 'longer time[frame]' or periods in history are not entirely synonymous with longer view. Analyses which embody longer view thinking are not looking at time (and its passage) per se, and are looking instead to embrace the conceptual connections which can be made between past, present and future. This reflects the regard amongst historians for these different temporal reference points all being part of the same continuum. This line of reasoning is grounded in related and supporting ideas of multiple future possibilities, and of agency in how these choices might (or might not) prevail. Importantly, this approach actively foregrounds the importance of understanding law in its present and current state. In looking to direct legal analysis in this way it is recognised that even analyses of law which appear to be entirely present-focused are either explicitly or implicitly future oriented, and undertaken with an 'eye' to future development or to highlight unintended consequences etc. And even though much scholarly interest in law is located in the 'here and now', and whilst individual views will vary on influences brought to bear on legal stasis and legal change, law's capacity to change is universally recognised. Foregrounding law 'as [it] is' is thus logical and

[18] See the temporal range showcased in H Wells (ed), *Research Handbook on the History of Corporate and Company Law* (Cheltenham, Edward Elgar, Research Handbooks in Corporate Law and Governance series, 2018).

[19] ibid, with Wells' collection also taking very wide jurisdictional perspectives in the dedicated pursuit of historical perspective.

[20] ibid, with Wells' collection also pointing to the appeal of collections of perspectives, and to the scope for this trend to continue through shared interests in understanding the diversity and versatility of the corporate form and the need for continuing openness in understanding its immense economic and societal significance.

[21] But not necessarily at the temporal extremes of this, such as centuries-long overviews that are evident in, eg, CM Reinhart and KS Rogoff, *This Time Is Different: Eight Centuries of Financial Folly* (Princeton, Princeton University Press, 2011) and W Scheidel, *The Great Leveler: Violence and the History of Inequality from the Stone Age to the Twenty-first century* (Princeton, Princeton University Press, 2017).

necessary for much legal analysis, but this does not have to make legal scholarship chronocentric. Here, longer-view analysis does question legal scholarship's present-focused tendences, and does so through scrutinising law through the significance attached by historians to longer views. The emphasis of long-view analysis is thus on patterns of continuity and change across time, rather than isolating particular points in time.

This approach has been given the working moniker of a law and history approach. It is considered a working title *mainly* because, as to date, theoretical underpinnings and possible applications have been set out only tentatively, and its further development needs must be worked through.[22] What follows now is an overview of how this vision of law and history is positioning itself in relation to traditional legal history, and how the differences it looks to emphasise pertain to how it recognises and looks to embed theoretical and ideological reference points used by historians. In turn, this is being conceived as a manifesto for legal scholarship across a range of individual research interests, and beyond this it is considered to have applications for teaching.[23] Law school teaching, like much legal scholarship is strongly present-centric, if not consciously chronocentric. From this emerges a proposition that whilst there are clear reasons why legal education is oriented as such, that legal education conducted without 'historical sensitivity' excludes the same enrichment possibilities that are said to attach to academic scholarship conducted without 'longer view' perspective.[24] It is also the case that legal education lacking 'historical sensitivity' attracts similar concerns to those expressed around legal scholarship showing these traits, and in some quarters is seen as a root cause of a perceived persistent resistance to history shown in legal scholarship.[25]

What follows is an account which looks to pull these threads together as they apply to legal analysis broadly, and then briefly speak to them using to key reference points in corporate law specifically. To try to promote some concreteness in how such a new approach might apply to corporate law specifically, there is an example of how the core ideas have been applied to long view analysis of Britain's experiences of unlawful behaviours commonly termed 'financial crime'. The approach taken in *The Origins of Modern Financial Crime*[26] posited that richer and more satisfying analyses of law can be achieved through engaging with law beyond the present, and across longer timeframes than are conventionally found

[22] See S Wilson, 'Law and Equity, and 'Law and History' as a resource of critique' [2017] *Pólemos: Journal of Law, Literature and Culture* 23.

[23] See S Wilson, 'Value and Values in Higher Education: Some Reflections From the UK on the Subversive Dimensions of Historical Approaches in the Study of Law' in M Duffy, H Gibbon, B Golder, L Lixinski, M Nehme, and P Vines, *Critical Legal Education as a Subversive Activity* (Abingdon, Routledge, Emerging Legal Education Series, 2022) 149.

[24] ibid.

[25] As considered below in the main text, from n 81 and text thereto.

[26] S Wilson, *The Origins of Modern Financial Crime in Britain: Historical Foundations and Current Problems* (Abingdon, Routledge, Criminology, 2014).

in legal scholarship *if* this is approached in particular ways. The basic premise of this 2014 analysis was that (seemingly) perpetual concerns that financial crimes remain unpunished would benefit from fresh and not entirely present-based understandings of the perceptual and enforcement challenges at play in twenty-first century Britain. It was underpinned by a rationale that understandings of 'the past' must be built in particular ways, and in ways closely aligned with the discipline of history. And from this that building these understandings required accepting that engaging with the past as part of our current and unfolding societal 'story' is not intended to provide answers for the present, and instead what is being sought through historicising present-day challenges is *insight*; insight into what might underlie seemingly entrenched challenges, and insight which might not be possible to attain from adopting a purely present-focused analysis.

What this requires in turn is an openness to possibility as far as insights is concerned. Openness to 'finding' such insights in societies whose experiences long predate us, and openness to evaluating how they might be applied to times and societal conditions which are very different from ones in which they arose. Thereby this analysis of problematics associated with financial crime across a long timeframe also proposed that theoretical aspirations for this 'law and history' approach could be applied widely across legal scholarship research agendas. Corporate law scholars might or might not wish to configure perpetuality in their research agendas. However corporate law study *does* expose multiple challenges arising from how corporate law seeks to 'manage' the needs of business and to do so in ways which recognise the social as well as economic significance of business, and which might be considered longstanding challenges, or even persistent ones. Indeed, one can reflect on the new directions taken in the Companies Act 2006 as recognising longstanding challenges, and embodying legal willingness to try to address them. These include highly profiled attempts to promote greater nuance in balancing the economic significance and realities of business with greater overall accountability for business decision-making across a wider community of interests. This is evident at macro level and also at micro level, approaching this 'from within' rather than seeking to 'superimpose social obligations' upon corporations.[27]

The former – macro – is most prominently evidenced in the rhetorical adoption of enlightened shareholder value (ESV) as a model for business decision-making, which was a highly symbolic move away from the traditional shareholder-centred Anglo-American model,[28] even if this more pluralistic orientation might remain somewhat symbolic, or even illusory. In analyses of

[27] Thereby embodying certainly the spirit behind Mitchell's *Progressive Corporate Law*, published in 1995 at the turn of the 'second century' of corporate law; see Mitchell (n 1) xiv.

[28] With this considering the corporation as embodying the interests of its shareholders, and in turn profit-maximisation goals for this particular interest group; with the traditional application of this to UK company law (namely, prior to the Companies Act 2006) embodied in, eg, *Re Smith and Fawcett Ltd* [1942] Ch 304.

the reforms to UK company law embodied in the Companies Act 2006,[29] the adoption of ESV is most closely associated with the reframing of the duty of loyalty as the s 172 duty to 'promote the success of the company'.[30] Whilst these changes in rhetoric are widely believed to promote stronger continuities with a traditional shareholder-centred, profit-maximising, orientation for corporate decision-making than departures from it,[31] they do acknowledge scope for conflict between profit-maximisation and a wider constituent of interests affected by a business. These changes even recognise the risks to the longevity of the business itself emanating from short-termist thinking around privileging the interests of the company's members.

When these perspectives on conflicts between the widely accepted need for business to generate profit and the realistic limits on reimagining business decision makers as 'moral, political, or economic arbiters'[32] dating from the reform movement are joined together with current events, it seems likely that ideas of persistent challenges for corporate law will dominate corporate law scholars' thinking. For this, the mass sackings of 800 ferry staff by P&O in 2022 and replacement of them with much cheaper overseas agency workers serves to illustrate continuing commitment to shareholder-centred profit maximisation.[33] Moreover, similar observations are evident in the currently highly-profiled affairs of Thames Water, first breaking in June 2023 with the sudden departure of Chief Executive Sarah Bentley amidst concerns about the company's indebtedness and its ability to continue to provide key water services to its 15 million customers.[34] In December 2023 Thames Water's new executive team warned Parliament that the company was unable to repay a loan amounting to £190 million falling due in April 2024, with seeking an extended repayment period

[29] See the extensive documentation generated by the reform movement leading to the Companies Act 2006, commencing with Company Law Review Steering Group, *Modern Company Law for a Competitive Economy: Developing the Framework* (London, Department of Trade and Industry, 2000).

[30] See, eg, G Wilson, 'From black box to glocalized player? Corporate personality in the 21st century and the scope of law's regulatory reach' [2011] *NILQ* 433.

[31] See, eg, A Keay, 'Moving Towards Stakeholderism? Constituency Statutes, Enlightened Shareholder Value and More: Much Ado About Little?' [2011] *European Business Law Review* 1.

[32] Company Law Steering Group (n 29) para 2.1.

[33] J Hills, 'P&O Ferries sacks 800 staff as part of 'necessary' cuts and replaces them with agency workers', *ITV News*, 17 March 2022 www.itv.com/news/meridian/2022-03-17/p-and-o-ferries-suspends-all-sailings-ahead-of-major-announcement.

[34] The commentary generated by the June 2023 revelations engages with Thames Water being a profit making corporate entity with shareholders in different ways. See, eg, different perspectives offered below (in nn 39 and 40), and the financial economics analysis of 'over privatisation' making direct reference to the distribution of sizable profits as dividends to shareholders in A Mullineux, 'Drowning in debt: the 'over-privatisation' of England's water', 30 August 2023, www.birmingham.ac.uk/news/2023/drowning-in-debt-the-over-privatisation-of-englands-water. Alongside this, Thames Water's own operational narrative looks to orient the importance of shareholders for investments which the company needs to make to serve its customers and deliver *What Customers, Communities and Stakeholders Want* in its Report in September 2023 (version 18.3) www.thameswater.co.uk/media-library/home/about-us/regulation/our-five-year-plan/pr24-2023/what-customers-communities-stakeholders-want.pdf.

appearing inevitable.[35] When Thames Water presented its revised business plan to Ofwat in April 2024,[36] the knock on implications of continuing difficulties for customers feared since December 2023 started to concretise around widely predicted bill increases.[37]

The P&O scandal and its aftermath also signal high levels of business confidence in the absence of consequences for business decision-making, even where this (by the company's own admission) contravenes the law.[38] More recently, it would appear that – unlike P&O's Peter Hebblethwaite's quick call to Parliament, Thames Water's summons did not even occur until 5 December 2023,[39] several months after the June 2023 revelations. It also appears unlikely that Sarah Bentley will be required to explain her abrupt departure, and the poor state of the business appearing to prompt this. Thus, Ms Bentley does not appear even to have experienced the extent of the reprimand given to Peter Hebblethwaite in his very public parliamentary 'grilling' and the encouragement given to him by then Transport Secretary Grant Shapps to 'reflect on' his 'position'.[40] This would of course have to be retrospective in Ms Bentley's case given her resignation, but it seems unlikely that any formal condemnation will follow for her. For Thames Water and its new executive team, there does not appear to be a response which is equivalent with Government ability to terminate the 'one of a kind' arrangement which subsisted with P&O.[41] Given this,

[35] Appearing before the Parliamentary Committee for Environment, Food and Rural Affairs Committee (EFRA), on Tuesday 12 December 2023, involving the new executive team led by new Chair Sir Adrian Montague. See S Jack, 'Thames Water says it can't pay back £190m loan', *BBC News*, 12 December 2023, www.bbc.co.uk/news/business-67696645.

[36] See Thames Water Utilities Limited (TWUL) PR24 business plan update, 22 April 2024 https://www.thameswater.co.uk/news/pr24-business-plan-update.

[37] See A Lawson 'Thames Water could raise bills to £627 a year to help fix leaks', The Guardian, 22 April 2024 https://www.theguardian.com/business/2024/apr/22/thames-water-bills-fix-leaks#:~:text=Thames%20Water%20could%20raise%20bills%20to%20as%20much%20as%20£,over%20the%20next%20five%20years.

[38] With the manner of the sackings (including the highly reported video call, and escorting workers off ships and premises carrying plastic bags), also attracting much consternation. For an account of how the sackings were actually unlawful, as well as being more generally repugnant, see, eg, N Lancefield, 'Bosses at P&O Ferries confident of avoiding fine for mass sackings', *The Independent*, 25 April 2023, www.independent.co.uk/business/bosses-at-p-o-ferries-confident-of-avoiding-fine-for-mass-sackings-b2326314.html. Here it was reported that the company's annual report said its directors 'think an ongoing inquiry by the Insolvency Service will not result in punishment'.

[39] With this being clear from EFRA's own parliamentary webpages; see 'EFRA Committee calls Thames Water in to give evidence, following concerns over its finances', UK Parliament Committees, 5 December 2023, committees.parliament.uk/committee/52/environment-food-and-rural-affairs-committee/news/198844/efra-committee-calls-thames-water-in-to-give-evidence-following-concerns-over-its-finances/.

[40] Which was presented as being untenable. See P Walker, 'P&O Ferries refuses plea to reverse sackings', *The Insider*, 29 March 2022, www.insider.co.uk/news/po-ferries-refuses-plea-reverse-26581610.

[41] Referring to the government contract between the Home Office which was terminated following the mass sackings, together with calls for P&O to repay £11 million received by P&O in Government furlough support during the pandemic; see P Davies 'Government terminates contract with P&O Ferries', *Travel Weekly*, 31 May 2022, travelweekly.co.uk/news/tourism/government-terminates-contract-with-po-ferries.

and how even talk of re-nationalisation has been seized upon by all political colours as a scandal centred around the payment of 'huge executive salaries and dividends while failing to invest in services',[42] it will be interesting to observe formal reactions to the latest revelations of continuing indebtedness and likely further fall out of its travails for its customers.

These examples suggest that corporate law scholars who are minded to configure crises in corporate decision-making as raising a research imperative underpinned by the pursuit of 'better business'[43] are unlikely to be short of material for making such a case. They also suggest that challenges arising from corporations being 'both private and public simultaneously'[44] are longstanding, and might properly be considered persistent. However, whilst problematising corporate law challenges in this way is at the heart of how a newer approach, and one which is less fully developed, which can be termed 'law and history' projects itself and its capabilities, doing so is not actually centre stage for this analysis. Instead, interest in a law and history analysis lies in explaining how exploring *law* through reference to history can provide a resource for *society* for navigating uncertain times. This might be considered to embody theorising with 'historical sensitivity' but it is a particular 'face' of this which not even the most enlightened works of legal history have engaged with theoretically to date. Explaining how engaging with history in analysing law might be able to achieve this begins initially with proposing that the early part of the twenty-first century suggests that, as a society, we are likely to experience the present and near future as times of challenge, unease, and upheaval, and continues by asking where ideas on history's importance for reacting to this might actually originate from. The latter begins with why, as the vision for law and history which is presented here develops its own identity, a law and history approach regards what is known as legal history in legal scholarship as a useful and necessary reference point for proposing how law should engage with the discipline of history, but does not consider it sufficient for doing so.

III. CORPORATE LAW HISTORY, LEGAL SCHOLARSHIP, AND LEGAL HISTORY: 'LAW AND HISTORY' AS A NEW ANALYTICAL DIRECTION

Legal history is an established, highly respected branch of legal scholarship, and a long-standing approach to legal analysis. The vision of law and history

[42] See B Marlow 'Thames Water's negligence deserves to be remembered as a national scandal', *The Telegraph*, 28 June 2023, www.telegraph.co.uk/business/2023/06/28/thames-water-is-a-disaster-zone-and-a-reckoning-is-overdue/.

[43] V Adebowale, 'Thames Water crisis presents an opportunity for better business: Nationalisation dominates the debate, but there are other viable alternatives', *The Guardian*, 19 July 2023, www.theguardian.com/business/2023/jul/19/thames-water-crisis-presents-an-opportunity-for-better-business.

[44] See Mitchell (n 1), xiv, citing classic work A Wolfe, 'The Modern Corporation: Private Agent or Public Actor?' [1993] *Wash & Lee Law Review* 1673, 1692.

presented here considers that it manifests important differences from legal history, but that it is also predicated on analysis widely identified with (and indeed, as) legal history. Explaining these nuances of difference and connection requires explaining what legal history is, but even this is not entirely straightforward. This is because, as noted by one of this generation's most outstanding legal historians, as is often the case in academic communities, there is perhaps much more disagreement than consensus.[45] Notwithstanding this, David Ibbetson proposes that legal history can be productively understood as the *history of* 'legal categories, concepts and doctrines; the mechanisms used by lawyers to organize their thoughts'.[46] Ibbetson also suggests that studying law's history allows legal scholars greater degrees of certainty in describing the state of law than can be achieved in studies of 'law today',[47] with this pointing to further overall agreement that legal history is regarded as being distinguishable from law 'as law', and so thus that it is most productively and persuasively considered to be history rather than law.[48] Beyond this, a further – and still related – point of agreement lies in assessments of law (as is) as being 'fluid and dynamic', with legal historians configuring legal history as the study of legal change.[49] Beyond this consensus, Ibbetson suggests that there is much disagreement amongst legal historians, on the forces at play, and influences brought to bear on this dynamism and fluidity, and thus what might encourage legal change or resistance to this.

Differing views on why law changes – or does not change – at particular points in time closely track key analytical traditions evident in legal scholarship, depending on whether the analysis is considered to be doctrinal, contextual, critical, or socio-legal. This range of perspectives found in legal history maps that which is found across legal scholarship generally, and which in turn can be found in the sphere of corporate law specifically. For the UK, the doctrinal analytical tradition is considered the dominant tradition, with widely recognised additional traditions – centrally 'contextualism', 'critical legal studies', and 'socio-legal studies' – very strongly configured as alternatives to this dominant approach.[50] Indeed, it is a scholar of corporate law who explains for us that doctrinal study is essentially 'doctrine-based study'.[51] Exactly what amounts to 'doctrine' for these purposes has inspired differentiation between internal and external approaches to legal history, with this premised on reference to source material which is purely that of law, or where some extrinsic sources which are proximately very close to law will be

[45] Ibbetson (n 15) v.
[46] ibid.
[47] ibid vi.
[48] JH Baker, 'Why the History of English Law Has Not Been Finished' [2000] *CLJ* 62; 64.
[49] ibid 63.
[50] Wilson (n 22) see, eg, 30.
[51] Mark (n 10) 79.

recognised as legal doctrine for these purposes.[52] Here corporate law scholarship itself can be called upon to explain the attraction of purist doctrinal study, highlighting legal change as emanating from law's internal 'rationalising process' with its own dynamic – one which 'tempers the overt pressures on doctrine and in doing so alters the pace of external events'.[53] This particular account is US generated, but it chimes very closely with UK-originated reflection on law's strong self-identification with an inherent internal coherence and logic, self-evident rationality, and lack of susceptibility to external 'non-legal' influences.[54] Through understanding how doctrinal analysis has been the dominant tradition for both the UK and US, key differences between how each has reacted intellectually to the perceived limits of such doctrine-based analysis can now be explained.

As a general idea, what is known as contextualism looks to showcase external 'human' influences brought to bear on law and legal institutions, rather than to minimise their significance, or downplay their ability to impact law's development. In the British legal tradition, contextualism has become defined strongly through reference to acknowledging social, economic, and political influences brought to bear on legal change (and legal stasis).[55] But whilst the impact of a phenomenon on 'society at large' is a grand tradition within American historiography,[56] contextualism applied to corporate law has become 'law and economics' dominated. For observers of this, 'law and economics' – based on welfare-maximising assumptions for human behaviour – is ahistorical, and actually consciously so.[57] In contrast, critical legal studies (CLS) is thought to have historicising tendencies. CLS is widely considered to build on contextualism, through interrogating key assumptions of inclusiveness, autonomy and individual action etc which are built into acknowledging human influences.[58] Its perceived historicising tendencies are evident in claims that CLS has (*probably*) devoted '... more pages to historical description ... than to anything else,[59] with assertions made from within corporate law scholarship specifically that in setting out to demonstrate the contingent nature of legal

[52] Though not for doctrinal purists, through these sources lying beyond 'the law' itself; see Wilson (n 22) 29.

[53] Mark (n 10) 79.

[54] eg, as explained in Roger Cotterrell's classic work, R Cotterrell 'Power, Property and the Law of Trusts: A Partial Agenda for Critical Legal Scholarship' [1987] *JLS* 77; 78.

[55] Wilson (n 22) 30. For understanding this approach generally see F Cownie and A Bradney, 'Socio-legal studies: a challenge to the doctrinal approach' in D Watkins (ed), *Research Methods in Law* (London, Routledge, 2013) 34. An example of contextualism applied to legal history specifically see Michael Lobban's reference to social and economic upheaval during the nineteenth century in M Lobban, 'Nineteenth-Century Frauds in Company Formation: *Derry v Peek* in Context' [1996] *LQR* 287.

[56] Mark (n 10) 73.

[57] ibid 80.

[58] See Wilson (n 22) especially 30, 39–40.

[59] RW Gordon, 'Critical Legal Histories' [1984] *Stanford Law Review*, 57; 57.

change, CLS is by its very nature 'historical in character'.[60] And beyond CLS, the socio-legal studies movement could plausibly embrace historical perspectives as part of this 'broad church movement' looking at enriching law drawing on theoretical and empirical dimensions of cognate disciplines.[61]

Building on stated Socio-Legal Studies' core aims of making connections between law and sociology and social policy, and looking to bridge divisions between law and the discipline of economics,[62] clearly this movement shows that law *has* ventured into social science well beyond this, and also into the space it claims to provide for law to meet with humanities.[63] However, notwithstanding the strengths of both CLS and Socio-Legal Studies, even if they are not considered to be ahistorical, it is argued that for mapping law and history, they are not historical *enough*. This is because for aspirational law and history, neither of them very obviously engages with the discipline of history. For CLS, this is because notwithstanding possibly devoting more pages to historical description than to anything else, as one of its key critics has argued, CLS manifests 'criticism from within' (the discipline of law),[64] and thus the pursuit of 'the contingent nature of legal change' which for some makes CLS historical in character renders it for others only a partial agenda for legal scholarship.[65] And although the socio-legal studies movement has achieved much in promoting what Roger Cotterrell termed legal scholarship's exposure to the 'wider currents of systemic knowledge associated with other intellectual disciplines',[66] overall it has not produced far-reaching historical perspective engagement, and certainly not the extensive reach evident in legal scholarship's intellectual partnering with Sociology and Philosophy.

There is perhaps more socio-legal oriented corporate history than there is 'socio-legal historical perspective' to be found across law's wider sweep of interest. This scholarly disposition in the corporate law field can be found across legal history's characteristic pluralistic tendencies in embracing accounts of legal change which are both 'top down' (through focus on narratives of key legal system actors, or institutions or systems)[67] or 'bottom up', in regarding ordinary people as agents of legal change.[68] Overall, even where legal scholarship does embrace historical perspective, the argument can be made that this is not enough to satisfy law and history's appetite for embracing the discipline of history

[60] Mark (n 10) 81.
[61] See slsa.ac.uk/.
[62] ibid.
[63] ibid.
[64] Cotterrell (n 54) 77.
[65] ibid.
[66] ibid.
[67] See, eg, R McQueen, *A Social History of Company Law: Great Britain and the Australian Colonies 1854–1920* (Aldershot, Ashgate, 2009).
[68] See, eg, V Barnes, 'Legal Transplants, Law Books, and Anglo-American Corporate Fiduciary Duties' [2020] *Hastings Business Law Journal* 145.

methodologically and intellectually. This is either because individual examples do not reflect on the significance of historical analysis sufficiently, or because where this does happen it does not happen often enough, or in ways which are systematic or well-theorised. Perhaps from this it can be argued that what is here presented as law and history embodies the underpinning part of Cotterrell's ambition for legal scholarship's exposure to 'wider currents of systemic knowledge associated with other intellectual disciplines'.[69] For Cotterrell, this was the goal for legal scholarship's eventual integration with these external influences, which could only be achieved through eventual confrontation with them.[70]

IV. CORPORATE LAW AND THE 'WIDER CURRENTS' OF INFLUENCE: ENCOURAGEMENT FOR LOOKING *BEYOND* THE DISCIPLINE FROM *WITHIN*

Cotterrell's views on the value *for* law of engaging with different disciplines, and indeed the perceived necessity of doing so, do amount to important support for mapping law and history, and for shining a light on how conversations between it and legal scholarship more broadly might, or should be, framed. However, this developmental phase for law and history to date has been far more influenced by the strengths of legal scholarship than so by its limitations, taking much which is positive from its intellectual versatility and significant openness to approaches from 'without' as well as from within. It has also drawn much inspiration from where these evident strengths of legal scholarship can be identified within legal history itself. What law and history suggests is that these strengths provide strong foundations for encouraging law to engage more extensively with not simply 'the past' as it might be embodied in events from the past, or even interpretations of these events, but to do so embracing the craftsmanship of history. This advocates that what Cotterrell has termed 'more adequate understanding of law'[71] can flow from legal scholarship acquiring greater understanding of what it means to be an historian, and what working as one entails – and what it can *achieve*. From this premise, nascent law and history has long argued that for all its undoubted intellectual richness and pluralism, legal history remains very strongly identifiable as '*law*'s history'.[72]

The core idea of legal history as 'law's history' is of course most plainly evident in legal history written in the doctrinal tradition, and where in its purest form this scholarship will only ever engage with law itself. In the UK tradition, (where contextualism has a different face from US 'law and economics') however richly law and legal change are contextualised through reference to the

[69] Cotterrell (n 54) 77.
[70] ibid.
[71] ibid.
[72] Wilson (n 22).

prevailing social, economic, intellectual, and political conditions which produced (or otherwise influenced) them, analysis appears to be strongly motivated by wishing to understand more about law itself. However thoroughly assumptions surrounding the capacity to exert influence over law's operations are questioned, it has been argued that CLS is, and remains highly law-centric, and unrivalled even in considering law to be 'at the very center of its universe',[73] even if CLS might also be (inherently) 'historical in character'.[74] And whilst the Socio-Legal Studies movement *has* enabled extensive exposure of legal scholarship to other intellectual disciplines, overall it has been characterised by much more emphasis of the *legal* (in socio-legal) than the *socio* (in socio-legal).[75] Clearly lawyers will, by definition, be interested primarily in building understandings of law, and this is where their training and expertise lie. But with much legal analysis beyond doctrinal study in different ways looking to engage with themes of 'law and social change' and thus with the reflective and reflexive nature of law as a 'living thing' within society,[76] there is so much scope for directing these understandings of law towards enriched understandings of society itself. These understandings of society might be considered enriched and also *enriching* through how they can shine a light on what kind of society we are, and how this has become shaped and influenced by hopes and aspirations, by fears and concerns, and by the adoption of some values and ideologies, and the rejection of others. This can help to strengthen the pursuit of 'confident law reform', but it can also provide insight into how 'the pursuit of history' can help to generate wider societal resource for navigating uncertain times.

For this, what this analysis presents as a vision for law and history has long advocated that there are many benefits for legal scholarship where there is openness to historians' perspectives on society and social change across time.[77] Being willing to embrace this helps to showcase the value of analysing law and legal change across much longer timeframes than is conventionally apparent in legal scholarship. It thus helps to showcase the value of the 'long view' for legal scholarship. Much legal scholarship which does engage with the past manifests the continuing separation of 'past and present'. For this work, which includes much legal history, the idea is that history is just that, rather than looking to make connections between past and present. This separation of the past from

[73] This is so in providing a theory of society which 'puts law at its very center': see C Tomlins 'What Is Left of the Law and Society Paradigm after Critique: Revisiting Gordon's 'Critical Legal Histories'' [2012] *Law & Social Enquiry* 155; 157.

[74] Mark (n 10) 81.

[75] With this being a key premise for D Feenan (ed), *Exploring the 'Socio' of Socio-Legal Studies* (Basingstoke, Palgrave Macmillan, Socio-Legal Studies book series (PSLS), 2013).

[76] A Gearey, ''We Want to Live': Metaphor and Ethical Life in F.W. Maitland's Jurisprudence of the Trust' [2016] *JLS* 105; 110.

[77] By way of balance, it also suggests that law could be more vocal in reminding historians of the reliance which their research places on sources which are generated from law and legal processes. See Wilson (n 22).

the present is also to be found within the discipline of history, where for many historians the goal of 'being historical'[78] is satisfied through achieving richer understandings of the past.[79] Here, law and history is attracted to what historians themselves consider to be the 'more exotic' applications of their insights; exploring how understandings of the past can help to make sense of the present.[80]

For law and history, this latter face of historical enquiry has tremendous scope for supporting understandings of the dynamics between law and society, which do, in different ways, underpin many research agendas in legal scholarship. From this flows possibilities for 'more adequate understanding' of law, achieved through enriched understanding of society itself. Understanding of societal conditions might seem an obvious ingredient for achieving competent understanding of law, and 'confident law reform' as advocated by legal history scholarship. Nevertheless, legal scholarship has shown significant 'resistance to history'.[81] And if 'history' in this sense means the work and craft of historians, then this can even be said for much legal history scholarship. By way of example, Sir John Baker has noted that as amongst legal historians the 'father' of modern legal history FW Maitland was unusual in working as an historian, in terms of contextualising law through reference to prevailing social and intellectual conditions, and drawing on extraneous primary source material in order to do so.[82] Clearly contextual approaches in legal history are more common today, but on such views, the consensus in legal history is that it amounts to being 'history' by virtue of being distinct from law 'as is', but also that this mostly stops short of fully embracing the craft and practices of history.

From this, and for this, it is important to understand that this concern about continuing resistance to history within legal scholarship actually emanates from within legal history itself. This proposition has been advanced with reference to a purported pattern of 'sidelining' of what has been termed 'historical sensitivity'[83] in legal scholarship. It has been argued that this sidelining has become embedded within legal analysis through dominant trends in legal education, where 'most if not all topics … are taught either without any historical sensitivity … or with but a passing nod to the 'origins' of some area of doctrine that is only ever at best recommended reading'.[84] Law and history suggests that legal scholarship could profitably respond to this through engaging with key perspectives in theorising history and its relevance for twenty-first century living. In some quarters at least legal history is confounded by this continuing resistance within a subject 'that so clearly lends itself to historical enquiry, and where there is

[78] Zundel, Holt, and Popp (n 13).
[79] Tosh (n 12) viii–ix.
[80] ibid.
[81] Del Mar (n 17) 4.
[82] See Baker (n 48) 64; see also Baker's account of Maitland's 'two logics' (also at 64).
[83] Del Mar (n 17) 4.
[84] ibid.

arguably so much overlap between legal thought and the practice of history'.[85] This is a very strong entreaty from within legal history for legal scholarship to embrace the theory and practice of history, and to do so in ways which are readily apparent in Philosophy's recognition of the value of historical enquiry.[86] Given this, it may well be that legal history could evolve to take up the cause of mainstreaming historical perspective which is underpinned by theory and practices of the discipline of history within legal scholarship, and which is currently being championed by law and history as it is presented in this analysis. If this transpires then law and history may not become a fully-fledged approach for legal scholarship. Movements within legal history to regard law as an 'object of enquiry', and presenting it as one which inter alia persists through time (across time and places) and which can be explored 'via multiple temporalities',[87] are very encouraging, and *could* render law and history as an idea redundant. However, this is likely to occur over time, and is unlikely to transpire very soon. Moreover, it may not even occur in the same way which this vision for law and history is currently developing.

V. 'LAW AND HISTORY' AND APPROACHING HISTORICAL PERSPECTIVE THROUGH THE DISCIPLINE OF HISTORY

In now continuing to explore how a law and history agenda might serve as a resource for navigating uncertain times, it is important to understand that this draws on particular visions of history. Just as it has been noted that there is much disagreement amongst scholars of legal history on what actually legal history is, the discipline of history considers that it is more readily characterised by 'heated argument' than 'consensus of expert opinion', with this very much evident in relation to the 'objectives and limitations of historical study'.[88] From this, in searching for a vision of history which can provide the most persuasive support for legal analysis, law and history engages with perspectives which are characterised broadly in two ways. First, it seeks perspectives appearing to foreground the importance of the 'social' – embodied in interest taken in society and social change. Second, it seeks perspectives looking to encourage thinking across long timeframes rather than encouraging separation of 'past and present', and thereby embracing temporal continuities, rather than effacing them.[89] From this, a vision of history as a resource can start to take shape.

For this vision, two perspectives stand out when encouraging legal scholarship to celebrate its strengths and look to build on these through celebrating the

[85] ibid.
[86] ibid.
[87] ibid 6.
[88] Tosh (n 12) ix.
[89] Per Rock (n 11).

'overlap between legal thought and the practice of history'. They are rooted in the expressed importance of society and the dynamics of social change within both the legal academy and the discipline of History. The first relates to historians' lament that the contributions their 'complex and many-sided' understanding of the 'temporalities of social life' could make to social science theory are barely acknowledged within social science.[90] The second relates to perceived scope for mutual enlightenment which can be achieved through bridging 'disciplinary divide[s]' also being largely ignored.[91] In bringing these two ideas together, John Tosh makes a powerful case for how relevant historians and their work are for living through the present, and for envisioning possible futures. This is championed through Tosh asking us to imagine how we might understand collective societal journey across time through reference to the significance we attach to 'the past' in our individual life stories:

> Because our species depends more on experience than on instinct, life cannot be lived without the consciousness of a personal past … As individuals we draw on our experience in all sorts of different ways- as a means of affirming our identity, as a clue to our potential, as the basis for our impression of others, and as some indication of the possibilities that lie ahead. Our memories serve as both a data bank and as a means of making sense of an unfolding life story. We know that we cannot understand a situation without some perception of where it fits into a continuing process or whether it has happened before. The same holds true of our lives as social beings. All societies have a collective memory, a storehouse of experience which is drawn on for a sense of identity and a sense of direction.[92]

The value which Tosh sees in understanding this sense of collective journey across a 'trajectory' on which past, present, and future lie on the same continuum, and are part of a journey which is still unfolding, and is not pre-determined is several-fold. But Tosh insists that the past is not intended to provide a blueprint for living through the present and anticipating the future. Working with the past in this way allows us to be aware of multiple possibilities of what lies ahead – an 'inventory of alternatives'. Access to these 'alternatives' requires on our part an openness to how all that we can, or even need, to understand about ourselves and our 'lives lived' today might not be possible to glean through looking only at the present (albeit mostly with an eye to the future in some way). As Tosh explains

> As a memory bank of what is unfamiliar or alien, history constitutes our most important cultural resource. It offers a means- imperfect but indispensable- of entering into the kind of experience that is simply not possible in our own lives. Our sense of the heights to which human beings can attain, and the depths to which they may sink, the

[90] WH Sewell, *Logics of History: Social Theory and Social Transformation* (Chicago, University of Chicago Press, 2005) see especially 1 and 6.
[91] ibid.
[92] Tosh (n 12) 33.

> resourcefulness they may show in a crisis, the sensitivity they can show in responding to each other's needs- all nourished by knowing what has been thought and done in the very different contexts of the past ... History reminds us that there is usually more than one way of interpreting a predicament or responding to a situation, and that the choices open to us are often more varied than we might have supposed ... The point is not to find a precedent, but to alert to possibilities. History is an inventory of alternatives, all the richer if research is conducted with half an eye to our immediate situation in the present.[93]

VI. CONCLUSION (BUT TO BE CONTINUED) ...

Clearly, there is more to history's potential contributions to this vision for law and history than this alone. And the application of historical 'thinking' to legal analyses of law 'as is' (as well as to law's past) involves explaining why we should not accept ideas of 'meta history' (configuring history as providing 'the answers' for current concerns and anxieties),[94] and acknowledging that not all will be persuaded that history has any value at all for lives lived in the twenty-first century, either fundamentally or because as an idea 'looking backwards' is antithetical to modernity.[95] It also requires observance of key 'rules' for making connections between points in time which are separated by a 'gulf of time'.[96] These are considerations relating to how to conduct the kind of analysis envisioned by law and history as well as underpinning why we might wish to. Had this analysis looked to foreground how to undertake the kind of corporate law scholarship which nascent 'law and history' is looking to encourage then greater attention would have been paid to the example of this undertaken in *The Origins of Modern Financial Crime*.[97] This approach would look to problematise chosen subject matter within the corporate law sphere in the same way which would ground any more conventional approach taken in legal scholarship (whether this is present-focused, or an intended study of the past). Whilst what is being presented as law and history is not likely to appeal to purist doctrinal scholarship, it can have a wide appeal across different applications of contextualism and critical perspectives. Within this, the starting points for present-focused analysis and that which embraces historical perspective are thus the same, whether these are 'familiar faces' for corporate scholars, or more novel problematics. Beyond this, the 'how' conversation is one for another day.

As for wrapping up this discussion which has focused on the 'why' question, and directed it towards the value of resource for navigating uncertain times,

[93] ibid.
[94] ibid 40.
[95] See Wilson (n 22) 38.
[96] Tosh (n 12). See discussion of Tosh and the three principles of historicism, 36–37.
[97] Wilson (n 26).

the insights from Tosh's 'trajectory thinking' are now presented as offering a vision for legal scholarship within which engaging with law through the prism of how historians analyse society and social change can convey an understanding of our current social character and condition. It is from this that messages of hope and societal resilience in uncertain times can emerge. It is argued that configuring historical approaches in this way can be part of a message that even the very worst of times can be times when positive societal choices are made, and that this is a message which legal scholarship framed in this way can help to convey and transmit. With its unfolding to date and even short-term future forecasting, suggesting that experiencing the present and near future is likely to be characterised by challenge, unease, and upheaval, this is an important moment for conveying messages of hope and resilience. Here, corporate law's extensive substantive interest reach could play an important role in communicating that even the worst of times we can choose to continue to strive for social justice, equality, and human rights. That we can choose politics which aspires to be progressive and inclusive and long-termist rather than divisive and popularist. And in the face of the demise of the age of 'global warming' and arrival of the era of 'global boiling',[98] we can choose to respond to the climate emergency by taking responsibility to halt environmental destruction rather than passing the burden of doing so to future generations.

Perhaps by returning to earlier reference to the P&O and Thames Water scandals, little more needs to be said about why corporate law analysis might benefit from 'trajectory thinking'. There is a rich history of the emergence of the corporation and capitalist ethos which can help us to make sense of the relentless pursuit of (primarily shareholder-driven) profit which can help us to understand both the egregious behaviours of these two businesses, and an apparent lack of legal accountability for unacceptable behaviour,[99] especially where we choose to configure this rich history as part of the pattern of social change and solidification of 'values'. The same can be said about the history of directors' duties, and the traditional imbalance between expectations relating to skill, care, and diligence and ones attaching to fiduciary propriety,[100] and connections which have been made between this and law's apparent queasiness around regulating entrepreneurship.[101]

Applying these known strands of corporate law's history to the latest corporate 'scandals' can help us to understand why we should not be surprised that it

[98] Reflections from the UN secretary general, António Guterres; see A Niranjan, 'Era of global boiling has arrived,' says UN chief as July set to be hottest month on record', *The Guardian* 27 July 2023, www.theguardian.com/science/2023/jul/27/scientists-july-world-hottest-month-record-climate-temperatures.

[99] See, eg, A Hudson, 'Law as Capitalist Technique' [2018] *King's Law Journal* 58.

[100] See B Pettet, *Company Law* (Essex, Pearson Press, 2001) 173.

[101] See S Wilson, 'Tort law, actors in the "enterprise economy", and articulations of nineteenth-century capitalism with law: The Fraudulent Trustees Act 1857 in context' in TT Arvind and J Steele (eds), *Tort law and the legislature: Common law, statute and the dynamics of legal change* (Oxford, Hart Publishing, 2012) 353.

was considered acceptable simply to rebuke P&O management and to encourage its highest placed corporate officers to reflect on their position as being untenable, with no further consequences attaching to admitted lawbreaking. And why we should not be surprised by the little by way of further comment upon the news that Peter Hebblethwaite not only defied calls to resign, but has been promoted to other roles within the organisation, with this occurring with virtually no media coverage even.[102] The same can be said of how little condemnation has followed from there being no word even from Sarah Bentley since her spectacular resignation as the most recent Thames Water scandal broke (with this being part of an ongoing 'story', involving multiple instances of law breaking and regulatory breaches, and relating to leak target breaches, leaking and dumping sewage and health and safety breaches for workers).[103] Situating these points in time together, and looking to understand them as part of an unfolding social journey also allows us to take stock of them, and reflect on how the society we are, and want to be, should react to such behaviours, and whether we might want to pursue a different kind of societal journey. Clearly, calling out capitalism's capacity to impoverish our lives through its embeddedness[104] using egregious corporate behaviours is far from simple. Engaging with history's core messages at least presents us with reasoned choices around whether we should attempt to do so.

[102] Except in the union-focused commentary where the coverage was clearly of a particular ilk; see E Stone, '"A complete insult to workers": Union hits out at P&O Ferries boss Peter Hebblethwaite's "'promotion"', *National World*, 9 May 2022.

[103] With this catalogue of breaches all occurring recently, within the timeframe from 2019.

[104] Mitchell (n 1),n xiii.

4

The Unexpected Origins of the US Limited Liability Partnership

HARWELL WELLS*

I. INTRODUCTION

IN 1991 THE United States (US)[1] gained a new type of business organisation, the limited liability partnership (LLP).[2] The LLP's origins are seemingly well-known: it was created as a response to staggering malpractice claims from the previous decade that pushed partners in large American law firms, almost all organised as general partnerships, to seek a shield from personal liability for their firms' or fellow partners' debts.[3] As this chapter will show, however, that account is incomplete. The LLP's invention lies at the tail end of a much longer story, that of American lawyers' stiff resistance to corporations practicing law. Since the beginning of the twentieth century the legal profession had laboured to protect lawyers' self-image and fend off competition by (among other things) forbidding corporations from offering legal services; the LLP appeared when lawyers decided that, despite this longstanding opposition, they needed one of the advantages of incorporation: limited liability. The LLP was thus the product not only of economic demands, but of the peculiarities of

* My thanks for helpful comments to participants at the Society for Legal Studies' Seminar on the Origins of Company Law; to Robert Thompson; and for research support to Temple University's James E Beasley School of Law.

[1] The US LLP shares a name with the UK limited liability partnership, but they are very different entities. See J Freedland, 'Limited Liability Partnerships in the United Kingdom: Do They Have a Role for Small Firms?' in J McCarehy, T Raaijmakers, and EPM Vermeulen (eds), *The Governance of Close Corporations and Partnerships: US and European Perspectives* (Oxford, Oxford University Press, 2004).

[2] One could quibble as to whether the LLP is a 'new business form' inasmuch as in most states it is governed by the Uniform Partnership Act and is in the eyes of the law a general partnership that has elected limited liability for its partners. Uniform Partnership Act (2013) § 102(9). In my judgment, however, the addition of limited liability to an entity long distinguished by the lack of limited liability justifies the term.

[3] See, eg, R Hamilton 'Registered Limited Liability Partnerships: Present at the Birth (Nearly)' (1995) 66 *University of Colorado Law Review* 1065.

the American legal profession and its conflicted relationship with the corporate form and the modern corporation. This longer and more complicated history of the birth of a new form of business organisation, one encompassing economics, politics, and the culture of a profession, is the one recounted here, and it begins not at the end of the twentieth century but at the end of the nineteenth.

II. THE MODERN CORPORATE LAW FIRM AND FEAR OF THE MODERN CORPORATION: BATTLING 'THE CORPORATE PRACTICE OF LAW'

Lawyers once did not need any business form beyond the venerable general partnership. Throughout the nineteenth century almost all lawyers in the US practiced either as solo practitioners or occasionally in two-man partnerships with one partner as courtroom lawyer and the other the 'office man' drafting legal documents.[4] Law firms were rare and large ones non-existent. This fit with lawyers' self-image as independent actors bound only by their duties to clients and public roles as 'officers of the court'.[5] This independence – imagined or not – also fit with lawyers' frequent role as civic leaders, playing a role on the local or national stage.[6] There was also little reason for lawyers to join together into larger economic organisations; the general partnership, easily formed and dissolved and amenable to private ordering, sufficed. Almost all lawyers were generalists, so there was no advantage to be gained from division of labour made possible by larger organisations, and solo practitioners had little need for the special advantages offered by incorporation such as lock-in of investors' capital or limited liability.[7]

In the late nineteenth century legal practice began to change in response to changes in the nation's economy. The growth of giant corporations created new demand for specialised legal work as railroads and other large firms routinely sought aid in areas such as corporate reorganisation and securities issuance. While the vast majority of lawyers continued in solo practice, law firms of unprecedented size appeared in New York and a few other cities. In New York, for example, a 1913 survey counted ten lawyers at the Cadwalader firm and 13 at Cravath, small numbers today but shockingly large then.[8] Though still organised as partnerships, the new firms were also organisationally innovative; partners

[4] W Hurst, *The Growth of American Law* (Boston, Little Brown, 1950) 302–06; LM Friedman, *A History of American Law*, 4th edn (Oxford, Oxford University Press, 2019) 619–623.

[5] R Gordon, 'The Independence of Lawyers' (1988) 68 *Boston University Law Review* 1.

[6] Friedman (n 4) 619.

[7] See, eg, M Blair 'Locking In Capital: What Corporate Law Achieved for Business Organizers in the Nineteenth Century' (2003) 51 *UCLA Law Review* 387; H Hansmann, R Kraakman, and R Squire 'Law and the Rise of the Firm' (2006) 119 *Harvard Law Review* 1333; 'The Practice of Law by Corporations' (1931) 44 *Harvard Law Review* 1114.

[8] R Gordon, 'The American Legal Profession 1870-2000' in M Grossberg and C Tomlins (eds), *The Cambridge History of Law in America III* (New York, Cambridge University Press, 2008); Hurst (n 4) 303.

could specialise in one area such as tax or securities, several associates and partners might work together as a team on major matters, and compensation was pooled rather than paid directly to individual partners, which encouraged partners and clients to see legal services being provided by the firm rather than individual members.[9] The new firms were later dubbed 'law factories.'[10]

The rise of the corporate law firm challenged the nation's legal elite. In the previous century the best-known lawyers were orator-statesmen who earned their reputation in the courtroom and represented an array of clients in a variety of legal matters, but by the beginning of the twentieth century that was no longer the case.[11] As early as the 1880s, notes Robert Gordon, a coterie of lawyers in New York had begun to specialise 'as legal brokers and intermediaries between large American corporations trying to attract new capital ... and the investment banking communities of Wall Street and Europe'.[12] In 1909 the legal scholar Roscoe Pound would comment that the leaders of the American bar had become 'chiefly client caretakers ... Their best work is done in the office, not in the forum'.[13] This provoked worries, reiterated ever since, that lawyers were losing the social leadership roles they once played and that law was declining from a once-noble and independent profession to a presumably servile business.[14] In 1906 Louis Brandeis would warn that lawyers were allowing 'themselves to become adjuncts of great corporations.'[15] The extreme version of this fear was voiced in a 1913 *Yale Law Journal* article which claimed that '[t]he lawyer's former place in society as an economical factor has been superseded by this artificial creature of his own genius, for whom he is now simply a clerk on a salary',[16] a comment that combined fears of social diminishment with economic dependency. In response, at least a few leaders of the bar began to craft for themselves a new self-image as trusted counsellors who advised corporations while keeping a distance from them.[17] This desire for independence may also explain why most corporate lawyers chose to remain as partners at law firms rather

[9] W Henderson, 'Three Generations of US Lawyers: Generalists, Specialists, Project Managers' (2011) 70 *Maryland Law Review* 373, 376.

[10] See, eg, K Llewellyn 'The Bar Specializes – With What Results?' (1933) 167 *Annals of the American Academy of Political and Social Science* 177.

[11] Hurst (n 4) 302–03.

[12] R Gordon '"The Ideal and the Actual in the Law": Fantasies and Practices of New York Lawyers, 1870–1910' in GW Gawalt (ed), *The New High Priests: Lawyers in Post-Civil War America* (Westport, Greenwood Press, 1984).

[13] M Galanter and T Palay, *Tournament of Lawyers: The Transformation of the Big Law Firm* (Chicago, University of Chicago Press, 1991) 6 quoting R Pound 'The Etiquette of Justice' (1909) 3 *Proceedings of the State Bar Association* 231.

[14] See R Hofstadter, *The Age of Reform* (New York, Vintage, 1960) 140–46; JS Auerbach, *Unequal Justice: Lawyers and Social Chance in Modern America* (New York, Oxford University Press, 1976). Whether or not lawyers were actually suffering an economic or social decline during this period is debatable, but many clearly thought they were. See M Galanter, 'Lawyers in the Mist: The Golden Age of Legal Nostalgia' (2017) 122 *Dickinson Law Review* 267, 270.

[15] LD Brandeis, 'The Opportunity in the Law' (1906) 3 *Commonwealth Law Review* 22, 26.

[16] GW Bristol, 'The Passing of the Legal Profession' (1913) 22 *Yale Law Journal* 590, 590.

[17] See R Gordon, 'The Return of the Lawyer-Statesman?' (2017) 69 *Stanford Law Review* 1731, 1736–41.

than becoming employees within their corporate clients, an arrangement which allowed them to work 'outside the managerial hierarchies' then springing up across the nation.[18] Lawyers advised the new specialised, hierarchical corporations, but they worked within flexible, egalitarian partnerships.[19]

While the legal elite fretted over their status, they also feared social change within the legal profession. The nineteenth century bar had been dominated by lawyers from Protestant backgrounds and established immigrant groups, but beginning in the 1880s, new waves of immigration began to alter its demographic base.[20] An increasing number of lawyers were first- or second-generation immigrants with roots in southern and eastern Europe, and, in a development that produced a particularly ugly nativist response, Jewish.[21] The new influx of lawyers produced challenges both economic and cultural. Economic, in that more lawyers meant more competition; 'bar admissions increased fourfold between 1900 and 1929, and the practicing profession nearly doubled between 1890 and 1930'.[22] Cultural, in that many leaders of the bar reacted with horror at the new lawyers and, to keep their numbers down imposed new character and fitness and educational requirements for bar admission.[23] In 1908 the American Bar Association (ABA), controlled by elite lawyers, adopted a Canon of Ethics to rein in the increasingly competitive legal market.[24] Canon 27 for instance banned advertising, while Canon 28 barred lawyers from hiring 'agents or runners' to obtain clients.[25]

At the beginning of the 1910s, we then find the upper echelons of the bar trying to navigate between their reliance on corporations for work and status and their insistence that they operated at a remove from their corporate clients and the market economy more generally. Imagine leading lawyers' shock when they found that corporations were practicing law. In 1909 New York lawyer Henry Marsh discovered that several corporations had been organised 'to institute and prosecute legal proceedings for the collection of claims of various kinds'.[26]

[18] Gordon (n 8) 93; see also O Zunz, *Making America Corporate 1870-1920* (Chicago, University of Chicago Press, 1990).

[19] At this time in the US the only real organisational choice for most businesses with multiple owners was between the partnership and the corporation. Unlike some European countries, the US had not developed business entities that combined elements of the two. N Lamoreaux, 'Partnerships, Corporations, and the Limits on Contractual Freedom in U.S. History: An Essay in Economics, Law, and Culture' in K Lipartito and D Sicilia (eds), *Constructing Corporate America: History, Politics, and Culture* (New York, Oxford University Press, 2004).

[20] See, eg, Auerbach (n 14) 19–25.

[21] ibid 125–27.

[22] RL Abel, *American Lawyers* (New York, Oxford University Press, 1989) 108.

[23] See, eg, Auerbach (n 14) 12.

[24] MS Ariens, *The Lawyers' Conscience: A History of American Lawyer Ethics* (Lawrence, University Press of Kansas, 2023) 128–134.

[25] American Bar Association, *Canons of Professional Ethics* (Baltimore, MD American Bar Association, 1908).

[26] BA Green 'The Disciplinary Restrictions on Multidisciplinary Practice: Their Derivation, Their Development, and Some Implications for the Core Value Debate' (2000) 84 *Minnesota Law Review* 1115, 1120. I draw here on Green's account of this episode.

The Cooperative Law Company, eventual target of the bar's ire, was hiring lawyers to perform legal services for its clients, including 'the prosecution and defence of suits; incorporation of business enterprises; drawing of contracts, leases, and agreements; drawing and probating of wills; management of estates, etc'.[27] The exact size of this burgeoning industry is not clear, but one corporation claimed (improbably) to employ 6,000 attorneys across the nation.[28] The bar's response was swift. Within a few months it had persuaded New York's legislature to pass a sweeping law forbidding a corporation from practicing or appearing

> as an attorney at law for any person other than itself in any of the courts of this State, or [holding] itself out to the public as being entitled to practice law, or [rendering or furnishing] legal services or advice, or to furnish attorneys or counsel, or to render legal services of any kind in actions or proceedings of any nature.[29]

The Cooperative Law Company challenged this statute, and the case that resulted, *In re Cooperative Law Company*, would establish a ban on legal practice in the corporate form that would last to the present day.[30]

The Cooperative Law Company led with a technical argument that its activities were not covered by the new statute. That Act included several exceptions, including one for 'a corporation lawfully engaged in a business authorised by the provisions of any existing statute'. Since the Cooperative Law Company had been chartered in 1901 under New York's corporation statute, which allowed incorporation for 'any lawful purpose', it argued it was lawfully engaged in a business authorised by an existing statute, in this case the corporations law.[31] The company lost before the state's highest court in a decision that would be cited for decades.[32] According to the court, the corporation act was not dispositive because corporations had *never* been allowed to practice law – even in 1901 the practice of law was not a lawful purpose for a corporation. In its very nature the practice of law was limited to natural persons. 'The practice of law is not a business open to all', the court announced, 'but a personal right, limited to a few persons of good moral character, with special qualifications ascertained and certified after a long course of study'. Practicing law required taking an oath of office and becoming an 'officer of the court, subject to its discipline, liable to punishment for contempt in violating his duties as such, and to suspension or removal'.[33] It was the lawyer's dual role, as not merely an advocate for an individual but as an officer of the court, that made practice of law by corporations impossible.

[27] *In re Cooperative Law Co*, 92 NE 15 (1909).
[28] *Matter of Assoc Lawyers' Co*, 119 NYS 77 (App Div 1909); Green (n 26) 1121.
[29] *Matter of Assoc Lawyers' Co*, 119 NYS 77. The act also included certain exceptions for title insurance companies and in-house counsel, among other things.
[30] *In re Cooperative Law Co*, 92 NE 15 (1909) 16.
[31] ibid.
[32] See, eg, *United States v Pierre*, 2023 WL 4493511 (SDNY July 12, 2023).
[33] *In re Cooperative Law Co*, 92 NE 15 (1909) 16.

The case also turned, however, on the clash between the attorney-client relationship and the nature of the corporation. According to the court, the attorney-client relationship was direct and intensely personal, 'master and servant in a limited and dignified sense'.[34] Were the lawyer an employee of a corporation, however, his loyalties would lie elsewhere. His 'master would be not the client but the corporation … organized simply to make money and not to aid in the administration of justice'. In the end, there would be 'no guide except the sordid purpose to earn money for the stockholders'.[35] Although unstated here, the partnership was presumably an acceptable organisation for lawyers because at this time its legal nature fundamentally differed from the corporation's. A corporation was a separate legal person ultimately controlled by its shareholders.[36] A partnership in contrast was not in the eyes of the law a separate legal person at all but a mere aggregate of its members, each with a direct responsibility to his clients and none of whom had the right to direct the actions of his fellow partners.[37] Under this logic, all corporations were incapable of practicing law.

While upholding the 1909 legislation, the court's ruling also turned on a peculiarity of American law: the inherent powers doctrine, under which regulation of the legal profession is the responsibility not of a state's legislature but of its highest court (in some states the court delegates this power to a bar association).[38] This meant the next few decades' fights over the corporate practice of law would as often occur in front of the courts or the state bar to which courts assigned regulatory responsibility as in front of the legislatures, giving lawyers fighting off competition a field tilted in their favour.

The ban on the corporate practice of law would be a major issue for the rest of the century as the bar invoked it time and again to fend off incorporated organisations offering legal services.[39] It was a major aspect – perhaps the most important one – in courts' and bar associations' ongoing campaigns against the unauthorised practice of law, in which lawyers wielded their regulatory power to shut down competitors attempting to provide legal services.[40] Title companies handling property transfers, trust companies drafting wills for clients, credit associations collecting debts owed to members, and automobile associations advising drivers on minor accidents were typical targets of bar complaints.[41]

[34] ibid.

[35] ibid. Similar arguments were made in this period against the corporate practice of medicine. See 'Right of Corporations to Practice Medicine' (1938) 48 *Yale Law Journal* 346.

[36] H Wells, 'The Personification of the Partnership' (2001) 74 *Vanderbilt Law Review* 1835.

[37] ibid.

[38] American Law Institute, *Restatement of the Law Governing Lawyers* (2023) § 1 Cmt c.

[39] See, eg, G Bundick, 'The Corporate Practice of Law' (1931) 37 *Case & Comment* 4.

[40] Sometimes however the complaint was that nonlawyers were preparing legal documents. See, eg, FC Hicks and ER Katz, *Unauthorized Practice of Law: A Handbook for Lawyers and Laymen* (New York, American Bar Association, 1934) 70–72.

[41] See, eg, American Bar Association, 'Report of the Standing Committee on the Unauthorized Practice of Law' (1937) 62 *Annual Report of the American Bar Association* 769, 772–76; 'The Unauthorized Practice of Law Controversy' (1938) 5 *Law & Contemporary Problems* 1.

Why the practice of law by corporations and similar associations was targeted is a more complex question than may initially appear. Undoubtedly the chief driver of the campaign against unauthorised practice was sheer self-interest.[42] Whatever the economic realities, lawyers concluded they were facing increasing competition from both a rising number of lawyers and from nonlawyers trespassing on their turf.[43] New restrictions on advertising and soliciting and new barriers to bar admission helped control internal competition, while external competition was attacked through the campaigns against unauthorised practice.[44] Also, there were genuine questions as to what constituted the practice of law.[45] Arguing before a court was surely the practice of law, but was preparing a document such as a deed or dunning a debtor to pay back a loan?[46] (Lawyers' response was of course 'yes'.)

Yet something more lurked behind challenges to the corporate practice of law: fear of the modern corporation. There is a reason that opposition to unauthorised practice so often was cast as opposition to *corporate* practice. As early as 1913 one commentator in the *Yale Law Journal*, writing of corporations, warned that 'the lawyer is being devoured by his own Frankenstein'.[47] The Cooperative Law Company had been unusual in offering clients a range of legal services, but most targets of the bar's campaign were taking a more focused approach. In the 1920s and 1930s the organisations accused of engaging in the corporate practice of law were specialists; title insurance companies, for instance, handling land transfers, trust companies drafting wills. Like other large corporations they promised to lower the cost of their product by routinising and standardising specific tasks, bringing the methods of mass production to the law. The fear then was not just that the corporations would compete for business with lawyers, but by applying corporate methods and organisation they would be better at it. Observers recognised this, a few even arguing for the social benefits to be reaped thereby. In a 1921 debate on the topic before the New York bar, one speaker argued that whatever corporations could 'do better and cheaper, and with no countervailing disadvantage to the public, is supported by economic principal'.[48] Another speaker at the same event, admittedly president of a trust company, warned that 'economy and efficiency are demanded' and that lawyers

[42] Abel (n 22) 112–15; Hurst (n 4) 313–323; D Rhode, 'Policing the Professional Monopoly: A Constitutional and Empirical Analysis of Unauthorized Practice Prohibitions' (1981) 34 *Stanford Law Review* 1, 6–11.

[43] YB Smith and JG Rogers, 'The Overcrowding of the Bar and What can be Done about it' (1932) 7 *American Law School Review* 565.

[44] Auerbach (n 14) 102–29; Ariens (n 24) 155–57.

[45] 'What Constitutes the Practice of Law' (1918) 31 *Harvard Law Review* 886, 887–88. The answer is still not always clear. See, eg, L Sudeall, 'The Overreach of Limits on "Legal Advice"' [2022] *Yale Law Journal Forum* 637.

[46] Hurst (n 4) 319–20.

[47] Bristol (n 16) 611.

[48] 'Address of Charles A. Boston' in *Lectures on Legal Topics 1920-1921* (New York, Macmillan, 1924) 547, 555.

'cannot reject the corporate principle'.[49] A few years later a commentator in the popular *American Mercury* argued that the practice of law would benefit from what the corporate form could provide: 'economy through standardization and large scale production, efficiency, continuity, financial responsibility'.[50] In 1931 the legal scholar Karl Llewellyn would tell a symposium on unauthorised practice that corporations were intruding on law practice because they had

> worked out machinery for handling with maximum use of pattern, forms, routine, and concentration of expensive executive decision, a semi-mass production of legal transactions or legal services in a very limited field. Given the mass of roughly similar units of business, production can have its price cut in legal matters.[51]

Opposition to corporate practice thus wove together several fears held by otherwise disparate groups of lawyers and united lawyers at different levels of what had become a stratified profession. Many lawyers of course opposed it simply because they did not want more competitors. Others feared corporate practice because they believed corporations might prove better competitors, offering a cheaper product by standardising legal work. Yet opposition was also born out of a fear of lost status; lawyers feared corporate practice would erode their social positions. Elite lawyers certainly did; quips might be made about law factories, but even at large law firms dependent on corporate work the partners insisted on their position as independent professionals, and one can speculate that lawyers in more workaday practices might also have valued their membership in a profession and their role as something other than a mere corporate employee.

The campaign against corporate practice gathered steam in the 1920s and really took off in the 1930s when the Great Depression cut spending on legal services; while 58 reported cases were filed alleging unauthorised practice before 1920, 149 were filed between 1921 and 1934.[52] In 1927 the ABA amended its Canons to make clear the limits on work lawyers could do for corporations and with nonlawyers generally. New Canon 35 stated that a lawyer could be employed by 'association, club, or trade association', but forbid him from providing 'legal services to the members of such an organization in respect to their individual affairs',[53] while new Canon 33, 'Partnerships', stated that 'no person should be admitted [to a law partnership] who is not a member of the legal profession,

[49] 'Address of Clarence A. Kelsey' in *Lectures on Legal Topics 1920–1921* (New York, Macmillan, 1924) 564, 567.

[50] M Dawson, 'Frankenstein Inc' (1930) 19 *American Mercury* 274, 278.

[51] K Llewellyn, 'The Bar's Troubles, and Poultices – and Cures?' (1931) 5 *Law & Contemporary Problems* 104, 113.

[52] Abel (n 22) 113; Ariens (n 24) 156.

[53] 'Report of the Special Committee on Supplements to the Canons of Professional Ethics' (1927) 50 *Annual Report of the American Bar* Association 372, 379. See also M Steinitz, 'The Partnership Mystique: Law Firm Finance and Governance for the 21st Century American Law Firm' (2022) 63 *William and Mary Law Review* 939, 951–52.

duly authorized to practice, and amenable to professional discipline'.[54] In 1930 the ABA formed a Committee on the Unauthorized Practice of Law in response to fears that the bar would soon be 'controlled by corporations and lay agencies', and by the end of the decade, 400 local bar associations would have similar committees.[55] The next few years saw a wave of statutes banning unauthorised practice[56] and several prominent cases where state supreme courts invoked their inherent powers to bar non-lawyers from activities perceived to impinge on legal practice.[57] By 1938 one compendium of *Unauthorized Practice Decisions* would run to 800 pages.[58]

By the end of the 1930s, the bar's campaign against practice of law by corporations had largely succeeded in stymieing attempts by corporations and similar associations to offer legal services to customers and clients.[59] Memorialising these victories, the bar entered into a series of agreements with professional organisations where the organisations promised not to offer their members legal advice.[60] The ABA soon signed such 'statements of principles' with organisations representing collection agencies, trust companies, auto insurance adjusters, realtors, and life insurance adjusters sharply limiting the activities each would undertake; the trust companies, for instance, agreed that their members would not prepare wills for clients.[61] A clear line had been drawn between corporations and the practice of law.

III. THE GOLDEN AGE, ITS END, AND THE PC

There things stood for almost 40 years. While bar associations would continue battling unauthorised practice into the postwar years, the urgency of the 1920s and 1930s was missing.[62] The principle that corporations could not practice law was well-established and the economic fears fuelling the campaigns had subsided. After World War II, the legal profession, and particularly the law firms housing most of its leaders, entered what observers have called its 'Golden Age.'[63] Competition eased as the number of lawyers per capita actually dropped slightly

[54] 'Report of the Special Committee' (n 53) 379.

[55] Hicks and Katz (n 40) 4; Abel (n 22) 113.

[56] G Giesel, 'Corporations Practicing Law Through Lawyers: Why the Unauthorized Practice of Law Doctrine Should Not Apply' (2000) 65 *Missouri Law Review* 151, 162.

[57] See, eg, *People ex rel Ill State Bar Ass'n v People's Stock Yards State Bank*, 176 NE 901 (Ill 1931); *In re Opinion of the Justices*, 194 NE 313 (Mass 1935).

[58] G Brand (ed), *Unauthorized Practice Decisions* (Detroit, Detroit Bar Association, 1937).

[59] Largely but not completely; there were constant skirmishes, and bar committees targeting unauthorised practice always seemed to find work to do. Abel (n 22) 113–14.

[60] Hurst (n 4) 324.

[61] Q Johnstone, 'The Unauthorized Practice Controversy: A Struggle Among Power Groups' (1955) 4 *Kansas Law Review* 1, 22–24.

[62] Ariens (n 24) 178.

[63] Galanter and Palay (n 13) 20.

in the 1940s and 1950s.[64] The vast majority of lawyers practiced either as solo practitioners or in small firms, and while the number and size of the big partnerships increased, they did so slowly. As late as 1960, only 38 US firms had more than 50 lawyers, and 21 of those were in New York.[65] While legally a partnership was insubstantial, technically dissolvable at the whim of any partner, these firms became established institutions relying on a steady stream of income from longtime clients and able to offer those who made partner what was effectively lifetime employment. For these firms, in the words of Marc Galanter and Thomas Palay, mid-century 'was a time of prosperity, stable relations with clients, steady but manageable growth, and a comfortable assumption that this kind of law practice was a permanent fixture of American life'.[66] Perhaps because of their economic insulation, leading lawyers were also able to fully embrace a conception of their role that emphasised their positions as counsellors to prominent businessmen and their professional independence from their clients.[67]

The campaign against corporate practice had left lawyers unable to incorporate their firms, but there still seemed to be little demand for the distinctive benefits provided by incorporation such as capital lock-in and liability shielding.[68] Law firms needed little capital, and at the time legal malpractice claims were so rare that lawyers practicing in firms did not need to worry about malpractice liability for either their own or their partners' errors.[69] So it is surprising to find that after World War II some lawyers did began to demand incorporation, until one realises the source of that demand: the tax code.

During World War II many corporations, prevented from raising salaries by wage controls, started offering their employees benefits such as retirement plans, which the Federal government encouraged by allowing corporations and employees to deduct contributions to a pension plan from their taxable income. But law firms could not offer these to their partners since partners of the firm were owners not employees.[70] Galled by missing out on this benefit, lawyers lobbied for the creation of a new kind of entity into which they could organise, the Professional Corporation (PC). Some version of the PC was adopted in every state during the 1950s and 1960s, and lawyers were eventually able to use them to reap the retirement plan tax benefits.[71] But as a corporation the PC was

[64] Abel (n 22) 281.

[65] Galanter and Palay (n 13) 24.

[66] ibid 36.

[67] RW Gordon, 'The Citizen Lawyer – A Brief Informal History of a Myth with Some Basis in Reality' (2009) 50 *William and Mary Law Review* 1169, 1182–84. As Gordon's title indicates, there were elements of myth to this, but it was a widely accepted myth.

[68] Blair (n 7) 427–33; Hansmann, Kraakman and Squire (n 7) 1337–39.

[69] Abel (n 22) 154.

[70] JR Nicholson, 'Pensions for Partners: Tax Laws are Unfair to Lawyers and Firms' (1947) 33 *American Bar Association Journal* 302, 303; RJ Gilson, 'Unlimited Liability and Law Firm Organization: Tax Factors and the Direction of Causation' (1991) 99 *Journal of Political Economy* 420, 421.

[71] HB Jones, 'The Professional Corporation' (1958) 27 *Fordham Law Review* 353; RW Hamilton, 'Professional Partnerships in the United States' (2001) 26 *Journal of Corporation Law* 1045, 1048–52.

less than what met the eye. Lawyers' use of PCs was hemmed in by the existing prohibitions on the corporate practice of law, meaning PCs lacked many of the benefits of incorporation. In most states a professional corporation could only pursue the profession of its owners, and in every state all its owners had to be members of the same profession, so nonlawyer ownership or investment was out. Relations among shareholders of a PC were often governed by partnership law, as courts treated them as 'really' partnerships with unusual tax treatment.[72] In a particularly sharp departure from corporation law, in many states a PC did not provide its owners limited liability.[73] Sometimes this was because state supreme courts used their inherent powers to forbid law firms from limiting their liability, but in a number of jurisdictions it appears the question was simply never litigated, demonstrating how rare major lawsuits against law firms were.[74] Except when it came to taxes, the PC was hardly a corporation at all.

The Golden Age ended in the 1970s, as a cascade of developments pushed lawyers into a new competitive environment. First the bar's control over competition weakened. Though the bar kept its ability to control entry to the legal profession, its ability to suppress competition between lawyers was eroded in a series of US Supreme Court decisions. The 1960s saw a few cases where the Court clipped bar regulations, notably *NAACP v Button*, where it struck down as violating the First Amendment a Virginia statute that purported to limit lawyer solicitation of clients but had the effect of stopping a major civil rights group from assisting parents challenging racial segregation.[75] In the 1970s the Court struck more directly at anti-competitive rules. In 1975 it held, in *Goldfarb v Virginia State Bar*, that Federal antitrust laws applied to bar regulations and overturned mandatory minimum fee schedules imposed by local bar associations.[76] *Goldfarb* led bar associations to abandon the anti-competition agreements they had entered into with other occupations in the 1930s.[77] Two years later in *Bates v State Bar of Arizona* the Court held that sweeping bans on lawyer advertising violated the First Amendment.[78] *Bates* had an unexpected consequence: the creation of a new legal press. Once lawyers were allowed to

[72] RW Hillman, 'The Impact of Partnership Law on the Legal Profession' (1998) 67 *Fordham Law Review* 393, 393 n1.

[73] JJ Johnson, 'Limited Liability for Lawyers: General Partners need not apply' (1995) 51 *Business Lawyer* 85, 94–96.

[74] SE Kalish, 'Lawyer Liability and Incorporation of the Law Firm: A Compromise Model Providing Lawyer-Owners with Limited Liability and Imposing Broad Vicarious Liability on Some Lawyer-Employees' (1987) 29 *Arizona Law Review* 563, 564 and n 6; CW Wolfram, 'Inherent Powers in the Crucible of Lawyer Self-Protection: Reflections on the LLP Campaign' (1998) 39 *South Texas Law Review* 359, 378–80.

[75] *NAACP v Button*, 371 US 415, 423–26 (1963).

[76] *Goldfarb v Virginia State Bar*, 421 US 773, 783–88 (1975) (also rejecting claim that a 'learned profession' is exempt from Federal antitrust laws).

[77] Giesel (n 56) 163.

[78] *Bates v State Bar of Arizona*, 433 US 350, 381–82 (1977) (finding First Amendment right to lawyer advertising).

advertise, their advertising dollars went to new legal publications such as the *American Lawyer* magazine which in turn closely covered the culture and economics of the legal profession.[79]

There were also more lawyers. After decades of slow growth the number of lawyers increased by over 50 per cent between 1970 and 1980, a development attributable both to the growth of higher education and a new influx of women and minorities into the profession.[80] Law firms saw rapid growth, and as they grew their internal structures changed. From the 1940s to the 1970s law firms had grown slowly, usually had offices in only a single city, and had partners most of whom had spent their entire careers at the firm. No more. As Richard Abel observes, 'in the eleven years from 1968 to 1979 the average size of the twenty largest law firms nearly doubled (from 128 to 234); in the nine years from 1979 to 1987, it more than doubled again (to 527)'.[81] Much of that growth came from lateral hiring of partners and associates who were lured to new firms by generous pay packages, which meant that fewer partners strongly identified with a single firm or saw it as a lifetime employer.[82] Changes in the larger corporate economy, especially the takeover boom of the 1980s, also resulted in more competition for clients between law firms. Corporate general counsel, facing demands to control their budgets, either moved legal work in house or put it up for bids from different law firms, which in turn put new responsibilities for business generation on law firm partners whose value came from their ability to draw clients (the term rainmaker, used to describe a partner who brings in lots of business, appears only at the end of the 1970s).[83] The sum of all these developments was that by 1989 'the large law firm increasingly resemble[d] its corporate clients far more than the traditional ideal of the independent professional'.[84]

Finally – and here our story bends back to questions of law firm organisation and strictures against the corporate practice of law – starting in the 1970s, lawyers began to face increased risk of personal liability for professional errors. Before the 1970s malpractice suits were uncommon and mainly targeted marginal attorneys in solo practice.[85] In the 1970s however legal malpractice suits began to skyrocket, for reasons still not completely understood, though certainly including new attention paid to legal ethics after the Watergate scandal, changing attitudes towards suing other lawyers within the profession, and an across-the-board loss of faith in professionals.[86] Such 'claims doubled in the

[79] Henderson (n 9) 380.

[80] T Morgan, *The Vanishing American Lawyer* (New York, Oxford University Press, 2009) 80.

[81] Abel (n 22) 183.

[82] Gordon (n 8) 115–116.

[83] Galanter and Palay (n 13) 54.

[84] Abel (n 22) 202.

[85] JS Dzienkowski, 'Legal Malpractice and the Multistate Law Firm: Supervision of Multistate Offices; Firms as Limited Liability Partnerships; and Predispute Agreements to Arbitrate Client Malpractice Claims' (1995) 36 *South Texas Law Review* 967, 981; MR Ramos, 'Legal Malpractice: The Profession's Dirty Legal Secret' (1994) 47 *Vanderbilt Law Review* 1657, 1659–63.

[86] Abel (n 22) 154–56.

seven years between 1979 and 1986, and the average settlement increased from \$3,000 to \$42,000'.[87] Prominent law firms were not immune; in 1986, for example, the giant law firm of Rogers and Wells paid \$40 million to settle a claim arising from a client's bankruptcy while in an even clearer sign of changing mores another 'white shoe' firm, Cadwalader, Wickersham, and Taft, 'took the unprecedented step of naming another New York firm – Fried, Frank, Harris, Shriver, and Jacobson, as codefendant' in a case arising from insider trading.[88] These however could be dismissed as outliers; the event that brought home changes in lawyer liability was the Savings and Loan (S&L) crisis.

IV. THE S&L CRISIS AND THE BIRTH OF THE LIMITED LIABILITY PARTNERSHIP

At least in the US, the story is well-known. S&Ls were government-insured financial institutions that had traditionally taken savings deposits at regulated rates and used them to make home mortgage loans.[89] At the end of the 1970s however, depositors seeking higher rates went elsewhere, which led regulators to relax the rules about the kinds of loans S&Ls could make and to take a 'hands-off' approach to oversight.[90] Many S&Ls, especially in the American Southwest, extended huge loans to real estate speculators and oil and gas deals and, when real estate and oil prices collapsed in the late 1980s, so did many S&Ls.[91] The Federal government wound up paying at least \$200 billion closing bankrupt S&Ls and making whole their depositors, and to recoup its losses created a temporary agency, the Resolution Trust Company (RTC). The RTC then began suing parties involved in S&L collapses – including the S&Ls' law firms.[92] As early as 1989 Federal and state regulators had sued over two dozen lawyers and law firms who formerly represented S&Ls, claiming they committed either malpractice (the RTC having stepped into the shoes of the S&Ls) or aided and abetted client fraud, and won, often through settlements, then-staggering amounts.[93] Large law firms settling claims in just that year included Philadelphia's Blank Rome, which settled claims for \$50 million,[94] and Baltimore's Venable, Baetjer, which

[87] Gordon (n 8) 122.

[88] Abel (n 22) 155.

[89] M Mayer, *The Greatest-Ever Bank Robbery: The Collapse of the Savings and Loan Industry* (New York, Collier Books, 1992); D Mason, 'Savings and Loan Industry, US' (EH.Net Encyclopedia, 2003) eh.net/encyclopedia/savings-and-loan-industry-us/.

[90] Mason (n 89).

[91] See generally WK Black, *The Best Way to Rob a Bank is to Own One* (Austin, University of Texas Press, 2005).

[92] Other government agencies including the Federal Deposit Insurance Corporation (FDIC), the Office of Thrift Supervision (OTS), and state agencies, also filed suits, but in lawyers' eyes the RTC was the main player.

[93] LP Campbell, 'U.S. suing lawyers to recoup S&L Losses' *Chicago Tribune* (20 November 1989).

[94] ibid.

paid a settlement of $27 million.[95] By 1992, 'the [RTC or related agencies] had suits pending against major law firms' in Minneapolis, New York City, Dallas, Cleveland, and Los Angeles.[96] Two years later '[f]our of the six largest legal malpractice settlements in history, totalling $100 million', would stem from the S&L crisis.[97]

Particularly chilling for many law firm partners was that the RTC aggressively sought potential judgments that might reach their personal assets. Under partnership law, partners' personal assets were always of course available to satisfy their firm's debts, but for most law firm partners this had never been a real danger. In the past firms were rarely sued for malpractice, and malpractice insurance existed to cover any potential loss. The S&L lawsuits showed these protections might no longer apply. When the RTC sued the law firm of Kaye Scholer in 1992 over representation of a failed S&L, it sought an immediate freeze on all the firm's assets, forcing the firm to swiftly settle for $41 million, and because this exceeded the firm's liability insurance between $5 and $10 million came from the assets of the partners themselves.[98] When the RTC sued the Dallas firm of Jenkens & Gilchrist in 1989 it was for losses stemming from a former partner's representation of an S&L. Even though that partner had left the firm in 1983, the RTC opened its presentation to the law firm's partners by showing slides estimating the personal assets of each firm partner, even those retired, recently promoted to partner, or who had nothing to do with the S&L representation, as a way of calculating total sums that might be available.[99] Plaintiffs' attorneys suing over S&L collapses apparently borrowed this tactic and opened settlement negotiations at a sum equal to a firm's malpractice insurance plus partners' estimated personal assets.[100] 'Needless to say, … [this] caught the attention of the hundreds of law firms that had represented banks or thrifts during the 1980s.'[101] Rising S&L litigation also caught the attention of insurance companies, which raised law firm malpractice premiums across the board and began refusing to write policies for claims arising from securities or banking work.[102]

Lawyers were suddenly forced to confront the downside of the ban on the corporate practice of law. As the S&L cases show, the odds had risen of a law firm partner being held vicariously liable for her partners' malpractice, but the

[95] Abel (n 22) 155.

[96] JA Hughes, 'Law Firm Kaye, Scholer, Lincoln S&L and the OTS' (1993) 7 *Notre Dame Journal of Law, Ethics, and Public Policy* 177, 177.

[97] Ramos (n 85) 1677 and n 138.

[98] S Walsh, 'Law Firm Settles S&L Complaint' *Washington Post* (9 March 1992).

[99] Hamilton (n 3) 1069–71.

[100] Wolfram (n 74) 364.

[101] Hamilton (n 3) 1071.

[102] 'Lawyers' Responses: Shifting the Costs of Liability' (1994) 107 *Harvard Law Review* 1651, 1652. The rise in malpractice insurance rates cannot be laid solely at the feet of the S&L crisis, as malpractice claims had been rising since the 1970s. See generally Ramos (n 85).

bar on corporate practice made it impossible for firms to readily reorganise as corporations, the only available business form guaranteeing limited liability. The professional corporation was available, but in most states the PC was not guaranteed to shield its owners from tort liability, and even in states where it did provide some liability shield (including Texas, ground zero for S&L litigation) unfavourable tax treatment had led law firms to avoid organising as PCs.[103] A new unincorporated business form, the limited liability company (LLC), had been adopted in a few states, but it was not yet clear what tax treatment it would receive nor whether state authorities would allow lawyers to use it.[104]

There were also significant advantages still to be wrung from bans on corporate practice. The same concerns that motivated the bar in the 1920s and 1930s still existed in the 1980s, as small firm lawyers, who represented mainly individual clients, still feared larger organisations would standardise and routinise the legal task that were the bulk of their practice, while in a new development big firm lawyers found the ban useful in staving off competition from the big accounting firms.[105] When in 1983 an ABA Committee proposed new Model Rules of Professional Conduct (to replace the Model Code, which replaced the Canons in 1969),[106] the original draft of Rule 5.4 would have weakened the ban on corporate practice by allowing a lawyer, subject to certain limits, 'to be employed by an organization in which a financial interest is held or managerial authority is exercised by a nonlawyer, ... such as a business corporation [or] insurance company'. The ABA's House of Delegates rejected the proposal. Were the rule adopted, one delegate complained, it would allow 'Sears, ... H&R Block, or the Big Eight accounting firms to open law offices in competition with traditional firms.'[107]

How could the legal profession square its opposition to corporate practice with partners' growing fear of the consequences of unlimited liability? Enter the limited-liability partnership, and its unexpected origins. Before 1991 there appeared to be no serious movement underway to provide lawyers improved liability shields that would abrogate traditional rules making partners vicariously liable for other partners' torts.[108] Yet that summer, the Texas legislature

[103] Hamilton (n 3) 1065 n 3.

[104] Until 1998 the LLC was hemmed in by Federally-imposed limits related to its pass-through tax status. See SP Hamill, 'The Origins Behind the Limited Liability Company' (1998) 59 *Ohio State Law Journal* 1459, 1469–84.

[105] On the growing bifurcation of the bar from the 1970s to the 1990s, see generally JP Heinz and EO Laumann, *Chicago Lawyers: The Social Structure of the Bar*, rev edn (Chicago, Northwestern University Press, 1994).

[106] See generally Ariens (n 24).

[107] TR Andrews, 'Nonlawyers in the Business of Law: Does One who has the Gold Really make the Rules?' (1989) 40 *Hastings Law Journal* 577, 593 (citation omitted).

[108] In 1977 the ABA did propose a Professional Corporation Supplement to the Model Business Corporation Act, which gave several possible options for liability for lawyer-owners, from corporation-style limited liability to liability for 'all corporate debts as if they were partners'. Kalish (n 74) 569–70. In 1987 an academic article argued that law firms should be allowed to incorporate and provide limited liability – ibid. Neither mustered any support.

adopted the first statute providing for a limited liability partnership. Luckily for historians, present at the creation of the LLP was University of Texas law professor Robert Hamilton.[109]

It is only a slight exaggeration to say that without Texas there would be no limited liability partnership in the US. As Hamilton recounts, that there was a legislative path open for the LLP at all was due to recent changes in how business legislation was developed in the state. Traditionally, changes to Texas's business statutes were formulated by the state bar's Business Law Section then reviewed by the bar association's board before being 'packaged and presented by the Bar's registered lobbyist to the state legislature'.[110] This process however created a problem for business lawyers, as the need for approval by a committee representing the entire bar, and not just business lawyers, gave plaintiffs' attorneys the opportunity to lobby against and sometimes defeat proposed pro-business legislation. So in 1988 leading business lawyers formed a separate organisation to propose business-related legislation, the Texas Business Law Foundation (TBLF), which hired its own lobbyist.[111] This opened direct lines of influence between Texas's business lawyers and legislators. Texas's treatment of professional corporations also made a new business form particularly desirable. Unlike in many states, Texas law provided lawyer-shareholders in PCs some shielding against vicarious liability for other lawyer-shareholders' malpractice. Yet Texas imposed a 4.5 per cent franchise tax on PCs – a tax not imposed on partnerships – while many of the Federal tax benefits PCs once enjoyed had been eliminated in the early 1980s.[112] All this meant a great many Texas law firms were still organised as general partnerships and would face an economic penalty if they reorganised as PCs.

The actual idea for a partnership with limited liability, however, originated not with leaders of the bar or legal scholars, but from a completely unexpected source. In early 1991 a state senator from Lubbock, a midsize city in west Texas, forwarded a proposal he had received from a 20-person law firm in that city for a limited liability partnership.[113] Clearly a reaction to the S&L crisis, the law firm's idea was for the state to provide in statute for a general partnership, open only to professionals, in which partners would not be vicariously liable for their partners' torts; in the words of the act as eventually adopted, partners were not liable for 'errors, omissions, negligence, incompetence, or malfeasance committed in the course of the partnership business by another partner or a representative of the partnership not working under the supervision or direction of the first partner'.[114] (Later iterations of the LLP would shield partners from

[109] See generally Hamilton (n 3). As should be clear, the account presented in the following paragraphs rests on Hamilton's account.
[110] ibid 1071.
[111] ibid 1072.
[112] Gilson (n 70); Hamilton (n 3) 1065 n 3, 1073 n 22.
[113] Hamilton (n 3) 1073.
[114] SS Fortney, 'Am I My Partner's Keeper – Peer Review in Law Firms' (1995) 66 *University of Colorado Law Review* 329, 330 n 6 quoting Tex Rev Civ Stat Ann art 6132b, § 15(2) (West Supp 1993).

both contract and tort liability.[115]) To become an LLP an eligible general partnership did not need to go through the troublesome process of dissolving and reforming, it simply required a majority of partners to vote to convert to an LLP and for the partnership to register and pay a fee to the state.[116]

Initial responses to the proposal were mixed, perhaps because the idea of a general partnership with limited liability seemed an oxymoron; in traditional partnership law, one of the defining features of the general partnership was partners' unlimited liability.[117] This might explain early academic hostility; the University of Texas's Robert Hamilton, chair of the TBLF's legislative committee, wrote of his initial negative reaction to the LLP proposal, and the idea was also criticised by perhaps the nation's leading partnership law scholar, Alan Bromberg of Dallas's Southern Methodist University.[118] Texas business lawyers, however, loved the idea and pushed hard for Texas to adopt the LLP. While there was pushback during legislative hearings over the new Bill, with one legislator accurately calling it 'a help-a-lawyer bill', it also garnered great support.[119] Eventually the new LLP provisions were 'quietly attached to an omnibus bill', and Texas Governor Ann Richards allowed the Bill to become law without her signature in June 1991.[120] Inside a year, 1,200 Texas law firms registered to become LLPs.[121]

V. THE LLP WINS THE FIELD

Within little more than a decade the LLP was adopted by legislatures in all 50 states[122] and was included in the model Revised Uniform Partnership Act (1997).[123] Its acceptance was confirmed in 1994 when three of the then-big six accounting firms reorganised as Delaware LLPs.[124] While many states soon allowed law firms to organise in the other new unincorporated business form, the LLC, as well,[125] not all did,[126] and the LLP appeared a particularly good

[115] See, eg, Uniform Partnership Act (2013) § 306(c). By 2013 42 out of the 50 states provided LLPs with both tort and contract shielding. A Martin-Rhodes, RW Hillman, and P Tran, 'Law Firms' Entity Choices Reflect Appeal of Newer Business Forms' (2014) 16 *Business Entities* 16, 16.

[116] NS Murphy, 'It's Nothing Personal: The Public Costs of Limited Liability Partnerships' (1995) 71 *Indiana Law Journal* 201, 213.

[117] See, eg, Uniform Partnership Act (1914) § 6.

[118] Hamilton (n 3) 1073–74.

[119] ibid. The Bill was sponsored by Steven Wolens, a prominent Democratic legislature from Dallas. C Harlan, 'Texas and Louisiana Move to Shield Personal Assets of Law-Firm Partners' *Wall Street Journal* (13 March 1992).

[120] Hamilton (n 3) 1074.

[121] ibid 1065.

[122] RW Hillman, 'Organizational Choices of Professional Service Firms: An Empirical Study' (2003) 58 *Business Lawyer* 1387, 1394.

[123] Revised Uniform Partnership Act (1997) § 1001.

[124] Hamilton (n 3) 1065–66.

[125] By 1995 22 states specifically authorised lawyers to form LLCs. DG Christensen and S Bertschi, 'LLC Statutes: Use by Attorneys' (1995) 29 *Georgia Law Review* 693, 696–97.

[126] See, eg, Calif Corp Code § 17701.04(d) (2023).

fit with preexisting law firm organisation and ethos.[127] As mentioned above, a law firm organised as a general partnership could adopt limited liability with a simple filing, maintaining its existing structure and avoiding possible unfavourable tax consequences of reorganising into a different business form.[128] The LLP also allowed lawyers to retain the title of partner, a status often won after many years of labour and which distinguished them from mere employees. There were some reasons for lawyers to prefer the LLC, in particular the fact that LLC statutes initially offered owners limitation on both tort and contract liability, whereas many early LLP statutes only limited tort liability.[129] Yet for lawyers thinking of adopting one of the new limited liability forms, two important questions remained open. Would they be allowed to use the new legal entities? And, would they choose to do so?

For a brief time some state bar authorities or supreme courts invoked their inherent powers to prevent lawyers from organising in the new limited-liability forms.[130] In the early 1990s, for example, Nebraska's bar held that that lawyers could not organise in an LLC, reasoning that vicarious liability was needed to protect firm clients,[131] while the Kentucky Supreme Court reached the same conclusion by a different route, holding that limited-liability practice would violate the well-established ethical rule preventing lawyers from seeking a prospective waiver of malpractice liability.[132] The trend however was clearly in the other direction.[133] In 1996 the ABA issued an Ethics Opinion stating that lawyers could, if allowed by state law, practice in an LLP or other form shielding them from vicarious liability so long as clients had notice of this.[134] That same year one of the leading cases holding that lawyers could not limit their liability for firm debts, Georgia's *First Bank & Trust Co v Zagoria*, was overturned by the Georgia Supreme Court, which held in *Henderson v HIS Financial Services* that shareholders in a PC were not personally liable for damages stemming from another shareholder's misdeeds.[135] Protections for clients were not completely abandoned; many states required either through state law or bar rules that law firms adopting a limited liability form purchase

[127] Some jurisdictions limit LLPs to professionals. KB Gutting, 'Keeping Pace with the Times: Exploring the Meaning of Limited Partnership for Purposes of the Internal Revenue Code' (2011) 60 *University of Kansas Law Review* 89, 115 and n 138.

[128] Hillman (n 122) 1394–95.

[129] Martin-Rhodes et al (n 115) 20.

[130] Hillman (n 122) 1395–96.

[131] Christensen and Bertschi (n 125) 696 citing Nebraska State Bar Association (1994) *Ethics Opinion* 94-1.

[132] EC Woodford, 'The Ethical Implications of the Limited Liability Status in the Practice of Law' (1998) 87 *Kentucky Law Review* 489, 489–90.

[133] See, eg, JJ Johnson, 'Limited Liability for Lawyers: General Partners Need not Apply' (1995) 51 *Business Lawyer* 85, 101.

[134] American Bar Association (1996) *Formal Opinion* 96–401.

[135] *Henderson v HSI Fin Servs Inc*, 471 SE2d 885, 886 (Ga 1996) reversing *First Bank & Trust Co v Zagoria*, 302 SE2d 674 (Ga 1983).

malpractice insurance, presumably to replace the personal assets of partners once available to satisfy firm debts.[136] The doors however were opening wide for limited liability practice.

Over the following decade law firms drifted towards the LLP and the LLC. A 2002 study by Robert Hillman charted the spread of the new business forms. Among all law firms for which data was available, he found the older forms stubbornly hanging on, with 53 per cent of firms organised as PCs and 29 per cent as general partnerships, with 8 per cent as LLCs and 10 per cent as LLPs.[137] Since many of the PCs may have been sole proprietorships, this may understate the adoption of the LLP by larger firms.[138] (Some firms may have remained PCs because of potential tax liabilities if they reorganised as LLPs or LLCs.) A follow-up study a decade later showed older forms still surviving, with 51 per cent of law firms still PCs and 16 per cent general partnerships, while LLPs were only 11 per cent and LLCs 22 per cent (the authors were not sure how to explain these patterns).[139]

Intriguingly, the LLP was particularly popular among large law firms. In the 2002 study, of the 748 law firms in the US with 50 or more lawyers the LLP was the most popular choice, with 48 per cent of the firms LLPs, 9 per cent LLCs, 29 per cent professional corporations, and only 14 per cent general partnerships.[140] The larger the firm, the more likely it was an LLP; of the 139 largest firms, 65 per cent were LLPs.[141] The move of larger law firms to the LLP also appeared to follow a pattern, as shown by an illuminating 2005 study by Scott Baker and Kim Krawiec, who looked at the organisational choices over time of New York's 147 largest law firms (those with 25 or more lawyers).[142] Again, the LLP predominated; 99 of the firms were LLPs, 2 LLCs, 27 PCs, and only 19 general partnerships.[143] Particularly noteworthy is that the move to limited liability form occurred in two waves connected to firms' perceived exposure to liability, and was also shaped by reputational concerns. The first wave occurred in 1994–95 immediately after New York adopted its LLP statute, when many of what the authors characterise as less elite firms adopted the LLP form.[144] The 'elite firms' remained

[136] For example, California state law requires professional LLPs to maintain liability insurance. Cal Corp Code § 16956 (2023), while in Kentucky a similar requirement is imposed by the rules of the state supreme court. Rules of the Kentucky Supreme Court (2023) 3.024.

[137] Hillman (n 122) 1408.

[138] ibid 1398.

[139] Martin-Rhodes et al (n 115).

[140] Hillman (n 122) 1401. His study surveyed all law firms listed in the Martindale-Hubbard database. ibid 1404. As he points out, the exact form is not always dictated by free choice; a PC may face a significant tax hit if it reorganises as an LLC or LLP, locking some firms into the older form, while in some states such as California law firms were not allowed to organise as LLCs. ibid 1393.

[141] ibid 1401.

[142] S Baker and K Krawiec, 'The Economics of Limited Liability: An Empirical Study of New York Law Firms' [2005] *University of Illinois Law Review* 107.

[143] ibid 128.

[144] ibid 128.

reluctant to become LLPs, apparently because their partners believed any limits on liability would send a 'negative signal' to clients and competitors; as the authors observe, 'law firms are extraordinarily conservative and are reluctant to take actions that may distinguish them from their competitors'.[145] In 2001–02 however, Enron and several other giant firms collapsed and their law and accounting firms were soon embroiled in lawsuits; in 2002 the accounting firm Arthur Anderson LLP collapsed following a criminal conviction related to its representation of Enron.[146] These events rekindled partners' fears of personal liability and provoked a second wave of conversions to LLPs, which led most of the remaining large general partnerships to become LLPs by 2003.[147] Law firms and other businesses still have a range of organisational choices, but the LLP is now the entity of choice for most large law firms in the US.[148]

VI. CONCLUSION

The account presented in this chapter demonstrates the complexity and contingency attending on of the birth of a new business form. It shows how the US limited liability partnership, while created only in 1991, was fundamentally shaped by a century of legal wrangling over the corporate practice of law. Since the early 1900s, the American bar had rejected the idea of corporations practicing law for reasons rooted in both self-interest and self-image and drew from this the conclusion that it was impossible for a corporation to engage in legal practice. For much of the century this was not a problem, as lawyers were content to practice in general partnerships or as solo practitioners and saw little need for the benefits offered by incorporation. When legal malpractice claims became a major threat in the 1980s, however, the ban on corporate practice stood in the way of lawyers reorganising their practices in liability-limiting forms. The invention of the LLP made it possible for America lawyers to square their opposition to corporate practice with their need to obtain one of the traditional features of the corporation, limited liability.

[145] ibid 146, 147.

[146] K Eichenwald, 'Anderson Guilty in Effort to Block Inquiry on Enron' *New York Times* (16 June 2002).

[147] Baker and Krawiec (n 142) 129.

[148] For instance, an informal survey by this author found that almost all the law firms that were general partnerships in Baker and Krawiec's 2005 study had by 2023 either become LLPs or disappeared, and of the top 50 most profitable law firms in the US, as listed by the *American Lawyer* magazine, at least 47 are LLPs.

5

Upending the State's Power to Regulate Corporate Separateness

ROBERT B THOMPSON*

I. INTRODUCTION

THE CORPORATE FORM embodies core characteristics that permit participants to achieve what would not be possible in an individual capacity. This chapter develops how the most prominent of these relate to the corporation's separateness – the law's recognition of the entity as distinct from the individuals who create it, direct it, and benefit from the corporation's activities. As illustrated in section II, limited liability, perhaps the most visible characteristic, permits entrepreneurs and others to separate themselves from the debts of the entity and reallocate the risks of the enterprise to suppliers, employees, or other creditors. That section also identifies a set of efficiency-producing internal governance rules – hierarchy, role specialisation, centralised control, and 'lock-in' of investments – that also accrue to the modern corporate form. Additionally, autonomy, magnification, and anonymity flow from separateness and permit individuals to achieve advantageous results via use of the corporation. These characteristics have made the corporation one of the most powerful actors in modern society.

Corporate law's centuries-old embrace of the beneficial effects of separateness has consistently been coupled with the recognition that, in some settings, those effects inappropriately shift costs and risks to outsiders, a bookend introduced in section II. To control these externalities, the state or sovereign, used the chartering power to check misuse, and after general incorporation became the norm, used other levers such as the common law doctrine of piercing the veil or extensive regulation of corporations to address these misuses. Corporations,

* My thanks to Elizabeth Pollman, Ann Lipton, Margaret Blair, and Morgan Ricks for their incisive and helpful comments. A forthcoming book project on Corporate Separateness in the United States explores in a broader context some of the topics covered in this chapter.

as separate entities, have long had rights eg, to hold and transfer property, to contract, and to sue and to be sued, found in early British and American sources identified in section II. But these separate entities historically lacked an equivalence to the constitutional or other rights of individuals.

Twenty-first century decisions by the United States Supreme Court upended this longstanding approach. In *Hobby Lobby* in 2014, the Court ruled that the federal government cannot require closely held corporations to provide health care coverage for employees when that violated the controlling family's religious beliefs.[1] In *Citizens United* in 2010, the Court ruled that government cannot ban corporations from making independent expenditures for candidates for federal office.[2] In each case, the Court's focus was on protecting individual rights from government, while ignoring the issues related to state regulation of corporations. In *Hobby Lobby*, for example, the Court described the corporation as 'simply a form of organization used by human beings to achieve desired ends'[3] whose 'purpose' is to 'provide protection for human beings' (presumably protection of those who form a corporation against an overreaching government).[4] The corporation as a separate and powerful legal entity is seemingly superfluous.[5] Corporations have the same rights as individuals and to deny the corporation any of the rights that the individuals who formed it had before incorporation would be 'discrimination' and 'forfeiture'.[6] Individuals who already have the right to free speech, to give money to political candidates, and to exercise their religion now gain the additional right to also speak separately through a corporation, to also to give money through a corporation, and also to practice religion through a corporation. The only effect of corporate law in this analysis is to provide what knowledgeable corporate commentators have called a 'one way ratchet' that expands rights of the entity to take in all rights of individuals who own and control it, but ignores long-standing corporate law concerns of overreaching that can follow from the corporate form and its enhanced powers.[7] This chapter develops how much the modern American judicial approach departs from earlier conceptions of the corporation.

[1] *Burwell v Hobby Lobby Stores, Inc*, 573 U.S. 682 (2014).

[2] *Citizens United v FEC*, 558 U.S. 310, 347 (2010).

[3] *Hobby Lobby* (n 1) 706.

[4] ibid.

[5] Similarly the Court's 2023 decision, *303 Creative LLC v Elenis*, 600 US 2298 143 SCt 570, 577–78 (2023) permitting an entity to exercise the free speech rights of its sole member, hardly mentions the entity at all, making dozens of references solely to the individual, 577–587.

[6] *Hobby Lobby* (n 1) 706. See also AA Scwartz, 'The Perpetual Corporation' (2012) 80 *George Washington Law Review* 764, 773 ('In the premodern era, perpetual existence was viewed as the leading attribute of corporations').

[7] See LE Strine, 'Corporate Power Ratchet: The Courts' Role in Eroding 'We the People's' Ability to Constrain Our Corporate Creations' (2016) 51 *Harvard Civil Rights-Civil Liberties Law Review* 423.

II. THE ORIGINS OF CORPORATE SEPARATENESS IN CORPORATIONS LAW

A. Antecedents to the American Experience

i. Continuity

One of the simplest and oldest benefits of an entity's separateness is the continuity that separateness provides to facilitate holding property across generations and the simple conveyancing and contracting as to that property.[8] Early illustrations can be found in religious uses of corporations so that property remained for the charitable use of monasteries or bishoprics beyond the lives of the original actors and was not transferred to the heirs of a particular person. Individual families similarly used a separate entity to keep property within the family, even as individual members died.[9]

ii. Autonomy and Self-Governance

Autonomy has long been a prized benefit that the corporate form could provide. The early religious entities that permitted simple cross-generational control of real property, as already discussed, could be paired with broader rights of self-governance such as to specify rules of behaviour of the faithful living in monasteries or members of a particular order. Incorporation of municipalities often was associated with the capacity to set rules within a geographic space.[10] Guilds acquired autonomy as to conduct of trades or crafts. Several of the Americans colonies were corporations, at least for a while, which brought them governmental powers important to those undertaking the settlement of the new world.[11]

Those autonomy-driven examples derive from the non-business sector but autonomy was also prized in commercial enterprises. The British and Dutch East Indies Companies, for example, were given broad autonomy over foreign trade ventures, and perhaps more importantly, gained some protection against the sovereign's sudden removal of private control. Dari-Mattiacci, Gelderblom, Jonker, and Perotti effectively show how limits on the government expropriation

[8] M Blair, 'Corporate Personhood and the Corporate Persona' [2013] *University of Illinois Law Review* 785, 787.

[9] See D Ciepley, 'Governing People or Governing Property? How Dartmouth College Assimilated the Corporation to Liberalism by Treating it as a Trust' (2 March 2021). Available at SSRN: ssrn.com/abstract=3796298 (discussing medieval Europe's viewing corporations through the lens of property, while failing to include the principal purpose of improving governance of people and property).

[10] See Blair (n 8) 787 ('self-governance is one of the earliest purposes of incorporation').

[11] See JS Davis, *Essays in the Earlier History of Corporations* (Cambridge, Harvard University Press, 1917) 48 (describing the Virginia Company and the Massachusetts Bay Company of the early 17th century).

of private assets were a necessary precondition to the development of a corporation with the indicia of separateness that we associate with the modern corporation and how the Dutch and then the British were first able to achieve this in the seventeenth century.[12] Elizabeth Pollman has shown how a parallel development of protection from removal of self-governance developed for corporations in America as the nineteenth century unfolded.[13]

To gain such autonomy, one had to get the sovereign's consent to the creation of a corporation. The number granted was small and the recipients were not equally spread across the realm – the sovereign's friends would be included; dissidents less so.[14] Whatever autonomy there was (and there still were not very many corporations at the time), came from the sovereign and then from the American states that succeeded to the monarch's sovereignty after the revolution.[15]

iii. British Precedent for American Concepts of Separateness

The American concept of corporations and their rights reflected British precedent attributing a common set of rights in corporations even when the explanations for them were still developing. Blackstone's *Commentaries*, for example, cited a corporation's capacity to hold and transfer property and sue and be sued as common corporate rights.[16] Stewart Kyd, a Scottish commentator of the same period, wrote of the policy of the law as endowing the entity 'with the capacity of *acting in several respects* as an individual, particularly of taking and granting property, contracting obligations and suing and being sued'.[17]

This common package of rights attached to the entity, relating to property, contracting and suing, suited the needs of the often-simple corporate forms of the period – eg, to facilitate property remaining within a collective even as individual participants came and went.[18] Entities oriented to active management of a fluid business, which would also value these same corporate rights, were not yet a frequent user of the corporate form as America became independent. This early set of rights developed during the time before general incorporation when

[12] G Dari-Mattiacci, O Gelderblom, J Jonker and EC Perotti, 'The Emergence of the Corporate Form' (2013) 23 *Journal of Law, Economics and Organization* 193 (hereinafter '*Emergence*').

[13] E Pollman, 'Corporate Personhood and Limited Sovereignty' (2021) 74 *Vanderbilt Law Review* 1727 (constitutional protection – like lock-in or asset partitioning – added to the stability of the business enterprise by enabling the corporation to make credible commitments and helping to ensure that firm-specific investments would be protected).

[14] NR Lamoreaux and J-L Rosenthal, 'Corporate Governance and the Plight of Minority Shareholders in the United States Before the Great Depression' in E Glazer and C Golden (eds), *Corruption and Reform, Lessons from America's Economic History* (Chicago, University of Chicago Press, 2006) 127 (in 19th century pressure mounted to 'prevent a favored few from engrossing' the benefits of corporations).

[15] Davis (n 11) (describing business corporations 'on the whole as of no great significance').

[16] W Blackstone, *Commentaries on the Law of England* (Buffalo, Wm S Hein Co, 1765), 463, 464.

[17] S Kyd, *A Treatise on the Law of Corporations* (London, Butterworth, 1793) 13 emphasis added).

[18] See DA Ciepley, 'Member Corporations, Property Corporations, and Constitutional Rights' (2017) 11 *Law and Ethics of Human Rights* 31.

corporateness was granted usually for a limited time and limited purpose, both for business corporations and the more numerous not-for-profits. The state's ability to regulate corporations qua corporations was not disputed either before or after the creation of the new American constitutional system. As American states disestablished churches after independence, for example, state laws added limits on church wealth and proscribed governance of these corporations that empowered lay members.[19]

The drafters of the American Constitution saw no need to address corporations, or their rights. The founders rejected James Madison's suggestion that incorporation be included among the powers of the national government.[20] Madison was no more accommodating to the efforts of various state ratifying conventions that sought a ban on federal incorporations as part of what became the Bill of Rights.[21] Corporate rights were not important enough to be resolved at this point. It can be argued, as in modern Supreme Court opinions, that the framers of the First Amendment knowingly accepted more speech as the answer to the danger of bad speech,[22] but it cannot be said that the founders had in any way decided the extent of rights a corporation possessed.

B. Across the Nineteenth Century

Corporations at the end of the eighteenth century, whether non-profit or business, lacked most of the characteristics associated today with the corporate form – there was no limited liability, entity permanence, or right to form a corporation without the government granting its approval; governance was very flat with no centralised control or hierarchy.[23] Each of these characteristics was added during the nineteenth century, usually by action of the state.

[19] SB Gordon, 'Religious Corporations and the Disestablishment, 1780-1840' in M Schwartzman, C Flanders and Z Robinson (eds), *The Rise of Corporate Religious Liberty* (Oxford, Oxford University Press, 2016) 64 ('Disestablishment thus established freedom of conscience from state control but not freedom of institutional religion from state oversight', 68).

[20] See, eg, DB Robertson, *The Constitution and America's Destiny* (Cambridge, Cambridge University Press, 2005) (describing Madison's unsuccessful proposal in 1787 to add specific national powers to charter corporations).

[21] States ratifying the Constitution sometimes submitted a list of desired amendments which included provisions that Congress shall 'erect no company of merchants with exclusive advantage of commerce'. See www.usconstitution.net/rat_mass.html. Representative Madison coordinated which of these various proposals would be included in the Bill of Rights, a list that did not include the corporations amendment.

[22] *First National Bank v Bellotti*, 435 US 765, 792 (1978) ('if there be any danger that the people cannot evaluate the information and arguments advanced by appellants, it is a danger contemplated by the Framers of the First Amendment.').

[23] See O Handlin and MF Handlin, 'Origins of the American Business Corporation' (1945) 5 *Journal of Economic History* 1, 2 ('The test of experience had not yet proved that corporations were "business bodies of enviable efficacy," or "that they offered the most suitable form for the management of capital."' (quoting S Livermore, *Early American Landed Companies: Their Influence on Corporate Development* (New York, The Commonwealth Fund, 1939) 258)).

i. Limited Liability

A visible illustration of separateness in contemporary corporate law has been limited liability for shareholders. Insulating shareholders from business risks encourages them to pursue business activity. Limited liability opened a broad new range of choices for allocating risks in doing business – sometimes having the risks carried by the insiders but at other times shifting these risks to creditors, customers, neighbours, or society. Parties likely will have different risk preferences, different capacities to bear risk, different information about risks, or varying capacity to prevent harm. Using the corporate form permits allocation to the cheapest risk bearer so long as creditors can adjust their price in dealing with a separate corporation to reflect the degree of risk being transferred.[24] Paul Halpern, Michael Trebilcock and Stuart Turnbull have argued that that limited liability produced a standardisation of rights in equity shares that facilitated the commodification of ownership interests important to creation of a public market for shares.[25]

Limited liability of shareholders was not in evidence for American corporations until Massachusetts and other New England states added that element to their corporation's code between 1815 and 1830.[26] Recognition of the concept expanded state by state through the ensuing decades, becoming almost universal later in the century.[27] The most common setting in which limited liability is contested today – in corporations with only one shareholder who seeks to avoid the entity's liabilities – was not possible through most of the nineteenth century when law required a minimum number of shareholders (eg, seven makes a corporation).[28] It was only after the *Salomon v A Salomon & Co* decision in the UK in 1897 and adoption of similar holdings by American courts in the twentieth century and passage of American statutes authorising corporations to own stock in another corporations that the full reach of the modern insulation flowing from separateness and limited liability took shape.

ii. Hierarchy and Role Specialisation

Statutory provisions as to internal governance increased the entity's value as compared to a similar business undertaken by individuals outside a corporation.[29] Unlike limited liability that focuses on the interaction between

[24] FH Easterbrook and DR Fischel, 'Limited Liability and the Corporation' (1985) 52 *University of Chicago Law Review* 89.

[25] P Halpern, M Trebilcock and S Turnbull, 'An Economic Analysis of Limited Liability in Corporation Law' (1980) 30 *University of Toronto Law Journal* 117, 124 (limited liability is indispensable to the functioning of an efficient capital market).

[26] PI Blumberg, 'The Corporate Entity in an Era of Multinational Corporations' (1990) 15 *Delaware Journal of Corporation Law* 283.

[27] See E Hilt, 'Early American Corporations and the State' in NR Lamoreaux and WJ Novak (eds), *Corporations and American Democracy* (Cambridge, Harvard University Press, 2017).

[28] *Salomon v A. Salomon & Co* [1897] AC 22. Statutes or rules such as that expressed in *Salomon* that seven make a corporation, soon disappeared, a deletion that left little apparent impact.

[29] Easterbrook and Fischel (n 24) (limited liability facilitates the efficient separation of function in publicly held corporations), 117.

corporation and 'outsiders' who contracted with it, hierarchy and role specialisation create value by ordering relations among three internal sets of actors (directors, officers, and shareholders) whose distinct roles, rights and duties are specified by corporation statutes.[30] This means the money providers do not have to also possess management skills and day-to-day managers can be hired separately from those providing oversight.

The law's contribution to efficient governance was not limited to specialisation. Hierarchy followed naturally with statutes providing clear rules for efficient decision-making in complex entities.[31] The mid-nineteenth century reflected a move to reallocate key corporate powers away from the general meeting of shareholders to boards of directors.[32] Not surprisingly, the business judgment rule (a broad judicial deference to the decisions of the centralised board of directors in making corporate decisions) began to spread in this environment.[33]

iii. Lock-in

'Lock-in', an important efficiency generating governance characteristic of the corporation, reflects the overlap of the governance and partitioning space. In contrast to traditional partnership rules of 'easy exit' for members who wished to depart – a manifestation of how fragile the separateness characteristics were in those entities – the corporate form conditioned return of any participant's investment in the entity on the approval of the board. This provided important stability to the firm and often facilitated the growth of large business.[34] Lock-in and a more stable asset base for creditors' lending that followed were key contributors to the magnification of business operated in the corporate form. Such a structure enabled corporations to supplant partnership as the key businesses by the mid-nineteenth century.[35]

[30] See Mod Bus Corp Act § 8.01 as to directors, § 8.41 as to officers, and § 7.01 et seq as to shareholders.

[31] See Mod Bus Corp Act § 8.01 ('all corporate powers shall be exercised by or under the authority of the board of directors ...').

[32] See AD Chandler, Jr, *The Visible Hand, The Managerial Revolution in American Business* (Cambridge, Belknap Press, 1977) (seeing decentralised governance shared by all participants through the 1840s); EM Dodd, 'Statutory Developments in Business Corporation Law, 1886–1936' (1936–1937) 50 *Harvard Law Review* 27, 40 (tracing broadening powers for directors over the 19th century); MJ Horwitz, 'Santa Clara Revisited: The Development of Corporate Theory' (1985–1986) 88 *West Virginia Law Review* 173, 182 (identifying a shift from shareholders to directors such that after 1900 directors were treated as the equivalent of the corporation).

[33] See RB Thompson, 'Why New Corporate Law Arises: Implications for the 21st Century' in SD Solomon and R Thomas (eds), *The Corporate Contract in Changing Times: Is the Law Keeping Up?* (Chicago, University of Chicago Press, 2019) 4–9.

[34] MM Blair, 'Locking in Capital: What Corporate Law Achieved for Business Organizers in the Nineteenth Century' (2003) 51 *UCLA Law Review* 387, 423–24; M Ricks, 'Organizational Law as Commitment Device' (2017) 70 *Vanderbilt Law Review* 1303, 1306. See also, Dari-Mattiacci, et al (n 12) (showing the added value of lock-in in providing durable capital to take on long-term projects such as seafaring trade with the far east by Dutch and English entrepreneurs in the 17th century).

[35] RC Clark, *Corporate Law* (Boston, Little Brown and Co, 1986) 1.

iv. Duration and Purpose

The nineteenth century also brought a change in the duration of the corporation. While a long-lasting duration was possible when granted by the sovereign, the small number of corporations and the use of limited duration as well as limited purpose for many early corporations limited the reach of this characteristic prior to general incorporation. The reforms of the 1890s saw erosion of limits on corporate purposes as well as duration.[36]

v. Asset Partitioning

Henry Hansmann and Reinier Kraakman developed a parallel but broader illustration of separateness useful in larger business entities and corporate groups, that has proved to be particularly helpful in facilitation of debt on favourable terms.[37] Modern corporate groups often contain hundreds of separate entities under centralised control, but each partitioned into a separate corporation with its own assets, and liabilities to gain the efficiency (and also perhaps opportunistic risk shifting) that comes from that.[38] Creditors can gain efficiencies by limiting their information gathering and their monitoring only to industries they know.[39] A similar capacity to focus monitoring can improve director performance and permit shareholders to follow only a specific market segment. Such specialisation of the efforts of each of these groups can produce overall gains over those that might exist without such partitioning leading Hansmann and Kraakman to conclude that partitioning was the essential part of separateness.[40]

This use of separateness prospered in the new financial world that grew out of the creation of corporate groups and the post-World War II development of large corporations with hundreds of separate subsidiaries. Such a regime was not possible until New Jersey and then other states changed their corporation statutes in the late 1800s to permit corporate entities to own shares in another corporation.[41]

These mostly statutory changes across the nineteenth century facilitated both a much broader and larger role for corporations in society and increased risks to parties affected by those corporations.

[36] Clark (n 35) 16–19.

[37] See H Hansmann and R Kraakman, 'The Essential Role of Organization Law' (2000) 110 *Yale Law Journal* 387, 403 (pointing out that similar monitoring economies result from affirmative asset partitioning).

[38] PI Blumberg, KA Strasser, NL Georgeakopoulos and EJ Gouvin, *Blumberg on Corporate Groups*, 2nd edn (New York, Wolters Kluwer, 2005) § 1.1 (hereafter '*Corporate Groups*').

[39] AJ Casey, 'The New Corporate Web: Tailored Entity Partitions and Creditors' Selective Enforcement' (2015) 124 *Yale Law Journal* 2680.

[40] See Hansmann and Kraakman (n 37).

[41] 1888 NJ Laws 385, 445; 1889 NJ Laws, 414.

C. American Law's Struggles to Keep Up with Entities with Enhanced Separateness

The industrial revolution dramatically increased the distances across which Americans could interact and the scale on which products could be produced.[42] The legal 'technology' reflected a similar transformation particularly in increasing the capacity of corporations to take advantage of these changes. Limited liability, entity permanence, general incorporation, and hierarchical control were each on their way to becoming standard features of American corporations and other features such as a corporation's ability to own shares in another corporation, were just over the horizon.[43] The number of American business corporations exceeded the number of not-for-profits by 1820 and grew dramatically in the middle decades of the nineteenth century.[44]

The initial American judicial opinions on the rights of corporations fit well within the Blackstone view of corporations focused on the limited and practical issues of transferring property, contracting as to corporate assets, or the entity's capacity to sue and be sued. The Supreme Court's opinion in *Bank of the United States v Deveaux* in 1809, the first US Supreme Court case to deal with corporate personhood, had to decide the corporation's access to federal courts under jurisdiction based on diversity of citizenship. Chief Justice John Marshall in that case pointed to English cases looking beyond the corporate name to notice the character of the individuals.[45] Two years later, in an opinion written as a circuit judge, (in *Dixon v US*), Marshall drew on the descriptions from Blackstone and Kyd as rights 'incidental to a corporation to sue and be sued, to convey and to take property'.[46]

Marshall's decision for the Court in the *Dartmouth College* case in 1819, showed the evolution of his thinking about corporateness beyond the right to hold and transfer property. This opinion, like his two earlier opinions just described, starts with a view of corporateness drawn from Blackstone and Kyd's recognition of the state's power to create the entity and limit the entity's powers:

> A corporation is an artificial being, invisible, intangible, and existing only in contemplation of law. Being the mere creature of law, it possesses only those properties which the charter of its creation confers upon it, either expressly or incidental to its very existence.[47]

[42] See J Ellis, *The Quartet: Orchestrating the Second American Revolution* 1783–1789 (Westminster, Knopf Doubleday Publishing Group, 2015) (describing a change in the size of the world Americans viewed as relevant for their political and social life from perhaps 30 miles at the time of the revolution to considerably larger by the writing of the Constitution).

[43] See Thompson (n 33).

[44] Blumberg (n 26) 301.

[45] *Bank of United States v Deveaux*, 5 Cranch 61 (1809), 84–85.

[46] *Dixon v United States*, 7 F Cas 761(CC D Va 1811), 763.

[47] *Trustees of Dartmouth College v Woodward*, 17 US 518 (1819), 659.

From there, the opinion takes a broader turn that shows how his understanding of the corporation was beginning to expand. The 'incidental rights' that Marshall was willing to recognise for the not-for-profit Dartmouth College corporation looked beyond the passive holding of property, contracting or suing. As a charitable college, there were no shareholders as in *Deveaux* to guide the examination of entity rights. Instead, Marshall looked to the donors and what they sought to accomplish by forming the corporation; it is their rights which would be impaired by the action contemplated by the New Hampshire legislature.[48]

These early cases provided protection for corporations but still incomplete comfort for groups of entrepreneurs increasingly making use of the corporate form. Throughout this period, corporations faced regular restrictions on their separateness status. The breadth of the contracts clause protection for corporations provided in *Dartmouth College* dissipated in subsequent decisions;[49] states took advantage of the flexibility suggested in Justice Story's separate opinion in *Dartmouth College* permitting them to claw back state power via language in corporate charters reserving to the state the power to make subsequent amendment to the entity's charter.[50] The corporation's ability to claim access to diversity jurisdiction in federal courts remained,[51] but a series of cases, each seemingly using different reasoning, failed to deliver certainty in predicting future cases or expanding the doctrine for use in other areas.[52] A decision written by Chief Justice Roger Taney in 1839, denying corporations the protection of the privileges and immunities clause of the Constitution when they operated out of state, adversely affected insurance companies and other corporations seeking to do business in a growing national economy.[53] Limits on corporate purpose and corporate duration continued.

[48] ibid 642. See M M Blair and E Pollman, 'The Derivative Nature of Corporate Constitutional Rights' (2015) 56 *William & Mary Law Review* 1673, 1683.

[49] See *Charles River Bridge v Warren Bridge*, 36 US (11 Pet) 420 (1837) (adopting a stricter test of impermissible state actions that impermissibly interfere with charters).

[50] *Dartmouth* (n 47).

[51] The US Constitution (in Art III, s 2, cl 1) defines the judicial power of the federal government to include deciding controversies between citizens of different states (ie, showing diversity in the citizenship of the parties) so that access to federal courts for cases involving corporations depends on the court's decision as to the place to which the corporation was associated for purposes of this clause.

[52] Compare *Bank of United States v Deveaux*, 9 US 61 (1809), 84–85 (appropriate to look at character of the individuals for purposes of jurisdiction by diversity – without discussing the specific shareholders) with *Louisville, C & C R Co v Letson*, 43 US 497 (1844), 509 (corporation shareholders considered as citizen of state of incorporation to determine diversity) and *Marshall v Baltimore & O RR*, 57 US 314, 6 How 314 (1853) (presuming all shareholders are citizens of the state of incorporation for purposes of determining complete diversity).

[53] *Bank of Augusta v Earle*, 38 US (13 Pet) 519 (1839), 586. Art IV, s 2 of the US Constitution protects a citizen's privileges and immunities against government – a way to protect the fundamental rights of citizens; thus Taney's restrictive reading of the privileges and immunities of corporations closed off an avenue for corporations to assert rights protected against government intrusion.

Advocates seeking to provide a more accommodating approach for corporations had been trying for decades to find more effective arguments, but with mixed success. Efforts to develop the 'law of the land' as a due process type limit on the power of state governments offered some hope but was not sustained.[54] Ultra vires, a traditional claim alleging acts as beyond the power of an entity, remained as a vulnerable point of attack against broadening corporate powers throughout the nineteenth century.[55]

D. Efforts to Use the 14th Amendment to Achieve Equal Rights for Corporations

Given the uneven success of corporate legal arguments for greater entity protection in the antebellum period, the adoption of the 14th Amendment to the US Constitution in the late 1860s produced an unexpected opening to corporation litigators. Adopted to protect formerly enslaved people, the Amendment's clause entitling persons to equal protection of the law quickly became a vehicle which litigants sought to extend the rights of corporations as persons. As in the original Constitution and the Bill of Rights, the 14th Amendment does not mention corporations. Yet as described in the remainder of this section, the Court quickly seemed to resolve that a corporation was a person under the amendment, using language that the contemporary Supreme Court has cited in providing corporations with broad rights to free speech and religious liberty.[56] While it may be argued that the 14th Amendment had been diverted from its original purpose,[57] the focus here is the weak foundation these late nineteenth-century developments provide for the Supreme Court's recent willingness to erase the separateness between entities and the individuals associated with them.

Efforts to use the 14th Amendment to protect corporations began soon after the Amendment was ratified but with little initial success. A California property tax enacted in 1880 seemed to offer a golden opportunity since the law did not permit corporations to deduct mortgages from the valuation of their property when such exclusion was permitted to individuals. Railroads claimed the

[54] HJ Graham, 'The "Conspiracy Theory" of the Fourteenth Amendment' (1938) 47 *Yale Law Journal* 171, 177 (discussing efforts in state court in the decades prior to the Civil War to use the 'law of the land' doctrine under state law to develop protections for corporations, after contract clause arguments had begun to suffer limitations).

[55] *Cf State v Standard Oil*, 49 Ohio St 137, 30 NE 279 (1892) (finding acts by Standard Oil pursuant to trust agreements were ultra vires).

[56] See, eg, *First National Bank of Boston v Bellotti*, 435 US 765 (1978).

[57] A Winkler, *We the Corporations: How American Businesses Won their Civil Rights* (New York, Liveright, 2018). He includes data from Charles Wallace Collins published in 1912 showing the Supreme Court's 14th Amendment cases involving the rights of African Americans by that date totalled 28 versus about 300 cases on the rights of corporations. CW Collins, *The Fourteenth Amendment and the States* (New York, Little, Brown, and Company, 1912) 129–138.

difference denied them equal protection of the law under the 14th Amendment.[58] This case was tried before Supreme Court Justice Stephen Field riding circuit to hear federal claims arising in California.[59] Field's lengthy and detailed circuit court opinion invoked, but went well beyond, Chief Justice Marshall's opinion in *Dartmouth College* and voiced conclusions repeated in *Hobby Lobby* and *Citizens United*: 'It would be a most singular result if a constitutional provision intended for the protection of every person against partial and discriminatory legislation would cease to exert such protection at the moment the person becomes a member of a corporation.'[60] Field declared the amendment 'a perpetual shield against injustice against the despised laborer from China, or the envied master of millions'.[61]

When the case moved to the Supreme Court (with Field participating as was the practice at the time), the railroads recruited Roscoe Conkling, a long-time Senator and political boss in New York, to argue their case. At oral argument, Conkling emphasised another part of his biography, his service as a congressman on the joint Congressional committee (the only surviving member at that time) drafting the 14th Amendment. He told the justices that the 14th Amendment as originally proposed had referred to 'citizens', but that the Congressional committee had changed it to 'persons' so as to protect corporations as well as former slaves and that he had a journal to prove it.[62] Twentieth-century scholar Howard Jay Graham, has shown the journal said no such thing and that 'person' had always been the term used.[63] Conkling's lie and Field's passion failed to sway the rest of the Court,[64] leading to a second railroad case also initially decided at the circuit level before Field. This produced a second Field opinion (again at the circuit court level) even more supportive of the railroad position, and a second Supreme Court decision in which Field's colleagues again chose not to take up his framing of the case, again declining to reach the constitutional questions.[65]

[58] The financial reality was that the different characteristics of railroads and individuals effectively erased any special benefit to individuals as compared to the corporations in question. The railroad property was so heavily mortgaged that the railroads would effectively owe no income and the mortgage holders, many located out of state, would escape state taxation on their property. Individuals, who Field asserted were benefiting, were usually required by their in-state lenders to pay the lender's taxes due on the mortgages. See P Kens, *Justice Stephen Field: Shaping Liberty from the Gold Rush to the Gilded Age* (Lawrence, University of Kansas Press, 1997) 240.

[59] Through most of the nineteenth century the Supreme Court justices, in addition to meeting collectively in Washington DC to hear the court's dockets, also would travel individually to their assigned federal circuit to hear claims filed in that circuit. Such decisions could then be appealed to the Supreme Court on which the circuit riding justice would sit with his colleagues to hear any appeal of his decision at the circuit level.

[60] *San Mateo County v Southern Pacific RR. Co*, 13 Fed CC (1885), 744. This presaged the modern use of this argument in first amendment cases that mere incorporation was causing a loss of 1st amendment rights. See introduction above.

[61] ibid 741. Field had asserted a similar breadth for the 14th Amendment a decade before in his dissent in the *Slaughter-House Cases*, 83 US 36 (16 Wall) (1873) (on the losing side of a 5–4 decision as to the reach of the amendment).

[62] See Graham (n 54); Winkler (n 57).

[63] See Graham (n 54).

[64] See *San Mateo County v So Pacific RR Co*, 116 US 138 (December 21, 1885).

[65] *Santa Clara County v Southern P R Co*, 118 US 394 (1886), 421.

Having failed twice on the substance, the corporations gained a back-handed victory in *Santa Clara*. A now-famous headnote had been added to the published opinion by the Court's reporter describing a comment made by Chief Justice Morrison Waite just before the oral argument: 'The court does not wish to hear argument on whether the 14th Amendment applies to these corporations. We are all of the opinion it does.'[66] Field milked this for all it was worth – repeatedly citing this headnote in subsequent cases which he described as a 'holding of the Court' that corporations are persons within the meaning of the 14th amendment.[67] Yet none of these decisions dealt with the broad issue left unresolved in the earlier cases – whether corporations had a right not to be taxed differently from individuals. Each of the cases was closer to the earlier and narrower nineteenth century holdings ensuring the corporation's right to protect its property or to be sued in the corporate name and the earlier writings of Blackstone and Kyd[68] than they were to the twenty-first century opinions where Justice Field's language would reappear.[69]

Field (and the railroads) had sought a broad definition of a corporation's rights as matching those of individuals. Field had described the impact of corporations in monumental terms: 'A large proportion of our people are members of some corporation [citing religious, education, manufacturing and others] … [A]ggregate wealth amounts to billions upon billions of dollars [that] furnishes employment, comfort and luxuries to all classes and thus promotes civilization and progress.'[70] Two trips to the Supreme Court, however, failed to gain a majority for such a broad claim, leaving only an abstract statement of personhood. The point for which modern Supreme Court cases cite *Santa Clara* was clearly placed before the justices and the Court of the 1880s let it pass. Field's recurring citations of *Santa Clara's* holding did not advance the law.

Morton Horwitz described the *Santa Clara* decision 'not as an innovation, but … as following a long line of cases going back almost 70 years to the *Dartmouth College* cases'.[71] The focus was property rights and contracts

[66] ibid Headnote 1. See Winkler (n 57).

[67] *Pembina Consol Silver Mining & Milling Co v Pennsylvania*, 125 US 181, 183, 8 S Ct 737, 31 L Ed. 65 (1888) ('associations of persons … permitted to do business under a particular name and have a succession of members without dissolution ….The equal protection of the laws which those bodies may claim is only such as accorded similar associations within the jurisdiction of the sate'); *Missouri Pacific R Co v Mackey* 127 US 205 (1888); *Minneapolis & St Cloud R Co v Beckwith*, 129 US 26 (1889) ('guaranty to persons the enjoyment of property or afford to them the means of protection'); *Charlotte, C & A R Co v Gibbes*, 142 US 386 (1892), 390.

[68] Each of the cases supported liability of a corporation, usually a railroad, that was not applied to individuals or regulation of a corporation's conduct. See *Pembina* (n 67) (a state licence tax on foreign corporations not a violation of the privileges and immunities clause); *Missouri Pacific* (n 67) 207 (corporation's responsibility for the conduct of its agent); *Minneapolis* (n 67) (state could impose damages on a railroad for failure to erect a fence leading to death of animals' in adjoining lands); *Charlotte* (n 67) 390 (corporations' liable for salaries of a railroad commission).

[69] E Pollman, 'Reconceiving Corporate Personhood' [2011] *Utah Law Review* 1629, 1659 ('The notion of corporate personhood in constitutionals jurisprudence is rooted in concerns protection contract and property.').

[70] *San Mateo* (n 60) 404–405.

[71] Horwitz (n 32) 221.

rights of the Blackstone era. Academics looking at this era see this jurisprudence of corporate personhood as still embracing a long line of cases drawing on a corporation's close linkage to partnership and not yet coming to grips with the ascendant business form of the late nineteenth century. Horwitz, for example, concludes 'Up until the 1880s there was a strong tendency to analyze corporations' law not very differently from the law of partnership.'[72] Victor Morawetz's 1888 treatise treated corporations 'as virtually indistinguishable' from partnership.[73] As Herbert Hovenkamp described this period, 'only thirty or forty years of hindsight can attach great consequences to the substantive protection produced by the *Santa Clara* decision'.[74]

E. The Lochner Era and the New Deal

The decades after Field's retirement from the Court were called the *Lochner* era.[75] The liberty of contract that the Court followed for most of the next four decades owes much to Field's jurisprudence.[76] The corporate sector was the biggest beneficiary of the *Lochner* approach, but the doctrine was broader than corporateness and did not need any of the developing sense of corporate separateness to achieve its ends. And when the New Deal Supreme Court supplanted the *Lochner* era with a constitutional view that permitted more government control over business, that depended more on one's view of the constitutional power under the interstate commerce clause than a particular understanding of corporate personhood.[77] In both the *Lochner* and the New Deal eras, successive Supreme Court opinions developed areas of constitutional rights affecting corporations without having a consistent theory of personhood to support it. For example, in *Hale v Henkel* the Court found a corporation could claim rights against production of documents but not the right against self-incrimination.[78]

[72] ibid.

[73] V Morawetz, *A Treatise on the Law of Private Corporations* (Boston, Little, Brown, 1882).

[74] H Hovenkamp, 'The Classical Corporation in American Legal Thought' (1988) 76 *Georgetown Law Journal* 1643.

[75] The *Lochner* era describes a period during which the US Supreme Court repeatedly struck down economic regulations as unconstitutional. The namesake case, *Lochner v New York*, 198 US 45 (1905), struck down state legislation limiting weekly working hours. See generally VF Nourse, 'A Tale of Two Lochner's: The Untold History of Substantive Due Process and the Idea of Fundamental Rights' (2009) 97 *California Law Review* 751, 754 n 16 (noting various definitions for the Lochner Era, including 'the period from 1900 until World War I' and 'the period from1890 until 1937'); CR Sunstein, 'Lochner's Legacy' (1987) 87 *Columbia Law Review* 873, 873–75.

[76] *Lochner v New York*, 198 US 45 (1905).

[77] *West Coast Hotel Co v Parrish*, 300 US 379 (1937), 400 (overruling a prior *Lochner* era decision and marking the beginning of greater Supreme Court deference to the legislation of the New Deal).

[78] *Hale v Henkel*, 201 US 43 (1906), 43–44, 74–75 ('It would be a strange anomaly to hold that a state, having chartered a corporation to make use of certain franchises, could not in the exercise of its sovereignty, inquire how these franchises had been employed, and whether they had been abused, and demand the production of the corporate books and papers for that purpose.').

The Court developed a long list of cases protecting media corporations and later protection for commercial speech without going deep into entity theory.[79]

In the 1890s and thereafter, there was a dramatic change in the regulation of corporations in response to the existential crisis brought about by their bigness and the seemingly shared conclusion that the large size of corporations was inevitable.[80] As Horwitz noted there was 'stunning reversal in American economic thought' in this period to 'defend and justify as inevitable' the emergence of large-scale corporate concentration. For some, this belief led to a conclusion that 'legal forms cannot interfere with the natural evolution of the economy', expressed in support of general incorporation acts that did not restrict corporations.[81] The enabling approach to state corporate law that has prevailed since the late nineteenth century is consistent with this view. Led by New Jersey in the 1890s and soon replicated elsewhere, states abandoned their traditional regulatory approach to corporations in favour of enabling statutes that no longer restricted corporations.[82]

The regulatory impulse did not disappear, however, but rather moved to common law of piercing the veil and to the actions of the federal government. For progressives of the day, the inevitability of bigness led to more support for intense federal regulation in antitrust and railroad regulation from the late nineteenth century,[83] in the Tillman Act of 1907 that prohibited corporate political contributions,[84] and in the tax laws of 1936 subjecting corporations to a less favourable tax.[85] This federal oversight intensified in the new regulatory state instituted by the New Deal with a particular attention to the new and growing power of corporations and the need for social control over their broad power. This continued willingness to regulate corporations differently reflected the recognition that their characteristics produced a different set of risks to outsiders and to society at large.

Through this long evolution, separateness remained subject to limitations. In *U.S. v Milwaukee Refrigerated Transit Co.*, for example, in 1905, a federal

[79] See, eg, the cases cited in *Citizens United* (n 2) 342.

[80] Horwitz (n 32).

[81] C Bostwick, *Legislative Competition for Corporate Capital* (New York, son, 1899).

[82] Professor Joel Seligman termed it a 'revolution wrought in the law of corporations' that 'turned corporate law inside out'. J Seligman, 'A Brief History of Delaware's General Corporation Law of 1899' (1976) 1 *Delaware Journal of Corporation Law* 249, 264, 273. Professor (later Supreme Court Justice) Wiley Rutledge described this period as 'destined eventually not only to reverse the historic policy of the states toward corporations but also to place state policy fundamentally in opposition to that of the Federal Government'. WD Rutledge, 'Significant Trends in Modern Incorporation Statutes' (1937) 22 *Washington University Law Quarterly* 305, 307.

[83] See, eg, the Sherman Act of 1890, 26 Stat 209 (prohibiting activities that restrict interstate commerce and competition in the marketplace); the Interstate Commerce Commission Act of 1887, Pub L 49-104 (requiring railroad rates to be reasonable and just).

[84] See the Tillman Act of 1907, Pub L No 59-36, 34 Stat 864.

[85] S Bank, 'Corporate Managers, Agency Costs, and the Rise of Double Taxation' (2002) 44 *William & Mary Law Review* 167 (describing enactment of the 1936 act, the first full double taxation of corporate income).

circuit court disregarded separateness to prevent a corporation from being inserted to receive rebates that would have avoided the federal law prohibiting rate discrimination. Within a few more years there had been enough cases of disregard of corporate separateness that Maurice Wormser was able to launch the new field of 'piercing the veil' that continues undiminished today.[86] The reality is that the corporate world in the nineteenth century produced two distinct streams of law in response to the rise of the large corporation: state laissez-faire corporations' law that today's corporate bar would still recognise as familiar and a distinctively more regulatory federal law that has continued to grow over more than a century.[87]

The through line is that the post-Civil War period brought a significant change in what corporations could do and the regulation to which they were subjected. Phillip Blumberg and his coauthors in a multi-volume treatise on corporate groups charts the development of dozens of subject matter areas in which statutes were developed disregarding the separateness of entities.[88] More recently Marianna Pargendler has compiled various areas of regulatory partitioning from antitrust to international sanctions that dot corporate law.[89] The indicia of corporation rights of the early nineteenth century to some extents were constitutionalised, and thus more firmly entrenched as rights of corporations against government.[90] But even as the Court moved toward liberty rights for corporations and addressed more complex issues of speech and religion, these rights coexist within a system that permits broad regulation of corporations, including regulation explicitly based on how corporations differ from individuals.

III. AMERICAN LAW'S CONSISTENT WILLINGNESS TO REGULATE CORPORATIONS DIFFERENTLY THAN INDIVIDUALS

This section shows the consistent pattern in American law across multiple eras to regulate corporations to balance the advantages and harms that flow from separateness. The government has regulated these separate entities in different ways at different times, but never going so far as to say that corporations must have the same rights as individuals that recent Supreme Court cases have suggested.

[86] IM Wormser, 'Piercing the Veil of Corporate Entity' (1921) 12 *Columbia Law Review* 496.
[87] See Thompson (n 33) 4–9.
[88] Blumberg et al (n 38).
[89] M Pargendler, 'Veil Peeking: The Corporation as a Nexus for Regulation' (2021) 169 *University of Pennsylvania Law Review* 717.
[90] See E Pollman, 'Constitutionalizing Corporate Law' (2016) 69 *Vanderbilt Law Review* 639.

A. Separateness Consequences that Provide a Basis for Differential Regulation

This subsection discusses three prominent consequences of corporate separateness that have been a recurring basis for legal regulation: (1) use of the corporate form to inappropriately shift the risk of the entity's business to parties interacting with the entity who did not bargain to carry that risk; (2) magnification of corporate entities, as compared to individual actors performing similar acts, that skews the economic and social impact to favour the corporate actors; and (3) targeted settings in which the separateness of the corporate form combines with other attributes such as anonymity or autonomy, to permit arbitrage in ways that hinder or block general government regulation.

i. Corporate Separateness Shifting Risk to Parties Not Bargaining for that Risk

Limited liability and other forms of asset partitioning often create a win-win where the creation of a separate entity reflects an explicit bargain between the parties as to which one is willing to accept particular risks of the transaction usually because one party can more efficiently bear the risk and/or evaluate the risk and possible losses. This allocation is more troubling, however, when only one party has participated in the decision to reallocate the risk and the other has not had an opportunity to adjust its conduct or its price. The result may well create a moral hazard where the insider may be able to keep the fruits of the transaction if the deal goes well, but avoid the liabilities if the deal does not.[91] Courts have long regulated this misuse of separateness by piercing the corporate veil, an ex-post use of law.[92]

ii. Magnification of Corporate Entities

Attributes such as perpetual life, limited liability, and lock-in permit incorporated entities to prosper more than similarly situated individuals in a way that may provide the corporation's principals with an inappropriate advantage. Many of the earliest business corporations in the US were given a monopoly, such as to operate a bridge or a turnpike, in ways that led to efforts to regulate corporations. The massive change in the scale of American business in the period after the Civil War and the massive growth in the power of corporations was accompanied with corporations (eg, railroads) gaining special privileges

[91] See, eg, H Hansmann and R Kraakman 'Toward Unlimited Shareholder Liability for Corporate Torts' (1991) 100 *Yale Law Journal* 1879; C Goodhart and R Lastra 'Equity Finance: Matching Liability to Power' (2021) 7 *Journal of Financial Regulation* 1.

[92] RB Thompson, 'Unpacking Limited Liability: Direct and Vicarious Liability of Corporate Participants for Torts of the Enterprise' (1994) 47 *Vanderbilt Law Review* 1.

from government. These include the right to eminent domain, or land grants for the railroads, that provoked renewed calls to regulate these emerging large corporations.[93]

iii. Arbitrage

A third setting where corporate attributes may produce inappropriate advantage can be seen in anonymity or autonomy that operate in particular settings to frustrate regulation. There may be ordinary societal transactions regulated by government such as building permits or political contributions. If a corporation were to undertake the project or to make the contribution, the separateness of the corporate form would provide anonymity that the individual would not have.[94] This results not from the affirmative grant of a corporate right such as with limited liability, but rather the law providing benefits without requiring disclosure of the shareholders who are behind any corporation.[95] The law's recognition of the separation of the entity from its humans has what may be an unintended effect. A recent hot spot for anonymity in the corporate form has been anti-money laundering regulations in an age of terrorism where financial institutions have been required to report suspicious activity and identify their customers.[96] The use of entities with undisclosed owners remains a point of concern to undermining the effectiveness of these efforts.

B. Through a Corporate Lens: What an Alternative Would Look Like

In failing to address corporate separateness, the twenty-first century Supreme Court ignores the concern of corporate size recognised by its predecessors of the 1870s and 1880s. The great economic power of these large entities created actors so large as to be both possible oppressors of individuals in society and important vehicles for recognising individual rights against the state. Stephen Field had made up his mind – an approach that viewed corporations as different from individuals was 'the essence of tyranny'.[97] His colleagues on the Court were unwilling to go that far. They understood that corporations had transformed their society. The majority of the Court of that era upheld recurring limits on these newly-powerful organisations that threatened large parts of society.[98]

[93] Horwitz (n 32).

[94] *New York Times*, 'Towers of Secrecy, Piercing the Shell Companies', December 2014–February 2015.

[95] Mod Bus Corp Act § 2.02 (requiring name of some corporate agents but not its shareholders).

[96] See 'Anonymous, Inc.' viewable at www.cbsnews.com/news/anonymous-inc-60-minutes-steve-kroft-investigation/; www.cbsnews.com/news/lawmakers-call-for-change-after-60-minutes-report/.

[97] ibid.

[98] See section II.D above.

After Field's death, the Court adopted his view on limiting state power generally, but not based on corporateness.[99]

The Court of the 2010s in *Citizens United* and *Hobby Lobby* ignored the dual-facing impact of the corporate form, having clearly come down on the side of corporate rights to establish bulwarks against the power of the state. Even so, the two principal cases, one involving a not-for profit corporation and the other owned by a single family, represent a small slice of corporations generally. The justices and the executive branch have been willing to expand the bulkhead in these two cases to apply to corporations of all types. *Citizens United's* language with its focus on hearers as opposed to speakers to define freedom of speech would easily encompasses publicly held corporations and Justices Stevens and Scalia in their separate opinions, previewed the vigorous debate as to speech of large entities that has since ensued.[100] *Hobby Lobby's* holding was limited to closely held corporations where the government was unable to enforce a broad accessibility provision to limit behaviour of the business in accordance with their owners' individual religious belief. The regulation in question, initially written to apply only to closely held corporations, was soon extended to all included all health care providers including publicly held entities that did not reflect the tight connection between an owner's religious belief and the policy being implemented.[101]

This part explores what a judicial approach to corporate constitutional rights would look like if the Court applied corporate law as well as constitutional law principles. This requires simultaneously recognising the corporation's role in helping safeguard individuals against possible government tyranny and the power of the modern corporation to create a large space for overreach by the organisation itself and the individual acting through it. Such an approach would expressly recognise three specific aspects of learning from corporate law and would push judicial review away from the depth of judicial deference that recent cases seem to prefer.

First, corporations are endowed by the state with beneficial characteristics different from human actors and these differences can operate to the disadvantages of those affected by the corporation.[102] This has been a traditional concern of corporate law that regularly permits courts or legislatures to disregard the corporate separateness in appropriate circumstances and otherwise regulate corporations.[103]

[99] See M Ross, *Justice of Shattered Dreams, Samuel Freeman Miller and the Supreme Court During the Civil War Era* (Baton Rouge, LSU Press, 2003) 251–253 (describing how the Court moved closer to Field's view that eventually led to *Lochner*).

[100] See the separate opinions of Justices Stevens and Scalia in *Citizens United* (n 2) 385 and 393 onwards focusing on the application of the Court's analysis to publicly held corporations.

[101] See 45 Code of Federal Regulations 147.132(a)(1)(iv).

[102] See section III.A.

[103] See section III.A.i.

Second, all corporations are not the same such that there will be some differences in how corporate rights can be limited in different kinds of entities. This leads, for example, to different analysis in close versus public corporations and profit versus non-profits. The strength of the argument for separateness differs depending on the extent the insiders to the corporation are using separateness to transfer risk to others who have not had a chance to bargain or the degree to which the state has indicated a clear desire to assert a rule maintaining or disregarding separateness.[104] In determining rights in these different general circumstances, corporate law should reflect learning as to organisational behaviour in adjacent behavioural disciplines.[105] Corporateness can change the relationship between the entity and the individuals who are part of it in ways that can diminish the capacity of the entity to exercise the full breadth of individual rights in particular circumstances. The opaqueness and impenetrability that can follow corporateness as entities become more complex weakens the tie between entity and individuals that can reduce the breadth of the corporation's capacity as a rights-holder for the individuals.[106]

There is a third dimension in the consideration of corporation rights that becomes clearer once the first two dimensions are in focus: the separateness of the corporate entity means that sometimes (but not always) the individual who seeks to assert rights in the corporate form remains able to assert some or all of those rights individually outside of the corporation. The breadth of the corporation's claim should consider the extent to which the individuals already have the capacity to exercise an overlapping right closely related to the right that the individual also seeks to pursue through the entity.[107]

The combination of these three elements suggests an intermediate scrutiny that would involve a balancing of sometimes counter-directional concerns.

i. A Corporation's Separateness Characteristics should be Front and Centre in Analysing its Constitutional Rights

Separateness is the key legal characteristics of corporations and can produce both benefits to those who form the corporation (and to society) as well as disadvantages to those who may be affected by these corporate add-ons. To determine corporation rights by looking only at the 'protection' for insiders that follows from the introduction of a separate entity into a relationship blocks society (through legislatures or judges) from using a dual-facing approach to regulating that separate entity when harm to others may follow. Corporate law has long rejected a one-way ratchet. There have been hundreds, even thousands, of cases

[104] See generally, RB Thompson, 'Piercing the Veil: An Empirical Analysis' (1991) 76 *Cornell Law Review* 1036 ((describing differences in close vs. public corporations and tort vs. contract claims and other factors).

[105] See section B.i below.

[106] See section III.B.ii.

[107] See section III.B.iii.

in which courts disregard the separateness or pierce the veil of a corporation because of the adverse impact of separateness.[108] There are recurring examples of statutes and regulations limiting corporate acts and constraining particular uses of corporate separateness.[109] To exclude similar considerations from rights discussions would let the individuals who have unilaterally chosen the corporate form to 'have their corporate veil and pierce it too'.[110]

The basis for this government intrusion can be for any of the reasons discussed in section III – blocking inappropriate transfer of risk, magnification, or specific settings when autonomy or anonymity or other ancillary effects of corporate separateness frustrate generally applied public policy.[111] Insiders have been permitted, by state provided rules, to determine the key elements of the corporate form, the risks it will undertake, and the asserts available to cover those risk in ways that can overreach outsiders adversely affected by the entity. In such settings government regulation has long been a reality.[112]

ii. Rights should Differ for Different Types of Corporations Taking into Account the Opaqueness or Impenetrability of the Corporate Form

Stephen Field in the 1880s eloquently expressed the impact that the change in the scale of the corporation had on society but did not delve into how the corporations of that era also fundamentally changed the corporation's relationships to the humans who were connected to it. Adolf Berle and Gardiner Means in 1932 took on this challenge.[113] They describe a separation of ownership and control in American corporations showing the growing power of managers, but as importantly, presenting a new understanding of shareholders in large business corporations as passive and disconnected. Their evidence does not fit well with a view of personhood that assumes an equivalence of the entity and the individuals. Shareholders in the Berle and Means corporation had a more tangential and less-involved role in the entity that weakens efforts to make the individuals relationship the only source for defining corporation rights.

As Berle and Means showed, publicly held entities look fundamentally different than closely held ones on matters of corporateness. Even before their book, the economic reality of public corporations meant corporateness could not realistically turn on viewing the entity as an association of individuals.[114]

[108] This an American description. The UK, for example, has adopted a different approach that is more reticent to pierce the veil.

[109] Blumberg et al (n 38); Pargendler (n 89) (developing the idea of regulatory partitioning).

[110] *Hobby Lobby Stores, Inc v Sebelius*, 723 F3d 1114, 1179 (10th Cir 2013) (opinion of Matheson J, concurring in part and dissenting in part) rev'd 573 US 682 (2014).

[111] See, eg, section II.B.ii.

[112] See Blumberg (n 26).

[113] AA Berle, Jr and GC Means, *The Modern Corporation and Private Property* (New York, Macmillan, 1932).

[114] Blair and Pollman (n 48) 1683 ('by the end of the century, much larger corporations emerged, with features that could no longer support a characterization as associations of identifiable people.').

The Supreme Court in *Hobby Lobby* limited its holding to closely held corporations, but the general thrust of its explanation was to treat all corporations the same and to worry only about how the entity protects individuals who are insiders but not about how enhanced corporate characteristics may harm those outside the corporation.[115]

Legal philosopher Meir Dan-Cohen identifies two key criteria for determining the corporation (or other collective entity) as an appropriate rights holder, criteria which also suggest significant differences in the corporateness treatment of publicly and closely-held entities. He focuses on: (1) the extent to which an entity can appropriately be viewed as a vehicle for individual autonomy; and (2) the social utility of recognising the entity as a rights holder.[116] In Dan-Cohen's view, the organisational reality of corporations and similar entities means the connection to individuals is looser and more complex. He sees this as 'dramatically constricting the moral vocabulary at the disposal of organization as compared to that available to individuals as the basis of organizational [rights]'.[117] As a result, 'broad areas of organizational activity are only of marginal interest to advocate of individual autonomy … [so that rights in this space] may be determined by considerations of utility, uninhibited by moral constraints imposed by the ideal of individual autonomy'.[118] In this 'utility' space, a number of the prominent corporate characteristics addressed earlier – externalisation, magnification, anonymity, and arbitrage become more relevant to the personhood discussion and operate to limit organisational rights.

James Nelson has taken these ideas of affiliation, identity, and detachment deeper into the corporate structure, looking at the modern role of shareholders (and particularly institutional shareholders that now own the largest portion of most of American public corporations), directors, officers, employees and customers.[119]

These possible limits on organisational rights also correlate with key differences among different kinds of corporations – eg, the difference between for profits and not for profits. Participants in nonprofits lack the financial commitment that have become the most visible connection for the individual to the business corporations. Instead, they may desire to join for an expressive purpose. Members may drift away and come and go at will. Their relationship with the entity and with other members may be intense or distant, without the metric to measure commitment that would come from the purchase of stock.

[115] See *Hobby Lobby* (n 1) fn 23 citing Blackstone that there is no sharp divide among capacity of corporations to exercise religion and its discussion in Part IIIB4 of the opinion dismissing concern about ascertaining sincere beliefs because of 'numerous practical constraints that would likely prevent that from occurring'.

[116] See M Dan-Cohen, *Rights, Persons, and Organizations: A Legal Theory for Bureaucratic Society*, 2nd edn (Berkeley, University of California Press, 2016) 51.

[117] ibid 51.

[118] ibid 113.

[119] JD Nelson, 'Conscience, Incorporated' (2013) *Michigan State Law Review* 1565, 1587, 1610.

Some not-for-profits may essentially lack any members as market relations with donors may determine the entity's structure and its duration. Defining rights centred on individual autonomy becomes more difficult in such a setting.

Dan-Cohen has noted that in many non-profits '[t]he essential contributors have increasingly become the professional staffs and their counterparts in the foundations or government agencies that provide funds and the relevant incentives are those to which staffs and agencies respond.'[120] In this world, nonprofits, like their for-profit cousins, see their claim as a rights-bearing entity dissipate. Mancur Olson's attack on the adequacy of aggregation of individuals as an account of membership organisation parallels similar concerns about aggregation explanations for business corporations discussed above.[121] The same complexity, impenetrability, and opaqueness that appears in a large business corporation also weakens the claim to rights-bearing states for some non-profits.

Dan-Cohen's philosophical frame is supported by modern learning in sociology, behavioural economics, and cognitive psychology as to group behaviour, ideas not present in earlier eras but coming to be appreciated in the modern setting. Changes in the nature of corporations and the dramatic increase in scale of corporations in American society, as discussed above, overwhelmed simplistic explanations for rights based on equivalence to individual actors. The ways in which corporations are different than individuals are much better understood today than at the founding or in the early days of real entity theory in the late nineteenth and early twentieth centuries. There are significant differences between publicly held and closely held business corporation and between all of those and not for profit corporations or different kinds of not for profits ranging from colleges, hospitals, religious institutions, membership coops, fellowship entities, or various organisations organised for expressive purposes.

iii. Separateness as Permitting Two Personas for Individuals to Exercise the Same or Similar Rights

For some rights, such as freedom of speech or free exercise of religion, incorporation can provide individuals with two separate personas by which to exercise the same or similar rights. This contrasts to the earliest corporate rights – to hold or transfer property, to contract about such property, and to sue and be sued, discussed in Part I. Such rights can be easily transferred from one holder to another. When the transfer is to a corporation of other entity, all essential elements can be conveyed – nothing is left behind. Thus, when a corporation is formed and property or rights transferred, the entity becomes solely empowered to act in that space – even a sole shareholder could not act as to that property

[120] Dan-Cohen (n 116) 19.

[121] M Olson, Jr, *The Logic of Collective Action: Public Goods and the Theory of Groups* (Cambridge, Harvard University Press, 1965) (In the large organisation, unlike the small one, membership cannot be explained merely in terms of mutual interest in the collective good.).

and rights except through exercising the mechanisms of corporate authority.[122] Such separation is often efficient and useful to both insiders and outsiders to the corporation. The rights ascribed to the entity in such a setting will track more closely the rights of individuals if they were holding the same property in their personal capacity.

Rights to freedom of speech or free exercise of religion are not so easily cabined. Individuals can speak (including speaking via contributing money) about politics or any social issue. An individual can speak or exercise religion and if, owning a corporation, can do the same thing a second time through the corporation. Doing it in one place does not exhaust it or prevent it from being essentially replicated in another. For this corporateness discussion, if the corporation were to be cabined in its exercise of speech or religion for one of the policy reasons already discussed, that impact could well be limited or ameliorated by the continued capacity of the individual to exercise those same rights in an individual persona. For example, a person could individually make the same political contribution that could otherwise be made through a corporation in which the individual was the only shareholder. It may be that the action through the corporation may be magnified by resources accumulated over an unlimited duration, enhanced by being gathered from a collective group instead of just one person, or shielded by anonymity not easily available to individual speakers, differences that can justify disparate treatment. Even if so limited, the capacity of the individual to make the same speech as would be made by the corporation can remain as a realistic alternative to ensure the speech is heard while avoiding the externalities of corporateness.

We have seen in the prior discussion that the strength of separateness can rise or fall in different corporate contexts. If, for example, the effect of separateness is to transfer risk to an outsider who lacked the opportunity to bargain about taking on that risk, courts have long found it appropriate to disregard entity boundaries and separateness. The more specific a legislative or agency finding has been to disregard separateness for a general regulatory purpose, the less reason to continue to respect the initial set point of corporateness generated by the initial planning of the insiders. If the entity (acting through those that control it under the default governance rules of corporate law) seeks to speak for and assert autonomy or rights like speech and religion on behalf of a larger group of shareholders or employees, but the reality of the relationship is layered, distant and with less intense common interests, there is less justification to make the corporation the bearer of individual rights. The limitations arising from the reality of the individual/entity overlap in the speech/religion space raised in this section may interact with the policy directions of the two preceding sections just above, to support a decision to disregard the entity's exercise of speech or religious rights for individuals who make up the corporation.

These are difficult and complex questions that make for hard cases, but prior law provides some guidance. There are parts of free exercise of religion, for

[122] FH O'Neal and RB Thompson, *O'Neal and Thompson's Close Corporations*, 3rd edn (Chicago, Thomson Reuters, 2021), §1.15, 58–59.

example, where collective assertion of constitutional rights by an entity has been affirmed with little controversy. Autonomy in worship and in picking ministers have long been protected.[123] This is like the corporate assertion of property, contract and suing found in the earliest American cases; the entity's role as the focus of these rights is widely accepted. More difficult questions arise for assertions of religious belief that limit behaviour outside of worship and affecting outsiders. In *Hobby Lobby*, for example, the interference with free exercise was that the individuals who owned that corporation believed that what happened at work – coverage of employees under the company's plan as required by the law – would make the humans complicit in an immoral act. That the corporation was owned by a single family as in *Hobby Lobby* suggests, per the analysis in the prior section, a stronger claim to the entity as a permissible receptacle to express individual rights such as these. To the extent the rights in questions relate not to the internal relations of the entity but more outward looking conduct directly impacting employees in their private behaviour or those who interact with the entity in a public accommodation setting, the corporation right to exercise religious rights would be less deserving of an expansive interpretation.

Citizens United, like *Hobby Lobby*, can make a plausible case of alignment between the corporation and its members so as to avoid concerns such as those in section ii above. There are no members who are likely to complain. Indeed, there may be no members beyond the litigant. Donors who are putting up all of the money for the not-for profit's work appear content to see their money spent in a predictable pattern the organisers have told them it would be. Thus, all the insiders are likely happy. Less so the outsiders who see Citizens United as a collection point for large cash amounts being spent for controversial public issues making use of the anonymity that the corporate form can provide. One result has been an explosion of 'dark money' in a national political conversation that is becoming increasingly combative such that national legislators have sought to rein in such spending.[124] If, as a result of that legislation, corporate contributions were banned for these reasons, these same member[s] and donors could continue make these same expenditures for these same causes, just without the anonymity or other benefits flowing from the corporate form.

IV. CONCLUSION

There is a beguiling simplicity to the Supreme Court's current approach to the constitutional rights of corporations: A corporation exists to protect shareholders; to do that, corporation rights have been interpreted as equivalent to what shareholders, directors, officers (and perhaps employees) had as individuals

[123] See *Hosanna-Tabor Evangelical Lutheran Church and School v EEOC*, 565 US 171 (2012) (confirming government cannot contradict church's determination of who can act as ministers).

[124] See J Mayer, *Dark Money: The Hidden History of the Billionaires Behind the Rise of the Radical Right* (New York, Doubleday, 2016).

before incorporation. To continue to apply that equivalence principle requires the Court to disregard several key aspects of modern corporate reality and law's historical approach to corporateness. First, the corporate form gives humans using it real advantages over acting outside of the corporate form and this disparity sometimes harms those who deal with or are affected by the corporation. Second, changes visible in modern society mean the relationship between corporations and their humans have changed dramatically so that the corporation is sometimes less suited to exercise individual rights. Third, where individuals are able to exercise much of the same rights as the corporation seeks to replicate, there is less reason to expand corporate rights, especially if one or both of the first two factors are flashing red. The presence of these three factors argues against the equivalence assumption of the current Court and its approach of subjecting challenges to corporate regulation to a strict scrutiny framework that give short shrift to corporate reality.

6

Salomon *and* Sequana: *The Central Significance of Separate Legal Entity*

SUSAN WATSON

I. INTRODUCTION

IN 2022 THE UK Supreme Court in *BTI 2014 LLC v Sequana SA* considered the duties that directors owe to actual or contingent creditors. The Court determined that, if a company approaches insolvency, it is the interests of creditors collectively (as the contributors of debt capital) that become increasingly significant.[1] The shift to what could broadly be termed the Antipodean approach[2] means *Sequana* is a landmark case for UK company law. But the wider significance of *Sequana* lies in the discussion of the conceptual underpinnings of the company. The Supreme Court re-affirmed that companies are separate legal entities from their shareholders with the duties of directors owed to the company as an entity, not its shareholders. The alternative paradigm, which is to see companies contractually based on their shareholders at any time in the same way a partnership is based on its partners, was rejected.[3] By affirming the entity approach, the Supreme Court confronted what could be termed the *Salomon* paradox. *Salomon v Salomon & Co Ltd* has been used as authority to support both competing conceptualisations of the modern company; that a company is comprised of its shareholders, and that a company is a separate legal entity from its shareholders.

This chapter is about the significance of separate legal entity to company law. In the second section the path that led to *Salomon v Salomon & Co Ltd* becoming the source of the paradox is set out before focus shifts to the outcome of the case in the wider context of how the courts in the late nineteenth century viewed the relationship between the company, its shareholders, and its directors.[4] What Lord Briggs had to say about separate legal entity in *Sequana* is discussed in the

[1] *BTI 2014 LLC v Sequana SA* [2022] UKSC 25, [2023] 2 All ER 303.

[2] *Walker v Wimborne* (1976) 50 ALJR 446; *Nicholson v Permakraft* (N.Z.) Ltd [1985] 1 NZLR 242.

[3] H Wells, 'The Personification of Partnership' (2021) 74 *Vanderbilt Law Review* 1835.

[4] *Salomon v Salomon & Co Ltd* [1897] AC 22 (HL).

context of the legal landscape of the mid-to-late nineteenth century as are the conclusions reached in *Sequana*. The third section of the chapter identifies how the concept of separate legal entity entered the common law with the receipt of the canonist *persona ficta* by the common law. The final section briefly considers how fully realising the implications of the company as a separate legal entity and an 'infinite game' may aid corporate decision makers to incorporate ESG considerations in a principled way whilst ensuring the company endures.

II. *SALOMON* AND *SEQUANA*[5]

A. The Path to *Salomon*

Salomon is a watershed company law case in many common law jurisdictions.[6] It is authority for the foundational principle that by 1897 a modern company was an entity legally separate from its shareholders. In case law that principle is most commonly tested when courts are considering whether or not to 'lift the corporate veil' and impose liability on shareholders for the obligations of the company.[7]

The modern corporate form did not emerge first in the late nineteenth century. Once the English East India Company (EEIC) acquired permanent capital in 1657,[8] it shared all the key features that the modern companies incorporated through general incorporation statutes had acquired by the time *Salomon* was decided. Those characteristics were drawn from first 'the old incidents of incorporation': the right to sue and be sued; the common seal; entering into transactions as a corporation; making bylaws as internal rules and perpetual succession. And second, from the contractual joint stock company: capital contributed by shareholders as the corporate fund separated through double entry bookkeeping from shareholders.[9] Most significantly status as a *persona ficta* or artificial legal person meant the EEIC was a separate legal entity from its incorporators and investing shareholders.

In the taxonomy of the time, the EEIC was a type of corporation – a business corporation.[10] Corporations, which were incorporated though charters or similar instruments, dominated medieval England. After 1612 all forms of corporation, including business corporations like the EEIC, were treated by

[5] This section is derived in part from the author's book: S Watson, *The Making of the Modern Company* (Oxford, Hart Publishing, 2022).

[6] *Salomon* (n 4). See R Grantham and C Rickett (eds), *Corporate Personality in the Twentieth Century* (Oxford, Hart Publishing, 1998) and A Dignam and P Oh, 'Rationalizing Corporate Disregard' (2020) 40 *Legal Studies* 1.

[7] *Prest v Petrodel Resources Ltd* [2013] UKSC 34, [2013] 2 AC 415.

[8] See Watson (n 5) ch 3.

[9] ibid.

[10] Corporate charters had to be granted for a public purpose. During the reign of Elizabeth I corporate charters were granted for the advancement of enterprise. See Watson (n 5) ch 2.

the law as *persona ficta* or artificial legal persons. The *persona ficta* concept, derived from Canon law, was received by the common law in 1612 by Coke CJ in *The Case of Sutton's Hospital*.[11] The *persona ficta* corporation existed in the abstract separate from its members as a creation of the law. Its transplantation into the common law is discussed in more depth in the next section.

The business corporation differed from other forms of corporation because, although it was a *persona ficta* corporation, it had permanent capital. This permanent capital, which can be termed the Corporate Fund[12] was seeded by capital contributed by but separated from shareholders both legally (because the *persona ficta* corporation existed separately from its shareholders) and through the accounting mechanism of double-entry bookkeeping.

A contractual form of unincorporated company based on shareholders that was at common law a partnership existed in parallel with the incorporated *persona ficta* business corporation.[13] When the general incorporation statutes were introduced in the mid-nineteenth century,[14] initially the modern company was considered to be based on an association of shareholders in the same way as the unincorporated form.[15] A change in that understanding of the modern company developed through the second half of the nineteenth century culminating in the House of Lords in *Salomon* determining that a company is a separate legal entity from its shareholders.

That outcome would have been unlikely 20 or 30 years earlier. The reference in the Companies Act 1862 to the persons being 'associated' would then have been interpreted as requiring an association of shareholders with the company based on those shareholders[16] as seen in cases like *Re Wincham Shipbuilding, Boiler and Salt Co*[17] discussed below. And the speeches in *Salomon* are not entirely consistent about the legal separation of shareholders from the company. They created an ambiguity that has led to the paradox discussed in this chapter and in *Sequana* itself: *Salomon* has been seen as authority for a modern company being based on its shareholders *and* authority for a company being a separate legal entity from its shareholders.

[11] *The Case of Sutton's Hospital* (1612) 10 Co Rep 23a, 77 ER 960. See Watson (n 5) ch 2.

[12] S Watson, 'The Corporate Legal Entity as a Fund' (2018) 6 *Journal of Business Law* 467.

[13] See Watson (n 5) chs 2, 8 and A Televantos, *Capitalism Before Corporations* (Oxford, Oxford University Press, 2021).

[14] Joint Stock Companies Act 1844 (7 & 8 Vict c 16); Companies Act 1856; Companies Act 1862 (25 & 26 Vict c 89).

[15] HN Butler, 'General Incorporation in Nineteenth Century England: Interaction of Common Law and Legislative Processes' (1986) 6 *International Review of Law and Economics* 169.

[16] See, eg, the series of nineteenth century treatises of writer and jurist Nathanial Lindley where he initially termed company law as a branch of partnership law and companies as an 'association of many persons': N Lindley, *Supplement to a Treatise on the Law of Partnership Including its Application to Joint-Stock and Other Companies*, 5th edn (London, W Maxwell, 1863) and the debates in Hansard involving Robert Lowe and others set out in Watson (n 5) 134–136.

[17] *Re Wincham Shipbuilding & Boiler Co.* (1878) 9 Ch D 322; *Re Dronfield Silkstone Coal Co.* (1881) 70 Ch D 76; *Bank of Toronto v Cobourg, Peterborough and Marmora Ry* (1885) 10 OR 376 (CA).

In *Re Wincham Shipbuilding, Boiler and Salt Co*, shareholder directors ordered that money they paid on their shares be used to eliminate the company's overdraft and therefore their own guarantees of that overdraft.[18] Bacon V-C at first instance held that the payments were a breach of trust by the directors, because the payments served the interests of the directors rather than the interests of the company.

Allowing the appeal, Jessel MR said:

> The Vice-Chancellor decided the question on this ground, that the directors were trustees of all their powers. So, no doubt, they were. … But it appears to me that the question is, for whom were they trustees? … It has always been held that the directors are trustees for the shareholders, that is, for the company. … But directors are not trustees for the creditors of the company. The creditors have certain rights against a company and its members, but they have no greater rights against the directors than against any other members of the company. They have only those statutory rights against the members which are given them in the winding-up.[19]

Lord Briggs, discussing *Wincham* in *Sequana*, said:

> … what stands out for present purposes is the way in which Jessel MR equated the company with its shareholders for the purpose of his analysis of the directors' duties in the phrase: 'the directors are trustees for the shareholders, that is, for the company'. No-one now contends that directors owe duties direct to shareholders (in the sense that shareholders can enforce them directly) or, for that matter, directly to creditors. It is common ground that their duties are owed to the company and to no-one else. But this passage is illuminating, from a historical perspective, in suggesting that it was the perception in the mind of judges like Jessel MR that for these purposes the company and its shareholders were one and the same that led to their view that, in the discharge of duties to the company, directors needed only to have regard to the interests of shareholders, so that they did not owe a duty to consider or act in accordance with the interests of creditors.[20]

Many nineteenth century judges considered directors either to be trustees or akin to trustees. Conceptions of who or what they were trustees for shifted through the nineteenth century.[21] Lord Briggs in *Sequana* highlights how Jessel MR considered that shareholders comprised the company in 1878 when he decided *Wincham*. If so, it appears that Jessel MR's own conception of the modern company shifted as the century progressed. In 1882 in *Re Exchange Banking Co* (also called *Flitcroft's case*)[22] directors presented untrue accounts and declared dividends based on those accounts. Jessel MR considered the action by the liquidator against the directors:

[18] ibid.

[19] *Sequana* (n 1) [134] citing *Re Wincham Shipbuilding, Boiler and Salt Co* (n 17).

[20] ibid [134]–[135].

[21] See the discussion in S Watson, 'How the Company Became an Entity: A New Understanding of Corporate Law' (2015) 2 *Journal of Business Law* 120.

[22] *Re Exchange Banking Co* (1882) LR 21 Ch D 519 (CA).

> The creditor has no debtor but that impalpable thing the corporation, which has no property except the assets of the business. The creditor … gives credit to the company on the faith of the representation that the capital shall be applied only for the purposes of the business, and he has therefore a right to say that the corporation shall keep its capital and not return it to the shareholders, though it may be a right which he cannot enforce otherwise than by a winding-up order. It follows then that if directors who are quasi trustees for the company improperly pay away the assets to the shareholders, they are liable to replace them. It is no answer to say that the shareholders could not compel them to do so. I am of opinion that the company could in its corporate capacity compel them to do so, even if there were no winding-up. … [D]irectors in each case are to be declared jointly and severally liable and not only jointly liable.[23]

Here Jessel MR, by describing the corporation as an 'impalpable thing' with 'no property except the assets of the business' and by referring to the directors as quasi trustees paying away assets to shareholders, appears to view shareholders as separate from the company.[24]

Lindley LJ was a member of the English Court of Appeal in *Broderip v Salomon*[25] overturned in *Salomon v Salomon & Co Ltd* in the House of Lords. In an earlier incarnation Lindley LJ authored a series of leading treatises on company law and partnership law. The transition in understanding of the modern company incorporated through a general incorporation statute can be traced through the nineteenth-century treatises. Lindley's treatise on company law started life as an 1863 supplement to his treatise on partnership law.[26] Reflecting lineage from the contractual and unincorporated form of company, Lindley initially treated modern company law as a branch of partnership law subject to its principles.[27] In the text he describes companies as partnerships incorporated by registration and companies as a form of partnership.[28] In the introduction to the text, Lindley defined a company as an 'association of many persons who contribute money or money's worth to a common stock and employ it in some trade or business'.[29]

Lindley did nevertheless recognise the hybrid lineage of the modern company that drew on the earlier business corporation form, saying in an earlier 1860 edition of his partnership treatise:

> Companies are associations of persons intermediate between corporations known to common law and ordinary partnerships, and partaking of the nature of both; and the

[23] ibid 533–34.

[24] Also in *Imperial Hydropathic Hotel Co, Blackpool v Hampson* (1882) 23 Ch D 1 (CA) decided in 1882 Lord Jessel MR analysed the requirements of the Companies Act 1862 by referencing corporations' law and municipal corporations. The courts consistently considered statutory corporations to be separate legal entities.

[25] *Broderip v Salomon* [1895] 2 Ch 323 (CA).

[26] Lindley (n 16).

[27] N Lindley, *A Treatise on the Law of Companies, considered as a branch of the Law of Partnership*, 5th edn (London, Sweet & Maxwell, 1889).

[28] ibid 8.

[29] ibid 1.

> law relating to companies depends as well on the principles which govern ordinary partnerships, as on those which are applicable to corporations strictly so called.[30]

Lindley did not at that time offer an opinion about whether companies were separate from their shareholders, or comprised of their shareholders. By the third edition of his treatise in 1873, Lindley acknowledged the implications of incorporation of a modern company. '[A] company which is incorporated, whether by charter, special act of Parliament, or registration, is in a legal point of view distinct from the persons composing it',[31] concluding 'and is therefore regarded by lawyers somewhat as a firm is by non-lawyers'.[32] (By a firm, Lindley presumably meant a partnership.) Lindley may have been somewhat Delphic, because on the face of it the legal separation of shareholders from the modern company made inconsistent statements which he continued to make elsewhere in his treatise that a company was an association of shareholders. Even in the statement excerpted in this paragraph, Lindley refers to persons composing a company as well as saying that the company is legally separate from those persons.[33] As set out in a later section of this chapter, the ambiguity has its origins far back in the history of the development of the modern company.

B. *Salomon*

The distinguished Bench that considered *Broderip v Salomon* in the Court of Appeal included Lindley LJ. They were, probably unexpectedly, overturned by the House of Lords in *Salomon v Salomon & Co Ltd*.[34] In *Broderip v Salomon*, Lindley LJ, describes directors as trustees.[35] Despite finding against Salomon (or, in reality, the mortgagee of the debenture), and consistent with the most recent edition of his treatise, Lindley LJ in his judgment accepted that the incorporation of the company could not be disputed, citing section 18 of the Companies Act 1862.[36] However, Lindley LJ also concluded it was intended that the seven persons associated together carry on the business of the company. What was not intended was, as here, six people making it possible for the seventh person to operate the business:

[30] N Lindley, *A Treatise on the Law of Partnership: Including its Application to Joint-Stock and Other Companies*, vol 1 (Philadelphia, T & JW Johnson, 1860) 67.

[31] N Lindley and S Dickinson, *A Treatise on the Law of Partnership Including its Application to Companies*, vol 1, 3rd edn (London, W Maxwell, 1873) 227.

[32] ibid.

[33] See P Ireland, 'Limited Liability, Shareholders Rights and the Problem of Corporate Irresponsibility' (2010) 34 *Cambridge Journal of Economics* 837.

[34] *Broderip* (n 25). See the discussion in Watson (n 21) and Watson (n 5) 139–141. The authors of the Davey Report, which analysed English corporate law and governance at the end of the nineteenth century, were so certain that *Broderip v Salomon* would not be overturned in the House of Lords that they appended a copy of the Court of Appeal judgments to their Report.

[35] *Broderip* (n 25) 338.

[36] ibid 337.

> There can be no doubt that in this case an attempt has been made to use the machinery of the Companies Act, 1862, for a purpose for which it never was intended. The legislature contemplated the encouragement of trade by enabling a comparatively small number of persons – namely, not less than seven – to carry on business with a limited joint stock or capital, and without the risk of liability beyond the loss of such joint stock or capital. But the legislature never contemplated an extension of limited liability to sole traders or to a fewer number than seven.[37]

As we know from the debates in *Hansard*, the driving motivation behind the general incorporation statutes was *not* primarily to enable a small number of traders to form companies.[38] The statutes were intended to encourage investment by the middle classes in larger companies, with partnership remaining the favoured form of organisation for small ventures.[39] It was only later in the century, facilitated by the publication of Palmer's precedents[40] where the benefits of limited liability for small traders were highlighted, that incorporation became favoured over forming a partnership by sole traders or small groups of traders.[41] In the debate leading to the passing of the Joint Stock Companies Act 1856, Robert Lowe, known as the father of modern company law, said that no one would form a company to avoid liability for their debts.[42] The first part of Lindley LJ's statement around the purpose of the Companies Act 1862 being to enable trade by a small number of persons may not therefore be correct. But the second part about not contemplating the extension of limited liability to small groups of traders is undoubtedly true.

In the pleadings to the Court of Appeal in *Broderip v Salomon*, Buckley QC argued that the assets belonged to the corporation and the creditors needed to look to them for their security: 'The corporation has always a separate existence from the shareholders.'[43] Lindley LJ did not disagree but concluded that '[t]he company must, therefore, be regarded as a corporation, but as a corporation created for an illegitimate purpose'.[44] To Lindley LJ by 1895 a company incorporated pursuant to a general incorporation statute (Companies Act 1862) was a form of corporation. Prior to the enactment of the general incorporation

[37] ibid.
[38] See Watson (n 5) 128–143.
[39] ibid.
[40] FB Palmer, *Company Precedents for Use in Relation to Companies subject to the Companies Acts 1862 to 1880,* 2nd edn (London, Stevens & Sons, 1881); FB Palmer, *Company Precedents for Use in Relation to Companies subject to the Companies Acts 1862 to 1883,* 4th edn (London, Stevens & Sons, 1888); FB Palmer, *Company Precedents for Use in Relation to Companies subject to the Companies Acts, 1862 to 1890* vol 1, 6th edn (London, Stevens & Sons, 1895–96); FB Palmer, *Company Precedents for Use in Relation to Companies subject to the Companies Acts, 1862 to 1900* vol 1, 8th edn (London, Stevens & Sons, 1902); FB Palmer, *Company Precedents for Use in Relation to Companies subject to the Companies Acts, 1862 to 1907* 10th edn (London, Stevens & Sons, 1910).
[41] Watson (n 5) ch 12.
[42] HC Deb 1 February 1856, vol 140, cols 111–26.
[43] *Broderip* (n 25) 333.
[44] ibid 337.

statutes, corporations were granted charters or equivalent if they could establish they had a public purpose.[45] The furtherance of commerce was regarded as a public purpose for business corporations. By questioning the purpose for which the company was established with the purpose now found in the statute rather than a charter, Lindley LJ may have been drawing on principles of corporations' law where courts would look to the charter of a corporation to determine its purpose. The general incorporation statute could be viewed as equivalent to the charter. Lindley LJ accepted that Salomon & Co Ltd was a corporation, 'but as a corporation created for an illegitimate purpose',[46] 'an instrument for cheating honest creditors'.[47] Lindley LJ's primary objection may well have been that the Companies Act 1862, which could be seen as akin to the charter of the company, was used by Mr Salomon to create a corporation to protect himself from liability; a purpose which the Act never intended.

When the appeal reached the House of Lords Lord Macnaghten disagreed with Lindley LJ's depiction of the company as a trustee.[48] But it was only because Lindley LJ had concluded that the company was established for an illegitimate purpose, that he then regarded the company as a trustee:

> I should rather liken the company to a trustee for him – a trustee improperly brought into existence by him to enable him to do what the statute prohibits. It is manifest that the other members of the company have practically no interest in it, and their names have merely been used by Mr Aron Salomon to enable him to form a company, and to use its name in order to screen himself from liability. … In a strict legal sense the business may have to be regarded as the business of the company; but if any jury were asked, Whose business was it? they would say Aron Salomon's, and they would be right, if they meant that the beneficial interest in the business was his.[49]

As Lord Briggs points out in *Sequana*, emphasising that a company is a separate legal entity from its shareholders by the House of Lords in *Salomon* 'arose from the need for the House of Lords to disapprove the reasoning of the Court of Appeal that, in the circumstances of that case, the separate personality of the company should be ignored'.[50] *Salomon* nevertheless is widely regarded as the foundation case for modern company law with judicial recognition that a company is a separate legal entity from its shareholders.[51]

Turning to the paradox, *Salomon* has also been seen as authority for the contrary principle that at least for some purposes shareholders can be equated

[45] See Watson (n 5) 18–19. For abuse of the process see M Patterson and D Reiffen, 'The Effect of the Bubble Act on the Market for Joint Stock Shares' (1990) 50 *Journal of Economic History* 163.

[46] *Broderip* (n 25) 337.

[47] ibid 339.

[48] '… the company is in not in law the agent of the subscribers or trustee for them' *Salomon* (n 4) 52–53.

[49] *Broderip* (n 25) 338.

[50] *Sequana* (n 1) [136].

[51] See, eg, *Sevilleja v Marex Financial Ltd* [2020] UKSC 31, [2021] AC 39 [32], [102].

with the company. In a series of cases courts have held that shareholders (presumably viewed as principals) can ratify wrongs by directors (presumably viewed as agents).[52] In *Sequana* Lord Briggs discussed *Salomon* as the earliest of these ratification cases, acknowledging that those cases:

> … do tend to support the respondents' thesis that, for certain purposes, shareholders may be regarded as the equivalent of the company ('the corporators' as counsel put it) … The justification which has emerged for the ratification principle from the authorities is that the unanimous decision of a company's shareholders about a matter within its corporate capacity makes the decision the company's 'own act' about which neither it nor its liquidator on its behalf can thereafter complain. If the relevant decision was originally made by the directors, then its subsequent ratification by the shareholders releases the directors from any liability for breach of duty.[53]

Lord Briggs is unequivocal though when he concludes that a modern company is a separate legal entity from its shareholders:

> I would start by accepting that the original, historical, justification for regarding the general duty of directors to their company as being to manage its affairs for the benefit of its shareholders arose from a perception that, as its corporators, shareholders could for that purpose be equated with the company itself. … But the law has since moved on a long way from a view that the interests of others in relation to the company, and its relationships with others, are altogether irrelevant. Put shortly, of the two strands in the reasoning in the *Salomon* case, namely the company as a separate entity with its own interests and responsibilities and the company as an abstract equivalent of its shareholders, it is the first which has clearly prevailed over time.[54]

So the company is a separate entity with its own interests and responsibilities rather than an abstract equivalent of its shareholders. The significance of *Sequana* for English law is that it establishes that in the zone of insolvency directors owe a duty to creditors as a class. The wider significance of *Sequana*, that may ultimately mean it is regarded as a landmark case in corporate law, is that the Supreme Court picked one side of an ancient debate as to what a company is, finally laying the question of the primary conceptual origins of the modern company to rest. A modern company is separate from its shareholders; a modern company is not comprised of its shareholders.

What are the conceptual origins of the modern company? In the next section of this chapter, the emergence of the concept that the corporation is a separate legal entity and its relationship to the *persona ficta* concept which holds that a corporation is an artificial legal person that exists in the abstract separately from its members, is discussed.

[52] *Re Duomatic Ltd* [1969] 2 Ch 365; *Julien v Evolving Tecknologies and Enterprise Development Co Ltd* [2018] UKPC 2, [2018] BCC 376; *Ciban Management Corp v Citco (BVI) Ltd* [2020] UKPC 21, [2021] AC 122, cited in *Sequana* (n 1) [24].

[53] *Sequana* (n 1) [136].

[54] ibid [139].

III. TWO TYPES OF CORPORATENESS

A. *Societas* and *Universitas*

Legal organisations either are primarily based on and derive their corporateness from the people who comprise them, or from the state in some form with the antecedent legal organisational forms that preceded the modern company, the partnership and the corporation, differing in their source of corporateness.

The distinction is of long standing. In Roman law there were two kinds of association: the *societas* and the *universitas*. One kind of association, the *societas* referred to a general category of contractual relationships between members.

Like the modern partnership, the assets of the *societas* were owned by the members based on the terms of the contract that bound them.[55] Unlike the modern partnership, contracting parties had obligations to make contributions to a shared goal, but those obligations did not affect third parties. Unlike a modern partnership, there was no mutual agency between partners in a *societas*.[56] Liability of partners was not joint and several; it was pro rata. The links between modern partnerships based on the legal relationship of the partners to each other and a conception of the company as based on an association of shareholders are therefore clear. The links between the early *societas*, and the conception of the company as being based on shareholders, are therefore also apparent. It follows that if the company is comprised of its shareholders, the assets of the company are considered to be the property of those shareholders. It also follows that in the absence of statutory limited liability shareholders, as the company, will be pro rata liable for the debts of the company.[57]

The second kind of association, the *universitas*, which is the origin of the corporation form, derived its legal status from the state.[58] The *universitas*, as a legal entity, could hold property. It had rights and obligations that were distinct from those of its members.[59] The Romans had the idea of corporate separateness, which they may have derived from the Greeks.[60] The *universitas* was

[55] R Scruton and J Finnis, 'Corporate Persons' (1989) 63 *Proceedings of the Aristotelian Society, Supplementary Volumes* 239, 242.

[56] ibid.

[57] See Watson (n 5) ch 2 for a discussion of the evolution of the *societas* form to the contractual Joint Stock Company.

[58] M Weber, *The History of Commercial Partnerships in the Middle Ages: The First Complete English Edition of Weber's Prelude to The Protestant Ethic and the Spirit of Capitalism and Economy and Society* (Lutz Kaelber tr, Washington, Rowman & Littlefield Publishers, 2003) 60.

[59] ibid.

[60] JK Angell and S Ames, *Treatise on the Law of Private Corporations Aggregate*, 7th edn (Boston, Little Brown and Co 1861) 34–35.

therefore a separate legal entity, although probably not a separate legal entity from its members.[61]

Lawyers from the thirteenth century 'have been wont to attribute to the *universitas*\corporation a "personality" that is "fictitious" or "artificial"'.[62] As Maitland puts it:

> Every system of law that has attained a certain degree of maturity seems compelled by the ever-increasing complexity of human affairs to create persons who are not men, or rather (for this may be a truer statement) to recognize that such persons have come and are coming into existence, and to regulate their rights and duties. In the history of medieval Europe we have to watch on the one hand the evolution of groups (in particular, religious groups and groups of burgesses) which in our eyes seem to display all or many of the characteristics of corporations, and on the other hand the play of thought around that idea of an *universitas* which was being slowly discovered in the Roman law books.[63]

The concept of a corporation with a separate pool of assets as well as separate legal personality is 'distinctly European',[64] even though its precise origins are contested. Roman law, which had, through Canon law, been interpreted in a contemporary context was drawn on.[65]

Legislators exploring Roman law slowly discovered the *universitas* and tried to distinguish it from the partnership and the group of co-proprietors. Churches with bishops at the head and canons as members, or abbots at the head and monks as members sought acceptance of the idea that a church was an *universitas* and the *universitas* was a *persona*.[66] It was a distinction that was not necessarily apparent by the thirteenth century when canonists were just beginning to proclaim that the *universitas* is a *persona* and a *persona ficta*.[67] In Gierke's view 'Innocent, the father of "the Fiction Theory," appears as a truly great lawyer. … he found the phrase, the thought, for which others had sought in vain. The corporation is a person; but it is a person by fiction and only by fiction.'[68] Gierke argues what was received was what Italian commentators had been elaborating. Those commentators were disposed to adopt a version of Roman law which fitted medieval life. 'In particular in the doctrine of corporations and communities, there was much which was Germanic.'[69]

[61] See Watson (n 5) ch 2 for a discussion of the evolution of separate legal entity, which is not a focus of this chapter.

[62] F Pollock and F Maitland, *The History of English Law: Before the Time of Edward I*, vol 1, Book II, 2nd edn (Cambridge, Cambridge University Press, 1898) 488.

[63] ibid 486.

[64] D Gindis, 'Conceptualizing the Business Corporation: Insights from History' (2020) 16 *Journal of Institutional Economics* 569, 570.

[65] Pollock and Maitland (n 62) 494.

[66] ibid 512.

[67] ibid 494.

[68] O Gierke, *Political Theories of the Middle Age* (Frederic Maitland tr, Cambridge, Cambridge University Press,1900) xix.

[69] ibid xv.

In England in the fifteenth century, words betokening corporateness became common.[70] Loose associations of persons had sought to be treated as collective entities and recognised as corporate and legal persons.[71] Examples were towns and guilds, with commercial corporate life beginning in towns as part of the struggle of private individuals to free themselves from ecclesiastical, feudal and political control.[72] By the end of the Middle Ages England was awash with forms of corporation used for ecclesiastical (religious) and lay purposes, with the latter further divided into eleemosynary (charitable) and civil purposes.[73]

Whether a legal person could exist separately from natural persons was debated in England in the fourteenth and fifteenth centuries. A nuisance action was brought in 1372 against both the Dean and Chapter of St Peter of Exeter, and also against a clerk named John Weliot. The record of the case records the plea from the counsel for the defendants that Weliot was being sued twice because he was also a member of the chapter, which was not allowed.[74]

In 1429, the mayor, bailiffs and commonalty of Ipswich, and also Jabe as an individual defendant, were sued for trespass.[75] The defendants pleaded that Jabe was being sued twice as he was one of the commonalty of Ipswich.[76] The court was divided: Justice Martin agreed that the writ should be thrown out, as if it were allowed, Jabe could be charged twice for the same wrong and Jabe's goods could be put in execution twice.[77] Chief Justice Babington and Justice Paston disagreed, on the basis that damages would only be collected from goods that were collectively owned.[78] Justice Strangeways agreed with Babington and

[70] Such as 'commonitas, perpetua, corpus political et corporatum'. CT Carr, *The General Principles of the Law of Corporations: (Being the Yorke Prize Essay for the Year 1902)* (Cambridge, Cambridge University Press, 1902) xiii.

[71] The doctrine of the German fellowship (*Genossenschaft*) developed, where corporate status can be obtained by a resolution of members given recognition by the Crown or the state. In the early Middle Ages, some corporations formed freely by their members were recognised as juridical persons. The City of London Corporation is the most famous example of a Corporation that exists without a known charter. AB Levy, *Private Corporations and their Control* (London, Routledge, 1950) 12. The real entity theory of the modern company expounded by Gierke and others is based on this understanding of corporate personality.

[72] CA Cooke, *Corporation, Trust and Company: An Essay in Legal History* (Cambridge, Harvard University Press, 1951) 19.

[73] ibid 51. See also JP Davis, *Corporations: A Study of the Origin and Development of Great Business Combinations and of Their Relation to the Authority of the State*, vol 1 (New York, GP Putnam's Sons, 1905). Municipal and ecclesiastical corporations existed after the Middle Ages and were numerous throughout Europe: Levy (n 71) 12. The Edwardian Statutes of Mortmain, aimed at limiting the land held by corporate bodies, were extended during the reign of Richard II to include 'Mayors, bailiffs, and commons of cities, boroughs and other towns that have a perpetual commonalty': Carr (n 70) xii.

[74] Quoted in (1372) YB Mich 46 Edw III, fo 23b–24a, pl 7 (as cited in DJ Seipp, 'Formalism and Realism in Fifteenth-Century English Law: Bodies Corporate and Bodies Natural' in PA Brand and J Getzler (eds), *Judges and Judging in the History of the Common Law and Civil Law: From Antiquity to Modern Times* (Cambridge, Cambridge University Press, 2012) ch 2, endnote n 11).

[75] Seipp (n 74) 45–46.

[76] ibid 46.

[77] ibid.

[78] ibid.

Paston, saying that 'no individual person is the commonalty'.[79] Strangeways said '[s]ingular goods are not goods of the commonalty, and no person by himself is the commonalty, but "this aggregate and this body"'.[80]

'Maitland saw here the first stirrings of limited liability, and the separation of corporate assets from individual assets for some purposes.'[81] Clear evidence exists that some judges viewed the members as individuals separate from the commonalty.[82] In a jury challenge case involving Lincoln Cathedral,[83] Prat challenged the inclusion of a juror who was a brother of one of the canons of Lincoln Cathedral, and therefore a brother of one member of the chapter. The court was split. Four serjeants, one apprentice and one justice said that the canon's brother should not be struck off the jury.[84]

Four serjeants, four justices and one serjeant[85] pleaded that the canon's brother should be struck from the jury for presumed bias.[86] Even though the justices said during argument that this question was evenly poised, four of the five justices favoured striking the canon's brother from the jury. Any other outcome would be counterintuitive: Seipp terms it the realist outcome.[87] In fact earlier Yearbook cases had struck brothers or other relatives of monks or nuns from juries when the abbot and convent were on trial.[88]

That the argument was considered tenable at all in the Lincoln case may be an indication that the concept of the corporation as a legal entity separate from the natural persons who comprised it was gradually taking hold in England.[89] Seipp considers the most obvious and proximate source of the arguments using the metaphor of a disembodied incorporeal yet corporate body composed of

[79] ibid.

[80] ibid.

[81] ibid 46.

[82] Quoted in (1429) YB Mich 8 Hen VI, fo 1a–1b, pl 2 (as cited in Seipp (n 74), ch 2, endnote n 13). See also (1429) YB Mich 8 Hen VI, fo 14b–15a, pl 32.

[83] A series of cases in the Yearbook Reports from 1478 to 1482 are described by Frederic Maitland as 'the most interesting cases in all the Year Books': F Pollock and FW Maitland, *A History of English Law*, vol 1, 2nd edn (Cambridge, Cambridge University Press, 1898) 491.

[84] Arguments put forward were 'that the dean-and-chapter as a collective entity could not have a brother or any other relative, that the canon himself was a stranger to the action and not a party or privy to it, that the canon's death or excommunication or a release from the canon would not affect the lawsuit, that if the collective body lost a judgment the canon's own goods would not be executed upon, as was said in 1429, and finally that the canon had no advantage or individual benefit or interest if the collective body won. The collective entity of dean-and-chapter was completely separate, completely estranged from the canons who made up the chapter'. Seipp (n 74) 47–48.

[85] Who became a justice while argument continued: ibid 47.

[86] ibid. 'Some of the arguments were that the canon was a party or privy to the action and not a stranger, that he had advantage by the collective body's recovery to their common use, and that the canon's brother would be permitted to appear in court and give evidence (if he had any), as a family member not barred by the law of maintenance, so that as to the dean and chapter he was family.' The most common argument was 'simply that the brother of one of the canons could be presumed to be biased when the dean and chapter were a party'.

[87] ibid.

[88] Quoted in (1450) YB Trin 28 Hen VI, fo 10a, pl 17 (as cited in Seipp (n 74) 47).

[89] Seipp (n 74) 46–47.

many natural bodies was the 'conciliarist' writing earlier in the fifteenth century by theologians and canonist lawyers, mostly in Paris, about the 'mystical body' (*corpus mysticum*) of the Church, based on 1 Corinthians chapter 12,[90] and the Church's *corpus politicum*.[91] These Church reformers sought to differentiate the Church as an ideal entity from the individual popes and prelates who led it at the time.[92] But as Maitland points out in his discussion of another case the concept of an entity separate from members was insecure at that time. 'So long as such a decision for such a reason is possible, the modern idea of a corporation is not secure; at any rate it is hampered by an inconsistent and older idea.'[93] Maitland here means the idea of the association of persons being a corporation. Elsewhere Maitland says, 'if we introduce the *persona ficta* too soon, we shall be doing worse than if we armed Hengest and Horsa with machine guns or pictured the venerable Bede correcting proofs for the press'.[94]

The *persona ficta*, the *universitas* or corporation as an artificial legal person that is not comprised of its corporators and which does not derive its legal personhood from its corporators, did not definitively enter the common law until 1612:

> It slowly stole from the ecclesiastical courts, which had much to say about the affairs of religious corporations, into our temporal courts, which, though they had long been dealing with English group-units, had no home-made theory to oppose the subtle and polished invader.[95]

Sir Edward Coke CJ, in his report on *The Case of Sutton's Hospital* in 1612, set out the classic exposition of the *persona ficta* theory of the corporation in the common law.[96] In the statement most often quoted from the case,[97] Coke CJ said that the corporation was 'invisible, immortal and rest[ing] only in intendment and consideration of the law'.[98] In a less quoted passage, useful for context, the statement was made to support the argument that:

> … an hospital in expectancy or intendment, or nomination, shall be sufficient to support the name of an incorporation when the corporation itself is only in abstracto,

[90] 1 Corinthians 12:12 KJV: 'For as the body is one, and hath many members, and all the members of that one body, being many, are one body: so also is Christ.'

[91] Seipp (n 74) 49.

[92] ibid.

[93] Pollock and Maitland (n 62) 429.

[94] F Maitland, *Domesday Book and Beyond: Three Essays in the Early History of England* (Cambridge, Cambridge University Press, 1907), 356; discussed in JR Cameron, *Frederic William Maitland and the History of English Law* (Westport, Greenwood Press, 1961) 4.

[95] Gierke (n 68) xiv.

[96] *The Case of Sutton's Hospital* (n 11).

[97] See, eg, EH Warren, 'Collateral Attack on Incorporation' (1908) 21 *Harvard Law Review* 305, 306 and PI Blumberg, 'The Corporate Personality in American Law: A Summary Review' (1990) 38 *The American Journal of Comparative Law* 49, 49.

[98] *The Case of Sutton's Hospital* (n 11) 973.

> and rests only in intendment and consideration of the law; ... and therefore ... cannot have predecessor nor successor ... They cannot commit treason, nor be ... outlawed, nor excommunicate, for they have no souls, neither can they appear in person, but by attorney.[99]

The common law *persona ficta* corporation as conceived or adumbrated by Coke CJ is, therefore, a creation of the law that exists as an artificial legal person in the abstract. Maitland, no fan of the concept, identified the *persona ficta* theory as being challenged in Europe and which 'English lawyers borrowed from medieval canonists [which] has never suited our English law very well.'[100] The Germanists would:

> ... tell us that a good deal of harm was done when, at the end of the Middle Ages, our common lawyers took over that theory from the canonists and tried, though often in a half-hearted way to impose it upon the traditional English materials.[101]

When considering the *persona ficta* conception of the corporation set out by Coke CJ, it is important to remind ourselves that the corporation that was the subject of *Sutton* was not a business enterprise. It did not contain a Joint Stock Fund which had shareholders\stockholders who owned shares in that fund. That development is discussed in the next section.

B. Joint Stock Funds

Joint Stock Funds are one of the foundations of modern capitalism. The development of Joint Stock that was perpetual and separate from shareholders for accounting purposes[102] was facilitated by double-entry bookkeeping.[103] Double-entry bookkeeping involves an accounting system that requires every entry in an account to have a corresponding entry in another account. Thus, investors' capital contribution would be shown in a capital or equity account, and a corresponding entry in an asset account of the firm would show an amount equal to the capital contributed as an asset of the firm. The business of the firm is on the assets side. This system, therefore, draws a clear distinction between investors' investments, on the one hand, and the firm's financial resources, on the other hand. From a commercial and accounting perspective, the firm has a distinct financial existence.[104]

[99] ibid.
[100] Pollock and Maitland (n 62) 489.
[101] F Maitland, 'The Corporation Sole' in HAL Fisher (ed), *The Collected Papers of Frederic William Maitland*, vol 3 (Cambridge, Cambridge University Press, 1911) 212.
[102] Weber (n 58) 26–27.
[103] ibid.
[104] For a discussion of the significance of double entry bookkeeping see J Gleeson-White, *Double Entry: How the Merchants of Venice Shaped the Modern World – and How Their Invention Could Make or Break the Planet* (Sydney, Allen & Unwin, 2011) 101.

Double-entry bookkeeping emerged in Italy in the sixteenth century and was first used for commercial partnerships.[105] Pacioli published *Summa de Arithmetica, Geometria, Proportioni et Proportionalita*, a 615-page work that set out the double-entry bookkeeping method, in 1494.[106]

As *The Economist* said in 2019:

> The book was revolutionary on more than one count. It integrated computation using Hindu-Arabic numerals with the logic of classic Greek geometry; it was written in the Italian of the marketplace rather than Latin; and it was circulated in large numbers thanks to the new technology of printing. Yet its greatest significance lay in a slim 'how to' chapter that described the double-entry accounting system used by Venetian merchants. With examples from dealers in butter to lemons to silk, Pacioli set out the method for tracking income and expenditure and the calculation of net profit or loss, which for the first time allowed an immediate snapshot of a firm's financial position. This slim section would facilitate the birth of the modern corporation.[107]

Summa de Arithmetica was not translated and published in England until 1543, delaying the use of Joint Stock Funds in England.[108] Joint Stock Funds were first used in partnerships. Double-entry bookkeeping was necessary for a separation of the accounts of the firm from the capitalist accounts of the capital partners.[109] Capital is creditor and cash is debtor.[110]

The concept of the firm entered European practice in the sixteenth and early-seventeenth centuries. The use of double-entry bookkeeping meant that the firm as a business enterprise had a form of separation from the partners.[111] Max Weber writes about the separate fund of the partnership in European partnerships, and the relation of the separate fund to personal creditors and the partners' personal assets.[112]

A contractual Joint Stock Company is at common law an association of shareholders that is a partnership based on a shared Joint Stock Fund. The key characteristic of contractual Joint Stock Companies was not the coordination of men but the combining in the holding of shares in a Joint Stock Fund. Over time in England, therefore, contractual Joint Stock Companies became separate accounting entities because the books of the firm were not the accounts of the partners as individuals.[113] Crucially, the later *legal* separation of capital from

[105] Cooke (n 72) 66.

[106] Pacioli was a true Renaissance Man who worked with Leonardo Da Vinci on a book on perspective that informed Da Vinci's *The Last Supper*. See LM Smith, 'Examining Intersecting Lives: Luca Pacioli, Father of Accounting, and his Friend, Leonardo da Vinci' (2022) 27 *Accounting History* 343.

[107] 'A revolutionary treatise goes on the block: The first folio of finance' *The Economist* (London, 4 June 2019).

[108] Cooke (n 72) 46.

[109] ibid.

[110] Gleeson-White (n 104) 101.

[111] Cooke (n 72) 48.

[112] Weber (n 58) 115–25.

[113] Cooke (n 72) 48.

investors in business corporations was 'supported (or perhaps led) by the notion of the business as a separate accounting entity'.[114]

Legally, like the *societas*, the holders of stock in a Joint Stock company were partners and the Joint Stock Company was based on them.[115] It was not incorporated and was not a legal person. The contractual Joint Stock Company was not a separate legal entity from its stockholders.

C. The Business Corporation

Coke CJ in *Sutton's Hospital* introduced into the common law the concept of *persona ficta*.[116] Corporations were therefore artificial legal persons that existed separately from their members. Business corporations has first been operated as Regulated Companies. A Regulated Company was incorporated through a charter, but its members each traded separately on their own account.[117] Over time some business corporations began to operate using Joint Stocks; 'the form of government, in its essentials, was copied from the regulated company [and] it was decided that, instead of each person participating by trading on his own capital, a joint stock should be established'.[118] For a period, the corporation as a legal form was a framework within which Joint Stocks were constituted for single terminating ventures.

The difference between operating ventures through the existing Regulated Company structure and using Joint Stock Funds was that Joint Stock ventures were carried on by the officers in the name of the corporation, rather than by the members themselves.[119] Participation was easier than in the Regulated Companies and the earlier guilds. In the Regulated Companies, individual traders could carry out their businesses either personally or through their factors within specified limits.[120] In a corporation operating using Joint Stock Funds, only a contribution of capital was needed by members.[121]

'[T]he Dutch and especially the English followed the Genoese example of combining private investment with state-granted monopoly privileges'.[122]

[114] ibid.

[115] ibid.

[116] Hobbes in *Leviathan* in 1633 considered and developed the concept of the trading corporation that aligned with it being *persona ficta*. See D Runciman, *Pluralism and the Personality of the State* (Cambridge, Cambridge University Press, 1997) citing T Hobbes, *Leviathan*, ed R Tuck (Cambridge, Cambridge University Press, 1991) 156.

[117] Levy (n 71) 13.

[118] W Scott, *The Constitution and Finance of English, Scottish and Irish Joint-Stock Companies to 1720*, vol 2 (Cambridge, Cambridge University Press, 1912) 36.

[119] Levy (n 71).

[120] Scott (n 118) 36.

[121] Levy (n 71) 23.

[122] H Hansmann, R Kraakman and R Squire, 'Law and the Rise of the Firm' (2006) 119 *Harvard Law Review* 1333, 1376.

The combination of a legal form derived from the state with a private Joint Stock Fund seeded by money provided by investors anticipated the modern company.

The English East India Company (EEIC) was chartered in 1600. Until 1657 it operated through a series of terminating Joint Stock Funds with proceeds of each voyage divided among investors at the end of that voyage. In its 1657 charter, Cromwell granted the EEIC permanent capital.[123] No copy of the 1657 Charter survives but an order by the Lord Protector at Whitehall on 6 November 1657 does survive; most significantly, the India Trade was to be reconstituted in 'one joint stock' – words that did not appear in any of the previous Royal Charters.[124] The notion of continuing Joint Stock had developed in the EEIC by the combination of voyages and by observation of the success of the Dutch East India Company (VOC). The concept of capital had emerged in an earlier 1650 parliamentary grant. The Company, under Cromwell's Charter, developed it further by using a continuous Joint Stock Fund as permanent capital.[125]

The governing body of the EEIC transitioned away from being personally accountable for property and consumable surplus to individual investors, and instead became responsible for a financial return on capital.[126] For that purpose, the Company began to recognise the need to distinguish capital from revenue: 'the greatest of accounting's responsibilities is to hold management accountable for the rate of return on capital employed'.[127] The Dutch used Hanseatic book keeping; the English used double-entry bookkeeping which had the effect of separating the capital contributed by shareholders for accounting purposes.[128] At law as a business corporation, the EEIC was a *persona ficta* that existed separately from its members. With the corresponding separation of capital from shareholders as the Corporate Fund, the EEIC became the first modern company.

To say the new legal and accounting form worked well for business would be an understatement. The EEIC experienced an economic boom over the next three decades completing 104 voyages between London and the East Indies between 1658 and 1688. In that period, sales increased eight-fold.[129] Profits were considerable.[130] Generous gifts to Charles II ensured widening powers in the

[123] See Watson (n 5) ch 3 for a discussion of developments in the EEIC in the first half of the 17th century.

[124] Lebrecht Music & Arts and Alamy Stock Photo, 'Autograph Note of Oliver Cromwell to a Petition of the East India Company, Given at Whitehall on 6 November, 1657' (Alamy, 1 February 2011) www.alamy.com/stock-photo-autograph-note-of-oliver-cromwell-to-a-petition-of-the-east-india-83336422.html.

[125] WW Hunter et al, *History of India: The European Struggle for Indian Supremacy in the Seventeenth Century* (London, Grolier Society, 1907) 283.

[126] RA Bryer, 'The History of Accounting and the Transition to Capitalism in England: Part 2, Evidence' (2000) 25 *Accounting, Organizations, and Society* 327.

[127] Hunter et al (n 125) 368.

[128] ibid.

[129] G Dari-Mattiaci et al, 'The Emergence of the Corporate Form' (2017) 33 *Journal of Law, Economics & Organization* 193, 236.

[130] Levy (n 71) 28.

EEIC's subsequent corporate charters.[131] By the end of the seventeenth century, the value of the EEIC's trade was fast catching up with that of the Dutch East India Company. Between 1657 and 1691, proprietors received 840 per cent in dividends on their original investment: 50 per cent dividends were paid in 1680, 1682, 1689 and 1691.[132] The EEIC's share price quadrupled from £60–70 in 1664 to £245 in 1677 and £300 in 1680.[133] In 1682, the original permanent capital was doubled by the issue of bonus shares.[134] Personnel sent to Asia increased from around 5,000 in 1657 to 10,000 in the first years of the eighteenth century.[135] The EEIC paid dividends of 60 per cent in the first seven years of permanent capital. Shares had become transferable,[136] and a secondary market for shares had developed. The EEIC became widely held, with the largest holding being £4,000 in nominal value of shares.

The EEIC was a business corporation and therefore a *persona ficta*. Like all *persona ficta*, it was legally separate from its members. The EEIC as a business corporation differed from other forms of corporation because it had a permanent fund of capital contributed by shareholders. Shareholders were entitled to a share in the surplus as a dividend.

The benefits of permanent capital in an entity separate from shareholders were realised by the EEIC. It may be going too far to attribute the success of the EEIC in the period after it acquired permanent capital solely to the advent of permanent capital as the Corporate Fund. But it seems clear that permanent capital was a contributing factor, or even major contributor, to that success because that capital as the Corporate Fund could exist in perpetuity making a perpetual business corporation possible. That permanent capital was separated through the accounting mechanism of double entry bookkeeping and through the legal mechanism of the *persona ficta* as a separate legal entity existing in the abstract from investing shareholders. As set out in this chapter, the form re-emerged after *Salomon*.

The ambiguity around separate legal entity and the more recent dominance of the contractual conceptualisation of the company in law and economics may mean that the implications and benefits of separate legal entity are not always fully realised.[137] The final section, therefore, considers the potential that could be realised through operating the modern company as a separate legal entity from its shareholders based on a perpetual Corporate Fund.

[131] SA Khan, *The East India Trade in the XVIIth Century in its Political and Economic Aspects* (Oxford, Oxford University Press, 1923) 148–50.

[132] N Robins, *The Corporation that Changed the World: How the East India Company Shaped the Modern Multinational*, 2nd edn (London, Pluto Press, 2012) 49.

[133] ibid 48–49.

[134] Levy (n 71) 27.

[135] Dari-Mattiaci et al (n 129) 233.

[136] Levy (n 71) 28.

[137] See, eg, FH Easterbrook and DR Fischel, 'The Corporate Contract' (1989) 89 *Columbia Law Review* 1416 and MC Jensen and WH Meckling, 'Theory of the Firm: Managerial Behavior, Agency Costs and Ownership Structure' (1976) 3 *Journal of Financial Economics* 305.

IV. THE POTENTIAL OF SEPARATE LEGAL ENTITY

Modern companies are separate legal entities from their shareholders. Both the fund of capital contributed by shareholders and the legal entity itself exist separate from all persons and could potentially exist forever. Whether or not a modern company endures is largely determined by the people who establish the rules of the game; its incorporators and those who operate it; its board and management, based on their understanding of the corporate form and their obligations to it. Incorporators have freedom of choice to set the rules of the game within the bounds of the incorporation statute. If incorporating shareholders agreed, companies could be established with the express intention that they will operate for a finite period of say five years and then be liquidated. But as has been proven over time the potential and power of the form offers more, with most companies incorporated without a planned end date of five years, 50 years, or even 500 years. But those who operate companies may not always make decisions that recognise the latent potential in the form because they do not fully understand it.

If the contractual paradigm is the dominant conception, companies therefore can be and have been operated as if they are contractually based on their shareholders at any time. The interests of current shareholders at any time will then dominate decision making potentially leading to short termism and a myopic focus on profit. For a perpetual entity an alternative mechanism might be to turn the focus to what the company is based on recognising that incorporators make a choice when they decide what the perpetual entity that exists in the abstract is based on. If it was overtly agreed that a modern for-profit company is based on a Corporate Fund that, like the entity itself, can exist in perpetuity, decision making would consequently shift. A focus on increasing the value of the perpetual corporate fund would facilitate the principled inclusion of ESG factors as corporate constituents shift from playing a finite game to an infinite game.

A. Finite and Infinite Games

James Carse's 1986 book *Finite and Infinite Games*[138] offers a key concept: '[t]here are at least two kinds of games. One could be called finite, the other infinite. A finite game is played for the purpose of winning, an infinite game for the purpose of continuing the play'.[139] The purpose of a finite game like chess or rugby is to win within a fixed set of rules; winners win while losers lose.

Through Carse's lens, if corporate managers adopt the contractual paradigm when operating a company, they play a finite, short-term game. This necessitates

[138] J Carse, *Finite and Infinite Games* (New York, Free Press, 1986).
[139] ibid 3.

extracting the maximum value possible at any time as profit for the sole benefit of the body of *current* shareholders. The contractual paradigm has dominated in recent decades with short-termism incentivising extreme risk, and arguably exacerbating harm to people and planet. When the contractual paradigm is adopted, those harms are called externalities because they are not viewed as the concern of the shareholders of the company at any time; they are something for others to bear.[140]

Sequana however affirms that modern companies are separate legal entities from their shareholders and from all other persons.[141] The entity fuelled by capital as the Corporate Fund operating in the world as an artificial legal person transcending current shareholders can potentially exist forever. This more expansive conception of the modern company opens the door for an infinite game where the primary purpose is to keep playing; the sustainable corporation. In order to keep playing the game, externalities which might be termed ESG considerations become relevant as the context in which the game is played becomes more significant.

The basis of decision-making shifts. Decisions that may not be in the interests of current shareholders in the sense that they may reduce profitability, may be in the interests of the perpetual entity. A concrete example may be paying employees more meaning that current shareholders receive a lower dividend in the year. However, adopting an infinite perspective, higher wages may ensure that the employees are retained by the company reducing recruitment and training costs. Those employees will develop trust and loyalty to the company and the reputation of the company will be enhanced with consumers. A growth in the value of the Corporate Fund will be an outcome. Another example is making decisions that are positive for the environment. In the short-term, this decision may cost the company money, reducing profitability. However, taking care of the environment may protect the company from being regulated, may enhance its reputation and customer base, and therefore its value.[142] Moreover, future generations are protected, because no one wins if planetary boundaries are exhausted[143] and the perpetual company ceases to exist. Once the infinite perspective is adopted climate risks come within the bounds of decision-making at all times.

Boards in fact often do make decisions adopting a perspective that recognises that share value is based on a market's understanding at any time of the

[140] It could be argued that this makes them not for company *law*, but for other areas of the legal taxonomy (eg, AK Sundaram and AC Inkpen, 'The Corporate Objective Revisited' (2004) 15 *Organization Science* 350) *cf* J Hardman 'Fixing the Misalignment of the Concession of Corporate Legal Personality' (2023) 43 *Legal Studies* 443.

[141] *Sequana* (n 1) [139].

[142] See B Sjåfjell and CM Bruner, 'Corporations and Sustainability' in B Sjåfjell and CM Bruner (eds), *Cambridge Handbook of Corporate Law, Corporate Governance, and Sustainability* (Cambridge, Cambridge University Press, 2019). See also Watson (n 5) ch 16.

[143] W Steffen et al, 'Planetary boundaries: Guiding human development on a changing planet' (2015) 347(6223) *Science*, www.science.org/doi/10.1126/science.1259855.

potential value of a company rather than short-term profitability reflected in dividend pay-outs.[144] For listed companies, share markets measure that value. Directors who believe they are operating within the contractual paradigm rationalise these decisions based on potential value by saying they are thinking about future shareholders. But using the contractual paradigm, why should directors care about future shareholders ahead of current shareholders? A better rationalisation that aligns with the company being a separate legal entity from its shareholders is simply for directors to say that they are acting in the interests of the company.

Intuitively entrusting other people with our money, as shareholders do when investing in shares should not be a path to riches. But owning shares in companies that can endure enriches individuals especially when the full potential of the form is realised. As set out in this chapter, the fortunes of the East India Company once it obtained all the characteristics of the modern form is a historical example. Vanguard Australia tracked how an initial investment of $10,000 in US shares in 1992 would have grown to a staggering $182,000 by August 2022 (investment in international shares over the same period would have led to a value of $94,188).[145]

A reality check. The object of an infinite game is simply to keep playing the game, not to erode the Corporate Fund as the capital base of the company to the extent that the company is no longer solvent and exits the game. Incorporators on incorporation through constitutions or similar could decide to base a company on anything at all, using the power of the form to drive for increase in non-financial form of value. Most companies however are incorporated and attract investors because they have the ultimate end of growing financial value. Moving beyond short-term profit maximisation for current shareholders will overall reduce externalities caused by companies, as context matters. But basing decision-making on the sustainability of the Corporate Fund as an engine for value creation is not a panacea that will make corporations a force for good. Business corporations at least currently are operated primarily as engines for financial value creation. As a tool they are not inherently ethical or moral. If taking care of the interests of stakeholders like employees will not, in the view of the directors, enhance the value of the Corporate Fund, then directors will not legitimately prioritise stakeholder' interests.

For many companies, in particular those that are consumer-facing, much of the value of the Corporate Fund is reputational meaning how they are perceived externally will impact value. Reputation affects value less for some companies

[144] For an example of the dominance of long-term decision making in the practice of directors see L Buckley, S Watson and L Eraković, '"My Responsibility is to the Company, it's Actually not to Shareholders": Director Interpretations of Their Duty to Act in Good Faith and in the Best Interests of the Company' (2024) 31 *New Zealand Universities Law Review* (forthcoming).

[145] www.vanguard.com.au/adviser/en/index-chart. The heading on the page states: 'It is the long term trend that really matters.'

than others. There are however limits on what activities society might permit through the corporate form; the social licence to operate. If a company continues selling tobacco or fossil fuels how will balancing of ESG factors ever solve the fundamental problem that the primary purpose of that corporation is deleterious to people and planet. For that reason, companies may transition or diversify from those activities to ensure the company endures.

V. CONCLUSION

The modern for-profit company is based on a Corporate Fund contributed by shareholders. In the latency of the permanent capital in the Corporate Fund held in the perpetual entity rests the potential of the form for value creation realised in modern companies since the EEIC acquired permanent capital in 1657. The finding in *Salomon* and the re-affirmation in *Sequana* that companies are separate legal entities unleashes the value-creating power of a legal form that has existed since 1657. Companies as *persona ficta* or artificial legal persons operate using 'other people's money'; the Corporate Fund. Although incorporators and successive shareholders set the rules of the game and retain influence or even indirect control through their ability to elect the board, whilst the company is extant, they relinquish direct control over the Corporate Fund to corporate governors.

Corporate governance discussion centres currently on corporate purpose when considering how companies might be operated in a way that aligns more with societal expectations. Purpose shifts the focus from the present and a focus on profit maximisation to a long-term focus with decisions aligning with an identified corporate purpose. But as a separate entity a company has the potential not just to exist in the long term but to exist forever. Decision-making need not be directed to a future focused outcome. Drawing on the dual roles of boards as guardians and drivers of value creation, a corporate sustainability perspective would mean decisions made at any time would ensure value creation through the Corporate Fund and that the entity above all endures.

7

Three Regimes: Corporations and Regulation in US History

NAOMI R LAMOREAUX[1]

REFORMERS TODAY BLAME 'the corporation' for a variety of social ills. They argue that an emphasis on shareholder primacy has led to practices that undermine workers' pay and working conditions, damage the environment, and hurt the communities in which firms operate. Somewhat contradictorily, they also argue that sky-high executive compensation, normally thought not to be in shareholders' interest, has increased inequality.[2] To remedy these ills reformers target corporations and propose changes in corporate-governance rules that would encourage, or even require, managers to take the social effects of their decisions into account.[3] Some have also turned to history, arguing that, once upon a time, governments granted charters to corporations for specific public purposes. Shareholders in these corporations could earn profits, but their charters were contingent on the fulfilment of their obligations to the public. According to this view, the shift to general incorporation laws disrupted this productive quid pro quo and ushered in a period of laissez faire. Reformers who embrace this perspective seek to return to a world where corporations once again must fulfil public purposes in exchange for the remunerative privileges they receive.[4]

[1] I am grateful to Eric Hilt and the editors for their helpful comments on this paper and to Ron Harris, Jean-Laurent Rosenthal, and John Wallis for the many conversations over the years that have shaped my ideas about corporations.

[2] A prominent example is J Bakan, whose book, *The Corporation: The Pathological Pursuit of Profit and Power* (New York, Free Press, 2004), was made into a popular documentary film by M Achbar, J Abbott, and Bakan. See also Bakan's sequel, *The New Corporation: How 'Good' Corporations are Bad for Democracy* (New York, Vintage, 2020).

[3] For a thoughtful example, see R Henderson, 'Moral Firms?' (2001) 152 *Daedalus* 198.

[4] As Eric Hilt has pointed out, this view traces back at least to AA Berle, Jr., and GC Means, *The Modern Corporation and Private Property* (New York, Macmillan, 1932). In addition to popular books such as *The People's Business: Controlling Corporations and Restoring Democracy* by Lee Drutman and Charlie Gray (San Francisco, Barrett-Koehler, 2004), see scholarly works such as D Ciepley, 'Beyond Public and Private: Toward a Political Theory of the Corporation' (2013) 107 *American Political Science Review* 139. See Hilt's critique in 'Early American Corporations and the State' in NR Lamoreaux and WJ Novak (eds), *Corporations and American Democracy* (Cambridge, MA, Harvard University Press, 2017).

As I argue in this chapter, this view gets the history backward. Contrary to the romantic notion that special charters fostered the public good, I show that they were primarily patronage instruments. The political relationships that businesspeople used to obtain charters in the first place also protected them from regulation. It was only when the special-charter era came to end – when legislatures were required to enact general incorporation laws and were prohibited from granting special charters to their political favourites – that governments gained the ability to regulate corporate behaviour. The advantages that the corporate form conveyed were still very real, however, and governments continued to use them to justify a variety of economic regulations. They also used them to justify tax policies and campaign finance legislation that treated corporations differently from businesses that took other organisational forms.

Today corporations are no longer uniquely privileged. In the late twentieth century, states began to enact enabling legislation for a variety of new organisational forms, including limited liability companies and limited liability partnerships, that extend to the businesses that adopt them advantages previously limited to corporations. Firms can now avoid regulatory restrictions on corporations by organising under one of these statutes, and they are doing so in ever larger numbers. Yet businesses that take these new, noncorporate forms can be responsible for the same social ills as corporations. They can even grow large; only the very biggest enterprises need a form that supports huge numbers of shareholders. Moreover, there is mounting evidence that unincorporated businesses account for a major proportion of the recent rise in inequality in the US.[5]

Reformers continue to seek new regulations to force corporations to behave in pro-social ways, but these policies are rooted in a by-gone era and might even be counterproductive. To the extent that such legislation binds, it is likely to encourage business to switch to other organisational forms. Anti-corporate rhetoric has long been (and still is) a powerful means of rallying political support for regulation, but to be effective in this new organisational environment, reformers need to find ways of cultivating support for solutions that target specific economic and social problems, not a particular business form.

I. REGIME 1: THE SPECIAL-CHARTER ERA

In the aftermath of the American Revolution, cash-strapped state governments began to charter corporations to provide badly needed public services. Some of these corporations were what we would today call non-profits and were created to found schools, hospitals, libraries, and various types of charities. But others,

[5] M Cooper et al, 'Business in the United States: Who Owns It, and How Much Tax Do They Pay?' in JR Brown (ed), *Tax Policy and the Economy*, vol. 30 (Chicago, University of Chicago Press, 2016); M Smith et al, 'Capitalists in the Twenty-First Century' (2019) 134 *Quarterly Journal of Economics* 1675.

such as banks, bridge companies, and turnpikes, aimed to turn a profit for their members. Like the charters awarded to non-profits, grants to for-profit enterprises were justified as serving the public good. Behind them was an explicit quid pro quo: in exchange for investing their wealth in infrastructural improvements that benefited society, shareholders in these corporations would be able to earn a reasonable profit.[6]

From early on, however, critics charged that the special charters legislatures were granting mainly benefited the favoured few who received them, not the public in general. Banks were a case in point. Promoters of banks promised that their institutions would provide all sorts of social benefits. For example, the founders of the Massachusetts Bank of 1784, the first bank chartered in that state, promised in their petition for a charter that the bank 'would prove beneficial to the Public in general & particularly to all Persons concerned in Trade' by granting credit at reasonable rates of interest and thereby ensuring that 'the enormous advantages made by the griping Usurer from the Necessities of those who want to borrow Money will be immediately checked & in great Measure Destroyed'.[7] In practice, however, the bank seems mainly to have lent its funds to a small group of elite merchants associated with the dominant Federalist political faction. Part of the problem was that the bank's resources were much too limited to meet the burgeoning demand for credit. When the legislature responded to the resulting pressure to create more banks, however, the new charters all went to the same kinds of people as had founded the Massachusetts Bank – that is, wealthy Federalist merchants. Elite members of opposing political factions, such as Democratic-Republic merchants in Salem, found their requests for charters repeatedly rebuffed, fuelling the belief that bank charters were awarded less for the good of the public than for the benefit of the Federalist party.[8]

This belief became self-fulfilling in New York in the runup to the election of 1800. Alexander Hamilton and other Federalist leaders associated with the Bank of New York had successfully blocked all attempts by rival political groups to organise their own banks. In 1799, however, Republican Aaron Burr cleverly exploited a loophole in the charter for a water works to start the Manhattan Bank. Burr's allies later credited the new bank with the destruction of the Federalist empire, crowing that it 'emancipated hundreds who were held in bondage by the old institutions'. Although the claim was overblown, there is no question that the Republicans made deliberate use of the bank to further the

[6] See especially O Handlin and MF Handlin, *Commonwealth: A Study of the Role of Government in the American Economy: Massachusetts, 1774-1861* (New York, New York University Press, 1947).

[7] Reprinted in NSB Gras, *The Massachusetts First National Bank of Boston, 1784–1934* (Cambridge, MA, Harvard University Press, 1937) 212–14.

[8] Q Lu, *From Partisan Banking to Open Access: The Emergence of Free Banking in Early Nineteenth Century Massachusetts* (London, Palgrave, 2017) 22–32; NR Lamoreaux, *Insider Lending: Banks, Personal Connections, and Economic Development in Industrial New England* (New York, Cambridge University Press, 1994) 11–18.

fortunes of their candidates, offering supporters accommodation in reward for their loyalty.[9] The Federalists responded in kind by denying credit to Republican merchants, and from that point on, the award of bank charters in New York was thoroughly politicised. As Howard Bodenhorn has shown, under the control of Martin Van Buren's Democratic political machine (the 'Albany Regency') in the 1830s, the legislature severely limited the number of bank charters and funnelled the resulting monopoly rents to supporters.[10]

Banking is an extreme example, but the idea that early corporations served the public interest is belied as well by conflicts over transportation companies such as the Charles River Bridge Company. The Massachusetts legislature had chartered the company in 1785 to build a bridge across the Charles River. At the time of the grant, it was not at all certain that the venture would succeed – that the bridge could be built at all or that it could be built and maintained at a reasonable cost. To compensate investors for their risk, the legislature granted the corporation the right to collect tolls for 40 years. In fact, however, the bridge earned handsome profits for its shareholders from the time it opened. Nonetheless, when the legislature chartered another bridge company at a different location in 1792, the original company's politically powerful investors complained that the new structure would cut into their returns, and the assembly extended the corporation's right to collect tolls for an additional 30 years. Despite the new bridge, the company continued to earn monopoly rents. Indeed, by 1814 the company's stock sold for an advance of 600 per cent over its original price. Residents who used the bridge chafed under tolls they regarded as excessive and finally prevailed upon the legislation to charter yet another bridge nearby. The new company would collect tolls for a maximum of six years (less if it recouped its investment sooner), at which point the bridge would become free. The Charles River Bridge Company sued to retain its monopoly position and famously lost in the US Supreme Court. Insisting that corporate charters must be construed narrowly, the Court ruled that the old company could not block the new bridge because its charter did not explicitly grant it a monopoly. There was nothing in the decision that prevented a state from granting a corporation a monopoly if it so chose, but it could no longer hide such a boon behind general rhetoric about the public good.[11]

Charters for manufacturing corporations sometimes also conferred extraordinary privileges during this early period. In one of the most extreme

[9] BP Murphy, ''A Very Convenient Instrument': The Manhattan Company, Aaron Burr, and the Election of 1800' (2008) 65 *William and Mary Quarterly* 233.

[10] H Bodenhorn, 'Bank Chartering and Political Corruption in Antebellum New York: Free Banking as Reform' in EL Glaeser and C Goldin (eds), *Corruption and Reform: Lessons from America's Economic History* (Chicago, University of Chicago Press, 2006); Bodenhorn, 'The Political Distribution of Economic Privilege in Van Buren's New York' (2021) 35 *Studies in American Political Development* 127.

[11] SI Kutler, *Privilege and Creative Destruction: The Charles River Bridge Case* (Baltimore, Johns Hopkins University Press, 1971); *Charles River Bridge v Warren Bridge*, 36 US 420 (1837).

examples, New Jersey granted a charter in 1791 to the Society for Establishing Useful Manufactures (SUM), a textile corporation associated with Alexander Hamilton, that exempted the company from property taxes and its workers from both taxes and militia service. The charter gave the company authority to build bridges, cut canals and improve existing waterways, and to charge tolls for the use of these improvements. It also enabled the company to raise funds by holding public lotteries.[12] To give another example, New York granted the New-York Manufacturing Company, a corporation formed in 1812 to manufacture iron and brass wire and cards to process cotton and wool, permission to operate a bank on the grounds it was difficult to induce 'persons to invest their money in untried enterprises, however important to the general welfare'.[13]

Although these kinds of boons quickly disappeared from charters for manufacturing companies, the advantages of the corporate form were valuable enough in and of themselves that businesses continued to seek them. What were these advantages? Much of the debate at the time revolved around limited liability, or what Henry Hansmann, Reinier Kraakman, and Richard Squire have called 'owner shielding'.[14] Shareholders, especially those with significant assets, wanted to be protected from creditors if their company was not able to pay its debts, but lenders worried that companies with limited liability would become havens for crooks. Because of lenders' opposition, many early corporate charters did not confer limited liability, and only later did owner shielding become routine.[15] However, there were other benefits of the form. Probably the most important were what Margaret Blair has called 'lock-in' – preventing members from withdrawing their investments – and what Hansmann, Kraakman, and Squire have called 'entity shielding' – protecting the assets of the firm from the creditors of its members.[16] These benefits corrected two major disadvantages of the partnership form of organisation: first, the ability of members to dissolve the enterprise at will and require the remaining partners to sell off valuable assets; and, second, the ability of creditors to force similar sales to collect on insolvent members of the firm. These risks of what Jean-Laurent Rosenthal and I have called 'untimely

[12] New Jersey, General Assembly, 'An Act to incorporate the Contributors to the Society for establishing useful Manufactures and for the further Encouragement of the said Society', 22 Nov 1791. Unless otherwise noted, all citations to state statutes are from Session Laws collection on heinonline.org.

[13] New York, Legislature, 'An Act to incorporate the New-York Manufacturing Company', 15 June 1812.

[14] H Hansmann, R Kraakman, and R Squire, 'Law and the Rise of the Firm' (2006) 119 *Harvard Law Review* 1333.

[15] Eg, the terms of all charters for manufacturing corporations granted by the Massachusetts legislature between 1809 and 1830 were set by 'An Act defining the general powers and duties of Manufacturing Corporations', 3 March 1809, which did not allow limited liability. The law was revised by the enactment on 23 Feb 1830 of a bill with the same title that made members 'jointly and severally liable for all debts and contracts made by such Corporation, until the whole amount of the capital stock … shall have been paid in'.

[16] MM Blair, 'Locking in Capital: What Corporate Law Achieved for Business Organizers in the Nineteenth Century' (2003) 51 *UCLA Law Review* 387; Hansmann, Kraakman, and Squire (n 14).

dissolution' were greatest for industrial enterprises with significant investments in firm-specific assets – that is, assets that could not easily be repurposed and hence lost much of their value if they had to be sold.[17] Moreover, they meant that partnerships faced serious size constraints. Because firms could not take on new partners without increasing these risks, it was rare to find partnerships with more than three members in the early nineteenth century, and most had only two.[18] In addition, the potential liabilities associated with adding new partners meant that firms could not reward valuable employees by giving them an ownership share. Thus, when George Corliss and Edwin J Nightingale wanted to grant top managers in their steam-engine business ownership stakes, they reorganised as a corporation, the Corliss Steam Engine Company.[19]

Even without additional perks, therefore, corporate charters conferred advantages that were valuable enough that political elites could use them as an important source of patronage. Complaints about the award of corporate privileges had a long history, but they soared in the early nineteenth century as rising political competition increased their use and turned them into a hot-button political issue. Elites out of power vociferously decried this form of corruption, asserting that the award of charters was fundamentally undemocratic, that corporations were 'incompatible with equality of rights'.[20] But they behaved in exactly the same way when they were in office, favouring supporters and freezing out opponents. To do otherwise would be to risk being ousted from power and losing access to these valuable privileges.[21]

In response to mounting criticism, legislatures began in the early nineteenth century to enact general incorporation statutes that ostensibly levelled the economic playing field by making the corporate form available to anyone who

[17] On the relative advantages of partnerships and corporations, see NR Lamoreaux and J-L Rosenthal, 'Legal Regime and Contractual Flexibility: A Comparison of Business's Organizational Choices in France and the United States during the Era of Industrialization' (2005) 7 *American Law and Economics Review* 28.

[18] On the size of partnerships in early nineteenth-century Boston, see NR Lamoreaux, 'The Partnership Form of Organization: Its Popularity in Early-Nineteenth-Century Boston' in CE Wright and KP Viens (eds), *Entrepreneurs: The Boston Business Community, 1750-1850* (Boston, Massachusetts Historical Society, 1997) 281. On financing constraints, see D Kim, 'Firm Financing, Ownership Structure and Market Competition in United States Manufacturing during the Nineteenth Century', unpublished Ph.D. Dissertation, University of California, Los Angeles (2003).

[19] For the award of shares to managers, see 'Business from 1847 to 1861', Box 4, Folder 6, George H. Corliss Papers, Ms. 80.3, John Hay Library, Brown University.

[20] From William Gouge's *Short History of Banking and Paper Money in the United States* (1833), quoted in JW Hurst, *The Legitimacy of the Business Corporation in the Law of the United States, 1780–1970* (Charlottesville, University Press of Virginia, 1970) 30. See also P Maier, 'The Revolutionary Origins of the American Corporation' (1993) 50 *William and Mary Quarterly* 51, 71–2; and LHartz, *Economic Policy and Democratic Thought: Pennsylvania, 1776-1860* (Cambridge, MA, Harvard University Press, 1948) 72.

[21] NR Lamoreaux and JJ Wallis, 'Economic Crisis, General Laws, and the Mid-Nineteenth-Century Transformation of American Political Economy' (2021) 41 *Journal of the Early Republic* 403.

registered under the terms of the act and paid the requisite fees.[22] So long, however, as legislatures retained the power to grant special charters, they could reward political favourites with privileges that those who secured charters under general laws did not possess. As a result, those who were politically well connected still sought special charters, and the number of corporations chartered under general laws stalled.[23] For example, five years after the enactment of Pennsylvania's 1849 general incorporation law for manufacturing less than a dozen companies had actually incorporated under it, while in 1855 alone the legislature passed 196 special bills chartering or amending the charters of for-profit business corporations. Many of these bills were sought by enterprises whose businesses were not yet covered by the general laws, but others allowed favoured corporations to escape restrictive features of the laws. Thus, in the iron industry, companies obtained special charters in order to buy stock in other companies (purchases that were otherwise prohibited), engage in lines of business not permitted by their charters (such as building a railroad or a telegraph), borrow money in amounts greater than allowed by the general statute, escape limits imposed on real estate holdings, and institute non-standard voting rules for elections for directors.[24]

It was not until states revised their constitutions to ban special charters that general incorporation prevailed. A small number of states modified their constitutions in this way in the antebellum years. These were mainly states that defaulted on their debts in the early 1840s and as a result had to call constitutional conventions that opened the way for more egalitarian reforms. Most other states followed suit over the next several decades. Whenever they took

[22] As Eric Hilt has shown, most states enacted this type of legislation in the 1840s and 1850s. See 'Corporation Law and the Shift toward Open Access in the Antebellum United States' in NR Lamoreaux and JJ Wallis (eds), *Organizations, Civil Society, and the Roots of Development* (Chicago, University of Chicago Press, 2017).

[23] An important exception to this generalisation was New York, which enacted a general incorporation law for manufacturing in 1811, before it was common to charter this type of corporation by special act. Even in New York, however, in the 1830s special charters outnumbered general ones in half the years. WC Kessler, 'A Statistical Study of the New York General Incorporation Act of 1811' (1940) 48 *Journal of Political Economy* 877, 879. See also E Hilt, 'When did Ownership Separate from Control? Corporate Governance in the Early Nineteenth Century' (2008) 68 *Journal of Economic History* 645.

[24] See, eg, Pennsylvania Legislature, 'AN ACT To enable the Sharon Iron Company, of Mercer county, to subscribe to the Stock of the Pittsburg and Erie Railroad Company', 5 April 1855; 'AN ACT To incorporate the Hopewell Coal and Iron Company', 7 May 1855; 'AN ACT To incorporate the Saucona Iron Company, in the county of Northampton', 8 April 1857; 'AN ACT To incorporate the Sullivan Coal and Iron Company', 2 March 1868; 'AN ACT To incorporate the Emaus Iron Company', 11 March 1870; 'AN ACT Relative to the Bloomsburg Iron Company', 12 March 1870; 'A Further Supplement To an act, entitled 'An Act to incorporate the Emaus Iron Company …" 2 April 1872. See also Hartz (n 20) 39–41. This discussion draws on NR Lamoreaux, 'Revisiting American Exceptionalism: Democracy and the Regulation of Corporate Governance: The Case of Nineteenth-Century Pennsylvania in Comparative Context' in WJ Collins and RA Margo (eds), *Enterprising America: Businesses, Banks, and Credit Markets in Historical Perspective* (Chicago, University of Chicago Press, 2015) 40.

this step, business use of the corporate form increased dramatically. Some idea of the magnitude of the effect can be obtained by comparing the number of incorporations in Ohio, which banned special charters in 1851, with those in New Jersey and Pennsylvania, which enacted general incorporation laws in the 1840s but did not ban special charters for three more decades. In the ten years following the Civil War, Ohio chartered 2.2 times as many corporations under its general law as New Jersey did under both its general and special laws. After New Jersey banned special charters in 1875, the gap began to close. During the 1880s (that is, before New Jersey's liberal revision of its general incorporation statute), the ratio of new corporations in Ohio relative to New Jersey fell to 1.5, at the same time as the numbers of corporations founded in both states rose dramatically. Although there are gaps in the data for Pennsylvania, the story there seems to have been much the same, with the number of corporations converging on the number in Ohio only after the imposition of the ban on special charters in 1874.[25]

As I argue in the next section, an unintended consequence of the shift to general incorporation was to facilitate economic regulation. Although regulatory provisions had sometimes been imbedded in special charters, they had little bite because the political connections recipients had used to secure the charters in the first place also protected them from enforcement actions. Significant efforts to enact and enforce economic regulations only began after it became routine to charter corporations under general laws.

II. REGIME 2: GENERAL INCORPORATION

The general incorporation laws that states began to enact in large numbers in the 1840s have often been viewed by scholars as marking a shift toward laissez-faire.[26] That is not a correct characterisation, however. The movement for general incorporation was certainly anti-government in the sense that it aimed to curb the power of legislators to award privileges to political favourites, but the statutes contained regulatory provisions that reflected proponents' fears that the same wealthy and powerful businesspeople who had benefited from legislative largess would reap disproportionate gains from the new regime. When the shift to general laws was coupled with a ban on special charters, moreover, the regulatory provisions would begin really to matter. Businesses organised

[25] GH Evans, Jr, *Business Incorporations in the United States, 1800–1943* (New York, National Bureau of Economic Research, 1948) 12, and App 3. This paragraph draws on Lamoreaux and Wallis (n 21) 426.

[26] For examples of the equation of general incorporation and laissez-faire, see Hurst (n 20); Hartz (n 20); RE Seavoy, 'Laissez-Faire: Business Policy, Corporations, and Capital Investment in the Early National Period' in JP Greene (ed), *Encyclopedia of American Political History: Studies of the Principal Movements and Ideas* (New York, Scribner, 1984).

to weaken their provisions, but other interest groups emerged and pushed to strengthen them. The relative strength of these groups varied from state to state, but as a rule, the scope of business regulation and the government's capacity to enforce the law increased everywhere in the late nineteenth century. Although some regulations applied to businesses regardless of organisational form, the special advantages that corporate charters conferred provided a powerful rationale for linking incorporation and regulation.

The general incorporation statutes that states enacted in the 1840s and 1850s contained numerous regulatory provisions that aimed to level the economic playing field and keep it as flat as possible. Most limited the size to which corporations could grow by restricting the amount of capital a company could raise or the amount of money it could borrow. Most denied incorporated enterprises perpetual life, insisting instead that they periodically secure the approval of their shareholders to extend their existence. Some imposed voting rules that curbed the power of the wealthiest shareholders. And most required corporations to submit regular financial reports. In addition, the statutes typically laid out detailed procedures that corporations had to follow to declare dividends or raise or lower their capital stock, making officers and directors personally liable if they failed to follow the law. Generally, mergers required the unanimous consent of all the stockholders in the affected companies, and corporations could not hold stock in other corporations.[27]

Most states revised their general incorporation statutes in the 1870s, at the height of what scholars have considered the laissez-faire policies of the Gilded Age. In some respects, the new statutes were less regulatory than their predecessors, but in other respects they were not. Ceilings on capital and duration gradually were relaxed, but most states still had them, and most states continued to limit corporate borrowing and require annual financial reports. Most states now mandated specific voting rules for electing directors, with an increasing number requiring that shareholders be allowed to cumulate their votes (a measure that aimed to increase the power of small shareholders).[28] Most states also continued to impose detailed procedures that corporations had to follow to declare dividends and increase or decrease their capital stock (again making directors personally liable for violations), to prohibit corporations from owning stock in other corporations, and to make mergers difficult to effect.[29]

[27] NR Lamoreaux, 'Antimonopoly and State Regulation of Corporations in the Gilded Age and Progressive Era' in DA Crane and WJ Novak (eds), *Antimonopoly and American Democracy* (New York, Oxford University Press, 2023) 122–25.

[28] Under cumulative voting rules, shareholders received as many votes as there were directors being elected and had the option of spreading them over an equal number of candidates, casting all of them for one candidate, or anything in between. By 1900, 17 states had such rules. CM Williams, *Cumulative Voting for Directors* (Boston, MA, Graduate School of Business Administration, Harvard University, 1951) 20.

[29] Lamoreaux (n 27) 125–28.

The regulatory provisions that states embedded in their general incorporation laws were meant to be self-enforcing in the sense that corporations that violated them risked lawsuits from shareholders and others with a stake in their provisions. However, once Standard Oil and other large companies demonstrated that it was possible to evade these provisions and monopolise their industries using ordinary contracts like the trust device, states responded by enacting antitrust laws that made such workarounds illegal, if they served anticompetitive purposes. At the same time, states began to invest in acquiring the bureaucratic capacity to enforce the antitrust statutes. In most cases that meant beefing up the office of the attorney general, but many western states established – sometimes by constitutional mandate, sometimes by statute – independent regulatory agencies called corporation commissions tasked with insuring that companies operating in their jurisdictions conformed to the law.[30]

In 1888, in response to a budgetary shortfall, New Jersey set off a chartermongering competition by liberalising its general incorporation laws to facilitate mergers and permit corporations to hold stock in other corporations. Standard Oil and many other large-scale enterprises responded by moving their corporate home to New Jersey, leading several other states to make similar changes to their corporate statutes in order similarly to attract charters. New Jersey's action, however, did not stimulate a full-blown regulatory race to the bottom. A 1903 study showed that, all told, only 13 states revised their laws to enable mergers, and a mere six allowed corporations to hold stock in other corporations. Even most of the states that liberalised their statutes in this way retained the regulatory provisions they had previously embedded in their general incorporation statutes. Moreover, although businesses that incorporated in New Jersey no longer had to conform to other states' corporate-governance strictures, they did have to obey the antitrust laws of the jurisdictions in which they operated, as well as any state labour, environmental, or tax regulations in effect.[31]

Businesses, of course, lobbied to forestall or weaken these regulations, but now opposition groups – 'the people's lobby' in the words of sociologist Elisabeth Clemens – emerged to counter those efforts.[32] As John Wallis and I have argued, these associations were themselves an outgrowth of the enactment of general laws, which granted voluntary associations access to the same organisational advantages that incorporated businesses could exploit.[33] Farmers were initially the most important beneficiaries of these developments, and the waves of organisations they formed in the last three decades of the century

[30] ibid 129–30.

[31] C Grandy, 'New Jersey Corporate Chartermongering, 1875–1929' (1989) 49 *Journal of Economic History* 677; Massachusetts, *Report of the Committee on Corporation Laws* (Boston, Wright & Potter, 1903) 157–204; Lamoreaux (n 27) 129–38.

[32] ES Clemens, *The People's Lobby: Organizational Innovation and the Rise of Interest Group Politics in the United States, 1890–1925* (Chicago: University of Chicago Press, 1997).

[33] Lamoreaux and Wallis (n 21) 429–32.

achieved notable success in securing legislation regulating railroads and other public service corporations. State after state formed commissions to regulate railroads and utilities, and the federal government followed suit with the creation of the Interstate Commerce Commission in 1887.[34]

More generally, once the rules to which corporations were subject were uniform and not a product of the privileged status of their owners, it was possible to set up bureaucracies to enforce them. In the case of banking, for example, regulatory authorities emerged quickly with the enactment of the first general incorporation laws – the so-called 'free banking' acts. New York's pioneering act of 1838 required banks to deposit government bonds and to file reports on their condition with the state controller, who had authority to sell off the bonds in the event of trouble.[35] Ohio's variant of New York's law, enacted in 1851, mandated that state officials order yearly examinations of all the banks in the state.[36] The federal government's National Banking Acts, enacted during the Civil War on the model of Ohio's statute, required banks to maintain reserves against deposits, limited the amounts they could lend to any single party, and restricted the purposes for which they could lend. These provisions were enforced by the newly created office of the US Comptroller of the Currency, whose staff of professional examiners was required to inspect the books of all banks in the system at least once each year, with more frequent inspections of institutions authorised to hold other banks' reserves. Of course, these measures did not eliminate bank failures, but they were an important start.[37]

Although some regulatory acts – for example, the antitrust laws – applied to all businesses regardless of organisational form, others applied only to corporations and were justified by the special advantages that charters conferred. A good example was the corporate income tax. Congress had passed a law imposing an income tax in 1894, but the Supreme Court overturned it the very next year in *Pollock v Farmers' Loan and Trust Company*, declaring that the Constitution required such direct taxes to be apportioned relative to population.[38] Congress tried again in 1909, enacting a corporate 'excise' tax that was in effect a levy on corporate income. The Court held this new tax constitutional in 1911 in *Flint v Stone Tracy Company* on the grounds that the 'thing taxed is not the mere dealing in merchandise … but … the privileges which exist in conducting businesses with the advantages which inhere in the corporate capacity of those taxed, and which are not enjoyed by private firms or individuals'. Corporations

[34] By the 1880s at least two dozen states had railroad commissions. See also WJ Novak, 'The Public Utility Idea and the Origin of Modern Business Regulation' in Lamoreaux and Novak (n 4).

[35] New York Legislature, 'An Act to authorize the business of banking', 18 April 1838.

[36] Ohio General Assembly, 'An Act to authorize free banking', 21 March 1851.

[37] On the National Banking Acts, see RS Grossman, *Unsettled Account: The Evolution of Banking in the Industrialized World since 1800* (Princeton, NJ, Princeton University Press, 2010) 230–43.

[38] *Pollock v Farmers' Loan and Trust Co*, 157 US 429 (1895); and *Pollock v Farmers' Loan and Trust Co*, 158 US 601 (1895).

were artificial entities granted privileges by the state, and it was their special advantages that justified the imposition of the tax.[39]

The ratification of the Sixteenth Amendment subsequently made this rationalisation unnecessary, but corporate privileges were invoked to justify other regulations, such as the prohibition on corporate campaign contributions. As Adam Winkler has shown, Congress passed the first federal campaign finance statute, the Tillman Act of 1907, at a time of rising concern about the rights of investors in corporations. In the wake of a scandal in the life insurance industry, the New York legislature held hearings in 1905 that uncovered many types of corporate malfeasance. But it was the revelation that the companies spent large sums on political contributions that provoked the most outrage. Commentators stressed the harm these expenditures inflicted on policy holders (the true owners of these companies). Not only were corporate funds being deployed to help elect politicians whose positions the owners did not necessarily support, but, still more galling, the executives were using the increased political influence they gained from these contributions to push for policies, such as weaker regulatory oversight, that were directly counter to policy holders' interests. Riding the wave of public outrage, Congress barred corporations from contributing to political campaigns for federal offices, and many states adopted similar laws around the same time.[40]

The first constitutional challenge to the Tillman Act came nearly a full decade later, in 1916, when several breweries that had been prosecuted under the law claimed that the act violated their First-Amendment rights. They did not prevail, and the opinion of the federal judge who heard the case again emphasised the special character of corporate privileges. Corporations were the creatures of government, 'artificial creatures, and 'must at all times be held subservient and subordinate to the government and the citizenship of which it is composed'.[41] The breweries did not appeal the decision, and there were no more challenges of this kind to the campaign finance law until the passage in 1947 of the Taft-Hartley Act, when labour unions, which were not corporations, challenged the act's extension of the prohibition against corporate campaign contributions to them.[42] In the end, the litigation over Taft Hartley led to a compromise, ratified

[39] *Flint v Stone Tracy Co*, 220 US 107 (1911) at 161–62. The Court subsequently faced many cases in which it had to decide whether particular taxes levied on corporations but not on other businesses were discriminatory. Sometimes, it found the taxes discriminatory; sometimes it did not. Contrast, for example, *Quaker City Cab Co. Pennsylvania*, 277 US 389 (1928) with *New Jersey Bell Telephone Co v New Jersey*, 280 US 338 (1930). See also RH Bloch and NR Lamoreaux, 'Corporations and the Fourteenth Amendment' in Lamoreaux and Novak (n 4) 305–6.

[40] A Winkler, "Other People's Money': Corporations, Agency Costs, and Campaign Finance Law' (2004) 92 *Georgetown Law Journal* 871; Bloch and Lamoreaux (n 39) 307–8.

[41] *United States v United States Brewers' Ass'n*, 239 F. 163 (1916) at 168; Bloch and Lamoreaux (n 39) 308.

[42] TR Mager, 'Past and Present Attempts by Congress and the Courts to Regulate Corporate and Union Campaign Contributions and Expenditures in the Election of Federal Officials' (1976) 1 *Southern Illinois University Law Journal* 338. There was one challenge on the very different

by the Supreme Court in 1972, that enabled unions to funnel voluntary contributions from their members through political action committees (PACs) that they organised and controlled. Corporations adopted similar strategies, and Congress legalised the use of PACS by both labour unions and corporations in the Federal Election Campaign Act of 1972.[43]

This compromise held until 2010, when the limits on corporate political donations were effectively repealed by the Supreme Court in the case of *Citizens United v Federal Election Commission*.[44] As the next section argues, the emergence of new organisational forms paved the way for this outcome by enabling businesses to secure corporate advantages without incorporating, thereby undercutting the quid pro quo that had justified these kinds of special regulations.

III. REGIME 3: NEW ORGANISATIONAL FORMS

The shift from special to general incorporation ushered in a long period of expanding economic regulation that culminated in the early 1970s with the creation of the Environmental Protection Agency, the Occupational Health and Safety Administration, and the Consumer Product Safety Commission, among other agencies.[45] During the last quarter of the twentieth century, however, this trend reversed, and deregulation became the order of the day. Much has been written about the revolt against excessive regulation, the ascendancy of neoliberalism, and the rise of the idea that corporations' primary goal should be to maximum returns for their shareholders.[46] What has less often been noticed is the spread during this period of new organisational forms that enabled unincorporated businesses to secure advantages traditionally reserved for corporations. The new forms were a response to dramatic shifts in the relative incidence of the corporate and personal income taxes. Their appearance undermined the idea that the corporations obtained special privileges from the state that, in turn, entailed special obligations.

Before the last decade of the twentieth century, American businesses effectively had two organisational forms from which to choose: partnerships and corporations. As already noted, corporations had important advantages over partnerships. But the corporate form also entailed disadvantages, the main one

grounds that Congress did not have the authority to regulate the selection of presidential electors, which was the responsibility of state legislatures. See *United States v Burroughs*, 65 F2d 796 (1933).

[43] For the history of PACs and campaign finance litigation, see A Winkler, '*Citizens United*, Personhood, and the Corporation in Politics' in Lamoreaux and Novak (n 4).

[44] *Citizens United v Federal Election Commission*, 558 US 310 (2010).

[45] D Vogel, 'The 'New' Social Regulation in Historical and Comparative Perspective' in TK McCraw (ed), *Regulation in Perspective: Historical Essays* (Boston, MA, Harvard Graduate School of Business Administration, 1981).

[46] For a recent survey of, and critical addition to, this literature, see G Gerstle, *The Rise and Fall of the Neoliberal Order* (New York, Oxford University Press, 2022).

being that controlling shareholders had full decision-making power and could run roughshod over the desires of minority owners. There was little the latter could do to increase their influence. The courts followed a business-judgment rule that gave controlling shareholders the benefit of the doubt unless they engaged in outright fraud, even if the results of their decisions were disastrous to the firm's bottom line.[47] Moreover, the rules prescribed by most states' general incorporation laws made the problem worse by ruling out governance structures that could mitigate the problem – for example by requiring supermajority votes for certain kinds of decisions. In Britain and on the European continent, such solutions were both available and in common use. In addition, on the continent there were other organisational forms that offered corporate advantages without such severe disadvantages. These ranged from the *commandite par action* in France (a limited partnership with tradable shares) to the *Gesellschaft mit beschränkter Haftung* (GmbH) in Germany (a limited liability company).[48] In the late nineteenth century, Pennsylvania and a few other states enacted legislation to allow similar forms in the US, but these alternatives did not thrive in the American legal environment of the time. Courts sometimes held limited partners fully liable for misstatements in the partnership agreement, and states did not always recognise the statutory innovations of other jurisdictions. Although the enabling statutes remained on the books until deep into the twentieth century, the forms were comparatively rarely used.[49]

The disadvantages of the corporate form meant that most multi-owner businesses continued to be organised as partnerships rather than corporations. As late as 1949, 61 per cent were partnerships and only 39 per cent corporations. By 1963, however, the percentages had almost completely reversed, and 41 per cent were partnerships and 59 per cent corporations.[50] At the root of the reversal was the persistence of extremely high personal income tax rates in the aftermath of the Second World War. Partnerships were 'pass-through' entities. That is, their profits passed through to their owners and were taxed as personal income. During the postwar decades, when the top marginal bracket for the personal income tax was 90 per cent or even higher, many successful business owners reorganised their enterprises as corporations, which paid a flat tax of 52 per cent on their income.[51] As more and more small businesses became

[47] NR Lamoreaux and J-L Rosenthal, 'Corporate Governance and the Plight of Minority Shareholders in the United States before the Great Depression' in Glaeser and Goldin (n 10).

[48] TW Guinnane, R Harris, NR Lamoreaux, and J-L Rosenthal, 'Putting the Corporation in its Place' (2007) 8 *Enterprise and Society* 687.

[49] The first year for which counts of limited partnerships are available is 1976, when they amounted only to about 2% of multi-owner firms. SB Carter et al, *Historical Statistics of the United States: Earliest Times to the Present, Millennial Edition* (New York, Cambridge University Press, 2006) Vol. 3, Tables ch 10, 13, 163. See also Guinnane et al (n 48).

[50] Carter et al (n 49) Vol. 3, Tables ch 10, 13. Limited partnerships are included in the figures for partnerships, but as noted above, they amounted to only a couple of percent of the total.

[51] WE Brownlee, *Federal Taxation in America: A Short History* (New York, Cambridge University Press, 1996) 89–129; T Piketty, *Capital in the Twenty-First Century* (Cambridge, MA, Harvard University Press, 2014) 639, 647–50.

corporations, their owners successfully lobbied state legislatures to revise their general incorporation statutes to allow close corporations to adopt supermajority voting rules or other governance structures that mitigated the potential for minority oppression. As a consequence, corporations whose shares were closely held were able to function internally more like partnerships, a change that further increased the popularity of organising as a corporation.[52]

After the Reagan tax cuts, however, personal income taxes fell relative to corporate income taxes, and the corporate form became less attractive again, especially for small- and medium-sized businesses. In 1958, Congress had given corporations with small numbers of shareholders the ability to file their taxes as 'S corporations' and pass their income through to shareholders as in partnerships. That option was not generally attractive when personal income tax rates were higher than corporate income tax rates, but in the 1980s filing as S corporations increased in popularity. More importantly, under lobbying pressure from small businesses, states began again to enact enabling legislation for limited liability companies (LLCs). After the Internal Revenue Service (IRS) signalled in 1988 that businesses organised as LLCs would be taxed as partnerships, the form exploded. This time the courts were supportive, and states followed with enabling legislation for a plethora of other pass-through forms: limited liability partnerships (LLPs), limited liability limited partnerships (LLLPs), business trusts, and so on. By the early twenty-first century, in most states a majority of new firms were registering as LLCs or other novel types of business entities rather than as corporations.[53]

One consequence of the changes in tax rates and the shift to new organisational forms was to make the corporate income tax in relative terms a diminishing source of revenue for the US government. In 1950, the amount of revenue raised from the corporate and personal income taxes were about the same. By 2022, revenue from personal income taxes was more than six times as great.[54] Progressives continue to defend the corporate income tax and even demand that it be raised, and there is a lot of popular support for that position. According to a 2019 Gallup poll, 69 per cent of respondents thought corporations paid too little tax.[55] But such a position may now be counterproductive. Although it is true that large publicly traded companies have little choice but to organise as corporations, they tend to operate globally and can take their

[52] FH O'Neal, 'Developments in the Regulation of the Close Corporation' (1965) 50 *Cornell Law Quarterly* 641; KH Dickinson, 'Partners in a Corporate Cloak: The Emergence and Legitimacy of the Incorporated Partnership' (1984) 33 *American University Law Review* 559.

[53] Guinnane et al (n 48) 721–2; Brownlee (n 51) 130–55; TB Petska and RA Wilson, 'Trends in Business Structure and Activity, 1980–1990' (1994) 13 *SOI Bulletin* 27; and Petska, 'Taxes and Organizational Choice: An Analysis of Trends, 1985–1992' (1996) 15 *SOI Bulletin* 86. The last sentence is based on my own compilation of data on business registrations that formerly were publicly available on the website of the International Association of Commercial Administrators (IACA).

[54] Brownlee (n 51) 107; 'Federal Revenue Trends Over Time', fiscaldata.treasury.gov/americas-finance-guide/government-revenue/#federal-revenue-trends-over-time, accessed 29 May 2023.

[55] In comparison, 62% of respondents think that upper-income people pay too little taxes. 'Taxes', news.gallup.com/poll/1714/taxes.aspx, accessed 29 May 2023.

profits in jurisdictions with lower corporate income tax rates. Other firms can shift their organisational form to one or another type of pass-through entity and reduce their tax burden accordingly. Moreover, though higher corporate income taxes are often justified on equalitarian grounds – excessive executive compensation is a perennial complaint – pass-through entities have become a more important driver of income inequality. Recently, researchers using IRS microdata have estimated that pass-through entities accounted for about 40 per cent of the rise in income equality between 1980 and 2014. In 2014, the top one per cent of the income distribution included about 10,000 corporate executives but about a *million* owners of other types of multi-owner firms. About 15,000 of the latter were in the top 0.01 per cent. Their total income alone was about three times that of *all* the executives in the top one per cent, even when perks like stock options were included in executive compensation.[56]

Since the mid-twentieth century, the use of the corporate form by nonprofit organisations has grown as well, further undermining the justification for regulations that specifically target corporations. Circa 2020, there were approximately 6.5 million business corporations in the US, but there were also about 1.5 million nonprofit corporations.[57] Nonprofit corporations included hospitals, colleges, charities, and the like, but they also included organisations formed for political purposes, such as Citizens United, a corporation created to aggregate small donations in service of a conservative political agenda. When Citizens United sought to fund the distribution of a film critical of presidential candidate Hillary Clinton during the 2008 primary season, the Federal Election Commission (FEC) objected that the action violated the campaign finance laws barring such spending by corporations. Although the FEC won in the lower court, the Supreme Court sided with the corporation, declaring that the First Amendment prohibited the government from censoring speech according to the identity of the speaker and thus effectively overturning the restrictions on corporate political contributions that had been in effect since 1907.[58] The Court had other options that would have left the restrictions in place. As Justice John Paul Stevens pointed out in his dissent, it had already created an exemption for nonprofit corporations formed to promote specific causes in a case involving Massachusetts Citizens for Life, an incorporated voluntary association dedicated to stopping abortions. This exemption, Stevens argued, could easily have been expanded to include entities like Citizens United.[59] However, the majority was unwilling to narrow the scope of its ruling. Indeed, as the Court would

[56] Cooper et al (n 5) 93; Smith et al (n 5) 1692.

[57] IRS, 'Corporate Income Tax Returns, Tax Year 2019', *Statistics of Income*, www.irs.gov/pub/irs-pdf/p5655.pdf, accessed 9 June 2023; and Statista, 'Nonprofit Organizations in the U.S. – Statistics & Facts', www.statista.com/topics/1390/nonprofit-organizations-in-the-us/#topicOverview, accessed 9 June 2023.

[58] *Citizens United v FEC*, 558 US 310 (2010).

[59] ibid at 406–8.

declare a few years later in interpreting the meaning of another statute, 'The term 'person' sometimes encompasses artificial persons, … and it sometimes is limited to natural persons. But no conceivable definition of the term includes natural persons and nonprofit corporations, but not for-profit corporations.'[60]

In response to the *Citizens United* decision, Senator Bernie Sanders proposed a constitutional amendment in 2011 that would make precisely that distinction. His draft amendment prohibited the extension of constitutional rights belonging to 'natural persons' to 'for-profit corporations' and, in recognition of the growing popularity of alternative organisational forms, extended the ban to limited liability companies and 'other private entities established for business purposes'.[61] Because Citizens United was a nonprofit corporation, however, the most the amendment could achieve would be to ratify the exemption from the campaign finance laws that Stevens had proposed. But even that outcome was unlikely, as a careful reading of the precedents for *Citizens United* shows. Historically, whenever the Court seemed to extend constitutional rights to corporations, it grounded its decisions in the rights of the people who constituted the entity – not in the rights of the entity itself. The most famous example was Justice Stephen J Field's application of the Fourteenth Amendment's due process protections for property to corporations. Siding with the Southern Pacific and other railroads against California's effort to tax railroad property differently from other property, he insisted that it would be 'a most singular result if a constitutional provision intended for the protection of every person against partial and discriminating legislation by the states, should cease to exert such protection the moment the person becomes a member of a corporation'.[62]

The growing use of the corporate form by small, closely held entities, as well as the popularity of alternative organisational forms with corporate advantages, has only reinforced the Court's determination to protect the rights

[60] *Burwell v Hobby Lobby Stores*, 573 US 682 (2014) at 708.

[61] 'Resolution Proposing an amendment to the Constitution of the United States to expressly exclude for-profit corporations from the rights given to natural persons …' www.sanders.senate.gov/wp-content/uploads/S.J.Res_.pdf, accessed 7 Dec 2023.

[62] *San Mateo v Southern Pacific Railroad Co.*, 13 F 722 (1882) at 744. For a similar statement, see *Santa Clara v Southern Pacific Railroad Co*, 18 F 385 (1883) at 398–9. These were district-court opinions that Field wrote while riding circuit. Although the Supreme Court ducked the constitutional issue when it decided the case in 1886 (see *Santa Clara v Southern Pacific Railroad*, 118 US 394), the reported version of the decision paraphrased a statement that Chief Justice Morrison R Waite made at the start of oral arguments: 'The Court does not wish to hear argument on the question whether the provision in the Fourteenth Amendment to the Constitution, which forbids a State to deny to any person within its jurisdiction the equal protection of the laws, applies to these corporations. We are all of the opinion that it does.' Field then used that statement to make his circuit court opinions into precedent. See MJ Horwitz, '*Santa Clara* Revisited: The Development of Corporate Theory' (1985) 88 *West Virginia Law Review* 173; MJ Horwitz, *The Transformation of American Law, 1870–1960: The Crisis of Legal Orthodoxy* (New York, Oxford University Press, 1992) 66–70; GA Mark, 'The Personification of the Business Corporation in American Law' (1987) 54 *University of Chicago Law Review* 1447; MM Blair and E Pollman, 'The Supreme Court's View of Corporate Rights: Two Centuries of Evolution and Controversy' in Lamoreaux and Novak (n 4) 252–6; and Bloch and Lamoreaux (n 39) 289–92.

of the members of corporations. This solicitousness was especially clear in its 2014 decision in the case of *Burwell v Hobby Lobby Stores*.[63] The owners of Hobby Lobby Stores, a closely held corporation, sued to block the government's attempt to force it to include coverage for contraception in the health insurance it provided its employees, as required by the Patient Protection and Affordable Care Act of 2010 (ACA). Congress had earlier enacted the Religious Freedom Restoration Act of 1993 (RFRA) to prevent the federal government from 'substantially burden[ing] a person's exercise of religion' unless in 'furtherance of a compelling governmental interest … [in] the least restrictive means'. Finding that there were less restrictive ways besides the contraception mandate for the government to fulfil the purpose of the ACA – ways that it already allowed nonprofit corporations to pursue – the Court noted that a person who operated a business as a sole proprietorship would be able to assert a free-exercise claim and escape the contraception mandate. Why was not Hobby Lobby, a closely held corporation 'owned and controlled by members of a single family', allowed to do the same, given that 'the sincerity of [the members'] religious beliefs' was not in doubt? The Court concluded that there was no good reason to require the family members to violate their beliefs just because they had used the corporate form to organise their affairs: 'we reject [the government's] argument that the owners of the companies forfeited all RFRA protection when they decided to organize their businesses as corporations rather than sole proprietorships or general partnerships'. The contraceptive mandate, the Court concluded, 'as applied to closely held corporations, violates RFRA'.[64]

Although the free-exercise clause would not, of course, be a limiting factor in the case of most regulatory legislation, the Court's language in *Hobby Lobby*, as in *Citizen's United*, was broader than it needed to be. Justice Samuel Alito's decision for the Court echoed Field's opinion in the *Railroad Tax Cases*:

> A corporation is simply a form of organization used by human beings to achieve desired ends. An established body of law specifies the rights and obligations of the *people* (including shareholders, officers, and employees) who are associated with a corporation in one way or another. When rights, whether constitutional or statutory, are extended to corporations, the purpose is to protect the rights of these people.[65]

The idea that a corporation was just 'a form of organization used by human beings to achieve desired ends' carried new conviction in a world where the overwhelming majority of corporations were closely held and where they were, for all practical purposes, indistinguishable from enterprises that took non-corporate forms.[66]

[63] *Burwell v Hobby Lobby Stores*, 573 US 682 (2014).
[64] *Burwell v Hobby Lobby Stores*, 573 US 682 (2014) at 691, 694–5, 717, 736.
[65] ibid at 706–7.
[66] When Field expressed a similar position in the 1880s, the railroads involved in the tax cases he adjudicated were closely held. Although they were important economic entities, they raised

IV. CONCLUSION

The last section of Sanders's proposed constitutional amendment declares in broad language, 'Congress and the States shall have the power to regulate and set limits on all election contributions and expenditures, including a candidate's own spending …'[67] A constitutional amendment that focused on this important principle would render the Supreme Court's *Citizens United* decision void, and Sanders could have led with it. But instead he prioritised his determination to deny for-profit corporations the rights of natural persons – a move that was not only more controversial but less likely to be effective. We cannot know why he chose this ordering, but the crowd-pleasing power of anticorporate rhetoric surely played a role. Antipathy to the corporation has a long history in American politics. During the special-charter era, corporations were an apt symbol of the corruption that pervaded state legislatures, and opposition to them helped propel the reforms that brought that regime to an end. Even after the adoption of state constitutional provisions banning special charters, however, the negative connotations of the word corporation persisted and so did the utility of anticorporate rhetoric. General incorporation laws still conferred advantages on companies that took the corporate form, and reformers could make effective use of popular antipathy to corporations to build support for regulations that reigned in the large-scale businesses that emerged in this period. Antipathy to corporations remains powerful in the present era, but it is much less useful in an environment where neither corporate advantages nor the evils reformers seek to eliminate are restricted to corporations. Of course, in some sense the word corporation is just a synonym for big business. But it is a synonym with the potential to mislead. Indeed, to the extent that reform proposals single out corporations, they are likely to miss their target. Thus, raising the corporate income tax will do little to reduce inequality now that pass-through entities are more important generators of the super-rich. Similarly, stripping corporate entities of their constitutional rights will do little to staunch the flow of money into electioneering. As the Supreme Court's decision in *Hobby Lobby* suggests, moreover, there is a real risk that a focus on corporations will render a regulatory policy ineffectual or, even worse, unenforceable.

capital by selling bonds, not equities, and consequently had small numbers of shareholders. See DH Bain, *Empire Express: Building the First Transcontinental Railroad* (New York, Viking, 1999); and R White, *Railroaded: The Transcontinentals and the Making of Modern America* (New York, Norton, 2011).

[67] 'Resolution Proposing an amendment to the Constitution'.

8

Early American Corporations and the Public Purpose

ERIC HILT

IN RECENT YEARS, scholars interested in corporate social responsibility have begun to ask whether corporations should have a purpose.[1] In the US, for-profit corporations typically have no explicitly stated purpose in their charters, and simply manage their operations to maximise shareholder value.[2] By contrast, some scholars and activists have argued that corporate charters should articulate a clear purpose, and that purpose should reflect the interests of the community or a broad set of stakeholders. For example, Senator Elizabeth Warren's proposed Accountable Capitalism Act would have required large corporations to obtain federal charters that would include an explicitly stated purpose of 'creating a general public benefit'.[3] Even the Business Roundtable Group, a lobbying organisation of CEOs, stated in 2019 that the purpose of corporations should include a 'fundamental commitment' to all stakeholders, not just shareholders.[4]

Some contributors to this debate have pointed to the early history of the American corporation as a source of inspiration for their proposed reforms. In the late eighteenth and early nineteenth centuries, American business corporations could only be created through special legislative act. Some scholars have argued that state governments limited access to the corporate form to businesses that provided some 'public service function', and wrote that function into

[1] See, eg, JE Fisch and SD Solomon, 'Should Corporations Have a Purpose?' (2021) 99 *Texas Law Review* 1310; E Pollman and RB Thompson (eds), *Research Handbook on Corporate Purpose and Personhood* (Cheltenham, Elgar, 2021); and C Mayer, *Prosperity: Better Business Makes the Greater Good* (Oxford, Oxford University Press, 2018).

[2] Fisch and Solomon note that 'most corporate charters contain a generic statement that the purpose of the corporation is to engage in any lawful activity'. Fisch and Solomon (n 1) 1316. The significance of corporate purpose clauses is explored in E Pollman, 'The History and Revival of the Corporate Purpose Clause' (2021) 99 *Texas Law Review* 1423.

[3] Accountable Capitalism Act, S. 3348, 115th Cong. § 5.

[4] www.businessroundtable.org/business-roundtable-redefines-the-purpose-of-a-corporation-to-promote-an-economy-that-serves-all-americans.

corporate charters.[5] Advocates for reform have argued that this suggests that corporations 'evolved from a limited and tightly controlled franchise incorporated to complete public improvement projects … to a sprawling, uncontrollable conglomerate',[6] and concluded that 'a corporation's duty to serve the public interest should be restored'.[7]

There is widespread agreement in the historical literature that early American corporations served a public purpose. For example, Oscar Handlin and Mary Flug Handlin characterise the early business corporation as an 'agency of government … designed to serve a social function of the state'; JW Hurst argues that 'public-interest undertakings practically monopolized the corporate form'; Pauline Maier discusses the 'requirement, based on English precedent, that corporations serve a public purpose'; and Naomi Lamoreaux and William Novak note that early business corporations were generally 'public service franchises'.[8] Yet the relevance of that early history for modern reform proposals is open to question. The political, economic, and social environments in which those early corporations operated were radically different from our modern world, and attributes of historical corporations that may seem benign by today's standards may have been understood very differently at the time. Some early business corporations were regarded as so powerful that they posed a threat to democracy itself; 'sprawling and uncontrollable' would have been regarded as an apt description of them by their critics. The fact that early corporations may have served a public purpose did not imply that they were widely regarded as socially beneficial. It seems unclear whether early corporations actually fit the conception of a public purpose envisaged by modern reformers.

In this chapter I explore the extent to which early American corporations served a public purpose. I begin by offering two possible definitions of a public purpose, with one based on the function of the corporation (what it does), and the other based on the benefits created by the corporation. These definitions, and variations that make them stricter or looser, are meant to serve as standards that can be applied to corporations to evaluate their role in society. Importantly,

[5] RE Seavoy, 'The Public Service Origins of the American Business Corporation' (1978) 52 *Business History Review* 59. See also A Berle and G Means, *The Modern Corporation and Private Property* (London, MacMillan, 1933).

[6] C Cray and L Drutman, 'Corporations and the Public Purpose: Restoring the Balance' (2005) 4 *Seattle Journal for Social Justice* 307.

[7] G Shepherd, 'Not Just Profits: The Duty of Corporate Leaders to the Public, Not Just Shareholders' (2021) 23 *University of Pennsylvania Journal of Business Law* 823. See also D Cieply, 'Can Corporations Be Held to the Public Interest, or Even to the Law?' (2019) 154 *Journal of Business Ethics* 1003.

[8] O Handlin and M F Handlin, *Commonwealth: A Study of the Role of Government in the American Economy: Massachusetts, 1774–1861* (Cambridge MA, Belknap Press of Harvard University, 1969) 22; JW Hurst, *The Legitimacy of the Business Corporation in the law of the United States, 1780–1970* (Charlottesville, University of Virginia Press, 1970) 15; P Maier, 'The Revolutionary Origins of the American Corporation' (1993) 50 *William and Mary Quarterly* 55; N Lamoreaux and W Novak (eds), *Corporations and American Democracy* (Cambridge MA, Harvard University Press, 2017).

they are not based in concepts such as the characteristics of the nonprofit corporation, or the distinction between public and private corporations, which had not yet developed in the early years of the nineteenth century. After presenting those definitions, I discuss the extent to which American corporations actually met them, using quantitative data on the charters granted by New York and Massachusetts, as well as narrative evidence.

My analysis indicates that a substantial share of early American corporations did not in fact meet either definition of a public purpose, and that the relative importance of those that did decline rapidly in the early nineteenth century. The most important reason for this decline is the rapid increase in the incorporation of manufacturing companies beginning around 1809. Those enterprises failed to meet any reasonably strong standard of a public purpose, and the fact that they became one of the most important categories of corporations suggests that the American states did not feel constrained to allocate corporate charters exclusively to businesses with a public purpose. The evidence also shows that some early corporations such as banks met some definitions of a public purpose related to their function, but were often viewed as failing to meet other definitions based on their benefits.

These insights do not imply that that the literature on historical corporations is incorrect. Instead, claims that early corporations served a public purpose need to be qualified. The notion that early American corporations served a broad public purpose is generally accurate for the late eighteenth century and the first few years of the nineteenth century, if we focus on the functional definition, but then it ceases to be correct for later years. The very earliest period of the American corporation was different from the years that followed, and it is important for analyses of the history of the corporation to contend with those changes. As businesses pursuing relatively large-scale manufacturing proliferated, state legislatures did not hesitate to offer them corporate charters.

An important special case with regard to the public purpose of early American corporations is found in federally chartered businesses. Nearly all early American corporations were incorporated by the states, but the federal government did charter two significant corporations as well. The supreme court interpreted the federal government's constitutional power to create corporations as being extremely limited, and required that federal corporations serve a public purpose as defined in a very strict and specific way. Yet over time those doctrines evolved, and far looser standards were applied to federal incorporations. I discuss the evolution of legal doctrines surrounding federal incorporations separately.

I. DEFINITIONS OF A PUBLIC PURPOSE

In order to evaluate whether a corporation served a public purpose, it is important to be clear about what is meant by that term. In this section I offer two definitions of a public purpose, with one focused on the corporations' function, and the other focused on its benefits. I also offer some variants of each.

A. Functional Definition

Although nearly all early American business corporations were granted charters by special legislative act, and were therefore public instrumentalities in a narrow sense, it is important to distinguish their function from their origin.[9] The functional definition of a public purpose focuses on a corporation's operations, and their relationship to the public sphere. If the operations of a corporation fall within the public sphere, or have some direct connection to the government, then it can reasonably be characterised as serving a public function, and therefore a public purpose. This would be true of a business corporation created to provide services to the government, or to provide services to the public on behalf of the government.

For example, a government that wishes to build or operate transportation infrastructure for the public, but chooses to incorporate a business for that purpose rather than providing it directly, has created a corporation that serves a public purpose. That transportation infrastructure might serve only a local community or a particular sector of the economy, but so long as it is provided by the corporation on behalf of the government, its function served a public purpose.[10] By contrast, a corporation chartered to engage in manufacturing would not meet this definition, since manufacturing is not part of the public sphere.

The ownership of a corporation is irrelevant to this definition. Some modern corporations meeting this definition are owned partly or completely by the state, but investment by the state is not necessary to meet this definition. A corporation owned by private shareholders can serve a public purpose if its operations are part of the public sphere.

B. Benefits Definition

An alternative definition of a public purpose for a corporation, which might encompass some corporations that fail to meet the functional definition, would focus on their benefits to society, rather than the nature of their operations. For example, one could argue that a corporation that serves the common good, in the sense of benefitting everyone, or at least benefitting a large portion of society without harming anyone, serves a public purpose. Some historians have defined

[9] As Hannah Farber has noted, early corporate charters 'bound merchants more closely to the state' than they would have been with unincorporated enterprises. Yet if being bound to the state via a special-act charter implied that a corporation served a public purpose, then all early business corporations would meet that definition, no matter what they did. H Farber, *Underwriters of the United States* (Chapel Hill, University of North Carolina Press, 2021) 85.

[10] This conception of a public purpose is broader than Miller and Gold's concept of a public purpose corporation. In their view, 'public purpose corporations are administered to advance purposes rather than to promote the interests of determinate persons … everyone in general, but no one in particular, has a reasonable expectation of benefitting from the advancement of its purposes' which would seem exclude corporations with localised benefits. PB Miller and AS Gold, 'Fiduciary Governance' (2015) *William & Mary Law Review* 57 513, 533.

the purpose of early business corporations in this way, and argued that they served the 'common interest'.[11]

The standard that everyone benefits, or at least no one is made worse off, is quite strict. Historical commentators stating that business corporations were created for the common good often did so in service of a legal argument that the state should be able to exercise greater control over them, rather than to characterise them as actually meeting that standard.[12] In that context the term was used to characterise the ideals that governed (or should have governed) the creation of corporations, rather than as a characterisation of their actual benefits. Other commentators who have claimed that early corporations served the common good may not have used it in the way that I have defined it. Instead of claiming that everyone benefitted from early corporations, they may have simply meant that early corporations produced benefits for society.

A weaker version of this definition might therefore be that a corporation's operations produce some benefit to the public. For example, if industrialisation is regarded as beneficial to society, corporations engaged in manufacturing might be deemed to benefit the public if they contribute to industrialisation. Alternatively, manufacturing corporations could be argued to meet this standard because they produce goods that the public values (in that they are willing to pay for them), or through the provision of employment. This would be true even if the interests of some members of society, such as competitors of the corporation, are harmed by the corporation's operations.

It is important to note that this latter version of the benefits definition is so weak that it is difficult to imagine any early nineteenth century business corporation that would fail to meet it. All businesses that produced goods or provided services or contributed to economic development could be said to benefit the public, even if their operations had other negative consequences. This weaker definition will therefore not figure prominently in the discussion that follows.

With the two definitions of a public purpose – one based on a corporation's function, the other based on its benefits to society – we can ask what share of early business corporations served a public purpose, and what relevance those corporations have for modern questions relating to the role of the corporation in society.

II. EARLY AMERICAN CORPORATIONS AND THE FUNCTIONAL DEFINITION OF A PUBLIC PURPOSE

I now turn to the functional definition of a public purpose, and investigate the extent to which early corporations met this standard. In the decades following the American Revolution, state legislatures began granting corporate charters

[11] Handlin and Handlin (n 8) 22.

[12] See, eg, D Henshaw, *Remarks Upon the Rights and Powers of Corporations, and of the Rights, Powers, and Duties of the Legislature Toward Them* (Boston, Beale and Greene, 1837).

to large numbers of businesses. Only a handful of business corporations had existed in colonial North America, in part due to the restrictions imposed by British colonial authorities, but once they obtained independence, the American states began to experiment with grants of corporate charters to businesses.[13] This process began slowly, but gradually accelerated over the following decades, and by the 1830s, there were likely more business corporations in the US than in any other nation.[14]

Table 8.1 Business Corporations Chartered in New York and Massachusetts, 1791–1820

	New York		Massachusetts	
Infrastructure	378	0.60	216	0.41
Finance	66	0.10	125	0.24
Manufacturing	193	0.30	187	0.35
Total	637	1.00	528	1.00

To describe this process in quantitative terms, I will present some data on early corporate charters and their distribution across industries. The data are for the two American states that accounted for the largest numbers of business corporations in the early nineteenth century, New York and Massachusetts. Both were great innovators in American corporate law, and the importance of both as sources of corporate charters is reflected in the fact that they have been the focus of major historical studies of the early history of business corporations.[15]

The number of charters granted to business corporations for the years 1791–1820 in both states is presented in Table 8.1.[16] Over these years, New York

[13] On colonial corporations, see JS Davis, *Essays on the Earlier History of American Corporations* (Cambridge MA, Harvard University Press, 1917).

[14] Total counts of American charters granted by year are presented in R Sylla, and RE Wright, 'Corporation Formation in the Antebellum United States in Comparative Context' (2013) 55 *Business History* 653. Those data understate the total number of American corporations because they exclude incorporations through general acts. On American general incorporation acts, see WC Kessler, 'A Statistical Study of the New York General Incorporation Act of 1811' (1940) 48 *Journal of Political Economy* 877, and E Hilt, 'Corporation Law and the Shift toward Open Access in the Antebellum United States' in N Lamoreaux and J Wallis (eds), *Organizations, Civil Society and the Roots of Development* (Chicago, University of Chicago Press, 2017) 147. As these sources show, the pace of American incorporations of businesses only accelerated after the 1830s.

[15] For Massachusetts, these include EM Dodd, *American Business Corporations Until 1860: with Special Reference to Massachusetts* (Cambridge MA, Harvard University Press, 1954), and Handlin and Handlin (n 8). For New York, see R Seavoy, *The origins of the American business corporation, 1784–1855: broadening the concept of public service during industrialization* (Westport, CT, Greenwood Press, 1982).

[16] The data used to create the table and subsequent figure for New York are from E Hilt, 'When Did Ownership Separate from Control? Corporate Governance in the Early Nineteenth Century' (2008) 63 *Journal of Economic History* 645. The data for Massachusetts are from Sylla and Wright (n 14).

incorporated 637 businesses, and Massachusetts incorporated 528.[17] In the table, the corporations are grouped into three main categories: manufacturing, which includes a small number of mining companies; finance, which includes banks, insurance companies, and a small number of securities exchanges; and infrastructure, which includes turnpike roads, bridges, canals, ferries, water companies and companies building wharves and docks.

Over the 29-year period covered by the table, infrastructure corporations accounted for the largest share of charters, 60 per cent in New York, and 41 per cent in Massachusetts. Manufacturing corporations were slightly less common, at 30 and 35 per cent, and financial firms accounted for 10 and 24 per cent in those two states. The small number of financial charters in New York, which developed into the nation's premier centre of banking and financial markets during this period, reflects that state's extremely restrictive approach to granting access to its banking industry, discussed below. The larger geographical area encompassed by New York likely contributed to the larger share of infrastructure companies; many more towns sought to be connected by turnpike roads, or sought bridges to span nearby rivers. The two states created roughly equal numbers of manufacturing corporations.

Figure 8.1 presents annual data for the two states. In both, total incorporations remained low until the beginning years of the nineteenth century, and then became persistently higher. The acceleration in grants of corporate charters suggests that state legislatures became more willing to incorporate businesses over time, as they gained experience and as political coalitions emerged that were supportive of incorporations. The expansion and development of the economy likely led to greater numbers of petitions for charters as well, as more towns were established and more business opportunities emerged.

In the first decade of the figure, corporations formed to build or operate infrastructure dominated both states' grants of charters, but over time other types of corporations became much more common. Manufacturing enterprises became increasingly important after 1809, when events leading up to the War of 1812 contributed to a rapid expansion of domestic manufacturing. Early American state governments actively used the law to stimulate economic development, and granted charters to manufacturing corporations because they felt that industrialisation was a desirable goal of public policy.[18] Finance

[17] The New York data include 129 business incorporated through the state's 1811 general incorporation act for manufacturing companies and excludes 3 corporations that do not fit into the three categories presented below; the Massachusetts data excludes one such company.

[18] See, eg, Handlin and Handlin (n 8), and JW Hurst, *Law and the Condition of Freedom in the Nineteenth Century United States* (Madison: The University of Wisconsin Press, 1956). William Novak argues this perspective understates the role of the state as fundamentally constitutive of the economic sphere. WN Novak, *The People's Welfare: Law and Regulation in Nineteenth-Century America* (Chapel Hill: The University of North Carolina Press, 1996.).

corporations were never very prevalent in New York, but increased in numbers over several particular years in Massachusetts, as political dynamics shifted.[19] These data suggest some clear patterns regarding the functional definition of a public purpose. Infrastructure corporations generally meet this definition. They built roads and bridges, and in some cases provided services such as access to water. These all clearly fall within the range of services that can generally be provided by the state.

Figure 8.1 Business Corporations Chartered in New York and Massachusetts by Year, 1791–1820

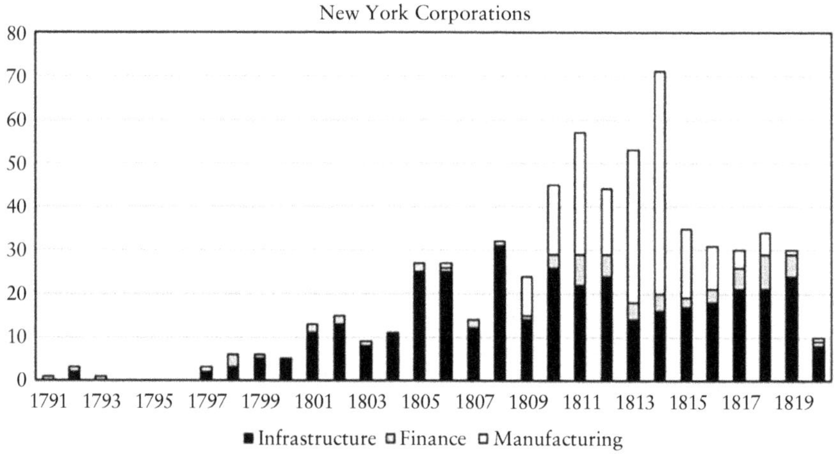

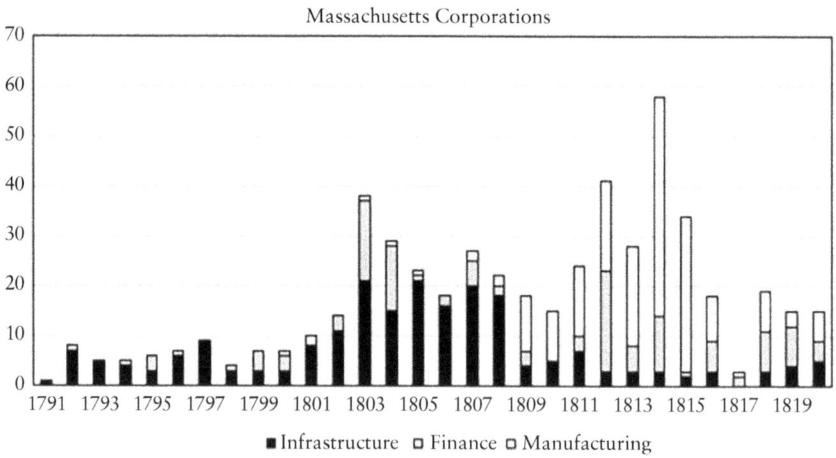

[19] See Q Lu and J Wallis, 'Banks, Politics, and Political Parties: From Partisan Banking to Open Access in Early Massachusetts' in N Lamoreaux and J Wallis (eds), *Organizations, Civil Society and the Roots of Development* (Chicago, University of Chicago Press, 2017).

The prevalence of these infrastructure companies reflects the limited administrative capacity of the early American states. Roads, for example, could be built and maintained by public road administrations, but they were poorly organised and managed. By contrast, the corporation was a superior organisational technology, and could be configured to build roads more successfully.[20]

Also, by raising money from local investors, corporations could overcome the limitations of early tax systems, and raise capital from the beneficiaries of their services. As one early commentator noted, regarding a harbour improvement corporation,

> It surely was better to have this work built by this individual association of wealth, than to have it undertaken by the state; for the citizens of other places who, in that case, would have been taxed for the purpose, would have derived little benefit from the improvement.[21]

With many infrastructure companies, the state lent its support to local initiatives to build a road or bridge by granting them corporate charters, which sometimes contained special legal privileges such as a process by which privately owned land could be taken. Their investors expected to receive dividends, but they were also motivated by the benefits they would enjoy from the services provided by the corporation.

Infrastructure companies accounted for just over 50 per cent of the total number of corporations created by Massachusetts and New York, and clearly served a public purpose. By contrast, it is difficult to make the case that manufacturing companies, which accounted for a third of the total corporations of the two states, served a public purpose by the functional definition. Those corporations were formed to produce products such as cotton textiles, iron nails, marble, slate, chemicals, leather, and machinery, activities that are not part of the public sphere, and have no direct connection to the state. The state supported those institutions, with charters and in some cases with other benefits such as subsidies, but those institutions did not serve a public purpose, by the functional definition.

Some of the financial corporations, particularly the banks, constitute an intermediate case. Some early banks did indeed provide financial services to state governments, which implies that they served a public purpose by one version of the functional definition. Yet this was only true of a small number of banks, and even for those, their transactions with the state may not have accounted for a significant share of their operations. On the other hand, incorporated banks were authorised to issue banknotes. Although those notes were not legal tender and were not officially backed by the state,

[20] See DB Klein and J Majewski, 'Economy, Community and the Law: The Turnpike Movement in New York, 1797–1845' (1992) 26 *Law and Society Review* 488.

[21] D Henshaw, *Remarks Upon the Rights and Powers of Corporations, and of the Rights, Powers, and Duties of the Legislature Toward Them* (Boston, Beale and Greene, 1837) 6.

they served as the main media of exchange locally and also circulated to distant locations. As the American states were constitutionally prohibited from issuing paper money, by chartering commercial banks state governments utilised business corporations to perform a function that at least some of them would have provided directly, meeting the standard of a public purpose.[22]

Figure 8.2 Share of Business Corporations Chartered in New York and Massachusetts with a Public Purpose (Functional Definition), 1791–1820

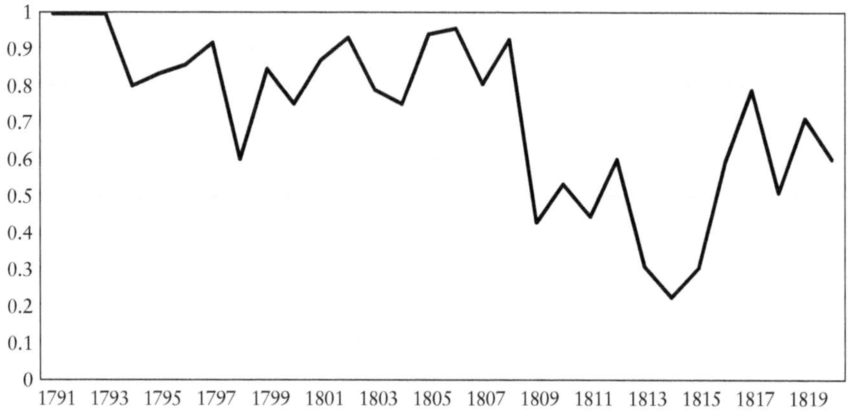

If we sum up the business corporations of New York and Massachusetts (1,165), infrastructure companies accounted for just over half of them (594), and commercial banks accounted for another nine per cent (105). By the functional definition, we can conclude that 60 per cent those states' corporations served a public purpose, whereas the remaining 40 per cent, mostly manufacturing and insurance companies, did not. This suggests that corporations with a public purpose were quite important in the years up to 1820, but a substantial minority did not meet that standard.

We can also use the data to study changes over time. In Figure 8.2, I present the share of corporations meeting the functional definition of a public purpose for New York and Massachusetts together, by year. That share is calculated as the number of infrastructure companies and banks divided by the total number of incorporations. In the figure the share is 1 for the years up to 1793, and remains very high, usually above 0.8, though 1808. Then in 1809 it shifts down

[22] Later reforms to state-chartered banks created state-administered insurance funds (eg, in 1829 New York implemented what was known as its safety fund) and eventually required that their notes be collateralised, often with government securities. This brought banks even closer to the state.

These preambles suggest that state legislators felt they needed to justify their grant of exclusive legal privileges to a business corporation by stating that doing so would benefit the public. On the other hand, the benefits that the preambles claimed would be produced – manufacturing development, employment, credit to commercial interests – were typically specific to a particular sector, and did not claim that the corporation would benefit everyone. Instead, the language suggests a weaker standard, that anything that advances economic development was regarded as a sufficient public benefit.

Over time, as the incorporation of businesses became increasingly routine, many charters included only cursory preambles, or no preamble at all. This suggests that the benefits of many business corporations were generally understood, and there was no longer any need for a recitation of public benefits in every charter. The later preambles of the charters of Massachusetts manufacturing corporations, for example, typically only mention that incorporation would help the business, pointing only to a private benefit.[32] New York's manufacturing charters generally continued to include preambles, but typically added only that the state was incorporating the business 'for the encouragement of … domestic manufactures', suggesting that promoting manufacturing was understood to benefit the public, and was a sufficient rationale for grants of corporate privileges.[33]

A few later charters sometimes did include lengthy preambles, however, and their contents are instructive. For example, in 1808 New York charted John Jacob Astor's American Fur Company. At the time Astor's trading interests had developed to the point that he had become one of the wealthiest Americans, and he sought a corporate charter for his fur trading operations which would ultimately expand to the west coast of North America in competition with the Hudson's Bay Company and other trading companies based in Canada and Europe.[34] The charter preamble begins by describing at length how incorporation would benefit the company, and enable it to pursue 'a fair competition with foreigners', and then claims,

> And whereas, such an establishment may be of great public utility, by serving to conciliate and secure the good will and affection of the Indian tribes toward the government and people of the United States, and may conduce to the peace and safety of our citizens inhabiting the territories bordering on the Indian tribes …[35]

[32] Eg, the 1799 charter of the Salem Iron Factory begins with the statement: whereas the founders have petitioned the government for a charter, 'with such powers, as may enable them, more conveniently and effectually, to execute the purposes' of 'carrying on the business of Anchor-Making …' 'An Act to Incorporate Ebenezer Beckford and Others …' *Acts and resolves passed by the General Court* (1798–1798) ch 80, 481.

[33] 'An Act to establish a company in the city of New-York …' *Laws of New York* (1809) ch 27, p 25.

[34] On Astor's business activities, see KW Porter, *John Jacob Astor, Businessman* (Cambridge MA, Harvard University Press, 1931).

[35] 'An Act to incorporate the American Fur Company' *Laws of New York* (1808) ch 140, 160.

It is possible that this claim was made in good faith. Yet it is also possible that this language was added simply to point to some kind of public benefit that might result from incorporating Astor's massive fur trading company.

B. Statements of Corporate Purpose

After their preambles, early American corporate charters contained a number of fairly standardised provisions. In addition to specifying the capital stock, elections of the board of directors, the legal rights of the corporation, and the corporation's name, the charter would state the lines of business the corporation was authorised to pursue, and its purpose. In some cases the purpose was embedded in the preamble, which would for example state that the incorporators 'intend to establish a manufactory of glass' or 'have associated themselves together for the purpose of establishing & carrying on the business of Anchor-Making, and other manufactures of iron …'[36] In other charters, particularly those of financial corporations, there would be a brief statement that the charter was 'for the establishment of a bank', but then later provisions would specify in detail the transactions the corporation was authorised to conduct, and what it meant to be a bank.

Recently legal scholars advocating for stronger standards of corporate social responsibility have ascribed great significance to these statements of corporate purpose. Whereas modern corporate directors 'owe duty only to their shareholders', these scholars have argued that early nineteenth century directors 'had a duty to serve the public', since they were required to fulfil the purpose specified in their charters.[37] This is true, but only in a narrow sense that may not be directly relevant to modern advocates for corporate social responsibility. The historical requirement that corporations serve a specific purpose mainly ensured that they could not switch industries; a glass manufacturing corporation could not produce cotton textiles without obtaining specific authorisation to do so through an additional special act of the legislature. This gave state governments a measure of control over the entry of new businesses into many industries, but not over their conduct within those industries. Corporations could and did engage in activities that were harmful to the interests of some of their stakeholders; they were merely constrained to do so within a particular industry. They served the public only insofar as operating in the industry stated in their charter meant serving the public.[38]

[36] The first quotation is from 'An Act to incorporate the stockholders of the Woodstock glass manufacturing society,' *Laws of New York* (1809, ch 84) 96. Even though it was not strictly necessary, that charter ended with the statement 'the company shall not apply any part of their capital to any other object than of manufacturing glass'. The second is from 'An Act to Incorporate Ebenezer Beckford and Others …' *Acts and resolves passed by the General Court* (1798–1798) ch 80, 481.

[37] Shepherd (n 7) 823.

[38] Some modern corporations in the US are similarly constrained to operate within a particular industry. Commercial banks, for example, are generally restricted from operating in most other industries or owning subsidiaries in other industries. Yet one might argue that the behaviour of some

The restriction that only corporations specifically authorised to engage in a particular activity in their charters could pursue that activity in fact led to significant political and economic problems in the early American states. Discretion over the allocation of charters with specific purposes might appear to be a mechanism through which the state legislature could ensure that corporations would serve the public. Individuals wishing to form a corporation to enter a specific industry had to petition their legislature for a charter, and the state governments could use their discretion to reject petitions from businesses that they felt did not benefit the public, and support petitions from those that did. They could also ensure that corporations did not shift into activities that did not benefit the public by enforcing the statements of corporate purpose included in the charters they granted.

Yet in practice, legislative discretion over access to corporate charters was sometimes used to advance private interests, rather than public interests. In some industries, control over grants of charters meant control over the entry of new firms – and therefore, the level of competition. Restricting the number of charters issued made an industry more profitable, and the resulting profits could be used to influence the political process and advance the interests of incumbent firms and their allies in government.

This problem was most acute in banking, where charters were tightly rationed, and states enacted legislation prohibiting unincorporated institutions from operating in the industry.[39] For example, in Massachusetts, every commercial bank was controlled by members of the Federalist Party until 1812. The Federalists and their allies in the industry blocked access to banking charters to other political factions, and carefully rationed charters to members of their own party, which both increased the profitability of banks and helped perpetuate the party's power.[40] In New York, the Federalist Party also initially maintained control over the banking system, but shifts in party politics and legislative manoeuvres by Aaron Burr resulted in a large Republican bank being chartered in 1799. Later in New York, a coalition of Republicans in the 1820s known by their detractors as the Albany Regency used control over bank charters to dominate the state's politics.[41] Some of the profits generated by restricting competition

corporations within that industry in the events surrounding the 2008 financial crisis illustrates the difference between fulfilling the requirement to operate within a particular industry, and serving the public. On bank chartering, see M Barr, H Jackson and M Tahyar, *Financial Regulation: Law and Policy* (St Paul MN, Foundation Press, 2021).

[39] Eg, in 1804 New York's legislature passed 'An Act to Restrain Unincorporated Banking Associations' (*New York Laws*, 1804, 615) in response to the opening of banks by groups who had been denied corporate charters for their institutions.

[40] Lu and Wallis (n 19) 109. In 1811–12, the Federalists' rivals, the Republicans, gained control of the legislature and threatened to shut down all the Federalist banks. This crisis was resolved by an agreement which led to broader access to banking charters and weaker ties between banks and political parties in that state.

[41] H Bodenhorn, 'Bank Chartering and Political Corruption in Antebellum New York. Free Banking as Reform' in C Goldin and E Glaser (eds), *Corruption and Reform: Lessons from America's Economic History* (Chicago, University of Chicago Press, 2006) 231.

in banking were used to advance the Republicans' agenda in government; the resulting limitations on bank entry likely impaired access to credit in some parts of the state. Far from generating public benefits, in these cases discretion over the allocation of corporate charters was distorted to serve private interests at the expense of the public.

Restricting access to charters in banking was of course not sufficient to maintain this system. Corporations whose charters did not include banking privileges also had to be excluded from entering the industry. In early nineteenth century New York, some insurance companies, whose charters granted them the right to conduct financial transactions that were somewhat similar to commercial banking operations, responded to the high profits of the state's banking sector by entering the industry. Deviations from the purpose stated in charters were regarded as ultra vires and state attorneys general could use the courts to restrain such behaviour when they became aware of it. And indeed, New York's Attorney General sued insurance companies for violating the terms of their charters by issuing banknotes.[42] The statements of a corporate purpose were thereby used to protect monopoly profits in an industry by restricting new entry, rather than to ensure that corporations had a duty to serve the public.

Critics noted that New York's system of restricting access to bank charters for economic and political gains was 'at variance with the great fundamental doctrine of democracy' and created banks 'for the benefit of the rich' that produced 'an amalgamation of their power'.[43] The banks that were incorporated within that system often provoked outrage when their charters were debated and ultimately approved. For example, one critic of the Bank of New York, chartered by the Federalists in 1791, stated that

> The present company which compose that body, are a combination of wealthy men, odious to the people, and formidable to the State … it is an institution formed for private emolument, injurious to the public welfare … and derogatory to the dignity of government.[44]

That bank was indeed owned by some of the wealthiest men in New York, and apparently used its influence in lending markets and in government to perpetuate the influence of the Federalist Party.[45]

To be sure, it is possible that some criticisms of early banks were motivated not by sincere concerns about the dangers posed by those institutions, but instead

[42] *People Ex Rel Attorney General v Utica Insurance Co* (1818, Supreme Court of New York, 15 Johnson 358).

[43] W Leggett (n 27) 98; D Raymond, *Elements of Political Economy* (Baltimore, Lucas and Coale, 1823) v 2, 120.

[44] 'Censor' in *New York Packet*, 21 January 1790.

[45] On the ownership of the bank, see E Hilt and J Valentine, 'Democratic Dividends: Stockholding, Wealth, and Politics in New York, 1791-1826' (2012) 72 *Journal of Economic History* 332. On the political and economic power of the Bank of New York, see B Hammond, *Banks and Politics in America From the Revolution to the Civil War* (Princeton, Princeton University Press, 1957).

by the frustrations of factions who had been excluded from the industry, and who would have felt very differently about the same banks if their own political parties controlled them. Nonetheless, the history of early American banks calls into question the notion that early corporations served the public good. Some Americans in the early nineteenth century felt that they did the opposite.

One might imagine that because of the uniquely powerful character of banks, those institutions were most likely to provoke opposition. Although banks certainly were among the most controversial early corporations, criticisms of early corporations were not confined to that industry. Anticorporate rhetoric was a mainstay of early American politics, and some factions felt that by granting corporate charters state governments were following 'the monarchical monopolizing plan of Britain', creating corporations whose interests were 'distinct from the general interest of the people, and in some cases probably opposed to it'.[46] Although we may doubt the analytical coherence of the claim that turnpike road companies were evidence of a transition 'from freedom toward despotism',[47] many corporations did provoke legitimate concerns about businesses receiving special legal privileges, about private business interests operating within the public sphere, and about the dangers of concentrated financial power for democracy.[48]

Even the grants of charters to corporations as seemingly innocuous as bridge companies could create problems. For example, in 1785 Massachusetts chartered the Charles River Bridge Company to build and operate a bridge connecting Boston with Charlestown, and that corporation enjoyed a near monopoly on transportation across that region of the Charles River and became enormously profitable. By the 1820s, it was widely believed that the corporation had become impediment to commerce and economic growth, and in response to popular demands in 1827 Massachusetts granted a charter to a new corporation, the Warren Bridge Company, to build a new bridge near the one operated by the Charles River Bridge Company. The Warren Bridge charter stipulated that once the company's construction costs were recovered, the bridge would revert to the state and become free to the public. The Charles River Bridge company sued to stop the construction of its competitor, claiming their vested rights were violated; in a celebrated decision, the Supreme Court ultimately ruled against them.[49] Through its tolls and near-monopoly status, the Charles River bridge imposed significant costs on society; a solution to that problem was found in creating a new corporation specifically to undermine the older one, a strategy

[46] 'Civis' quoted Klein and J Majewski (n 20).

[47] ibid 488.

[48] An insightful analysis of early American anticorporate rhetoric is presented in L Hartz, *Economic Policy and Democratic Thought: Pennsylvania, 1776–1860* (Cambridge MA, Harvard University Press, 1948).

[49] *Charles River Bridge v Warren Bridge*, 36 US (11 Pet) 420 (1837). The lasting influence of that decision is perhaps an indication of the prevalence of disputes created by corporations whose operations were deemed to impose substantial costs on society.

with an uncertain legal outcome. Even infrastructure companies could impose costs and create complex problems, and even if they were regarded as beneficial at the time they were created, they did not always remain so.

IV. FEDERAL INCORPORATIONS

The analysis thus far has focused on business corporations that received charters from the states. The federal government, however, chartered two business corporations in the late eighteenth and early nineteenth centuries, the Bank of the United States (1791–1811), and the Second Bank of the United States (1816–36). The first of these was modelled after the Bank of England by the author of its charter, Alexander Hamilton, and the second was its larger successor.

The importance of these institutions for the American economy and for American politics can hardly be overstated. Among the many controversies that resulted from the creation of those institutions were legal disputes focused on the question of whether they served a public purpose in a specific sense. They are therefore important to our analysis.

Most early state constitutions did not explicitly authorise the creation of corporations; the states asserted this power, with relatively little controversy.[50] The federal Constitution also does not explicitly authorise the government to create corporations.[51] The Constitution does, however, grant Congress the authority to 'make all Laws which shall be necessary and proper for carrying into Execution' its powers, and this clause became the basis for federal incorporations. Although that language might appear to grant the federal government very broad powers, it was interpreted in the context of corporations in a relatively restrictive way.

Both the Bank of the United States and the Second Bank of the United States were much larger than any other American banks at the time, with nation-wide branch networks. The banks lent to the federal government, helped facilitate the issuance of public debt, and acted as the government's fiscal agents. Yet their banking operations were quite extensive and most of the transactions they conducted were with the public and with other banks, rather than with the federal government. The power of those institutions to regulate and compete with state-chartered banks made them a target of opposition from the states, which at times sought to impose taxes on their notes or on the capital of their branches. Those taxes became the subject of complex legal disputes that clarified the legal basis for the banks' existence.

[50] See the discussion in Davis (n 13).

[51] At the Constitutional Convention in 1787, James Madison argued that Congress should be given the power 'To grant charters of incorporation where the public good may require them.' But Madison's proposal was never voted on, nor were most other proposals related to federal powers of incorporation. Davis (n 13) vol II, 13.

One of the Supreme Court's best-known decisions concerning these issues was *McCulloch v Maryland*.[52] At issue in that 1819 case was the State of Maryland's tax on the banknotes issued by a branch of the Second Bank of the United States, yet the case also raised the issue of whether the federal government had the constitutional authority to charter the bank. In its decision, the Court held that the bank was a 'convenient, a useful, and essential instrument in the prosecution of [the federal government's] fiscal operations',[53] and that its creation was indeed a necessary and proper exercise of the federal government's constitutional powers related to public finance. It also held that Maryland did not have the power to tax the federal bank's notes.

Less well known, but more illuminating on the issue of federal incorporation, is the Court's 1824 decision *Osborn v Bank of the United States*.[54] At issue in that case was another state tax imposed on the Second Bank, this time by the State of Ohio. In its decision, the Court revisited the question of the constitutionality of the bank's charter, and affirmed its holding in *McCulloch v Maryland*.[55] Yet it also clarified its reasoning regarding federal incorporations in important ways. The State of Ohio argued that it should be able to tax the bank since it was a corporation whose charter 'originated for the management of an individual concern, to be founded upon contract between individuals, having private trade and private profit for its great end and principal object'. Justice Marshall's decision denied this, and concluded that the bank was instead a 'public corporation, created for public and national purposes'. Yet he also concluded that if it were true that the bank had been created merely for the private benefit of individuals, Congress would not have had the constitutional authority to grant its charter: 'It has never been supposed that Congress could create such a corporation.'[56] The 'principal object' of any corporation chartered by the federal government must be a public purpose.

The decision also clarified the nature of the institution's public purpose. The State of Ohio argued that the broad banking powers granted in the charter of the Second Bank were not necessary for the services it provided to the government; its transactions with others were 'solely for the benefit of the members of the corporation'. Marshall's decision again conceded that if it were true that the institution's banking powers only had private benefits, they could not have been granted. Yet he concluded that the institution's banking powers were 'indispensable to the character and objects of the institution' and inseparable from the services it provided to the federal government.[57] The fact that the Second Bank acted as the government's fiscal agent and provided lending and payments

[52] 17 US 316 (1819).
[53] ibid 422.
[54] 22 US 738 (1824).
[55] 17 US 16 (1819).
[56] ibid 859–60.
[57] ibid 864–5.

services made it necessary for the institution to have banking powers, and therefore justified the charter's grant of those powers.

Thus with federal incorporations, a very specific public purpose was required. Congress could only charter businesses when it was necessary to do so to carry out its constitutional powers. Federally chartered corporations had to be direct instruments of the government, carrying out its policies. This standard is a particularly narrow and rigid version of the functional definition of the public purpose outlined above. It was much stricter than those applied to state-chartered corporations, where a public benefit of some kind was required.

Over time, as its role in the economy changed, the federal government began to assert broader powers to charter business corporations. For example, during the Civil War, the federal government enacted statutes that functioned as general incorporation acts for banks, known as the National Banking Acts of 1863 and 1864. Due in part to their provisions imposing significant taxes on the notes of state-chartered banks, these statutes induced most of the nation's commercial banks to reincorporate with federal charters, and over time, large numbers of new national banks were incorporated as well. The national banks' notes were collateralised with federal government debt, making the national paper money supply uniform and reliable. Although the US Treasury did deposit funds in some national banks, the vast majority of these institutions did not provide banking services to the government.

The constitutionality of the incorporation of those banks was repeatedly contested in subsequent litigation. For example, in the 1875 case *Farmers' & Mechanics' National Bank v Dearing*, the Court held that national banks were 'instruments designed to be used to aid the government in the administration of an important branch of the public service', and a 'means appropriate to that end', citing the reasoning of *McCulloch v Maryland* and *Osborne v Bank of the United States*.[58] Yet the public services provided by national banks were much more limited than the services provided by the Bank of the United States, and arguably consisted of little more than offering banking services to the public, which is exactly what the Court had previously held was justified only by the Second Bank's provisions of services to the federal government. Similarly, in *Davis v Elmira Savings Bank*, the Court held that 'National banks are instrumentalities of the federal government, created for a public purpose', even though that purpose was mainly banking services to the public.[59]

These cases arguably changed the meaning of the standards by which the public purpose of a federally chartered corporation would be judged. Rather than providing services to the government or playing a direct role in implementing government policy, the commercial banks chartered by the National Banking

[58] 91 US 29 (1875) 33.

[59] 161 US 275 (1896) 283. Similar reasoning is offered in *Owensboro National Bank v Owensboro*, 173 US 664 (1899).

Act were regarded as instrumentalities of the federal government mainly because they helped fulfil an objective that the federal government found desirable. Effectively, the extremely strict standard of a public purpose for federal corporations was weakened almost out of existence, in the interests of expanding federal powers.

V. DISCUSSION AND CONCLUSION

In recent years, scholars and activists have expressed interest in the concept of the corporate purpose as a means of reorienting corporate conduct in a more socially responsible way. Some of these scholars have noted that early business corporations had public purposes, and have suggested that the legal regimes governing early corporate charters might serve as a basis for modern reforms.

In this chapter I proposed two definitions of a public purpose, one based on a corporation's function, the other based on the benefits it created. Based on the functional definition, data on early charters indicate that about 60 per cent of early corporations in New York and Massachusetts up to 1820 served a public purpose, but the share declined dramatically around 1808. It is difficult to quantify the share that would meet the standard based on the benefits definition, but evidence was presented indicating that even some corporations that would seem innocuous by modern standards, such as turnpike road companies or bridge companies, were sometimes regarded as failing to meet a standard of serving the public good, and were thought to impose significant costs on society. Some of the banks chartered at the time were among the most intensely controversial organisations in American society, and even though they provided the vital services of issuing paper money and supplying credit, they were regarded as dangerous to the economy and to democracy. The legal requirement that only institutions whose corporate purpose included banking could enter the industry worsened the problem, since it served as the basis for restricting entry.

Early American corporations were complex and varied, and it is difficult to generalise about them. Yet the discussion in this chapter has shown that scholars and activists should not regard the business corporations of late eighteenth and early nineteenth centuries as serving the common good, being governed by a duty to act in the interests of society, or having clear public purposes that could serve as an example for modern reforms. The chartering of corporations by the states during that period was guided by doctrines that held that the public should benefit from their operations, but that benefit could come in the form of greater economic activity, and virtually any business from that time would meet that standard. Federal incorporations, by contrast, were initially by much stricter conceptions of a public purpose. Yet over time, those restrictions came into conflict with the expansion of the federal government's role in the economy, and were relaxed.

9

Capitalism as Personal: Brunner, Mond & Co Ltd (1881–1926)

LORRAINE TALBOT

THE ORIGINS OF modern company law lie in the unincorporated forms under which many Victorian entrepreneurs organised. Such businesses were owned and controlled by the original entrepreneurs, or family members in pursuit of their vision.[1] They were in this sense, personal organisations, closely connected (for good or ill) to the moral, political and cultural inclinations of the entrepreneurs. While they were undoubtably driven by profit, unlike large modern companies they did not have to be solely run for the financial interests of outside shareholders.[2] As such, they could be connected to philanthropic activities, including initiatives to benefit employees or the community, if the controlling owner so desired. Unlike modern companies they were under no pressure to do so through the market imperatives which underpin corporate social responsibility or governance initiatives to support human rights or the environment imposed by national or international bodies. The social leaning of these companies was derived from the entrepreneurs or closely held group of owners themselves.

There are a number of Victorian companies that are readily associated with the personal morality of its owners, Cadbury, Rowntree, Lever Bros, J. S. Fry & Sons Ltd and for the most part this reflects the controlling owners' non-conformist religious affiliations. I examine a company less commonly associated with the personal, Brunner, Mond & Company Ltd, established by John Brunner and Ludwig Mond, (themselves of the Unitarian and Jewish faith respectively).[3] The company existed from 1881–1926, their business partnership from 1873. The personal nature of the company will be demonstrated through a biographical

[1] PL Payne, *British Entrepreneurship in the Nineteenth Century*, 2nd edn (London, Macmillan, 1988) on the social origins and impact on industrial growth of such personal owner/entrepreneurs.

[2] Tech giants controlled by founders-entrepreneurs, through dual class share structures might be considered analogous as they may impose a highly personal vision of the company.

[3] Using company materials, literature about the company, its founders, their origin stories, and case material.

account of the influences on Ludwig Mond and John Brunner, how this affected their view on culture, politics and social welfare and how this was mirrored in the company's approach to employees and the wider community.

The company's legal life covers the period when key doctrines of modern company law developed. These doctrines reflect the general shift in the economy from owner-controlled businesses in the early Victorian period to large companies with numerous shareholders and a management board with low shareholdings by the end of the nineteenth century. The company's life encompasses the period when businesses shifted from personal organisations to impersonal, profit-making organisations existing for the enrichment of rentier shareholders. The latter are generally referred to as management-controlled companies, and while I shall utilise that phrase, I am using it in the sense of an organisation no longer able to pursue the personal interests of controlling or founder shareholders, rather than the more contestable claim that a professional, non-owning management determines corporate decision-making. This is a thesis most famously connected to *The Modern Corporation and Private Property*.[4]

Brunner, Mond & Co. Ltd conformed to these general economic developments, growing through increased capitalisation resulting in dispersed share ownership. Yet the company held on to the last vestiges of the personal as evidenced in *Evans v Brunner, Mond & Company* (1921).[5] As such, Brunner, Mond & Co Ltd reflects the personal capitalism of a typical Victorian company, in which the depersonalised demands of outside share ownership had not become generalised.

In this chapter, I will illustrate how Brunner, Mond & Co. Ltd manifested the owners' moral, political and cultural inclinations. In section I, I set out a brief history of Brunner, Mond & Co. Ltd from its emergence as a small entrepreneurial concern to one of the largest companies in England. In section II, I provide a short contextual biography of the two founders John Brunner and Ludwig Mond. I show how their often shared, moral, political, cosmopolitan and cultural outlook was expressed in their work and philanthropic activities. In some detail I show how Mond's life is connected to the complex history of antisemitism, which for him resulted in the pursuit of commercial interests in England while simultaneously retaining his cultural interests and connection to Europe. The latter is evidenced in his art collection, now the Mond Collection, donated to the National Gallery in London. Finally, I show how their joint social, moral and cultural vision was realised in the activities of the company, thus demonstrating the company as a continuation of their personal outlook. In section III, I show how their philanthropic impulses continued in the company

[4] A Berle and G Means, *The Modern Corporation and Private Property* (Harcourt, Brace & World Inc 1967, first edn 1932).

[5] *Evans v Brunner, Mond & Company* (1921) Ch 359.

even when it had become a huge multinational organisation with large numbers of shareholders. This is demonstrated in the contested ultra vires company gift giving case of *Evans v Brunner*, noted above, in which in Brunner's son Roscoe, continued the philanthropic impulses of his father through the company. I show how this judgment was astonishingly out of step with the prevailing law, and how this can be explained by the continuing personal character of Brunner, Mond & Co. Ltd – albeit on the cusp of change into an archetypal management company.

Throughout, I provide some context for developments in company law in the late nineteenth century and early twentieth century, specifically on corporate gift giving and the doctrine of ultra vires. In conclusion, I show that its merger with three other companies to form the chemical giant Imperial Chemical Industries completed its transition to a management controlled, shareholder value driven company with the (literal) death of the personal.

I. THE ORIGINS AND DEVELOPMENT OF BRUNNER, MOND & CO. LTD

Like many Victorian companies, it began as a business project organised as a partnership between professional acquaintances who shared a mutual interest, ambition and personal compatibility. John Brunner and Ludwig Mond were also friends. They met in 1862 while working for the firm John Hutchinson & Sons, chemical manufacturers in Widnes, where Brunner was office manager and Mond was developing the recovery of sulphur from Leblanc alkali waste in partnership with John Hutchinson.[6] Mond worked in Europe for some years and met Belgium chemist Ernest Solvay in 1872, from whom he bought a licence for a new process developed to produce soda crystals, more efficient than the Leblanc process.[7] Mond returned to England and entered into partnership with Brunner to exploit the licence. In 1873, they signed a deed of partnership to operate as the firm, Brunner, Mond & Co, with Brunner leading the management and finance side of the business and Mond the chemical process and research.[8] The partnership included a sleeping partner, Charles Holland, who invested £5,000 in return for one third of the profits. As Holland was a friend, the arrangement was intentionally 'framed under Bovill's Act' by Brunner to ensure that Holland was treated in law as a lender not a partner and thus protected from any liabilities.[9] Mond's Solvey licence became the partnership's property, and he

[6] SE Koss, *Sir John Brunner, Radical Plutocrat, 1842–1919* (New York, Cambridge University Press, 1970) 15.

[7] *The 50th Anniversary of Brunner, Mond &Co. 1873–1923* (Derby, Bemrose & Sons Ltd, 1923) 7.

[8] ibid 24.

[9] ibid 23. This was the most expedient way of achieving limited liability for a sleeping partner as the Limited Partnership Act was not passed until 1907.

invested a further £1,000.[10] Brunner invested £4,000 (borrowed from his mother in law).[11] These investments financed the purchase of Winnington Hall, an estate in Cheshire in which they set up their first manufacturing works, and brought their families to live in different parts of the estate.[12] They began production in 1874 and by 1875, the business had around 100 employees who represented around 10 per cent of capital expenditure. Like many businesses in the 1870s, they struggled to be profitable for some years but by 1880, the business was in a more stable position. On 1 January 1881 the business was registered as a company through the expedient of selling to the newly formed legal entity the works at Winnington.

The company was registered with five directors and nominal capital of £600,000 divided into 30,000 ordinary shares and 30,000 preference shares at 7 per cent. 18,000 ordinary shares were issued and Brunner and Mond were allotted 12,000 ordinary shares, two thirds of issued shares and more than enough to exercise absolute owner control. There were five directors, including Holland, Mond and Brunner. Under the Articles of Association Brunner and Mond were directors for life.[13] Thus, like many businesses at the time, though they registered as a company, the levels of share ownership and personal control by Mond and Brunner, together with personal acquaintance and friends, meant they conformed more to the quasi-partnership model, utilising the company form for administrative convenience, and to raise capital but with no intention of losing control and becoming outside investors. As Mond continued to develop new chemical processes and Brunner concentrated on the business, the company enjoyed a steady success and in 1884 its nominal capital was increased to £1.5 million, in the expectation of being sold. The company grew rapidly. Koss reports that its production of soda rose from eight hundred tons in 1874 to 18,000 tons in 1880, almost 130,000 tons in 1890, and 240,000 tons in 1903.[14] Company sponsored literature reported that by 1898 output had increased nine-fold from 1881, twelve-fold by 1903, and twenty-fold by 1920.[15]

The company bought such rights, business and lands as would enable it to utilise a vertical integration model, maximising productivity and control, which included mines, water ways and shipping to carry ammoniacal liquor. They built their first tank boats in 1880 and a considerable fleet of shipping over the years.[16]

[10] In a partnership, the assets, in this case the licence, are prima facie owned jointly by the partners. It is partnership property.

[11] '*The 50th Anniversary*' (n 7) 23.

[12] The paternalism of industrialists who lived adjacent to their works and identified their careers with the locality is a pattern noted in JM Lee, *Social Leaders and Public Persons* (Oxford, OUP, 1968).

[13] At this time and until the Companies Act 1948 there was no mandatory rule in company law requiring that directors could be removed by ordinary resolution. This meant that neither directors were able to remove the other by resolution as the stipulation in the articles was binding.

[14] Koss (n 6) 43.

[15] '*The 50th Anniversary*' (n 7) 43.

[16] ibid 50. By 1916, the total was 18 steamers, four motor boats, five liquor boats and eight barges.

The company steadily bought controlling interests in other companies such as Pennys Lane Mine in 1888.[17] In the twentieth century, Brunner, Mond & Co Ltd were expanding through the purchase of other companies and through networks at a national and international level. From 1916, purchases of controlling stakes in other companies escalated considerably including the Amonia Soda Company in 1916, Chance and Hint in 1917, Castner-Keller Ltd in 1920, and Boston Lime Firms in 1919.[18] From the 1900s, through a series of subsidiaries, controlling interests, agents and offices, Brunner and Mond had become a vast international concern. This included operations in Canada (Canadian subsidiary Brunner, Mond Canada Limited was formed in 1919); offices throughout China from 1901 later coordinated through the head office of Brummer & Mond Ltd (China) formed in 1920; Japan and Korea, through Brummer & Mond Co. (Japan) Ltd; Australia and New Zealand, through Brummer & Mond Co Limited, Sydney and Melbourne; South America, through Brummer & Mond Co, Limited, Buenos Aires, Mexico, Singapore and India through Brummer & Mond Co (India), Limited.[19]

By the beginning of the twentieth century, the company was among the largest in England. As early as 1881, Britain was beginning to lead the world in the emerging chemical industries in terms of output and employees, with Brunner & Mond as leaders in that field. For example, the company's production of alkali outstripped that of the leader, France, soon after becoming incorporated.[20] The company's nominal capital of £1.5 million in 1884, noted above, represents nearly one per cent of the total paid up capital of all industries in England in 1881.[21] And those largest companies were, for the most part, consistently conforming to the management-controlled model. Based on a study of ownership and management in the 337 largest companies on the London Stock Exchange in 1914, Foreman-Peck and Hannah demonstrate that 'the evolution of managerial control in the UK was substantially complete before 1914'.[22]

[17] '*The 50th Anniversary*' (n 7) 46.

[18] The state's relationship with companies substantially changed over the war period, to the disadvantage of many, but to the great advantage of some. Arnold claims that 'across the period 1913–24 the average total value added was 80 per cent above that for the immediate pre-war period'. AJ Arnold, 'Profitability and Capital Accumulation in British Industry during the Transwar Period, 1913–1924' (1999) 52 *The Economic History Review* 45, 62. Brunner, Mond & Co Ltd was among the success stories. It temporarily increased the working week for employees, and became a leading munitions manufacturer. There is not scope in this chapter, however, to examine this fascinating period in both the economy's and the company's development.

[19] '*The 50th Anniversary*' (n 7) 105–106.

[20] L Hannah and R Bennett, 'Large-scale Victorian manufacturers: Reconstructing the lost 1881 UK employer census' (2022) 75(3) *The Economic History Review* 830–856, 839.

[21] ibid 844.

[22] J Foreman-Peck and L Hannah, 'Extreme divorce: the managerial revolution in UK companies before 1914' (2012) 65 *Economic History Review* 1217, 218. There are different views about this. Cheffins, Mayer et al maintain that the separation of ownership from control took place in the UK later than in the US so in the 1950s or thereabouts. My own view is that this level of independent management control never occurred. For the purpose of this chapter, as noted earlier, I use the term 'management controlled' to designate an orientation away from the personal company, to one where

Management collectively owned only 3.4 per cent of the total share capital (of the 337 companies) and the average holding of a director was £2,113 – a tiny amount given the £1.926 million share value of the companies in the study.[23] Even this amount may have been artificially enhanced because the LSE's listing rules required that directors be shareholders.[24] Yet the vast increase in shareholders notwithstanding, Brunner, Mond & Co Ltd, I claim, retained much of its personal nature.

To be sure the drift to management control in the largest companies was not consistent. Unlike the largest companies today, in this period the variations between these companies in terms of shareholder numbers, director shareholding and share dispersal was much more pronounced even though the overriding outcome was a majority of management-controlled companies.[25] Shareholder numbers ranged from the lowest number of 170 (Martin's Bank) to 79,400 in Midland Railway.[26] In 136 companies, directors held substantial shareholdings averaging £144,118 per director.[27] Brunner, Mond & Co Ltd was among this group. It maintained high levels of director ownership, with family members dominating the board even as they relied on the expertise of professional management. In 1913, there were 15 directors on the board, eight of whom were from the Brunner, Mond and Solvay families.[28] From 1881 until 1921, there had been only 38 directors, of which 11 were from the family.[29] Nonetheless, the twentieth century was at a pivotal period for the company, balanced between the old personal ownership model in which the founding members' moral inclination were expressed, and the new impersonal model, in which shareholder value was the goal. This transitionary moment, I will argue, accounts for the case of *Evans v Brunner*. It also accounts for John Brunner's distaste for these developments in a letter to his banker in which he regretted that 'the men who make the profits get too little and the shareholders too much'.[30]

the interests of shareholders as a whole are paramount. For these purposes, the statistics offered in Foreman-Peck and Hannah's piece serve the purpose of that definition.

[23] ibid 1225. Accompanying this evolutionary separation of ownership from control were changes in top managerial personnel, in their selection and training, and in their function'. See ibid 1222.

[24] ibid 1225. They note that 'the average shareholding was probably worth about £1240' at a time when the average wage was £50/annum.

[25] ibid 1228. Though the question of owner control rests on the proportion of shares deemed necessary to retain control, owner control in the 337 companies was a minority. Hannah estimates that the most commonly adopted 20% ownership hurdle would mean that only 16 per cent were owner controlled while even the low 5% hurdle resulted in a 36% owner control.

[26] ibid 1223. The average number of shareholders was relatively substantial at 6,177.

[27] ibid 1225. Including, 'Guinness, Peter Walker, Whitbread, Coats, Imperial Tobacco, Lever Brothers, Barclays, and the Union of London & Smith's Bank'.

[28] '*The 50th Anniversary*' (n 7) 104.

[29] '*The 50th Anniversary*' (n 7) 105.

[30] Koss (n 6) notes 75% profits in 1889, 44.

II. IT'S PERSONAL – FROM PEOPLE TO THE COMPANY

A. Ludwig Mond (1839–1909)

Ludwig Mond was born in Kassel, Germany in 1839. He was a well-travelled, educated and cultured European with access to an elite and wealthy network[31] – all of which might have embedded him within the scientific and business community in Germany while giving him access to the art and culture he evidently sought. However, he was a Jewish man who was born into a continent historically riven with antisemitism and on the cusp of becoming much more pronounced and aggressive. Furthermore, it was a form of antisemitism which increasingly demonised science, finance and business which was non-traditional, cosmopolitan and unbound from the land. Everything which Ludwig Mond represented and pursued.

Antisemitism in Christian Europe[32] had for many centuries manifested in organised discrimination, mainly the regulation of Jewish people's habitation and practices. Until the Napoleonic Wars, detailed rules determined the movement and practices of Jews in many towns and cities, for example, the cities of Augsburg, Cologne, Nuremberg, and Strasbourg did not allow Jewish habitation until the end of the eighteenth century.[33] In Ravensburg, Lindau, Schaffhausen, Uberlingen, and Constance, towns of the Lake Constance region, and in Tubingen and Nambung, to name but a few, there was no Jewish presence until the mid-nineteenth century. In the Italian states, Jews had been confined in ghettos since the sixteenth century. Often, discriminatory legislation forbad Jewish people from otherwise ordinary activities, for example, in Hamburg, Jews were banned from coffee houses until 1798.[34]

However, Napoleon's victories in the Holy Roman Empire made regions to the left bank of the Rhine part of the French Republic and Napoleonic Empire for over 20 years, and to the East under the rule of the Napoleonic satellite states. In this, the Kingdom of Westphalia was established under the rule of Napoleon's brother Jerome, who spent huge sums trying to transform the region into a modern, cultural centre. Kassel was its capital city. The French revolutionaries' values of equality and fraternity inherited by Napoleon were legislated into these conquered German regions, to varying degree, removing much of the legal architecture of antisemitism from 1793–1813.

[31] JM Cohen, *The Life of Ludwig Mond* (London, Methuen 1956).

[32] Parts of Europe controlled by the Ottomans did not exercise antisemitic discrimination and many Jews fled to these areas. This is illustrated in the novel, Solmaz Kamuran, *Kiraze* (Garnet Publishing, 2015).

[33] HW Smith, *Nation, Religion, and Race across the Long Nineteenth Century* (Cambridge, CUP, 2008).

[34] ibid 124.

It was within this period of relative equality for Jewish people and in the City of Kassel, arguably at the centre of the modernising and emancipatory project, that Mond's parents were born, his father in 1811, and his mother in 1816 – products of French cultural transplants, enlightenment philosophy and the new liberties enjoyed by the Jewish community.[35] They were also products of the tumultuous periods which followed the defeat of Napoleon in central Europe in 1813 during which time Jewish emancipation partly unravelled. The Congress of Vienna 1815 brought the Kingdom of Westphalia to an end.[36] However, many of the Napoleonic-era reforms were continued, particularly the economic reforms enabling of capitalist industrialisation and economic liberalism.[37] This precipitated a particularly strong form of social dislocation, amplified by the geographically patchy progress of industrialisation in Germany. Jonathan Sperber argues that the first decades created, 'a large lower class, no longer part of an agrarian-artisan society but not yet integrated into an industrial world'.[38]

As a response to this, antisemitism developed in specific ways which would define German politics into the twentieth century. First, antisemitism operated as a stand in for the old social norms, the association of ordered discrimination as an important attribute of the pre-capitalist economy. Second, Jewish people were personally associated with the capitalist market economy and its negative impacts. As an economy driven by capital, rather than land, it naturally benefitted those of the Jewish community whose business was money lending or finance more generally – a vocation traditionally available to Jewish people as they were not subject to the Christian or Muslim prohibitions against usury, and because they were excluded from many other occupations and forms of advancement.

For many, antisemitism and anti-capitalism was synonymous so that the economic deprivation and social upheavals caused by capitalism precipitated violent attacks on Jewish people and property. This was particularly true for those who had availed themselves of freedoms of movement and settlement under French rule.[39] The series of riots which became known as the Hep Hep Riots were the first such reactions, initially erupting in Wurzburg in an attack on the house of the first Jewish family to get a residence permit since the expulsions of Jews in 1642.[40] The riots went on to affect another 40 cities and towns. The return of Jewish people to towns and cities that had expelled them was unpopular with much of the local population. The Hep Hep Riots 'thus represented the

[35] S Woolf, *Napoleon's Integration of Europe* (Abingdon, Routledge, 1991) 196–226.

[36] With the establishment of the German Confederation in 1815. J Whaley, War and Dissolution: The Reich, 1792–1806 Germany and the Holy Roman Empire: Volume II: The Peace of Westphalia to the Dissolution of the Reich, *1648–1806* (Oxford, Oxford University Press, 2012) 646.

[37] J Sperber, *Popular Catholicism in Nineteenth-Century Germany* (Princeton, Princeton University Press 1984).

[38] ibid 11.

[39] Smith (n 33) 123.

[40] ibid 124.

first uprising in Germany against emancipation, and especially against that part of emancipation that affronted local privilege'.[41] The riots started in the cities of southern and middle Germany and soon spread north. Frankfurt, for example, reintroduced the discriminatory laws that prevailed for centuries before French rule.

Nonetheless many Jewish communities, especially the wealthier, escaped much of this violence. Kassel remained relatively liberal, reformist, and tolerant of Judaism and continued the culture and philosophy of the French occupiers. Mond's mother was a committed Rousseau-ian, and a writer, interested in theories around education and Mond grew up learning the canon of French as well as German high culture.[42] However, their privileged bubble could not have been immune to the growing antisemitism which consolidated around a newly confected German identity as the natural inheritors of the Holy Roman Empire which specifically excluded the Jewish community.[43]

Jewish people were also associated with a new governing elite which accompanied the emerging capitalist market centred on urban areas and industrial sectors. New grievances emerged as 'New elites arising from these social transformations confronted existing ruling groups, demanding a share of political power.'[44] Ludwig Mond was just nine years old when antagonism connected to these social, political and economic dislocations came to a head in the Revolution of 1848. Smith characterises events in the lead up to and over the Revolution as 'the last great rebellion of wide classes on the basis of pre-industrial goals and anti-capitalist norms and values'.[45] The new elites and large-scale bureaucracies which symbolised the removal of the securities of the old regime were part of Mond's world. These elites were the backbone of Heidelburg University, where Mond studied chemistry in the late 1850s under the supervision of Robert Bunsen.[46] Many of his Professors supported liberal and democratic causes, some becoming members of the first freely elected German Parliament, the Frankfurt Parliament of 1848. The University was highly cosmopolitan, having the highest number of foreign students at the time from Britain, Russia, North America and Europe. In contrast, dislocated people in Germany sought the securities of the old order, which meant Jewish subordination. In 1849, there were at least 180 separate communities in which attacks on Jews occurred with 'flashpoints including Baden, Hessen, Bavaria,

[41] ibid 125.

[42] T Adams, *Transnational Philanthropy* (New York, Palgrave Macmillan Transnational History Series, 2016) 19.

[43] Whaley (n 36) 656.

[44] Sperber (n 37) 11.

[45] Smith (n 33) 131.

[46] Adam (n 42). Mond didn't complete a graduate degree having spent too much money on partying, but Karl Heinsheimer, Professor of law at the University of Heidelberg, argued that Mond had selected his alma mater because he considered this university not just a German institution but an institution that served the world. See ibid 25.

and Posen – all areas of small-town Jewish settlement where Christians and Jews lived in close proximity'.[47] When in December 1849, the lower house of Parliament in Bavaria passed a Bill granting equal rights to Christians and Jews there were at least '552 separate petitions from 1,762 Bavarian localities from Christians who feared the shift from Jewish people's designation as foreigner'.[48]

The antisemitic momentum was also evidenced in Conservative political parties across the board and at all levels of seniority, promoted through conservative newspapers and other conservative publications. For example, antisemitic propaganda was promoted in leading conservative newspaper the *Kreuzzeitung* from the mid-century, under the editorship of Hermann Wagener.[49]

Amongst the elite classes to which Mond would have mixed, a restrained form of antisemitism festered. Richard Wagner is a case in point. In his antisemitic essay 'Das Judentum in der Musik' first published in *Neue Zeitschrift für Musik* in 1850, he made spurious claims about culture (that it derived from geography and local language and therefore belongs to long-standing inhabitants) and the Jewish community (that they were a dislocated, Semitic race), to the conclusion that they lacked culture and so extracted culture from others. For Wagner, they constituted a 'transnational category of cultural parasites, merely imitating the various cultures in which they reside'. Wagner, like many of his class, did not publicise his hate speech until antisemitism had become more mainstream among respectable society. This essay was signed with the pseudonym K. Freigedank ('Free Thought'). And it was not until 1869 that he republished it under his own name.[50]

Nonetheless elite social networks in Germany continued to support Mond's career, in spite of his abrupt departure from university. Through his mother, a business venture was arranged between the nineteen-year-old Mond and the Jewish run bank, the Darmsradter Bank fur Handel, which funded industrial start-up companies – his father reluctantly arranging the contract.[51] After one year, Mond had developed a method for the recovery of sulphur from the waste in soda production which he patented in 1859.

However, his ambitions in Germany were limited by prejudice and ambivalence to commercialism, while England presented many commercial opportunities for Mond, particularly with its large number of chemical businesses. And so, in 1862 Mond moved to England, working, as noted above with John Hutchinson. From 1863, he sold licences for his sulphur recovery process

[47] Smith (n 33) 134.

[48] Citing research by James Harris, which he evidences a generalised aversion to Jewish emancipation. Smith (n 33) 131–2.

[49] J Retallack, 'Conservatives and Antisemites in Baden and Saxony' (1999) 17 *German History* 507.

[50] J Loeffler, 'Richard Wagner's 'Jewish Music': Antisemitism and Aesthetics in Modern Jewish Culture' (2009) 15 *Jewish Social Studies: History, Culture, Society* 2, 5.

[51] Adam (n 42) 28.

to 60 companies in England and Europe and received around £5,000[52] in net royalties from 1863 to 1876.[53] He made many returns to Germany and Europe maintaining close contract with his parents and extended family, in particular, his Aunt and cousin Frida. His friendship with Frida was in part formed from their shared love of literature, especially Goethe, which kept them in frequent communication, and they became secretly engaged when she was just 13 and he 21.[54] In 1866, on an extended business trip to Europe Mond married Frida, and they enjoyed a cultured and intellectual community in Utrecht.[55]

During this time, Germany went through significant changes with the creation of German National unity in 1866–71 and the introduction of universal, equal, and direct manhood suffrage.[56] A formal end to the discrimination of Jewish people was, on the face of it, a great opportunity to return home. This would have suited his wife, who expected to live in Europe indefinitely. Frida stayed in Utrecht when Mond made return trips to England, and when she became pregnant she lived in her parents' home in Cologne.[57] A highly cultured woman, Frida, like many Germans viewed England as being a commercially obsessed and culturally philistine country.[58] However, Mond chose to make England his primary residence and insisted that Frida join him there. He was in part drawn to England because of the ability of Jewish men to prosper on many different fields, and was particularly inspired by the political rise of Benjamin Disraeli.[59] Antisemitic legislation which prohibited Jewish men sitting in Parliament had been removed under the Jewish Relief Act 1858. Prior to that Lionel de Rothchild, of the banking dynasty, was in 1850, the first man of Jewish faith to take up a seat in the House of Commons. Thus, Mond became part of a new wave of wealthy, educated Jewish migrants that included Hugo Hirsch, Alfred Beit, and Ernest Cassel.[60]

It was not yet settled. The newlywed's family were not happy with this move, and Frida herself was very lonely in Winnington Hall. She was bereft of the rich intellectual and cultural life and community she had held in Germany. Thus, much continued which would have drawn the Monds back to Germany. However, any plans the Monds may have had about returning home would have

[52] Today this would be around £750,000. www.officialdata.org/1860-GBP-in-2017?amount=1000.

[53] Adam (n 42) 30.

[54] ibid 28.

[55] ibid 29.

[56] Sperber (n 37).

[57] JM Cohen, *The Life of Ludwig Mond* (London, Methuen, 1956) 115.

[58] Treitsche's extreme Anglophobia is discussed in J Hawes, *Englanders and Huns: How Five Decades of Enmity LED to the First World War: The Culture-Clash which Led to the First World War* (London, Simon & Schuster, 2014).

[59] Disraeli served as Chancellor of the Exchequer and Leader of the House of Commons in the 1850s and 60s, becoming Prime Minister in 1868.

[60] Cassel, who lived in England since 1869, quickly became one of the most influential bankers of London and his philanthropic donations included recipients such as the London School of Economics.

been tempered by the backlash against Jewish people following the stock market crash of 1873. If the association of Jewish people with capitalism was viewed negatively when the economy was in the ascendency, it reached predictably dire levels when capitalism started to fail. The crash of 1873, and the subsequent 'Great Depression' was for many in Germany the fault of the Jewish community. Crucially, this was a collapse in finance, thought by many to be Jewish businesses. As Hans Rosenberg notes, the fixed production associated with agriculture and the artisan and shopkeeper class was associated with German-ness, in contrast with the 'mobile capital' such as stocks and credit, associated with the Jewish community.[61]

In the wake of the crash, the classes who were prominently anticapitalistic and antisemitic in the 1848 revolution, sought with an 'attitude of growing belligerency' more state intervention to curtail the market, specifically to curtail 'mobile capital' through laws against usury. Rosenberg argues this 'found at least partial recognition in the German legislation of 188I, 1883, and 1897, and more drastically in the revision of the Austrian trade codes in 1883 and 1885'.[62] The antisemitism which was integral to the entire Conservative project, whether moderate or radical, intensified.[63] The *Kreuzzeitung's* long standing antisemitic positioning concretised around the so called 'Era Articles' in 1876, a series of five articles written by journalist Franz Perrot, under a pseudonym, in which he attributed the stock market crash to the continued presence of Jewish usury, and the share market as a quintessentially Jewish method of value extraction.[64]

The fallacious attribution of blame to Jewish people for the exploitation of agricultural and industrial labourers made through express or coded conspiracy theories became common from the 1870s, argues Retallack.[65] In a speech made in 1879, 'what we demand from modern jewry', Stoecker, founder of the Christian Social Party characterised the exploitation of labour by capital as being essentially the exploitation of true Germans by Jews. The economy and social class were racialised regardless of the inconvenient fact that most Jewish people were working class and the majority of wealth in Germany lay with non-Jewish, white Germans.[66] But it was a 'fake news' which resonated with the electorate and in the 1881 elections the Conservative Central Committee put

[61] H Rosenberg, 'Political and Social Consequences of the Great Depression of 1873–1896 in Central Europe' (1943) 13 *The Economic History Review* 58, 62.

[62] ibid 62.

[63] RS Levy, *The Downfall of the Anti-Semitic Political Parties in Imperial Germany* (New Haven, Conn., Yale University Press, 1975).

[64] F Perrot 'Era of Bleichröder-Delbrück-Camphausen', Neue Preußische (Kreuz-) Zeitung (Berlin), 29 June – 1 July 1875.

[65] J Retallack, *The German Right, 1860–1920: Political Limits of the Authoritarian Imagination* (Toronto, University of Toronto Press, 2006) 306.

[66] S Berger, *Social Democracy and the Working Class: In Nineteenth- and Twentieth-Century Germany* (Abingdon, Routledge, 1999); SM Lowenstein, 'Economic Life' in MA Kaplan (ed), *Jewish Daily Life in Germany, 1618–1945* (New York, OUP, 2005).

forward four anti-Semitic candidates, including Stoecker, and gained nearly one-third of the votes.

In the same period, historian and National Liberal Reichstag member Professor Heinrich von Treitschke redirected his anti-Catholic views toward Jews, 'displacing his venom from the flagging Kulturkampf onto the new discourse of "antisemitism"'.[67] Blaming the crash on Jews and adopting the old antisemitic tropes of material greed and absence of 'Volks' based Germanic spirit became Treitschke's dominant theme.[68] He reflected a world view that was the antithesis of Mond's person, as a Jewish man, concerned with commercial and scientific matters, shot through with cosmopolitan modernity and at ease in many countries. Treitschke's position was readily grasped by conservative politicians. Baron Heinrich von Friesen-Rötha, for example, a member of the Reichstag from 1887 to 1893 confirmed that the Conservative project was to redress Jewish emancipation, which was 'energetically opposed by the Conservatives in all German states'.[69] Treitschke's message was one that resonated in German society, and by the end of 1880 'A Word' had been printed in three editions.

Thus, Mond did not return to Germany. Instead, he put down more roots in England, formed the partnership with John Brunner, and joined their work and families together in Winnington Hall. His parents and extended family largely remained in Germany and Mond travelled between England and continental Europe regularly, maintaining the transnational links which would come to define the transnational character of Brunner, Mond & Co Ltd. Frida, as a Victorian wife and mother did not, however, have the same freedom of movement. Later, her isolation was mitigated by the arrival at Wilmington of her educated and cultured childhood friend Henrietta Hertz.

Mond's personal experience as a scientist engaged in cutting edge science, his humanism, his awareness of antisemitism and his love of European art, culture and knowledge, informed the philanthropy enabled by the economic success of Brunner, Mond & Co Ltd. Adams estimates that Mond spent over 30 per cent of his personal wealth on philanthropic activities, in England, Germany and Italy.[70] The breadth of donations was extensive but this brief list gives a flavour of the nature of his interests. This included the founding of the British Academy in 1901, donations to the Lister Institute of Preventative Medicine and to the Infants Hospital (both in London).[71] He established a laboratory which he endowed with £62,000 as the Davy-Faraday Laboratory to the Royal

[67] P Steinberg 'The Narcissism of Major Differences: Richard Wagner and the Peculiarities of German Antisemitism' (2022) 89 *Social Research: An International Quarterly* 21. The term was coined earlier in the decade by the journalist Wilhelm Marr Michael.

[68] PGJ Pulzer, *The Rise of Political Anti-Semitism in Germany and Austria* (London, Wiley, 1988) 508.

[69] Rosenberg (n 61) 517.

[70] Adam (n 42) 58.

[71] ibid 59.

Institution. In Germany, he donated £10,000 to create the Chemical Research Institute (later becoming the Institute for Chemical Research of the Emperor Wilhelm Society), £5,000 for the creation of the Henriette Mond Endowment in Kassell for convalescents of all faiths, and £4,000 to establish the M. B. Mond Endowment for the Relief of Jewish People in Distress for the Jewish community of Kassell in 1892, in memory of his father.[72] In Italy, Mond donated £7,480 to the Accademia dei Lincei in Rome for the endowment of the Cannizzaro Prize, after the Italian chemist Stanislao Cannizzaro.[73] Mond was, in turn, elected an honorary member of the Accademia dei Lincei in 1899.[74]

Establishing an art collection that could be enjoyed within the home, served both as salve for Frida's cultural isolation and a public service for the future. Mond began funding the purchase of art works for the collections in 1884.[75] He had specific requirements. He wanted the finest Old Masters, that were of public gallery quality and so worthy of being bequeathed to the nation.[76] And, to ensure their quality, he wanted to engage someone with expertise and keen artistic appreciation. Thus, he empowered renowned art dealer and historian of Italian art, Jean Paul Richter and Hertz to make the selection and for Richter to verify their authenticity. Writing an account of making the collection, Richter stated that

> the collection was to be representative of Italian art in general, and not of that of any particular school; that the pictures of which it was to be composed were to be of indisputable authenticity, and on a niveau of quality which would entitle them to an honourable place in any public gallery.[77]

Mond was particularly drawn to Richter because he adopted the scientific approach to authenticity of Giovanni Morelli, an Italian art critic.[78] Morelli was trained in natural science and used a scientific approach to medical symptoms to create his 'Morellian' approach to authenticity in paintings – concentrating on a series of minor traits in artist's techniques, such as hand details, rather than grand themes and compositions which were often adopted by the apprentices of the Masters. Though Morelli's approach was not recognised in English art authentication and scholarship until the end of the century, Mond was fully aware as his cultural interests and friendships were grounded in continental Europe, especially hubs of high culture such as Rome and Florence. Richter was given full power to establish price, provided authenticity and quality was ensured.

[72] ibid 59.

[73] ibid 59.

[74] ibid 60.

[75] T Stammers, 'Jewishness, antiquity and civilization: Alfred Mond, Lord Melchett (1868–1930) and the renewal of a collecting legacy' (2022) 34(3) *Journal of the History of Collections* 430.

[76] ibid 430.

[77] JP Richter, *The Mond Collection: an appreciation. Vol 1* (London, John Murray, 1910).

[78] J Vakkari 'Giovanni Morelli's "Scientific" Method of attribution and its reinterpretations from the 1960's until the 1990's' (2001) 70 *Journal of Art History* 46.

Ludwig Mond collected art which in a general sense expressed his cultural instincts and life experiences, and which he associated with being worthy of public exhibition. The artistic virtues of each piece and authentication methods were considered by Richter in two volumes on the Mond Collection, published in 1910. Richter's first volume considers the works of the Venetian, Paduan, Veronese and Vicentine school which included Raphael's altarpiece, The Crucified Christ with the Virgin Mary, Saints and Angels (The Mond Crucifixion) from Raphael's pre-Roman period.[79] Painted when he was 18, it hung in Citta di Castello for 300 years, and after passing through a number of hands in the nineteenth century it was bought by Richter for Mond in 1892. The first volume also covered notable pieces such as St Mark by Michele Giambono, two Madonnas and a Pieta by Giovanni Bellini, Titian's Virgin and Child, and Andrea Mantegna's Holy Family. The Second volume considers the works drawn from the Lombard, Tuscan, Umbrian, Bolognese and Ferrarese Schools including St John the Baptist, by Murillo, the Effects of Jealousy by Cranach and Moonlit Landscape, by Rubens.[80]

Mond's love of European art and culture were, of course, genuine, and he and his family spent much of the year in their home at the Palazzo Zuccari, in Rome.[81] Nonetheless, his investment in art for the public would certainly deflect antisemitic tropes of the uncultured money obsessed Jew. And, while there is no record of Mond complaining about antisemitism in England it was clearly there. When his son, Alfred, entered politics, he struggled to get a footing because of expressly stated antisemitic prejudice. He was criticised as a wealthy Jew when he stood for the Chester seat for the Liberals at the 1906 election, winning by a narrow margin.[82] In contrast, standing in the same election, Jack Brunner, son of John, suffered no such difficulty.

B. John Brunner (1832–1919)

John Brunner was early motivated by a combination of the strong moral and religious imperatives derived from his Unitarian background and an interest in commerce.[83] The former derived from his father, a Swiss Protestant minister

[79] Technique discussed in Roy, Ashok et al, 'Raphael's Early Work in the National Gallery: Paintings before Rome' (2004) 25 *National Gallery Technical Bulletin* 4.

[80] Richter (n 77).

[81] The family, including Richter and Hertz stayed there for a large portion of each year. Mond, on his death, left the Palazzo and the paintings in it to Henrietta. She in turn left it to the German Government. The Palazzo became the Bibliotéka Hertziana, now run by the Max Planck Institute as a centre for art-historical study. D Wardleworth, 'The 'friendly' Battle for the Mond Bequest' (2003) 4 *The British Art Journal* 87.

[82] RM Bevan, *The ICI Affair: Cheshire's most Sensational Murder Mystery* (RM Bevan & CC Publishing, 2017). 259.

[83] Koss (n 6) 8.

who migrated to Lancashire in 1832 and became a Unitarian, setting up a school in Liverpool, St George's House, which Brunner attended. His early interest in commerce was met by leaving school at the age of 15 to work in a Liverpool shipping office, and then the chemical firm, Hutchinson & Sons.[84] His ability to combine Mond's skills as a chemist into a functioning business gave him the wealth he needed to pursue his moral concerns as well as to operationalise them in Brunner, Mond & Co Ltd. He was dubbed by *The Times* the 'chemical Croesus'.[85]

Brunner took what might today be called a stakeholder approach to management. He was concerned with consumers, and focused on the quality of the company's products.[86] He maintained close relationships with employees, and when the workforce become too large for personal relationships, he, together with Mond, introduced recreational activities such as cricket and cycling, supplying a cricket ground and club house,[87] and building a bath house and housing.[88] As the person heading up personal and labour management in the company, and later as Chairman, from 1891–1918, he personally introduced many of the changes to improve the working lives of employees, noted in the next section.

Outside of the company, he served on the local education committee, funded the building of schools in Barnton, founded the Northwich High School for Girls and later secured its merger with the grammar school through funding new buildings and a playground. He provided scholarships for pupils to attend the grammar school.[89] He funded a library in Norwich, a village Hall in Halton, and Guildhalls in Winsford and Runcorn.[90] He endowed professorial chairs of Economics and Physical Chemistry to the University of Liverpool, and served as its Pro-Chancellor for five years. He financed a hospital in Bülach, the town of his father's birth in Canton Zürich.

His wealth allowed him to stand as a member of Parliament for the Liberal Party (1885–1910) and to pursue his radical progressivism in his political career. He introduced a Bill to provide compensation for those whose property suffered damage through subsidence caused by the pumping of brine, which was passed in 1891 as the Brine Pumping (Compensation for Subsidence) Act. He championed Home Rule for Ireland, the relief of poverty in Ireland, and promoted educational reform and the extension of state education.[91] To these causes, he contributed his own personal wealth.[92] He supported the trade union movement and maintained close political ties with trade-union leaders.[93] He supported

[84] Koss (n 6) 9.
[85] ibid 2.
[86] '*The 50th Anniversary*' (n 7) 2.
[87] ibid 93.
[88] ibid 84.
[89] *The Manchester Guardian*,18 January 1912, 4.
[90] ibid.
[91] Koss (n 6) 54–55.
[92] See Anon, 'Gift of Secondary School: Sir John Brunner's Generosity', *The Manchester Guardian*, 9 March 1907.
[93] Koss (n 6) 146.

legislation to provide compensation for injured workmen.[94] He was a generous contributor to radical newspapers and to the Liberal Party and its related causes.[95]

C. Brunner, Mond & Co Ltd (1881–1926)

Brunner, Mond & Co Ltd was an enlightened employer. This was not the norm for companies at the time, nor was it the direct result of legislation. The acts of the company in this respect were an extension of its founders' moral positions. Their belief in reasonable wages, lower hours and treating employees humanely, at all ages, and even into retirement was operationalised in the company as their beliefs were operationalised in their philanthropic activities, noted above. As such, it demonstrates that the company remained a personal company, even as it grew beyond personal relationships.

Mond and Brunner were not unique in their awareness of worker exploitation. That employees in factories were dangerously overworked was a known quantity in Victorian England and from 1833 a number of Acts were passed which restricted the hours that 'protected persons' (children, young people and women) could work.[96] Most notably, the Factory Act 1847, restricted the working week to 58 hours, or ten hours a day, for women and young persons (from 13–18 years). Subsequent legislation attempted to redress the many loopholes employers found, to reduce exceptions to its application and to extend its scope to more workplaces. For example, in 1867 the Factories Act was extended to all establishments employing 50 or more workers. So, when Brunner and Mond's partnership began works in Winnington, operating day and night in shifts of 84 hours a week for each adult male employee, they could not claim to be particularly progressive employers.[97]

In the early days, economic success was precarious and they undoubtedly relied on exploitative work practices. Nonetheless, sickness benefit was instituted in 1873 and houses were provided at low rents from 1879.[98] And, when the company became more successful, they adopted the more progressive practices which seem closer to their moral position. From 1884, all employees were given one week's paid leave.[99] A combined day and evening school was opened in 1886, and a sports ground for the workers was provided in 1890.[100] In 1889, they

[94] F Dick, 'Brunner, Sir John Tomlinson, (1842–1919)' Oxford Dictionary of National Biography (Oxford, 1993).

[95] Koss (n 6) 50.

[96] Despite the gradual extension of the franchise in 1832, 1867 and 1884, until 1918 factory workers did not have a right to vote, thus we can surmise that the Factory Acts demonstrate a concern by the upper and middle classes.

[97] '*The 50th Anniversary*' (n 7) 68.

[98] ibid 83.

[99] ibid. Although subject to condition of attendance which meant initially only 42% of men qualified, 76.

[100] Koss (n 6) 44.

reduced the length of shift from 12 to eight hours, with only a 10 per cent reduction in pay per shift, a change which, 'was not only absolutely unheard of in the chemical trade, but was also almost unknown in the country'.[101] In 1895, the working day was reduced from 55.5 hours a week to 48 hours for tradesmen and 49.5 hours for labourers, with no reduction in pay.[102] In an article published in the *Manchester Guardian* in 1913, Brunner stated that the company considered improving working condition and wages to be a duty and enjoyed good relations with trade union leaders.[103] In 1902, paid holiday was increased to two weeks.

Much later in the company's life, awards for long service were introduced. From 1913, a sliding reward scheme was introduced for all those who had worked fulltime for two years or more.[104] From 1898, the company introduced a pension like scheme, available to men who ceased work in old age and had not saved enough 'to enable him to live in comfort'. Each case was considered on its merits by the board of directors with the result that 495 were granted from 1898 to 1922.[105] Mond left a bequest of £20,000 to provide pensions for retired, long-term employees of the company, who became known as Mond pensioners.

These changes were particularly progressive given their application to non-protected persons, that is working men. Reforms were adopted by their moral inclination rather than mandated by law, which was in any case notoriously ineffective. The application of the various Factory Acts was widely acknowledged to have been thwarted by employers gaming the rules or engaging in outright noncompliance.[106] Oversight of compliance was known to be inadequate, and the TUC, in particular, made the increase in factory inspectors a plank of its campaigns.[107] Thus, the adoption by the company of its own schemes to provide a level of compassion for employees was rare and reflects the personal inclination of John Brunner and Ludwig Mond.

These personal inclinations, as has been demonstrated, were formed by their life and educational experiences. The tension in Mond's experiences of an elite, cosmopolitan culture and education and a new form of antisemitism grounded in anti-modernity, brought his commercial interests and above all his science to England. At the same time, his research and cultural interests were informed and grounded in Europe, and he remained a transnational citizen. All these

[101] '*The 50th Anniversary*' (n 7) 70. Koss argues that this may have been in response to the fact that in 1889 the prominent trade unionist Tom Mann obtained temporary employment at Brunner, Mond's works at Winnington and in a series of articles in the Labour Elector campaigned against the long hours worked.

[102] '*The 50th Anniversary*' (n 7) 70.

[103] Anon, 'Sir John Brunner on the position', *The Manchester Guardian*, 31 May 1913, 14.

[104] '*The 50th Anniversary*' (n 7) 2 years' service gave 1 shilling per week, 6 years' service 3 shillings per week. 75.

[105] '*The 50th Anniversary*' (n 7) 76. Of these, 36 payments were stopped for reasons other than death.

[106] BL Hutchins and AH Spencer, *A history of factory legislation* (London, PS King, 1926).

[107] URQ Henriques, *The Early Factory Acts and Their Enforcements* (London, The Historical Association, 1971).

attributes are reflected in Brunner, Mond & Co Ltd. Similarly, the commercial literacy and social concerns of Brunner, son of an immigrant with wider horizons than England, informed by an anti-conformist religion which valued education and the improvement of working people's lives became part of the company. The company's character as an entrepreneur, owner-controlled company is evidenced by the extension of many aspects of Brunner and Mond's character into the company's activities, over and beyond the enhancement of shareholder value. In the next section, we consider a case which heralds the end of this era, and the coming of the company as a management controlled, shareholder value business.

III. EVANS v BRUNNER, MOND & CO LTD: THE FINAL HURRAH OF THE PERSONAL

John Brunner and Ludwig Mond's embrace of philanthropy underpinned the well-known case of *Evans v Brunner, Mond & Co Ltd* on ultra vires and corporate gift giving. The case is illustrative of the wider developments in the economy and corporate organisation which was reflected in evolutions in the doctrine of ultra vires and gratuitous payments, set out in the plaintiff's objections.[108] However, as the judgment did not reflect the prevailing position on ultra vires and gift giving it is indicative of an understanding of the company as embedded in the persons involved. Though the company was now chaired by Roscoe Brunner, the youngest son of John Brunner, his decision-making was informed by the founders' philanthropy.

Of all of Brunner and Mond's sons, only Roscoe showed any real interest in the business. Alfred Mond wanted a political career, Robert Mond's interests lay in science and archaeology and Jack Brunner became an MP for the Liberal Party. All the sons took seats on the board but only Roscoe Brunner was involved in management, which he undertook from 1898.

A. The Case

On 4 August 1920, a resolution authorising the directors 'to distribute to such universities, or other scientific institutions in the United Kingdom as they may select for the furtherance of scientific education and research the sum of 100,000*l*. out of invested surplus reserve account' was passed at an extraordinary general meeting of the company. William Wynne Evans, a minority shareholder of the

[108] LE Talbot, 'A Contextual Analysis of the Demise of the Doctrine of *Ultra Vires* in English Company law and the Rhetoric and Reality of Enlightened Shareholders' (2009) 30 *Company Lawyer* 323; LE Talbot, 'Critical Corporate Governance and the Demise of the *Ultra Vires* Doctrine' (2009) 38 *Common Law World Review* 170.

company suing on behalf of himself and other minority shareholders, claimed a declaration that the resolution was ultra vires the objects and powers of the company and therefore void under the common law doctrine of ultra vires.

Under the memorandum of association, the company's primary object was to purchase and carry on the business of chemical manufacturers. Various objects and powers were ancillary to the main object, concluding with one(s) whereby the company was enabled to do 'all such business and things as may be incidental or conducive to the attainment of the above objects, or any of them'. The plaintiff contended that as the paramount object of the company was to carry on the business of chemical manufacturers, this was not enabled by this gift. And, while the ancillary object enabled actions which were incidental or conducive to the main object, this donation was too general and not sufficiently bound to the promotion of chemical manufacture. Indeed, he claimed that the proposed expenditure principally benefited the community at large, and only benefitted the company to an insignificant extent so that it essentially provided a general benefit to rival companies.

The plaintiff's position entirely reflected the prevailing doctrine of ultra vires and gratuitous payments and had every expectation of success. As noted earlier, by this time the largest companies which composed the greater part of the economy were management controlled rather than entrepreneurial companies. Brunner, Mond & Co. Ltd had 23,713 shareholders at the time of this case.[109] The evolution of larger companies was recognised in the doctrine of ultra vires which accommodated the reality of members' diminishing involvement in the business as they become numerous, possessed a smaller proportion of voting rights and were not part of management. Devoid of day-to-day control, the doctrine of ultra vires allowed shareholders (and creditors) to have a contract declared void if it didn't reflect the business they had intended to invest in, (or lend to). The nature of that business was set out under the objects clause in the company's constitution.[110] By fixing the company's business in this way, the doctrine of ultra vires went some way to concretising the company as an entity with a fixed business identity, setting some of the scene for the judgment in *Salomon v Salomon*.[111]

A strict approach characterised early formulations of the doctrine, but later, and by the time of *Evans*, the doctrine had become flexible in respect of business activity, though remained strict in respect to profit making and prohibited actions which reduced returns to shareholders, principally gratuitous payments.

[109] *Evan v Brunner*, 359.

[110] The 1856 Companies Act introduced an objects clause into the company constitution of a registered company, the purpose of which was to state the business capacity of the company. However, it was not until the last quarter of the nineteenth century that the courts clearly asserted the scope and effectiveness of the ultra vires doctrine.

[111] *Salomon v Salomon Co Ltd*. (1897) AC 22 and discussed in LE Talbot, *Critical Company Law* (Abingdon, Routledge, 2015) ch 4.

The strict approach to business activity is demonstrated in *Ashbury Railway Carriage & Iron Co v Riche* (1875) which held that any contract entered into involving business which did not fall under a company's objects clauses was outside the company's capacity and therefore ultra vires the company and void.[112] In *Ashbury* a contract to finance the construction of a Railway in Belgium was held by the House of Lords to be ultra vires because although the substance of this contract was within the normal business activity of a railway company, it fell outside its exact business purposes under the constitution which was 'to make, sell, lend or hire, railway carriages, wagons plant machinery etc'. To further underline the separateness of the company from the members, the court also held that any ratification of the contract would have been ineffective regardless of a clause purporting to empower members to extend company business beyond that specified in the objects 'in pursuance of a special resolution'. The case conceived of the company as a distinct, reified productive entity whose purpose was to do that business set out in the constitution to the letter. Judgments around this period show the courts developing the doctrine as a way of providing members and creditors with a mechanism to actively protect their investment in a context where such opportunities were limited.[113]

This strict approach was also taken in cases involving agreements by the company to make gratuitous payments. When challenged by a shareholder or creditor, gratuitous payments were consistently declared to be ultra vires. Judicial antipathy to corporate gifts is most famously contained in the dictum 'there shall be no cakes and ale except such as are required for the benefit of the company'.[114] The key was whether payment would enhance the interests of the company. Thus, in an earlier case, a bonus to servants was held to be intra vires because it helped 'ease the friction between master and servant' in an ongoing business which was reliant on a compliant workforce.[115] Furthermore, there would be 'no cakes and ale' even if the company had an express clause in its objects so allowing. So, in *Lee Behrens*[116] the liquidator successfully challenged the validity of payments by the company to a widow of a former director notwithstanding that the memorandum included an express power to provide for the welfare of persons in the employment of the company as well as their

[112] *Ashbury Railway Carriage & Iron Co v Riche* (1875) LR 7 HL 653. *Re Amalgamated Syndicate* [1897] 2 Ch 600.

[113] LE Talbot, 'Critical Corporate Governance and the Demise of the *Ultra Vires* Doctrine' (2009) 38 *Common Law World Review* 170 and 'A Contextual Analysis of the Demise of the Doctrine of *Ultra Vires* in English Company law and the Rhetoric and Reality of Enlightened Shareholders' (2009) 30 *Company Lawyer* 323.

[114] *Hutton v West Cork Railway Co* (1883) LR 23 ChD 654.

[115] *Hampson v Price's Patent Candle Company* (1876) 45 LJ Ch 437, where the Master of the Rolls held that the directors of *Price's Patent Candle Company* were at liberty to make payments to their servants when there had been a very good year, by giving each of them in their service and of good character a gratuity equal to a week's wages. This 'helped ease the friction between master and servant'.

[116] [1932] 2 Ch 46.

widows and children. The court held that such gifts should be subjected to a three-part test; was the payment for a purpose which is reasonably incidental to the company's business, was it bona fide and would it promote the prosperity of company? As the company was in liquidation, such a payment could no longer be justified as being in the interest of the company. Similarly, redundancy payments were successfully challenged by a shareholder as no longer for the benefit of the company as the company had ceased trading.[117] Indeed, it was not until 1970 that the court finally allowed that a gift was intra vires if there was an express object in the memorandum without the need to provide *Lee Behrens* type proof.[118] And it was not until 1983 that the courts allowed corporate gifts to be made absent an express clause.[119]

The economic rationale was clear. Gratuitous payments were declared ultra vires because they reduced profit and diminished shareholder returns, and it was shareholders who challenged these payments.[120] In contrast, if agreements entered into by the company were profitable, but were ultra vires according to the *Ashbury* construction, the courts became increasingly willing to allow them. In *A-G v Great Eastern Railway Co*[121] a contract was held not ultra vires if it was 'reasonably incidental' to the main objects. For a short period thereafter, the courts continued to uphold the 'main objects' rule.[122] However, when that rule hampered profitability, it too was jettisoned. Thus, in *Cotman v Brougham*[123] the House of Lords upheld an objects clause which allowed multi-clauses to be treated as independent clauses rather than ancillary to a main clause. By this time, the courts had ceased to view ultra vires as a way for shareholders to control the actual business, merely to judge their risk; 'the narrower the objects expressed in the memorandum the less is the subscriber's risk'.[124]

These developments in ultra vires show how the company was increasingly seen as an investment vehicle, whose purpose was to generate profit, rather than a productive organisation in which the *kind* of business it engaged in was protected. This was characteristic of a management-controlled company. A company that was no longer a personal or purposeful business, reflecting the skills, inclinations or moral position of the owners.

Thus, it would have been expected that the payment in *Evan v Brunner* would be declared ultra vires and void. Perhaps to be seen as a misguided attempt to express the family's philanthropy through a legal vehicle, the company, which was designed to deliver shareholder value and not the personal interests of the owners. And yet the court decided against the plaintiff's suit, declaring the

[117] *Parke v Daily News* [1962] Ch 927.
[118] *Charterbridge Corp Ltd v Lloyds Bank Ltd* [1970] Ch 62, also followed in *Re Halt Garage* (1982) 3 All ER 1016 and *Re Horsley and Weight Ltd* (1982) Ch 442.
[119] *Simmonds v Heffer* (1983) BCLC 298 provided they were incidental to the company's purpose.
[120] Or creditors for companies in liquidation.
[121] *AG v Great Eastern Railway Co* (1880) 5 App Cas 473.
[122] *Re German Date Coffee* (1882) 20 Ch D 169.
[123] *Cotman v Brougham* [1918] AC 514.
[124] ibid 520.

payment to be ancillary, incidental and conducive to the main or paramount purpose for which the company was formed, because it was,

> to encourage and assist men who will cultivate the scientific attitude of mind, and be prepared to devote their time and abilities to scientific study and research generally. According to the evidence that is the class of men for whom the company is constantly looking out, a class of men of which the supply is very inadequate.[125]

Encouraging scientific study, at least for men, was not too remote a benefit for a chemical company, notwithstanding that the benefit may be enjoyed by different and rival businesses. Indeed, the question of whether it was for the company's benefit or too remote, the generalised approach of the common law, was secondary to the question, particularised to the company of whether it was intra vires the constitution. And, because the *board* believed the payment to be intra vires – evidence by an affidavit by Roscoe Brunner – it was intra vires.[126] Thus not only were 'cakes and ale' provided without the need to show benefit to the company, but an assessment of the intra vires nature of the payment was a matter for the subjective view of management (who claimed benefit to the company). The courts declined to take the objective view evident in previous and subsequent cases in which ultra vires reflected the emerging view of the company as a capital enhancing entity able to take on most contracts provided they were potentially profitable, which generally excluded donations and other gratuitous payments.

The company conformed to many of the attributes of a management company, as noted in section one, with attendant depersonalised pursuit of shareholder value – it had 23,713 members but only 89 voted on the disputed resolution, indicating huge shareholder passivity. Yet, the court treated Brunner, Mond & Co Ltd as an owner-controlled company in which the personal views of the principal owners were the views of the company. Brunner, Mond & Co Ltd continued to be an extension of the personal views of the Brunner and Mond family, long since committed to the philanthropic support of science, art and education, and the court treated it as such.[127]

IV. CONCLUSION AND AFTERNOTE

For most of its existence, the company Brunner, Mond & Co Ltd was the expression of the views and skills of its two founding members. Mond's education,

[125] *Evans v Brunner* (1921) Ch 359.

[126] The affidavit stated that the company occupied a leading position in the chemical manufacturing industry throughout the world, and that the development of that industry depended increasingly upon the advance of pure science. The company's greatest difficulty was to find men sufficiently equipped by their previous studies to undertake research work' *Evans* (1921) Ch 359 at 368.

[127] This case can also be read through the lens of class bias. The judge seemed content to allow considerable funding for an Oxbridge College, in contrast to the no cakes and ale approach of previous gift cases. It also indicates the prevailing view of women, who have no role in science and the intellectual progress of society. Only men of science are required.

innovative boldness, transnational cosmopolitanism, humanist sympathies and response to prejudice met Brunner's philanthropism and social conscience. These dispositions were operationalised together, separately and through the company. The shaping of the company in their own image was so profound that it transcended the massive growth in ownership and internationalisation of its operations. This is evident in the case of *Evans v Brunner*. While many companies became impersonal organisations for the expansion of capital, an economic reality reflected in the development of company law doctrines such as ultra vires and gratuitous payment, Brunner, Mond & Co Ltd continued to act philanthropically and the courts upheld the right of the company to continue as a personalised company.

Nonetheless, this was a pivotal moment for the company, and the contradictions of the company's persona with the realities of its economic context could not be maintained. When the case of *Evans* was heard it was just a few years from the machinations of Alfred Mond, son of Ludwig Mond, which would see Roscoe Brummer removed as chairman, and the merger of Brunner, Mond & Co Ltd with three other companies to create the colossus company, the Imperial Chemical Industries (ICI). No less dramatically, it was short years away from the murder/suicide of a broken Roscoe, who killed himself and his wife, Ethel.

After serving as an MP from 1906 under Lloyd George, Alfred Mond was finally voted out in the 1923 election. He had been an unpopular MP, partly for his wealth and attitude but also because of antisemitism.[128] He had opposed the First World War and was in consequence accused of betraying the country as a 'German Jew' in national newspapers.[129] And, when a catastrophic explosion in Brunner Mond's TNT purifying works in London's Dockland killed 73 people, injured 400, and damaged 70,000 homes, there were widely held claims that this was deliberate sabotage by Mond, and that the works were 'a nest of German agents'.[130] Less catastrophic but perhaps more damaging for Mond was that at the beginning of the war the Mond Nickel Company[131] distributed 300 preference shares (1 per cent of total) to German relatives, in breach of the Trading with the Enemy Act 1914.[132] Notices were placed around London claiming that 'Sir Alfred Mond is a traitor; he allotted shares to Huns during the war.'[133]

After losing his seat, Alfred henceforth turned his ambitions to Brunner, Mond & Co Ltd. He had long resented the company's domination by the 'Brunner side', John and Roscoe, after his father's death in 1909 and had earlier insisted the Mond family be represented on the board by his cousin Emile Mond.

[128] Bevan (n 82).
[129] ibid 351.
[130] ibid 365. An official enquiry concluded it was an accident.
[131] In 1884, Ludwig Mond set up the Mond Nickel Company for the recovery of nickel through a new process he had developed.
[132] Bevan (n 82) 319 (Kindle).
[133] ibid.

Later, Alfred Mond took advantage from the fall out of a costly legal dispute between Lever Bros and Brunner, Mond & Co Ltd over a promise to supply alkali at a cheap rate, a key raw material for the production of soap which was almost entirely controlled by Brunner, Mond & Co. Ltd. Roscoe denied the agreement which was evidently made by the junior director James Gold without the knowledge of senior management. The ensuing dispute cost the company £1 million. This scandal and Roscoe's resulting illness over this year, took him away from the business and Alfred Mond replaced him on a supposedly temporary basis. Roscoe returned to work in January 1926 but then abruptly resigned in March having been persuaded by Mond to take a different role in a new multinational business made up of the company's interests in America and a German partner. Mond announced his departure in a brief statement at the company meeting as thus, 'Mr Roscoe Brunner has unfortunately been feeling for some time the strain of the responsibilities of the position he has occupied for a considerable time, and I understand he intends taking a well- deserved vacation.'[134] Mond meanwhile agreed a merger with Harry McGowan MD of Nobel Industries Ltd, to include Brunner, Mond & Co., United AlkaliCo., Nobel Industries and the British Dyestuffs Corporation. Mond and McGowan agreed to be Chairman and MD of a new company Imperial Chemical Industries (ICI), with the major shareholders of the merging companies to serve on the board. Pointedly, and unexpectedly, Roscoe was excluded. After over 28 years working for the company as his father moved into politics, he was removed without ceremony. Six months later, Roscoe Mond and his wife Edith[135] were found shot at their home.[136] As the modern argot goes, no other person was involved. ICI become the management company par excellence. It resulted in the death of the personal and of persons. But that's business. It's not personal.

[134] Anon, 'Company Meeting. Brunner, Mond &Co. LTD', *The Manchester Guardian* 15 May 1926, 10.

[135] While a politician Brunner (snr) established a friendship with Arthur Houston through whom Roscoe met and married Houston's daughter Ethel.

[136] Anon, 'Death of Sir John Brunner: Career of Great Industrialist' *The Manchester Guardian* 17 January 1929, 3. It was first reported as a poisoning.

10

The Corporate Share: From Membership to Financial Interest to Contractual Design

RON HARRIS[1]

THIS CHAPTER SURVEYS the history of corporate shares. It shows that the attributes we identify today as fundamental to every corporate share were not in place from the start and are not inevitable, intrinsic, or essential. Each of these attributes was formed through a centuries-long, non-linear process. The chapter follows the creation of the key attributes that were attached to the corporate share and their alternation from their origins to their current form. These attributes include transferability, voting rights, liability of shareholders to corporate creditors, priorities of shares in insolvency, dividend rights, the possibility to create more than one class of share, and who could own shares (only natural humans or also corporations). The concluding part of the chapter will offer a preliminary overall proposition with respect to the overall periodisation and causation of the development of the various attributes of the corporate share.

Table 10.1 Attributes of Corporate Shares

Playing with:	
Transferability	Could shares be transferred from one investor to another? Like real or personal property?
Voting Rights	Who could vote? Were voting rights correlated with money invested?
Liability	Unlimited liability, pro-rata liability, partly paid shares, double and triple liability, reserved liability, full limited liability.

(continued)

[1] I would like to thank Naomi Lamoreaux for comments and for sharing with me sources on general legislation and chartering in the US, the organisers of the York conference and editors of this volume Victoria Barnes and Jonny Hardman on useful suggestions that improved this chapter,

Table 10.1 *(Continued)*

Priority in Insolvency and Liability	Equity (bonds) > Preferred Shares > Shares.
Dividends	Preferred Shares Vs. Common Shares.
Classes of Shares	Founders' shares, management shares / class 'A' and 'B' shares.
Share Ownership	Only natural humans or could legal entities such as companies own shares?

The chapter focuses on Britain with an excursion to the US, and on the period between 1600 and the early twentieth century. It offers a periodisation of this history and aims at suggesting an initial causal explanation for the history of the development of share attributes.

Corporate shares were not born with the corporation. In the first few centuries of their history, corporations had members and not shareholders. Members of corporations were termed 'brethren', 'fellows', 'at freedom' or 'at liberty'.[2] Different names were used in universities, municipal corporations, guilds, livery corporations, and regulated corporations. The concept of corporate shares was conceived for the first time with the creation of the first joint-stock corporations.

The formation of the first joint-stock companies, the Russia Company (1553), Levant Company (1581), English East India Company – EIC (1600), and Dutch East India Company – VOC (1602) challenged the understanding that corporations were associations whose base was membership.[3] Let's take the prime example, the EIC. Its 1600 charter of foundation, listed its members by name, defining 'every one above-named to be of the said Company fellowship as all others hereafter to be admitted, or free of the said Company' as the members of the company. Its governance structure was based on general meetings of all its members in which each member had one vote.[4] The charter did not refer at all to the fact that the company raised joint stock equity and intended to distribute its profits based on investment. Soon a dissonance was created between the charter that was based on the same template as those of previous guilds and regulated corporations and the financial reality of the EIC. In reality, the company invited

Dor Mana, Alona Gueta, Bruria Friedman and Tal Yakobi for the excellent research assistance, and the ISF for Grant 1427/22 that funded this research.

[2] Lord Leycester Hospital had 'Master' and 'Bredren', University College Oxford 'Master' and 'Fellows', the Draper Company, one of London's livery companies had 'Master', 'Wardens', 'Brethren' and 'Sisters', the Corporation of the City of London had 'Lord Mayor', 'Alderman' and 'Freeman', the Spanish Company 'President, Assistants' and 'Fellowship of Merchants'.

[3] For the history of the first two joint-stock companies, whose joint-stock phase was short, before they reverted to the conventional regulated company model see: AC Wood, *A history of the Levant Company* (Oxford, Oxford University Press, 1935); TS Willan, *The early history of the Russia Company, 1553–1603* (Manchester, Manchester University Press, 1956).

[4] East India Company and J Shaw, *Charters Relating to the East India Company from 1600 to 1761* (Madras, Government Press, 1887); East India Company, *Charters Granted to the East-India Company from 1601* (London, 1774).

investments from the public to fund its voyages to Asia and opened subscription books. Different individuals subscribed to invest different sums of money in the EIC under the assumption they would receive a share in the future profits of the company in proportion to their investment. The subscribers/investors were called 'adventurers' rather than 'members'. As we can see in Table 10.1, a discrepancy was soon evident between the number and identity of members of the EIC named in the charters, and the number and identity of the shareholders reflected in the subscription books.[5]

Table 10.2 Number of Members/Investors in East India Company, 1599–1609[6]

List of Members	Year	Number of Members/Adventurers
1st Meeting	1599	132
1st Charter	1600	218
Subscription to 1st Voyage	1601	232
Subscription to 3rd Voyage	1607	208
Subscription to 4th Voyage	1608	56
2nd Charter	1609	275

I. TRANSFERABILITY

Two sets of questions arose from this discrepancy. The first, could those who invested transfer their interest in the company to another investor, be it a member, a shareholder, or a newcomer? Second, and the most direct problem: who could vote? Only members, also shareholders, what about members who did not invest or stopped investing? Also, would voting rights take into account the sum invested or be based on membership alone? The first question will be discussed in this section and the second and third in the next section.

Initially investments in the EIC were recorded in subscription books and in the company's register according to names of investors and their respective money investment in the company. Initially the possibility that the interest of

[5] Names were taken from lists recorded in two types of sources: Royal Charters and EIC Court minutes. Lists are available for six points in time: those present at the first official meeting (22 September 1599), the list of names in the first Charter (31 December 1600), the list of adventurers in the first voyage (21 March 1601) and the amounts they subscribed for, the list of adventurers in the third voyage (1607) and the amounts they subscribed for, the list of adventurers in the fourth voyage (1608) and the amounts they subscribed for, and the list of names on the second Charter (31 May 1609). No lists of adventurers survived for any of the other nine voyages. For more about the sources and their analysis See: R Harris, 'The Formation of the East India Company as a Cooperation-Enhancing Institution' (2005) ssrn.com/abstract=874406; R Harris, *Going the Distance: Eurasian Trade and the Rise of the Business Corporation, 1400–1700* (Princeton NJ, Princeton University Press, 2020) chs 9–11.

[6] Based on R Harris, *Going the Distance: Eurasian Trade and the Rise of the Business Corporation, 1400–1700*, (Princeton NJ, Princeton University Press, 2020) 298.

one person would be sold and transferred to another was not envisioned.[7] Soon a secondary market in which interests were sold and transferred emerged as an exit option for the original investors.[8] Once interest was sold, the new holder of interest was recorded in the EIC register.[9] The mandatory approval by the directors of the company for such a transfer soon became symbolic. The interest in the joint-stock of the company was termed 'several parts', 'proportions', 'interests' and eventually 'shares'. In the next stage, the company issued certificates to the investors indicating the sum of their investment. These were the first share certificates. Next arose the question of whether these certificates were analogous to bills of exchange. Were they classified legally as an obligation or chattel? The actual transactions in share certificates had to be classified legally. Could they be endorsed and freely transferred? Once they were, the corporate share was born.

The process of legalising share transfer was better recorded with respect to the VOC than the EIC. VOC directors promulgated a rule that regulated how investors could ascertain and convey share ownership in the subscription book.[10] Title to a share could be transferred by means of official registration. This procedure was similar to the procedure for transferring immovable goods such as real estate, meaning that the law initially classified shares as immovable property. *Van Balck v Rotgans* (1622) marks an important step in clarifying the rules for ownership of a share. The Court confirmed the legal status of transfers in the stock registers. The lawsuit of *Adriaen van der Heijden and Daniel van Genegen v Abraham Abelijn* (1614) shows that the VOC ceased to be a party to share transfers. Shares could be simply endorsed from seller to buyer and the endorsement transferred the rights in the shares. Property rights in shares were

[7] When Edward Coke discussed corporations, not long after the formation of the EIC he still did not refer to joint-stock or shares or their transferability. See: E Coke, *The First Part of the Institutes of the Laws of England, Or, A Commentary Upon Littleton in 1628* (London, 1832) ch XIII; Interestingly William Blackstone who compiled his Commentaries on the Laws of England 140 years later, while devoting a full chapter, ch 18, to corporations he did not refer to joint-stock or to the status and transferability of shares. See: W Blackstone, *Commentaries on the Laws of England: Book the Second*, Vol 1 (Oxford, Clarendon Press, 1765) ch18; The first legal treaties devoted to corporations, referred to stock only in bypassing, offering no analytical discussion of its legal status. See: S Kyd, *A treatise on the law of corporations* (London, Butterworths, 1793).

[8] R Harris, 'The Formation of the East India Company as a Deal between Entrepreneurs and Outside Investors' (2004) papers.ssrn.com/sol3/papers.cfm?abstract_id=567941; Harris, 'Cooperation-Enhancing Institution'(n 5); O Gelderblom and J Jonker, 'Completing a Financial Revolution: The Finance of the Dutch East India Trade and the Rise of the Amsterdam Capital Market, 1595–1612' (2004) 64(3) *The Journal of Economic History* 641, 641–72; O Gelderblom et al, 'The Formative Years of the Modern Corporation: The Dutch East India Company VOC, 1602–1623' (2013) 73(4) *The Journal of Economic History* 1050, 1050–76.

[9] East India Company, *The Dawn of British Trade to the East Indies as Recorded in the Court Minutes of the East India Company, 1599–1603* (London, 1886); East India Company, *The Register of Letters of the Governor and Company of Merchants of London Trading into the East Indies 1600–1619* (London, 1893).

[10] E Gepken-Jager, et al, *VOC 1602–2002: 400 Years of Company Law* (Alphen aan den Rijn, Kluwer Legal Publishers, 2005) 17–38: Dutch transcript 17–28, English translation 29–38. FS Gaastra, 'The Organization of The VOC' in L Balk et al (eds), *The Archives of the Dutch East India Company (VOC) and the Local Institutions in Batavia (Jakarta)* (Leiden, Brill, 2007).

now clearly defined, and a legal certainty with respect to how to perform share transactions in the secondary market reduced the chance of disputes and court litigation.[11]

In some respects, such as intergenerational transfer, the nature of shares as real or personal, had to be determined in order to define inheritance modes. Shares are confusing. They reflect interest in corporations whose property consisted of both tangible and intangible assets, in legalese real and personal property, in different blends. An early view of the character of shares held by a shareholder in a joint stock company's property is that the company held the property in trust for the shareholders as beneficiaries (the company has the legal estate and the shareholders the equitable interest in the land).[12] This is a non-trivial legal construction given the fact that the corporation had a legal entity separated from that of the shareholders and that legal entity owns the corporate assets. The notion that shareholders have a direct legal relationship with the corporate assets is also reflected in the English word 'share' that alludes to assets that are somehow shared among the shareholders. Could shareholders hold common law property rights in the shares and at the same time equitable rights as beneficiaries in the corporate assets?

The judicial discussion on the classification of shares as real or personal property focuses on land-dominated corporations, specifically water supply companies, and more specifically the New River Company that supplied water to parts of London. This company had a unique shareholding structure called moiety (division into parts) that resembles part-ownership in property such as ships.[13] The question was extended in the 1760s to shares in Canal Companies, whose major property was real estate but whose financial structure was joint-stock, and not part-ownership like the New River. In all cases reviewed, most of which took place in the 1700s, it was concluded that shares in such companies represented fractions in real property.[14] In order to overcome the complications that result from this classification, with the progression into the canal era, a standard clause was included in most canal incorporation acts, and the incorporation acts of bridges, water supply and other utility companies. It read: 'All

[11] L O Petram, *The World's First Stock Exchange: How the Amsterdam Market for Dutch East India Company Shares Became a Modern Securities Market, 1602–1700* (New York, Columbia Business School Publishing, 2011).

[12] For a survey of eighteenth and nineteenth century cases and the confusion reflected in them, see: P Ireland, 'Capitalism without the capitalist: The joint stock company share and the emergence of the modern doctrine of separate corporate personality' (1996) 17(1) *The Journal of Legal History*, 41, 41–73.

[13] J Williams, *Principles of the Law of Personal Property* (Philadelphia, 1872) 210; C Stebbings, 'The Legal Nature of Shares in Landowning Joint Stock Companies in the Nineteenth Century' (1987) 8(1) *The Journal of Legal History* 25, 25–35; B Rudden, *The New River: A Legal History* (Oxford, Oxford University Press, 1985) 50. R Harris, *Industrializing English Law: Entrepreneurship and Business Organization, 1720–1844* (Cambridge, Cambridge University Press, 2000).

[14] *Drybutter v Bartholemew* [1723] 2 P WMS 127, 24 ER 668; *Townsend v Ash* [1745] 3 ATK 336, 26 ER 995; *Lord Sandys v Sibthorpe* [1778] Dickens 545, 21 ER 382; *Buckeridge v Ingram* [1795] 2 Ves Jun 652, 30 ER 824; *Howse v Chapman* [1799] 4 Ves Jun 542, 30 ER 824.

Shares in the Undertaking shall be Personal Estate, and transmissible as such, and shall not be of the Nature of Real Estate.'[15]

In the US the situation was more varied due to the multitude of jurisdictions. In New Jersey the act that incorporated the Washington Canal Company in 1822 included the following clause: 'And be it enacted, That the shares or stock in said canal shall be taken, deemed and considered personal property and be transferred in such manner as the directors may appoint.'[16] On the other hand, in Massachusetts textile companies, such as the Finsburg Cotton Manufactory had old style clauses 'any share may be alienated by the proprietor thereof … by deed under the hand and seal acknowledged in a book kept for that purpose … be entitled to a new certificate … certifying the property in such share …'.[17] Despite the fact that this Massachusetts textile company was not as real estate dominated as the New Jersey canal company, transfer of shares in it required a deed, and the transfer was constituted by recording in a book and issuing certificate by the company, much like in seventeenth-century companies.

The issue of the nature of the share was finally settled in the general incorporation acts. While the very first act of 1844 did not refer to the legal nature of shares, the Companies Act of 1856 was the first to define shares as personal estate, and the 1862 Act reiterated the classification and made transferability of shares purely contractual: 'The Shares or other Interest of any Member in a Company under this Act shall be Personal Estate, capable of being transferred in manner provided by the Regulations of the Company.' This settled, once and for all, an issue that vexed jurists for nearly 300 years.

In New York State the issue was settled earlier with its, and in fact the world's, very first general incorporation act, that applied only to manufacturing companies, and was passed as early as 1811: 'And be it further enacted, That the stock of such company shall be deemed personal estate, and be transferable in such manner as shall be prescribed by the laws of the company.'[18]

II. VOTING RIGHTS

How was the tension between the original membership-based voting paradigm and modern investment-based voting paradigm reconciled? The answer in short is that the route was long. I'll follow the first part of this route through the history of voting rights in the EIC. The first and second charters

[15] *The Vauxhall Bridge Company* [1821] 1 G & J 101; *The Lancaster Canal Company* [1832] Mont & Bl 94; *Bligh v Brent* [1837] 2 Y & C Ex 268, 160 ER 397.

[16] State of New Jersey, An act to incorporate the Washington Canal Company [1822].

[17] Laws of the Commonwealth of Massachusetts, c. 33 An act to incorporate Peter Snow and others, by the name of the Fitchburg Cotton Manufactory Corporation [1807].

[18] The Act relative to incorporations for manufacturing purposes passed by the 34th New York State Legislature on 22 March 1811. See: Laws of the State of New-York, c. 67 An act relative to incorporations for manufacturing purposes.

(1600 and 1609) followed the traditional corporate pattern of one member one vote. In the 1661 Charter the idea that membership, shareholding and voting rights can be separated, first appeared, and a voting scheme was set. In this Charter, 500 shares were equated to one voting right. Shareholders with more than 500 shares, could have several votes – one per every 500 shares, while shareholders with less than 500 could pool together their shares to obtain the option of a communal vote.[19] In the 1693 Charter a new voting scheme was introduced; a shareholder received one vote for every 1,000 shares, and up to 10 votes. A shareholder with less than 100 shares could not vote.[20] The 1698 Charter introduced for the first time a scaled voting scheme: one vote for holders of £500 shares, two votes for holders of £1,000, three votes for holders of £2,000, four votes for holders of £3,000 and five votes for holders of any amount over £4,000.[21] In 1773 the voting rights were set for the first time by parliamentary legislation, the East India Regulating Act rather than via charter. This legislation raised the minimum qualification to vote in the Court of Proprietors from £500 to £1,000. Also, shareholders with £3,000 received two votes, with £4,000 had three votes, and those with £10,000 or more received four votes.[22] Allegedly, in the specific case of the EIC this was done in order to empower directors and shift power from shareholders towards the British Government. Between 1661 and 1773 the EIC experimented with various schemes of non-linear, graduated or capped voting rights. Many of the companies that were formed during this period, beyond EIC, by charters or private acts of parliaments, notably canal and utility companies, had graduated (scaled) voting schemes of different variations. Some of the companies had separate schemes for electing directors and for business related decisions.

The first general incorporation act of 1844 in its Schedule A, set the default voting rule: 'where it is not provided that each Shareholder is to have a Vote in respect of each Share, the Appointment of the Number of Votes to be given by Shareholders in respect of any Number of Shares held by them'.[23] The Clause Consolidation Act of 1845, which applied to railways and other companies incorporated by private acts, set a different default:

> Every Shareholder shall be entitled to vote according to the prescribed Scale of voting, and where no Scale shall be prescribed every Shareholder shall have One Vote for every Share up to Ten, and he shall have an additional Vote for every Five Shares beyond the First Ten Shares held by him up to One hundred, and an additional Vote for every Ten Shares held by him beyond the First Hundred Shares.[24]

[19] East India and Shaw (n 4).
[20] ibid 107.
[21] ibid 122.
[22] B Buchan, 'The East India Company 1749-1800: The Evolution of a Territorial Strategy and The Changing Role of the Directors' (1994) 23(1) *Business and Economics* 52–61.
[23] Joint Stock Companies Act 1844 (7 & 8 Vict c. 110).
[24] Railways Clause Consolidation Act 1845 (8 & 9 Vict).

The 1844 Act offered a default of one vote per one share while the 1845 Act offered a default of scaled voting. The 1862 Companies Act set the following default: 'Every member shall have one vote for every share up to ten: he shall have an additional vote for every five shares beyond the first ten shares up to one hundred, and an additional vote for every ten shares beyond the first hundred shares.'[25] This was the default for the next 45 years until the 1908 Companies Act opted for one share one vote for votes by poll approach (but not show of hands): 'On a show of hands every member present in person shall have one vote. On a poll every member shall have one vote for each share of which he is the holder.'[26]

Those companies that opted out of these defaults wrote into their incorporation documents different and varied schemes. One vote per share was far from being the majority voting approach for nineteenth-century companies:

Table 10.3 Shareholder Voting Rights – Samples of Early US Corporations[27]

	Dunlavy Sample, 1825–35 (*N* = 1233)	New York, 1790–1825 (N = 812)
One vote per share	35	48
Graduated voting rights	27	45
One vote per shareholder	38	2
Not specified	–	5

The idea of one share one vote was anything but natural and obvious throughout the first 300 years of joint-stock companies.

Figure 10.1 Evolution of Shares Structures

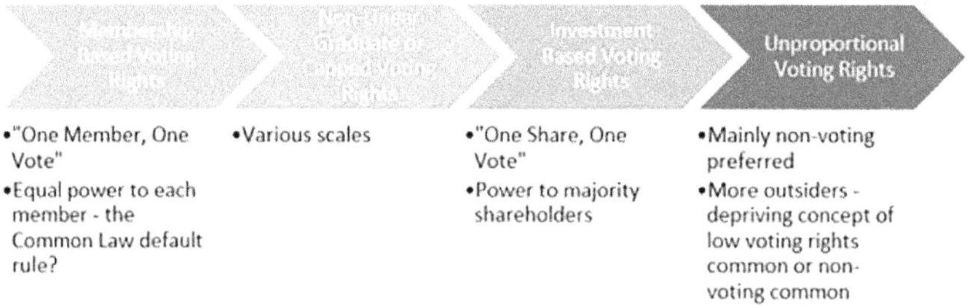

[25] Companies Act 1862 (25 & 26 Vict c. 89).

[26] Companies (Consolidation) Act 1908 (8 Edw. 7 c. 69).

[27] E Hilt, 'Shareholder voting rights in early American Corporations' (2013) 55(4) *Business History Review* 620, 622–623; CA Dunlavy, 'Social Conceptions of the Corporation: Insights from the History of Shareholder Voting Rights' (2006) 63(4) *Washington & Lee Law Review* 1347.

While the convergence from various graduated schemes to one share one vote, was slow to materialise, a new and interesting development began, the use of dual and even multiple types of shares with different voting rights. This development became possible after the transition from the chartering era to the general incorporation and contractual freedom era. In Britain, the 1844 Companies Act stated that the Deed of Settlement should set 'The Division of the Capital (if any) into equal Shares, and the total Number of such Shares' (clause 7). The assumption here is that all shares are going to be equal. The 1856 Limited Liability Companies Act stated that the Memorandum of Association should contain: 'The number of Shares into which such Capital is to be divided; and the amount of each share' (clause 5). This allowed the creation of shares with different nominal par value. The 1908 Companies Act stated that a company authorised to do so by its Memorandum may by Special Resolution alter its shares in various ways. Clause 45 refers explicitly to 'shares of different classes'. This reflects a clear recognition of the possibility of multiple shares in the same company. The enabling acts were followed by the growing creation of dual class companies. Sometimes one class was called 'management shares' or 'founders' shares' and the other 'ordinary shares', maybe as an indication for the motivation behind the share structure, either to extend the capital of the company by allowing differential share payment plans[28] or for the founders to maintain control of the company.[29] Sometimes one class was called 'A Shares' and the other 'B Shares'. Dual class shareholding was first used by companies in Britain in the middle of the nineteenth century. In the US, dual-class shares were first used in the early twentieth century.[30]

In 1926, the New York Stock Exchange started to prohibit the issuance of new non-voting securities.[31] As a result the number of dual stock companies listed on the NYSE declined to only ten in the following 60 years.[32] Interestingly,

[28] The British and African Steam Navigation Company used dual class shares to infuse cash into the company. See PN Davies, *The Trade Makers: Elder Dempster in West Africa 1852–1972* (London, Allen & Unwin, 1973) 56–57.

[29] The Railway Debenture Trust Company is an example for a company using dual class shares to maintain founder control. See E Hutson, 'The Early Managed Fund Industry: Investment Trusts in 19th Century Britain' (2005) 14 *International Review of Financial Analysis* 439.

[30] Some of the first companies to adopt dual class shares were: P&O (1840), Grand Trunk Railway (1853), Suez Canal Company (1858), and The Imperial Ottoman Bank (1864).

[31] See: JW Howell, 'The Survival of the U.S. Dual Class Share Structure' (2017) 44 *Journal on Corporate Finance*, 440, 444–446. Note that a formal prohibition was only announced in 1940. The Congressional Research Service paper explains that in 1940, NYSE adopted a rule that, with few exceptions, barred listed firms from issuing non-voting stock and prohibited superior-voting stock from constituting more than 18.5% of all outstanding common shares. According to various sources, these effectively limited most multi-class NYSE listings.

[32] ibid. An interesting exception brought by Howell is Ford Motor Company. It managed to bypass the prohibition by issuing not a non-vote stock, but an inferior one. The Ford family kept controlling Ford with class B stocks, holding a total of 40% voting power but only 5.1% of the total equity. Howell notes that similar proportional voting structures were used in other firms such as JM Smucker and American Family.

the AMEX and NASDAQ did not prohibit the listing of dual stock but this type of company was not popular in these exchanges in that period.[33] In 1985 the NYSE lifted the prohibition on listing new dual class companies.[34] Dual stock expanded again in the twenty-first century with the rise of super-star entrepreneurs and information companies. The use of dual class in Britain declined from the 1960s due to the expectation of institutional investors that public corporations adopt higher standards of corporate governance with regards to protection of public investors.

III. LIABILITY

The level of liability of shareholders to the debts of the corporation is an important attribute of the corporate share. Interestingly, as I have argued in a recent article, the history of the liability attribute should be divided into three periods.[35] In the first period, from the appearance of the first joint stock corporation to the early nineteenth century, the liability attribute could not be separated from legal entity attribute. In the second period, from the early nineteenth century to the early twentieth century, this attribute developed into a dimension with a variety of liability regimes. Only in the third period, the twentieth century, a convergence from a variety of liability regimes to limited liability in the modern sense, which means no liability, occurred.

The early semi-public corporations, municipalities, guilds, universities, and hospitals were member corporations, having no joint-stock and no significant debt finance. In those cases, shareholders' liability was irrelevant. The early joint-stock business corporations, such as the EIC and other chartered trading corporations, relied on equity finance and used credit only on the margins and on a short-term basis, such as trade credit, credit from suppliers or wage owed to employees. They were not leveraged in any way. They could lose money, potentially the entire investment made by the shareholders but could not go bankrupt while owing money to creditors. The question whether the creditors can collect their debts from the shareholders could not even become relevant. Corporate creditors had to collect from the corporation and not from the shareholders because the corporation was a legal entity separated by law from its shareholders. The company and not the shareholders owed money. The separate legal entity of the corporation, and not a limited liability attribute, created asset partitioning between the corporate assets and the shareholders' personal assets.

[33] ibid. By 1985, Seligman estimated that about 7% of AMEC firms, and more than 2.5% of NASDAQ firms were dual class.

[34] J Seligman, 'Equal Protection in Shareholder Voting Rights: The One Common Share, One Vote Controversy' (1986) 54 *George Washington Law Review*, 687, 694, 700.

[35] R Harris, 'A New Understanding of the History of Limited Liability: An Invitation for Theoretical Reframing' (2020) 16(5) *Journal of Institutional* Economics, 643, 643–664.

The legal entity created what Hansmann and Kraakman term entity shielding and shareholder shielding.[36]

The decoupling of limited liability from legal entity and its distinction as a separate attribute with a spectrum of liability regimes took place around 1800. It resulted from a few causes. The most fundamental is the increased use of debt finance as a long-term tool for financing corporations whose main aim was to construct a large lump-sum project in either the transportation or utility sectors. The mixture of significant debt finance with equity finance created, for the first time, a major conflict of interest between shareholders and bondholders in the same corporation. Other factors that drove the liability of shareholders to the forefront were: the experience gained by the design of unincorporated and thus unlimited companies, the drafting of a growing number of incorporation acts in the canal era and with other utilities all leading up to the railway era, the drafting of general incorporation acts (1837, 1844, 1856, 1862), and the creation of a mechanism for winding-up insolvent corporations.

All these developments taken together gave rise to the discussion on the extent of shareholder liability to corporate debts in case of insolvency. The unincorporated company demonstrated the possibility of forming joint-stock enterprises whose shareholders were liable for their debts, like in partnerships. The drafting of specific and general incorporation acts forced the drafters to explicitly address the issue of shareholder liability in one way or another. The shift from incorporation by the state to general incorporation gave rise to the question, which was muted in the chartering era, how would corporations be dissolved? And once the legal entity dissolved, could the creditors collect from shareholders?

Shareholder liability kicked in only upon dissolution. During the life of the corporation, corporate debt was owed only by the corporate legal entity and corporate creditors could not collect from shareholders. But in dissolution a whole new dimension of liability regimes opened-up. Some companies were incorporated with unlimited shareholders' liability, namely that each shareholder was liable at dissolution to all corporate debt. Some were incorporated with a pro-rata shareholders' liability, which means that each shareholder was liable to debt in proportion to their stake in the total share capital. Others were incorporated with double or triple liability, which meant that each shareholder was personally liable at dissolution to debts two or three times the par value of their shares. While another group was incorporated with limited liability, which meant that shareholders were not liable to corporate debts beyond their committed investment. For the banking sector, due to its unique financial structure, having significant debt to customers-depositors and because of a high leverage ratio, the liability regime was of paramount importance. From the table below

[36] H Hansmann and R Kraakman, 'Toward Unlimited Shareholder Liability for Corporate Torts' (1990) 100 *Yale Law Journal* 1879.

one can see that while unlimited liability disappeared in the UK between 1849 and 1889, reserve liability banks were more common even in 1889 than fully limited liability banks.

Table 10.4 Liability Regimes in UK Joint-Stock Banking, 1849–1889[37]

Region	Type of Liability Regime	1849	1869	1889
England & Wales	Chartered	1	1	1
	Unlimited Liability	113	73	2
	Limited Liability	0	41	40
	Reserve Liability	0	0	62
Scotland	Chartered	3	3	3
	Unlimited Liability	18	9	0
	Limited Liability	0	0	0
	Reserve Liability	0	0	7
Ireland	Chartered	1	1	1
	Unlimited Liability	10	7	0
	Limited Liability	0	1	0
	Reserve Liability	0	0	8
UK Total	Chartered	5	5	5
	Unlimited Liability	141	81	2
	Limited Liability	0	42	40
	Reserve Liability	0	0	77

The committed investment was the nominal capital of the shares they subscribed for. However, the common practice in most nineteenth-century companies was that the nominal capital was not fully paid upon the allocation of shares. It was often the case, particularly with project-based companies (canals, railways, gas, water supply, etc) that the capital was called in instalments as the construction of the project progressed. The initial call was often no more than 5 or 10 per cent of the nominal value of the share. In dissolution the uncalled capital could be called by the liquidator of the corporation in order to pay corporate debts to its creditors. Shareholders were liable to debts up until the nominal capital of their shares. In some companies uncalled capital was designed as reserve capital, for the protection of corporate creditors.

The common wisdom, that views the Limited Liability Act of 1855 as a watershed, before which shareholders were liable to debts and after which

[37] Based on G Acheson et al, 'Does Limited Liability Matter? Evidence from Nineteenth-Century British Banking' (2010) 6(2) *Review of Law and Economics* 250.

they were not liable to debts, is mistaken for two reasons. First, because it only enabled but did not impose and did not even set full liability as a default rule. The 1862 Companies Act that incorporate the 1855 Act into the general law stated:

> The Liability of the Members of a Company formed under this Act may, according to the Memorandum of Association, be limited either to the amount, if any, unpaid on the Shares respectively held by them, *or to such amount as the Members may respectively undertake by the Memorandum of Association to contribute* to the Assets of the Company in the event of its being wound up.[38]

The 1862 Act did not set a default rule. Liability had to be drafted by the incorporators into the Memorandum. This enabled the incorporators to design the desired level of liability by determining the level of nominal capital and varying the percentage of that capital that was actually paid up. This drafting also opened the way for the use of reserve liability, to which we will turn later. The Act did not mandate or encourage though default rule a specific shareholders' liability regime. As we have seen above, most companies did not in fact converge over a full liability regime until the early twentieth century, and when they did this, it was not because of legislation.

Second, because the default rule was not no shareholder liability, but rather liability that was limited by the nominal capital and not by the paid-up capital. In most companies the shares were not fully paid and thus in insolvency and dissolution they were liable for the balance. In the late nineteenth century, the issuance of fully paid shares, whose shareholders paid the nominal par value of the shares upon issuance, became common both in Britain and the US. In 1912, after long debates, New York State legislated an act that permitted the issuance of shares with no par value. Many other states took similar steps over the next decade. The issuance of shares with no par value became a widespread practice after the turn of the twentieth century. Such shares had no unpaid balance and as a result shareholders in them bore no liability to corporate debt. Another confusion resulted from a wrong reading of the canonical *Salomon v Salomon* case decided by the House of Lords in 1897.[39] Some jurists understand the case to declare basic principles of separate legal personality and limited liability. In fact the case dealt with a case that was still exceptional at the time, a company created by a single shareholder accompanied by six nominal shareholders. It was held that such a company was legal based on the Companies Act of 1862. It was further decided that the same person can be at the same time a shareholder of a company and its creditor.[40] The Salomon case did not legalise the concept of full limited liability and did not lead to its spreading.

[38] Companies Act 1862 (25 & 26 Vict c 89, sec 7).

[39] *Salomon v Salomon & Co Ltd* [1897] AC 22.

[40] R Harris, 'The private origins of the private company: Britain 1862–1907' (2013) 33(2) *OJLS* 339–378.

In the first 200 years of the history of the joint-stock businesses, the attribute of liability of shareholders was not yet formed. The pre-conditions for its formation did not exist. Those who believe that this attribute was there from the start mistook some of the effects of separate legal entity to limited liability. After 1800, the preconditions for its existence gradually emerged one-by-one. The emergence of shareholders' liability as an identified attribute created a full spectrum of liability regimes from unlimited liability through various regimes of pro-rata liability, partly paid shares, double and triple liability, and reserved liability, to full limited liability. Only in the early twentieth century was there a convergence to a single liability regime of full limited liability, which in fact meant no liability beyond the initial investment of the original shareholders.

IV. DIVIDENDS

The development of preferred shares is built upon the development of the shareholder voting rights attribute and the shareholders' liability attribute. Initially preferred stock was used in order to vary the income generated by the stock, from common stock on the one hand, and bonds on the other, usually bearing fixed interest for a few years and then having a share in the distributed profits. Later in its development, preferred stocks were also used to vary priority in bankruptcy. Preferred stock, in some companies, had higher priority than common stock but had lower priority than bonds. The development of preferred shares blurred the distinction between shares and bonds.

Figure 10.2 Creditors Priority in Bankruptcy

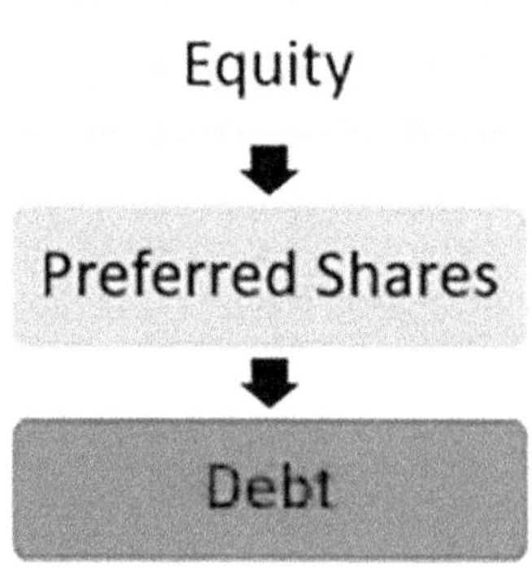

Preferred shares were first used on a small scale in the eighteenth century in canals and were widely used in the nineteenth century in railways. Preferred stock could initially be created by incorporation acts (canal and railway incorporation acts). After the enactment of general incorporation in the middle of the nineteenth century they could be designed contractually in the corporate memorandum and articles (charter and bylaws in the US). They were tailored specifically to the needs of different companies. Preferred shares were used in order to raise additional funding for the completion of the railway projects. Typically, the original capital was raised in return for common shares. Once it was understood that the costs of the project would be higher than originally estimated, and additional investment was needed, the second round of investment had to offer different terms. One of the early examples for the use of preferred shares is the Aberdeenshire Canal. In 1801, six years after its incorporation, the company ran out of money before the completion of the canal, and it turned again to Parliament which authorised the issue of preference shares:

> And they are hereby authorized and empowered to raise the paid sum of twenty thousand pound, or so much thereof as shall be necessary for completing the paid navigation, by creating new or additional shares of twenty pounds pre share; and that the respective proprietors of any share or shares which ... may be created by virtue of this act, *shall be entitled to receive an annual dividend of twenty shillings pre share, should the tolls of the canal produce so much, before the proprietors of the original shares be entitled to any interest or dividend*; but ... whenever the dividends shall amount to twenty shillings per share on the new shares, the remainder shall be divided among the proprietors of the original shares until they receive an annual interest or dividend of fifty shillings per share; and after the above mentioned payments of twenty shillings and fifty shillings for each share respectively, the remaining net profits arising from the canal shall be divided share and share alike among the proprietors both of the old and new shares.[41]

These terms were packaged in what came to be known as preferred stock, a financial instrument between equity and debt. In the railway era the use of preferred stock expanded considerably. The resort to preferred stock was often done because of statutory restriction on the level of borrowing permitted to companies. As can be seen from the table below by the late 1850s, 18 per cent of the financing for British railway companies was done through preferred stock.

[41] An act for better enabling the company of proprietors of the Aberdeenshire canal navigation to complete the fame (41 Geo 3 ciii, s 2). Emphasis added.

Table 10.5 Funds Raised by Railways[42]

Year	Total paid-up shares and loan capital £	Ordinary Shares paid-up capital %	Preferred Shares paid-up capital %	Debt capital %
1849	229,747,778	69	9	22
1850	240,270,745	63	14	23
1851	264,165,672	62	14	24
1852	273,324,672	61	15	24
1853	273,324,514	60	16	24
1854	286,068,794	58	17	25
1855	297,583,284	57	18	25
1856	308,775,894	57	18	25
1857	315,989,826	57	18	25

The first use of preferred stock in the US was in the context of canal and railway bailout. The State of Maryland was willing to invest in lines that failed to complete only through preferred stock and not through regular loans or grants. These lines included the Baltimore and Ohio Railroad Co., Chesapeake and Ohio Canal Co., Eastern Shore Railroad Co., Maryland Canal Co., and Annapolis and Potomac Canal Co.[43] The preferred stock in these companies was entitled to a fixed 6 per cent return (like interest on bonds) in preference over the common shares right for dividends. Variations between companies existed in the detail. In some, the preferred stock participated in the distribution of the profits. It was then entitled to a share in the profits through dividends and as much as above 6 per cent would be distributed (like a dividend on common stock). In others, the fixed return continued even once the company became profitable. In all companies the preferred stock was entitled to vote like common stock. In some companies the state required in addition the right to appoint a director that would protect its interest. By the 1840s the use of preferred stock expanded from state investors to private investors.

In the middle of the nineteenth century, both in Britain and the US, preferred stock was seen as a short-term emergency solution for railway projects in crisis. It offered fixed returns on investment until the completion and maturation of the project, and once this was reached, the return on preferred and common stock would be equated. For this reason, preferred stock was initially granted voting rights equal to those of common stock. Howell, in his research, reviews the early

[42] Based on GH Evans, *British Corporation Finance, 1775–1850: A Study of Preference Shares* (Baltimore, John Hopkins Press, 1936) 82–83.

[43] GH Evans, 'The Early History of Preferred Stock in the United States' (1929) 19(1) *The American Economic Review* 43–58; GH Evans, 'Preferred Stock in the United States 1850–1878' (1931) *The American Economic Review* 56–62.

history (1898–1926) of the dual-class structure in the US, and concludes that until 1898 voting rights were bundled with the cash flow, meaning, both common and preferred stock were given full voting rights.[44] In Britain, the playing with voting rights began earlier than in the US where the questions of voting rights and variations in voting rights of preferred shares, non-voting, limited voting and full voting, became common practice only later on. Two earlier examples in Britain are from the telegraph sector and from managing agencies. In both of these sectors a small group of entrepreneurs wished to raise capital from the public through prospectuses while retaining their own control. For example, the project that aimed at connecting India with Britain created a series of companies in the 1860s and 1870s, and the movers of the project wanted to maintain control in order to secure their ability to direct the project and to merge the various companies upon its completion. They allocated to themselves deferred or founding shares with lower dividend rights and higher voting rights, than those of the common shares. Managing agencies were an organisational model that was used in India from the second half of the nineteenth century. The managing agency, typically a partnership among British, incorporated new joint-stock companies in sectors such as tea plantations, jute mills, coal mines, and textiles. It raised money from investors in India and Britain. The managing agency did not want to hold large equity stakes in these companies. Thus it kept to itself founders shares with superior voting rights than the common stock.[45]

One way to capture the change is to examine the general incorporation acts of various states in different years. The Massachusetts Corporations Act of 1879 and the New York Business Corporations Act of 1890 are written based on the assumption that a corporation has only one class of shares. The Massachusetts Act of 1903 abandoned that assumption and replaced it with: 'Every corporation may create two or may be more classes of stock with such preferences, voting powers, restrictions and qualifications thereof as shall be fixed in the agreement of association.'[46] This act, in various sections, not only acknowledges the possibility of a corporation having more than one class of shares, but also that shares can vary not only in dividend but also in voting rights and rights in dissolution. The process seems to have been that initially the assumption was that corporations can have only one class of shares and acts were drafted in singular. Next a practice emerged of creating another class of shares, typically with preference in dividends. This was done initially as a necessity when more investments had to be attracted in railroad reorganisation. This was done by taking advantage of the drafting of the legislation that did not expressly prohibit the creation of more than one class. Last, the practice was reflected in the legislation. Generally

[44] Howell (n 31).

[45] R Harris, *Empire Ltd.: Capital Flows, Multinationals and Investor Protection in the First Era of Globalization (1850–1914)*, (draft book manuscript).

[46] Laws of the Commonwealth of Massachusetts, c 437 An Act Relative To Business Corporations [1903].

speaking, US corporation law was more restrictive than British corporation law. It had more mandatory rules with respect to governance. British law was more contractual from its inception in 1844.[47] Because of this and the uncertainty it created with respect to how far the practice can expand without violating the law, the spread of dual class was slower in the US.

V. WHO COULD OWN SHARES?

Another attribute of corporate shares dealt with the issue of who could own shares. The issue itself is somewhat perplexing. Isn't it clear that anyone can own shares upon investing in the equity capital of a company? Going back in time to members' corporations like guilds and colleges, it becomes evident that only a human could be a guildsman or college fellow. The shareholders of the early joint-stock corporations, such as the EIC, were all humans and were listed by name in the relevant charters. By the eighteenth and nineteenth centuries, corporations invested, though rarely, passively, and marginally, in the shares of other corporations. In theory the EIC could subscribe to a small number of shares on the Bank of England or the Leeds and Liverpool Canal. The ability of corporations to invest in the stock of other corporations was so marginal that it was not yet a legal issue. Upon general incorporation, the first Companies Acts of 1844, 1856, 1862 did not restrict the ownership of the shares of one business corporation by another business corporation. From then on no one in Britain questioned this practice. By the last quarter of the nineteenth century corporations started establishing subsidiaries, some of which were fully owned, and others partly owned (with other shares being held by individuals). Soon corporate groups were created with parent or holding company at their head.

In the US, it seems as though there was an assumption, possibly based on the conception that corporations were associations of individual human beings, that corporations could not hold shares in other corporations. Later this conception was enhanced because of the idea that corporate groups create corporations that are too big at the expense of small businesses and consumers, while compromising the integrity of the political process. In the second half of the nineteenth century voting agreements and voting trusts were used to bypass the prohibition on the ownership of corporate shares by corporations. The agreements and trusts were used in order to form de-facto corporate groups. New Jersey was the first jurisdiction to permit in 1888, 1889, and 1896 the holding of corporate

[47] R Harris and NR Lamoreaux, 'Opening the black box of the common-law legal regime: Contrasts in the development of corporate law in Britain and the United States in the late nineteenth and early twentieth centuries' (2019) 61(7) *Business History Review* 1199–1221. TW Guinnane et al, 'Contractual Freedom and Corporate Governance in Britain in the Late Nineteenth and Early Twentieth Centuries' (2017) 91(2) *Business History Review* 227–77.

shares by another company. This allowed the formation of holding companies and eventually corporate pyramids in which the holders of a minority of the equity investment could control the group by holding share up the pyramid. After more than half a century of divergence between Britain and the US, the two converged to a consolidated legal rule that allowed corporations to hold stakes, even majority stakes, or the whole of the shares, in other companies.

VI. CONCLUSION

By way of conclusion, I would like to offer a periodisation of the development of corporate shares attributes. The first period was that of the very first joint-stock companies in which it became apparent that shares in joint-stock equity investments are different from membership in corporations. This led to questions of transferability and voting rights. The second was the period of the construction of major projects such as canals and railways. The new challenge led to mixed investment of common shares, and the new financial instruments of corporate bonds and preferred shares. These were used in order to play with the distribution of profits and the setting of priorities in bankruptcy. Next, the drafting of a growing number of incorporation acts and then general incorporation acts opened the discussion on the extent of liability of shareholders. The transition to the era of freedom of contract allowed companies to design more freely their share characteristics and attributes. The growing flexibility of shares made possible in this last period increased the impetus to raise capital from the public while control remained in the hands of the few. This was done by using dual class shares with different voting rights, and corporate groups and pyramids in order for control to remain in the hands of the holders with only a minority equity stake. On a higher level of generalisation, the transition was from viewing shares as membership of a corporation to viewing them as representing the financial stake in the corporation, and finally, as an instrument that can be flexibly moulded in any way that is beneficial to the shareholders as a whole or to the controlling shareholders specifically in detachment from financial stakes. The causal chain that led to the changes in the nature of the corporate share seems to run from new business and financial reality, to learning by doing in the face of legal ambiguity, whose lessons were implemented on the individual company level, and finally to a legal regulation that follows and reflects the corporate practice. This chapter has offered an overview of the path of development of the various attributes of the corporate share, but still leaves much room for further investigation of the interplay between the various attributes and of the causal chain.

11

Natural Unity? The Origins of the Principle of Inseparability of Voting Rights from Shares across Jurisdictions

JENNIFER TRINKS

I. INTRODUCTION

SHAREHOLDERS ARE OFTEN said to be the owners of a company.[1] This contentious metaphor[2] tells, however, little about their role in a company. While some scholars acknowledge that shareholders in particular in publicly-held companies are rationally apathetic,[3] others try to engage shareholders as stewards for the benefits of the economy, the environment and the society.[4] Nowhere is this ambiguity seen more than in the regulation of their 'noblest right',[5] their voting right. This chapter therefore follows one distinct attribute of shareholder voting rights to its roots: the principle of inseparability of voting rights from shares.

[1] See, eg, JD Baumann, RB Stevenson, Jr and RJ Rhee, *Business Organizations Law and Policy, Materials and Problems*, 10th edn (St Paul, West Academic Publishing, 2022) 555.

[2] See also on the economic model MM Blair and LA Stout, 'A Team Production Theory of Corporate Law' (1999) 85 *Virginia Law Review* 247, 259 ff.

[3] AA Berle Jr and GC Means, *The Modern Corporation and Private Property* (New York, Commerce Clearing House Inc, 1932) 81; more recently on the separation of ownership and control for the UK, BR Cheffins, 'Does Law Matter? The Separation of Ownership and Control in the United Kingdom' (2001) 30 *Journal of Legal Studies* 459, 466 ff; furthermore, BR Cheffins, 'The Rise and Fall (?) of the Berle-Means Corporation' (2019) 42 *Seattle University Law Review* 445.

[4] *Cf* FRC, The UK Stewardship Code 2020, 4; further JG Hill, 'Good Activist/Bad Activist: The Rise of International Stewardship Codes' (2018) 41 *Seattle University Law Review* 247.

[5] J Haselberger, *Das Stimmrecht des Aktionärs* (München, Schweitzer, 1906) 60; see also T Hergenhahn, *Berufung und Thätigkeit der Generalversammlung der Aktiengesellschaften nach dem Reichsgesetz betreffend die Kommanditgesellschaften auf Aktien und die Aktiengesellschaften vom 18. Juli 1884* (Berlin, Vahlen, 1888) 118; in Italy eg, Tribunale di Genova 21 November 1927 [1928] *Il Foro Italiano* I.313, 317.

Voting rights in the shareholder meeting are usually only granted to shareholders, and not to other stakeholders.[6] Many jurisdictions tighten this link between voting rights and shareholding by declaring voting rights inseparable from the underlying shares (the 'inseparability principle').[7] In essence, this means that shareholders cannot transfer or trade their voting rights to another person without simultaneously transferring the underlying shares; even unanimously, shareholders cannot consent to such a transaction. English law might be 'particularly liberal' in this respect.[8] The prohibition is still common, however, in civil law jurisdictions.[9]

In its basic form, the inseparability principle has a limited scope of application: it only prevents the independent and isolated transfer of shareholder voting rights. The prohibition, for instance, does not apply to proxy voting. With a proxy, a shareholder only allows another person to exercise their voting rights, but they do not transfer the title to these rights. Nonetheless, the inseparability principle makes a proxy's position precarious: the proxy's mandate must remain revocable in order to distinguish it from vote trading.[10] Most jurisdictions similarly permit non-shareholders to contract for influence on the exercise of voting rights but such influence is usually limited: following the inseparability principle, they control and eventually void agreements which could harm the company.[11] As a result, the inseparability principle does not *prevent* the invention of new financial instruments, but it influences their regulation. For example, so-called

[6] See only § 7.21(a) MBCA (Model Business Corporation Act; model act developed and periodically amended by the American Bar Association): 'Only shares are entitled to vote.'

[7] See also on indivisibility as a common trait J Van Ryn, 'II. Securities and Securities Holders' in A Conard and D Vagts (eds), *International Encyclopedia of Comparative Law. Volume XIII. Business and Private Organizations. Part 1* (Tübingen, Mohr Siebeck, 2006) no 5–98.

[8] P Cordonnier, 'L'actionnaire peut-il céder son droit de vote?' [1927] *Journal des Sociétés* 5, 30 fn 3: 'solutions particulièrement libérales de la coutume anglaise'; however for US corporate law, FH Easterbrook and DR Fischel, *The Economic Structure of Corporate Law* (Cambridge, HUP, 1991) 74; on the other hand, for voting-only shares in the US, eg, *Lehrman v Cohen* 222 A2d 800, 805 f (Del 1966); *Stroh v Blackhawk Holding Corp* 272 NE2d 1, 6 (Ill 1971).

[9] For France, Italy and Germany see only, C Coupet, *L'attribution du droit de vote dans les sociétés* (Issy-les-Moulineaux, LGDJ, 2015) no 42; GP La Sala, '2347' in P Abbadessa and GB Portale, *Le società per azioni. Codice civile e norme complementari. Tomo I* (Milan, Giuffrè, 2016) no 2, 510 ff; H Wiedemann, *Gesellschaftsrecht. Band II. Recht der Personengesellschaften* (Munich, CH Beck, 2004) 215.

[10] Eg, Art 2372 III 1 Codice civile; § 7.22(d) MBCA; W Bayer, 'Zur Dogmatik der unwiderruflichen Vollmacht' [2020] *Deutsche Notar-Zeitschrift* 373, 379: 'Verbot der verdrängenden Vollmacht'; Y Guyon, 'Assemblées d'actionnaires' in *Répertoire des sociétés*, edn April 2023 (Paris, Dalloz, September 2022) no 123; O Rieckers, '§ 134 AktG' in G Spindler and E Stilz (eds), *Aktienrecht. Band 2*, 5th edn (Munich, CH Beck, 2022) no 51.

[11] See, eg, RG 10 January1928 – II 173/27, *Entscheidungen des Reichsgerichts in Zivilsachen* (RGZ) 119, 386, 388; RG 11 June 1931 – II 398/29, RGZ 133, 90, 93; GF Campobasso and M Campobasso, *Diritto Commerciale. 2 Diritto delle società*, 9th edn (Milanofiori Assago, Wolters Kluwer Italia, 2015) 339 ff; Coupet (n 9) no 47 ff; K Schmidt, *Gesellschaftsrecht*, 4th edn (Köln, Carl Heymanns, 2002) § 21 II 4, 616 ff; S de Vendeuil, 'Fasc. 136-6: Assemblées d'actionnaires SA non cotée. Règles communes à toutes les assemblées. Vote des résolutions' in *JurisClasseur Sociétés Traité* (Paris, LexisNexis, 13.7.2022) nos 47 ff, 56 ff.

empty voting, ie, voting without any financial interest in the company,[12] remains possible, but its limits are determined by considerations linked to the inseparability principle.[13]

Overall, the ramifications of the inseparability principle are often incalculable, its contours blurred. Uncertainty surrounds its foundations and its justification. The principle mostly stands as a general but unwritten rule; courts and scholars take it for granted and generally give no specific explanation. The diagnosis formulated by Rudolf Müller-Erzbach in 1948 thus still holds true:

> One indeed agrees in Germany and abroad that the voting right cannot be separated from the shareholding. However, there is no clarity wherein this inseparability is founded.[14]

This chapter traces the origins of the inseparability principle searching for its roots in scholarship and case law. Taking Müller-Erzbach as a starting point, it focuses on debates which took place in the beginning of the twentieth century in Germany (II), France (III) and Italy (IV). They, in turn, lead to early US case law (V). From these sources, key aspects and the prevalent justifications of the principle will be compared, yielding three implications (VI): that the discussion centred around the alignment of shareholders' interests, that similar concerns arose in different socio-economic contexts, and that ideas circulated easily in early comparative company law.

II. GERMANY

When modern scholarship discusses the German prohibition on separating voting rights from shares, the so-called *Abspaltungsverbot*, it generally refers

[12] HTC Hu and B Black, 'The New Vote Buying: Empty Voting and Hidden (Morphable) Ownership' (2006) 79 *Southern California Law Review* 811.

[13] Eg, C Osterloh-Konrad, 'Gefährdet "Empty Voting" die Willensbildung in der Aktiengesellschaft? Überlegungen zur Proportionalität zwischen Stimmrechtseinfluss und wirtschaftlicher Betroffenheit der Aktionäre' [2012] *Zeitschrift für Unternehmens- und Gesellschaftsrecht* 35, 44 f, 57 ff; G Sandrelli, *Innovazione finanziaria ed esercizio del voto. Il fenomeno dell'*empty voting *nella prospettiva delle società quotate* (Milan, EGEA, 2017) 86; distinguishing however the transfer of voting rights from mere contractual arrangements, M Bione, 'Le azioni' in GE Colombo and GB Portale (eds), *Trattato delle società per azioni. 2* Azioni. Gruppi* (Turin, UTET, 1991) 32; see attacking the principle, D Schmidt, '*Empty Voting* et cession du droit de vote' [4/2011] *Revue Trimestrielle de Droit Financier* 90, 92.

[14] R Müller-Erzbach, *Das private Recht der Mitgliedschaft als Prüfstein eines kausalen Rechtsdenkens* (Weimar, Hermann Böhlaus Nachfolger, 1948) 241: 'Daß das Stimmrecht nicht von der Mitgliedschaft getrennt werden kann, darüber ist man sich zwar im In- und Ausland weithin einig. Worin diese Unlösbarkeit begründet ist, darüber besteht indes keine Klarheit', referring to German, Italian and French sources; see also in Italy, Tribunale di Genova 21 November 1927 [1928] *Il Foro Italiano* I.313, 317: 'un principio universalmente ammesso, sebbene non espressamente dichiarato dalla legge, che trova unanimi tutte le autorità dottrinali nel proclamarlo'; C Angelici, 'Sulla "inscindibilità" della partecipazione azionaria' [1985] *Rivista del diritto commerciale* I.123: 'spesso presentato in modo assiomatico'; Bione (n 13) 31; pointed and critical, C Baj, 'La cessibilité du droit de vote' [4/1996] *Cahiers de droit de l'entreprise* 16: 'Principe d'autant plus sacré qu'il prend naissance dans le mystère.'

to a decision by the Federal Court of Justice dated 25 February 1965.[15] While this might indeed have been the first time the Court applied this prohibition, its roots go far further back.[16] Following the line of references, one reaches a 1896 decision by the German Imperial Court[17] – which, however, dealt with the criminal prohibition against vote selling (section A below). The exact moment of birth of the *Abspaltungsverbot* as an unwritten, general principle thus remains in the dark. The scholarly debates equally do not reveal the prohibition's origin (section B below).

A. Criminal Prohibition against Vote Selling

The German Imperial Court in civil matters decided in 1896 that the assignment of the sole voting right without the underlying share was invalid. The case centred on a very particular share sale and resale agreement: the seller transferred the shares but retained the right to dividends, the buyer had the option to hand back the shares instead of paying the purchase price, and the buyer further obliged herself to return the shares if the seller required her to do so.[18] Such an arrangement, the Court held, ultimately amounted to stock lending. As the buyer had simultaneously promised to arrange for the seller's lease over a restaurant to be prolonged, this stock lending agreement was deemed to be made against payment, and it was thus criminally sanctioned as a kind of vote selling.[19] In consequence, the agreement did not bind the parties.[20]

Whilst this was a company law dispute, the decisive argument drew on a criminal law provision, the prohibition against vote selling. At first sight, the decision has therefore little to say about the German inseparability principle as a company law rule. The Court however explained the rationale of the criminal law provision. It first distinguished stock lending against payment from mere proxy voting. The statute allowed for such proxy voting, the Court said, because it assumes that the proxy would exercise the voting rights in line with the shareholder's interests. This assumption no longer holds if the third party grants the shareholder some benefit in consideration for the right to exercise their voting

[15] BGH 10.11.1951 – II ZR 111/50, *Entscheidungen des Bundesgerichtshofs in Zivilsachen* (BGHZ) 3, 354; see, eg, K Heider, '§ 8 AktG' in W Goette, M Habersack and S Kalss (eds), *Münchener Kommentar zum Aktiengesetz. Band 1. §§ 1–75*, 5th edn (Munich, CH Beck, 2019) no 89; C Schäfer, '§ 717 BGB' in FJ Säcker, R Rixecker, H Oetker and B Limperg (eds), *Münchener Kommentar zum Bürgerlichen Gesetzbuch. Band 7. Schuldrecht Besonderer Teil IV. §§ 705–853. Partnerschaftsgesellschaftsgesetz. Produkthaftungsgesetz*, 8th edn (Munich, CH Beck, 2020) no 7.

[16] Explicitly, eg, RG 31 March 1931 – II 222/30, RGZ 132, 149, 159; on the importance and the need to look at public companies in particular see J Trinks, *Stimmrechtszuordnung beim Nießbrauch an Gesellschaftsanteilen. Ein deutsch-französischer Rechtsvergleich* (Berlin, Duncker & Humblot, 2021) 295 f.

[17] RG 17 December 1896 – I 201/96, RGZ 38, 257.

[18] RGZ 38, 257, 258.

[19] Art 249f *Allgemeines Deutsches Handelsgesetzbuch*; later § 318 *Handelsgesetzbuch*.

[20] RGZ 38, 257, 259 f.

rights. Such consideration, the Court reasoned, suggests that the third party wants to use the voting rights to their own benefit. As the third party furthermore has no financial interest in the company, being able to return the shares at will, their interest does not necessarily align with the 'company's interest'.[21] The Court concluded from the criminal sanction that 'the law does not want such contracts'.[22]

Just like the phrase 'the law does not want such contracts', the reasoning transcends criminal law.[23] Once non-shareholders vote, the foundations of shareholder resolutions start to tremble: shareholders have made a specific type of long-term investment in the company; in order to protect this investment, they generally want the company's business to flourish. Non-shareholders, without a financial interest in the company's overall profit, do not necessarily share this common interest. As there is no financial incentive to set boundaries for their self-interested behaviour, non-shareholders might use such a vote to foster their own projects which could harm the company's business.[24] Introducing a criminal sanction for vote selling, the legislator prohibited at least the most egregious cases of third-party influence on shareholder resolutions. Beyond this, cases where no payment was involved might not deserve criminal prosecution. In view of the underlying rationale, some have, however, argued that gratuitous transfers of voting rights to non-shareholders should be unenforceable even if not criminal.[25] The German inseparability principle therefore shows ties with the statutory, criminal prohibition of loaning stock against payment, or put differently, selling votes.[26]

B. Legitimationszession as Test Case

Links to the statutory framework also lingered in the academic debate in respect of the so-called *Legitimationszession* in the 1920s. In a *Legitimationszession*,

[21] RGZ 38, 257, 259 f; confirming this Haselberger (n 5) 67; generally also H Horrwitz, *Das Recht der Generalversammlungen der Aktiengesellschaften und Kommanditgesellschaften auf Aktien* (Berlin, Franz Vahlen, 1913) § 29 B I 2, 3, 140, 142; furthermore E Schreib, *Aktionär und Generalversammlung* (Straßburg, Dissertation, 1912) 54 f.

[22] RGZ 38, 257, 260: 'Solchen Vertrag will das Gesetz nicht'.

[23] *Cf* also the general formulation at RGZ 38, 257, 258: 'gesetzlich unzulässige bloße Abtretung des Stimmrechtes der Aktien'.

[24] See the reference to the true will of the company Hergenhahn (n 5) 118, 127 f.

[25] M Hachenburg, 'Einleitung' in *Düringer-Hachenburg. Das Handelsgesetzbuch vom 10. Mai 1897. III. Band. 1. Teil*, 3rd edn (Mannheim, Deutsches Druck- u Verlagshaus, 1934) no 79; E Jacobi, 'Stimmrecht in fremden Aktien auf Grund unwiderruflicher Vollmacht' (1910/11) X *Bank-Archiv. Zeitschrift für Bank- und Börsenwesen* 81, 82; W Nord, 'Die "Legitimationsübertragung" von Aktien zur Ausübung des Stimmrechts' [1926] *Juristische Wochenschrift* 530, 531; later also, G Püttner, *Das Depotstimmrecht der Banken* (Berlin, Duncker & Humblot, 1963) 51; explaining the distinction with the need to protect the possibility of proxy voting, Horrwitz (n 21) § 29 B I 2, 140; critical however, G Frohner, *Aktiensonderdepot und Legitimationsübertragung* (Hamburg, Friederichsen, de Gruyter & Co mbH, 1929) 100; H Weiß, *Die Legitimationsübertragung zur Ausübung des Aktienstimmrechts* (Calw, Ölschlägersche Buchdruckerei, 1930) 49 f.

[26] *Cf* Horrwitz (n 21) § 28 II 7, 134.

the shareholder keeps their legal title, but authorises a third party to exercise their rights (in particular their voting rights) in the third party's own name.[27] It thus goes beyond mere proxy voting, where the proxy exercises voting rights in the name of the shareholder.[28] In Germany, the practice is tightly linked to banks exercising their depositories' voting rights.[29] It was in widespread use, and German courts held it to be valid already around the turn of the century.[30] Some authors even considered this to be customary law.[31] Today, its validity is implicitly acknowledged in the German Stock Corporation Act.[32]

Nevertheless, the *Legitimationszession* caused a heated scholarly debate at the start of the twentieth century. The instrument tests the inseparability principle, at least theoretically, as it allows a non-shareholder to exercise voting rights in their own name and interest.[33] The *Legitimationszession* thus could have led to a substantial discussion of the inseparability principle. But most authors only brought forward a technical argument:[34] with a *Legitimationszession*, the shareholder would temporarily provide the exercise of their rights to another person, but – similarly to the case of proxy voting – they would not irrevocably transfer them.[35] Authors could thus avoid in-depth engagement with the inseparability principle because, technically, there was no actual separation of voting rights from shares. As a result, many did not even mention the principle. Where they did, some simply explained it with the inextricability of share rights,[36] some

[27] RG 4 November 1927 – II 135/27, RGZ 118, 330, 331.

[28] Eg, F Will, *Die Legitimationsübertragung im deutschen Aktienrecht unter besonderer Berücksichtigung des Bankenstimmrechts* (Altenburg Thür, Thallwitz, 1928) 43.

[29] See, eg, Nord (n 25) 530; Püttner (n 25) 16 ff; furthermore, J Mohamed, *Die Legitimationszession im Aktienrecht. Eine Untersuchung zu den Legitimations- und Strukturfragen der anonymen Repräsentanz* (Cologne, Carl Heymanns, 2018) 15 ff; U Noack, 'Die Legitimationsübertragung – eine dubiose Rechtsfigur' in M Habersack, K Huber and G Spindler (eds), *Festschrift für Eberhard Stilz zum 65. Geburtstag* (Munich, CH Beck, 2014) 439, 440 f.

[30] Eg, RG 23 November 1892 – I 266/92, RGZ 30, 50, 51; RG 10.11.1897 – I 235/97, RGZ 40, 80, 82 f; *cf* the more explicit decision in 1927 RGZ 118, 330; looking back, eg, Püttner (n 25) 15 f; HA Troeltsch, *Legitimation und Legitimationsübertragung im Aktienrecht* (Borna-Leipzig, Universitätsverlag von Robert Roske, 1929) 39; on the *Legitimationszession* as an exception to the principle made necessary by the widespread practice, J Flechtheim, 'Vorbem §§ 222 und 223' in *Düringer-Hachenburg. Das Handelsgesetzbuch vom 10. Mai 1897. III. Band. 1. Teil*, 3rd edn (Mannheim, Deutsches Druck- u Verlagshaus, 1934) no 7; see also Nord (n 25) 530; Mohamed (n 29) 61 f; critical as to the meaning of these early decisions, B Grunewald, 'Die Rechtsstellung des Legitimationsaktionärs' [2015] *Zeitschrift für Unternehmens- und Gesellschaftsrecht* 347, 349.

[31] K Andreae, *Das Stimmrecht in der Aktiengesellschaft* (Cologne, Dissertation, 1930) 13; see also, W Deuß, *Die Ausübung des aktienrechtlichen Stimmrechts durch Dritte* (Cologne, Dissertation, 1963) 98 f; today § 129 III 1 *Aktiengesetz*; see, eg, Noack (n 29) 452.

[32] § 129 para 3 *Aktiengesetz*.

[33] Explicitly, Grunewald (n 30) 352: 'Bei Lichte besehen ist die Legitimationszession nichts anderes als die stets verteufelte Abspaltung des Stimmrechts von der Rechtstellung des Aktionärs'.

[34] Eg, P Gieseke, *Das Aktienstimmrecht der Banken (Depotaktie und Legitimationsübertragung)* (Berlin, Carl Heymanns Verlag, 1926) 18; Jander, 'Die Legitimationsübertragung' [1913] *Juristische Wochenschrift* 471 ff.

[35] Frohner (n 25) 98; Troeltsch (n 30) 42, 45; Will (n 28) 26.

[36] Horrwitz (n 21) § 28 II 7, 134; H Planitz, *Die Stimmrechtsaktie. Ein Beitrag zur Reform des Aktienrechts* (Leipzig, Felix Meiner, 1922) 17; Will (n 28) 26.

portrayed a share as a complex, coherent unit,[37] and some merely pointed to French sources.[38] Others linked shareholder voting rights to the company as an organisation: these rights could only be seen in relation to the organisation that a company is, and they thus needed to remain with its members.[39] Ultimately, this links back to the financial investment of shareholders as a minimum common interest and as a key feature of companies.[40] In the case of the *Legitimationszession*, many scholars found reassurance in banks being contractually bound to their customers' and thus to the shareholders' interests when exercising voting rights related to the latter's shares.[41]

Beyond these conceptual accounts, the prohibition against separating voting rights from shares also appeared as a mandatory design feature of the German statutory regime of the public company.[42] Some scholars contrasted the explicit statutory acknowledgment of proxy voting to the silence around the transfer of voting rights.[43] Others drew on the indivisibility of shares.[44] Finally, where authors focused on the development of company law, they noted the relatively late emergence of shareholder voting rights, hinting at the legislator's design choices in shaping these rights and, ultimately, in laying the foundations for the inseparability principle.[45]

III. FRANCE

French scholars did not face a test case like the *Legitimationszession*. Still, a number of contributions dealt with the inseparability principle in the early

[37] R Fischer, 'Drittes Kapitel. Die Personenvereinigungen' in V Ehrenberg (ed), *Handbuch des gesamten Handelsrechts. Dritter Band. I. Abteilung* (Leipzig, OR Reisland, 1916) 146 f; H Röhricht, *Das Problem der Zulässigkeit der sog. Legitimationszession von Aktien zum Zwecke der Ausübung des Stimmrechts* (Bresslau, Dissertation, 1935) 11, 42.

[38] Especially, HV Simon, 'Die Vertretung eigener und fremder Aktien in Generalversammlungen' in R Alexander-Katz, W Benedict and others (eds), *Festgabe für Richard Wilke* (Berlin, Franz Vahlen, 1900) 255, 262, 275.

[39] Deuß (n 31) 71, 90; see also Röhricht (n 37) 10, 17 f, linking it beyond that to National Socialist ideas of a *Volksvermögen* at 39 f, 56.

[40] Also using this to justify the rule of the majority over the minority see R Müller-Erzbach, 'Das Aktiengesetz vom 30. Januar 1937 und das Aktienrechtsproblem' (1937/38) 87 *Jherings Jahrbücher* 73, 96 f; K Wolferstätter, *Das Bankenstimmrecht und seine Regelung im Aktiengesetz vom 30. Januar 1937* (Munich, Hansadruckerei, 1939) 65; *cf* Hachenburg (n 25) no 78.

[41] Differentiating, Gieseke (n 34) 48, 51; Will (n 28) 44 f; see also, Weiß (n 25) 61; critical, Nord (n 25) 530; in detail, Püttner (n 25) 60 ff.

[42] K Drewes, *Die Generalversammlung der Aktiengesellschaft* (Stuttgart, J Hess, 1933) 74; *cf* also, Fischer (n 37) 186.

[43] § 252 II 1 *Handelsgesetzbuch*; Frohner (n 25) 89, 97; Gieseke (n 34) 19; Planitz (n 36) 14, 16 f; Troeltsch (n 30) 52 f; later also, Püttner (n 25) 50 f.

[44] § 179 I *Handelsgesetzbuch*, today § 8 V *Aktiengesetz*; see Fischer (n 37) 146 f; Röhricht (n 37), 19; also, Deuß (n 31) 77; critical, Planitz (n 36) 11 ff; see also on every shareholder's right to vote pursuant to § 252 I 1 *Handelsgesetzbuch* Andreae (n 31) 18; Haselberger (n 5) 10, 29.

[45] Eg, Haselberger (n 5) 3 ff; J Matsuda, 'Kollektivismus und Individualismus im Aktienrecht (unter besonderer Berücksichtigung des Wesens der Aktie)' (1931) 96 *Zeitschrift für das Gesamte Handelsrecht und Konkursrecht* 239, 246.

twentieth century, fuelled by comparative sources.[46] Already in 1897, an essay about producers' cartels in France and the US mentioned the issue.[47] Later, an Italian case was translated and published in a French journal, opening the question again.[48] Similar to the German debate, the French discussion reflects the importance of the statutory regime of public companies (section A below), and it seems to have drawn on comparable underlying ideas (section B below).

A. Democratic Principles vs Statutory Interpretation

French company law is often associated with democratic principles and terminology, especially when it comes to the public company, the *société anonyme* (SA).[49] The company is presented as a republic, and the shareholders are its citizens which are to be treated equally and have civic rights such as the right to vote. Authors often consider this idea as a legacy of the French Revolution, and many claim it has spread to other jurisdictions.[50] This analogy could have served as a beautiful explanation for the inseparability principle – after all, citizens are not allowed to trade their voting rights either, be it against payment or gratuitously.[51] The differences between civic voting and shareholder voting are salient, however, and scholars themselves explicitly acknowledged this.[52] The democratic principle therefore seems to be less important than it initially seemed.

Instead, focus was on the interpretation and application of statutory provisions.[53] French law lacks an explicit rule on the inseparability principle. The ensuing scholarly discourse around possible statutory foundations impressively

[46] See later, Tribunal de commerce de la Seine 8.3.1928 [1928] *Journal des sociétés* 670, 675 f; on the essential nature of voting rights, Cassation civile 7.4.1932 [1933] *Dalloz* I.153, 156.

[47] J Percerou, 'Des syndicats de producteurs. Essai sur leur fonctionnement et leur forme juridique' [1897] *Annales de droit commercial* 271, 297 in favour of a separability; also R Michel, *Le contrôle économique des sociétés et ses rapports avec leur nationalité* (Poitiers, Société française d'imprimerie, 1923) 68; against the separability under French law later, J Percerou, 'Req. 3 mai 1911' [1912] *Dalloz* I.33 (note).

[48] Tribunale di Napoli 6 August 1909 [1910] *Recueil Sirey* IV.1 with a note by Albert Wahl; see the references by, eg, H Mazeaud, *Le vote privilégié dans les sociétés de capitaux* (Paris, Dalloz, 1924) 100.

[49] See, eg, R Rousseau and F Amiot, 'Les restrictions conventionnelles au droit de vote des actionnaires' [1913] *Gazette des Sociétés* 119.

[50] Matsuda (n 45) 246; Troeltsch (n 30) 78 f; on the idea of equality further F Klein, *Die neueren Entwicklungen in Verfassung und Recht der Aktiengesellschaft* (Vienna, Manz, 1904) 7 f.

[51] *Cf* Cordonnier (n 8) 12 f; Rousseau and Amiot (n 49) 121: 'suffrage universel'.

[52] C Royer, *Traité théorique et pratique des sociétés anonymes. Tome deuxième*, 3rd edn (Paris, Dalloz, 1925) no 381bis, 196; Cordonnier (n 8) 13.

[53] Cordonnier (n 8) 14 ff; A Jauffret, *Du droit de souscrire par préférence à des actions nouvelles* (Paris, Recueil Sirey, 1926) 132; A Wahl, 'De la cession du droit de souscrire par préférence aux actions émises en augmentation du capital' [1912] *Journal des sociétés* 337, 339; critical, however, as to the interpretation of individual company law rules, A Wahl, 'Trib. de Naples 6 août 1909' [1910] *Recueil Sirey* IV.1 f (note); regarding the articles of association, A Wahl, 'Des mandataires aux assemblées générales dans les sociétés par actions' [1905] *Journal des sociétés* 97, 103; later referencing Art 10 *décret-loi du 31 août 1937*, H Solus, *La réforme du droit des sociétés par les décrets-lois*

illustrates the ambiguity of interpretation. A prominent example is the express statutory admission of proxy voting. For some, it contained an implicit ban on every other form of voting by non-shareholders while others saw it as a mere non-exhaustive example.[54] Scholars therefore tried to go beyond individual provisions and to explain the inseparability principle through the wider context of legal reforms in contemporary company law. One relevant reform allowed shareholders to join forces to overcome a minimal shareholding requirement for voting.[55] Furthermore, a 1913 act guaranteed each shareholder a voting right proportional to their shares for amendments to the company's constitution.[56] Authors understood statutory rules like these to express the law's willingness to protect shareholder voting rights, and the inseparability principle furthered this protection.[57]

B. Supporting Arguments and Underlying Ideas

The discussion did not stop at statutory provisions, however. French proponents of the inseparability principle underpinned their argument with more fundamental, conceptual considerations. For instance, they also highlighted the connection between voting rights and financial interest. The shareholders' common interest in the success of their investment, ie, the success of the company, would guide their vote.[58] Scholars also argued that this commonality of interest was a basic operational principle of company law, essential for the functioning of a company as a legal institution.[59]

de 1935 et 1937 (Paris, Recueil Sirey, 1938) no 323, 290; for the validity of assigning voting rights individually, R Michel, 'De la cession du droit de vote attaché aux actions' (1926) 3 *Recueil juridique des sociétés* 80, 81 ff.

[54] Art 27 *loi de 1867*; Cordonnier (n 8) 15 f, 27; Mazeaud (n 48) 98 f; L Mazeaud, *Le problème des unions de producteurs devant la loi française* (Paris, Dalloz, 1924) 154; L Mazeaud, 'Coalitions et sociétés (suite et fin)' [1924] *Revue des sociétés* 187, 197; L Mazeaud, *Die rechtliche Behandlung der Unternehmenszusammenfassungen in Frankreich* (Rudolf Jsay tr, Berlin, Carl Heymanns, 1927) 42; see also, Royer (n 52) no 381bis, 196; Wahl 'Naples' (n 53) 3; see also the ambiguity on the question of indivisibility of shares, Rousseau and Amiot (n 49) 121: 'indissoluble'; critical, Wahl 'De la cession' (n 53) 338 f; today, Art L 228-5 *Code de commerce*; *cf* for Germany above at n 43.

[55] Art 4 *loi du 1er août 1893*; Cordonnier (n 8) 16; Rousseau and Amiot (n 49) 119 ff; with a different interpretation, Percerou 'Des Syndicats' (n 47) 297.

[56] *Loi du 22 novembre 1913 portant modification à l'article 34 du Code de commerce et aux articles 27 et 31 de la loi du 24 juillet 1867* (amendement of Art 31 *loi du 24 juillet 1867*); on this, Cordonnier (n 8) 16 f.

[57] Cordonnier (n 8) 16; P Cordonnier, 'Civ. 7 avr. 1932' [1933] *Dalloz* I.153, 154 (note); Rousseau and Amiot (n 49) 121; see also Wahl, 'Naples' (n 53) 3.

[58] Solus (n 53) no 323, 290; Rousseau and Amiot (n 49) 121 quoting Percerou; referencing US law, Mazeaud (n 48) 100 f; going further for a social conception of shareholder voting rights, Mazeaud (n 48) 102; Rousseau and Amiot (n 49) 124.

[59] A Amiaud, *Les nouvelles formes d'ententes entre producteurs devant la loi pénale* (Paris, Recueil Sirey, 1914) 133 f fn 1; C Houpin and H Bosvieux, *Traité général théorique et pratique des sociétés civiles et commerciales et des associations, Tome deuxième*, 6th edn (Paris, Recueil Sirey, 1929) no 1165; Mazeaud, *Le Problème* (n 54) 155; Mazeaud 'Coalitions' (n 54) 200; Mazeaud, *Die rechtliche* (n 54) 43 f; in relation with the freedom of voting, Cordonnier (n 8) 10 f, 31 f; *cf* also, Tribunal de commerce de la Seine 8 March 1928 [1928] *Journal des sociétés* 670, 674 f.

However, this by-now familiar argument received a special spin in France. Scholars stressed the intensity of this connection between voting rights and financial interest, and argued that they were, and should be seen as completing each other.[60] A shareholder would receive voting rights in return for having made their contribution. From then on, the voting rights would serve as a guarantee of the shareholders' financial interest, the instrument through which shareholders can assert their interests and ensure the company's prosperity. Voting rights were thus seen as a protective tool for the individual shareholder.[61] The principle of inseparability consequently developed a different flavour in France: focusing on the shareholder as an individual – a perspective which seems to again align with Revolutionary ideas.

IV. ITALY

Italy saw a number of court decisions in the early twentieth century which commented on the role and function of voting rights including their inseparability from shares (section A below). These contributions quickly became an important anchor point for the scholarly debate which rejected some arguments, elaborated on similar aspects as the German and French debates, and ultimately highlighted another consideration: the mechanics of majority rule (section B below).[62]

A. Contributions by Courts

In the early twentieth century, Italian courts saw a number of cases related to the distribution of power in a company and contractual manipulations of voting rights. While the facts and legal contexts varied, judges often took the opportunity to develop general principles of shareholder voting. In doing so, they touched upon the inseparability principle. One of the earliest cases, a decision by the Court of Naples of 6 August 1909,[63] gained significant traction. It was translated to French, published in a well-known French law journal, and commented on by a renowned French scholar.[64] However, this decision was ultimately reversed by the Court of Appeal of Naples.[65]

[60] Pointed, Cordonnier (n 57) 154: 'Le simple bon sens découvre que ces deux droits se complètent'; also Wahl, 'Naples' (n 53) 3: 'un des attributs de l'action'.

[61] Cordonnier (n 8) 13 f, 17, 32; Houpin and Bosvieux (n 59) no 1165; Rousseau and Amiot (n 49) 119; Solus (n 53) no 323, 289; on the corresponding prohibition to renounce voting rights Cassation civile 7 April 1932 [1933] *Dalloz* I.153, 156; Rousseau and Amiot (n 49) 121; see also Wahl, 'Naples' (n 53) 3; for modern discussion see Trinks (n 16) 344 f.

[62] On the majority principle in Germany, eg, Wolferstätter (n 40) 64 f.

[63] Tribunale di Napoli 6 August 1909 [1909] *Il Foro Italiano* I.1298.

[64] Tribunale di Napoli 6 August 1909 [1910] *Recueil Sirey* IV.1 with a note by Albert Wahl.

[65] Corte d'appelo di Napoli 10 January 1910 [1910] *Il Foro Italiano* I.510.

The facts of the Naples decision related to a common Italian practice of the time: debt financing was often linked to some form of influence on the company's business.[66] The creditor in this case held shares in pledge, and she had agreed with the shareholder that as the pledgee, she would exercise the relevant voting rights. Such attribution of voting rights deviated from general principles. Contemporary scholarship agreed that the pledgor, ie, the shareholder, should keep their voting rights as a general rule.[67] The Court of Naples accepted this basic principle, and held the contractual attribution of voting rights to the pledgee to be invalid. Its main argument was, however, based on the law of pledges holding the arrangement to have the pledgee exercise the shareholder's voting rights to amount to an illicit *patto commissorio*. Its effects reached even further: while such a *patto commissorio* provides that the pledgee becomes owner of the pledged assets upon default, granting voting rights to the pledgee would have them immediately exercise powers characteristic of the shareholder – even prior to default.[68] An arrangement which has the pledgee exercise voting rights had thus to follow the same rules as a *patto commissorio* and be declared null.[69]

This reasoning was not only overturned by the Court of Appeals, it was also criticised in scholarship. Some authors did not approve of extending the prohibition of the *patto commissorio* to this context.[70] Others focused on the typical pledgee's interests: as a general rule, it is in a pledgee's own interest to secure the value of the shares that serve as security, in other words to promote the success of the company. Furthermore, the pledgee is generally bound to respect the pledgor's interests. This typical alignment of interests should then justify transferring voting rights to the pledgee – either directly or as an irrevocable mandate.[71] The Court of Naples had adhered to a strict interpretation of the law.

[66] See the widespread discussions of pledges of shares or the usufruct of shares in several continental countries' legal literatures, eg, L Lordi, 'Tribunale di Napoli. Udienza 6 agosto 1909. Corte d'appello di Napoli. Udienza 10 gennaio 1910' [1910] *Il Foro Italiano* I.1564, 1574 (note); A Lucci, 'Tribunale di Napoli – 6 agosto 1909' [1910] *Rivista del diritto commerciale* II.88 (note); distinguishing usufruct from pledge agreement, I La Lumia, 'La cessione ed il vincolo del diritto di voto nelle società per azioni' [1915] *Rivista del diritto commerciale* II.68, 69 f; regarding voting rights in the case of a usufruct of shares, eg, Cordonnier (n 8) 28 f; Wahl, 'Naples' (n 53) 1 f.; on the German and French debates, eg, Trinks (n 16) 64 ff, 70 ff; for Italy see the references in AM Luciano, 'Usufrutto di partecipazioni sociali ed esercizio dei diritti amministrativi nelle società di capitali' (2015) 42 *Giurisprudenza Commerciale* I.194 f.

[67] Comparing also French and German law, A Gambardella, 'Tribunale di Napoli. Udienza 6 agosto 1909' [1909] *Il Foro Italiano* I.1298 f (note); Lucci (n 66) 89 f; see also C Vivante, *Trattato di diritto commerciale. Volume II. Le società commerciali*, 5th edn (Milano, Dottor Francesco Vallardi, 1923) no 497bis.

[68] See the full argument at Tribunale di Napoli 6 August 1909 [1909] *Il Foro Italiano* I.1298, 1301; also Lucci (n 66) 92.

[69] Tribunale di Napoli 6 August 1909 [1909] *Il Foro Italiano* I.1298, 1302.

[70] Gambardella (n 67) 1301; Lordi (n 66) 1564: 'motivo sentimentale'; F Messineo, *I titoli di credito* (Padua, CEDAM, 1928) 229; also La Lumia (n 66) 70; for further arguments Lordi (n 66) 1566 f; from the French perspective Wahl, 'Naples' (n 53) 4.

[71] Gambardella (n 67) 1302; Lordi (n 66) 1566 f; see also similarly in the German debate above at n 41; from a US perspective, § 7.22(d)(1) MBCA; FA Gevurtz, *Corporation Law*, 3rd edn (St Paul, West Academic Publishing, 2021) 503.

Quoting the statutory rule according to which each share must entail a voting right in the general meeting, the Court concluded that not only could there be no shares without voting rights, but voting rights must also only be given to shareholders or their representatives.[72] The voting right could not be separated from the position of shareholder, and an assignee in particular could not exercise such right – at least not without another legal act which could support the assignee's voting right as an accessory.[73] The Court of Naples did however not accept the pledge of shares as a basis for such an agreement.[74]

Other court decisions added to the wider debate about the role and function of shareholder voting rights, and most drew more or less loosely from the statutory foundations of company law.[75] Again, the expressly allowed proxy voting was contrasted with the not mentioned, and therefore illegitimate, separate transfer of voting rights.[76] The rule which ensured that every shareholder had the right to vote further led to conceptualising voting rights as an integral part of each share.[77] Thus, voting rights were seen as inseparable from the underlying shares.[78] They quickly became infused with grander ideas: shares without voting rights would become a kind of incomplete property;[79] voting rights would represent personal rights which cannot be the object of separate rights and do not form part of commerce;[80] voting rights were even attributed ethical and moral importance.[81] In this line of grand ideas, some courts stressed the freedom of voting which ultimately led to comparisons with democratic structures and civic voting. Even though differences exist,

[72] Art 164 *Codice di commercio* 1882; Tribunale di Napoli 6 August 1909 [1909] *Il Foro Italiano* I.1298, 1302.

[73] Tribunale di Napoli 6 August 1909 [1909] *Il Foro Italiano* I.1298, 1302: 'interesse legittimo'.

[74] Tribunale di Napoli 6 August 1909 [1909] *Il Foro Italiano* I.1298, 1301 f.

[75] Corte d'appello di Milano 12 December 1911 [1912] *Rivista del diritto commerciale* II.314, 316 f; see also the reference in Tribunale di Roma 14 July 1914 [1915] *Rivista del diritto commerciale* II.68, 73 f; T Ascarelli, 'La liceità dei sindacati azionari' [1931] *Rivista del diritto commerciale* II.256, 267, 270 f.

[76] See Art 160 *Codice di commercio* 1882; Corte d'appello di Milano 12 December 1911 [1912] *Rivista del diritto commerciale* II.314, 315; Tribunale di Roma 14 July 1914 [1915] *Rivista del diritto commerciale* II.68, 74; see also Tribunale di Genova 21 Novembeer 1927 [1928] *Il Foro Italiano* I.313, 317 f; Ascarelli (n 75) 269; La Lumia (n 66) 72; Vivante (n 67) no 499bis.

[77] Tribunale di Napoli 6 August 1909 [1909] *Il Foro Italiano* I.1289, 1302; more generally also Tribunale di Roma 14 July 1914 [1915] *Rivista del diritto commerciale* II.68, 73 regarding voting agreements; see further C Vivante, 'Gli azionisti non possono alienare o vincolare il loro diritto di voto' [1914] *Rivista del diritto commerciale* I.173, 175.

[78] Corte d'appello di Milano 12 December 1911 [1912] *Rivista del diritto commerciale* II.314; Tribunale di Genova 21 November 1927 [1928] *Il Foro Italiano* I.313, 317.

[79] *Cf* Tribunale di Napoli 6 August 1909 [1909] *Il Foro Italiano* I.1298, 1302; see also Tribunale di Genova 21 November 1927 [1928] *Il Foro Italiano* I.313, 317; Vivante (n 77) 174.

[80] Corte d'appello di Milano 12 December 1911 [1912] *Rivista del diritto commerciale* II.314 f; also Anonymous, 'Corte d'appello di Milano – 12 dicembre 1911' [1912] *Rivista del diritto commerciale* II.314 (note); La Lumia (n 66) 71; similarly in Germany Nord (n 25) 531.

[81] Tribunale di Roma 14 July 1914 [1915] *Rivista del diritto commerciale* II.68, 72; also Corte d'appello di Milano 12 December 1911 [1912] *Rivista del diritto commerciale* II.314.

shareholder voting rights would hold similar importance and equally be personal rights which cannot be traded or transferred.[82]

B. Assessment in the Scholarly Debate

One early scholarly contribution classified shareholders' voting rights instead as a kind of property right.[83] However, this approach was soon replaced by the common conception of unity of voting rights and shares. Nonetheless, it exposed the weakness of many of the concepts and terms used. They could ultimately be turned in either direction.[84] Pointedly, authors criticised the focus on shareholders and the strict protection of their voting rights as following from mere democratic prejudice.[85]

The statutory framework of corporate decision-making supported arguments in favour of a stricter regime for shareholder voting rights and the inseparability principle.[86] After all, shareholders need the general meeting to voice their opinion, and most important decisions are generally left to this body. Like in Germany and France, Italian literature therefore stressed the importance of well-guided decisions –which depended on a certain alignment of interests and, more precisely, on having only shareholders vote.[87] Shareholders, of course, needed to be free to vote as they thought fit.[88] However, Italian scholars also framed voting rights as duty-bound.[89] As a minimum, shareholders would be obliged to respect the terms agreed upon, so were forbidden from promoting their personal interests over the common interest of all shareholders.[90] This resembled the German focus on voting rights as a responsible decision-making mechanism. Nonetheless, Italian scholarship added an important consideration:

[82] Tribunale di Roma 14 July 1914 [1915] *Rivista del diritto commerciale* II.68, 72; stressing differences Ascarelli (n 75) 268; see further A S, 'Corte d'appello di Milano Udienza 12 dicembre 1911' [1912] *Il Foro Italiano* I.181, 182 (note).

[83] Lordi (n 66) 1567, 1569 f.

[84] Eg, Lordi (n 66) 1569: 'un'eresia giuridica'; *cf* from the French perspective, Wahl, 'Naples' (n 53) 1; see further above at n 54.

[85] Lordi (n 66) 1570; *cf* cautiously distinguishing S (n 82) 182.

[86] See S (n 82) 182: 'illiceità giuridica'; *cf* today, Art 2347 *Codice civile* on the indivisibility of shares; on this link and attributing it ultimately to Vivante, see Bione (n 13) 30 n 99.

[87] A Asquini, 'Conflitto d'interessi tra il socio e la società nelle deliberazioni di assemblee delle società per azioni' [1919] *Rivista del diritto commerciale* II.652, 661; Vivante (n 77) 173 f; Vivante (n 67) no 499bis; similarly, Anonymous (n 80) 315; La Lumia (n 66) 71 f; S (n 82) 182; C Vivante, 'Un progetto di legge sulle società anonime' [1905] *Rivista del diritto commerciale* I.212, 217; see also in contrast to proxy voting Lucci (n 66) 89.

[88] Anonymous (n 80) 315; S (n 82) 182; Vivante (n 67) no 499bis; see with a view to voting agreements Ascarelli (n 75) 272; La Lumia (n 66) 74: 'cessione indiretta'.

[89] Anonymous (n 80) 314; La Lumia (n 66) 71; Vivante (n 67) no 499bis: 'dovere collettivo'; see also Asquini (n 87) 662 referencing Otto Gierke's *Genossenschaftstheorie* (1887); furthermore Ascarelli (n 75) 261, 263.

[90] Explicitly, Asquini (n 87) 661; Vivante (n 77) 174; see also on the impossibility for shareholders to abandon their voting rights, Ascarelli (n 75) 268.

linking the inseparability principle with majority rule.[91] Majority rule applied to most shareholder resolutions, allowing the majority to determine the outcome of a decision while necessarily disregarding the votes of the minority. This mechanism could only be justified if majority decisions integrated basic interests of all shareholders, including the minority. Limiting voting rights to shareholders at least ensured that those who voted exercised these rights with regard to their financial investment and the success of the company. The inseparability principle thus also served a protective function for the minority.[92]

V. US

Common law jurisdictions generally seem to take a more relaxed stance vis-à-vis the unity of voting rights and underlying shares, and concerns in respect of third-party influence on shareholder resolutions. Some early US court cases and journal articles, though, connected with the European debates.[93] In particular, the 1890 decision in *People v N Riv Sugar Ref Co*[94] spurred the debate in France[95] and showed similar arguments in favour of the necessary alignment of interest of the voting shareholders (section A below). Looking at later developments and even more so from today's perspective, the ties between European and US legal thoughts about separating voting rights from shares need, however, to be put into perspective (section B below).

A. Relatable Reasoning in an Early Case

The decision in *People v N Riv Sugar Ref Co* dissolved a voting trust and explicitly condemned shareholders abandoning their voting rights to trustees.

[91] *Cf* mentioning the protection of the minority, Tribunale di Roma 14 July 1914 [1915] *Rivista del diritto commerciale* II.68, 73 f; see also the German contributions referred to in n 40.

[92] Anonymous (n 80) 315; S (n 82) 182; Vivante (n 77) 174; Vivante (n 67) no 499bis.

[93] *Cf* M Sarfatti, 'Sulla validità o invalidità della cessione del diritto di voto nelle assemblee di società anonime nell'America del Nord' [1911] *Rivista del diritto commerciale* 71, 73; SD Thompson and JW Thompson, *Commentaries on the Law of Corporations. Volume 2*, 3rd edn (Indianapolis, Bobbs-Merrill, 1927) § 946, 313; pointed, *Harvey v Linville Imp Co* 118 NC 693: 'In short, all agreements and devices by which stockholders surrender their voting powers are invalid' (however referring to 'real ownership' which probably meant beneficial ownership); similar, *Sheppard v Rockingham Power Co* 150 NC 776; see on the early scepticism vis-à-vis shareholder voting agreements SE Baldwin, 'Voting-Trusts' (1891) 1 *Yale Law Journal* 1; with a detailed overview over cases, M Finkelstein, 'Voting Trust Agreements' (1926) 24 *Michigan Law Review* 344, 353 ff; JW Lilienthal, 'Corporate Voting and Public Policy' (1897) 10 *Harvard Law Review* 428; for today's perspective, Gevurtz (n 71) 499; for the prohibition on vote buying, eg, § 609(e) NY Bus Corp Law; *Schreiber v Carney* 447 A2d 17, 22 ff (Del Ch 1982); for an overview, JD Cox and TL Hazen, *Business Organizations Law*, 5th edn (St Paul, West Academic Publishing, 2020) 391 f.

[94] *People v N Riv Sugar Ref Co* 121 NY 582 (1890).

[95] Percerou 'Des Syndicats' (n 47) 296; for a more general reference to the voting trust, also Michel (n 53) 85.

Finch J explained that '[the corporation's] stockholders, retaining their beneficial interest, have separated from it their voting power, and so parted with the control which the charter gave them and the State required them to exercise'.[96] The issue thus lay more specifically in the separation of voting rights from beneficial ownership, in voting rights being exercised by somebody who had no financial interest in the company.[97] In this vein, the decision might have been a precursor to the broader discourse linking shareholder voting rights to shareholders' specific interests.[98]

However, this idea ultimately only played a small part in the decision. The case concerned a sugar cartel which was organised in the form of a trust. The shareholders of the individual sugar refining companies had signed over their shares to trustees who were designated as members of the cartel's board; in return, the shareholders received trust certificates. While the individual companies were formally kept separate, all decisions were made by the cartel on the level of its board.[99] Without going into the debate over monopolies and cartelisation, the court held this form of business combination unlawful. Not only did the corporations circumvent the interdiction to enter into a partnership; they also avoided the statutory ways of combining corporations.[100] Giving up their 'separate activity' and their 'free and independent action', they ultimately violated their charters.[101]

Concerns about separating voting rights from beneficial ownership of shares were thus expressed in a very specific context.[102] They could hardly be extended to a general principle of US company law. Nonetheless, like in Germany, France and Italy, these concerns linked back to statute: the corporate charter.[103] The court criticised that shareholders 'parted with the control which the charter gave them' and that they thereby 'wasted and perverted

[96] *People v N Riv Sugar Ref Co* 121 NY 582, 623 (1890).

[97] Eg, *Griffith v Jewett* 9 Ohio Dec Reprint 627, 631 (1886); Berle and Means (n 3) 77: 'The voting trust, more completely than any device we have hitherto considered, separates control from all ownership interest'; see even the use of the term 'stockholders' in *Warren v Pim* 66 NJ Eq 353, 381 (1904); similar for the term 'owner' *Bryson v Bryson* 62 CalApp 170, 174 (1923); for such an interpretation of early US law, also Percerou 'Des Syndicats' (n 47) 295 ff; Percerou '3 mai' (n 47) 33 f; quoted by Mazeaud (n 48) 100.

[98] See also, *Bostwick v Chapman (Shepaug Voting Trust Cases)* 60 Conn 553, 24 A 32, 40 f (1890); *Cone v Russell* 48 NJ Eq 208, 213 f (1891); *Warren v Pim* 66 NJ Eq 353, 382 f (1904); this latter decision was also quoted by Sarfatti (n 93) 73; also WK Tuller, 'The Rules Which Determine the Validity or Invalidity of Voting Agreements of Corporate Stock' (1910) 44 *American Law Review* 663, 665 f; differentiating, TJ André Jr, 'A Preliminary Inquiry into the Utility of Vote Buying in the Market for Corporate Control' (1990) 63 *Southern California Law Rev* 533, 541 ff.

[99] See *People v N Riv Sugar Ref Co* 121 NY 582, 611 ff (1890).

[100] See *People v N Riv Sugar Ref Co* 121 NY 582, 623 (1890): 'It has helped to create an anomalous trust which is, in substance and effect, a partnership of twenty separate corporations.'

[101] *People v N Riv Sugar Ref Co* 121 NY 582, 625 f (1890).

[102] See for the specific context of the right to vote for directors, *Haldeman v Haldeman* 197 SW 376, 382 (Kentucky 1917).

[103] Illustrated by early legislative acts granting the status of corporation: see Eric Hilt, ch 8 in this volume.

the privileges conferred by the charter'.[104] The connection between voting rights and beneficial ownership did thus not merely follow from general considerations; it stood because it was embedded in the internal structure of contemporary company law.[105]

B. An Exceptional Decision

Despite the parallels to the European debates, the situation in the US was much more complicated than the decision in *People v N Riv Sugar Ref Co* suggests. First, the case did not technically involve the separation of voting rights from the underlying shares. Especially French scholars read some US cases as instances of isolated transfers of shareholders' voting rights to a trustee with the shareholders keeping legal title to the shares.[106] In practice, though, trustees normally received legal title to the entire shares.[107] The voting rights thus remained with the person who formally was the shareholder.[108] As such, these trusts would not trigger the inseparability principle.[109] Nonetheless, the inseparability principle highlights the risks and dangers of exercising voting rights with no financial interest – of separating voting rights from beneficial ownership. Its rationale might consequently influence how such manipulations of shareholder voting rights are treated under general rules.[110]

[104] *People v N Riv Sugar Ref Co* 121 NY 582, 623 (1890).

[105] See also *Warren v Pim* 66 NJ Eq 353, 364 (1904): 'such a power – a practically irrevocable voting power, uncoupled with any ownership or interest in the stock itself – is obnoxious to the plain terms and spirit of our general corporation act', further 378 f; on statutory rules, eg, *Bostwick v Chapman (Shepaug Voting Trust Cases)* 60 Conn 553, 24 A 32, 41 (1890); *Carnegie Trust Co v Security Life Ins Co of America* 111 Va 1, 28 ff (1910); statutory provisions as one strand of argument, WM Fletcher, *Cyclopedia of the Law of Private Corporations. Volume III* (Chicago, Callaghan and Company, 1917) § 1710, 2883 ff; for a changing interpretation with changing law, *Schreiber v Carney* 447 A2d 17, 25 (Del Ch 1982); Lilienthal (n 93) 432.

[106] Michel (n 47) 66; see also Amiaud (n 59) 135; Mazeaud, *Le Problème* (n 54) 151; also Mazeaud 'Coalitions' (n 54) 197 quoting the Pure Oil trust; *cf* Sarfatti (n 93) 74; also *Brown v Pacific Mail S S Co* 5 Blatchf 525: 'irrevocable power of attorney'; for a certain separation of decision-making power and legal title to vote *Bostwick v Chapman (Shepaug Voting Trust Cases)* 60 Conn 553, 24 A 32, 41 (1890); classifying an actual separation as a younger phenomenon, TW Watkins, 'The Development of Voting Trust Legislation' (1958) 35 *University of Detroit Law Journal* 595, 611; see further, J Willenberg, *Voting Trust und Stimmrechtsbindung. Funktionsverwandte Institute zur Beherrschung von Aktiengesellschaften im amerikanischen und im deutschen Recht* (Hamburg, Dissertation, 1965) 44 f.

[107] *People v N Riv Sugar Ref Co* 121 NY 582, 583 f (1890); Fletcher (n 105) § 1705, 2873; see also § 7.30(a) MBCA; furthermore, Baumann, Stevenson and Rhee (n 1) 221: '[The certificates] are, in effect, shares of stock shorn of their voting power.'

[108] Gevurtz (n 71) 505; IM Wormser, 'The Legality of Corporate Voting Trusts and Pooling Agreements' (1918) 18 *Columbia Law Review* 123, 134.

[109] See on proxy voting and other generally admissible instruments above at n 10 to n 13.

[110] See for the general revocability of proxies under US law, Baumann, Stevenson and Rhee (n 1) 222; more generally, also Gevurtz (n 71) 501 f.

Second, voting trusts were and are accepted in US company law.[111] Quite early on, several courts held voting trusts valid as long as they served legitimate ends.[112] This, in turn, led many state legislators to explicitly allow and regulate voting trusts, starting with New York in 1901.[113] Today, most states, as well as the Model Business Corporation Act, contain rules on voting trusts. Many statutes fix a maximum duration for voting trusts.[114] Such persisting limitations on voting trusts might be seen as signs of continuing disquiet with the separation of voting rights from the beneficial ownership of shares. However, this separation is less pronounced in voting trusts than it seems at first sight.[115] The trust agreement and fiduciary duties typically bind the trustee to the beneficiary's will and best interest.[116] The interest and incentive structure of the beneficial owner is thus mirrored onto the trustee.[117] This argument resurfaces in most European jurisdictions: where they provide for a similar alignment of interests, trust-like constructions usually receive a favourable welcome on the continent, too.[118]

VI. IMPLICATIONS

What seemed self-evident from a European civilian perspective – prohibiting the separation of voting rights from shares – becomes thus less obvious when

[111] Baumann, Stevenson and Rhee (n 1) 221: 'Virtually all jurisdictions permit voting trusts'; see on the development of case law, eg, Fletcher (n 105) § 1707, 2876: 'change of opinion', in detail, § 707 ff, 2876 ff; Willenberg (n 106) 97 ff; *cf* Wormser (n 108) 123: 'industrial necessities'.

[112] *Brightman v Bates* 175 Mass 105, 111 (1900); *Chapman v Bates* 60 NJ Eq 17 (1900); *Chapman v Bates* 61 NJ Eq 658 (1900); for the distinction, also *Griffith v Jewett* 9 Ohio Dec Reprint 627, 630 (1886): 'Perhaps the most important point is to determine, if we can, what is its real purport and effect'; *Bostwick v Chapman (Shepaug Voting Trust Cases)* 60 Conn 553, 24 A 32, 41 f (1890); *Cone v Russell* 48 NJ Eq 208, 215 f (1891); *White v Thomas Inflatable Tire Co* 52 NJ Eq 178, 185 f (1893); *Kreissl v Distilling Co of America* 61 NJ Eq 5, 14 f (1900); *Clowes v Miller* 60 NJ Eq 179, 185 ff (1900); *Warren v Pim* 65 NJ Eq 36, 53 (1903); see albeit the different opinions in *Warren v Pim* 66 NJ Eq 353 (1904); Tuller (n 98) 663 ff; posing however the condition that voting trusts are valid 'without an absolute separation of the voting power from the ownership of the stock', Thompson and Thompson (n 93) § 991, 372; in conclusion, Finkelstein (n 93) 346: 'In nearly every case, where a voting trust agreement was held to be against public policy, the court was opposed, not to the voting trust agreement, *per se*, but to the objects of the contracting parties'; similarly already *Smith v San Francisco & NP Ry Co* 115 Cal 584, 606 f (1897); to the development also *Carnegie Trust Co v Security Life Ins Co of America* 111 Va 1, 20 ff (1910).

[113] See in detail Watkins (n 106) 595; on pushback led by the Pujo Committee 1913, Wormser (n 108) 126 ff; generally, WCP Bartos, 'The Voting Trust' (1959) 34 *New York University Law Review* 290, 294: 'modern business necessities'.

[114] Eg, § 706(b)Cal Corp Code (10 years); § 302A.453(1) Minnesota Statues (15 years); § 14A:5-20 NJ SA (21 years); see also the former limit of ten years in § 7.30 MBCA; critical, Gevurtz (n 71) 507.

[115] See also Berle and Means (n 3) 78.

[116] See *Kreissl v Distilling Co of America* 61 NJ Eq 5, 14 (1900); *Bryson v Bryson* 62 CalApp 170, 175 f (1923); Fletcher (n 105) § 1666, 2804 f; on the importance of this, *White v Thomas Inflatable Tire Co* 52 NJ Eq 178, 183 ff (1893); Gevurtz (n 71) 504 f.

[117] See also the lack or exclusion of such duties in *Warren v Pim* 66 NJ Eq 353, 377, 394 (1904); *cf* Lilienthal (n 93) 438: 'dry trusts'.

[118] See only the discussions above at n 41 and n 71.

looking at common law jurisdictions. Nonetheless, it is interesting to note that, at least in the US, some courts and scholars harboured similar concerns as their European counterparts. To some degree, the inseparability principle thus developed as an international phenomenon. Its origins remain uncertain, however. With this said, the material examined in this chapter has three key implications.

A. Shareholder Voting Rights and Shareholders' Role

First, it sheds light on the role of shareholders and the function of their voting rights. Tempting as it may be to draw a parallel to civic voting and democratic principles, these ideas ultimately are of little help in explaining the inseparability principle.[119] Of course, the idea of the company as a republic has been voiced, especially in France and Italy.[120] Nonetheless, where courts and scholars employed democratic ideas, these arguments were quickly qualified, the differences between civic and shareholder voting were promptly stressed. A democratic conception of companies therefore remains a mere matter of speaking, a metaphor – albeit a powerful one, giving the discussion a more fundamental spin. Conclusions drawn from this metaphor will still hardly be perceived as authoritative arguments.

The debates around the inseparability principle rather seem to have had another focus: the alignment of interests between shareholders. As diverse as their interests might be,[121] all shareholders at least have made a certain type of financial investment that they want to protect. This common interest in the success of their company allows for coherent, target-oriented decisions. In contrast, third parties are not bound by a similar incentive structure. They are more prone to pursue different personal interests and shall thus be kept from interfering with the voting process. The inseparability principle accordingly prevents the transfer of voting power to disinterested third parties and thereby protects the decision-making process in the general meeting.[122] This reasoning has prominently reappeared in the economic analysis of company law and, more specifically, of shareholder voting.[123] However, the early legal debates add specific flavours. In France, for instance, scholars highlighted the protection of the individual shareholder as the flip side of this collective, interest-based analysis.[124] In Italy, on the other hand, shareholders' common interest served as an added

[119] See however state charters as a link, Baldwin (n 93) 2.

[120] In Germany, eg, Gieseke (n 34) 49; Matsuda (n 45) 247, 253 f; Will (n 28) 45: 'Aktiendemokratie'; in detail, Püttner (n 25) 21 ff; also, Planitz (n 36) 5 f; in the US see, eg, *Sheppard v Rockingham Power Co* 150 NC 776.

[121] See on shareholders' divergent interests, eg, I Anabtawi, 'Some Skepticism About Increasing Shareholder Power' (2006) 53 *UCLA Law Review* 561, 577 ff.

[122] See in more detail in the German context, Trinks (n 16) 301 ff.

[123] Easterbrook and Fischel (n 8) 67 ff; also Baumann, Stevenson and Rhee (n 1) 556 f.

[124] Voting rights as a means of special protection afforded to and needed particularly by shareholders in comparison to other stakeholders, Easterbrook and Fischel (n 8) 67, 69; see also Blair and Stout (n 2) 314: 'compensation for shareholders' unique vulnerabilities'.

justification of the majority principle.[125] Ultimately, the conception of shareholders voting in a common interest to foster their company's business begs the question whether and to what degree shareholders are bound by this interest in casting their vote.[126]

B. Similar Considerations in Different Circumstances

As idiosyncratic as some arguments seem to individual jurisdictions, the debates mostly evolved around a common core. This is all the more remarkable as the debates related to different economic realities in the different jurisdictions. They originated in the context of cartelisation and monopolisation in the US and to a certain extent in France. In contrast, in Germany and Italy, the inseparability principle mostly linked to questions of credit and financing.[127] These issues furthermore appear in a different light with the heated debates over the *Legitimationszession* and the influence of banks in Germany.[128] Due to these different socio-economic contexts, arguments and even the content of the principle itself could well have varied. Nonetheless, all these considerations turned around the allocation of voting rights – ultimately illustrating the importance of shareholder voting rights as an instrument of power.

Despite the different contexts, this function as an instrument of power finally traces back to the same foundations in all jurisdictions: the statutory framework of what a company is. Wherever they get the chance, judges and authors have specific legal norms support their reasoning. Even in a discussion with such far-reaching conceptual implications as that around the inseparability principle, many arguments thus imply the interpretation of rather prosaic statutory rules. This might speak to an intrinsic desire to apply law instead of changing it – or, at least, to appear to do so. Even more so, this concern for the statutory foundations shows that the inseparability principle is neither self-evident nor inevitable but that it results from a specific construction of company law.[129] As widespread as it seems in civil law jurisdictions, the principle thus applies only because it is built into the respective company law systems.

[125] See also the argument in *Cone v Russell* 48 NJ Eq 208, 212 ff (1891); *Warren v Pim* 66 NJ Eq 353, 387 (1904); based on a duty to vote in good faith, Tuller (n 98) 676, 685.

[126] See, eg, Tuller (n 98) 666; *cf Bostwick v Chapman (Shepaug Voting Trust Cases)* 60 Conn 553, 24 A 32, 41 (1890).

[127] See, however, the examples given by Vivante (n 77) 173; Vivante (n 67) no 499bis; in contrast, comparison to the pledge of shares, *Warren v Pim* 66 NJ Eq 353, 385 f (1904); Baldwin (n 93) 4.

[128] On banks' rising powers in Italy, A Arcangeli and T Ascarelli, 'Moderne Gestaltungen und Lösungen im italienischen Aktienrecht (insbesondere der Minderheitenschutz)' (von Kaemmerer tr) (1932) 6 *Zeitschrift für ausländisches und internationales Privatrecht* 342, 347; Asquini (n 87) 652.

[129] See Ascarelli (n 75) 268: 'nel sistema del nostro codice'; furthermore, Matsuda (n 45) 247; today explicitly, Bione (n 13) 35; see generally, also Fischer (n 37) 185 f; *cf* in contrast arguments relating to the nature of the question, A Renaud, *Das Recht der Aktiengesellschaft*, 2nd edn (Leipzig, Verlag von Bernhard Tauchnitz, 1875) 461.

C. Interjurisdictional Discourse and Comparativist Refinement

Without insisting on the many merits of comparative legal research, I will simply conclude by highlighting the ease with which texts and arguments from other jurisdictions were received in the early twentieth century.[130] Translations of court decisions and references to foreign articles appeared in general law journals and were not only a matter for comparativists or internationalists. Admittedly, the various interjurisdictional references rarely amounted to a full comparative analysis of the subject matter. They rather offered snapshots of foreign law, and these were not always updated.[131] For instance, the variety of US case law on voting trusts was only reflected indirectly in some scholarly contributions in France, and also the appeal against the decision of the Court of Naples of 6 August 1909 does not seem to have been printed in a French journal. It is furthermore astonishing that an Italian journal article on US law[132] was regularly quoted in France – but mostly with the same French translation of the originally Italian title.[133] While it is important to keep such limitations in mind, the origins of the inseparability principle show how even a summary glance at other jurisdictions enriches the discussion and the development of common principles of company law.

[130] See, eg, Anonymous (n 80) 316 f; Ascarelli (n 75) 264, 271; Asquini (n 87) 653 f; Cordonnier (n 8) 30; Cordonnier (n 57) 154; Mazeaud (n 48) 100 f; Müller-Erzbach (n 14) 241; Nord (n 25) 531; Planitz (n 36) 19; for an example of references to foreign law in legal proceedings, Tribunale di Napoli 6.8.1909 [1909] *Il Foro Italiano* I.1298, 1302; on the different sources of the public company Klein (n 50) 10.

[131] See for rather short, imprecise insinuations of foreign law, Michel (n 53) 85.

[132] Sarfatti (n 93) reporting Tuller (n 98).

[133] Eg, Amiaud (n 59) 133 f fn 1; Percerou '3 mai' (n 47) 33.

12

From Managerialism to Shareholder Primacy: The Role of the Cohen Committee and the Bank of England

ANDREW JOHNSTON

I. INTRODUCTION

BERLE AND MEANS concluded their seminal 1932 work by imagining the possibility of management developing into a 'purely neutral technocracy, balancing a variety of claims by various groups in the community'.[1] In contrast, this chapter highlights the strong efforts made by policymakers and legislators which had the effect of putting managers back in their box and shareholders back at the centre of large companies. This history confirms that 'the tenacity and the flexibility of the corporate form' allows it to accommodate both 'benevolent capitalism' and 'shareholder value'.[2] Which of these companies pursue is influenced by (among other things): the way in which company law allocates control rights; whether or how those control rights are exercised, bought or sold; and the way boards are structured. At a time when there are ever more discussions around whether and how the company can make a contribution to sustainability,[3] and whether changes to corporate purpose will be sufficient to bring about the necessary change in orientation,[4] it is timely to remind ourselves that the current system of shareholder primacy is neither a fact of

[1] AA Berle and GC Means, *The Modern Corporation and Private Property* (New York, Macmillan, 1933) 312. This work is widely described as seminal, see, eg, HG Manne, 'The "Higher Criticism of the Modern Corporation' (1962) 62(3) *Columbia Law Review* 399, 399; GW Dent, 'Toward Unifying Ownership and Control in the Public Corporation' [1989] *Wisconsin Law Review* 881.

[2] S Wheeler, 'Gone and Almost Entirely Forgotten: the Watkinson Report' (2008) 60(2) *NILQ* 263, 278.

[3] A Johnston, 'Integrating Sustainability into Corporate Governance' in C Bruner and M Moore (eds), *A Research Agenda for Corporate Law* (Cheltenham, Edward Elgar, 2023).

[4] ibid.

nature, nor the outcome of bargaining between shareholders and companies. Rather it is the outcome of a number of deliberate choices that brought with them a series of intended and unintended consequences.

This chapter highlights the emergence of managerialism during the first half of the twentieth century in the UK, and argues that the pushback against it began immediately after World War II, with the Cohen Committee's Report and the reforms to the Companies Act of 1947–48. Those reforms weakened the position of management, particularly in listed companies, by opening them up to hostile takeover. As control of these companies became contestable, managers began to prioritise the interests of shareholders, selling off real property and raising the dividend. Managers also experimented with a range of takeover defences, which were controlled at first by case law developed by the courts. But from the end of the 1960s, the Bank of England made ever more frequent interventions in the corporate governance space, beginning with its efforts to set up the City Code and Panel to regulate takeovers more strictly. A further wave of policy interventions accompanied the economic downturn of the early 1970s, with the Bank of England once again at the heart of the action, encouraging institutional investors to intervene in companies and promoting the use of non-executive directors (NEDs). It was another two decades before these efforts were formalised and made public in the Cadbury Report and ultimately the UK Corporate Governance Code. But the Bank worked very hard behind the scenes to promote its agenda during the 1970s and 1980s.

Overall, the chapter highlights the strong efforts to constrain managerialism and enhance the position of shareholders during the second half of the twentieth century. It also highlights that much of the apparatus of shareholder primacy, in the form of hostile takeovers, NEDs and institutional investor engagement, was put in place quite some time before shareholder value theories were formalised, and even longer before they became mainstream. Hence this confirms Ireland's argument that, 'historically, contractual theories of the corporation, with their emphasis on efficiency-based justifications, emerged as an attempt to defend and legitimate the rights and privileges of *rentier* shareholders in face of the increasing difficulties involved in characterising corporations as private property and shareholders as corporate "owners"'.[5]

The rest of this chapter is divided into four parts. Section II examines the development of managerialism during the first half of the twentieth century, and its reception in the literature. Section III explores the beginning of the pushback, from the Cohen Committee's Report of 1945 to the emergence of the hostile takeover. Section IV briefly looks at the role of the Bank of England in shaping the modern system, which contributed significantly to putting managerial accountability to shareholders back at the forefront of corporate governance. Section V concludes.

[5] P Ireland, 'Defending the Rentier: Corporate Theory and the Reprivatization of the Public Company' in J Parkinson, A Gamble and G Kelly (eds), *Political Economy of the Company* (Oxford, Hart Publishing, 2001) 144–5.

II. THE EMERGENCE OF MANAGERIALISM

The precise timing of the separation of ownership and control in large public companies remains contested. Chandler argued that the UK maintained a system of 'personal capitalism' for much longer than the US and Germany, with family members continuing to play 'a larger role in middle- and top-management' until well after World War II.[6] However, Foreman-Peck and Hannah's empirical analysis suggests that dominant shareholders did not control boards during the first half of the twentieth century, and that the 'evolution of managerial control in the U.K. was substantially complete before 1914'. As a result, directors increasingly held office 'by virtue of their skills, knowledge, and networks, and promotion or recruitment to the board, not because they held preponderant ownership stakes'.[7]

One result of this separation was the emergence of a system of managerial capitalism, or 'managerialism', in which managers had significant financial and decisional autonomy. Marris highlighted managerial freedom to retain corporate income and to use it to expand the business.[8] Davis highlighted how managerialism depended on 'vertically integrated production and managerial indifference to financial markets'.[9] Others highlighted the implications of managerialism for the ways companies were run. Keynes referred to the 'tendency of big enterprise to socialise itself', so that 'the general stability and reputation of the institution are more considered by the management than the maximum of profit for the shareholders'.[10] Lynn Stout noted directors and executives 'viewed themselves as stewards or trustees charged with guiding a vital social and economic institutions in the interests of a wide range of beneficiaries. Certainly they looked out for investors' interests, but they also looked out for the interests of employees, customers, and the nation as well'. Whilst not perfect, she says, managerialism produced good outcomes for all these interests over a period of decades.[11]

These developments during the first half of the twentieth century did not occur in a legal or policy vacuum. By the end of the 1920s, rationalisation was high on the political agenda. Although ill-defined, it generally referred to encouraging the development of larger scale enterprises through mergers and other means in order to improve efficiency and competitiveness.[12] The 1926 Greene Committee on Company Law Reform recommended the introduction

[6] AD Chandler, *Scale and Scope: The Dynamics of Industrial Capitalism* (Cambridge, Belknap Press, 1990) 240.

[7] J Foreman-Peck and L Hannah, 'Extreme Divorce: The Managerial Revolution in UK Companies before 1914' (2012) 65 *Economic History Review* 1217.

[8] R Marris, *The Economic Theory of Managerial Capitalism* (London, Macmillan, 1964) 13.

[9] GF Davis, *Managed by the Markets: How Finance Re-Shaped America* (Oxford, Oxford University Press, 2009) 10–11.

[10] JM Keynes, 'The End of Laissez-Faire' in *Essays in Persuasion* (London, Macmillan, 1933).

[11] L Stout, 'On the Rise of Shareholder Primacy, Signs of its Fall, and the Return of Managerialism (in the Closet)' (2012) 36 *Seattle University Law Review* 1169, 1171.

[12] J Greaves, *Industrial Reorganization and Government Policy in Interwar Britain* (Abingdon, Routledge, 2017) ch 2.

of a court sanctioned scheme to facilitate amalgamations without liquidation, and to allow the purchaser of 90 per cent of a company's shares compulsorily to acquire the remaining 10 per cent on the same terms, subject to protection against oppression by the courts.[13] This intervention in the property framework was justified on the basis that such hold outs were 'in effect an oppression of the majority by a minority', but certainly also chimed with wider political debates about the need for larger enterprises that could exploit economies of scale.[14] The 1920s witnessed a great deal of concentration through both mergers and internal expansion, with large companies coming to dominate areas such as chemicals, electrical engineering, food and drink, and tobacco, although firms in other sectors remained small or medium-sized.[15] However, directors of many companies, both large and small, were able to resist rationalisation, preferring to maintain control over being a small part of a larger amalgamation. As Hannah puts it, '[i]n the case of private firms, of course, little could be done if the owner-directors of a firm standing in the way of rationalization did not wish to sell their shares.'[16] Indeed, even for listed public companies, with a separation of ownership and control, 'takeover bids contesting the views of incumbent directors were virtually unknown before 1950'.[17] Control of many of these companies would only become contestable after the 1948 reforms to the Companies Act, as we will see in the next section.

On the 'ownership' side, shareholder dispersal began to increase from the late nineteenth century, as the stock market enabled companies to raise more capital and shareholders to trade shares. Yet, as Hannah points out, this dispersal reflected not a democratisation of share ownership, but rather a decision by the wealthiest families to diversify their assets by spreading them over a wider range of companies, in part driven by tax considerations, and in part by a desire to gain some of the benefits of scale.[18] As theorists of managerialism highlighted, this left boards of directors with greater discretion as to how they ran companies. Yet company law did little to assist shareholders: with its longstanding refusal to intervene in the affairs of companies,[19] it left the question

[13] *Report of the Company Law Amendment Committee* (Cmd 2657, 1925–26), paras 84–5, implemented in Companies Act 1929, ss 154–5.

[14] J Tomlinson, 'The Labour Party and the Capitalist Firm, c. 1950–1970' (2004) 47(3) *The Historical Journal* 685, 692; Greaves (n 12).

[15] H Gospel, *Markets, Firms and The Management of Labour in Modern Britain* (Cambridge, Cambridge University Press, 1992) 44–5.

[16] L Hannah, *The Rise of the Corporate Economy*, 2nd edn (London, Methuen, 1983) 129–30.

[17] ibid 130.

[18] ibid 56–8. For empirical evidence that shareholding was not democratised in the late nineteenth and early twentieth centuries, see J Maltby, J Rutherford, DR Green, S Ainscough and C van Mourik, 'The Evidence for "Democratization" of Share Ownership in Great Britain in the Early Twentieth Century' in DR Green (ed), *Men, Women and Money: Perspectives on Gender, Wealth and Investment 1850–1930* (Oxford, Oxford University Press, 2011).

[19] *Re Smith & Fawcett Ltd* (1942) Ch. 304. For a historical overview of the case law, see D Kershaw, 'The Foundations of Anglo-American Corporate Fiduciary Law' (Cambridge, Cambridge University Press, 2018) ch 2.

of how intensely directors pursued the interests of shareholders in the hands of the general meeting subject to the company's articles. Most companies adopted articles incorporating the Table A default rule that the shareholders could only change the directors with a 75 per cent majority,[20] and the courts required the same majority before shareholders could interfere with the management powers granted to boards of directors in the articles.[21] These provisions made it very difficult for shareholders to intervene or put pressure on directors, yet they willingly bought shares on terms providing for effective entrenchment of the directors and management team. Nor does this practice appear to have caused any concern, either in practitioner manuals[22] or on the part of the London Stock Exchange.[23] One reason for this may have been the growing legitimacy of professional management. Another was that directors did not neglect shareholders entirely: before World War II, alignment between shareholders and directors was increased through requirements that directors hold 'qualification' shares, whilst directors and managers were often paid profit-related salaries or bonuses when profits were high.[24] However, as managers were not wealthy, they still tended to focus on increasing their salaries and prestige through the growth of their firms.[25] So, generally speaking, dispersed shareholders had to be 'satisfied with conventionally adequate dividends'.[26]

On the control side, managerial hierarchies developed very rapidly from the end of the nineteenth century.[27] This is largely invisible in the doctrines of company law, which remained narrowly focused on directors, although the key actors, managing directors and general managers do pop up in the case law, as the courts wrestled with the limits of their authority.[28] It is true that some historical accounts have focused on the fact that most of the larger firms were organised along holding company lines until the 1930s, with subsidiaries having

[20] Eg, the 'overwhelming majority' of companies incorporated in 1892, regardless of size, adopted the Table A default rule: TW Guinnane, R Harris and NR Lamoreaux, 'Contractual Freedom and Corporate Governance in Britain in the Late Nineteenth and Early Twentieth Centuries' (2017) 91 *Business History Review* 227, 244. For further discussion of the obstacles to removing directors before 1948, see A Johnston, B Segrestin and A Hatchuel, 'From Balanced Enterprise to Hostile Takeover: How the Law Forgot About Management' (2019) 39 *Legal Studies* 75, 81–2.

[21] *Automatic Self-Cleansing Filter Syndicate Co Ltd v Cunninghame* [1906] 2 Ch 34.

[22] Eg, Stiebel's 1920 book, which recognised the practical reality of delegation to directors and spent several pages dealing with the question of qualification shares, simply stated that the articles 'should empower the company to remove directors by extraordinary or special resolution': See A Stiebel, *Company Law and Precedents*, 2nd edn (London, Sweet & Maxwell, 1920) 396 and 423.

[23] As late as 1945, the London Stock Exchange only required that all directors of listed companies be removable by extraordinary resolution: see *Minutes of Evidence Taken Before the Company Law Amendment Committee* (HMSO 1943–1944), Appx X at 350.

[24] Johnston et al (n 20) 84; Hannah (n 16) 67.

[25] Hannah (n 16) 68.

[26] Keynes (n 10).

[27] Johnston et al (n 20) 78.

[28] See, eg, *Nelson v James Nelson & Sons Limited* (1913) 2 KB 471; *Horn v Henry Faulder & Co* (1908) 99 LT 524; *Re County Palatine Loan and Discount Company. Cartmell's Case* (1874) LR 9 Ch App 691.

considerable autonomy.[29] The result was that the groups in question obtained some but not all the benefits of rationalisation.[30] Likewise, there was ongoing concern about the 'availability of sufficient managers with capacity to control these new larger enterprises'.[31] However, questions about the form of the hierarchical structure and the quality of management do not mean that large managerial hierarchies below board level were absent.[32] During this period, the proportion of administrative, technical and clerical staff increased dramatically, from 8 per cent of the workforce in 1907 to 15 per cent in the mid-1930s and to 20 per cent by 1948.[33]

A less appreciated aspect of the development of managerial control of companies is that managers did not simply fill the void left by passive, dispersed shareholders; the managers who took control did so because they possessed the necessary specialist and managerial expertise to build successful enterprises at a time of rapid technological change. In some cases, the managers in question concentrated on ways of increasing productivity. The theory and practice of Taylorist scientific management was gradually accepted by the British engineering profession during the early part of the twentieth century,[34] as the job of the engineer was transformed from 'a purely technical one, to one with a commercial/managerial dimension'.[35] While the UK may have lagged its rivals in this regard, growing numbers of engineers in management positions attested to the importance of innovation in competitive advantage.[36] The largest companies established research labs and these investments in R&D led to a succession of innovations.[37] In turn, the larger companies which developed extensive technical expertise and knowledge of markets were better able than the stock market to evaluate proposals and make investments in smaller companies.[38] Diversification also allowed managers to protect themselves against risk.[39] All this pushed in the direction of larger companies, more shareholder dispersal and increased managerial control.

[29] Gospel (n 15) 46. ICI led the way in developing a decentralised divisional structure, with a head office controlling capital allocation.

[30] L Hannah, 'Managerial Innovation and the Rise of the Large-Scale Company in Interwar Britain' (1974) 27(2) *The Economic History Review* 252, 264–5.

[31] ibid 254.

[32] For discussion of managerial hierarchies in the 1890s, see L Urwick and EFL Brech, *The Making of Scientific Management Volume II: Management in British Industry* (London, Management Publications Trust, 1949) 81.

[33] Gospel (n 15) 48.

[34] K Whitston, 'The Reception of Scientific Management by British Engineers, 1890–1914' (1997) 71(2) *The Business History Review* 207.

[35] K Whitston, *Scientific Management in Britain, A History* (Unpublished PhD thesis, University of Warwick, 1995) 74.

[36] P Armstrong, 'Engineers, Management and Trust' (1987) 1 *Work, Employment & Society* 421; S Keeble, *The Ability to Manage: A Study of British Management 1890–1990* (Manchester, Manchester University Press, 1992).

[37] Hannah (n 16) 113.

[38] ibid 63.

[39] ibid 65.

These changes in organisation and the rapid growth of managerial hierarchy raised questions about the legitimacy of the new managerial class. There was growing public debate about management as an emergent profession and the social responsibilities associated with this.[40] For example, Tawney highlighted that, for industry to be organised as a profession, 'it should cease to be conducted by the agents of property-owners for the advantage of property-owners, and should be carried on, instead, for the service of the public' and 'the responsibility for the maintenance of the service should rest upon the shoulders of those, from organizer and scientist to labourer, by whom, in effect, the work is conducted'.[41] Managers highlighted their social responsibilities for productivity and progress, and their ability to mediate relations between labour and capital.[42] These claims were even endorsed by a 1919 government publication, which stated that:

> In the past management has often been somewhat mechanical in its tendency, ignoring the human element in production and distribution. Today, more than ever, it is realised that the welfare of the worker is not only a vital matter for the community, but also from the point of view of the employer a matter of expediency. There is thus the double stimulus – the good employer profits by his 'goodness'.[43]

As late as 1955, Professor Gower commented that 'it has become almost an accepted dogma that management owed duties to 'the four parties to industry' (labor, capital, management, and the community) – a dogma which is repeated indiscriminately in the speeches of right-wing company chairmen and left-wing politicians'.[44] However, the purpose here is not to claim that managerialism was a panacea. Indeed, Quail has highlighted that we cannot know the extent to which these claims were reflected in practice in large firms,[45] and there were important dissenters at the time, such as Veblen, who argued in the US context that 'the rule of the technicians does not go all the way … in deference to the paramount claims of absentee ownership'.[46] What is clear is that these claims were loudly and publicly advanced to legitimise managerialism and that shareholders, presumably knowingly, bought shares on terms that empowered and

[40] For an overview, see J Child, *British Management Thought: A Critical Analysis* (London, Allen and Unwin, 1969) 51–3.

[41] RH Tawney, *The Acquisitive Society* (London, Bell, 1920) 111.

[42] Eg, FW Taylor, *The Principles of Scientific Management* (New York, Harper, 1919) 10; ET Elborne, 'Lecture 3: The Organisation of Brains in Industry (September 1924)', *The Rowntree Business Lectures and the Interwar British Management Movement* available at rowntree.exeter.ac.uk/items/show/546.

[43] Ministry of Reconstruction, *Scientific Business Management*, Reconstruction Problems 28, (London, HMSO, 1919).

[44] LCB Gower, 'Corporate Control: The Battle for the Berkeley' (1955) 68 *Harvard Law Review* 1176, 1190.

[45] J Quail, 'Visible Hands and Visible Handles: Understanding the Managerial Revolution in the UK' (2002) 5 *Journal of Industrial History* 1, 5.

[46] T Veblen, *Absentee Ownership and Business Enterprise in Recent Times* (London, Routledge, 1923) 273–4.

often entrenched management. However, as we will see next, none of this made any impact on the company law reform process which began in 1943.

III. THE PUSHBACK AGAINST MANAGERIALISM

The Cohen Committee's report of 1945 marked the beginning of a concerted pushback against managerialism. The Committee had been asked 'to consider and report what major amendments are desirable in the Companies Act, 1929, and, in particular, to review the requirements prescribed in regard to the formation and affairs of companies and the safeguards afforded for investors and for the public interest'.[47] However, with its focus very firmly on the separation of ownership and control, the Committee paid little or no attention to the public interest, and it never discussed anything related to managerialism or the balancing of competing interests at stake in the company. One of the Committee's stated aims was to give shareholders 'greater powers to remove directors with whom they are dissatisfied'.[48] This aim did not form part of the Committee's explicit mandate. The initial Board of Trade memorandum to the Committee in June 1943 highlighted the gap between theory and practice in company law, with 'the small shareholder in a large concern … generally both unable and unwilling to exercise the control which is theoretically vested in him', although it did not include changes to shareholder rights among its non-exhaustive list of important matters for discussion.[49] Perhaps Cohen envisaged increasing the powers of shareholders from the beginning. In his first draft of the questionnaire for those giving evidence, Cohen added 'Shareholders Control' as one of nine areas for investigation, asking 'Is the theory of shareholders' control over the powers of management effective in practice and is reform desirable and, if so, what?' By the time this was circulated to the Committee for discussion, the heading had become 'Shareholders' Control and modification of rights of shareholders', and the question was '[a]re reforms necessary to safeguard the interests of shareholders or minorities of shareholders?'[50]

Ultimately, this question prompted the Committee's crucial recommendation that 'there should be a provision, overriding anything to the contrary in the articles of a company, that any director, whether under a service contract or not, should be removable by ordinary resolution, without prejudice to any

[47] *Report of the Committee on Company Law Amendment* (Cmd 6659, 1945) (Cohen Report) 7; for further discussion of how the Committee's mandate was watered down before Cohen was appointed, see B Clift, 'The Labour Movement and Company Law Reform 1918–1945' [1999] *Sheffield Political Economy Research Centre Research Paper No.1*, 34–7.

[48] Cohen Report, ibid para 130. The Committee of course made many other recommendations which became law, including modernising accounting (see Recommendations on pp 58–63) and prohibiting the use of undisclosed reserves, which companies had used to 'avoid violent fluctuations in its published profits or its dividends' (para 101).

[49] 'Historical and General Memorandum by the Board of Trade', CL1, BT 146/4.

[50] Meeting to be held on Thursday 8th July, CL3, BT 146/4.

contractual right for compensation'.[51] The precise origin of this recommendation is, however, obscure. There is no doubt that Cohen was well aware of the vulnerable position in practice of minority shareholders, and it was Cohen himself who suggested the introduction of an oppression remedy.[52] He was also familiar with practice in larger companies.[53] Yet, despite its prominence in the questionnaire, it appears that the Committee rarely discussed increasing shareholder powers.[54] It was only at the 32nd meeting that there was a discussion about possibly requiring all directors to be subject to annual re-election, suggesting that the Committee was considering different ways of giving shareholders greater powers over directors and making director entrenchment more difficult. At the 33rd meeting, it was agreed to drop the annual re-election requirement and 'to recommend instead that shareholders should be given the power to remove directors, including directors under service contracts, by ordinary resolution'.[55]

Beyond Cohen's influence on the scope of discussions, a number of suggestions were made to the committee about how shareholder interests could be better protected. A memo from the Association of British Chambers of Commerce argued that there was 'no case for a general alteration of the existing rights of shareholders, since shareholders could ascertain their rights at the time when they subscribed or bought their shares', and instead each director should be submitted for re-election separately.[56] A solicitor called Stephen Gordon noted that '[m]anagements in this country, at all events have a very strong sense of service to the entity which they manage and they tend to put the Company before the shareholders.' One of his recommendations to bring the shareholders into 'closer relation with the company's affairs' was that '[s]hareholders should be entitled, subject to any contract, to remove any Director by a bare majority (on a poll).'[57] This may have found favour with Cohen, whose thinking was clearly going in the same direction from the beginning. A first draft of the section of the final report, entitled 'Shareholders' Control', recommended that 'there should be a provision, overriding anything to the contrary in the articles of a company, that any director, whether under a service contract or not, should be removable by an ordinary resolution'.[58]

[51] Cohen Report (n 47) para 130.

[52] ibid para 60, recommending that the court be given a far-reaching power to protect minorities. In fact, very few witnesses mentioned the problems facing minorities, and it was Cohen himself who, based on what he had observed 'in practice', suggested the introduction of the minority oppression remedy: see *Company Law Amendment Committee, Minutes of Evidence 1–26* (London, HMSO, 1943) paras 4064–69.

[53] See observation of Justice Cohen that directors tended to hold all the proxies: *Minutes of Evidence* ibid para 7071.

[54] Unfortunately, the minutes of the first 13 meetings of the Committee, BT 146/3, are missing from the National Archives.

[55] 'Minutes of 33rd meeting, 19/9/44', para 1, BT 146/4.

[56] CL72, BT 146/5, para 11A.

[57] CL 11A, BT 146/5.

[58] BT 146/9.

On its way to becoming law,[59] this recommendation gave rise to little political controversy, other than in relation to the amount of notice the director should receive.[60] It was presented to Parliament as 'urgently necessary' because 'the relationship between management and ownership in limited liability companies has tended progressively to be more and more shadowy'.[61]

In trying to explain the emergence of the hostile takeover in the early 1950s, commentators have highlighted the growth of institutional investors, the high rate of taxation of dividends, the greater availability of finance and increased transparency in company accounts after 1948.[62] The contribution of the majority shareholder removal power has been much less discussed.[63] It is strongly arguable that the section made a (probably unintended but still) very important contribution to the emergence of the hostile takeover, a few short years later. When this provision came into force in 1948, the control of many companies became contestable overnight. Before 1948, a bidder who acquired more than 50 per cent but less than 75 per cent of the shares would, at the very least, have to wait two years to take control of the board.[64] Moreover, they would be unable to amend the articles, and would therefore often be unable to remove directors.[65] After 1948, none of these devices would have worked against a new majority shareholder, and the old technique of directors and their supporters keeping hold of between a quarter and a third of the shares on flotation would no longer have been effective to guarantee control either.[66] Suddenly, anyone who could gain control of a majority of the shares was able to replace the directors and then the management team.

Charles Clore's early hostile bids, which were among the very first, illustrate the significance of this change in the legal framework. His bid for J. Sears & Co

[59] Companies Act 1947, s 29, subsequently recodified as Companies Act 1948, s 184.

[60] *Hansard*, HL Deb, vol 146, cols 727–8 (25 March 1947); HC Deb, vol 441, cols 194–5 (28 July 1947); HL Deb, vol 151 cols 955–75 (5 August 1947).

[61] *Hansard*, HC Deb, Vol 438, cols 585–6 (6 June 1947) (speech of Sir Stafford Cripps, President of the Board of Trade).

[62] Eg, D Kynaston, *The City of London Volume 4* (London, Pimlico, 2002) 62–3.

[63] For a fuller discussion see Johnston et al (n 20).

[64] By default, boards were 'staggered' with one third of the directors required to retire each year but available for re-election by the general meeting: Companies Act 1862, Table A, Arts 58 and 60; Companies Act 1906, Table A, Arts 78 and 80; Companies Act 1929, Table A, Arts 73 and 75.

[65] Many companies retained the default rule, allowing companies to appoint managing directors, who were exempted from retirement by rotation: see Companies Act 1906, Table A, Art 72; Companies Act 1929, Table A, Art 68. In Guinnane et al's samples the vast majority of companies adopted this provision, so that 'by designating themselves managers, directors could perpetuate their power indefinitely' (Guinnane et al (n 20) 244). Some companies made no provision for removal of directors whatsoever, which meant that the shareholders had to pass a special resolution to change the articles before they could vote on removal of directors: see *Imperial Hydropathic Hotel Co v Hampson* [1882] 23 CD 1 and Cohen Report (n 47) para 130. Finally, it was common practice for the founders of the company to provide that they would remain directors for life or for a certain number of years provided they satisfied a shareholding requirement: see FB Palmer, *Company Precedents for Use in Relation to Companies Subject to the Companies (Consolidation) Act 1908 (Volume 1)* (London, Stevens, 1906) 981–2.

[66] L Hannah, 'The "Divorce" of Ownership from Control from 1900 Onwards: Re-calibrating Imagined Global Trends' (2007) 49 *Business History* 404, 415–7.

was assisted by the fact that the Sears family had had to sell off the majority of their majority shareholding,[67] which had the effect of loosening their control of the board under the new post-1948 rules. Motivated by gaining control of Sears' 900 properties, which were greatly undervalued in the accounts, Clore bought up shares on the market covertly through a nominee.[68] Once news of the bid broke, the Sears board trebled the dividend,[69] but it was too late and Clore acquired sufficient shares to gain control of the general meeting.[70] He then removed the incumbent chairman and managing director, and appointed himself as chairman and his associates Leonard Sainer and Jack Gardiner as directors of both Sears and its subsidiary.[71] Clore then sold off the Sears freeholds to Legal & General, and leased them back.[72] The Sears family, having apparently been taken by surprise by Clore's gambit, then sold off the rest of their shares.[73] Clore's takeover of SMT followed a similar pattern. Clore acquired 53 per cent of SMT shares on 18 June 1953 in exchange for shares in Sears.[74] The directors of SMT accepted his offer for the shares they owned on 19 June. As *The Economist* noted after he had removed the incumbents and installed himself, Sainer and Gardiner on the board, 'Mr Clore now controls a majority of the SMT ordinary capital; and as director he can modify the use to which the company's assets have hitherto been put, for the benefit of the company, and of its shareholders, including himself.'[75] Clore then bought out a rival bidder, Fraser, and eventually squeezed out the remaining shareholders.[76] Similarly, when he bid for Lewis's in 1965, the target board raised the dividend, but, despite family shareholders owning over 30 per cent of the shares,[77] Clore still gained control of the general meeting and then made changes

[67] An online source reports that Caroline Sears had inherited a majority of the shares in 1916 on the death of her husband. When she died, her son Stanley was forced to sell her shares. 'The news of Caroline's death and Stanley's financial problems sent the value of the shares down on the London stock market.' (See 'The Sears Family and the story of the True-Form Boot Company' available at www.justcollingtree.co.uk/village-memories.php.) Elsewhere it is reported that her son was forced to sell the majority of her shares: G Gault, *Gentleman Jack: The Official Biography of Jack Sears* (Dorchester, Veloce Publishing, 2008) 19.

[68] D Clutterbuck and M Devine, *Charles Clore: The Man and his Millions* (London, Weidenfeld and Nicolson, 1987) 64.

[69] W Davis, *Merger Mania* (London, Constable, 1970) 21.

[70] It was reported at the time that Clore controlled 'substantially more than half the issued ordinary share capital' (see 'J. Sears Board Reconstituted', *Financial Times*, 16 February 1953) and that Clore became Chairman 'following the acquisition of more than half the issued ordinary capital' ('J. Sears Sells Freeholds', *Financial Times*, 1 December 1953). Later accounts claim with no authority cited that Clore secured 75% acceptances (Davis (n 69) 21) and that 'The City believed that Mr. Clore controlled about 75 per cent of the Sears equity' (Bull and Vice, *Bid for Power* (London, Elek, 1961) 122).

[71] Clutterbuck and Devine (n 68) 69.

[72] 'J. Sears Sells Freeholds', *Financial Times*, 1 December 1953.

[73] Clutterbuck and Devine (n 68) 69–70.

[74] 'Tactical Victory for Mr Clore', *The Economist*, 23 June 1956. This figure excluded any shares in SMT owned by Sears.

[75] 'Mr Clore's Victory', *The Economist*, 30 June 1956.

[76] Clutterbuck and Devine (n 68) 76–7.

[77] 'Cohen Family to Fight Clore Bid', *The Guardian*, 20 October 1965; FRJ Jervis, *The Economics of Mergers* (Abingdon, Routledge, 1971) 84.

to the board.[78] It was clear that acquiring a majority was critical: Sainer explained to the *Guardian* that Clore had increased his bid because he 'wanted to be sure that the acceptances would go "well over 50 per cent"'.[79]

Incumbent boards responded to the new threat by abandoning the balancing rhetoric and conservative management style that characterised managerialism in favour of keeping control through prioritising the shareholder interest. This involved taking actions that would persuade shareholders not to sell their shares to the bidder. Most obviously, boards increased the dividend, as the boards of Sears and Lewis's did in response to Clore. Boards sold off freeholds (which were significantly undervalued in the accounts[80]) to life assurance companies and leased them back.[81] This allowed them to increase distributions to shareholders, making it less likely that they would accept a bid. Moreover, the removal of the freehold from the balance sheet took away a large part of the bidder's motivation, namely being able to sell the undervalued property and lease it back.[82] Incumbent boards also began to explore the outer limits of their management powers, taking defensive measures against takeovers, including drawing up schemes to put key assets beyond the reach of the bidder,[83] or issuing shares to employee trusts.[84] When challenged before the courts, these defences were reviewed against the directors' duty to use their powers for proper purposes, and ruled unlawful where the aim was 'simply and solely to dilute the majority voting power'[85] or to 'ensure control of the company by the directors and those whom they could confidently regard as their supporters'.[86] Whilst this did circumscribe directors' ability to defend unwelcome takeovers, the litigation process was fundamentally uncertain and time-consuming, and far from conducive to hostile takeovers.[87] Others sought, often in vain, to solicit rival, and friendlier, bids.[88] Mechanisms that relied on the general meeting were

[78] Clutterbuck and Devine (n 68) 88.

[79] 'Mr Clore Raised Bid for Lewis's to £58.5m', *The Guardian*, 18 November 1965.

[80] 'London Stock Coup Stirs Fiscal Row', *New York Times*, 20 December 1953.

[81] The directors of Frederick Gorringe successfully headed off a bid from Clore, lobbying their shareholders to reject on a number of grounds, including that they would sell the company's premises; Clore's bid failed, attracting only 41% acceptances from ordinaries and 28% from voting preferences: Bull and Vice (n 70) 115–6.

[82] Some accounts put gaining control of property at the centre of the story. Clutterbuck and Devine comment that many companies had undervalued real estate assets, but life insurance companies 'could not realise those assets themselves. What they needed was an intermediary, a fixer who would shake up moribund, asset-heavy companies for them'. See Clutterbuck and Devine (n 68) 53 and 64.

[83] The directors of the Savoy Hotel Ltd appear to have been the first to have contemplated this with their Worcester Buildings Scheme: see ibid 29–46. The directors of SMT similarly made a belated and ultimately futile attempt to put the company's assets beyond the reach of Clore: see (n 75).

[84] *Hogg v Cramphorn Ltd* [1967] 1 Ch. 254.

[85] *Howard Smith Ltd v Ampol Petroleum Ltd* [1974] AC 821, 837.

[86] *Hogg v Cramphorn* [1967] 1 Ch. 254, 267.

[87] A Johnston, 'Takeover Regulation: Historical and Theoretical Perspectives on the City Code' (2007) 66(2) *Cambridge Law Journal* 422.

[88] Both Jones & Higgins and Hope Bros solicited bids from Macowards and Debenhams in a futile attempt to fend off bids from Wolfson's Great Universal Stores: Bull and Vice (n 70) 99; *Financial Times*, 2 September and 14 November 1957.

more successful. Having deterred Samuel and Clore, the Savoy Hotel directors then issued shares with multiple voting rights, effectively giving themselves majority control of the general meeting in perpetuity.[89] Likewise, the directors of Lyle & Scott were able successfully to head off a hostile takeover from Hugh Fraser because the company's articles included a provision that any shareholders 'desirous of transferring' their shares had to notify the company in order to give other existing shareholders the opportunity to purchase them. A majority of the shareholders, including a number of investment trusts, who were dissatisfied with the board's conservative dividend policy,[90] had accepted Fraser's offer to purchase up to 75 per cent of the shares. They had transferred share certificates and a general proxy in return for payment, despite having purchased their shares in 1949 on terms that they would offer first to existing shareholders.[91] The shareholders then tried to pass a resolution at the general meeting, removing three directors and replacing them with Mr Fraser and two nominees of Fraser's choice.[92] The incumbent directors and their supporters still controlled about one third of the shares,[93] but this was no longer sufficient to block a removal resolution. The company sought an injunction,[94] and ultimately the House of Lords ruled that the shareholders who had agreed to sell their shares had breached the articles.[95] The case offers a snapshot of the feverish 1950s hostile takeover wave,[96] and highlights how bidders quickly sought to take advantage of the 1948 reforms to contest control of companies that had previously been immune.

Ultimately, takeovers became normalised, the Jenkins Committee of 1962 endorsing them as a 'convenient method of amalgamation',[97] whilst a minority of that Committee, led by Professor Gower, went further, adding the gloss (and anticipating Manne's famous argument by three years[98]) that takeovers were a spur to managerial efficiency.[99] The balance of power in corporate governance had been transformed: before 1948, the directors and managers of companies had generally been firmly entrenched with broad discretion as to how they ran

[89] 'Savoy for Ever? Control Scheme by Directors', *The Manchester Guardian*, 3 May 1955. See also N Rollings, ch 13 in this volume.

[90] Bull and Vice (n 70) 118.

[91] ibid 117.

[92] *Lyle & Scott Ltd v Scott's Trustees* [1959] AC 763, 772–3 (Opinion of Viscount Simonds) 776 (Lord Reid).

[93] Bull and Vice (n 70) 117.

[94] *Lyle & Scott Ltd v Scott's Trustees* [1958] SC 230.

[95] *Lyle & Scott Ltd v Scott's Trustees* [1959] AC 763.

[96] Bull and Vice (n 70) 116 highlight trade union opposition as well as questions from Labour MPs in the House of Commons.

[97] *Report of the Company Law Committee* (Cmnd 1749, 1962) para 265.

[98] HG Manne, 'Mergers and the Market for Corporate Control' (1965) 73 *Journal of Political Economy* 110. In fact Manne's argument was also pre-empted in the academic literature by R Marris, 'A Model of the "Managerial" Enterprise' (1963) 77(2) *Quarterly Journal of Economics* 185, 190.

[99] Jenkins Committee (n 97) para 9 of the dissenting opinion: 'Efficient directors who have treated their shareholders fairly and frankly should have little to fear from a raider' and should not be allowed to protect themselves against this 'remote risk' by issuing non-voting shares and 'converting themselves into a self-perpetuating oligarchy.'

the business, whilst shareholders were passive and/or transient; after 1948, directors and managers were vulnerable to hostile takeover if they didn't keep the share price sufficiently high. Discussions about management professionalism and duties to a range of constituencies are very sparse in the literature after 1950 compared to the previous half century.

IV. THE ROLE OF THE BANK OF ENGLAND

The Bank of England also played an important role in the move from managerialism to shareholder primacy from the late 1960s. This section highlights a number of its interventions in the corporate governance space. The wider context for these interventions was, as Michael Moran highlighted, that the Bank of England's practice of 'esoteric politics' was coming under increasing threat from Whitehall interventions from the early 1970s. This system of 'meso-corporatism loosely coordinated by the Bank of England … involved a rejection of legal controls, on the grounds of their "rigidity" and "inflexibility"', with the Bank coordinating self-regulation by associations and institutions in City markets.[100] This was the Bank's approach to banking regulation until the middle of the 1970s, for example.[101] The Governor of the Bank of England told a 1970 Select Committee that:

> There is not any doubt at the present that the Bank is an arm of Government in the City … However, in the execution of policy, [the Governor] has of course to influence the conduct of many institutions. This has traditionally been done by persuasion as much as by instruction and statutory limitation … the Bank has an understanding of the legitimate interests and needs of City institutions … I am not the representative of the City but I do represent City interests when I think it right and proper to do so.[102]

This section offers a brief account of the Bank's well-known role in encouraging self-regulation in the City of London that supported hostile takeovers and further increased the pressure on managers to serve shareholders.[103] It then explores the Bank's less well-known role in promoting the use of non-executive directors and encouraging institutional investors to play a more active role in their investee companies. These activities might have been primarily intended to head off

[100] M Moran, *The Politics of the Financial Services Revolution: The USA, UK and Japan* (Oxford, Palgrave Macmillan, 1991) 56 and 63–5.

[101] JL Metcalfe, 'Self Regulation, Crisis Management and Preventive Medicine: The Evolution of UK Bank Supervision' (1982) 19(1) *Journal of Management Studies* 75.

[102] First Report from the Select Committee on Nationalised Industries, *Report, Minutes of Evidence and Appendices, Session 1969–70, Bank of England*, 5 May 1970, question 1986.

[103] Johnston (n 87); BAK Rider, 'Self-Regulation: The British Approach to Policing Conduct in the Securities Business, with Particular Reference to the Role of the City Panel on Takeovers and Mergers in the Regulation of Insider Trading' (1978) 1 *Journal of Comparative Corporate Law and Securities Regulation* 319, 320–3.

threats of regulatory encroachment on the Bank's turf, but they also highlight the Bank's strong opposition to managerialism and made a significant contribution to the return of shareholders to the centre of corporate governance. Indeed, the foundations of global corporate governance norms that promote managerial accountability to shareholders can be traced back to the Bank's efforts from the early 1970s to promote non-executive directors and shareholder engagement.[104]

A. Promoting Takeover Regulation

In 1959, the Governor of the Bank of England had become concerned about the public perception of takeovers, and Labour had been highly critical of the practices of Charles Clore, prompted primarily by his recent bid for the brewer, Watney Mann.[105] The Governor had pushed the Issuing Houses Association (IHA) to take the lead in drawing up a code of conduct, but the *Notes on Amalgamations of British Businesses* of 1959 and *Revised Notes* of 1963 had proven ineffective. At a City dinner in 1967, Prime Minister Harold Wilson had called on the City to publish 'formal and clear ground rules for takeovers, and ensure they were enforced'.[106] The Governor once again leaned on the IHA to reconvene their earlier working party, against a threat that he would advise the government to introduce 'a securities and exchange commission on the American model'.[107] The City Code on Takeovers and Mergers that resulted was to be enforced by a Panel and focused not only on ensuring fair treatment for shareholders, but also included a rule entirely prohibiting defensive measures.[108] This removed the uncertainty associated with the courts' use of the proper purposes duty to regulate takeovers, and rendered companies even more open to hostile takeover than they had been before. By closing off all management discretion in the face of an unwelcome bid, the City Code ensured that the hostile takeover would remain a fixture on the corporate scene.

Whilst prohibiting defensive measures was clearly in the interests of the financial institutions that drew up the rules,[109] it seems likely that the Bank's primary aim here was to avoid governmental intervention, given its long-standing

[104] For a detailed discussion, see A Johnston, 'The Bank of England and the Prehistory of Corporate Governance' (2024) *Business History* (https://doi.org/10.1080/00076791.2024.2319343).

[105] Kynaston (n 62) 240; Harold Wilson speech of June 29th 1959, *Hansard*, HC Deb 29 June 1959 vol 608 cols 34–52.

[106] Kynaston (n 62) 327.

[107] ibid 328.

[108] 'City Code on Takeovers and Mergers: Panel now Available for Consultations', *Financial Times*, 27 March 1968.

[109] The man in charge of drafting the code, and the Chairman of the IHA, was Michael Bucks of Rothschild, and he received a letter from the Governor, Sir Leslie O'Brien, stating that he would give the new code any necessary support: see 'New Rules "Close Most of the Loopholes"', *Financial Times*, 27 March 1968. On the background to the IHA, see R Roberts, 'What's in a Name? Merchants, Merchant Bankers, Accepting Houses, Issuing Houses, Industrial Bankers and Investment Bankers' (1993) 35(3) *Business History* 22, 31–4.

preference for self-regulation on the part of the financial institutions it oversaw in the City of London.[110] The Governor told a Parliamentary Select Committee in 1970 that the Bank was concerned with 'the good order of the financial system', something demonstrated by the Governor's initiatives in relation to takeovers, and that 'it remained to be seen whether a statutory system was what was needed'.[111] Indeed, the extent of the Governor's commitment can be seen from the considerable time he spent looking for a replacement for outgoing chair of the Panel and former deputy governor of the Bank, Sir Humphrey Mynors, eventually settling on 'legendary lawyer' Lord Shawcross, who had become 'almost a professional non-executive director', as non-executive Chair.[112]

B. Promoting Non-Executive Directors

As the 1960s takeover wave gave way to the economic difficulties of the early 1970s,[113] the Bank of England then embarked on a programme of behind-the-scenes corporate governance activity that lasted for over 20 years, culminating in the Cadbury Report, and leading eventually to the UK Corporate Governance and Stewardship Codes. Where the Cohen Committee had ignored managerialism, the Bank of England set itself firmly against it, viewing appointment of non-executive directors (NEDs) as an important way of reducing the autonomy of management.

The trigger for the Bank's involvement in corporate governance matters beyond takeovers was the financial collapse of Rolls Royce. The incoming Conservative government of 1970 had abolished the Industrial Reorganisation Corporation (IRC), which had been established by Labour to promote consolidation, and had even supported takeovers where they promised to create enterprises of large scale.[114] As a result, there was no government body to take the lead when Rolls Royce got into serious financial difficulties in 1970. The Governor put pressure on the private sector to provide finance, but the company was ultimately put into receivership in February 1971, with a government-owned company taking control of the assets.[115] The Bank's 1972 Annual Report states

[110] Moran (n 100).

[111] First Report from the Select Committee on Nationalised Industries, *Report, Minutes of Evidence and Appendices, Session 1969–70, Bank of England*, (London, HMSO, 1970) para 90. In his evidence (Q587), responding to a claim that his opposition to regulation was 'docrinaire', the Governor emphasised the inexpensive and efficient set of rules that had been put in place, as well as the efforts to repair deficiencies where they were revealed. He also (Q585) emphasised the Bank's backing for the City Code was essential for 'an effort in which all contribute'.

[112] Kynaston (n 62) 384.

[113] D Coates, 'Britain in the 1970s: Economic Crisis and the Resurgence of Radicalism' in A Cox (ed), *Politics, Policy and the European Recession* (Oxford, Macmillan, 1982).

[114] C Pass, 'The Industrial Reorganisation Corporation – A Positive Approach to the Structure of Industry' [1971] *Long Range Planning* 63, 66–7.

[115] F Capie, *The Bank of England 1950s to 1979* (Cambridge, Cambridge University Press, 2010) 789; M Holmes, *The Failure of the Heath Government*, 2nd edn (Oxford, Macmillan, 1997) 40–1.

that '[a] good deal of thought was given in the year under review by the Bank, by others in the City and by the Confederation of British Industry to improving the management of public companies.'[116]

By May 1971, behind its closed doors, the Bank had concluded that the 'rise of management and the decline of the proprietor left the large public company in a position of autonomy'.[117] Neither the notion that professional managers would act as 'enlightened trustees' nor the possibility of state annexation were acceptable responses to this situation. No explanation is given for the Bank's rejection of the managerial ideology of balancing competing interests, which had been so prominent during the first half of the twentieth century. Clearly, the Bank was having doubts about the competence of British management generally, but perhaps there was also an element of wanting to put financial institutions in charge, and even an implicit notion that shareholder control was the natural way of things. State annexation was probably even more unwelcome, removing private influence from companies entirely. Moreover, the Heath government had only reluctantly agreed to nationalise Rolls Royce, having been elected on a platform of less government intervention in the market.[118] As such, the Bank would work to improve 'managerial accountability within the existing form of the public company', by mobilising companies' 'principal owners' and developing rules or codes under which boards and managements operate, including ensuring 'the effectiveness of non-executive directors'. Another driver of action on the part of the Bank was the constant threat of legislation which would sideline the Bank. In June 1971, Brandon Rhys-Williams, a Member of Parliament, made the first of several attempts to introduce a Private Member's Bill requiring companies with net assets above £5 million or with over 1,500 employees to have at least three NEDs.[119]

In July 1971, a dinner was held at the Savoy Hotel, hosted by Lord Shawcross, chair of the City Panel, and Sir Reay Geddes, chair of Dunlop, and attended by the Governor of the Bank and a number of City luminaries. At the meeting, the Governor presented the Bank's paper, later telling the Secretary of State that the 'general consensus of opinion … had been that it would be desirable for something to be done to strengthen the position of the part-time director within the board of directors'.[120] As agreed, Sir Henry Benson, then of the Institute of Chartered Accountants, and later advisor to the Governor, produced a note recording the dinner and a wide-ranging discussion paper. In it, Benson noted consensus on the 'low standard of administration and management of a number of companies', and that discussion had included 'the role and function of part time directors', 'the role of the institutional investor', and 'the possibility

[116] Bank of England, *Annual Report 1972*, 25–26.
[117] 'Industrial Management and the Institutional Investor', 14.5.71 (7A19/1/79).
[118] Holmes (n 115) ch 3.
[119] Companies Bill of 9 June 1971, Bill 182, 45/1.
[120] Memo, 'The Secretary of State's Meeting with the Governor of the Bank of England', Meeting at 1 Victoria St, 28 July 1971 (7A19/1/124).

of establishing a code of practice in company management' which might be enforced by a panel similar to the City Panel. A special working party would be established, including the CBI, the British Institute of Management and the law and accountancy bodies, to consider 'the function and responsibilities of non-executive directors', with the ultimate aim of producing a code of practice, given that this subject was 'not suitable for legislation'.[121] Similarly, 'the role of the institutional investor … might well be studied by the institutions' and again 'a code of practice might be issued'.

A few months later, Lord Watkinson, at the time the Chair of Cadbury Schweppes, was appointed to chair a committee to review the responsibilities and accountability of public companies.[122] This was formally under the auspices of the Confederation of British Industry (CBI), but the Bank had been a driving force behind the establishment and composition of the Committee. Shawcross, Geddes and Benson, who had all been at the dinner at the Savoy, were all members. After his committee was publicly announced,[123] Lord Watkinson wrote to the Institute of Directors that he was in the dark as to the discussions leading to the formation of the committee, noting that it 'arose from long drawn out negotiations in the City in which the Governor of the Bank was deeply involved'.[124]

There was strong impetus from the beginning for NEDs to be a central part of the Committee's recommendations. Shortly after his appointment, Watkinson received a copy of Benson's memorandum, as well as a 1969 British Institute of Management (BIM) memorandum discussing the role of NEDs and focusing on the 'outside' director. It noted the need to move beyond appointing 'Grand-Dukes or other luminaries' and to appoint those who could bring experience, judgment, different perspectives and a willingness 'to ask the awkward question'.[125] At the second committee meeting, a report prepared for the BIM was circulated, highlighting that executives had 'effective control' and that 'non-executive directors are seen as playing a key role as the objective critics of executive directors on the board'. A survey of 250 large companies identified a consensus that NEDs' role was 'to act as a guarantor to the shareholders that the company was being run in a reputable and competent fashion with shareholders' interests to the forefront' and 'to act as an objective force on the board'.[126] It urged a strengthening of the NED to bring the UK into line with 'the practice

[121] 'Administration and Management of Business Enterprises: Note by Sir Henry Benson' dated 8/9/71 (MS.200/C/3/COM2/1).

[122] 'Talks at the City Round Table', *Daily Telegraph*, 16 March 1972.

[123] 'New CBI Committee on Company Affairs', 15 March 1972, P.29.72.

[124] Letter from Watkinson to Richard Powell, Institute of Directors, 17.3.72 (MS.200/C/3/COM2/1).

[125] BIM Board Room Discussion Meetings at Dunlop, 6 and 11 November 1969, 'The composition of a Board and the role of non-executive director in relation to the Chairman and executive directors' (COM 2/4). Sir Reay Geddes sent these discussions to Harry Gray, Director of Legal Affairs at the CBI on 11 April 1972.

[126] CBI, 'Summary of a Report Entitled "The Board of Directors: A Survey of its Structure, Composition and Role" prepared by PEP for the British Institute of Management', 3 (G.178A.72).

of other successful industrialised countries',[127] and suggested an obligation for companies of a certain size to have a minimum of three NEDs, with some method of appointing them to be set up. Finally, Lord Shawcross, himself a serial non-executive director, wrote a memorandum for Watkinson in which he noted the growing tendency for US boards to include outside directors and his belief that 'United Kingdom companies should be required to have outside directors in the proportion of not less than one third of the total.'[128]

Watkinson's interim report unsurprisingly concluded that 'inclusion on the board of non-executive directors is highly desirable' and that 'action should be taken to encourage more candidates to make themselves available',[129] recommendations which were endorsed by the Bank in its comments. These recommendations made it into the final Watkinson Report,[130] which was endorsed by the CBI Council on 19 September 1973.

Unlike later reports issued in the names of City luminaries,[131] the Watkinson Report as a whole seems to have made little impact.[132] It did, however, authoritatively endorse and formalise a commitment to appointing NEDs to boards at a time when the question of board structure was a matter of much debate. EEC accession was imminent, and there was much consternation in both the Bank and the CBI about the prospect of the Fifth Company Law Directive, which would have mandated employee representation on two tier boards. The arrival of Benson in 1975, as special advisor to the Governor with responsibility for encouraging institutional investor engagement,[133] and of David Walker in 1977,[134] gave fresh impetus to the Bank's efforts. Faced with an apparent shortage of candidates of the right calibre, Walker, who was strongly opposed to legislation, suggested a central register to get the 'great and the good' onto boards to help with the 'financial aspects of a company's business'.[135]

In 1980, the Wilson Committee endorsed the 'general view about the value of non-executive directors', adding that institutions discharging their responsibilities as 'part owners' should ensure boards 'include a number of competent directors of this sort'.[136] Perhaps making a jibe at Walker's efforts behind the

[127] ibid 5, citing with approval a speech given by Sir Charles Villiers at the Financial Times Conference in October 1971.

[128] 'The Company and the Community', 22 June 1972 (COM 2/6).

[129] CBI Company Affairs Committee, *Draft Interim Report: A New Look at the Responsibilities of the British Public Company*, para 2.39 (G.374.72).

[130] CBI, *A New Look at the Responsibilities of the British Public Company* (1973).

[131] S Wheeler, 'Non-Executive Directors and Corporate Governance' (2009) 60 *NILQ* 51, 54.

[132] J Boswell and J Peters, *Capitalism in Contention* (Cambridge, Cambridge University Press, 1997) 116; Wheeler (n 2).

[133] Bank of England, 'Savings and investment: recent developments in financing arrangements' (1977) Q3 *Quarterly Bulletin* 318.

[134] J Treanor and J Finch, 'Sir David Walker: "I'm a Man of the People, not a City Grandee"', *The Guardian*, 26 November 2009.

[135] Memo from Walker to Cooke, 22.8.79 (6A334/1).

[136] *Report of the Committee to Review the Functioning of Financial Institutions* (Cmnd 7937, 1980) para 917.

scenes, it added that in order to be effective, 'they should not be drawn solely from private lists of "the great and the good"', adding that executives in non-competing firms, as well as 'Academics, consumerists and public figures' and even trade unionists could be considered.[137] In 1982, the Bank established PRO NED to encourage companies to appoint NEDs and to offer their executives as candidates. Sir Adrian Cadbury, a long-time non-executive director at the Bank, was later appointed chair of PRO NED, which worked hard to identify candidates that companies could appoint as NEDs right up until the Cadbury Committee was set up.

C. Promoting Institutional Investor Engagement

Whilst the Watkinson Committee and PRO NED might have been the public faces of the Bank's drive for NEDs, the Bank itself did most of the leg work that led to the creation of the Institutional Shareholders' Committee (ISC). By August 1972, a 'Working Party on Industrial Management and the Institutional Investor' had been established. Its terms of reference were to examine and report on 'a possible structure and method of operation of a central organisation through which institutional investors, in collaboration with those concerned, would stimulate action to improve efficiency in industrial and commercial companies where this is judged necessary'.[138] The document referred to discussions that had been ongoing for several years, and cited support from institutional investors, one of whom had expressed concern about the Labour Party's plans for disenfranchisement of shareholders. There was also support from the Chairman of the Stock Exchange who told the Governor that 'Institutional investors would probably not claim to any special expertise in assessing management, but an organisation, such as envisaged in your paper, could make a valuable contribution to the cure for irresponsible and inefficient management.'[139] The Governor himself seems to have viewed action by institutional investors as a possible substitute for takeovers in terms of improving the efficiency of management.[140]

The Bank's first initiatives ultimately did not receive a high level of support from the institutions, and at a meeting between the Governor and the Committee of London Clearing Banks, Sir Reginald Verdon-Smith said 'that the lack of stronger support for the Initiative had done a good deal to fortify the thinking of the Watkinson Committee on the responsibilities of boards'.[141]

[137] ibid para 918.

[138] Working Party, Terms of Reference (7A19/4/28).

[139] 7A19/3/42.

[140] At his meeting with Insurance Company Chairmen and General Managers, 16 October 1972 (7A19/5/52), the Governor 'recognised the force of the takeover process but would not want to argue that this was the best way of improving the efficiency of British industry'.

[141] 7A19/5/2, 11 January 1973.

In particular, the British Insurance Association (BIA), which represented a very significant fraction of UK shareholdings in 1973,[142] had become 'much more cautious and there was a real danger of the possibility of effective action evaporating'.[143] The Governor highlighted to the insurance industry that there was a 'real need to bring shareholder influence to bear more effectively upon industrial managements'. If they were not willing to act, this would 'have to be done heavy-handedly by Government'.[144]

Three months later, in February 1973, a draft statement on the ISC was drawn up, with only the BIA holding out. The object of the ISC was to coordinate existing investment protection activities of investors where necessary 'with a view … to stimulating action by industrial and commercial companies to improve efficiency'.[145] The ISC was formally launched on 16 April 1973, but by May 1975 it was recognised within the Bank that the ISC had not really met the objectives of the Governor, Lord O'Brien.[146] The Governor had envisaged something along the lines of the City Panel, that is, a 'standing committee or panel of institutional shareholders', with a full time director-general and a small staff responsible for ensuring that action was taken as necessary.[147]

The idea that institutional investors should take action in relation to investee companies did not go away. In its submission to the Wilson Committee of 1977, the Bank said that 'it could bring nothing but good if institutional investors could be mobilised to take, directly or indirectly, an active concern in the commercial performance of the companies whose shares they held'.[148] The Bank maintained its position that there was a need for a 'constructively neutral' central organisation to 'gather together all the parties concerned and ensure that divergent interests can be combined'.[149] Later that year, a discussion paper 'Institutional Investors and Company Management' was circulated by David Walker, who had joined the Bank the previous year.[150] In his communications from 1978 onwards, Walker repeatedly highlighted the 'proprietorial gap', and also the potential for powerful shareholders to intervene with corrective action for inadequate managerial performance. Walker highlighted the limited role – emergency action – to date of the ISC, and set the objective of 'trying to give the institutions a more positive concept of their secondary role' which involved 'preventive medicine

[142] R Dobbins and T McRae, 'Institutional Shareholders and Corporate Management' (1975) 13(6) *Management Decision* 372, 379.
[143] 7A19/5/52.
[144] 'Governor's Meeting with Insurance Company Chairmen and General Managers', 16 October 1972 (7A19/5/52).
[145] 7A19/6/23, 26 February 1973.
[146] 7A19/7/64, 23 May 1975.
[147] Kynaston (n 62) 443.
[148] Bank of England, 'Savings and Investment: Recent Developments in Financing Arrangements' (1977) Q3 *Quarterly Bulletin* 316.
[149] ibid 317–8.
[150] 7A19/9, 3 July 1978.

and early diagnosis'. In October 1978, Walker suggested a code of conduct and responsibility, 'almost a Bank of England Green Paper' which

> would seek to embody an agreed view of 'best practice' in the handling of institutional relationships with companies. Such a paper might cover the case for the appointment of non-executive directors and wider use of audit committees … and suggest areas where it is helpful for institutional investors to intervene in company management and those which are unhelpful.[151]

It can be seen from this that the ideas that underpinned his recommendations relating to the Stewardship Code in 2009[152] were already fairly fully formulated in Walker's mind in 1978, some 31 years earlier, and in the context of a very different kind of crisis. During the decades that followed, the influence of institutional investors ebbed and flowed, but mostly ebbed. In its review of the ISC, the 1980 Wilson Report concluded that the ISC 'was adequate for any collective action that may be needed, though they would often be more effective if they acted at an earlier stage than has been common in the past'.[153] In the event, however, institutional investor engagement largely dropped off the Bank's policy agenda during the 1980s, with the market witnessing an enormous takeover boom, whilst the Bank focused on promoting NEDs. Perhaps as a result of the 1980s takeover boom, the ISC became 'virtually inactive'.[154] It was not until 1989 that internal discussions began again in the Bank of England,[155] Jonathan Charkham highlighting that, in the UK context, there was 'no alternative' to 'active shareholding' because company law had made shareholders 'technically supreme', yet shareholders had 'all but abdicated', doing little more than deciding on the success or failure of takeover bids.[156] Elsewhere, Charkham highlighted the pressure on institutional investors to take 'the lazy way out' and accept the premia offered in takeovers, which meant that 'a thoroughly competent management can be displaced by hostile takeover', so that there might even be a danger of 'excessive instability'.[157] Perhaps as a result of these musings,[158] the ISC was reactivated in 1989, and in 1991 issued a statement

[151] DAW memo dates 26 October 1978 (7A19/9).

[152] D Walker, *A Review of Corporate Governance in UK Banks and Other Financial Industry Entities: Final Recommendations* (London, HM Treasury, 2009) recommendations 16 and 17.

[153] (n 136) para 925.

[154] ISC, 'The Institutional Shareholders' Committee', 24 June 1991 available from the Cadbury archive: cadbury.cjbs.archios.info/_media/files/CAD-01221.pdf.

[155] After his early work with PRO NED, Charkham had been appointed a Chief Adviser to the Bank in 1985, working with David Walker.

[156] J Charkham, 'Corporate Governance and the Market for Companies: Aspects of the Shareholders' Role' *Bank of England Discussion Paper No44*, November 1989, 8.

[157] J Charkham, 'Corporate Governance and the Market for Control of Companies', *Bank of England Panel Paper No25*, March 1989, 11.

[158] ibid 9, highlighted the threat of 'political activity to make boards once again more accountable'.

on the 'Responsibilities of Institutional Shareholders in the UK', which committed to bringing about change in companies and was endorsed by the Cadbury Committee in 1992.[159]

V. CONCLUSION

This chapter has sought to highlight the extraordinary rise and fall of managerialism, and the way in which shareholder primacy corporate governance took its place. Managerialism was driven by the twin forces of shareholder dispersal and technical legitimacy. The emergence of shareholder primacy was the outcome of a complex bundle of forces that included law reform, policy activism on the part of the Bank of England and shifts in the availability of finance. It is hoped that the chapter serves as a limited corrective to accounts which suggest that shareholder primacy is efficient and legitimate because it is simply the outcome of market forces. Rather, it was driven in large part by a series of decisions that were highly contingent and could have been entirely different.

[159] A Cadbury, *Report of the Committee on the Financial Aspects of Corporate Governance* (London, Gee, 1992) paras 6.9–6.11.

13

'A Few Pike in a Trout River'? Hostile Take-Over Bids and Dividend Restraint: The Debate in Government in the 1950s

NEIL ROLLINGS

I. INTRODUCTION

THE SAVOY HOTEL case of late 1953 to mid-1954 has no legal standing but has been recognised as a significant staging post in the development of British company law. This is because it resulted in a critique of the steps taken by the Savoy Hotel Group board to defend the company against a hostile take-over bid. This chapter unpicks the development of this episode through the records of key government departments, the Prime Minister's Private Office, the Treasury and the Board of Trade, which were all at the heart of the government's response, first, to the emergence of hostile takeovers and, second, to the defensive measures adopted in the Savoy Hotel case. It shows that while technical legal considerations were always important, their interpretation by ministers and civil servants was driven by political, social and economic considerations which had little to do with company law per se. As such, this contributes to the existing literature on the political economy of the company, notably the idea that 'the history of the company is inseparable from political conflicts over how the powers and responsibilities of the company should be defined, what should be its licence to operate'.[1] In this case, however, the conflict is not so much between Labour and Conservative thinking, which has been the focus of much work in this field,[2] but between different strands of thinking within the Conservative government and its officials.

[1] A Gamble, G Kelly and J Parkinson, 'Introduction: The Political Economy of the Company' in J Parkinson, A Gamble and G Kelly (eds), *The Political Economy of the Company* (Oxford, Hart Publishing, 2000) 7.

[2] B Clift, A Gamble and M Harris, 'The Labour Party and the Company' in J Parkinson, A Gamble and G Kelly (eds), *The Political Economy of the Company* (Oxford, Hart Publishing,

In the middle of the episode, in February 1954, with the prospect of a debate in the House of Commons on the new phenomenon of hostile take-overs, a stockbroker in the City wrote to Reginald Maudling, the Economic Secretary to the Treasury in Winston Churchill's Conservative government: '[T]here is a good deal of ignorant and faulty thinking on this subject, even amongst people who one might class as reasonably intelligent'. He continued,

> I think it is fair to say that assets should be employed to the greatest possible advantage, even though it may be immoral to-day to say so – I use the word 'advantage' to mean profit. Therefore, it follows that many of the bids are based on the theory that these assets can be employed to a more useful purpose, or, alternatively, by Management that can make greater profit out of them .... I feel convinced that 'a few pike in a trout river' are a very valuable asset, and I equally feel that a great many Boards in this country to-day come well within my description of 'trout'.[3]

This shareholder-dominated view of the company and the concept of a market for corporate control in which hostile takeovers form an important disciplining tool for company boards is one commonly associated with UK corporate governance over the last 50 or so years.[4] It was given theoretical substance in the work of Robin Marris and Henry Manne in the early 1960s and became the predominant narrative for thinking about corporate governance in the UK.[5] This position was markedly different from the pre-Second World War period where it is commonly agreed that shareholders had strictly limited powers over company boards and, while there were mergers, these were agreed and consensual.[6]

As a result, the period from the end of the Second World War to the early 1960s has been highlighted as marking this shift towards the shareholder view of the company and the creation of a market for corporate control.[7] Typically, the Companies Act 1948 is flagged as a crucial factor here as it increased company financial transparency and increased the power of shareholders.[8] Crucial here

2000) 51; J Tomlinson, 'The Labour Party and the Capitalist Firm, c. 1950-1970' (2007) 47 *Historical Journal* 685.

[3] TNA T233/2001, CW Garnett to Maudling, 9 February 1954.

[4] Eg, CM Bruner, *Corporate Governance in the Common-Law World: The Political Foundations of Shareholder Power* (Cambridge, Cambridge University Press, 2013); J Armour and DA Steel, 'Who Writes the Rules for Hostile Takeovers, and Why? The Peculiar Divergence of US and UK Takeover Regulation' (2007) 95 *Georgetown Law Journal* 1727.

[5] R Marris, 'A Model of the "Managerial" Enterprise' (1963) 77 *Quarterly Journal of Economics* 185 and H Manne, 'Mergers and the Market for Corporate Control' (1965) 73 *Journal of Political Economy* 110.

[6] L Hannah, 'Takeover Bids in Britain before 1950: An Exercise in Business "Pre-History"' (1974) 16 *Business History* 65; L Hannah, 'The Shareholders' "Dog" That Did Not Bark: Contested Takeover Bids in Long-Run Comparative Perspective' in D Green, A Owens, J Maltby and J Rutterford (eds), *Men, Women and Money: Perspectives on Gender, Wealth and Investment 1850–1930* (Oxford, Oxford University Press, 2011).

[7] Eg, A Johnston and L Talbot, 'Why Is Modern Capitalism Irresponsible and What Would Make It More Responsible? A Company Law Perspective' (2018) 29 *King's Law Journal* 111.

[8] P Bircher, *From the Companies Act of 1929 to the Companies Act of 1948: A Study of Change in the Law and Practice of Accountancy* (New York, Garland, 1991) and various works by A Johnston

are the requirements for increased transparency of the accounts, providing shareholders with information about the financial state of the company which they previously did not have.[9] One significant reform here was the removal of hidden reserves in most sectors of the economy, that is secret reserves of capital and revenue which did not need to be declared in a company's published accounts.[10] In addition, the legislation now allowed shareholders to remove directors by ordinary resolution, making the process far easier than before.[11] Shareholders were given both the knowledge to understand how a company was performing and the means to discipline the board as well. Greater transparency of accounts also meant prospective bidders had a far more informed picture of which company's shares prices did not reflect the value of the company's assets. As Johnston et al suggest, 'It is no exaggeration to state that the Companies Act 1948 ushered in the modern era of financialised shareholder value corporate governance.'[12]

Added to this legal change was an economic environment which offered the possibility of significant profits. First, there was a tendency for directors not to distribute profits encouraged by fiscal discrimination – the tax on distributed profits was higher than that on undistributed profits[13] – and government appeals for voluntary dividend restraint.[14] Second, companies had built up considerable reserves during and after the war because of unspent depreciation provisions and an inability to invest because of the lack of raw materials. Third, many companies had not revalued their assets in a period of inflation so such assets, particularly property, could be sold for a quick profit. Access to such cash and assets was especially attractive given ongoing restrictions on borrowing, most notably the need to get approval from the Capital Issues Committee (CIC). The CIC was set up in 1939 to advise on applications to the Treasury for the issue of capital, the offer of securities for sale and on the renewal or postponement of

including A Johnston, ch 12 in this volume, which argues that the Cohen Report which led to the 1948 Act 'weakened the position of management, particularly in listed companies, by opening them up to hostile takeover'.

[9] Hannah, 'Takeover Bids' (n 6) 69–70, 75; H Callaghan, *Contestants, Profiteers, and the Political Dynamics of Marketization: How Shareholders Gained Control Rights in Britain, Germany, and France* (Oxford, Oxford University Press, 2018) 46; H Rose, *Disclosure in Company Accounts* (London, Institute for Economic Affairs, 1963) 23.

[10] AJ Arnold and P Collier, *The Evolution of Reserve and Provision Accounting in the UK, 1938–50* (Edinburgh, Institute of Chartered Accountants of Scotland, 2007) 22–26. One notable exception was the banking sector, see M Billings and F Capie, 'Transparency and Financial Reporting in mid-20th Century British Banking' (2009) 33 *Accounting Forum* 38.

[11] A Johnston, A Hatchuel and B Segrestin, 'From Balanced Enterprise to Hostile Takeover: How the Law Forgot about Management' (2019) 39 *Legal Studies* 75.

[12] ibid 92.

[13] M Daunton, *Just Taxes: The Politics of Taxation in Britain, 1914–1979* (Cambridge, Cambridge University Press, 2009) 200–04.

[14] JF Wright, 'The Capital Market and the Finance of Industry' in GDN Worswick and PH Ady (eds), *The British Economy in the Nineteen-Fifties* (Oxford, Clarendon Press, 1962) 464; Sir A Johnston, *The City Take-Over Code* (Oxford, Oxford University Press, 1980) 8–9; G Bull and A Vice, *Bid for Power* (London, Elek Books, 1958) 15–18. The following points in the text come from Wright.

the maturity date of securities for sale. This meant that until 1959, all significant borrowing (over £10,000 in 1947) had to be approved by the committee before it could be undertaken.

In these circumstances 'speculators' and 'takeover tycoons' like the infamous Charles Clore were able to discover companies with such underexploited resources and, to buy their shares.[15] Clore's first major target was J. Sears & Co., the parent company of Freeman, Hardy & Willis, the shoe shop chain, in early 1953.[16] Next came the Savoy Hotel case, 'one of the most fascinating financial struggles of this century which, before it was done, ousted world crises from the headlines, led to a government enquiry, and inspired one of the most disputed company schemes ever devised'.[17] At first, condemnation focussed on the bidders.[18] However, some opinion shifted once the defence device adopted by the Savoy board became known, quickly being established as a legal cause célèbre.[19] The case had potentially far-reaching implications for takeovers and more generally for the relationship between boards of directors and shareholders.[20] In response to the threat of a takeover, the Savoy board transferred the Berkeley Hotel, which it was believed was the targeted undervalued asset, to a newly created company, the Worcester Building Co. whose equity was owned by the Savoy staff benevolent fund. All of this was done without prior shareholder knowledge let alone consent. The City and the press responded with hostility to this device and the Board of Trade set up an investigation into the board's activities.[21] The inspector's report concluded that the board 'genuinely believed that it was for the benefit of those Companies and of the stockholders of the Savoy Company to do so, and received clear legal advice that they were entitled to implement them. It was nevertheless in [his] opinion an invalid use of the powers of management'.[22] Although his conclusion had no legal force, it marked an important check on boards' perceived ability to defend themselves against hostile takeovers and an important step towards acceptance of hostile takeover bids.

[15] For accounts of Clore's career see D Clutterbuck and M Devine, *Clore: The Man and His Millions* (London, Weidenfeld & Nicolson, 1987); C Gordon, *The Two Tycoons: A Personal Memoir of Charles Clore and Jack Cotton* (London, Hamish Hamilton, 1984). The best contemporary account of the phenomenon in the 1950s is Bull and Vice (n 9).

[16] R Roberts, 'Regulatory Responses to the Market for Corporate Control in Britain in the 1950s' (1992) 34 *Business History* 183, 186–187.

[17] Bull and Vice (n 14) 29.

[18] Roberts (n 16) 189.

[19] LCB Gower, *The Principles of Modern Company Law*, 3rd edn (London, Stevens & Sons, 1969) 521 fn 35. It is still mentioned in the 2021 11th edition – PL Davies, S Worthington and C Hare, *Gower Principles of Modern Company Law*, 11th edn (London, Sweet & Maxwell, 2021) 990.

[20] LCB Gower, 'Corporate Control – The Battle for the Berkeley' (1955) 68 *Harvard Law Review* 1176.

[21] Bull and Vice (n 14) 36–42.

[22] Board of Trade, *Report of Mr. E Milner Holland, The Savoy Hotel Limited and the Berkeley Hotel Company Limited: Investigation* (London, HMSO, 1954).

Accordingly, it is common to refer to a shift from the mid-1950s in attitudes towards takeovers.[23] Thereafter, led by City opinion, it is believed, the Bank of England and the government came to accept hostile takeovers as part of the UK system of corporate governance such that by the end of the decade and the start of the next wave of mergers and takeovers there had been a 'profound change' in attitudes and 'a turning point' in the development of the takeover.[24] Crucial here were the 'Notes on Amalgamations', issued in 1959 to provide self-regulatory guidelines on mergers and takeovers, which re-affirmed the principle of shareholder control, later reinforced in the 1968 City Code.[25]

Roberts' research, just cited, has been highly influential in constructing this understanding of these changes and, in particular, the regulatory response of government to such takeovers in the 1950s. Two features of his account are worthy of emphasis: first, the Bank of England and government were critical of hostile takeovers in the early 1950s, siding clearly with directors defending their companies and, second, that, led by City opinion, the Bank and the government had come to terms with such takeovers by the end of the 1950s. This chapter, by focussing on government discussions around the notorious Savoy Hotel case and its aftermath will show that this is an oversimplified and, in some respects, misleading account. The main reason for this is that Roberts draws heavily on the records of the Bank of England supplemented by two files from the Prime Minister's Office. This fails to take into account material held by the Treasury and the Board of Trade. As will be shown, both were important actors in this field – the Treasury because of its concern over the policy of voluntary dividend restraint and the Board of Trade because it was the government department responsible for company law – and both need to be incorporated into accounts of the episode. Despite the wealth of existing literature exploring these issues from a range of disciplines – accounting historians,[26] financial historians,[27] legal historians,[28] business and economic historians,[29] and political economists[30] – this

[23] Johnston et al (n 11) 96.

[24] Roberts (n 16) 193 and 194. For restatements of this position, all based on Roberts' account see A Johnston, 'The Shrinking Scope of CSR in UK Corporate Law' (2017) 74 *Washington & Lee Law Review* 1001, 1018–19; D Kershaw, *Principles of Takeover Legislation* (Oxford, Oxford University Press, 2016) 79–80, and Hannah, 'The Shareholders' "Dog"' (n 6) 244.

[25] Bruner (n 4) 149–150.

[26] Eg, AJ Arnold and DR Matthews, 'Corporate Financial Disclosures in the UK, 1920-50: The Effects of Legislative Change and Managerial Discretion' (2002) 32 *Accounting and Business Research* 3; and J Maltby, 'Was the Companies Act 1947 A Response to a National Crisis' (2000) NS 5 *Accounting History* 31.

[27] Eg, D Kynaston, *The City of London Volume IV: A Club No More 1945–2000* (London, Chatto & Windus, 2001) 62–65; and Roberts (n 16).

[28] Eg, B Cheffins, 'Does Law Matter? The Separation of Ownership and Control in the United Kingdom' (2001) 30 *Journal of Legal Studies* 459–484; A Johnston, 'Takeover Regulation: Historical and Theoretical Perspectives on the City Code' (2007) 66 *CLJ* 422–460; and A Johnston (n 24).

[29] Eg, Hannah, 'Takeover Bids' (n 6); and Hannah, 'Shareholders' "Dog"' (n 6).

[30] Eg, Callaghan (n 9) 39–67; and J Parkinson, A Gamble and G Kelly (eds), *The Political Economy of the Company* (Oxford, Hart Publishing, 2000).

source material has not previously been exploited. Using these records, the rest of the chapter develops a chronological narrative of the Savoy Hotel case and its aftermath, highlighting in particular the different positions taken by the Bank of England and the Treasury on the one hand and the Board of Trade, notably its President, Peter Thorneycroft, before drawing some conclusions.

II. THE EMERGENCE OF TAKEOVER BIDS

From the outset the Treasury was involved in assisting the defence of company boards against hostile takeover bids. As early as January 1953 it was advising J Sears & Co. on making an application to the CIC to use funds to make a bonus issue to shareholders and 'doing as much as we legitimately can to help them'.[31] Its oversight of the independent CIC was one reason for the Treasury's interest in takeover bids, but the main one was its responsibility for the policy of voluntary dividend restraint. This was introduced by the Federation of British Industries in 1948 as a response to the then Labour government's call for restraint in return for voluntary wage restraint by trade unions. Despite the breakdown of wage restraint in 1950 and the replacement of the Labour government by a Conservative one in 1951, the Conservative Chancellor of the Exchequer, RA Butler, continued to emphasise the need for voluntary dividend restraint. Companies, however, complained that their adherence to the voluntary dividend restraint policy was exacerbating their exposure to a possible takeover bid.[32] Within the Treasury there were concerns for the implications for maintaining the policy. Robert Hall, the Chief Economic Adviser to the Government, voiced these concerns:

> The reason for this policy is undoubtedly the relation with wage policy: there seems to be no way of combining wage restraint with high employment except by voluntary co-operation by the Unions.
>
> From this point of view, it does not matter a great deal why Mr. Clore and his friends make their moves – the papers show that Sears Board put up their dividends and paid a bonus because they wanted to anticipate Mr. Clore (though they were not successful). If this happened generally, the Unions would certainly argue that dividend limitation was being frustrated by speculators and that they were going to give up wage limitation too ….
>
> While our policy is in favour of restraint generally, surely H.M.G. ought to let it be known that they disapprove of such bids.[33]

Nevertheless, despite their anxiety about such events, Treasury, Bank and Board of Trade policy was to emphasise the voluntary nature of dividend limitation

[31] TNA T233/2000, Lees to Compton, 9 January 1953, added handwritten note by Compton.
[32] Eg, TNA T233/2000, John Bedford, Debenhams Ltd to Maudling, 29 May 1953.
[33] TNA T233/1392, Hall to Compton, 3 March 1953.

and that the government should not intervene to guide the City in individual cases where a takeover bid was threatened.[34]

III. THE SAVOY BID

The issue of hostile takeovers was reignited in government in the autumn of 1953 when the Savoy Hotel Group came under pressure. Hugh Wontner, its Managing Director and Chairman, was extremely well connected and used these connections to gain exceptional access to ministers and civil servants to make his case and to test possible defence devices. Winston Churchill, the Prime Minister, for one, had a special relationship with the Savoy Hotel and its board. Churchill would often take his Cabinet there for meals, it was where one of his favourite dining clubs met and when he was recovering from illness a suite at Claridge's, owned by the Savoy Hotel Group, was put at his disposal.[35] Wontner had even arranged the wedding breakfast at 10 Downing Street for Anthony Eden, the Foreign Secretary, in 1952 at Churchill's specific request.[36]

Wontner turned to Churchill when the Savoy Board realised that the company's shares were being bought up. Churchill pointed him towards the Board of Trade.[37] Wontner asked about possible investigations but also raised the possibility of the government requisitioning either property or shares as a way of defeating the bidder. About two weeks later Wontner saw Churchill again to update him and to ask for further advice.[38] Seeing Churchill at 10 am, by 11.30 am Wontner was meeting Thorneycroft.[39] Wontner strongly suspected that Clore was behind the bid: if Clore gained control his likely actions would not 'be to the real interest of the country, since the Savoy was a national asset and earned very substantial amounts of dollars'.[40] He then asked the Board of Trade to appoint an enquiry into the bidder's identity. Thorneycroft was sympathetic to 'companies who have pursued a conservative policy, partly at any rate in response to the Treasury's appeal for dividend limitation, and then find themselves at the mercy of "take-over bidders"'. He also considered the Savoy as a 'national asset': 'if in fact the result of Mr. Clore's securing control would be to impair the services it offers, we ought, if we properly can, to try to prevent that'.[41]

[34] TNA T233/2000, Compton to J Marshall, 9 July 1953.

[35] Callaghan (n 9) 50, and B Davies, 'Corporate Control: The Savoy Hotel Re-Visited' (1972) 3 *Cambrian Law Review* 34.

[36] Churchill Archives Centre, Churchill Papers, CHUR2/198, Wontner to JR Colville, 9 February 1952 [online version available by subscription from www.churchillarchive.com].

[37] TNA BT58/634, J Cowan, 'Note of a Meeting: The Savoy Hotels Group', undated but meeting held 23 October 1953.

[38] TNA PREM11/656, Colville to Churchill, 6 November 1953.

[39] TNA PREM11/656, Colville to Lt-General Sir Frederick Browning, 6 November 1953.

[40] TNA BT58/634, Ian Gray, 'Mr. Clore and the Savoy Hotel', 10 November 1953.

[41] ibid.

Accordingly, Thorneycroft saw the chairman of the Stock Exchange, Sir John Braithwaite, the next day to discuss appointing an investigation under section 172(3) of the Companies Act 1948. Braithwaite was not keen on an investigation but that if the requisite number of shareholders made an application 'we should have to consider it carefully and interpret a tricky piece of legislation'.[42] The President broadly agreed and sought legal advice, with officials concerned that any investigation might set a precedent leading to a deluge of applications for investigations, necessitating legislative reform.[43] The legal advice was that there was no reason to turn down the application for an investigation.[44] With this in mind Thorneycroft met Wontner, explaining that the enquiry might take more than three months and that announcing the enquiry might damage the Savoy share price (both points raised by Braithwaite) but Wontner insisted that the enquiry should proceed. To this end, JB Lindon QC was appointed as the inspector on 18 November. Two days before the announcement representatives of Harold Samuel, who was the main bidder disclosed by the Lindon enquiry (with Clore separately acting as a second purchaser of Savoy shares), met Board of Trade officials in order to disclose their client's identity 'as perfectly reputable persons engaged in a perfectly legitimate transaction' but which the Board of Trade officials present interpreted as an attempt (to no avail) to get the Board of Trade to call off the appointment of an enquiry.[45]

Meanwhile, the Economic Secretary to the Treasury, Reginald Maudling, was asked to provide Churchill with a note on takeover bids. Maudling set out the Treasury's perspective:

> All this is rather distasteful because it is liable to involve the disruption of existing business. It creates a bad public impression when large capital profits are seen to be earned by mere financial manipulations. It is also a danger to the Chancellor's policy of voluntary restraint, both of wages and dividends. The Boards of companies whose shareholders are likely to be approached in this manner are tempted to increase their dividend distributions substantially in the hope of increasing the Stock Exchange valuation of their shares, so making the take-over bid less attractive, though in some cases this can be bad from the long-term interests of their companies.
>
> But while the process is distasteful, and may be politically embarrassing, it is difficult to see anything that the Government can do about it. It is impossible by legislation to prevent individuals offering to buy the property of other individuals. Yet, short of such legislation, there is really nothing that would hamper the process, not is it possible to do anything to dry up the sources of finance for the speculators concerned.
>
> I have consulted the Governor of the Bank of England, who shares our dislike for many of these operations, but tells me that so far he himself, despite much thought

[42] TNA BT58/634, FW Glaves-Smith, 'Note of a Meeting: "Take-over bids"', 11 November 1953.

[43] TNA BT58/634, FW Glaves-Smith, 'The Savoy Hotel', 11 November 1953.

[44] TNA BT58/634, RWA Speed, 'Mr Clore and the Savoy Hotel', 12 November 1953.

[45] TNA BT58/634, unsigned, 'Savoy Hotel Limited', undated note of a meeting held on 16 November 1953.

on the subject, has reached the same conclusion, that there is no action that either the Government or the Bank can properly take in the matter.[46]

As Roberts has argued, there is a clear consensus by the middle of November 1953 among the key government actors in the Treasury and the Board of Trade (as well as the Bank of England) that hostile takeovers were broadly distasteful but there was little that the government could do to stop such activities.[47]

Once Lindon's enquiry was published – it took only two weeks rather than the three months mentioned by Braithwaite[48] – the names of the two bidders were in the public domain but there was little else directly the government could do.[49] However, the Governor of the Bank of England did follow up by reminding the banks and insurance companies to avoid lending to speculators.[50] Roberts' discussion of the Savoy case ends here because on 10 December 1953 Samuel sold his shareholding to the Savoy Board and the takeover bid was over. However, this was by no means the end of the discussion on the issue within government with a clear split between the Treasury and Bank of England on the one hand and the Board of Trade on the other over how to respond to the Savoy Board's actions.

IV. REACTION IN GOVERNMENT TO THE SAVOY HOTEL GROUP'S DEFENCE

The first inklings of difficulties to come preceded the Savoy Board's defensive actions at the start of December. On 27 November Wontner met Thorneycroft. Wontner wanted to issue a statement to the Savoy Hotel Ltd's shareholders 'to the effect that, in view of the importance of the tourist trade, the Government would not like to see any change in the present policy of the Savoy Hotel Co. or in the present user of their properties'.[51] Thorneycroft refused and, when Wontner asked what he could put in such a statement about the government's attitude, Thorneycroft made clear that 'so far as he was concerned Mr. Wontner had no authority to say anything at all about the Government's attitude'. Even worse, since no one else was present at the meeting Thorneycroft immediately afterwards asked for a letter to be drafted as 'he did not wish there to be any possibility of Mr. Wontner's misinterpreting what he had said' and the letter was delivered by hand that afternoon.[52] Wontner responded in forthright terms: 'I was surprised to receive your letter, sent by hand to me at the Savoy within

[46] TNA PREM11/656, Maudling to Churchill, 13 November 1953.
[47] Roberts (n 16) 188–189.
[48] TNA T233/2000, Board of Trade, 'The Savoy Hotel Limited Investigation: Interim Report of JB Lindon, QC', 28 November 1953. The report was published on 1 December.
[49] TNA BT58/634, Thorneycroft to Churchill, 30 November 1953.
[50] Roberts (n 16) 189.
[51] TNA BT58/634, I Gray, 'The Savoy Hotel', 27 November 1953.
[52] ibid.

two hours of my conversation with you. As it was quite unnecessary for you to confirm what you had just told me, I can only regard your letter as a reflection on my integrity.'[53] In his fury he sent the correspondence to Churchill setting out his astonishment at Thorneycroft's refusal. Also, given that he saw Thorneycroft at 12.15 pm and the letter arrived at 1.50 pm, 'I must regard it as a most unpleasant reflection upon my integrity.'[54] Churchill's private secretary, wrote calming words, what a Board of Trade official described as 'the polite brush off'. Thorneycroft ignored Wonter's letter.[55]

Nor was this Wontner's only gambit as he sought to find a defence device. He also wrote to the Financial Secretary to the Treasury, John Boyd-Carpenter.[56] His letter referred to one device but in his meeting and a subsequent meeting with Maudling (both apparently immediately before his heated argument with Thorneycroft) he set out a different idea. Wontner had seen counsel, Denys Buckley, the night before. Buckley had suggested that 'it would be possible to create a special type of share to be vested in a publicly appointed person or persons, which would carry with it the right to prevent radical changes in the running of Claridges'.[57] On the basis of the archival evidence, he did not refer to this idea in his later meeting with Thorneycroft. The Treasury felt it should be ready to examine such a proposal but it was left for Wontner to develop the idea and that he would need to re-direct his discussions to the Board of Trade, something Wontner was reluctant to do.[58] A few days later the Worcester Buildings Co. scheme was announced.

This announcement completely changed the situation and brought disagreements within government out into the open. Samuel's initial reaction was to demand an enquiry into the actions of the Savoy board under section 165 of the Companies Act 1948 and that this should be appointed as a matter of urgency.[59] However, with the sale of his shareholding he no longer required an investigation.[60] Thorneycroft met his officials to discuss whether, among other things, the government should initiate an investigation into the Savoy board's actions over the Worcester Building Co.[61] It was felt that a wide-ranging enquiry would be difficult but that, '[t]he implications of some of the

[53] TNA PREM11/656, Wontner to Thorneycroft, 28 November 1953.

[54] TNA PREM11/656, Wontner to Colville (Churchill's private secretary), 28 November 1953.

[55] TNA PREM11/656, Colville to Wontner, 30 November 1953, and TNA BT58/634, FW Glaves-Smith handwritten comments on Colville to Glaves-Smith, 30 November 1953 and Wontner to Thorneycroft, 28 November 1953.

[56] TNA T233/2137, Wontner to Boyd-Carpenter, 26 November 1953.

[57] TNA T233/2137, Boyd-Carpenter to H Brittain (Treasury official), 27 November 1953.

[58] TNA T233/2137, H Beer (Board of Trade) to Compton, 1 December 1953, and TNA T233/2137, Compton, 'Savoy', 27 November 1953.

[59] TNA BT58/634, Gray, 'The Savoy Hotel', 4 December 1953, and R Woodley (Board of Trade official) to Glaves-Smith, 'Savoy Hotel', 4 December 1953.

[60] TNA BT58/634, Leslie Nathanson & Co to Beer, 11 December 1953.

[61] TNA BT58/634, Glaves-Smith, 'Note of a Meeting: Take-over Bids and "Hiving Off"', 15 December 1953.

measures taken recently were very serious for the whole Company system'.[62] It was agreed that the Law Officers should be asked for an opinion on the actions of the Savoy board, with the possibility of launching an investigation.

In the meantime, Wontner had contacted Maudling because the Savoy board needed to find the funds to buy out Samuel. The banks were 'very sympathetic' but he also needed further assistance: would the Treasury either lend some money or, if not, guarantee a loan made by someone else?[63] Maudling offered sympathy but declined. Nevertheless, he and others in the Treasury did consider the issue of the need for CIC approval for the financing.[64] The chairman of the CIC, Lord Kennet, advised that the case for rejection was clear and that giving consent would set a 'very bad precedent … and he hopes that the Treasury will not weaken'.[65] Under the standard procedure, the Board of Trade were asked for their opinion on the Savoy Group's application (under the name Clairville Investments Ltd) to the CIC. The Board's opinion was lukewarm at best towards the Savoy application, specifically stating that the Board of Trade could make no judgement on whether the group under the current board would contribute more to the national interest than any other board. In addition, Thorneycroft wished to discuss the case with Maudling before any decision was announced.[66]

On 23 December the Financial Secretary, Boyd-Carpenter, met Thorneycroft on Maudling's behalf. Despite the CIC's rejection of the application, as expected, Boyd-Carpenter informed Thorneycroft that Treasury official opinion, with which he agreed, was that the CIC recommendation should not be accepted. Thorneycroft expressed his surprise at this decision. His personal view was that the committee's advice should not be rejected without very strong reasons and as far as he could tell there were insufficient reasons. The Board of Trade saw no problem with the committee's conclusions nor any Board of Trade reasons in favour of the application which were outside its remit. Despite this clear difference of opinion, the Chancellor of the Exchequer approved the application later that day: he had 'decided in favour of the Treasury view and against that expressed by the President'.[67]

Why had the Treasury taken this unusual position, in opposition to the Committee and the President of the Board of Trade? Edward Bridges, the Permanent Secretary, summed up the situation as follows:

> Wontner and his friends have behaved in some way foolishly and stupidly. The fact remains, however, that they have been assaulted by the take-over emergence and that their attempt to retain control of the undertaking depends on this application. If the application is rejected, two things will happen. First, it will be a victory for the

[62] ibid.
[63] TNA T233/2137, Maudling, 'Note for the Record', 10 December 1953.
[64] TNA T233/2137, RT Armstrong (Treasury), 'Note for Record', 18 December 1953.
[65] TNA T233/2137, Compton, 'Savoy', undated but mid-December 1953.
[66] TNA BT58/634, Glaves-Smith, 'The Savoy Hotel', 21 December 1953.
[67] TNA BT58/634, Glaves-Smith, 'The Savoy Hotel Case', 23 December 1953. The quote is a handwritten note added 29 December.

> take-over bid side, secondly, so far as I can see, it probably means personal disaster for the Savoy Board, who will inevitably fail to carry out their undertaking to purchase the shares.
>
> In a sense the ordinary person will regard the fact that C.I.C. consent is required for borrowing from the Bank of England in this case as somewhat of a technicality. The Treasury and the Government will get all the blame for the fall of the Savoy Board and the victory of the take-over bid merchants.
>
> This seems to me to override all the other points. I just cannot see how Ministers could face this and hope to get away with it.
>
> I should add that Mr. Governor also feels this very strongly indeed. He wholly recognises that this is a decision for Ministers: but he has been at pains to be very helpful in unravelling the problem and to give us the City's reactions. He tells me that the City would not have understood it at all if the application to the C.I.C. was rejected.
>
> To sum up, it is a difficult case and by no means all the merits are on one side: but I am convinced that the application to borrow the money must be approved, although in terms which will [be] related to this specific case and will not commit us to do the same in other cases.[68]

He added the handwritten comment, 'Mr. Governor, to whom I spoke, said that rejection would result in A HELL OF A RUMPUS in the City, which he thought would spread to Westminster'[69] [emphasis in original]. In other words, political considerations plus the recognised special status of the Savoy Hotel Group lay behind the decision.

V. THE SECOND ENQUIRY

From this point on relations between the Board of Trade, particularly the President, Thorneycroft, and the Treasury became worse. Churchill also became unhappy with Thorneycroft.[70] The key issue here was whether the Board of Trade should launch an investigation against the actions of the Savoy Board. Bridges did not think that it should and Boyd-Carpenter went further, 'all this is now settled, and I think it would be rather rough to pursue them for an ill[-]advised act taken in stress of an emergency which, in the event, has hurt no one', 'the less we now do on this subject the better'.[71] In contrast, 'it is very clear from my discussion with Mr. Beer [Board of Trade] that the President is disposed to be less critical of take-over operations than we are, and has some inclination towards thinking that Mr. Governor may have put a foot wrong with his reminder to the banks of their duty'.[72]

[68] TNA T233/2137, Bridges, 'Savoy', 23 December 1953.
[69] ibid.
[70] TNA PREM11/656, Churchill to Thorneycroft, 7 February 1954.
[71] TNA T233/2001, Boyd-Carpenter, 'Take-over Bids', 7 January 1954.
[72] TNA T233/2001, S Lees (Treasury) to Compton, 'Take-over Bids', 1 January 1954.

This was the context in which Thorneycroft met with Maudling, the Attorney General, the Solicitor General, and others on 8 January. Maudling argued that since no one had been harmed by the action 'it would be best to let the matter rest there, and not re-excite the public'.[73] Thorneycroft said he would make a decision on an enquiry once he had the final opinion of the Law Officers. Although it was decided not to have a broader enquiry into take-over bids, Thorneycroft took the opportunity to air the arguments in favour of such an enquiry: 'There was a good deal of public misunderstanding about take-over bids and an enquiry might help to make it clear that such transactions were not necessarily bad, and were, indeed, an essential part of the working of the capitalist system.' From the Treasury's point of view the meeting was 'not a success':

> In the Board of Trade camp there was no trace of the advice given to Sir M. Dean [Board of Trade] by Sir E. Bridges and Sir N. Brook [Cabinet Secretary] to procure a Law Officers' opinion on the type of transaction exemplified by the Savoy Directors promotion of the Worcester Building Company, not on the Worcester transaction itself.[74]

It was clear that the Law Officers would advise that there were grounds to appoint an enquiry and that the Board of Trade:

> [W]ill advise him to do so on grounds of Board of Trade policy i.e. they are convinced it is necessary to prove that the Worcester transaction was not only improper but also illegal and the Savoy inspection is the way to establish that in public. The Treasury view on the other hand (which was expressed at the meeting, but is not recorded in the Board of Trade note) is that a decision to inspect would look vindictive. It would also be inconsistent with the Chancellor's attitude to the Savoy case which was that Government powers should not be used to frustrate the arrangements which the Savoy Directors had made to restore their control over the Company. An inspection based on a formal decision by the Board of Trade that (in the words of the Statute) there were circumstances suggesting 'that the persons concerned with the management of its affairs have in connection therewith been guilty of fraud, misfeasance or other misconduct' must discredit the Company and spoil its chances of securing the finances required to carry on the business after buying back the shares from Mr. Samuel. Finally, from the standpoint of public policy on take over bids, Parliament and the public would sharply contrast the critical attitude of the Chancellor and the Governor on the one hand, and the apparent determination of the Board of Trade to punish a concern that defended itself even after it had undertaken to wash out the transaction which had given offence.[75]

Maudling decided to hold fire in the meeting but that he and Treasury officials should be ready to make their case as soon as Thorneycroft received the Law Officers' report. Two weeks later that legal opinion was provided, saying, as

[73] TNA T233/2001, 'Glaves-Smith', 'Note of a Meeting: Take-over Bids and "Hiving Off"', 9 January 1954.

[74] TNA T233/2001, Compton, 'Take-over Bids and the Savoy Case', 11 January 1954.

[75] ibid.

expected in the Treasury, that there were circumstances entitling the President to appoint an inspector.[76] However, the Treasury had clearly been at work on the Board of Trade. It was recognised that there was a difference of opinion between the Treasury which believed 'the attitude to take-over bids should be selective and we should be critical of the speculative type' while Thorneycroft 'likes speculation as being good for markets and the efficiency of business':[77]

> The President thinks that speculation should be encouraged for the sake of an active share market and to stimulate business. His principal concern is to see that shareholders are protected and that the Companies Acts are efficiently operated for this purpose. From this standpoint, he is an enemy of dividend limitation and generally of any action taken by the boards of companies to prevent shareholders from getting full value out of their property by big dividends or break-up of assets.[78]

However, a compromise was proposed: the Board of Trade would approach the Savoy board about what they had to say about the Berkeley device and whether it had been undone. 'If the answer is satisfactory (as it is bound to be) then the President will feel justified in concluding that he need not order an inspection but can close the case.'[79]

Thorneycroft then updated Churchill. He simply noted that the action of the Savoy board 'raises a matter of substantial importance in Company law affecting the whole basis on which the existing Companies' system operates'.[80] He now had the Law Officers' opinion that the board's actions did appear to be misfeasance or other misconduct, and possibly even fraud. He added that the Chancellor agreed that the Board of Trade should act as it normally would in such cases by writing to the Savoy board stating that there was a prima facie case to appoint an inspector and inviting its observations.[81]

Neither the Treasury nor Churchill were happy with this letter. The Treasury believed the report was misleading because it made no mention of the compromise that the case would be dropped if the Savoy board apologised. Moreover, there was a concern that Churchill would ask Butler how he had come to agree a course of action which 'looks like victimising Mr. Wontner and his fellow directors'.[82] Instead, it would appear that Churchill's ire was focussed on Thorneycroft. He should consider, Churchill wrote:

> [T]he great provocation they have received and the fight they were making to preserve the character of their business. This should be set against legal technicalities. After all as soon as they realised they were infringing the law did they not withdraw the new

[76] TNA T233/2001, Beer to Compton, 26 January 1954. A copy of the opinion is attached to the letter.
[77] TNA T233/2001, Compton, 'Notes', 29 January 1954.
[78] TNA T233/2001, Compton, 'Take-over Bids in Parliament', 29 January 1954.
[79] TNA T233/2001, Compton, 'Notes', 29 January 1954.
[80] TNA PREM11/656, Thorneycroft to Churchill, 2 February 1954.
[81] ibid.
[82] TNA T233/2001, Compton, 'The Savoy Hotel', 4 February 1954.

> Company and cancel it, so that no shareholders were in fact damaged? There will be a certain amount of sympathy in the House of Commons (not one side only) with the case of employees who had worked for 20 years in the Berkeley Hotel and were to be cleared out for the sake of a profit-making ramp by speculators.[83]

It was not until almost one month later that the observations of the Savoy board were received.[84] It consisted of a 14-page robust defence of the actions of the board. It quoted the debate in the House of Commons on 11 February 1954, discussed the reputation of the Savoy and refuted the suggestion that the board's actions had not served the shareholders well. Moreover, these actions 'were not measures taken by the directors in panic at the last minute … but they were examined in great detail and with care by Counsel and ourselves, as well as by the directors of the Company'.[85] The counsel used was Denys Buckley and he advised that:

> [S]o long as the directors acted bona fide in what they believed to be the best interests of the Company, they would be fulfilling their duty, and this, he pointed out, did not mean they should take into account only a sectional interest (it might be the majority) of the present members, or even, in his opinion, the interest of all the present members, but of present and future members. He continued that … the Board should, in his opinion, conduct the Company's business upon the footing that it would be continued as a going concern and accordingly should balance a long[-] term view against short term interests of the present members.
>
> Mr. Buckley also advised that the objects of The Berkeley Hotel Company Limited included the sale of any part of its property for shares and that, by the Articles, that power was delegated to the Board. Decisions on all matters so delegated were for the Board alone, with whose discretion the Company in general meeting could not interfere, so long as the directors acted bona fide in what they believed to be the best interests of the company.
>
> Mr. Buckley further advised that such a sale as he outlined (and which was the one carried into effect) was intra vires the directors of The Berkeley Hotel Company Limited, and that the transaction would be one upon which they could properly embark if they were bona fide of opinion that it would be in the better interests of their Company that the new state of affairs, as he indicated, should be brought into existence, rather than that the risk, then existing, should continue of the sale of their freehold site for cash.[86]

Accordingly, the Savoy board believed that there was no case for the appointment of an inspector given that they had acted on the basis of counsel and believed that their actions were bona fide in the best interests of the company.

[83] TNA PREM11/656, Churchill to Thorneycroft, 7 February 1954.

[84] TNA BT58/635, Fladgate & Co., 'The Savoy Hotel Limited: The Berkeley Hotel Company Limited', 4 March 1954.

[85] ibid 6.

[86] ibid 9–10. Buckley's opinion is attached to this letter. Ironically, Buckley was also advising the Board of Trade on aspects of the Companies Act 1948 at about the same time as he was giving his opinion to the Savoy board.

In contrast, Board of Trade officials did not agree the Savoy board's response was satisfactory. Action had to be taken because the letter showed no contrition.[87] Having examined the possibilities they concluded that an enquiry under section 165 (b) of the Companies Act 1948 was the next step. Before he had seen the Savoy's response, Thorneycroft 'doubted whether he would be able to let things rest with the Savoy reply' as 'it seemed necessary to establish whether it [the Savoy's actions] were legal or not' and that, as an enquiry would not do this, wondered if there was any alternative path of action to settle the issue of legality.[88] Having read the official analysis of the options available he came round to the idea of proceeding with an enquiry, though he did not wish to tell Churchill this until he had received advice from the Law Officers confirming this approach in order to avoid an exchange of correspondence with the Prime Minister at this stage.

The Law Officers' further opinion was sent on 8 April 1954. They did not differ on the general principles set out by Buckley but felt that Buckley had defined the board's discretion too widely as what the Savoy board had done:

> [A]ppears to be a quite unprecedented exercise of the powers of Directors: we are unable to find any reported cases where directors, by exercising their powers of sale, have removed from the control of the Company its principal asset on terms in any way resembling what was done here: and we think that the mere fact that the transaction had this unprecedented result may well be said to require from the Directors a high standard of proof that they did act bona fide in what they considered to be the best interests of the Company. If this principle be of such wide applicability as to cover this kind of case, it is obvious that Directors have great scope for defeating the aspirations of their members by merely saying that in their opinion what they did was in the best interest of the Company, and such operations would henceforth be extremely difficult to prevent.[89]

In light of this, if there was to be an enquiry they recommended that it be by an inspector appointed under section 165(b) rather than anything more general and that it should be carried out by 'someone of the highest status and reputation', a judge of the High Court.[90]

In the Treasury there was both dismay and a sense of throwing in the towel: the Savoy board's response had forced the Board of Trade into this action. Had the Savoy board admitted that they had been misguided it would have been possible:

> [T]o follow the Governor's advice to let bygones be bygones. The Board of Trade would then [have] take[n] up the position in public that they had been advised that the device was illegal, but that, as it had been undone by the Savoy Board and

[87] TNA BT58/635, RWA Speed, 'Savoy Hotel Limited', 11 March 1954.
[88] TNA BT58/635, Glaves-Smith, 'The Savoy Case', 10 March 1954.
[89] TNA BT58/635, 'Savoy Hotel Limited: Note by Law Officers', 8 April 1954.
[90] TNA BT58/635, 'Savoy Hotel Limited: Note by Law Officers', 8 April 1954.

condemned by public opinion, there was no need to proceed further with the Savoy case or to amend the law.[91]

There was no alternative but to agree with the Board of Trade that the appointment of an inspector was inevitable. As the Chancellor noted, 'This is v[ery] awkward and unnecessary'.[92]

Thorneycroft then wrote to Churchill to inform the Prime Minister of this decision. Churchill was not impressed. Thorneycroft was told that there would be a delay of a day or two before he got a reply.[93] This was a stalling device while Churchill asked his good friend Lord Swinton, then the Secretary of State for Commonwealth Relations, and known critic of takeover bids, for his private comments on Thorneycroft's letter. Swinton felt that an enquiry was the only way to answer the legal question of whether the Savoy board's action was legal. On the question of the moral justification for the action he noted, 'Here I would imagine that the result of what was done was in the national interest: indeed, that was why the Governor of the Bank and others helped. It is more doubtful if what was done was in the shareholders' interest.'[94] In light of this Churchill did not send his initial note of response – he had written on Swinton's letter, 'P[resident] of B[oard] of T[rade] .... I don't like your legalism and still less your language'.[95] Nevertheless, on the same day Churchill approved the press notice announcing the appointment of an inspector.

The next day the Savoy board's legal representative, Fladgate's, was informed of the decision and that there were two names in mind to be appointed as inspector and 'it was for him and his clients to choose' which was appointed.[96] The legal representative also asked if the announcement of the appointment could be deferred until the start of May as the company AGM was due to take place on 30 April. On hearing this, Thorneycroft 'reacted strongly against the suggestion' and that 'it would be tantamount to HMG conniving at deception of the shareholders'.[97] Nevertheless, Fladgate's wrote to the Board of Trade asking for the announcement to be delayed and also to be consulted on the wording of the press notice.[98] A relatively long notice setting out the reasons why the inspector was being appointed suggesting that the enquiry was more about reaching a legal position than investigating the actions of the Savoy board. In this and in getting the announcement delayed they failed with a short succinct notice being issued on 23 April 1954 announcing the appointment of Mr Milner Holland QC

[91] TNA T233/2137, Compton, 'Savoy', 12 April 1954.
[92] ibid. Added handwritten note, 12 April 1954.
[93] TNA PREM11/656, AM Bligh to Churchill, 13 April 1954.
[94] TNA PREM11/656, Swinton to Churchill, 'The Savoy Hotel Case', 13 April 1954.
[95] TNA PREM11/656, Swinton to Churchill, 'The Savoy Hotel Case', 13 April 1954, handwritten comment by Churchill 14 April 1954. There is no copy of the initial response but one can guess at its tone given this comment after Swinton's letter had conceded the need for an enquiry.
[96] TNA BT58/635, RWA Speed, 'Savoy Hotel Limited', 15 April 1954.
[97] TNA BT58/635, Glaves-Smith to Henry Gregory, 15 April 1954.
[98] TNA BT58/635, Fladgate & Co. to Speed, 'The Savoy Hotel Limited', 21 April 1954.

as inspector. Fladgate's tried to get it withdrawn and rewritten (without success) as the form of the notice was 'of the greatest importance' to their clients because in its published form it impugned the integrity of their clients.[99]

Little seems to have happened in government thereafter until Milner Holland's report was completed in June 1954. On one level it drew a line under the case. On 22 June Thorneycroft wrote to Churchill with a copy of the report. Holland had found that the use of the directors' power was invalid but that they had believed that this was in the best interests of the Savoy's shareholders and on the basis of legal counsel. In Thorneycroft's opinion:

> I regard this as a very satisfactory outcome of the investigation. While the Inspector's Report has not the authority of a judgment in a court of law, I feel sure it will relieve the great anxiety felt in the city, Parliament and the press about the possibility that the transactions in question might be taken as a precedent for similar or even more undesirable acts by other boards of directors, and will reassure shareholders generally. At the same time, the Savoy directors are now exonerated from the suspicion of having acted from improper motives.[100]

He did not think any further government action was called for and Churchill did not reply.[101] The reaction in the Treasury was equally muted.[102]

On a different level the same underlying issues remained. While the President and the Attorney General initially agreed that no further action was required, in particular there was no need to reform the Companies Act, others disagreed.[103] The Savoy board noted that since legal opinion on the issue was not unanimous it was still not certain whether how they exercised their powers was invalid, a number of newspapers including *The Times* and *The Economist* called for reform of the legislation and the Institute of Directors called for an amendment to clarify the extent of directors' powers.[104] In light of these calls, Thorneycroft started to have second thoughts and made sure that his Parliamentary Answer on the government's report allowed the possibility of amending the Companies Act though nothing was to happen until the Jenkins Committee was appointed in 1959.[105]

In the longer term too, issues remained unresolved. Accordingly, in the conventional wisdom, based on Roberts, from this period on, led by City opinion, the government and the Bank of England gradually became more accepting of the role of hostile takeovers in the economy.[106] Certainly, there was

[99] ibid.
[100] TNA PREM11/656, Thorneycroft to Churchill, 22 June 1954. See also TNA LO2/1100, Thorneycroft to Lionel Heald, Attorney General, 22 June 1954.
[101] TNA PREM11/656, Thorneycroft to Churchill, 22 June 1954.
[102] TNA T233/2137, Compton to Bancroft, 1 July 1954.
[103] TNA LO2/1110, Speed to Heald, 'Savoy Hotel', 2 July 1954.
[104] ibid.
[105] TNA LO2/1110, Gregory to A Macdonald (Law Officers' Department), 'Savoy Hotel', 3 July 1954.
[106] See Johnston (n 24) 1017; Kershaw (n 24) both citing Roberts' depiction of the thaw in opposition to hostile takeovers.

an acceptance that evidence of the fears of severe damage to the economy had not materialised and that many takeovers were beneficial.[107] However, the situation was not so straightforward as this implies. First, in 1956 the Capital Issues Committee believed that:

> [I]t was time something was done to stop the activities of the "Clores" who by using share for share procedure were obtaining control of companies with ample liquid resources and using those resources for purposes which would not be approved if application to the Committee had been necessary.[108]

Second, nearly a year later the Cabinet invited the Chancellor of the Exchequer 'to consider what further intensification of the restriction of credit in the private sector might be possible, particularly in connection with "take-over bids"'.[109] Finally, when hostile takeover bids became a topic of public debate again in 1959, it is clear that the Treasury was more sanguine about the effects. However, some concerns still remained: for example, although it was not relevant at that time, takeover bids would raise issues if a policy of dividend restraint was reintroduced (as it was in 1961).[110] One Treasury official, commenting on the draft 'Notes on Amalgamations' was highly critical: 'More generally I would only say that the notes seem to ignore almost to the point of absurdity the element of self-interest which so often inspires the kind of bid which attracts unfavourable publicity.'[111]

The Governor of the Bank of England thought the Notes were 'quite sensible'.[112] However, only a few months earlier the Governor had been 'very concerned' about hostile take-over bids, 'but he finds it hard to know what, if any, action can be taken to control them'.[113] He recalled that no remedy had been found at the time of the Savoy Hotel case but was sufficiently concerned to put Bank staff to work on the question again. He was concerned about the situation in the insurance industry but 'The Governor's nightmare is that he might one day wake up to find that some successful bid had been made for one of the Banks.'[114] William Armstrong, at this time in the Home Finance Division of the Treasury, but later to become Permanent Secretary to the Treasury and the Head of the Home Civil Service, thought the chance of such an event was pretty

[107] TNA T233/2002, JA to Miss Littler, 'Take-over Bids', 24 June 1959, attached brief, 'Debate on the State of Industry' as example from the Treasury, and a Board of Trade brief for the President of the Board of Trade, sent to Steel, 26 June 1959. See also Roberts (n 16) 193.

[108] TNA T233/2002, Sangster to Lees, 'Capital Issues Committee: "Take-over Bids"', 26 October 1956.

[109] TNA T233/2002, AJC to Compton, 22 July 1957.

[110] TNA T233/2002, JA to Miss Littler, 'Take-over Bids', 24 June 1959, attached brief, 'Debate on the State of Industry'.

[111] TNA T233/2002, unclear signature to Armstrong, 15 October 1959.

[112] TNA T233/2002, Makins, 'Record of Conversation: Take-over Bids', 14 October 1959.

[113] TNA T233/2002, Makins 'Record of Conversation: Take-over Bids', 29 May 1959.

[114] TNA T233/2002, Makins, 'Record of Conversation', 19 June 1959 on the insurance industry and Makins 'Record of Conversation: Take-over Bids', 29 May 1959.

remote but Roger Makins, the then Joint Permanent Secretary to the Treasury, responded that the Governor 'did not share the view that nobody is likely to take over a bank for the real estate' as, under certain circumstances it might be very profitable.[115] Interestingly, Armstrong added, 'As regards banks we are, of course, much more interested in the preservation of the status quo and therefore of defending banks against the type of takeover bid that has for its aim the diversion of assets to quite different purposes.'[116]

In general, it remained the case that the government did not wish to intervene because it was 'almost impossible to distinguish between those take-over bids (probably the majority) which most people would regard as advantageous and those which many would think deplorable'.[117] This seems little different from the Treasury-Board of Trade paper from December 1953. As a Treasury official put it in looking back at that paper, it was clear that while some aspects of the paper had been rendered out of date, the paper's 'underlying philosophy is still valid'.[118] This was a paper over which the Treasury and the Board of Trade could not agree back in 1953 because of different views on the value of hostile takeover bids.

VI. CONCLUSION

Roberts' 1992 article has played a formative role in opening up our understanding of the regulatory responses in the 1950s to the emergence of hostile takeover bids.[119] Understandably, given the way regulation developed later, his focus was on the Bank and the City with less attention paid to government. This chapter has tried to show that adding a more detailed understanding of the debates in government does amend our view of the process by which the shareholder dominant view of the company came to predominate in the UK after the Second World War. First, it has shown how the Board of Trade and, in particular, its President, Peter Thorneycroft, were much more sympathetic to the benefits of a few pike in a trout river at a much earlier date than conventionally presented. This is important because it raises a broader issue about support for a free market at a time when some wartime controls and rationing were still in place. Thorneycroft became Chancellor of the Exchequer in January 1957 but only 12 months later resigned over the Cabinet's refusal to back his public expenditure cuts.

[115] TNA T233/2002, Armstrong to Padmore, 'Takeover Bids', 5 June 1954 and added handwritten comment 19 June.

[116] TNA T233/2002, Armstrong to Padmore, 'Takeover Bids', 5 June 1954.

[117] TNA T233/2002, Derick Heathcoat Amory (Chancellor of the Exchequer) to Sir John Barlow MP, 3 September 1959.

[118] TNA T233/2002, unclear signature to Lees, 'Take-over Bids', 4 June 1959.

[119] Roberts (n 16).

He was also concerned with the quantity of money in circulation, leading to his depiction by some as a 'proto-Thatcherite'.[120] The evidence here gives weight at an even earlier time to this notion. It is also significant because it questions the interpretation that the government was led by City opinion during the 1950s.

Second, the Treasury, and particularly the Bank of England's position in the early 1950s was as depicted by Roberts but they held a more consistent view over the 1950s than Roberts suggests. There had been movement in opinion both about takeovers and a shift away from talking about the national interest and employees (as Churchill did in the Savoy Hotel case) to focus on shareholder rights. Yet, fear of takeover close to home, like of a major bank, was still there, quick to re-surface when it became a potential issue. The Treasury's position also highlights the risks of adopting an overly narrow and discrete approach to examining policy and regulation. Certainly, at the start the Treasury's interest in takeovers was only partly driven by the phenomenon itself. Much more important was the potential impact on the maintenance of full employment without inflation via a breakdown of voluntary dividend restraint. This points to what Cairncross has called the 'seamless web' of policy.[121] At the same time, this case also points to a countervailing pressure to keep policy domains discrete. The straightforward solution to hostile takeovers was to introduce a capital gains tax but the Treasury refused to countenance this as they regarded this as off limits.[122]

Third, and finally, the case shows the importance of context. Hugh Wontner used his many connections with powerful people to lobby his case and his degree of access was highly exceptional. Few company directors could ever get the Prime Minister to arrange a meeting with another minister to take place in less than 90 minutes. Similarly, the Savoy Hotel Group was not just another company. Wontner described Claridge's as 'an annexe to Buckingham Palace'.[123] One Board of Trade official countered the argument that a change of management might not necessarily impact on the running of the hotels by emphasising the importance of luxury and that he doubted whether this would be maintained by new management: it would become 'a kind of Waldorf-Astoria'.[124] Similarly, Armstrong differentiated the banks from other companies as ones that should not be taken over. Against this, the Board of Trade argued that, 'the economic causes or effects of take-over bids are not within the province of Company Law, which is concerned only to ensure that the necessary

[120] C Cooper, 'Little Local Difficulties Revisited: Peter Thorneycroft, the 1958 Treasury Resignations and the Origins of Thatcherism' (2011) 25 *Contemporary British History*, 227.

[121] A Cairncross, 'The Managed Economy' in A Cairncross (ed), *The Managed Economy* (Oxford, Basil Blackwell, 1970) 20.

[122] TNA T233/2000, Compton, 'Take-over Bids', 9 December 1953.

[123] TNA T233/2137, Boyd-Carpenter to H Brittain (Treasury official), 27 November 1953.

[124] TNA BT58/634, AC Hill to I Gray, 21 December 1953.

mechanism exists and that there are adequate safeguards for the interests of present shareholders'.[125] Despite this desire to keep the consideration of company law discrete and framed by technical expertise it is clear that the Savoy Hotel case highlights the ways in which political, economic and social pressures influenced the perception of hostile takeovers in the early 1950s and the resulting contestation over their regulation.

[125] TNA BT58/721, Board of Trade written evidence to the Jenkins Committee, heading 16, Take-over Bids, 2.

14

The Right to Repose in Peace: The Making of Modern Company Law

PADDY IRELAND

IN *O'NEILL V PHILLIPS* in 1999, in a discussion of the background to section 459 of the Companies Act 1985 on 'unfair prejudice' (now s 994 of Companies the Act 2006), Lord Hoffmann sought to explain why in some circumstances 'equitable considerations' might make it unfair for those conducting the affairs of a company to rely on their strict legal powers. He did so by referring to the partnership origins of company law, arguing that 'company law ha[d] developed seamlessly from the law of partnership'.[1] Hoffmann was half right. Company law did indeed emerge from the law of partnership, but it did not do so 'seamlessly'. On the contrary, the emergence of 'company law' was the product of a series of conceptual and doctrinal ruptures in which the principles of the law of partnership were modified or abandoned in their application to joint stock companies (JSCs). These ruptures, this article suggests, were driven by a growing recognition that JSCs and JSC shareholders were fundamentally different in nature from partnerships and partners, and by a growing willingness not only to accommodate but to protect *rentier* investor-shareholders, whose interests were increasingly conflated with the wider public interest. By the end of the nineteenth century, so great were the modifications made to the law of partnership in its application to JSCs that 'company law' had emerged as a separate legal category. This chapter explores some of these ruptures.

I. THE NATURE OF THE JOINT STOCK COMPANY

Modern company law was a nineteenth century construct. The first book on anything resembling 'company law', Charles Wordsworth's *The Law Relating to Railway, Bank, Insurance, Mining and Other Joint Stock Companies*, did not

[1] *O'Neill v Phillips* [1999] UKHL 24.

appear until 1836.[2] As its title made clear, Wordsworth's book was assembled around the *economic* form of the JSC, not the corporate *legal* form, encompassing both incorporated companies (like railway companies) and *un*incorporated companies (like mining companies) and reminding us that what we now call 'company law' began life as 'joint stock company law', the laws applicable to JSCs, incorporated or not.

The distinguishing features of JSCs were identified by Adam Smith in *The Wealth of Nations* when he contrasted them with 'private co-partneries'.[3] 'Private co-partneries' were typically based around a small number of closely-related individuals who were active participants in the firm. By this time, the principles upon which such partnerships were based were well-established, so much so that William Paley was able confidently to assert (in 1785) that 'nothing upon the subject of partnership requires explanation, but in what manner the profits are to be divided when one partner contributes money, and the other labor, which is a common case'.[4] By the end of the century these principles had crystallised into an increasingly coherent, settled and important body of law. Specialist treatises on partnership duly began to appear: William Watson's treatise led the way in 1794, followed by Basil Montagu's *Digest* in 1815, Niel Gow's treatise in 1823 and John Collyer's in 1832.[5]

Under the law of partnership, partners were seen as having voluntarily placed themselves in 'a peculiar relation with regard to each other'.[6] They could bind one another contractually (the doctrine of mutual agency); were seen as joint owners of the partnership property; and were deemed to be jointly and severally liable for partnership debts to 'their last shilling and acre'. As these principles made clear, private partnerships were assumed (and expected) to be associations of people who knew one another, were active participants in firms willing to share in profits and losses, and who displayed what was referred to, rather extravagantly, as 'exuberant trust'.[7] These principles were regarded as both economically and morally sound. As James Taylor says, the law of partnership

[2] C Wordsworth, *The Law Relating to Railway, Bank, Insurance Mining, and Other Joint Stock Companies*, 1st edn (London, Butterworth, 1836; references are to 2nd edn, 1837). Stewart Kyd's two volume *Treatise on the Law of Corporations* appeared in 1793, but most of the text and citations related to non-profit corporations (churches, charities, universities and so on); joint stock business corporations figured only in the margins. The same was true of the first American text on corporations, J Angell and S Ames', *Treatise on the Law of Private Corporations Aggregate*, 1st edn (Boston, Hilliard et al 1832).

[3] A Smith, *Wealth of Nations* (1776, Liberty Fund 1982 ed by Campbell, Skinner & Todd), Vol II, 731–758. The section on JSCs appeared in the 3rd edition, published in 1784.

[4] W Paley, *Principles of Moral and Political Philosophy* (London, Rivington, 1785) vol 1, 176.

[5] W Watson, *Treatise of the Law of Partnership* (London, Strahan & Woodfall, 1794; 2nd edn, 1807); B Montagu, *A Digest of the Law of Partnership* (London, Butterworths, 2 vols, 1815); N Gow, *Practical Treatise on the Law of Partnership* (London, Charles Hunter, 1823); J Collyer, *Practical Treatise on the Law of Partnership* (London, Sweet, 1832).

[6] J George, *A View of the existing law affecting unincorporated JSCs* (London, Sweet, 1825) 5.

[7] See FW Clark, *A Treatise on the Law of Partnership and Joint Stock Companies according to the Law of Scotland* (Edinburgh, Clark, 1866) Vol 1, 182, 352.

was thought to be based on 'a coherent political economy' which had proved itself in practice. With its focus on trust and character, it was thought to encourage hard work and active and alert management, and to accord with the natural principles of justice.[8] Unlimited liability ensured that firms were well-run, that success was rewarded and failure punished and, as such, was 'divinely-ordained'.[9] 'In the scheme laid down by Providence for the government of the world', argued the economist JR McCulloch, 'there is no shifting or narrowing of responsibilities, every man being personally answerable to the utmost extent for all his actions'.[10] If people wanted to limit their risks, the argument ran, they should 'also limit [their] profits by, say, lending money at a fixed rate of interest instead of buying shares'.[11] Crucially, many believed that Britain's economic prosperity 'rest[ed] on the dynamism and integrity of the private partnership', and that the partnership system was the foundation of British economic success.[12] It was not by 'shirking responsibility and evading the risks inseparable from all undertakings', wrote McCulloch, 'that we attained to our pre-eminence in character, in wealth, and in manufacturing and commercial industry'.[13]

As Smith made clear, JSCs were seen as violating these principles. Based around a capital fund rather than specific people,[14] JSCs were composed of many more members most of whom were inactive, their interest in the firm being largely, if not wholly, financial. They were vehicles for not only productive activity but *rentier* investment. JSC 'proprietors', Smith explained, 'seldom pretend to understand anything of the business of the company; … and give themselves no trouble about it but receive contentedly such half yearly dividend or yearly dividend as the directors think proper to make to them'.[15] In JSCs, Marx later argued, 'the actually functioning capitalist' was transformed 'into a mere manager, [an] administrator of others people's capital' and the 'owner of capital [transformed] into a mere owner, a mere money capitalist'.[16] Viewing them 'through the prism of the large state-favoured corporation', Smith associated JSCs with 'privilege and monopoly, inefficiency and "Old Corruption"'.[17] He was not enamoured of them. Composed of inactive *rentier* shareholders and run by directors managing 'other people's money', he argued, they were inevitably characterised by 'negligence and profusion'. Moreover, they violated the partnership principles of trust, personal responsibility and character. For Smith, limited liability 'exempted a particular set of dealers from some of the general

[8] J Taylor, *Creating Capitalism* (London, RHS/Boydell, 2006) 15.
[9] ibid 31.
[10] JR McCulloch, *Considerations on partnerships with limited liability* (London, Longman, 1856) 10.
[11] B Hilton, *The Age of Atonement* (Oxford, Clarendon, 1991) 261.
[12] Taylor (n 8) 22.
[13] McCulloch (n 10) 26.
[14] CA Cooke, *Corporation, Trust and Company* (Manchester, Manchester UP, 1950) 79.
[15] Smith (n 3) 741.
[16] K Marx, *Capital Vol III* (London, Lawrence & Wishart, 1977) 436.
[17] Taylor (n 8) 22.

laws' and gave them a 'total exemption from trouble and risk'.[18] His antipathy towards JSCs was thus rooted not only in their alleged inefficiency but in *moral* objections to the way they facilitated and encouraged inactive and often speculative *rentier* shareholding, undermined personal responsibility and weakened the connection between work and reward.

Smith was well aware that to function smoothy JSCs needed corporate status and that unlimited liability was a potential problem for passive JSC shareholders,[19] but argued that 'exemptions from the general law' should be granted only in special circumstances: in industries where the capital required was beyond the capacity of private partnerships and the risks unusually great; where the operations of the business could be reduced to a routine; and where there was an identifiable public benefit.[20] Crucially, his views were highly influential and for many years shaped public opinion and state policy. For much of the eighteenth century, nearly all JSCs were incorporated by Royal Charter or Special Act of Parliament and were relatively few in number.[21] Despite industrialisation and the growing attractions of joint stock enterprise, corporate privileges were granted only grudgingly and sparingly well into the nineteenth century. The result, extensively documented by Armand DuBois, was a growth in *un*incorporated JSCs organised around complex deeds of settlements in which a mix of contract and trust law was used to try to replicate the benefits of incorporation.[22] It was for this reason that Wordsworth organised his book around the JSC as an *economic* form and encompassed both incorporated and unincorporated companies.

II. JOINT STOCK COMPANIES AS PUBLIC PARTNERSHIPS

In reality, the line between the private partnership and the JSC was fuzzy. 'In the eighteenth century', DuBois writes, 'the distinction between a partnership and a

[18] Smith (n 3) 741, 755–58. See also Taylor (n 8) 32–37. As Taylor explains, 'notions taken for granted today were entirely alien' in the early nineteenth century. The ideas that 'any collection of individuals associating in the form of a company should be able to sue in the courts as an autonomous entity, that individuals should be able to transfer in and out of the company at will, that they should bear only a limited responsibility for the actions of the company, that such responsibility should cease immediately on the sale of the their shares and that such companies should continue to exist after all the original members had long since died, were alarming and unfamiliar concepts' at this time: (n 8) 12.

[19] Limited liability does not seem to have become one of the principal reasons for seeking incorporation until the nineteenth century. In the eighteenth century, many corporations had no fixed capital and members were subject to assessments (levitations), often without stated limit. Getting monopoly privileges, corporate status and protecting corporate property from the personal creditors of members seem to have been the main motivations.

[20] Smith (n 3) 757–58.

[21] Incorporation by special act became more common in the second half of the century. P Mirowski, 'The Rise (and Retreat) of a Market' (1981) 41 *Journal of Economic History* 559.

[22] AB DuBois, *The English Business Company after the Bubble Act 1720-1800* (New York, Commonwealth Fund, 1938).

JSC was primarily a matter of size', partnerships 'shad[ed] imperceptibly' into JSCs 'when the individuals concerned and the capital were increased'.[23] Many firms emerged with relatively large memberships, a separation of ownership and management and (purportedly) transferable shares: some were able to incorporate, some were not. But many of them were more like extended partnerships than the much purer JSCs that emerged as the nineteenth century progressed, their shareholders often participating in governance and having more than a purely financial interest in the enterprises concerned.[24] Moreover, JSCs shares were far from being the liquid assets they are today: there was still no developed share market, restrictions on the free transferability of shares remained common, and the legal efficacy of share transfers in unincorporated companies was questionable.[25] These material realities contributed to the perception, which continued well into the nineteenth century, of *all* JSCs (incorporated *and* unincorporated) as types of partnership. In the jargon of the day, JSCs were 'public', rather than 'private', partnerships – terminology which emphasised their quantitative rather than qualitative distinctiveness. 'The first great division', wrote William Watson in his treatise, was between 'public and private partnerships', the latter being 'usually called companies or societies'.[26] JSC shareholders were frequently described as 'partners'.

Wordsworth's book reflected and gave expression to these perceptions. He depicted all JSCs as large partnerships and as, in principle, subject to partnership law, including incorporated companies, notwithstanding their 'confirmation by public authority'.[27] He saw them, like 'ordinary' partnerships, as essentially contractual affairs irrespective of their legal status, treating Acts of Parliament, charters from the Crown, letters patent and other instruments of incorporation as akin to deeds of settlement, as simply one of the instruments by which 'the *partnership* between directors and shareholders is constituted and governed'.[28] As this suggests, incorporation did not yet provide anything resembling a fully-fledged alternative legal form for business enterprises. On the contrary, as Samuel Williston observed, in relation to 'the points which belong exclusively

[23] ibid 242.

[24] See M Freeman, R Pearson and J Taylor, *Shareholder Democracies* (Chicago, University of Chicago Press, 2012). Many early JSC shareholders invested to benefit their communities as well as to receive financial benefits.

[25] See *Duvergier v Fellowes* (1828) 5 Bing 267. See P Ireland 'Capitalism Without the Capitalist: The Joint Stock Company Share and the Emergence of the Modern Doctrine of Separate Corporate Personality' (1996) 17 *Journal of Legal History* 41. For a succinct summary of the legal problems facing unincorporated JSCs, see M Lobban, 'Corporate Identity and Limited Liability in France and England' (1996) 25 *Anglo American Law Review*, 397–440 at 401–06.

[26] Watson (n 5) 2nd edn 1807, 3–5.

[27] Wordsworth (n 2) 109.

[28] CFF Wordsworth, *The Law Relating to Railway, Bank, Insurance, Mining and Other Joint-Stock Companies*, 2nd edn (London: Butterworth, 1837). At this time, instruments of incorporation were usually bespoke documents, those sponsoring the company commonly being intimately involved in the drafting process, statutory or otherwise. Perceptions of the early incorporated trading companies were rather different as they were quasi-governmental in nature.

to the conception of the business corporation', as opposed to the conception of corporations in general, 'the law [was] formed very largely after 1800'.[29] For Wordsworth, all incorporation did was partially displace the operation of the normal principles of partnership, particularly those relating to dealings with third parties, the degree of displacement depending upon the precise terms of and privileges granted by the instrument of incorporation. Thus, in his exposition of the law, Wordsworth tended to present the general principles of the law of partnership, while noting the gradual emergence within that law, mainly as a result of decisions by the courts of Chancery, of rules specifically applicable to companies. He then sought to outline the derogations from these (partnership) principles in the companies found in different areas of productive activity, devoting separate chapters to railway, mining, banking, and insurance companies. He treated it as more or less axiomatic that joint stock companies, incorporated and *un*incorporated, were governed by the 'general law of partnership' except in those important respects in which the latter had been '*superceded*' (sic) or '*limited and restrained*' either by the granting of corporate privileges or by the judiciary.[30]

John William Smith adopted a very similar approach in his *Compendium of Mercantile Law*. For Smith, a JSC was 'a partnership consisting of a very large number of members' and the rights and liabilities of these members

> would be precisely the same as those of any other sort of partner did not their multitude oblige them to adopt certain peculiar regulations for the government of the concern, which are ordinarily contained in an instrument called a deed of settlement to which is frequently added an act of parliament expressly for that purpose.

Where a company existed under an act of Parliament or letters patent it 'certainly differ[ed] … from an ordinary firm' but only to the extent provided by the act or patent; in all other respects it was 'governed by the ordinary law of partnership'. Joint stock companies were thus 'nothing but partnerships of a peculiar kind' and the law relating to them could, therefore, be 'conveniently be distributed under the same heads' as the law of partnership.[31]

[29] S Williston, 'History of the Law of Business Corporations Before 1800' (1888) 2 *Harvard LR* 105 at 113.

[30] Wordsworth (n 2) 35, 64, 101–4. He adopted the same approach in the third edition of the book in 1842, modifying it only after the passing of the 1844 JSC Act.

[31] JW Smith, *Compendium of Mercantile Law*, 1st edn (London, Benning, 1834) 35–42. The second edition (1838) extended its coverage of JSCs and corporations: 57–76. This view was also to be found in the US. Thus in *Bissell v The Michigan Southern & Northern Indiana Railroad Cos* (1860) 22 NY 259 (New York Court of Appeals), Comstock CJ asserted that 'a private or trading corporation is essentially a chartered partnership, with or without immunity from personal liability beyond the capital invested, and with certain other convenient attributes which ordinary partnerships do not enjoy'. See HL Wilgus, *Cases on the General Principles of the Law of Private Corporations* (Indianapolis: Bowen-Merrill, 1902) vol II, 1187.

III. THE RUPTURES

The perception of JSCs as types of partnership persisted. The 1844 Joint Stock Companies Act, for example, was based on the supposition that companies were types of 'modified partnership',[32] using the term 'JSC' to cover 'every partnership' whose capital was divided into shares and 'every partnership' with 25 members or more.[33] Moreover, the shareholders of the 'quasi-corporations' created under its auspices continued to be denied the important privilege of limited liability, something which contributed to their continuing, partnership-style identification with their shareholders.[34] In the words of Peter Stein, the registered company 'was still thought of as a special sort of partnership rather than as a special sort of corporation'; the members of these companies did not simply associate, they associated as partners, something particularly evident when firms failed.[35]

It is clear from Wordsworth's text, however, that by this time the law of partnership was already being modified and relaxed in its application to JSCs. This was the result not only of the more frequent granting of corporate privileges to JSCs but of judicial innovations. For example, the general rule that all those materially interested in the subject of lawsuits (meaning, under the law of partnership, all the partners) had to be made parties to them had by this time been 'modified when applied to the case of a company'.[36] Where a 'great many individuals' were involved, the courts were prepared to 'permit a few to represent the whole and sue on their behalf'.[37] This judicial change was, in effect, formalised and generalised by the 1844 Act which made corporate status available on mere registration.

Very soon, however, even more fundamental changes were being made to the law of partnership as it applied to JSCs. Some of these changes were effected legislatively, others judicially, still others by a combination of both. Collectively, they gradually established a very different set of founding principles for JSC law. The doctrinal and conceptual ruptures involved were many and varied. In what follows I focus on just a few: the re-conceptualisation of the JSC share; the erosion of the partnership conception of the JSC; the collapse of the doctrine of mutual agency; the demise of unlimited liability and introduction of general

[32] M Lobban, 'Nineteenth Century Frauds in Company Formation: *Derry v Peek* in Context' (1996) 112 *LQR* 287 at 299.

[33] 7&8 Vict c110, s 2.

[34] The term 'quasi-corporation' was used to refer to companies which had been granted the right to sue and be sued in the name of an officer and, later, to describe companies formed under the 1844 Act.

[35] P Stein, 'Nineteenth Century English Company Law and Theories of Legal Personality' (1982/83) 11/12 *Quaderni Fiorentini* 503 at 507.

[36] Wordsworth (n 2) 155.

[37] Gow (n 2) 109–10; Wordsworth (n 2) 155–6. Representative suits on behalf of partners had already been allowed in certain circumstances: see, eg, *Adair v New River Company* (1805) 11 Ves 429; *Meux v Maltby* (1818) 2 Swanst. 277; *Lloyd v Loaring* (1802) 6 Ves 773.

limited liability; the development of the doctrine of ultra vires; and the rise of de facto no-liability shareholding and consequent emergence of the modern doctrine of separate corporate personality.

IV. THE RE-CONCEPTUALISATION OF THE JSC SHARE

Throughout the eighteenth and early nineteenth centuries, shares in both incorporated and unincorporated JSCs were deemed to be equitable interests in the property of companies. It followed that JSC shareholders were the equitable owners of the company's assets. This meant, amongst other things, that if a company owned real estate, its shares were considered to be, in part, an interest in land, giving rise to questions about their devolution on intestacy, transfer by will and devise to charity. It also complicated their transfer, as a result of which companies seeking corporate privileges commonly sought to have their shares declared personal property in their instruments of incorporation.[38]

One of the key material underpinnings of this view was the absence at this time of a developed share market, a product of the fact that JSCs were still relatively few in number and small in size. With the growth in canal, docks, insurance, gas and waterworks companies, the volume of shares began gradually to grow, but as late as the 1820s, dealings in them remained relatively infrequent outside short-lived boom periods. This was all changed by the rise of the railways from the mid-late 1820s. Railway companies had, by the standards of the day, very large numbers of shareholders, most of whom were *rentiers*. Their rise saw a rapid growth in the number of shares and shareholders, and generated the emergence for the first time of a developed share market.[39] As a result, shares emerged as not only much more widely held but much more liquid forms of property. Beginning in the 1830s, their legal nature was reconceptualised. In 1837, in *Bligh v Brent*, a case involving an incorporated waterworks company, it was explicitly held that JSC shares conferred on their holders no direct interest, legal or equitable, in a company's assets. They were mere rights to profit, autonomous forms of intangible personal property. Shareholders were portrayed as providers of a 'joint stock of money' which companies converted 'part into land, part into goods' with a view to obtaining 'a clear surplus profit' for division among the shareholders. Moreover, Baron Parke suggested, shares in *un*incorporated companies were also mere rights to profits, not interests in

[38] For a detailed exploration of the case law, see P Ireland, 'Capitalism Without the Capitalist: The Joint Stock Company Share and the Emergence of the Modern Doctrine of Separate Corporate Personality' (1996) 17 *Journal of Legal History* 41.

[39] See MC Reed, *Investment in Railways in Britain, 1820-1844* (Oxford, OUP, 1975); MC Reed, 'Railways and the growth of the capital Market' in MC Reed (ed), *Railways in the Victorian Economy* (Newton Abbot, David & Charles, 1969); Ireland (n 38).

the assets of companies, notwithstanding the absence of a corporate entity.[40] This was confirmed in 1854 in *Watson v Spratley*, a case involving an unincorporated joint-stock mining company. The court drew a clear distinction between 'ordinary' partnerships and JSCs. The shares in *all* JSCs, incorporated or not, Baron Martin argued, were freely transferable, with 'each shareholder or partner [having] the right at his pleasure to sell his share, and insist upon his vendee being accepted as a member of the partnership in his place or stead'. This right did not exist in 'ordinary partnerships' and was the 'great essential difference between them and 'joint stock partnerships'. The case turned on 'the essential nature and quality of a share in a JSC'; in 'substance and reality', the interests of *all* JSC shareholders were 'exactly the same' – 'an interest in ultimate profits'; the 'right to receive the dividends payable on [their] shares'.[41] By the 1860s, any *direct* links between the assets of JSCs, incorporated and unincorporated, and their shares had been severed. JSCs now involved two quite distinctive pieces of property: shares, intangible revenue rights owned by shareholders, and assets, now wholly owned by 'the company' either through a corporate entity (incorporated companies) or through trustees (unincorporated companies).[42]

V. THE EROSION OF THE PARTNERSHIP CONCEPTION OF THE JSC

The reconceptualisation of the JSC share contributed to the subtle changes that were taking place in the way JSCs were perceived. Business associations had long had a limited legal existence separate from their constituent members as a result of the process of 'affirmative asset partitioning' whereby their property was treated as separate estates shielded to some degree from the creditors of the members of the firm as individuals.[43] Affirmative asset partitioning did

[40] *Bligh v Brent* (1837) 160 ER 397. When discussing an *un*incorporated deed of settlement company, Baron Parke asserted that 'the company are as much distinct from the proprietors of shares as one man is from another'.

[41] *Watson v Spratley* (1854) 156 ER 424.

[42] See Ireland (n 38).

[43] Affirmative asset partitioning is distinguishable from the 'defensive' asset partitioning associated with limited liability. See H Hansmann and R Kraakman, 'The Essential Role of Organizational Law' (2000) 110 *Yale LJ* 387; H Hansmann and R Kraakman, 'Organisational Law as Asset Partitioning' [2000] *European Economic Review* 807; H Hansmann, R Kraakman and R Squire, 'Law and the Rise of the Firm' (2006) 119 *Harvard Law Review* 1333; J Getzler and M MacNair, 'The firm as an entity before the Companies Acts' in P Brand et al (eds), *Adventures of the Law* (Dublin, Four Courts Press, 2005) 267. As Hansmann and Kraakman point out, while it is possible to try to achieve some degree of defensive asset partitioning (limited liability) through contract, affirmative asset partitioning 'cannot feasibly be created by contract" but requires the promulgation of a rule of law'. On this see, P Ireland, 'Property and Contract in Contemporary Corporate Theory' (2003) 23 *Legal Studies* 453. The ability of firms to become separate entities even in this limited sense, however, was and is limited wherever the firm's creditors are not confined to the members property but can go beyond it to reach the members themselves: see SJ Stoljar, *Groups and Entities* (Canberra, ANUP, 1973) 79–87.

not, however, prevent the firm's assets from being seen as the property of its members, or prevent firms, even if incorporated, from being identified, partnership-style, with their members. Deep into the nineteenth century, even incorporated companies were seen, like partnerships, as aggregations of individuals, the corporate entity being seen as the company's members merged into one legally distinct entity, 'a collection of many individuals united into one body', as Stewart Kyd put it.[44] This was reflected in the way English lawyers and judges regularly referred to both incorporated and unincorporated companies as 'theys'.[45] Indeed, the conceptualisation of JSCs as aggregates of people, as 'theys', was not confined to the English. Merrick Dodd noted in his book on the history of American business corporations that in the early nineteenth century American judges also 'frequently refer[red] to a corporation as 'they' rather than it',[46] something since confirmed by Naomi Lamoreaux: 'During the early nineteenth century, … [American] judges invariably referred to partnerships in ways that focused attention on the people who made them up rather than on the enterprises as entities ….[and] during this early period, judges often referred to corporations in the same way they did partnerships'.[47]

The reconceptualisation of shareholders and companies as owners of quite different forms of property drove a wedge between them. Shareholders were being re-designated as money-capitalists, passive, money-providing 'investors', *external* to 'the company' and the process of production and, as such, as qualitatively rather different from active, asset-owning partners.[48] Concomitantly, both incorporated and unincorporated companies were being established as separate, property-owning entities in their own right, cleansed of, and distinguishable in new ways from, their share-owning shareholders; as not merely quantitatively but *qualitatively* different from partnerships. This shift was exemplified by a subtle change in the wording of the Companies Acts. The Joint Stock Companies Act 1856 permitted seven or more persons to 'form *themselves*' into an incorporated company, implying that the company was made *of* them, that the shareholders *were* the company. By contrast, the Companies Act 1862 permitted seven or more persons to 'form a company', implying that the company was an object external to them, a 'thing' made *by*, but not *of*, them.[49]

[44] S Kyd *Treatise on the Law of Corporations* (London, Butterworth, 1793) Vol I, 1, 7.

[45] For examples, see Ireland (n 38).

[46] EM Dodd, *American Business Corporations until 1860* (Cambridge MA, Harvard UP, 1954) 66.

[47] N Lamoreaux, 'Partnerships, Corporations and the Limits on Contractual Freedom in US History' in K Lipartito and D Sicilia (eds), *Constructing Corporate America* (Oxford, OUP, 2004) 29 at 44–45. One American commentator thought the 'persistent' references by English 'pleaders, legislators and judges' to the corporation as a 'they' was evidence that 'the English have never been strong on corporation grammar': EH Warren, 'Safeguarding the Creditors of Corporations' (1923) 36 *Harvard LR* 509 at 510.

[48] See P Ireland, I Grigg-Spall and D Kelly, 'The Conceptual Foundations of Modern Company Law (1987) 14 *JLS* 149.

[49] 19 & 20 Vict c 47, s 3 (1856 Act); 25 & 26 Vict c 89, s 6 (1862 Act).

VI. THE DEMISE OF MUTUAL AGENCY

Growing recognition of the qualitative differences between JSCs and partnerships was reflected in a further series of legal ruptures. One of these was the demise of the principle of mutual agency. Under the law of partnership, each partner was deemed to be an agent of the firm with implied authority to bind it in contracts within the ordinary scope of the partnership business. 'By entering into the partnership', Gow explained, 'each party reposes confidence in the other, and constitutes him his general agent as to all the partnership concerns', so that '… partners are bound universally by what is done by each other in the course of the partnership business'. The general rule that only those privy to contracts were bound by them was 'not contravened by the liability of partners, since they may be imagined virtually present at and sanctioning the proceedings they singly enter into in the course of trade'.[50]

When Wordsworth wrote the second edition of his text in 1837, he was in 'no doubt that where a member or shareholder of a company becomes a party to a negociable (sic) security', as long as the transaction was 'bona fide and in or for the concerns of the company' the act of the shareholder 'pledge[d] the whole credit of the company and consequently render[ed] the whole body liable to any third party [holder of the security] … unless .. express notice should have been given to him of the want of authority in the shareholder to bind the company'. 'These observations extend[ed] to include all cases of simple contracts.'[51] The 1844 Act, however, provided that it was 'lawful' for joint stock company directors to 'conduct and manage the affairs of the company' subject to the provisions of the deed of settlement 'or other special authority', adding, significantly, 'not so as to enable the shareholders to act in their own behalf in the ordinary management of the concerns of the company otherwise than by means of directors'.[52] Within a few years, it had been authoritatively held that third parties dealing with companies were deemed to know that only their managers had the power to act for them.

The questions surrounding who had the authority to bind registered companies were first considered judicially in *Ridley v Plymouth, Stonehouse & Devonport Grinding Co* and *Kingsbridge Flour Mill Co v Same* in 1848. In *Ridley*, a company with 400–500 members denied liability for two contracts,

[50] Gow (n 5) 2nd edn, 1825, 52–53. Gow moves on to 'consider in what instances, by virtue of the relation subsisting between them, the act of one shall be construed as the act of all'. In reality, of course, in many partnerships the day-to-day running of the firm had been delegated by agreement to specific people, hence the well-established distinction drawn between 'active' and 'dormant' partners. However, any such arrangement between the partners inter se – for example, to restrict the power and authority of (some) partners to bind the firm or to limit the liability of partners for partnership contracts – did not generally affect their position vis-a-vis third parties unless the latter had notice of the 'private arrangement': See Collyer (n 5) 2nd edn, 1840, 259–262.

[51] Wordsworth (n 2) 153.

[52] 7&8 Vict c110, s 27.

arguing that those who purported to enter them on the company's behalf lacked authority. In one of the cases the contract had been confirmed at a meeting of four directors when the deed stated that the quorum was five; in the other flour was ordered by the company's secretary and although the debt was acknowledged by a meeting of the directors, it was again inquorate. The claims against the company were rejected. While in an ordinary partnership, Parke argued, 'each individual partner has, by the common law and usage of trade, power to bind all his co-partners, … the same rule does not apply to JSCs'. Because the deed was registered, every person dealing with a company could 'ascertain [its] objects, … who the directors are …. [and] their powers as between them and the company'. Third parties seeking to enforce contracts against companies, therefore, had to show that the contracts were made by 'persons having the authority of the shareholders to bind them', either by reference to the deed or by showing that all the shareholders had 'sanctioned these persons' to act on their behalf. In *Kingsbridge* the plaintiffs argued that the company was bound because it had consumed the flour, but Platt J rejected their claim as they were unable to show that the persons who entered the contract were 'competent to bind the company'. 'The company', he argued, 'consists of many persons who may never be near the premises, and who do not consume goods, or contract for them, or know anything about them except through their agents. A man may very well trust five directors with power to trade for him and yet decline to trust a smaller number'.[53]

These principles were soon well established. The rationale behind them was elaborated by Lord Campbell in *Burnes v Pennell* in 1849. A distinction had to be made, Campbell argued, between joint stock companies and 'common mercantile partnerships'. No one could contend, he asserted, that a joint stock company would be liable on a bill of exchange drawn, accepted and endorsed by any one shareholder of a company because it was 'known that the power of carrying on the business of [a] company … is vested exclusively in directors'. Thus although a joint stock company was a partnership, it was

> a partnership of a different description, and attended with different incidents and liabilities from a partnership constituted between a few individuals who carry on business jointly, with equal powers and without transferable shares. All who have dealings with a joint stock company know that the authority to manage the business is conferred upon directors and that the shareholder, as such, has no power to contract for the company.

It was 'immaterial', he added, whether the company was incorporated or unincorporated.[54]

[53] *Ridley v Plymouth, Stonehouse & Devonport Grinding and Baking Co* (1848) 17 LJ Ex 252 at 255; 2 Ex 711 at 717–18. I have made use of both reports. See also *Smith v Hull Glass Company* (1849) 8 CB 668.

[54] (1849) 2 HLC 497 at 521.

This preference for shareholder over creditor protection was confirmed a few years later in *Ernest v Nicholls*. Parke, now Lord Wensleydale, reiterated the views he had expressed in *Ridley*, embedding the doctrine of constructive notice into English JSC law. It was 'obvious', he argued, that the partnership doctrine of mutual agency was 'inapplicable' to companies 'consisting of a great number of individuals contributing small sums to the common stock'. In such companies, 'to allow each one to bind the other by any contract which he thought fit to enter into, even within the scope of the partnership business, would soon lead to the utter ruin of the contributories'. The 1844 Act had solved the problem by incorporating these companies 'with special powers of management and liabilities', while at the same time providing through the registration of deeds 'accessible to all' that third parties had notice of who was authorised to bind 'the shareholders'. If third parties chose not to take notice of the deed and gave credit to unauthorised persons, 'it [was] their own fault'; they could 'look to them only, not to the company at large'. It followed that the stipulations of the deed regulating and restricting the authority of directors bound all dealing with the company: 'the directors can make no contract so as to bind the whole body of shareholders, *for whose protection these rules are made*, unless they are strictly complied with'.[55]

By the mid-century, then, the partnership principle of mutual agency had been abandoned in relation to JSCs to the advantage of the passive, rentier shareholders who increasingly populated them, enabling them more easily and effectively to limit the authority not only of their fellow-shareholders but of company directors. The effect was to shift monitoring functions and risk to creditors, enhancing the security of shareholders at their expense.[56] Notwithstanding its retention of unlimited liability and explicit conceptualisation of companies as types of partnership, therefore, the 1844 Act effected, with judicial assistance, a number of important modifications to the law of partnership in its application to companies.

VII. FROM UNLIMITED LIABILITY TO LIMITED LIABILITY

Finally, the principle of joint and several unlimited liability was comprehensively abandoned in relation to JSCs by the Limited Liability Act 1855[57] and Joint Stock Companies Act 1856.[58] During the later eighteenth and early nineteenth

[55] (1857) 6 HLC 401 at 417–21 (emphasis added).

[56] American commentators noted that in contrast to US law with its notion of the capital stock of corporations as a 'trust fund' for its creditors, English company law displayed less concern with the rights and interests of creditors than it did with those of shareholders. See, eg, SD Thompson, *Treatise on the Liability of Stockholders*, (St Louis, FH Thomas, 1879) vi–viii, 228–32.

[57] 18 & 19 Vict c 133.

[58] 19 & 20 Vict c 47. It was not until the early decades that the term 'limited liability' came into common use: see J Chaplin, 'The Origins of 1855/6 Introduction of Limited Liability in England' (2016, PhD, UEA) ch 1.

centuries, the desire of both JSCs and private partnerships with so-called 'sleeping' or 'dormant' partners to limit the liabilities of their members (or some of them) gradually grew.[59] With this, the principle of what was by then coming to be referred to as 'unlimited liability' was gradually compromised. It was undermined, first, by the growing number of JSCs incorporated by statutes containing explicit limited liability clauses (like railway companies[60]) and, second, by the piecemeal granting of corporate privileges under the Trading Companies Act 1834 and Chartered Companies Act 1837.[61] It was further undermined by unincorporated companies inserting limited liability clauses into their deeds of settlement and/or contracts with third parties. Although the legal efficacy of these mechanisms, particularly the former, was doubtful, as were the claims of some unincorporated companies to have freely transferable shares where shareholder liabilities terminated on transfer, they undoubtedly muddied the legal waters.[62] So far as JSCs were concerned, the 1855 and 1856 Acts decisively displaced the old partnership principle of joint and several unlimited liability. Indeed, it is in the context of this controversial change that the forces driving the ruptures come into sharper relief.

The legislative changes wrought by the Companies Acts 1844–56 clearly sought, in different ways and to different degrees, to encourage JSC formation and to provide greater protection for *rentier* JSC investments. The 1844 Act implemented the recommendations of a Select Committee set up to explore a series of frauds which highlighted the vulnerability of money invested in JSCs. It sought to facilitate JSC formation by making key corporate privileges available on mere registration and to protect shareholders by introducing a double system of registration and compulsory balance sheets and audits. Moreover, although it continued to characterise JSCs as types of partnership and to identify them with their shareholders and retained the partnership principle of unlimited liability, the Act interposed 'the company' between shareholders and creditors on insolvency. Whereas under the law of partnership a creditor who obtained judgment against a firm could immediately levy execution against any of the firm's partners, under the 1844 Act creditors could levy execution against shareholders only if due diligence had been undertaken to try to obtain satisfaction against

[59] *Waugh v Carver* (126 ER 525), decided in 1793, had confirmed that receipt of the profits of a partnership rendered one a partner for liability purposes.

[60] Limited liability was considered justifiable for railway companies on the Smithian grounds of capital need and public benefit.

[61] 4 & 5 Will IV c 94; 1 Vict, c 73. Between 1844 and 1853, the Board of Trade granted charters to 65 enterprises and Parliament passed 135 private Bills conferring limited liability, not including the many more railway acts that were passed: Taylor (n 8) 166.

[62] Deeds of settlement could contractually govern relations between the members inter se, but not their relations with outside third parties. Some courts and commentators pointed out that transferring contractual burdens was a legal impossibility without statutory intervention: see George (n 6). More generally, see R Harris, *Industrializing English Law* (Cambridge, CUP, 2000), especially chs 6 & 9.

the property of 'the company'.[63] The liability of shareholders, which continued for three years after transfer, thus remained unlimited but became a subsidiary liability.[64] The changes effected by the Act thus represented a step in the direction of general defensive asset partitioning, further enhancing the idea of companies as entities separate from their shareholders.

The hope underlying the 1844 Act was that mandatory incorporation coupled with 'publicity' (today's 'disclosure') would provide shareholders with the information they needed to make better informed investment decisions and to hold directors accountable.[65] For one enthusiastic commentator, George Farren, the Act 'rendered [joint stock companies] a safe medium through which to realise interest on surplus money'. In the future, he argued, men would be 'less hesitatory … about taking upon themselves the character of shareholders', for they would realise that 'a share in a JSC [i]s one of the most pleasurable means whereby to become recompensed for depositing surplus money in trust; because no *corporeal labour* is necessary to realise an income from such a source, but a mere judicious exertion of *mental faculties* at stated periods'.[66] That the Act did not succeed was due in part to the mistaken assumption that investors would, using their 'mental faculties', be able to protect themselves. Indeed, the complicated two-stage registration process seems to have deceived many into thinking that the companies concerned had been officially sanctioned and that there was, therefore, no need to exercise any faculties at all. During the railway mania of the 1840s, JSC fraud reached new heights. This contributed to the radical change in strategy of 1855–56. In a 'sharp', 'dramatic' and 'total' liberalisation, a much more permissive legal framework was introduced which combined free incorporation with general limited liability and abandoned much of the old regulatory framework.[67]

[63] Section 66.

[64] Section 66. For a contemporary discussion of the section, see JH James, *A Practical Application of the Joint-Stock Companies' and Friendly Societies' Acts* (London, Simpkin, Marshall & Co, 1851) 84–87.

[65] Some were optimistic it would achieve these goals. James Burchell and Charles Rann Kennedy thought it would enable 'honest persons safely to enter into engagements with a view to fair profit and benefit either to themselves or families …': J Burchell and CR Kennedy, *The Joint Stock Companies Registration Act* (London, Henry Butterworth, 1844) 2. J Taylor has highlighted the role of the press in this regard: 'Privacy, Publicity and Reputation: How the Press Regulated the Market in Nineteenth-Century England' (2013) 87 *Business History Review* 679.

[66] G Farren, *The Liabilities of Members of Existing and Future Public Companies and Partnerships* (London, Shaw & Sons, 1844) v–vi.

[67] PL Cottrell, *Industrial Finance, 1830-1914* (London, Methuen, 1980) 41–45. The 1855–56 Acts went further than many of the proponents of limited liability had been demanding. Most of the latter had sought only the introduction of continental, limited partnerships along the lines of the French *societe en commandite* in which passive, money-providing, sleeping partners got the benefit of limited liability while active managing partners remained unlimitedly liable. What they got was general limited liability with few regulatory strings.

VIII. WHAT DROVE THE RUPTURES?

Historians have variously seen the introduction of general limited liability as historically and technologically inevitable and thus in little need of explanation[68] or as rather puzzling.[69] It is clear that there were many different forces at work, some more visible than others. For example, in the face of claims of unfair competition, differential treatment and favouritism, the state itself was increasingly discomforted at having to decide when corporate privileges and limited liability should be granted. At the same time, in the late 1840s and early 1850s, with the poor enduring appalling conditions, Chartism was seen by many as a serious threat[70] and various groups, such as the Christian Socialists, lobbied for reform.[71] The hope was that limited liability would soothe class tensions by giving more people a stake in the capitalist future: it would make it easier for the industrious working classes to attract capital and set up businesses of their own and easier and safer for the middle classes to profitably invest their surplus money.[72] The pressure for reform was later led by the Law Amendment Society, an umbrella organisation which brought together disparate groups of reformers with different motivations.[73] What the Select Committees and Royal Commissions that preceded the 1855 Act reveal above all else, however, is the 'great contrareity of opinion' surrounding the possible introduction of French-style *en commandite* partnerships or, more radically, general limited liability; and the lack of concerted demand for either from industry.[74]

The main force at work, alluded to by Farren, was the growth, in an increasingly wealthy country, in the number of people searching for 'safe medium[s] through which to realise interest on [their] surplus money' with yields higher than those available from the 'Funds' (government debt). It was this that fuelled the increasingly heated debates about the liabilities that should be borne by investors, especially passive investors. Despite the railway mania and subsequent collapse, the habit of shareholding was spreading rapidly during this period. As share denominations began to fall and the number of shares in circulation rose,

[68] See, eg, BC Hunt: '… the history of the business corporation or JSC in England during the one hundred and fifty years following the statute of 1720 [the Bubble Act] is the story of an economic necessity forcing its way slowly and painfully to legal recognition …': *The Development of the Business Corporation in England 1800–1867* (Cambridge MA, Harvard UP, 1936) 13.

[69] See, eg, Cottrell (n 67) 45.

[70] The 1848 revolution in France was seen by some as a revolt of labour against capital.

[71] J Saville, 'The Christian Socialists of 1848' in J Saville (ed), *Democracy and the Labour Movement: Essays in Honour of Dona Torr* (London, Lawrence & Wishart, 1954) 135.

[72] For a while, for example, the Chartists were enthusiastic about the potential power of the JSC to economically enfranchise the working classes: see Taylor (n 8) 155.

[73] See DC Smith, 'The Mid-Victorian Reform of Britain's Company Laws and the Moral Economy of Free Competition' (2020) 22 *Enterprise and Society* 1103–39.

[74] The Royal Commission of 1854 admitted that it had been 'much embarrassed by the great contrariety of opinion': see Taylor (n 8) 151. Both sides claimed to be supported by the principles of free trade.

more and more people, mainly from the wealthier middle and upper class, were drawn into the growing share market as both investors and speculators.[75]

The supporters of general limited liability argued that unlimited liability, rather than generating productive investment, tended to generate excess and waste, encouraging creditors to lend recklessly and shareholders to engage in nothing-to-lose, speculative investments. By contrast, they argued, limited liability would facilitate JSC formation, increase investment, boost economic growth and bring forth a better class of long-term, non-speculative shareholder by facilitating the creation of more secure, less risky investment outlets for those with some money to invest but lacking the commercial contacts and networks that were enjoyed by the 'great capitalists'. 'Democratising investment', by enabling this group to claim a larger share of the growing economic cake, would also, some hoped, broaden the support for an increasingly volatile and polarised social order. More fancifully, others suggested that limited liability would bring capital and labour together by 'incorporating working men into public life' and enabling working people to become investors themselves.[76] Overall, therefore, there is more than a grain of truth in Jeffreys' claim that the Acts marked a 'victory for the investing classes over the industrialists',[77] for they do indeed reflect the important changes that were taking place in class relations and in the modes of generating and appropriating productive surpluses. More specifically, perhaps, they were in an important sense a victory for smaller money capitalist investors (the middle classes) over the so-called 'monied interest' – the 'great capitalists', 'overpowering money-aristocracy', 'London wealthy' – many of whom, with their insider connections, were opposed to extending limited liability.[78] The surrounding rhetoric was, of course, that of laissez-faire and of a society composed of free and equal individuals transacting in markets.

IX. SMITH, USURY AND UNPRODUCTIVE LABOUR

The growth in the number of people seeking to invest in JSCs in search of better pecuniary returns than those available from the 'Funds', ideally with minimum

[75] 'The acceptance of provisional directorships [by English gentlemen]', writes Kostal, 'was more akin to prostitution than seduction': RW Kostal, *Law and English Railway Capitalism 1825–1875* (Oxford, Clarendon, 1994) 57. According to Taylor, 'landed and town elites were drawn en masse into the world of share ownership and company direction': Taylor (n 8) 170.

[76] See D Loftus, 'Capital and Community: Limited Liability and Attempts to Democratize the Market in Mid-Nineteenth Century England' (2002) 45 *Victorian Studies* 93–110 at 95–105. Loftus points out that many of those, like Robert Lowe, who spoke the language of democracy in relation to investment and limited liability companies, opposed the extension of the franchise, 115.

[77] JB Jeffreys, 'Trends in Business Organisation in Great Britain since 1856' (University of London, PhD 1938) 53.

[78] Although they often benefitted for it in the form of shareholdings in statutory companies. See RA Bryer, 'Accounting for the Railway Mania of 1845: A Great Railway Swindle' (1991) 16 *Accounting, Organisations and Society* 439–86.

risk, was reflected in the changes in attitude towards JSC shareholders and – more abstractedly, less discernibly but equally importantly – towards money and its productive capacities. The early-mid nineteenth century saw different depictions of JSC shareholders vying for supremacy, depictions underlain by different ideas about their economic value, moral standing and entitlement to legal protection. These depictions were themselves in part reflective of different ideas about the productivity of money.

Historically, money had tended to be regarded as barren and sterile. This was reflected in the prohibition on usury, the taking interest on loans. Lacking, as Bentham put it, 'organs for generating any other such piece', money was seen as essentially *un*productive.[79] For Aristotle, for example, of all the modes of making money, charging interest on loans was 'the most unnatural' and 'contrary to nature'. Making of money from money encouraged greed, undermined justice in exchange, corrupted social relations and subverted the ethical roots of social order.[80] These ideas informed Dante's *Divine Comedy* in which usurers were consigned to the seventh circle of hell.[81] Gradually, however, as commerce and (often contorted) ways around the usury prohibition were developed, attitudes began to soften and by the eighteenth century, usury had come to refer not to taking interest but to taking excessive interest. With this, caps on interest rates were enacted: people could make money from money but there were limits on the extent to which they could not only ethically but legally do so. The doubts about money's productive capacities continued, however, underlying the contemporary hostility towards banking[82] and so-called 'monied men' – people who made money from lending to governments. In France, this group was referred to as 'capitalists', a term which eventually crossed the channel.[83] Based in London, the 'monied interest' was widely depicted as parasitical and *rentier* in nature. Indeed, for some, like David Hume, the rise of this cosmopolitan and self-interested group posed a serious threat to the traditional social order.[84]

Adam Smith was less critical, seeing government debt, being relatively secure and liquid, as having something of the character of money and the market for it as stimulating commercial activity. But he remained suspicious of the making of money from money, something reflected in his 'notorious' support for

[79] J Bentham, 'Defence of Usury' (1787) in *The Works of Jeremy Bentham*, Vol III (New York, Russell and Russell, 1962) 16.

[80] See Aristotle, *Politics*, Book 1, chs 8–10. See S Miekle, 'Aristotle and Exchange Value' in D Keyt and F Miller (eds), *A Companion to Aristotle's Politics* (Cambridge Mass, Blackwells, 1991) 156.

[81] See JS Toffler, 'Capital in Hell: Dante's Lesson on Usury' (1979) 32 *Rutgers LR* 609.

[82] See B Christophers, *Banking Across Boundaries: Placing Finance in Capitalism* (Chichester, Wiley, 2013) 43–73.

[83] See F Rainer, 'Word Formation and word history: The case of CAPITALIST and CAPITALISM' in O Bonami et al (eds), *The Lexeme in Descriptive and Theoretical Morphology* (Berlin, Language Science Press, 2018) 43.

[84] M Daunton, *Trusting Leviathan* (Cambridge, CUP, 2001) 38–39.

usury laws.[85] Unlike Aristotle and medieval churchmen like Aquinas, Smith did not oppose the taking of interest on loans. 'As something can everywhere be made by the use of money', he argued, 'something ought everywhere to be paid for the use of it'. He did not, however, favour removing existing legal restraints on the chargeable rate of interest, expressing support for the existing usury laws, partly for ethical reasons (he referred to 'usury' as 'extortion' and an 'evil'), but mainly for practical and economic ones. Efforts to outlaw interest altogether or to set the maximum rate too low, he argued, would simply create a black market for money and raise the cost of borrowing.[86] The permissible rate of interest should be capped at a rate 'somewhat above [but] not much above the lowest market rate'. Endorsing the existing legal maximum of five per cent as having been made with 'great propriety', he argued that if higher legal rates were permitted '... the greater part of the money which was to be lent would be lent to prodigals and projectors'.[87] Without usury laws, they would outbid 'sober people' and 'a great part of the capital of the country' would end up not in the hands of those 'most likely to make a profitable and advantageous use of it' but in the hands of those 'most likely to waste and destroy it'. For Smith, the ceiling on interest rates helped to ensure that the 'capital of the country' was 'employed with advantage'. In response, Bentham famously wrote *Defence of Usury* to try to persuade Smith to change his mind.[88] But Smith was unmoved: subsequent editions of *Wealth of Nations* continued to support the usury laws.

Smith's views were, in part, a product of the distinction he drew between productive and unproductive labour. 'There is', he argued, 'one sort of labour which adds to the value of the subject upon which it is bestowed: there is another which has no such effect. The former, as it produces value, may be called productive; the latter, unproductive labour.'[89] The downside of government debt was that the sums borrowed by the government 'were deducted from the national stock of capital, so reducing private investment ... and shifting workers from productive to non-productive labour'.[90] Elaborating, Smith contrasted the productive labour of the manufacturer with the unproductive labour of the

[85] Samuel Hollander's description. Hollander observes that his support for the laws has bewildered and embarrassed many of Smith's free-market supporters, who have variously called it an 'aberration', a 'mistake' of 'not much consequence', the product of 'an incautious moment': see 'Making the Most of Anomaly in the History of Economic Thought' in A Arnon et al (eds), *Perspectives on Keynesian Economics* (New York, Springer, 2010) 15 at 16.

[86] Smith (n 3) Book 2, ch 4. The debtor, Smith argued, would be 'obliged to pay, not only for the use of the money, but for the risk which his creditor runs by accepting a compensation for that use. He is obliged, if one may say so, to insure his creditor from the penalties of usury'.

[87] Smith (n 3) Book 2, ch 4. The term 'projector' was common in the eighteenth century, and 'included a surprisingly broad range of innovative financial and real investors. Ponzi schemes and wild speculations could be advanced by projectors but so could real productive inventions': J Persky, 'From Usury to Interest' (2007) 21 *Journal of Economic Perspectives* 227 at 230.

[88] Bentham (n 79). Bentham and his brother were themselves prospective projectors who hoped to make money from their work on panopticons: see Persky (n 87).

[89] Smith (n 3) Book 2 ch 3.

[90] Daunton (n 84) 40.

'menial servant' whose work 'consists in services which perish generally in the very instant of their performance' and do not produce 'any vendible commodity which can replace the value of their wages and maintenance'. He 'classed artificers, manufacturers, and merchants among the productive labourers, and menial servants among the barren or unproductive', arguing that 'the labour of some of the most respectable orders in the society' was 'unproductive of any value'. The 'sovereign', 'the officers both of justice and war who serve under him' and 'the whole army and navy', were all 'unproductive labourers', 'servants of the public … maintained by a part of the annual produce of the industry of other people'. Smith ranked 'churchmen, lawyers, physicians, men of letters of all kinds; players, buffoons, musicians, opera-singers, opera-dancers, etc.' in the 'same class'. It followed that while he wrote of the 'great and general utility of the banking trade' and thought that, 'operated judiciously', banks were 'important facilitators of wealth creation', Smith did not consider them to be directly productive.[91] While earlier economists generally thought of capital as money which was invested to make more money, Smith tended to think of it productively as physical things.

X. COMPETING CONCEPTIONS OF THE SHAREHOLDER: PARTNER, SPECULATOR OR INVESTOR?

The negativity surrounding making money from money persisted well into the nineteenth century. The Napoleonic wars saw government debt reach unprecedented levels and growing complaints that higher taxes were seeing 'parasitical loan contractors and *rentiers* … sucking the blood of the productive classes'.[92] The identities of 'producers and parasites, debtors and creditors', Martin Daunton writes, 'were created discursively, through the use of rhetoric … A distinction was drawn between the "real" activities of land and production, and artificial monied interests and speculation which subverted the social order'.[93]

These identities pervaded the rhetorical struggles about how to characterise JSC shareholders in the early nineteenth century. For much of the eighteenth and early nineteenth centuries, JSC shareholders were not viewed in a positive light. As we have seen, Smith recognised that JSCs were not only vehicles for productive activity (necessary vehicles in certain areas of public interest

[91] Smith (n 3) Book 2, ch 3. For a discussion of this, see Christophers (n 81) 55–65 Marx gleefully observed that Smith's relegation of all those providing professional services to the status of 'unproductive' caused considerable discomfort: 'the great mass of so-called "higher grade" workers – such as state officials, military people, artists, doctors, priests, judges, lawyers etc. … found it not at all pleasant to be relegated *economically* to the same class as clowns and menial servants and to appear merely as people partaking in the consumption, parasites on the actual producers', *Theories of Surplus Value, Part 1* (London, Lawrence and Wishart, 1969 [1862–63]) ch 4.

[92] Daunton (n 84) 45.

[93] Daunton (n 84) 52–53.

where capital needs were great), but also vehicles for *rentier* investment, and that most shareholders were inactive and ignorant of business, their contribution to firms being largely, if not entirely, financial. Directors were managers of 'other people's money'. Ordinarily, it was regarded as permissible for dormant partners in firms to receive a return higher than the maximum rate of interest because they bore the risk of no returns or, indeed, of losses (unlike creditors, who were entitled to both interest and repayment whatever the firm's performance); and because, again unlike creditors, they did not relinquish ownership of their money or of the goods bought with it: as we have seen, JSC shareholders were regarded as the owners in equity of the company's assets. One of the objections to limited liability was precisely that it limited the risk of loss, hence the need for justifications for such 'exemptions from the general law' (like capital need and/or public good). Significantly, Smith's discussion of JSCs appeared in a section of the book on the 'Publick Works and Institutions' which supported 'commerce' and is followed by a discussion of educational and ecclesiastical institutions. Smith, who tended to assess the design of institutions in terms of their contribution to the 'wealth of nations', considered all these institutions to be troubled by organisational (and incentive) structures which adversely impacted on performance.[94] JSCs, he suggested, were structured in such a way that they managed 'their own affairs ill to the diminution of the general stock of society', rarely 'fail[ing] to do more harm than good'. This was because they broke 'the natural proportion … between judicious industry and profit … which, to the general industry of the country, is of all encouragements the greatest and the most effectual'.[95]

Smith's views of JSCs and their shareholders were widely shared in the early nineteenth century. Although JSC shareholders still tended to be regarded in law as 'partners', with all that implied in terms of mutual trust, active participation and self-protection, everyone was aware that this depiction was at odds with empirical reality. Shareholders were often depicted as passive, inactive and commercially ignorant *rentiers* interested only in financial returns[96] or as gamblers looking to make a fast buck from speculative share trading, a depiction fuelled by memories of the South Sea Bubble and the various early nineteenth-century booms in company promotion and subsequent collapses. These negative portrayals found expression in a series of articles in *The Times* in 1840. Echoing Smith, the articles lamented the continuing popularity of JSCs notwithstanding 'their repeated failures and embarrassments' and argued that they were 'incompatible with the true principles of partnership' and 'inconsistent with the solid

[94] See A Ortmann, 'The Nature and Causes of Corporate Negligence, Sham Lectures and Ecclesiastical Indolence: Adam Smith on Joint-Stock Companies, Teachers and Preachers' (1999) 31 *History of Political Economy* 297.

[95] Smith (n 3) 758.

[96] Preferably at little or no risk. Many of these 'adventurers' in JSCs, Smith wrote, 'would, upon no account, hazard their fortunes in any private copartnery': Smith (n 3) 741.

and wholesome principles of trade'. You simply couldn't expect JSC directors managing 'other people's money' to show the same levels of commitment and hard work as 'private traders'. There were some contexts, like 'heavy-wheeled trades', in which JSCs 'ought … to be used and promoted', but the 'proper occasions' warranting this were relatively rare. 'The whole system of JSCs', the articles argued, was 'a system of dormant partners' who wanted to 'share in the profits of trade without knowledge of trade …; without abilities, without character, without any attention or exertion …'. Thus, whereas in 'private partnerships', the members' choice of business associates was based on trust, character and skills, in JSCs the 'bond of connexion [was] money alone'. JSCs sought to 'substitute money for mind'. For most of their members, they were 'a means of making money [not only] in idleness', but 'in compulsory idleness', for while partners in a 'private partnership', even if not actively involved in management, tended at least to keep an eye on the conduct of the business, in these 'public partnerships' the 'proprietors' were not only 'ignorant of business' but actually excluded from 'intimate knowledge', something which they 'accepted as a privilege'. The members of JSCs sought to make money 'without attention or exertion', 'without the application of mind or labour'. JSCs were 'a tempting bait' made even more 'wholesome' when supplemented by limited liability. Likening shareholders to usurers, the articles concluded with a reminder that 'money cannot make money of itself', that it was 'motionless and lifeless'. While it was legitimate for people to seek to make money from money, they should expect only the modest returns available from government securities or loans to businesses. To seek more through the ownership of JSC shares, while benefitting from limited liability, was greedy and smacked of 'speculation'.[97]

Perceptions of JSC shareholders as either idle, parasitical, greedy quasi-usurers or as gamblers speculating for quick profits were not conducive to the abandonment of the partnership principles of individual responsibility and unlimited liability. If bad things happened to shareholders, it was their own fault. Indeed, sympathy for JSC creditors was also often in short supply. Faced by the procedural obstacles surrounding unincorporated JSCs, many took the view that if they were going to do business with joint-stock enterprises creditors also needed to protect themselves and carefully assess the risks involved. Thus, in 1825–26, when a boom in JSC promotions was followed by a collapse which revealed considerable fraud and mismanagement, the authorities displayed limited desire to help either the shareholders or the creditors of the collapsed concerns. Indeed, the rise of speculative shareholding persuaded many that the law should, as a matter of policy, continue to treat shareholders as 'partners' with all that that implied in terms of responsibilities, self-reliance and self-protection. Whatever their real nature and however they actually behaved,

[97] *The Times*, 9 October 1840; 22 October 1840. 9 November 1840. Probably written if not by, under the influence of, Thomas Alsager.

shareholders *should*, normatively speaking, be vigilant, active participants in the firms of which they were members. Indeed, negativity towards shareholders and lack of sympathy for them persisted deep into the century.[98] In the wake of the collapse of the Royal British Bank in 1856, for example, *The Economist* railed against members of 'the public' who 'want[ed] the security of Consols without submitting to the low interest' and 'the high profits of speculating businesses without incurring the risk attending them, and without taking the labour and trouble of looking after them'.[99] However, by the time the courts were muddling their way through the chaotic 'hurricane of litigation' that followed the railway panic of 1845, there are signs of greater sympathy for shareholders. They start to be depicted by some as gullible (if greedy) victims.[100] 'From around mid-century, writes James Taylor, 'the moral scales began to shift.'[101] What prompted this shift?

The rise of the railways saw the number of JSC shares and commercially ignorant, rentier shareholders rapidly grow. With this, it became ever harder to maintain the conception of shareholders as 'partners' in anything like the traditional sense. As Freeman, Pearson and Taylor document, activist shareholding steadily declined, and power gradually shifted from General Meetings to Boards of Directors. Within companies, shareholders were increasingly marginalised, often by design.[102] At the same time, the number of established and stable JSCs also grew, and this helped more positive conceptions of shareholders to begin to gain traction. The usury laws, which had already fallen into desuetude, were formally repealed in 1854, legitimating the unconstrained making of money from money.[103] Equally importantly, despite the bubbles, collapses and frauds, the public benefits brought by the development of the joint-stock economy (and particularly the railway system) began to feed into a much more positive perceptions of shareholders as worthwhile and valuable 'investors'. In *Bligh v Brent*, for example, shareholders are explicitly depicted as investors whose money makes possible the purchase of material productive resources – resources now deemed to be wholly owned by a 'company', a separate entity which puts them to productive use. Money wasn't a 'factor of production' as such, but it made possible the purchase of factors of production. While, therefore, shareholders

[98] In 1825–26 when, following the a boom in JSC promotions, the bubble burst and the authorities displayed little or no desire to help the shareholders of the collapsed concerns: see J Taylor, *Boardroom Scandal: The Criminalisation of Company Fraud in Nineteenth-Century Britain* (Oxford, OUP 2013) ch 2.

[99] J Taylor, 'Company Fraud in Victorian Britain: The Royal British Bank Scandal of 1856' (2007) 497(cxxii) *English Historical Review* 700 at 713.

[100] See Kostal (n 75) ch 2. Though there is considerable disagreement about the intra-class ascription of guilt and innocence amongst the creditors, scrip holders and provisional committeemen caught up in the mess.

[101] Taylor (n 98) 250.

[102] Freeman et al (n 24).

[103] Some saw the formal repeal of the usury laws as clearing the way for general limited liability and greater protection for valuable money-providing, investor-shareholders: see Chaplin (n 58) 210, 240.

are increasingly depicted as *external* to the company and the process of production and their passive nature recognised, they are also portrayed as people who give something valuable to (who 'invest in') companies and perform an important productive function. Crucially, while seeing them as speculators and gamblers pointed towards a non-interventionist policy of let-them-take-the-consequences, seeing them more positively as valuable but vulnerable investors suggested that greater legal protection was justifiable. Criticisms of shareholder inactivity and expectations of some degree of shareholder self-protection do not completely disappear (they still haven't), but by the third quarter of the century, they are beginning gradually to diminish.[104] The emerging view, as Taylor says, was that 'if they can't protect themselves, the law would have to do it for them'. Moreover, he adds, 'as the century wore on, … the interests of investors and the wider "public interest" became increasingly conflated'.[105] What was emerging is the idea of what Brett Christophers has called 'productive finance'. Finance was being 'made productive, not in a literal sense but rather in a perceptual sense'.[106]

The changes to the law of partnership as it was applied to JSCs were both expressions and reflections of these changes in societal attitudes towards JSCs, JSC shareholders and money's productive capacities. It was becoming possible for all money to be 'invested' to yield a return, so that it increasingly seemed to be 'a property of money to generate value and yield interest, much as it is an attribute of pear-trees to bear pears'.[107] With this, the social relational dimensions of the revenues accruing to invested money, central to the class-based economic narratives of Smith, Ricardo and Marx, began to slip from consciousness. Indeed, after the marginal revolution of the 1870s, social class more or less disappeared from mainstream economic thinking. The ability of money to make more money seemed to be one of its innate attributes: no longer were the pecuniary rewards accruing to it thought to derive from the labour of others.

XI. ULTRA VIRES AND THE RIGHT TO REPOSE IN PEACE

The greater sympathy felt towards shareholders was evident in Thomas Wilson's *Partnership en Commandite*, published in 1848. Using the parliamentary Blue

[104] That some still, against all the evidence, seem to hope that *rentier* shareholders can be made active, responsible 'owners' is evident in the recent tendency, in the face of egregious corporate social and environmental irresponsibility, to try to turn to them into the potential solution to our contemporary corporate governance problems by recasting them and their institutional representatives as 'stewards'. It is difficult to escape the conclusion that these attempts are an example of history repeating itself first as tragedy, then as farce and, in this case, then as tragedy again. See L Talbot, 'Why Shareholders shouldn't vote: A Marxist-progressive Critique of Shareholder Empowerment' (2013) 76 *MLR* 791.

[105] Taylor (n 98) 251–2.

[106] Christophers (n 82) 18, 43–4.

[107] Marx (n 16) 392.

Books which showed who had subscribed to railway projects, Wilson concluded that two-thirds of the money was

> disbursed, not by millionaires, but persons in the middle ranks of life .... Professional men, naval and military men, small manufacturers, shopkeepers, clerks, tradesmen, engineers, schoolmasters, clergymen, annuitants, pensioners, placemen, or by their widows, daughters and sisters. These, and not the great commercial men, risked their money in such speculations.

Some of these people were pure gamblers, but many had 'the bona fide intention of investing their means in what promised to yield them good returns'.[108] The 'industrious and lower middle classes' were thus ones who had suffered most, not the 'great capitalists', 'the overpowering money aristocracy'.[109] Indeed, many believed the latter, as 'insiders', had done well from the crisis, buying up the best shares on the cheap. The 'large fish', wrote one contemporary commentator, 'are swallowing the smaller with a vengeance. Seldom have the userers reaped a richer harvest ...'.[110] One of the subtexts of the intensifying debates about limited liability which followed was the fear of conflict between the middle classes and the 'great capitalists'. The introduction of general limited liability, it was hoped, would extend the appropriative power of finance to those further down the wealth pyramid and widen the base of support for industrial capitalism by encouraging business (and especially JSC) formation and creating more, less risky outlets for middle class investment in revenue rights.[111] State policy was also affected by the fact that a growing number of MPs were themselves now *rentier* shareholders as, indeed, were many members of the judiciary. William Gladstone's family, for example, were owners of large West Indian plantations and substantial slave owners and when slavery was abolished in 1833 they invested much of the compensation they received in railway companies[112] and about one quarter of MPs invested in railway shares during the railway mania.[113] In similar vein, there are reported cases involving railway companies

[108] T Wilson, *Partnership en Commandite* (Effingham Wilson, London, 1848) 72–3.

[109] Wilson (n 108) 133; Chaplin (n 58) 103.

[110] *Jerrold's Weekly Newspaper*, 2/10/1847, 1250. This prompted Marx to write of the 'great railway swindle' in Vol 3 of Capital: see Bryer (n 78). See also G Campbell and J Turner, 'Dispelling the Myth of the Naive Investor during the British Railway Mania, 1845–1846' (2012) 86 *Business History Review* 3–41, arguing that although there is no evidence to suggest less experienced investors were expropriated by railway insiders, they did tend to earn lower returns and lost more money during the downturn.

[111] JS Mill, for example, argued that partnership reform and limited liability were necessary to put small investors on the same footing (as money capitalists) as the very wealthy: *Principles of Political Economy* (London, Longmans Green, 1848) 582. It was also argued, more incidentally, that it would also make it easier for workers to join with capital to start their own firms, though the skilled and unskilled working classes contributed only 0.1% of the total capital pledged during the railway mania: Campbell & Turne (n 109) 12.

[112] See P Ireland, 'Making Sense of Contemporary Capitalism using Company Law' (2019) 33 *Australian Journal of Corporate Law* 379.

[113] Campbell & Turner (n 110) 12.

where judges recused themselves because they owned shares in the companies involved.[114] Manifold forces, then, added to the growing support for extending limited liability.

It wasn't, however, just a matter of protecting *people*, but of protecting *property*. As JSC shares became increasingly important as ways of laying claim to a share of the growing social product, so too did maintaining their integrity. This was highlighted by another area of law where the law of partnership was modified in its application to JSCs: ultra vires. The development of ultra vires, which famously culminated in *Ashbury Railway Carriage & Iron Co v Riche* in 1875,[115] was tortuous and complex. The dense case law, discussed only briefly here, vividly illustrates the continuing judicial disagreements about how to conceptualise JSCs (partnerships or qualitatively quite different sorts of association) and JSC shareholders (partners, speculators or investors).

Two bodies of law informed the development of the doctrine: the common law of corporations, under which corporations had traditionally been seen as having full legal capacity; and the law of partnership, under which the scope and purpose of partnerships was a contractual matter for the partners themselves to determine.[116] The decision in *Natusch v Irving* (1824), a case involving a company with 500–600 partner-shareholders, confirmed that in matters within the scope of a partnership agreement, the majority could bind the minority, but that in matters not within scope, the unanimous consent of all the partners was required.[117] Given the vulnerability of shareholders, the courts reasoned, strict adherence to partnership agreements was needed to provide 'security' for 'proprietors' against errant directors.[118]

The first traces of something resembling the modern doctrine emerged in cases involving statutory railway and canal companies endowed with special powers, most notably of compulsory purchase. Because of the potential impact of these powers on other property owners, the courts begin to place limits on their exercise.[119] By the 1830s, it had been established that incorporated statutory companies could be restrained from 'abuse of privileges' to protect third parties whose property rights might be affected.[120] In the 1840s, however, in

[114] See, eg, *Shrewsbury and Birmingham Railway Co v North-Western Railway Co* (1857), 6 HLC 114, where both Lord St Leonards and Lord Wensleydale (the former Baron Parke) withdrew as they were shareholders in one of the companies involved. Judges had traditionally been rather conservative investors, focusing on the 'Funds': see Taylor (n 97) 250. During the railway mania, however, legal professionals contributed nearly 8% of the capital invested: Campbell & Turner (n 110) 12.

[115] *Ashbury Railway Carriage & Iron Co v Riche* (1875) LR 7 HL 653.

[116] *See Const v Harris* (1823) 37 ER 1191.

[117] *Natusch v Irving* (1824) 47 ER 1196. 'The principles which a court would act upon in the case of a partnership of six', wrote Lord Eldon, 'must, as far as the nature of things will admit, ne applied to a partnership of 600'.

[118] See *Ex parte Morgan* (1849) 41 ER 1250 at 1257.

[119] See, eg, *Blakemore v Glamorganshire Canal Co* (1825) 23 ER 1092, 39 ER 639. *Webb v Manchester & Leeds Railway Co* (1839) 41 ER 46.

[120] Collyer (n 5) 2nd edn, 1840, 777–8.

another significant departure from partnership principles, the courts began to place limits on the capacity of *all* JSCs, incorporated and unincorporated, to expand or alter their objects, not to protect outside third parties but to protect shareholders and the share as a property form. Even in cases where third parties were not directly affected (and, indeed, in cases where the new doctrine operated to their disadvantage[121]), the courts came to hold that not even the unanimous shareholders could validate acts beyond the purposes and objects of companies.

The landmark case was *Colman v Eastern Counties Railways*, decided in 1846.[122] *Colman* involved a statutory railway company which proposed to offer financial support to a new steam packet company to increase traffic and profits. At the instigation of a rival steam-boat company, one of the railway company's shareholders sought an injunction to prevent the proposed extension. Counsel for the railway relied in part on the law of corporations (full capacity) and in part on the traditional principles of the law of partnership, arguing that what was proposed was an 'adjunct to the railway' not an 'entirely new trade', and as such a matter of 'practice' requiring only majority approval. Counsel for Colman agreed the case depended on 'the usual principles applicable to ordinary partnerships' but argued that what the company was proposing was not a mere matter of 'practice' but a change in object that required the consent of all the shareholders.

The Master of the Rolls, Lord Langdale,[123] found for Colman. There were two ways he could have done this without breaking new ground: by confining incorporated companies to their statutory purposes to protect third parties, or, as Colman's counsel had urged, by applying *Natusch* and requiring unanimous shareholder approval. The problem with the former approach was that the company did not need additional powers from Parliament to undertake the extension and no third party's property was directly and adversely affected. This did not prevent Langdale from asserting that the special nature and size of railway companies made it imperative they be confined to their stated objects. To treat 'these great combinations and companies' as 'subject to no greater vigilance than common partnerships', he argued, would 'be greatly to mistake' their power and potential impact on 'the public [and] the private rights of individuals'. Railway companies should have 'no right to enter into trades or businesses not pointed out by their acts'.

[121] See, eg, *Hawkes v Eastern Counties Railway Co* (1852) 42 ER 739.

[122] *Colman v Eastern Counties Railways* 10 Beav 1 (50 ER 481); 16 LJ Ch 73 (New Series). The two reports are substantially the same, one being more detailed in some parts, the other in other parts. In the following analysis I have drawn from both. 50 ER 481.

[123] Langdale (Henry Bickersteth, 1783-1851) 'friend of Austin and disciple of Bentham', was one of the small band of Benthamite radicals among leading lawyers and was a strong supporter of greater democracy and of Chancery reform': CHS Fifoot, *Judge and Jurist in the Reign of Victoria* (London, Stevens 1959) 59.

Langdale was concerned, however, not only with third party protection but with shareholder protection and this led him to abandon the partnership principle of unanimity in relation to JSCs. 'To suppose', he argued,

> that the acquiescence of railway shareholders for the last fifteen years in any transaction conducted by a railway company is any evidence whatever of their having a lawful right to enter into it, is, I think, wholly to forget the sort of frenzy which during that period the country has been in. There has been no project, however wild, which has not been encouraged by some one or more of these companies.

Moreover, shareholders had acquiesced in these projects, often 'from cupidity, hoping to gain extraordinary profits'.[124] The consent of shareholders to transactions beyond a company's stated purposes 'afford[ed] no ground whatever for the presumption of their legality'. Indeed, it is clear Langdale wanted to protect not only current shareholders (requiring unanimity would have done that) but future shareholders. He wanted to establish the share as an investment not a speculation and as a secure outlet for *rentier* investment. If there was 'any one thing which is more desirable than another, after providing for the safety of all persons who travel upon railways', he argued, it was that 'the property invested in railway companies should itself be safe; that a railway investment should not be considered, and not be a wild speculation exposing those who are engaged in it to all sorts of risks, whether they intended it or not'. Given 'the vast property which is now invested in railways, and how easily it is transferable', it was imperative that 'investment [in them] should be of such a safe nature that prudent persons might, without improper hazard, invest their monies in it'. In his view this could not be achieved if railway companies were at liberty to 'pledge their funds in support of any plausible speculations, not authorised by their legal powers …'. To do this required establishing shares as stable forms of property with a specific character – rights to revenues derived from a particular venture – rather than 'unspecified', 'wild' 'speculations'. A few years later, the US Supreme Court expressed similar sentiments when granting a shareholder an injunction to stop the company's directors from acting outside its charter. '[A]n investment in the stock of a corporation must by everyone', argued Wayne J 'be considered a wild speculation if it exposed the owners of the stock to all sorts of risk in support of plausible objects not set forth and authorized by the act of incorporation, and which may lead to extraordinary losses'.[125] Indeed, this became a regular theme in subsequent cases: if the integrity of the system of JSC investment was to be safeguarded, it was essential that the capital and profits of companies were applied only to the objects outlined in a company's instrument of incorporation. In *East Anglian Railways Co v Eastern Counties Railway Co* (1851), the defendants refused to pay the costs incurred by the plaintiffs under

[124] Here, Langdale highlights the, conceptually speaking, transitional nature of this period. He at the same time prises apart JSCs and their shareholders while seeing them as combinations of people.
[125] *Dodge v Woolsey* (1855) 18 Howard 331 at 342. *Colman* was cited approvingly by the court.

a contract they had entered into, arguing that the contract was void because it was outside the terms of their incorporating act. It was vital to the protection of shareholders, Counsel claimed, that the directors of the company be restrained. Every shareholder, he asserted, had 'a right to repose in peace ... upon the faith and confidence of which he has invested his money'.[126] The court agreed. 'Every proprietor, when he takes his shares', Jervis CJ explained, 'has a right to expect that the conditions upon which the act was obtained will be performed; and it is no sufficient answer to a shareholder, expecting his dividend, that the money has been expended upon an undertaking which at some remote period may be highly beneficial to the line'.[127]

XII. FROM LIMITED LIABILITY TO NO-LIABILITY: THE EMERGENCE OF THE MODERN DOCTRINE OF SEPARATE CORPORATE PERSONALITY

The development of the doctrine followed a rocky path after *Colman*, partly because of its adverse impact, as in *East Anglian*, on third parties and partly because the courts found it hard completely to abandon the partnership conception of JSCs as aggregates of individuals and the principle of unanimity.[128] The cases reveal growing recognition that most JSC shareholders are commercially ignorant rentiers, but continuing disagreement about whether some degree of self-protection should nevertheless be expected of them. The view that eventually prevailed in *Ashbury* (that even the unanimous shareholders could not authorise acts outside the objects of the company) acknowledged not only that JSCs were qualitatively different from ordinary partnerships but the increasingly *rentier* nature of JSC shareholding and detachment of shareholders from the companies in which they held shares. Conceptually, it prised company and shareholders even further apart, effectively placing 'the company' in certain respects beyond the will even of its unanimous shareholders, reinforcing the idea of it as something quite separate from them. Indeed, the legal historian, CHS Fifoot, considered the development of ultra vires to be central to the development of the modern doctrine of separate corporate personality. By 1875, Seward Brice was describing Kyd's definition of a corporation as 'a collection of many individuals united into one body' as 'fairly accurate' but arguing that it laid insufficient stress on 'its real characteristic in the eye of the law, ... its existence separate and distinct from the individual or individual composing it'.[129]

[126] *East Anglian Railways Co v Eastern Counties Railway Co* 138 ER 680 at 689.

[127] ibid at 695.

[128] This was especially true in relation to companies registered under the Companies Acts. On the persistence of partnership conceptions of JSCs, see Lobban (n 25).

[129] S Brice, *A Treatise on the Doctrine of Ultra Vires*, 2nd edn (London, Stevens & Haynes, 1877) 1–2.

It was not, however, until the final decades of the century that this 'complete separation' was fully realised. For much of the nineteenth century, shares carried high denominations and were only partly paid up, the uncalled capital giving companies a ready source of additional finance and acting as a comfort to creditors. But the residual liabilities attached to shares impeded transferability and also meant that links remained between shareholders and companies, and, indirectly, between shareholders and creditors. In the closing decades of the century, however, these links were all but severed as share denominations fell and the residual liabilities on shares were eliminated.[130] By 1885 only about 32 per cent of companies outside the banking, insurance and finance sectors had shares which weren't fully paid up; by 1913 this had fallen to just 5.4 per cent. This development was largely attributable to the growing and increasingly prosperous middle classes demanding 'safe equity' and a 'diversified portfolio of readily marketable stocks'.[131] By the 1870s, the wealthier among them were already diversifying their holdings through investment trusts, spreading the risks across a portfolio of investments. Having already delegated management of the company, they were now beginning to delegate management of their money.[132]

The result was that by the close of the century existing shares were no longer sources of additional capital for companies. Henceforth, neither directors nor shareholders had any particular need to check the financial wherewithal of new shareholders and creditors could look only to the assets of companies to meet debts. JSC shareholders really did now benefit from Smith's 'total exemption from trouble and from risk'. The de jure regime of limited liability had been turned into a de facto regime of no-liability. Corporate shareholding now entailed ownership of an unencumbered, free-standing right to revenue, external to the process of production and entailing no liabilities or obligations, contractual or otherwise, to the company or third parties. Standing outside the company, shareholders now received their returns in the form of interest, as a simple reward for owning money. They had become money capitalists who only ever stood to lose the money they had spent on their shares.[133] The foundations for the emergence of the doctrine of separate corporate personality in its modern form, with its conception of the business corporation as a depersonified, property-owning legal person 'completely separate' from its shareholders, had been cemented in place.

[130] A process facilitated by courts and legislature: 1867 Act; see S Thompson, *Treatise on the Liability of Stockholders in Corporations* (London, Thomas & Co., 1879).

[131] See Acheson, Turner & Ye, 'The character and denomination of shares in the Victorian equity market' (2012) 65 *Economic History Review* 862.

[132] See, eg, A Scratchley, *On Average Investment Trusts* (London, Shaw and Sons, 1875).

[133] See P Ireland, 'Corporate Schizophrenia: The Institutional Origins of Corporate Social Irresponsibility' in N Boeger and C Villiers (eds), *Shaping the Corporate Landscape* (Oxford, Hart Publishing, 2018) 13. The demise of residual shareholder liabilities and growth in financial institutions which enabled the wealthy to diversify their financial property (revenue rights) holdings rendered the protections offered by ultra vires less important. By the 1880s, the doctrine was already being eroded: *Attorney General v Great Eastern Railway* (1880) 5 App Cas 473.

XIII. EPILOGUE: THE IRONIES OF COMPANY LAW

By the second half of the nineteenth century, JSC law had deviated so much from the law of partnership that it started to be seen as a quite separate body of law. As early as 1863, it was becoming clear to some that a body of JSC law with its own quite distinctive conceptual structure was emerging. In his 1863 treatise, *The Law of Joint Stock Companies*, Leonard Shelford argued that although there were many valuable works on the law of partnership, a separate work specifically on JSCs was needed. 'The Law relative to JSCs', he argued, 'has not at present many rules in common with those on the law of partnership, but it has in fact been framed to supersede some of those rules, and to establish a separate system independent of the law of partnership.[134] The emergence of company law as a fully separate legal category took time, however. Nathaniel Lindley, author of the leading late nineteenth-century treatise on partnership, first published in 1860, revealingly entitled it *The Law of Partnership including its Application to Joint-Stock and other Companies.*[135] Not until the late 1880s did he finally break it up into two separate volumes, one dealing with partnership law, the other with company law.[136] By the end of the century, however, company law had clearly emerged as a separate legal category in its own right.[137]

There were, however, ironies. In many ways, the 'complete separation' of company and shareholders created a shareholder's paradise: a world of liability- and responsibility-free *rentier* shareholding. Companies came simultaneously to be seen as completely separate property-owning legal persons (for liability purposes) but also as objects of property 'owned' by their shareholders (for the purpose of determining corporate goals). The idea of shareholder ownership was (and still is) used to justify shareholder control rights and primacy. For shareholders, however, there was a potential downside to all this. Fully paid-up shares were no longer sources of new capital and new shareholders were no longer 'investors' who gave something to companies; they simply bought existing, fully paid-up shares. This prompted many commentators – Veblen, Tawney, Keynes, Berle, Galbraith, Goyder and others – to cast them in a negative light once again as functionless, vestigial *rentiers*, liability- and responsibility-free owners of rights to 'unearned incomes'. This led to calls for their rights to be pared down and, in some cases, for their relegation to the status of creditors. In similar vein, the rise of the JSC was emblematic of the fact that production

[134] L Shelford, *The Law of Joint Stock Companies* (London, Butterworths, 1863) 2.

[135] N Lindley, *Treatise on the Law of partnership including its Application to Joint Stock Companies*, 1st edn (London, Sweet & Maxwell, 1860).

[136] Sir N Lindley, *Treatise on the Law of Companies* (London, Sweet & Maxwell, 1889). Lindley was one of the judges who, in *Broderip v Salomon* [1895] 2 ChD 333, denied Aaron Salomon the benefit of limited liability.

[137] Exemplified by the texts of people like Palmer and Buckley. Palmer's *Company Law*, London: Stevens, first appeared in 1898.

was becoming a much less individual and much more social affair,[138] in which context shares appeared simply to be vehicles for the private appropriation of an increasingly social product and public corporations appeared to be much more like social or quasi-social institutions than purely private enterprises. Separate corporate personality, it was argued, should be taken *really* seriously and these corporations be run in the wider public interest. It has taken sustained political and ideological effort to stave off these threats and to maintain belief in the fundamentally private nature of public corporations and legitimacy of shareholder revenue and control rights.[139]

In a further irony, no sooner had company law separated itself from the law of partnership than it was invaded by partnerships from another direction. The decades around the turn of the nineteenth and twentieth centuries saw more and more small partnerships and one-man firms incorporate to get the protection of limited liability, a practice legitimated by the decision in *Salomon v Salomon & Co Ltd* in 1897.[140] Suddenly, a body of law designed for application to JSCs, where the separation of shareholders and company had a real-world, empirical basis was being applied to small, closely-held and subsidiary companies, where it didn't. This has been a source of a variety of ongoing problems, one of which is minority shareholder protection in small companies.[141] While unhappy shareholders in public companies can simply sell their shares and 'exit', this option is generally unavailable to shareholders in private companies. The legislature initially responded with s 210 of the Companies Act 1948 on 'oppression' and, when this didn't work, with s 459 of the Companies Act 1985, now s 994 of the Companies Act 2006, on 'unfair prejudice'. Through the latter, the courts have re-introduced partnership principles into company law in its application to some non-JSCs. And this, of course, brings us back to Lord Hoffmann and to where we began.

[138] Marx described them as representing the abolition of private property: K Marx, *Capital, Volume III*, (London, Lawrence and Wishart, 1959 [1885]) ch 27, 435–41.

[139] See P Ireland, 'Defending the Rentier: Corporate Theory and the Reprivatization of the Public Company' in J Parkinson et al (eds), *The Political Economy of the Company* (Oxford, Hart Publishing, 2001) 141–73.

[140] *Salomon v Salomon & Co Ltd* [1897] AC 22. See P Ireland, 'The Rise of the Limited Liability Company' (1984) 12 *International Journal of the Sociology of Law* 239–60.

[141] The other, of course, is the exploitation of separate corporate personality by large multinational enterprises and high net-worth individuals.

15

Epilogue

VICTORIA BARNES AND JONATHAN HARDMAN

THIS EPILOGUE SUMMARISES some of the main themes which have come together through the collection. The main one is perhaps obvious, given the book's motivation and the circumstances that prompted it. Policy-makers use the past and the history of corporate regulation to generate a legal approach. The ties that bind the chapters together are often the state and its role in private enterprise. The collection, while providing a range of methodological insights, also provides some opportunities and further avenues for exploration.

I. THE STATE AND PRIVATE ENTERPRISE

One theme that is ever present in company law scholarship is the role of the state.[1] To be clear, recent political discussions also underpinned the premise for this book and looking back at company law. How far should company law extend to encompass market activity? What should be left to individuals and their rights? Only one of the chapters discusses the theme of the state explicitly. That is Robert Thompson's chapter five. Most do not consider issues explicitly that are obviously or commonly allied to it, such as capitalism,[2] class interests,[3] profit,[4] power,[5] political economy,[6] or

[1] P Ireland, I Grigg-Spall and D Kelly, 'The Conceptual Foundations of Modern Company Law' (1987) 14 *Journal of Law and Society* 149.

[2] C Stanley, 'Corporate Personality and Capitalist Relations: A Critical Analysis of the Artifice of Company Law' (1988) 19 *Cambrian Law Review* 97; P Ireland, 'Capitalism without the Capitalist: The Joint Stock Company Share and the Emergence of the Modern Doctrine of Separate Corporate Personality' (1996) 17 *The Journal of Legal History* 41.

[3] ME Cain and A Hunt, *Marx and Engels on Law* (London, Academic Press, 1979) 62–68.

[4] CA Cooke, 'The Legal Content of the Profit Concept' (1936) 46 *Yale Law Journal* 436.

[5] DL MacPherson, 'Companies Gone Wild A Review of the Corporation: The Pathological Pursuit of Profit and Power' (2005) 31 *Manitoba Law Journal* 201; N Rollings, '"The Vast and Unsolved Enigma of Power": Business History and Business Power' (2021) 22 *Enterprise & Society* 893.

[6] J Parkinson, G Kelly and A Gamble (eds), *The Political Economy of the Company* (Oxford, Hart Publishing, 2000); PA McCoy, 'A Political Economy of the Business Judgment Rule in Banking: Implication for Corporate Law' (1996) 47 *Case Western Reserve Law Review* 1.

nationalisation/privatisation[7] to name a few. Lorraine Talbot's chapter nine is notable here as she considers the emergence of capitalism and its roots in Victorian Britain in a company called Brunner, Mond & Co Ltd. Here, she examines the company ownership, its leaders and the business culture of the time. She describes this as a 'personal' firm, where the entrepreneurial owners/managers were closely associated with the firm and they remained tightly bound to their kin and social groups. Religion played a role in shaping business leaders and the face of capitalism.[8] Victorian Britain represented a period before business became large-scale in size. It was also a time before management as a professional class came into play.[9] Talbot shows us the softer face of business and the antecedents of the modern capitalism firm.

These sub-themes surrounding the state may not be well represented as such, but they stem from what is often thought to be a wider political conflict.[10] Indeed, it is one that is what is often characterised as a distinction between the left and right. Yet, this theme is one of contesting ideologies. It is here in this collection. That is because it is, in truth, difficult to escape from. This theme appears here often in an implicit and subtle fashion with authors taking different views and frameworks. This is also because most authors have allowed their historical actors to speak for themselves and they have naturally used the language of their time as opposed to the language of our own. So this theme is at the background rather than being an overt, obvious and central unifying theme.[11] Perhaps one of the chapters that contributes to this discussion in this exact way is chapter thirteen by Neil Rollings. It is on the topic of hostile takeovers.[12]

Rollings writes about the first hostile takeover in modern company law, which focussed on the Savoy Hotel. The issue is, no doubt, political. The extent to which company law should allow such activity is moot. As Rollings points out, the question was linked rather inherently in the minds of policy makers to

[7] AW Bradley, 'Legal Aspects of the Nationalisations in Tanzania' (1967) 3 *East African Law Journal* 149; C Graham and T Prosser, 'Privatising Nationalised Industries: Constitutional Issues and New Legal Techniques' (1987) 50 *The Modern Law Review* 16; R Millward and J Singleton (eds), *The Political Economy of Nationalisation in Britain, 1920–1950* (Cambridge, Cambridge University Press, 2002).

[8] DJ Jeremy, *Capitalists and Christians: Business Leaders and the Churches in Britain 1900–1960*, 1st edn (Oxford, Clarendon Press,1990).

[9] For more in the historical emergence of management in Britain, see AD Chandler, *Scale and Scope: Dynamics of Industrial Capitalism: The Dynamics of Industrial Capitalism*, reprint (Cambridge, Harvard University Press, 1994).

[10] JG Deutsch, 'Corporate Law as the Ideology of Capitalism' (1983) 93 *Yale Law Journal* 395.

[11] Had the collection featured jurisdictions with a more explicit Marxist ideology, this may have been different. The studies on corporate law in China often consider these issues explicitly. See T Ruskola, 'Conceptualizing Corporations and Kinship: Comparative Law and Development Theory in a Chinese Perspective' (1999) 52 *Stanford Law Review* 1599; 'State Capitalism and Corporate Law: The Governance of State-Owned Enterprises in China' in R Tomasic (ed), *Routledge Handbook of Corporate Law* (Abingdon, Routledge, 2016); M Pargendler, 'State Ownership and Corporate Governance' (2011) 80 *Fordham Law Review* 2917.

[12] N Rollings, ch 13 in this volume.

the question of profits and dividends.[13] His chapter, borrows as its title, a quote he found in private correspondence from a stockbroker to Reginald Maudling (1917–79), who was the Economic Secretary from 1952 to 1955. He later became the Chancellor of the Exchequer in 1962 and Home Secretary in 1970. There in this letter, the stockbroker explained that he thought 'profit' ought to be used to the 'greatest possible advantage'.[14] The stockbroker's line was that companies were 'pikes' or 'trout' and 'a great many Boards in this country to-day come well within my description of "trout"'.[15] This, therefore, in his mind meant that businesses ought to be allowed to grow through mergers and acquisitions. Although the stockbroker does not state expressly what he thought companies ought to do with their profit, Rollings makes this clear. Dividends – the ideology of shareholder primacy – was the driver.[16] Linking corporate takeovers to the food chain, the stockbroker thought that predatory behaviour was acceptable and even natural. It was to be both encouraged and allowed. When Rollings's title is understood fully, it clearly speaks to the theme of the state; its role in regulating companies, setting the standard for business behaviour and in protecting weaker parties. He states that this 'shareholder-dominated view of the company … is one commonly associated with UK corporate governance over the last fifty or so years'.[17] The role of the state has changed over time and it differs through time period and jurisdiction.

While Rollings, Johnston,[18] Watson[19] and Harris[20] examine English law, British politics and the state, Lamoreaux, Hilt, Thompson and Wells focus on the US. This comparative element in the collection is important. The focus often limited to a single jurisdiction, namely the UK or US.[21] The exception here is an explicitly comparative chapter written by Jennifer Trinks, where she examines voting rights in Germany, France, Italy and the US. She notes the importance of translations as ways of contributing to interjurisdictional discourse.[22] There is good reason to think that the English-speaking/common law jurisdictions might share elements of company law. First, comparing jurisdictions has historically been understudied, especially in the field of company law.[23] Elsewhere in

[13] ibid.
[14] ibid.
[15] ibid.
[16] ibid.
[17] ibid.
[18] A Johnston, ch 12 in this volume.
[19] S Watson, ch 6 in this volume.
[20] R Harris, ch 10 in this volume.
[21] For a UK, US and European comparison, the literature on the varieties of capitalism is useful. See P Zumbansen, 'Varieties of Capitalism and the Learning Firm: Corporate Governance and Labour in the Context of Contemporary Developments in European and German Company Law' (2007) 8 *European Business Organization Law Review* 467; M O'Sullivan, 'The Political Economy of Comparative Corporate Governance' (2003) 10 *Review of International Political Economy* 23. There are now attempts to draw together a more global approach.
[22] J Trinks, ch 11 in this volume.
[23] LCB Gower, 'Some Contrasts between British and American Corporation Law' (1955) 69 *Harvard Law Review* 1369.

Europe, the comparativist tradition is far more common.[24] Second, the literature on historical development of company law is well mapped out in the UK.[25] It may be tempting to assume that the pattern we know so well and observe in company law in the UK is present elsewhere in the common law world. Third, given Britain's place within its empire, other areas of law did, indeed, follow a London-centric legal path. This closeness was, of course, intentional. The other apparatus of law, such as the use of legal precedent and hierarchical structure of the courts,[26] no doubt, helped strengthen legal bonds. It was not until the winds of change in post-colonial period that law and politics began to develop differently.[27] For the US, this came far earlier. Yet, as Robert Thompson shows us in this volume, there was still adherence to English legal ideas, after it had broken away formally from the empire.[28]

Lamoreaux, Hilt, Thompson and Wells show that, for the US, there was little in the way of parallel developments in company law. Harwell Wells shows us that in the US the Limited Liability Partnership came to be in 1991. This happened in the UK in 2001. Limited liability for companies incorporated by registration came in much more generally in the UK in the mid-nineteenth century. The literature, which maps this out in the UK is voluminous.[29] Lamoreaux and Hilt's chapters show how idiosyncratic the historical development of company law in England was by allowing the reader to contrast the chapters on the UK with that of the US. Hilt examines the process of chartering that existed in various US states around the turn of the eighteenth century.[30] This was at a point in time where there was little in the way of federal law which joined up thinking in contract and commercial law. Corporate law, on the other hand, remains regulated by states.[31] Lamoreaux provides a long run study, where she traces the way

[24] W Hug, 'The History of Comparative Law' (1931) 45 *Harvard Law Review* 1027; RB Schlesinger, 'The Past and Future of Comparative Law' (1995) 43 *The American Journal of Comparative Law* 477.

[25] See stalwart texts such as BC Hunt, *The Development of the Business Corporation in England, 1800–1867* (Cambridge, Harvard University Press, 1936); CA Cooke, *Corporation, Trust and Company: An Essay in Legal History* (Cambridge, Harvard University Press, 1951); R McQueen, *A Social History of Company Law: Great Britain and the Australian Colonies 1854–1920*, 1st edn (Abingdon, Routledge, 2009); P Johnson, *Making the Market: Victorian Origins of Corporate Capitalism* (Cambridge, Cambridge University Press, 2010).

[26] AP Poley, 'The Privy Council and Problems of Closer Union of the Empire' (1917) 17 *Journal of the Society of Comparative Legislation* 30; N Bentwich, 'The Limitation of the Jurisdiction of the Privy Council' (1935) 47 *Juridical Review* 330; P Mitchell, 'The Privy Council and the Difficulty of Distance' (2016) 36 *Oxford Journal of Legal Studies* 26.

[27] For some jurisdictions, there is still a path dependency and adherence to an earlier area of law.

[28] R Thompson, ch 5 in this volume. Section II.A.iii.

[29] HA Shannon, 'The Coming of General Limited Liability' (1931) 41 *The Economic Journal* 267; D Loftus, 'Capital and Community: Limited Liability and Attempts to Democratize the Market in Mid-Nineteenth-Century England' (2002) 45 *Victorian Studies* 93; DC Smith, 'The Mid-Victorian Reform of Britain's Company Laws and the Moral Economy of Fair Competition' (2021) 22 *Enterprise & Society* 1103.

[30] E Hilt, ch 8 in this volume.

[31] RK Winter, 'State Law, Shareholder Protection, and the Theory of the Corporation' (1977) 6 *The Journal of Legal Studies* 251.

this chartering process changed and developed from the American Revolution to the late twentieth century.[32]

These developments were entirely out of sync with Britain; they were both yards ahead of Britain in some respects and also lagging behind in others. Susan Watson's chapter is the closest in terms of exposing these themes in the British mirror. While the state was heavily involved in the company promotion process in the US in the eighteenth and nineteenth centuries, this resembled Britain, perhaps in some sense, in the sixteenth and seventeenth centuries. Susan Watson traces the path from the English East India Company to the modern company. She identifies that the provision of the corporate form enabled a corporate fund to sit in a perpetual vehicle. She argues – informed by this historical lineage – that these features provide considerable opportunity to reconceptualise the company in the modern day.[33] Her work makes an important contribution in the post *Sequana* world.

The role of the state is clearly a theme that is present in this collection, although not explicitly. It is a key part of the political debate. It will continue to be present as long as policy-makers engage in a process which either restrains the excesses of capitalism and attempts to make the modern corporation friendlier, or pushes for maximum growth. If politicians decide to pursue the latter, or leave businesses to themselves, again the state plays a role in refusing to regulate. Law, of course, is central here as it is the key mechanism through which politicians achieve their goals, and also a key determinant of business activity.[34] Legislation is now used to place boundaries on corporations and influence their operations. Aside from these points about how the collection influences this debate, it also shows that a number of avenues are open and worth exploring. We now turn to discuss some of the methods and styles of research.

II. SOURCES

This collection features a number of different sources, but there is little in the way of sources which legal historians would see instantly as being part of their craft. The typical method in English legal history is known as the 'manuscript tradition'.[35] It implies, as the name suggests, that scholars seek out manuscript (handwritten) documents from archives and other repositories. These are often original documents from court cases; they are important sources of law.[36] There

[32] N Lamoreaux, ch 7 in this volume.

[33] Watson (n 19).

[34] S Deakin, D Gindis, GM Hodgson, H Kainan and K Pistor, 'Legal Institutionalism: Capitalism and the Constitutive Role of Law' (2017) 45 *Journal of Comparative Economics* 188.

[35] DJ Seipp, 'The Law's Many Bodies, and the Manuscript Tradition in English Legal History' (2004) 25 *The Journal of Legal History* 74.

[36] JH Baker, *Baker and Milsom Sources of English Legal History: Private Law to 1750* (Oxford, Oxford University Press, 2010).

are a good number of archives and other repositories holding manuscripts through which a legal historian can find relevant sources.[37] That said, the task at hand is not a simple one. It is not the same as ordinary doctrinal research, which is desk based. With so many archival locations and so many documents within the single location, this style of research can be both time consuming and frustrating. The cataloguing can be lank and lacklustre meaning that pulling up documents can be the luck of the draw. When, and if, sources can be found, deciphering manuscripts is not necessarily simple either. A course in palaeography may be relevant.[38] Handwriting not only differs through time and by the hand itself, but so does legal language.[39] The need for extra specialist training reflects the typical background of a legal historian in the UK, where the background of the scholars here in this collection is often in law (rather than history).

The job of a legal historian is, for some, to apply the methods of law to the past,[40] also described as 'applied legal history'.[41] The use of concepts and theory is not especially common in this form of legal history, nor perhaps in legal history more generally.[42] Yet, in other jurisdictions, legal history is much more tied to the study of history than law. Sarah Wilson discusses the evolution of legal history as a sub-discipline exceptionally well in her chapter.[43] She notes that British legal historians, such as Andrew Lewis and Michael Lobban, characterise scholarship that speaks to law as 'internal' and the work to history as 'external'.[44] American legal history, on the other hand, strikes a balance between the two audiences. It is perhaps even swayed more towards history than to law. This, again, is a matter of training. Law in the US is a second degree. Legal historians based there usually have a first degree in history and a postgraduate degree in law. None of the chapters here engage in the use of manuscripts or factual and 'internal' description of the law as might be typical or prevalent among British legal historians.

There are but two chapters here, which use archives. That is the work of Neil Rollings, who surveys the National Archives for material relating to hostile takeovers.[45] Andrew Johnston uses archival material, connected with

[37] JH Baker, *Why the History of English Law Has Not Been Finished* (Cambridge, Cambridge University Press, 1999).

[38] J Rose, 'Learning to Be a Legal Historian: Reflections of a Nontraditional Student' (2001) 51 *Journal of Legal Education* 294.

[39] Lawyers used to use Law French, see JH Baker, *Manual of Law French* (Abingdon, Routledge, 2016).

[40] See the various methods, as discussed in M Lobban, 'The Varieties of Legal History' [2012] Clio@Themis. Revue électronique d'histoire du droit, journals.openedition.org/cliothemis/1727 (accessed 21 April 2024).

[41] AL Brophy, 'Introducing Applied Legal History' (2013) 31 *Law and History Review* 233.

[42] An exception here is AWB Simpson, *Legal Theory and Legal History: Essays on the Common Law* (London, Hambledon Press, 1987).

[43] S Wilson, ch 3 in this volume.

[44] A Lewis and M Lobban (eds), *Law and History: Current Legal Issues 2003 Volume 6* (Oxford, Oxford University Press, 2004).

[45] Rollings (n 12).

other sources. The remainder here solely or primarily use different sources, whether that be law books,[46] company histories,[47] or other sources. It is clear that there is much more in the way of archival that can be exploited to tell a story of the historical evolution of company law.

III. QUANTIFICATION

While trying to bring together frameworks and approaches from law and history, it is important to also acknowledge that not all branches of history are the same. Business and economic history have different roots, too. Business history has focussed on the use of qualitative evidence. Much like law, it uses case studies.[48] Those cases can then be used by those developing theory to do just that,[49] although some simply devote themselves to identifying and analysing the facts themselves. Again, Rollings's chapter here is an excellent example of that.[50] Economic history is, on the other hand, motivated more often than not by the collection of data, which is then analysed statistically. The adage here is that such a method is more objective and brings a wider viewpoint. Case studies can be seen as anecdotal or single issues that matter little to the collective. Of course, for the purposes of scholarship on entrepreneurship, for example, individuals thinking or behaving differently matter because they innovate and lead the market.[51] The same is true for law with its emphasis on landmark cases and following of legal precedents.[52]

Rollings sees the Savoy Hotel as one such incident that acted as a turning point. He notes that this marked a shift from past policy, where business dealings were hoped to be more consensual. After the Savoy Hotel, aggressive mergers were accepted. He considers that the Savoy Hotel case marks 'a significant staging post in the development of British company law'.[53] Hardman focuses on the way in which modern company lawyers utilise such historical details to advance their normative prescriptions, deploying repeated tropes and structures in order

[46] P Ireland, ch 14 in this volume.

[47] L Talbot, ch 9 in this volume.

[48] See the pioneering texts in the US and Britain respectively: NSB Gras and HM Larson, *Casebook in American Business History* (New York, FS Crofts & Co, 1939); C Wilson, *The History of Unilever: A Study in Economic Growth and Social Change*, 1st edn (London, Cassell, 1954).

[49] See for instance AD Chandler Jr, *The Visible Hand* (Cambridge, Harvard University Press, 1993).

[50] JA Schumpeter, *The Theory of Economic Development: An Inquiry into Profits, Capital, Credit, Interest, and the Business Cycle* (Cambridge, Harvard University Press, 1934); M Casson, *The Entrepreneur: An Economic Theory* (New York, Rowman & Littlefield, 1982).

[51] PL Payne, *British Entrepreneurship in the Nineteenth Century* (Basingstoke, Palgrave Macmillan, 1974).

[52] N Duxbury, *The Nature and Authority of Precedent* (Cambridge, Cambridge University Press, 2008).

[53] Rollings (n 12).

to do so.[54] These narrative histories of company law rely often upon the assessment of qualitative data. The alternative here is quantification.

There are just two studies that showcase quantitative methods. Barnes and Wheeler use a blend of quantification and case study as they count the number of cases in company law.[55] Hilt, too, calculates data by tabulating the number of corporations in cities in the US.[56] The empirical movement in law now gives rise to further studies that use statistics as a way to identify patterns.[57] It is important to note here, as this collection does, that the vast majority of studies are qualitative. So expectations about the reader's understanding of regression and other complex quantitative methods should not be high. Overall, this remains a promising area for new research.

IV. META-EPILOGUE

In the introduction we flagged the need for a multiplicity of methods and approaches to identify the core of the subject matter that the authors of chapters, and readers, of this book study. We believe that this collection helps shed light on alternative methodologies that can be deployed, and also how they will point to different outcomes. By allowing readers to compare and contrast these approaches, further work can be one in this field to help drive the discipline onwards. In other words, this book should be the origins of a renewed focus on the origins of company law.

[54] J Hardman, ch 2 in this volume.

[55] V Barnes and S Wheeler, ch 1 in this volume.

[56] Hilt (n 30).

[57] JB Gelbach and J Klick, 'Empirical Law and Economics' in F Parisi (ed), *The Oxford Handbook of Law and Economics: Volume 1: Methodology and Concepts* (Oxford, Oxford University Press, 2017); S Wheeler, 'Contracts and Corporations' in P Cane and HM Kritzer (eds), *The Oxford Handbook of Empirical Legal Research* (Oxford, Oxford University Press, 2010).

Index

Abel, Richard 82
account of profits by fiduciaries 16–17
accountability 56–7, 263, 265–6, 309
accounts
double entry bookkeeping 118, 119, 131–2, 134–5
English East India Company (EEIC) 134–5
hostile takeover bids 258–60, 275
separation of capital from income 133
transparency 258, 275
Adam, Thomas 195
advantages of the corporate form *see* **corporate privileges**
agencies, creation of government 153
agency law
authority to bind companies 305–7
constructive notice, doctrine of 307
law syllabus 21
mutual agency 296, 305–7
American Bar Association (ABA)
Canon of Ethics 74, 78–9, 85
Model Rules of Professional Conduct 85
statements of principles 79
vicarious liability 88
anonymity 91, 107, 108, 111–12, 115
anti-Semitism 184, 189–95, 200
capitalism, association of Jews with 190, 194
conspiracy theories 194–5
discriminatory legislation 189, 191, 193
England, in 193, 197, 206
Germany 189–95
elite, association of Jews with the 191
Napoleonic-era reforms 190
riots and attacks on Jews 190–2
usury 190, 194
Aquinas, Thomas 313
arbitrage 107, 108, 112
archives, use of 282, 332–3
argumentation structures 27–47
Aristotle 312–13
Armstrong, William 291–3
articles of association 253, 258, 261
Ashhurst, William Henry 21
asset-partitioning 98, 107, 218, 303–4
Astor, John Jacob 173–4
autonomy 61, 91, 93–4, 107, 111–14, 265

Baker, John 65
Baker, Scott 89
Balkin, Jack 36
Bank of England 250, 262–71
accountability 263
corporate governance 262–71
hostile takeovers 262, 277–9, 281, 290–1
institutional investor engagement, encouraging 250, 262–3, 266, 268–71
managerialism 262–5
meso-corporatism 262
non-executive directors (NEDs), promotion of 250, 262–3, 264–8, 270
policy activism 250, 271
self-regulation in City of London 262–4
shareholders 262, 265
state annexation 265
takeover regulation, promoting 263–4
banks *see also* **Bank of England**
charters 143–4, 174–7
competition 175–6
elites 143–4
federal incorporations and the public purpose 178–81
free banking acts 151
hostile takeovers 291–2, 293
inseparability principle 234, 247
politicisation 143–4
public purpose 167, 169–70
reserve liability 220
self-regulation 262
Beit, Alfred 193
benefits definition of public purpose 162–3, 164–5, 171–8
Benson, Henry 265–7
Bentham, Jeremy 312–13
Bentley, Sarah 57–9, 70
Berle, Adolf 111, 184, 249, 325
Blackstone's *Commentaries* 94, 99, 103–4
Blair, Margaret 145
Blumberg, Phillip 106

Board of Trade 273, 276–89, 292–4
Bodenhorn, Howard 144
bonds 219, 222, 227
Boyd-Carpenter, John 282–4
Braithwaite, John 280–1
Brandeis, Louis 73
Brice, Seward 323
bridge companies 107, 143–5, 167–9, 177–8, 181, 213
Bridges, Edward 283–5
British Insurance Association (BIA) 269
Bromberg, Alan 87
Brunner, Jack 197, 201
Brunner, John 183–6, 195, 197–201, 206
Brunner, Mond & Co Ltd (1881–1926) 183–207
- anti-Semitism 184, 189–95, 200, 206
- art collection 184, 196–7
- Brunner, John, biography of 197–9
- capitalism 184, 190, 194, 328
- chemical industry 183–207
- cosmopolitanism 184, 189, 195, 200, 206
- culture 184, 192, 195–7, 200, 328
- employees, treatment of 198–201, 203–4
- *Evans v Brunner, Mond & Co Ltd* 185, 188, 201–6
- gift-giving by corporations 185, 188, 201–6
- growth and expansion of company 186–7, 206
- ICI, mergers to become 185, 206–7
- international expansion 185, 187, 195, 207
- large companies, shift from owner-controlled businesses to 184, 187–8
- management-controlled model 184–5, 187–8, 201, 205, 207
- mergers 185, 206–7
- Mond, Ludwig, biography of 189–97
- moral inclinations of owners 184, 195–201, 206
- non-conforming religious beliefs 183, 197–8, 201
- objects of the company 201–6
- ordinary shares, issue of 186
- origins and development 185–8
- personal nature of company 183–6, 188–207, 328
- profits 183–6, 188, 202, 204–5, 329
- public purposes 183, 201–6
- quasi-partnership model, using a 186
- registration of the company 186
- religion 189–95, 328
  - anti-Semitism 184, 189–95, 197, 206
  - non-conforming religious beliefs 183, 197–8, 201
  - Unitarianism 183, 197–8, 201
- rentier shareholders, move to 194
- shareholders
  - directors, holdings of 188
  - dispersal of ownership 184
  - minority shareholders and corporate gift-giving 185, 188, 201–6
  - numbers 185, 188, 206
  - ordinary shares, issue of 186
  - ultra vires 185, 188, 201–6
  - value 188, 201
- social inclinations 184, 328
- stakeholder approach 198
- subsidiaries 187
- sulphur recovery process 185, 192–3
- ultra vires doctrine and corporate gift-giving 185, 188, 201–6
- vertical integration model 186

Brunner, Roscoe 185, 201, 205–7
Bryer, RA 7
Buckley, Denys 282, 287–8
Bunsen, Robert 191
Burr, Aaron 143, 175
business corporations
- democracy, as threats to 162
- joint-stock companies 133–4, 304
- permanent capital 119
- private investment with state-granted monopoly privileges, combining 133
- public purpose 161–2, 164–74, 181
- Regulated Companies 133
- separate legal personality 133–5, 138
- social function of the state, performing the 162

business-judgment rule 97, 154
business vehicles, choice of 28, 40–7
Butler, RA (Rab) 278, 286

Cadbury, Adrian 268 *see also* **Cadbury Report**
Cadbury Committee 268
Cadbury Report 250, 264, 271
Cairncross, Alec 293
campaign finance
- Federal Election Campaign Act of 1972 153
- freedom of speech 156
- general incorporation statutes 152–3

new organisational forms, era of 156–7, 159
political action committees (PACs) 153
Taft-Hartley Act of 1947 152–3
Tillman Act of 1907 152–3
trade unions 152–3
canal companies
bailouts in United States 224
compulsory purchase powers 320
dividend rights, history of 223–4
general incorporation statutes 219
joint-stock companies 320
shareholders, liability of 219
transferability of shares 213–14
ultra vires 320
voting rights, history of 215
Cannizzaro, Stanislao 196
capital
lock-ins 72, 80, 91, 97, 107, 145
permanent capital 118–19, 134–5, 139
revenue, distinguished from 134
shareholders 324
Capital Issues Committee (CIC) 275–6, 278, 283–4, 291
capitalism 184, 190, 194, 251, 319, 328
***Carlen v Drury* (1812)** 16, 18–20, 22–5
Carr, EH 4–6
Carse, James 136–9
cartels 236, 243, 247
Cassel, Ernest 193
Chandler, Alfred D 251
***Charitable Corpn v Sutton* (1742)** 16, 17, 19–20, 23–5
Charkham, Jonathan 270
Charles II, King 134
Charles River Bridge Company 144, 177–8
charter corporations 134, 171–80
banks 143–4, 174–7
bridge companies 177–8
competition 150
federal incorporations and the public purpose 178–80
general incorporation statutes 142, 146–50
joint-stock companies 298
misuse, checking 91
monopolies 177–8
ownership of shares 226
patronage 141–2
politics 141–2, 175–7
preambles 172–4
public purpose 141–2, 161–2, 164, 165–8, 171–8, 181
Regulated Companies 133
restrictions 176
Salomon v Salomon case 118, 122, 124
separate legal personality 91
shareholders, liability of 218–20
special charters 148–50
special legislative acts, corporations created by 164, 165–8, 181
United States 1, 141–8, 159, 330–1
voting rights, history of 214–15, 217
chemical industry 183–207
Christophers, Brett 318
chronocentricity 51, 53, 55
Churchill, Winston 274, 279, 282, 284, 286–90, 293
cities, charters for 17–18, 20–1
City Code on Takeovers and Mergers 250, 263, 277
Clark, George 4–5
class tensions 310–11, 318
Clause Consolidation Act of 1845 215
Clemens, Elisabeth 150
climate change 69
Clinton, Hillary 156
Clore, Charles 258–61, 263, 276, 279–81
closely-held companies 92, 108, 111–13, 157–9 *see also* **family companies**
codes of practice
City Code on Takeovers and Mergers 250, 263, 277
non-executive directors (NEDs), promotion of 266
UK Corporate Governance Code 250, 264
UK Stewardship Code 264
Cohen Committee, role of the 249–71
archives, use of 332–3
Bank of England 250, 262–71
Cadbury Report 250
institutional investor engagement 250
managerialism 250–62, 264, 271
shareholder primacy 249–50, 271
Coke, Edward 130–1
Collyer, John 296
common law
hierarchy of courts 12
inseparability principle 242–6
Joint Stock Companies Act of 1844 8–9
law reporting 22
legislation, advantages of 8
Limited Liability Act of 1855 8–9
persona ficta concept 118, 130–1, 133
Salomon v Salomon case 120–1

separate legal personality 118, 130–1, 133
ultra vires 320
commonality of interests 235, 237, 241, 246–7
communitarianism 49–50
Companies Act 1862 42–3, 119, 122–4, 216, 221, 226, 304
Companies Act 1948 56–7, 250, 252, 261, 274–5, 280, 282, 290
Companies Act 2006 8, 17, 19, 43–4
comparative law 9, 13, 23, 231, 236, 248, 329–30
competition 71, 74, 76–81, 85, 90, 146
compulsory purchase powers 320
Conaglen, Matthew 19
concession theory of the corporation 20–1
conflicts of interest 219
Conkling, Roscoe 102
constitutional law/constitutions 21, 95, 100–16, 147–8
context/contextualism 28, 40, 53, 60–5, 68
contract
corporation, contractual concept of the 135, 136–8
freedom of contract 217, 227
joint-stock companies 132–3
rights of companies 94, 99–100, 103–4
societas 126
transferability of shares 214
voting rights 238–9
Corliss, George 146
corporate form *see also* **corporate privileges; incorporation**
choice between legal forms 28, 40–7
joint-stock companies, legal form of 296, 302
new organisational forms, era of 142, 153–8
opaqueness or impenetrability of corporate form 111–13
Corporate Fund 119, 134–5, 136, 137–8
corporate governance
Bank of England 262–71
disputes, intervention in 19–20, 24
efficiency-producing internal governance rules 91
environmental, social and governance (ESG) factors 118, 136–7, 139
historic cases 19–20, 24
hostile takeovers 274–7
managerialism 261
Rolls Royce, collapse of 264–5
separate legal personality 139
shareholder primacy 271
UK Corporate Governance Code 264
corporate practice of law in United States 72–85
campaigns against corporate practice 76–80
fear of the modern corporation 77–8
prohibition on corporations practising law 71, 75–85
corporate privileges 153–8
abuse 320–1
alternative forms with corporate advantages 157–8
charter corporations 141–7, 298
Crown's role in determining corporate privileges 17–18, 20–1
disadvantages 153–5
general incorporation statutes 148, 151–3, 159
joint-stock companies 298, 300, 301, 320–1
modern company law, making of 310
monopoly privileges 133
public purpose, benefits definition of 171–3
small and medium-sized enterprises 155
ultra vires 320–1
without incorporation 163
corporate social responsibility (CSR) 161, 174, 183
corruption 146, 159
cosmopolitanism 184, 189, 195, 200, 206
Costello, Kevin 20
Cotterrell, Roger 62–3
Court of Chancery 24
criminal law *see also* **fraud, self-dealing and mismanagement**
anti-money laundering regulations 108
corruption 146, 159
financial crime 55–6, 68
vote selling 232–3
critical legal studies (CLS) 61–2, 64
Cromwell, Oliver 134
culture 74, 184, 192, 195–7, 200, 328
customary law 234

Dan-Cohen, Meir 112–13
Daria-Mattiacci, Giuseppe 93–4
Daunton, Martin 314–15
Davis, Gerald F 251

defensive measures to takeovers
Cohen Committee 271
fraud, misfeasance or misconduct 286
hostile takeovers 273, 276–7, 281–90
regulation, promoting 263–4
Savoy Hotel takeover 276, 281–90
democracy 162, 240, 241, 246
deregulation 153
Dignam, Alan 10 *see also* **Dignam, Alan & Lowry, John.** ***Company Law***
Dignam, Alan & Lowry, John. ***Company Law*** 13, 14–15
directors/boards of directors *see also* **non-executive directors (NEDs)**
account of profits 16–17
accountability 309
Brunner, Mond & Co Ltd 186, 188
creditors, duties to 117, 125
discipline by shareholders 274–5
diversity 9
employee representation 267
excessive executive compensation 59, 141, 156
hierarchy 97
historic cases 9, 16–17
hostile takeovers 257, 272–7
interlocks (board to board ties) 9
majority shareholders 258
managerialism 251–3, 261–2
ratification of wrongs by shareholders 125
removal of directors by ordinary resolution 256–8, 261, 275
Savoy Hotel takeover 276, 285–90
shareholders 188, 274–6
discipline 274–5
relationship with 276
removal of directors by ordinary resolution 256–8, 261, 275
Disraeli, Benjamin 193
dissolution of corporations 18, 145–6, 219–21, 225
dividend rights, history of 209–10, 222–6
bonds, blurring of distinction between shares and 222
canal companies 223–4
dual-class structure 225–6
general incorporation statutes 223, 225–6
hostile takeovers 275, 277–9, 329
preference shares 222–5
railway companies 223–5
priorities 222
tax 257
voluntary restraints 275, 277–9, 329
voting rights 222, 225
wage restraints 278
doctrinal analytical tradition 60–4
Dodd, Merrick 304
double entry bookkeeping 118, 119, 131–2, 134–5
dual class shares 217–18, 225–7
DuBois, Armand B 298–9
Dutch East India Company (VOC) 93–4, 134–5, 210, 212–13

early corporations in United States and the public purpose 161–81
business corporations 161–2, 164–5
charter corporations 1, 141–8, 159, 161–2, 243–4, 330–1
federal incorporations 163–4, 178–81
manufacturing corporations 163, 164, 165
patronage 141–2
political relationships 141–2
private and public organisations, distinction between 163
public purposes
benefits definition 162–3, 164–5, 171–8, 181
definition of 162–78, 181
functional definition 162–3, 165–71, 181
quantitative methods 163, 166, 171, 334
shareholders 161
social function of the state, performing the 162
stakeholders 161
states limiting access to businesses providing a public service function 161
East India Companies *see* **Dutch East India Company (VOC); English East India Company (EEIC)**
ecclesiastical purposes, corporations used for 128
Eden, Anthony 279
efficiency 33–4, 35–6, 44–5, 91, 97–8
eleemosynary (charitable) purposes, corporations used for 128
elites 9, 73–4, 78, 89–90, 143–4
employment
big business, emergence of 2
boards, representation on 267
productive and unproductive labour, distinction between 313–14
public purpose, benefits definition of 165, 172–3

trade unions 152–3
treatment of employees 198–201, 203–4
wage restraints 278
English East India Company (EEIC)
accounting 134–5
autonomy 93–4
certificates, issue of 212
charter 134, 210–11
double-entry bookkeeping 134–5
formation 210–11
governance structures 210
members/subscribers, number and identity of 211
monopolies 171
persona ficta concept 134–5
public purpose, benefits definition of 171
Salomon v Salomon case 118–19, 331
separate legal personality 134–5, 138, 139, 331
shareholders 211, 218
shares 210–12, 214–15
history of 210–11
ownership 226
registration 211–12
transferability 211–12
value 135
voting rights 210, 214–15
English Reports 22, 24
enlightened shareholder value (ESV) 56–7
entity approach 117
entity shielding 145, 219
environmental, social and governance (ESG) **factors** 118, 136–7, 139
equal rights 2, 101–4, 141–2, 171–2
equity 3, 16, 17, 213, 302
European Union
Brexit 2
EEC, accession to 267
Fifth Company Law Directive 267
excessive executive compensation 59, 141, 156

Factories Acts 199–200
family companies 158, 183, 188, 206–7 *see also* **Brunner, Mond & Co Ltd (1881–1926)**
hostile takeover bids 259–60
managerialism 251, 259–60
personal capitalism 251
state, power of the 92, 93, 109, 115, 158
Farren, George 309, 310
federal incorporations (United States) **and the public purpose** 163–4, 178–81
fiduciary duties 16–17, 19
Fifoot, Cecil HS 323
Fifth Company Law Directive 267
finance corporations *see* **banks**
financial crime 55–6, 68
Foreman-Peck, James S 251
forgotten cases 10, 11, 12, 20, 21–2, 25
forms of organisation *see* **new organisational forms, era of**
founders' shares 217, 225
France
corporate privileges 154
democratic principles 246
inseparability principle 235–8, 329
Court of Naples judgment, influence of 238–9, 248
supporting arguments and underlying ideas 237–8
United States law, influence of 242, 244, 248
public companies (*sociétés anonyme* (SAs)), statutory regime governing 236
Fraser, Hugh 259, 261
fraud, self-dealing and mismanagement
fiduciary duties 17
general incorporation statutes 152
historic cases 16–17, 19
joint-stock companies 309, 317
railway companies 302
Savoy Hotel takeover 286
freedom of contract 217, 227
freedom of speech 92, 95, 101, 105–6, 109, 113–15, 156
Freeman, Mark 317
fully paid up shares 221
functional definition of a public purpose 162–3, 165–71
banks 167, 169–70
business corporations 164, 165–70, 181
charters by special legislative acts, corporations created by 164, 165–8, 181
finance corporations 166–70
government, services to the 164
infrastructure corporations 164, 166–9, 181
manufacturing corporations 166–71
number of corporations 166–71
transportation infrastructure 164, 166–9, 181

Galanter, Marc 80
Galbraith, John Kenneth 325
Gardiner, Jack 259–60
Geddes, Reay 265–6

Gelderblom, Oscar 93–4
general incorporation statutes
19th century 148–9, 223
banks 151
campaign finance 152–3
canal companies 219
charter corporations 142, 146–50
corporate income tax 151–2, 159
corporate privileges 148, 151–3, 159
corporation commissions 150–1
dividend rights, history of 223, 225–6
laissez-faire 148–9
liability of shareholders 227
mergers 149–50
minority oppression 154–5
opposition groups 150–2
patronage 148
perpetual entities, companies as 149
politicisation 148, 152–3
Salomon v Salomon case 118–19, 121, 123–4
shareholders, liability of 219
Taft-Hartley Act of 1947 152–3
Tillman Act of 1907 152–3
transferability of shares 214
United States 142, 148–53, 159, 225–6
voting rights 149, 217
Germany
anti-Semitism 189–95
banks 234, 247
corporate privileges 154
credit and financing 233–5
criminal prohibition against vote selling 232–3
inseparability principle 231–5, 247, 329
criminal prohibition against vote selling 232–3
German Imperial Court 232–3
Legitimationszession 233–5, 247
Stock Corporation Act 234
Legitimationszession 233–5, 247
Stock Corporation Act 234
Getzler, Joshua 23
Gierke, Otto von 127
Gladstone, William 319
Gold, James 207
Golden Age of legal profession in United States 79–81
good faith in financial law 21
Gordon, Robert 73
governance *see* **corporate governance**
Gow, Niel 296, 305
Gower, Laurence CB 255, 261 *see also* ***Gower's Principles of Modern Company Law*** 13
Goyder, Mark 325
Graham, Howard Jay 102
gratuitous payments 185, 188, 201–6
Greene Committee 251–2
groups of companies 98, 106, 226–7
guilds 93, 128, 133

Hall, Robert 278
Halpern, Paul 96
Hamilton, Alexander 143, 145, 178
Hamilton, Robert 86–7
Handlin, Mary Flug 162
Handlin, Oscar 162
Hannah, Leslie 187–8, 251–2
Hannigan, Brenda 13–15
Hansmann, Henry 98, 145, 219
Hay, Douglas 21
Heath, Edward 265
Hebblethwaite, Peter 58, 70
Hertz, Henrietta 195–6
hierarchy of courts 12
Hill, Jennifer 19
Hillman, Robert 89
historicisation 49–59, 61–2
holding companies 226–7, 253–4
Holland, Charles 185
Holland, Milner 289–90
Horwitz, Morton 103–5
hostile takeover bids 273–94
1950s, debate in UK government on 273–94
accounts, transparency of 257
archives, use of 282, 331–3
Bank of England 262, 277–9, 281, 290–1
banks 291–2, 293
Board of Trade 273, 276–89, 292–4
boards of directors 274–7
discipline by shareholders 274–5
relationship with shareholders 276
removal by shareholders 275
Savoy Hotel takeover 276, 285–90
Capital Issues Committee (CIC) 275–6, 278, 291
borrowing, approval by 276
Savoy Hotel defence, approval of funding for 283–4
Treasury, oversight by the 278
City Code on Takeovers and Mergers 277
Companies act 1948 274–5, 280, 282, 290

Conservative government and officials, thinking within the 273–94
control, market for corporate 274
corporate governance 274–7
defensive measures 273, 276–7, 281–90
departments 273–94, 332
dividends
high rate of tax 257
voluntary restraints 275, 277–9, 329
wage restraint, voluntary 278
economic considerations 273, 294
emergence of takeover bids 278–9
finance, increase in availability of 257
identity of bidders 279–81
institutional investors 270–1
investigations 276, 279–80, 282–92
majority shareholders 258–9
managerialism 257–62
Notes on Amalgamations 1959 277, 291
political considerations 273–94, 328–9
Prime Minister's Private Office 273, 277
profits 275, 280, 287, 292
qualitative evidence 333
regulation 263
Savoy Hotel takeover 273, 276–8, 294, 328–9, 333
background 279–81
defensive measures 276, 281–90
directors, role of 276, 285–90
fraud or misfeasance/misconduct 286
investigations 276, 279–80, 282–92
law officers' opinion 283, 285–6, 288
Lindon Inquiry 280–1
national asset, as 279, 281, 283–4, 293
second enquiry 284–92
Worcester Buildings Co scheme 276, 282–3, 285–6
self-regulation 262, 277
shareholder-dominated view 274
shareholders
board of directors 274–6
control 277
increase in power 274, 292
institutional investors 270–1
transparency 274–5
value 275
social considerations 273, 294
speculators and takeover tycoons 276
transparency 274–5
Treasury 273, 277–81, 283–6, 290–3
Hovenkamp, Herbert 104
Howell, Jason W 224–5
Hume, David 312
Hurst, JW 162
Hutchinson, John 185, 192–3
hypothetical bargaining 33, 35–6, 44–5

Ibbetson, David 60
ICI 185, 206–7
incorporation *see also* **general incorporation statutes**
common seal 118
competition for incorporations 28, 41
equitable interests 302
federal incorporations 163–4, 178–81
horizontal market for incorporation 28, 41, 45
incidents 118
joint-stock companies 118, 296, 298, 302–4, 306, 308–9
mandatory incorporation 309
railway companies 296, 309
registration 309
small partnerships and one-person companies, increase in 326
tax 80
individuals, rights of 92, 114–16
Industrial Reorganisation Corporation (IRC), **abolition of** 264
Industrial Revolution 2, 99
inherent powers doctrine 76, 88
inseparability principle 229–48
academic scholarship 231–5, 239, 241–2
agreements on influence over voting 230
alignment of interests between shareholders 246
beneficial ownership from voting rights, separation of 243–4
cartels 236, 243, 247
civil law jurisdictions 231–42, 246–7
common law jurisdictions 242–6
commonality of interests 237–8, 246–7
compensatory agreements 239
consideration 232–3
contractual attribution of voting rights 238–9
credit and financing 233–5, 247
criminal prohibition against vote selling 232–3
customary law 234
democratic principles 240, 241, 246
empty voting 230–1
financial interests and voting rights, connection between 237–8

France 235–8, 329
Court of Naples judgment, influence of 238–9, 248
democratic principles 246
public companies (*sociétés anonyme* (SAs)), statutory regime governing 236
supporting arguments and underlying ideas 237–8
United States law, influence of 242, 244, 248
Germany 231–5, 329
banks 234, 247
credit and financing 233–5
criminal prohibition against vote selling 232–3
German Imperial Court 232–3
Legitimationszession 233–5, 247
Stock Corporation Act 234
interjurisdictional discourse 248, 329
Italy 238–42, 329
courts, contributions by 238–41
France, influence of Court of Naples judgment in 238–9, 248
patto commissorio (compensatory agreements) 239
majority principle 238, 242, 247
minority protection 242
monopolisation 236, 243, 247
new financial instruments 230–1
personal rights, voting rights as 241
pledges 239–40
proxy voting 230, 232, 233–4
public companies 235, 236
role of shareholders 246–7
statutory interpretation 236–7, 239–40
stock lending agreements 232–3
transfer of voting rights 230
United States 242–5, 329
beneficial ownership from voting rights, separation of 243–4
cartelisation and monopolisation 236, 243, 247
corporate charters 243–4
France, influence in 242, 244, 248
Model Business Corporation Act 245
People c N Riv Sugar Ref Co 242–5
voting trusts 242–4, 248
voting trusts 242–4, 248
insolvency 117, 125, 209–10, 219, 221, 227
institutional investors 250, 262–3, 266, 268–71
Institutional Shareholders' Committee (ISC) 268–71
insurance
insurable interests 18, 21
malpractice claims 84
marine insurance 18, 21
purpose 176
interest rates 312–13
Interstate Commerce Commission (ICC) 151
Ireland, Paddy 250
Italy, inseparability principle in 238–42, 329
courts, contributions by 238–41
France, influence of Court of Naples judgment in 238–9, 248
patto commissorio (compensatory agreements) 239

J Sears & Co, takeover of 258–60, 276, 278
Jeffreys, James B 311
Jenkins Committee 261–2
Jerome Bonaparte 189
Johnson, Boris 1
Johnston, Andrew 275
joint-stock companies (JSCs) 295–307
activist shareholders 317
affirmative asset partitioning 303–4
agency
authority to bind companies 305–7
constructive notice, doctrine of 307
demise of mutual agency 305–7
mutual 296, 305–7
charter corporations 298
common law 8–9
company law, emergence of 325–6
constructive notice, doctrine of 307
contractual JSCs 118, 132–3
corporate privileges 298, 300, 301, 320–1
deeds of settlement 298, 299
distinguishing features 296
double entry bookkeeping 118
economic form of JSCs 296, 298
equitable interests 302
formation of JSCs 210–11
fraud 309, 317
incorporated companies 296, 298, 302–4, 306, 308–9, 326
Joint Stock Companies Act 1844 8–9, 43–4, 214, 216–17, 226, 301, 305, 307–9
Joint Stock Companies Act 1856 42–4, 214, 226, 304, 307
Joint Stock Funds 131–4

legal form of JSCs 296, 302
limited liability 297–8, 301–2, 307–11
managing agencies 225
mining companies 296, 303
moral objections 297–8
mutual agency, doctrine of 296
Napoleonic wars, government debt arising from 314
nature 295–8, 302–3
no-liability shareholding, emergence of 302
objects, expansion of alteration of 321–2
partnerships 295–306, 315–18, 320–3, 325–6
  mutual agency, doctrine of 296, 305–6
  public partnerships, JSCs as 298–300, 316
  qualitative differences 299, 304, 305
  quantitative differences 299, 304
  trust and character, focus on 296–8, 305, 315–16
  types of partnership, JSCs as 298–301, 306, 315–17, 320
  ultra vires 302, 320–3
  unanimity rule, abandonment of 322
private co-partneries, as 296
profits 296–7, 302–3, 316–17, 321–2
property, protection of 320
public benefit 298, 317, 326
public partnerships, as 298–300, 316, 326
quasi-corporations 301
railway companies 296, 302, 309, 317, 319–23
re-conceptualisation of JSC share 302–3
Regulated Companies distinguished 133
rentier shareholding 297–8, 302, 307, 311–12, 314–16, 319–20, 325
separation of ownership and management 299, 302, 325
separate legal personality 133–4
shareholders
  competing conceptions 314–18
  liability of 218, 220–2
shares
  market, absence of a share 302
  transferability of shares 212–14, 299, 303
single terminating ventures, for 133
small partnerships and one-person companies, increase in 326
speculators 314–18, 320
'they', reference to JSCs as 304
transferable shares 299, 303
treatises
  company law, on 325
  partnerships, on 296, 325
trust and character, focus on 296–8, 305, 315–16
ultra vires 302, 318–23
unincorporated companies 296, 298, 302–4, 306
unlimited liability 297, 298, 307–10, 316
usury, repeal of prohibition on 317
voting rights, history of 216
Jonker, Joost 93–4
JSCs ***see*** **joint-stock companies (JSCs)**
judiciary
  biography 21
  opinions 99–100

Keech v Sandford **(1726)** 16–17, 19–20, 22–5
Kennet, Wayland (Lord Kennet) 283
key cases 10, 12, 21, 24, 25
Keynes, Maynard 251, 325
King, Peter (Lord Chancellor) 24
Koss, Stephen E 186
Kraakman, Reinier 98, 145, 219
Krawiec, Kim 89
Kyd, Stewart 94, 99, 103, 304, 323

laissez-faire 141, 148–9, 311
Lamoreaux, Naomi R 145–6, 162, 304
landmark case, use of term 10–11
Langbein, John 23
large corporations
  big business, emergence of 2
  capital lock-in 97
  economic power 108
  lifting the corporate veil 105
  managerialism 254, 257
  owner-controlled businesses, shift from 184, 187–8
  regulation 105, 108
  separate legal personality 105–9, 113
law and economics analysis 53, 61, 135
'law factories' 73, 78
law firms ***see*** **limited liability partnership (LLP) structure for law firms in United States, origins of**
lay purposes, corporations used for 128
legal change, study of 60–3
legal forms, choice between 28, 40–7
law matters thesis 9
law reports

authorisation 22
common law 22
doctrines, principles and rules 22
editing 22, 24
English Reports 22, 24
formalisation 11
historic cases 11, 22–5
length and complexity 24
Nominate Reports 22
scholarship 22–3
social and economic context 23
standardisation 22
unreported cases 11
legal scholarship 50–69 *see also* **textbooks**
chronocentric, as 51, 53, 55
historical perspectives, with 50–3
historical sensitivity 59, 65, 68
historicisation 50–9
inseparability principle 231–5, 239, 241–2
law reports 22–3
legal history 59–66
past and present, separation of 64–5, 67–8
present, ideological importance of 51
resource, history as a 52
social change 67
Levant Company 210
Lewis, Andrew 332
liability of shareholders, history of 209, 218–22
19th-20th century 218
asset partitioning 218
charter corporations 218–20
conflicts of interest between shareholders and bondholders 219
debt finance for large projects 219
default rule 221
dissolution of corporations 219, 221
double liability 222
entity shielding 145, 219
general incorporation statutes 219, 227, 229
joint-stock companies 218, 220–2
large projects in transport or utility sectors 219
legal entity attribute 218
limited liability 209, 218–22
nominal capital 220–1
periodization 218
pro-rata liability 219, 222
reserve liability 220, 222
separate legal entity concept 221–2
triple liability 222
unincorporated corporations 219
unlimited liability 219–20, 222
variety of regimes 218
lifting the corporate veil 91–2, 105–6, 107, 111, 118
limited liability 7–9, 330 *see also* **limited liability partnership (LLP) structure for law firms in United States, origins of**
19th century 96–7
accounting firms 85, 87, 90
banks 220
campaign finance laws 157
capitalists 319
charter corporations 145
class tensions 310
common law 8–9
general limited liability 309–11
joint-stock companies 297–8, 301–2, 307, 309, 311
Limited Liability Act 1855 7–9, 220–1, 310
Limited Liability Act 1955 307
Limited Liability Companies (LLCs) 85–9, 142, 155, 157
limited liability limited partnerships (LLLPs) 155
limited liability partnerships (LLPs) 142, 155
medieval period in England 129
modern company law, making of 307–10, 311
no-liability companies 323–4
risk shifting to parties not bargaining for that risk 107
Salomon v Salomon 96
separate legal personality 91, 96–7, 107
shareholders, liability of 209, 218–22
social ills, causing 142
unlimited liability, from 307–10, 311
limited liability partnership (LLP) structure for law firms in United States, origins of 71–90
admissions, increase in 74
adoption of LLPs in all states 87–8
advertising 74, 77, 81–2
anti-competition agreements 79, 81
attorney-client relationship 76
birth of LLPs 83–7
capital lock-in 72, 80
competition 71, 74, 76–81, 85, 90
Cooperative Law Company 75, 77

corporate practice of law 72–85
campaigns against 76–80
fear of the modern corporation 77–8
prohibition on corporations practising law 71, 75–85
cultural challenges 74
demands for incorporation 80
economic challenges 71–4, 77
efficiency 77–8
elite firms 73–4, 78, 89–90
fear of the modern corporation 77–8
general partnerships 72–3, 80, 87–90
Golden Age of legal profession 79–81
historical background 72–9
immigrant lawyers 74
independence of lawyers 72, 73–4, 78, 80
inherent powers doctrine 76, 88
large law firms 71, 78, 89
'law factories' 73, 78
liability shielding 71–2, 80, 90
Limited Liability Companies (LLCs) 85–9
malpractice claims 71, 80, 82–6, 88–90
modern corporate law firms 72–9
personal liability 84–5, 90
practice of law, definition of 77
Professional Corporation (PC) form 80–1, 85, 89
prohibition on corporations practising law 71, 75–85
Savings and Loan (S&L) crisis 83–7
birth of LLPs 83–7
Resolution Trust Company (RTC) 83–4
self-image 71, 72, 73, 90
separate legal personality 76
size of partnerships 72–3, 75, 80
social change within the profession 74
social position 72–3, 78, 80
solo practitioners 72, 80, 90
specialisation 72–3, 77
standardization 78
tax treatment 80–1, 85
Texas, legislation on LLPs in 85–7
unauthorised practice, statutes banning 79
vicarious liability 84–6, 88
World War II 79–80
limited partnerships 154
Lindley, Nathaniel 20, 22, 119, 121–124, 325
Lindon, JB 280–1
listed companies 252
Llewellyn, Karl 78
Lloyd George, David 206
Lobban, Michael 332
lock-ins 72, 80, 91, 97, 107, 145
Lowe, Robert 42, 123
Lowry, John 13–15, 21

McCulloch, JR 297
MacGowan, Harry 207
McQueen, Rob 7
Madison, James 95
magnification of corporate entities 91, 107–8, 111–12
Maier, Pauline 162
Maitland, FW 65, 127, 129, 130–1
majority shareholders
hostile takeovers 258–9
inseparability principle 238, 242, 247
minority oppression 154–5
shareholders, removal of 258
supermajority rules 154–5
voting rights, history of 216
Makins, Roger 292
malpractice claims 71, 80, 82–6, 88–90
managerialism 250–62, 271
accountability 263, 265
administrative, technical and clerical staff 254
articles of association 253, 258, 261
Bank of England 262–5
Clore, Charles, takeover bids by 258–61
Cohen Committee 250–62, 264, 271
Companies Act 1948 252, 261
corporate governance and balance of power 261
directors 251–3, 256–8, 261–2
diversification 254
emergence 250, 251–6, 271
Greene Committee 251–2
hierarchies 253–5
holding companies 254
hostile takeovers 257–62
income, retention of corporate 251
institutional investors 257
Jenkins Committee 261–2
large companies 254, 257
legitimacy of managerial class 255
mergers 251
minority oppression 257
non-executive directors (NEDs), promotion of 262
opposition 262, 264–5
politics 251–2
profession, management as a 253, 255, 262
pushback 250, 256–62, 271

rationalisation 251–2
risk, protection against 254
separation of ownership and control 251–2, 256
shareholders
control 256–61
dispersal 252–4
minority shareholders 257
primacy 260, 262
social responsibilities 255
Taylorist scientific management 254
vertical integration 251
management-controlled model 184–5, 187–8, 201, 205, 207
Manne, Henry G 261, 274
manufacturing corporations 144–5, 163–73
marine insurance 18, 21
Marris, Robin 251, 274
Marsh, Henry 74
Marx, Karl 5, 297, 318
Massachusetts, United States
banks 143, 175
Charles River Bridge Company 144, 177–8
charter corporations 163, 166–73, 175, 177–8, 181
Constitution 172
dividends 225
freedom of speech 156
limited liability 96
number of corporations 166–70
transferability of shares 214
Maudling, Reginald 274, 280–6, 329
Mayson, Stephen W, French, Derek & Ryan, Christopher. *Company Law* 13–16, 20
Means, Gardiner 111–12, 184, 249
medieval England 118, 128–31, 133
members and shares 210–11, 227
mergers 149–50, 185, 206–7, 251
meso-corporatism 262
methods, open and diversity in 4–6
mining companies 296, 303
minority shareholders
business-judgment rule 154
Cohen Committee 256–8
disadvantages of the corporate form 154–5
general incorporation statutes 154
gratuitous payments 185, 188, 201–6
groups of companies 226–7
inseparability principle 242
managerialism 257
oppression 154–5, 257, 326
protection 242, 326
small companies 326
supermajority rules 154–5
mismanagement *see* fraud, self-dealing and mismanagement
mistake argument 27–8, 37–40
counter-arguments 46
major changes 27, 37–40, 47
path dependence 38–9
perception 37–8, 40
politics 40
reform 37–9
shareholder control 38
state/governmental intervention 39
substance and form 38
trajectory argument 37, 38–9, 46–7
Mitchell, Lawrence E 49–50
Mond, Alfred 201, 206–7
Mond, Emile 206
Mond, Frida (neé Löwenthal) 193, 195
Mond, Ludwig 183–201, 205–6
Mond, Robert 201
money as unproductive 312, 316, 317–18
money laundering 108
monopolies 2, 133, 171, 177–8
charter corporations 144, 177–8
general incorporation statutes 150
inseparability principle 236, 243, 247
regulation 107
Montagu, Basil 296
morality 184, 195–201, 206, 297–8
Morawetz, Victor 104
Morelli, Giovanni 196
Müller-Erzbach, Rudolf 231
municipalities 93
Mynors, Humphrey 264

Napoleon Bonaparte 189–90, 314
Napoleonic wars, government debt arising from 314
Nelson, James 112
new financial instruments 230–1
new organisational forms, era of 142, 153–8
agencies, creation of government 153
campaign finance law 156–7, 159
closely held corporations 157–9
corporate income tax 153, 155–6
corporate privileges 153–8
deregulation 153
disadvantages of corporate form 153–5

limited liability companies (LLCs) 142, 155, 157
limited liability limited partnerships (LLLPs)
limited liability partnerships (LLPs) 142, 155
limited partnerships 154
non-profit organisations 156–7
partnerships 142, 153–4, 159
personal income tax 153, 154–6
New York, United States
banks 143–5, 151, 175
charter corporations 143–5, 163, 166–76, 181
dividends 225
general incorporation statutes 214, 225
law firms 72–5, 77, 80, 83–4, 89
liability of shareholder 221
malfeasance 152
New York Stock Exchange (NYSE) 217–18
number of corporations 166–71
public purpose 163, 166–71, 181
voting trusts 245
Nightingale, Edwin J 146
no-liability shareholdings 302, 323–4
Nominate Reports 22
non-executive directors (NEDs)
Bank of England 250, 262–3, 264–8, 270
code of practice, proposal for 266
Cohen Committee 250
managerialism 262
minimum number of NEDs, obligation to have a 267
PRO NED 268
promotion 250, 262–3, 264–8, 270
non-profit organisations 95, 100, 109–10, 112–13, 115, 156–7, 163
normative company law, using history in 27–47
argumentation structures 27–47
legal forms, choice between 28, 40–7
limits 30–1
mistake argument 27–8, 37–40, 44–7
qualitative data, assessment of 333–4
semiotics 28–9, 40
trajectory argument 27–8, 32–7, 44–7
non-profit organisations 142–3
Notes on Amalgamations. Issuing Houses Association 263, 277, 291
Novak, William 162

obiter dicta 12
objects of companies *see* **purposes and objects of companies**
O'Brien, Leslie (Lord O'Brien) 269
obsolete cases 10, 11, 12, 21–2
Oh, Peter 10
Oldham, James 20–1
Olson, Mancur 113
one-person companies 72, 80, 90, 326
organisation forms *see* **new organisational forms, era of**

Pacioli, Luca 132
Palay, Thomas 80
Paley, William 296
P&O scandal 57–9, 69
Panel on Takeovers and Mergers 250, 264
Pargendler, Marianna 106
partly paid shares 222
partnerships 142, 153–5 *see also* **limited liability partnership (LLP) structure for law firms in United States, origins of**
agreements 320
changes in partnership law 318
charter corporations 145–6
company law, origins of 295, 301–4
conception, erosion of the partnership 295, 301, 303–4
general law of partnership 300
joint and several liability 296
joint-stock companies 132, 295–301, 315–18
distinguished from partnerships 298–9, 303, 304, 306, 325
public partnerships, JSCs as 298–300, 316, 326
qualitative differences 299, 304, 305
quantitative differences 299, 304
types of partnership, JSCs as 298–301, 306, 315–17, 320
ultra vires 320–1
limited liability limited partnerships (LLLPs) 155
limited liability partnerships (LLPs) 142, 155
limited partnerships 154
maximum number 42–4, 46–7
multi-owner businesses 154
mutual agency, doctrine of 296, 305–6
partnership law 320–1
pass-through entities, as 154, 156, 159

personal income tax rate 154
public partnerships, JSCs as 298–300, 316, 326
quasi-partnership model 186
reorganisation as corporations 154–5
ruptures 295, 301–2, 305, 310–11
S corporations 155
shareholders as partners 314–18, 320
small partnerships and one-person companies, increase in 326
societas 126
trust and character, focus on 296–8, 305, 315–16
ultra vires 302, 320–3
unanimity, principle of 322–3
unlimited liability 297
path dependence 2, 33–6, 38–9, 44–6
patronage 141–2, 146–8
Pearson, Robin 317
permanent capital 118–19, 134–5, 139
Perotti, Enrico 93–4
perpetual entities, corporations as 107, 118, 136–9, 149, 331
Perrot, Franz 194
***persona ficta* concept** 118–19, 125, 130–1, 137, 139
personal nature of companies 183–6, 188–207, 328
Pettet, BG 13–15, 21
philanthropy 184–5, 188, 195–6, 198–205
piercing the corporate veil 91–2, 105–6, 107, 111, 118
pledges 239–40
political action committees (PACs) 153
politics *see also* **campaign finance**
anti-corporate rhetoric 142, 159
argumentation structures 29
Bank of England 262
banks 143–4, 175–7
Brunner, Mond & Co Ltd 184
charter corporations 141–9, 175–7
general incorporation statutes 148, 152–3
hostile takeovers 273–94, 328–9
managerialism 251–2
mistake argument 40
non-profit organisations 156–7
path dependence 35–6
public purpose 168
regulation 141–2, 159
significance of corporations 50
trajectory arguments 36
Pollman, Elizabeth 94
Posner, Richard 33, 45
postmodernism 5
Pound, Roscoe 73
precedents 11, 12, 20
preferred shares 227
Prime Minister's Private Office 273, 277
priorities 209–10, 222, 227
private partnerships 299
privileges *see* **corporate privileges**
Professional Corporation (PC) form 80–1, 85, 89
profits
account of profits 16–17
Brunner, Mond & Co Ltd 183–6, 188, 202, 204–5, 329
charter corporations 141–4, 147, 175–9, 210–11
community of interest 233
Corporate Fund 139
dividends 222–4, 227, 329
hostile takeovers 275, 280, 287, 292
joint-stock companies 296–7, 302–3, 316–17, 321–2
managerialism 251, 253, 255–6
maximisation 57–9, 60
profit corporations versus non-profit corporations 110, 112–13
rentier investors 184
separate legal personality 134–8
short-termism 136, 138
tax 154–6, 275
property
joint-stock companies 320
private property, corporations as 251
rights of corporations 94, 99, 103–4, 113, 212–13
proxy voting 230, 232, 233–4
public companies
accountability 266
autonomy 265
Bank of England 264–7
inseparability principle 235, 236
separate legal personality 110–13
public partnerships 298–300, 316, 326
public purposes
banks 167, 169–70
Brunner, Mond & Co Ltd 183
business corporations 164, 165–70, 181
charter corporations 141–5, 164, 165–8, 181
federal incorporations 163–4, 178–81
finance corporations 166–70

functional definition 152–3, 165–71
government, services to the 164
infrastructure corporations 164, 166–9, 181
instrumentalities 164
joint-stock companies 298, 317, 326
manufacturing corporations 166–71
number of corporations 166–71
politicisation 168
private shareholders 164
public purpose, definition of 162–78, 181
regulation 141
rentier investors 295
shareholders 319
state, investment by the 164
transportation infrastructure 164, 166–9, 181
United States, early corporations in 161–81
purposes and objects of companies *see also* **public purposes**
alteration 321–2
Brunner, Mond & Co Ltd 183, 201–6
Cohen Committee 249–50
main objects rule 204
proper purposes duty, use of 263
reasonably incidental activities 204–5
Salomon v Salomon case 124
separate legal personality 98, 100, 107
takeover regulation, promoting 263
ultra vires 201–6, 321–2

Quail, John 255
quasi-corporations 301
quasi-partnership model 186

***R v Pasmore* (1789)** 16, 17–18, 20–1, 23
railway corporations
bailouts in United States 224
compulsory purchase powers 320
crisis, in 224
dividend rights, history of 223–5
fraud 309
incorporated companies 296, 309
joint-stock companies 296, 302, 309, 317, 320–3
judges as investors 319–20
middle-class investors 319–20
MPs as investors 319
objects, alteration of 321–2
railway mania 309, 310, 317
rentier investment 302
shareholders 319–20
Rajak, Harry 24
Reagan, Ronald 155
real entity theory 113
redemption, equity of 16
reform 50–3, 57, 64
registration of companies 186, 211–12, 309
regulation 1–2
campaign finance 142, 159
charter corporations 141–8, 159, 330–1
corporate privileges 141–2
deregulation 153
differential regulation, basis for 107–8
general incorporation statutes, era of 142, 148–53, 159
individuals, different regulation of corporations from 106–15
large companies 105, 108
monopolies 107
new financial interests 230–1
new organisational forms, era of 142, 153–8, 159
politics 141–2, 159
Regulated Companies 133
separate legal personality 106–15
social ills, corporations as causing 141–2
state's power 91–116, 327–8
tax policies 142
United States history, in 141–59, 330
Reisberg, Arad 13–15, 21
religion
anonymity 115
anti-Semitism 184, 189–95, 197, 206
autonomy 93, 115
Brunner, Mond & Co Ltd 183, 189–95, 197–8, 201
closely-held corporations 158–9
continuity 93
freedom of religion 92, 101, 106, 109, 113–15, 158–9
non-conforming religious beliefs 183, 197–8, 201
self-governance 93
rentier investors 310–16
Brunner, Mond & Co Ltd 194
Cohen Committee 250
joint-stock companies 297–8, 302, 307, 311–12, 315–16, 325
judges and MPs as rentiers 319–20
monied interests 311, 312, 314
productive and unproductive labour, distinction between 313–14
public purposes 295

railway companies 302
separate corporate personality 323
reputation 138–9
res ipsa loquitur 45
Research Excellence Framework 6
reserve liability 220, 222
Resolution Trust Company (RTC) 83–4
Retallack, James 194
Rhys-Williams, Brandon 265
Richards, Ann 87
Richter, Jean Paul 196–7
Ricardo, David 318
rights of corporations in United States 92, 94, 99–116
Bill of Rights 95, 101
Constitution 95, 100, 110–16
contracting 94, 99–100, 103–4
different types of corporation, different rights for 111–12
equal rights 101–4
federal incorporation, state bans on 95
judicial opinions 99–100
opaqueness or impenetrability of corporate form 111–13
property, capacity to hold and transfer 94, 99, 103–4, 113, 212–13
sue and be sued, capacity to be 94, 99, 113
UK precedent 94–5, 99
risk shifting 107, 110, 111, 114
Rix, MS 7
Roberts, Richard 277, 281, 290–2
Rolls Royce, collapse of 264–5
Roman law 126–31
Rosenberg, Hans 194
Rosenthal, Jean-Laurent 145–6
Rothschild, Lionel de 193
Russia Company 210

S corporations 155
Sainer, Leonard 259–60
***Salomon v Salomon* case** 117–25
19th century 118–20
background 118–25
business corporations 119
charter corporations 118, 122, 124
common law 120–1
general incorporation statutes 118–19, 121, 123–4
incidents of incorporation 118
lifting the corporate veil 118
limited liability 96
persona ficta concept 118–19
purpose of corporations 124
ratification of directors' wrongs by shareholders 125
Salomon paradox 117, 124–5
separate legal personality 10, 117–25, 139
Sequana decision 124–5
shareholders, liability of 221
textbooks 121–2
ultra vires doctrine 202
unincorporated corporations 119
Samuel, Harold 280–3
Sanders, Bernie 157, 159
Savings and Loan (S&L) crisis 83–7
Savoy Hotel takeover 273, 276–8, 294, 328–9, 333
background 279–81
defensive measures 276, 281–90
directors, role of 276, 285–90
fraud or misfeasance/misconduct 286
investigations 276, 279–80, 282–92
law officers' opinion 283, 285–6, 288
Lindon Inquiry 280–1
national asset, Savoy as a 279, 281, 283–4, 293
second enquiry 284–92
Worcester Buildings Co scheme 276, 282–3, 285–6
scholarships *see* **legal scholarship**
Sealy, Len & Worthington, Sarah. *Text, Cases and Materials in Company Law* 13–15
Seipp, David J 129
self-dealing *see* **fraud, self-dealing and mismanagement**
self-regulation 262–4, 277
seminal cases 10, 12–13, 21, 25
semiotics 28–9, 40
separate corporate personality *see also* ***Salomon v Salomon* case**
19th century 95–106, 118
alternatives 108–15
anonymity 91, 107, 108, 111–12, 115
antecedents to the US experience 93–5
arbitrage 107, 108, 112
asset partitioning 98, 107
autonomy 91, 93–4, 107, 111–14
capital, benefits of permanent 135
centralised control 91
charter corporations 91
closely held corporations 92, 109, 111–13
codification 10
common law 118, 130–1, 133

continuity 93
contractual concept of the corporation 135, 136–8
Corporate Fund 134–5, 136, 137–9
corporateness, two types of 126–35
decision-making, change in basis of 137–8
double-entry bookkeeping 131–2, 134–5
duration of companies 98, 100, 107, 136–9
Dutch East India Company (VOC) 134–5
English East India Company (EEIC) 134–5, 138, 139, 331
enhanced separateness, entities with 99–101
entity approach 117
England, medieval period in 128–31, 133
equal rights 101–4
ESG (environmental, social and governance) factors 118, 136–7, 139
externalities 112, 118–19, 137, 139
Finite and Infinite Games. Carse 136–9
freedom of speech 92, 95, 101, 105–6, 109, 113–15
groups of companies 98
hierarchy 91, 96–7
individuals
  regulation 106–15
  rights of 92, 114–16
Joint Stock Funds 131–4
large corporations, rise of 105–9, 113
limitations 105–6
limited liability 76, 91, 96–7, 107, 302, 323–4
Lochner era 104–6
lock-in of investments 91, 97, 107
magnification of corporate entities 91, 107–8, 111–12
misuse 91–2
modern doctrine 302, 323–4
New Deal 104–6
non-profit corporations 95, 100, 109–10, 112–13, 115
non-liability companies 323–4
opaqueness or impenetrability of corporate form 111–13
origins 93–106
partnerships 126, 132
perpetual entities, companies as 107, 136–9, 331
persona ficta concept 101–4, 118–19, 125, 130–1, 134–5, 137, 139
piercing the corporate veil 91–2, 105–6, 107, 111
potential of separate legal entity 136–9
power of corporations 107–9
public corporations 110–13
real entity theory 113
regulation 91–116, 327–8
religion 92, 101, 106, 109, 113–15
rentier shareholders 323
reputation 138–9
rights of corporations 92, 94, 99–116
risk shifting to parties not bargaining for that risk 107, 110, 111, 114
role specialisation 91, 96–7, 98
Roman law 126–31
Salomon v Salomon 10, 117–25, 139
same or similar rights, separateness as permitting two persons for individuals to exercise 113–14
self-governance 93–4
Sequana decision 117–18, 124–5, 137, 139
significance 117–39
shareholders 221–2, 323–4
societas 126–31, 133
state, power of the 91–116, 327–8
textbooks 10, 132
transferability of shares 324
ultra vires 323
unanimity, principle of 323
universitas 126–31
United States 91–116
  Constitution 95, 100–4, 110–16
  Fourteenth Amendment to use equal rights, efforts to use 101–4
  large corporations, rise of 105–9, 113
  state, power of the 91–116, 327–8
  Supreme Court 92, 104, 106–12, 115–16
  United Kingdom precedent for US concepts of separateness 94–5, 330
separation between ownership and control 2, 251–2, 256, 299, 302, 325
separation of voting rights from shares *see* **inseparability principle**
***Sequana* decision** 117–18, 124–5, 137, 139
Shapps, Grant 58
shareholders *see also* **dividend rights, history of; inseparability principle; liability of**
shareholders, history of; majority shareholders; minority shareholders
  activist shareholders 317
  Bank of England 262, 265

Brunner, Mond & Co Ltd 184–5, 188, 201–6
capitalists, as 324
class tensions 318
competing conceptions 314–19, 325
control 38, 256–61, 265, 277, 325
directors 125, 188, 274–6
dispersal of ownership 184, 252–4
enlightened shareholder value (ESV) 56–7
external, shareholders as 318
great capitalists, tensions with 319
hierarchy 97
hostile takeovers 274–7, 292
increase in power 274, 292
institutional investors 250, 262–3, 266, 268–71
investors, as 314–18, 320
joint-stock companies 314–19
limited liability 96, 319
managerialism 256–7, 262
maximum number 42, 43–4, 46
middle-class investors 319
money from money, negativity towards 314
no-liability shareholdings 302, 323–4
partners, as 314–18, 320
primacy 249–50, 262, 271, 325
public purpose 161, 318
railway shareholders 319–20
ratification of directors' wrongs 125
rentier investment 314–16, 319–20
separate corporate personality 323–4
shareholder-dominated view 274
shielding 219
speculators, as 314–18, 320
transparency 274–5
ultra vires 185, 188, 201–6, 318–19
usury, repeal of prohibition on 317
value 135, 188, 201, 275
shares, history of 209–27 *see also* **inseparability principle; transferability of shares, history of; voting rights, history of**
attributes of shares 209–27
bonds 222
class of share, creation of more than one 209–10
distribution of rights 227
dividend rights 209–10, 222–6
dual class shares 217–18, 225–7
equitable rights 213
founder shares 225
freedom of contract, period of 227
fully paid up shares 221, 324, 325
groups and pyramids 227
joint-stock companies 210–11, 227, 299, 303
liability of shareholders 209, 218–22, 227
major projects, period of construction of 227
market, absence of a share 302
members 210–11, 227
no par value, shares with 221
ownership of shares 209–10, 226–7
partly paid shares 222
periodisation 209, 227
preference shares 222–5
priorities in insolvency 209–10, 227
voting rights 209, 210, 214–18, 227
Shawcross, Hartley (Lord Shawcross) 264–5, 267
Shelford, Leonard 325
Simpson, Brian 6
small and medium-sized enterprises (SMEs) 155
Smith, Adam 296–8, 312–15, 318, 324
Smith, John William 300–1
social considerations
change 67
class tensions 310–11, 318
corporate social responsibility (CSR) 161, 174, 183
environmental, social and governance (ESG) factors 118, 136–7, 139
historic cases 23
hostile takeovers 273, 294
imposition of social obligations on corporations 56
law reporting 23
law firms in United States 72–4, 78, 80
limited liability as causing social ills 142
managerialism 255
regulation 141–2
rights of companies 112
social function of the state, performing the 162
social ills, corporations as causing 141–2
social significance of corporations 50
societas 126–31, 133
socio-legal studies 9–10, 60, 62–3
Society of Legal Scholars' Annual Seminar 1–2
sole practitioners 72, 80, 90, 326
Solvay family 185, 188

sources 331–3
archives, use of 282, 331–3
legal historians, training of 332
manuscript tradition 331–2
South Sea Bubble 315
speculators 276, 314–18, 320
Sperber, Jonathan 190
Squire, Richard 145
stakeholders 138, 161, 174, 198
statements of corporate purpose in charters 174–8
states
annexation 265
churches and limits on wealth, disestablishment of 95
family companies 92, 93, 109, 115, 158
intervention 39, 263–4
power of the state 91–116, 327–8
public purpose 161–2, 164
regulation 91–116, 327–8
social function of the state, corporations performing the 162
statutory interpretation 236–7, 239–40
Stein, Peter 301
stock lending agreements 232–3
Stoecker, Adolf 194–5
Stout, Lynn 251
subsidiaries 187, 254, 309
sue and be sued, capacity to be 94, 99, 113

takeovers *see also* **defensive measures to takeovers; hostile takeover bids**
City Code on Takeovers and Mergers, advent of 263
defensive measures 250, 263–4
governmental intervention, avoidance of 263–4
hostile takeovers 263
Panel on Takeovers and Mergers 264
proper purposes duty, use of 263
public perception 263
regulation 142, 263–4
self-regulation 264
Tawney, Richard H 255, 325
tax
corporate income tax 151–3, 155–6, 159
dividends 257
general incorporation statutes 151–2, 159
limited liability partnership (LLP) structure for law firms in United States 80–1, 85
personal income tax 153, 154–6
Taylor, James 296–7, 317–18
Taylorist scientific management 254
telegraph sector 225
textbooks
double-entry bookkeeping 132
financial crime 55–6, 68
historic cases 9–10, 13–15, 20–5
joint-stock companies 296, 325
separate legal personality 10, 132
Salomon v Salomon case 121–2
Thames Water scandal 57–9, 69–70
Thorneycroft, Peter 278, 279, 281–90, 292–3
Tosh, John 67–9
Toynbee, Arnold J 31
trade unions 152–3
trajectory argument 27–8, 32–7, 52–3, 67, 69
hypothetical bargaining 33, 35–6, 44–5
incrementalist, as 27, 35
intertemporal aspects 34–5, 45
legal efficiency theory 33–4, 35–6, 44–5
optimal, current law as 33, 36, 45
path dependence 33–6, 44–6
political character 35–6
status quo 27, 33, 36–7, 39, 47
transferability of shares, history of 209, 211–14, 227, 324
classification of shares 212–14
contractual, as 214
equitable rights in shares 213
intergenerational transfer 213
joint-stock companies 212–14, 299, 302
land-dominated companies 213
major projects 213–14
property rights in shares 212–13
real or personal property, shares as 213–14
voting rights 211
transparency 56, 257–8, 274–5
transportation corporations *see also* **canal corporations; railway corporations**
charter corporations 144
public purpose 164, 166–9, 181
shareholders, liability of 219
Treasury 273, 277–81, 283–6, 290–3
Trebilcock, Michael 96
trust 3, 242–4, 248
breach of trust 17, 23
partnerships 296–8, 305, 315–16
Turnbull, Stuart 96

UK Corporate Governance Code 250, 264
UK Stewardship Code 264
ultra vires 318–23

abuse of privileges 320–1
canal companies 320
common law of corporations 320
gratuitous payments 185, 188, 201–6
objects, expansion of alteration of 321–2
partnership 302, 320–3
purpose/objects of companies 201–6
railway companies 320–3
Salomon v Salomon case 202
separate corporate personality 323
shareholders 185, 188, 201–6, 318–19
unanimity, principle of 322–3
unfair prejudice 295
unincorporated businesses 119, 142, 219
Unitarianism 183, 197–8, 201
United States *see also* **early corporations in United States and the public purpose; limited liability partnership (LLP) structure for law firms in United States, origins of; Massachusetts, United States; New York, United States; separate legal personality in United States**
banks 143–4
beneficial ownership from voting rights, separation of 243–4
Bill of Rights 95, 101
business corporations 304
campaign finance 142, 152–3, 159
canal corporations 214
capital lock-ins 145
cartelisation and monopolisation 236, 243, 247
charter era 141–8
bans under state laws 147–8, 159
competition 146
dissolution 145–6
manufacturing corporations 144–5
state constitutions, revision of 147–8
colonies 93–4
corporate privileges 141–7
corruption 146, 159
dividend rights, history of 224–6
doctrinal analytical tradition 61
dual-class structure 225–6
elites 143–4
English historic cases 23
entity shielding 145
Federal Election Campaign Act of 1972 153
Federalists 143–4
France, influence in 242, 244, 248
fully paid up shares 221
general incorporation statutes 142, 146–53, 225–6
historical background 141–2, 330
historiography 61
inequalities 141–2
inseparability principle 242–5, 329
beneficial ownership from voting rights, separation of 243–4
cartelisation and monopolisation 236, 243, 247
charters 243–4
France, influence in 242, 244, 248
Model Business Corporation Act 245
People v N Riv Sugar Ref Co 242–5
voting trusts 242–4, 248
law and economics analysis 53
limited liability 145
manufacturing corporations 144–5
Model Business Corporation Act 245
monopolies 144
new organisational forms, era of 142, 153–8, 159
no par value, shares with 221
non-profit corporations 142–3
patronage 141–2, 146–7
People v N Riv Sugar Ref Co 242–5
political action committees (PACs) 153
politics 141–8, 152–3, 159
preference shares 224–5
public purposes 141–5
railway companies 224–5
regulation 141–59
shareholders, liability of 221
social effects, taking into consideration 141–2
Taft-Hartley Act of 1947 152–3
tax policies 142
Tillman Act of 1907 152–3
transferability of shares 214
transportation companies 144
trusts, law of 23
ultra vires 322
voting rights 216–18, 225, 242–4, 248
voting trusts 242–4, 248
universitas 126–31
unlimited liability
corporate governance 19
historic cases 19
joint-stock companies 297, 298, 307–9, 316
limitation of liability 307–10, 311

partnerships 297
shareholders, liability of 219–20, 222
subsidiary liability 309
unreported cases 11
usury
anti-Semitism 190, 194
prohibition 312–13, 317
shareholders 317
utility companies 215, 219

value of historical narratives 4–6
Van Buren, Martin 144
Veblen, Thorstein 255, 325
veil, lifting the corporate 91–2, 105–6, 107, 111, 118
Verdon-Smith, Reginald 268–9
vicarious liability 84–6, 88
von Friesen-Rötha, Heinrich 195
von Treitschke, Heinrich 195
voting rights, history of 209, 214–18 *see* **inseparability principle**
charter corporations 214–15, 217
dividend rights, history of 222, 225
dual class shares 217–18, 227
evolution of shares structures 216
freedom of contract era 217
general incorporation statute period 149, 217
general meetings 210
graduated/scaled voting schemes 215–17
investment-based voting rights 209, 211, 214–15
joint-stock companies 216
Limited Liability Companies Act 1856 217
majority voting 216
management shares 217
membership based voting rights 216
one share, one vote approach 216–17
ordinary shares 217
polls 216
show of hands 216
transferability of shares 211
unproportional voting rights 216

Wagener, Hermann 192
Wagner, Richard 192
Walker, David 267–70
Wallis, John 150
Warren, Elizabeth 1, 161
Watkinson, Harold (Lord Watkinson) 266–8
Watson, William 296, 299
Weber, Max 132
White, Hayden 30
Williston, Samuel 299–300
Wilson Committee 267–70
Wilson, Harold 263
Wilson, Thomas 318–19
***Wilson v Tooker* (1714)** 16, 20, 23
Winkler, Adam 152
***Wolff v Horncastle* (1798)** 16, 18, 21, 23–4
Wontner, Hugh 279–83, 286, 293
Wordsworth, Charles 295–6, 298–301, 305
Wormser, Maurice 106